SPECIAL EDUCATION LAW AND PRACTICE IN PUBLIC SCHOOLS

SECOND EDITION

Larry D. Bartlett
The University of Iowa

Susan Etscheidt
University of Northern Iowa

Greg R. Weisenstein
University of North Dakota

PEARSON
Merrill
Prentice Hall

Upper Saddle River, New Jersey
Columbus, Ohio

Library of Congress Cataloging in Publication Data

Bartlett, Larry Dean.
    Special education law and practice in public schools / Larry D.
Bartlett, Susan Etscheidt, Greg R. Weisenstein.—2nd ed.
      p. cm.
    Includes index.
    ISBN 0-13-220714-1
    1. Special education—Law and legislation—United States. 2. Children
with disabilities—Education—Law and legislation—United States.
3. United States. Individuals with Disabilities Education Act. 4. Inclusive
education—United States. I. Etscheidt, Susan Larson.
II. Weisenstein, Gregory R. III. Title.
KF4209.3.B365 2006
344.73′0791—dc22

                                                      2006019262

Vice President and Executive Publisher: Jeffery W. Johnston
Executive Editor: Ann Castel Davis
Editorial Assistant: Penny Burleson
Production Editor: Sheryl Glicker Langner
Production Coordinator: Vijay Kataria, *Techbooks*
Design Coordinator: Diane C. Lorenzo
Cover Design: Bryan Huber
Cover Image: Fotosearch
Production Manager: Laura Messerly
Director of Marketing: David Gesell
Marketing Manager: Autumn Purdy
Marketing Coordinator: Brian Mounts

This book was set in Franklin Gothic and Palatino by *Techbooks*. It was printed and bound by
R. R. Donnelley & Sons Company. The cover was printed by R. R. Donnelley & Sons Company.

Pearson Education Ltd.
Pearson Education Singapore Pte. Ltd.
Pearson Education Canada, Ltd.
Pearson Education—Japan

Pearson Education Australia Pty. Limited
Pearson Education North Asia Ltd.
Pearson Educación de Mexico, S.A. de C.V.
Pearson Education Malaysia Pte. Ltd.

10 9 8 7 6 5 4 3 2 1
ISBN: 0-13-220714-1

*This book is dedicated to school leaders and
educators who strive to provide a quality education to all children.*

I would like to also dedicate my effort on this book to my
wife, Gayle Luck, who is herself an educator worthy of emulation.

L. D. B.

I would like to also dedicate this book to my husband,
Randy, and daughter, Courtney, for their support and
encouragement. And to my mom and dad . . . for a life I cherish.

S. E.

I would like to also dedicate this book to my wife, Sandra, daughters, Michelle
and Alyson, and my son, Adam, for the lessons they continually teach me and for
their unwavering support of my work.

G. R. W.

PREFACE

A public policy proclaimed nearly 30 years ago assured students with disabilities the right to a free appropriate public education in the least restrictive environment (LRE). This public law required that students with disabilities be educated with non-disabled peers to the maximum extent appropriate. Removal from general education environments was permitted only when the educational needs of the child could not be met in that environment, even with the provision of supplementary aids and services.

This public policy emerged in response to a recognition of the history of segregation and exclusion of children with disabilities from the public schools. The common school had been established to educate only those children of acceptable intellect and social status, and any children with physical, mental, or behavioral disabilities were excluded. Our nation's early response to many children with disabilities was exclusion, institutionalization, and segregation.

Parents and advocates began to challenge this "separate but equal" structure of education in the early 1970s, and "right to education" court cases led Congress to adopt the public policy confirming the right of *all* children to a public education conferring meaningful benefit. This policy was first enacted in 1975 as the Education for All Handicapped Children Act (EAHCA).

The implementation of the EAHCA resulted in access to public school programs for millions of children with disabilities who had been historically excluded. Yet, within the public schools, the education of students with disabilities remained largely segregated. Self-contained special classes were the predominant placements for students with disabilities, and only children with mild, often invisible, disabilities were mainstreamed into general education settings. In the late 1980s and 1990s, parents and advocates again challenged the "separate but equal" structure calling for more inclusive placements. Court interpretations clarified and emphasized the LRE mandate, finding that Individual Education Program (IEP) placement teams must first discuss how a child with disabilities could be educated in the general education environment if provided supplementary aids and services. If efforts to provide those aids and services were inadequate or insufficient, courts ruled against school districts. In what seems to be baby steps, given the 30-year-old mandate, school districts began to explore inclusive environments for all students with disabilities and to fortify supports and services to ensure compliance with the LRE mandate.

Most important, no court interpretation or administrative agency interpretation of special education law has held that full inclusion (all children with disabilities should be educated in the regular education environment) is required under law. Although full inclusion is a laudable goal for school district policy, the law clearly requires only that children with disabilities be provided an appropriate program in the least restrictive environment appropriate for each child. The regular education environment may not be an appropriate setting for some students with disabilities, who may require more intensive services. The Individuals with Disabilities Education Act (IDEA) requires an individualized determination of each child's needs and services.

Despite the clarity and intent of this policy, the implementation of the LRE mandate has been challenging. Barriers to the successful inclusion of children with disabilities range from competing political pressure to the appropriate preparation of school personnel.

Many barriers have been overcome in schools due to an increased awareness of the legal requirements for students with disabilities and to intensified efforts to comply with those requirements. Professional development activities have focused on the why and how of inclusive practices, and current state and district policies reflect an improved understanding of the schools' obligations concerning inclusion. Yet many questions remain.

We believe that this text answers these questions. It is designed to provide background information on legal mandates, current interpretations of the law, and appropriate responsive school policy and practices. Our book presents scientifically based strategies and best practices for implementing the IDEA. Also provided are recommended readings, questions for thought, selected websites, and other resources to help school leaders access pertinent information. Reference to the Interstate School Leaders Licensure Consortium Standards is highlighted.

We have attempted to provide both an understanding of law and information on appropriate practice for implementation so that educational leaders will have the knowledge and skills to effectively meet the legal requirements of the IDEA and provide all students with a quality education.

This book was designed and organized to provide educational leaders with a clear understanding of student disabilities, relevant legal mandates, and research-based implementation strategies and best practices. As school leaders expand their understanding of special education law and practice, schools become good places for all students.

Acknowledgments

We would like to thank the reviewers of this text for their constructive comments: Judy L. Bell, Furman University; Lynda A. Cook, Shippensburg University; Placido A. Hoernicke, Fort Hays State University; Cindy Marble, Arizona State University Polytechnic; Connie J. Pollard, Black Hills State University; Sarah J. Templin, Purdue University; Richard P. West, Utah State University; and Jane M. Williams, Towson University.

DISCOVER THE MERRILL RESOURCES FOR SPECIAL EDUCATION WEBSITE

Technology is a constantly growing and changing aspect of our field that is creating a need for new content and resources. To address this emerging need, Merrill Education has developed an online learning environment for students, teachers, and professors alike to complement our products—the *Merrill Resources for Special Education* Website. This content-rich website provides additional resources specific to this book's topic and will help you—professors, classroom teachers, and students—augment your teaching, learning, and professional development.

Our goal with this initiative is to build on and enhance what our products already offer. For this reason, the content for our user-friendly website is organized by topic and provides teachers, professors, and students with a variety of meaningful resources all in one location. With this website, we bring together the best of what Merrill has to offer: text resources, video clips, web links, tutorials, and a wide variety of information on topics of interest to general and special educators alike. Rich content, applications, and competencies further enhance the learning process.

The *Merrill Resources for Special Education* Website includes:

- Video clips specific to each topic, with questions to help you evaluate the content and make crucial theory-to-practice connections.
- Thought-provoking critical analysis questions that students can answer and turn in for evaluation or that can serve as basis for class discussions and lectures.
- Access to a wide variety of resources related to classroom strategies and methods, including lesson planning and classroom management.
- Information on all the most current relevant topics related to special and general education, including CEC and Praxis™ standards, IEPs, portfolios, and professional development.
- Extensive web resources and overviews on each topic addressed on the website.
- A search feature to help access specific information quickly.

To take advantage of these and other resources, please visit the *Merrill Resources for Special Education* Website at

http://www.prenhall.com/bartlett

TEACHER PREP

MERRILL
PRENTICE HALL

Teacher Preparation Classroom

See a demo at
www.prenhall.com/teacherprep/demo

Your Class. Their Careers. Our Future. Will your students be prepared?

We invite you to explore our new, innovative and engaging website and all that it has to offer you, your course, and tomorrow's educators! Organized around the major courses pre-service teachers take, the Teacher Preparation site provides media, student/teacher artifacts, strategies, research articles, and other resources to equip your students with the quality tools needed to excel in their courses and prepare them for their first classroom.

This ultimate on-line education resource is available at no cost, when packaged with a Merrill text, and will provide you and your students access to:

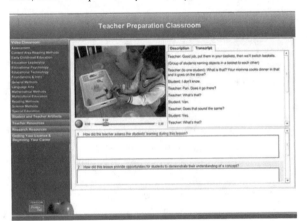

Online Video Library. More than 150 video clips—each tied to a course topic and framed by learning goals and Praxis-type questions—capture real teachers and students working in real classrooms, as well as in-depth interviews with both students and educators.

Student and Teacher Artifacts. More than 200 student and teacher classroom artifacts—each tied to a course topic and framed by learning goals and application questions—provide a wealth of materials and experiences to help make your study to become a professional teacher more concrete and hands-on.

Research Articles. Over 500 articles from ASCD's renowned journal *Educational Leadership.* The site also includes Research Navigator, a searchable database of additional educational journals.

Teaching Strategies. Over 500 strategies and lesson plans for you to use when you become a practicing professional.

Licensure and Career Tools. Resources devoted to helping you pass your licensure exam; learn standards, law, and public policies; plan a teaching portfolio; and succeed in your first year of teaching.

BRIEF CONTENTS

CONTENTS

Note: Every effort has been made to provide accurate and current Internet information in this book. However, the Internet and information posted on it are constantly changing, and it is inevitable that some of the Internet addresses listed in this textbook will change.

SPECIAL EDUCATION LAW AND PRACTICE IN PUBLIC SCHOOLS

PART I

LEGAL AND POLICY ISSUES

CHAPTER 1

THE FOUNDATION OF INCLUSIVE PRACTICES

CHAPTER PREVIEW

Focus

In little more than 30 years, major federal laws have revolutionized the treatment of persons with disabilities in the United States and have had far-reaching effects on public schools. The new requirements for education of students with disabilities, especially within the regular education environment, place demands on school principals and staff members for which they often have not received adequate professional training.

The Law

The three most important laws that directly impact the education of children with disabilities are: The Individuals with Disabilities Education Act (IDEA), first enacted in 1975 and implemented in 1977; Section 504 of the Rehabilitation Act of 1973, also implemented in 1977; and the Americans with Disabilities Act (ADA), enacted in 1990.

The early IDEA legislation established education as an entitlement for those children with disabilities who need special education and related services in states that accepted federal funds for that purpose. The other two statutes guarantee basic civil rights by prohibiting discrimination against persons with disabilities, including children. Both Section 504 and the ADA are somewhat broader in scope than the IDEA in that they apply to program access, higher education, and discrimination in employment opportunities, as well as education. As antidiscrimination laws, Section 504 and the ADA are not special education laws and remain the responsibility of the entire education community.

Although all three laws contain many similar provisions that affect educational programs, only the IDEA provides funding for education programs. It also goes into considerable detail covering many substantive and procedural requirements, including free appropriate public education (FAPE), individualized education programs (IEPs), the least restrictive environment (LRE), and parental safeguards. Basic principles of special education under the IDEA, Part B include the following:

- All children over age 3 who are identified as having potential disabilities are entitled to a full, nondiscriminatory assessment of their educational needs and a determination of eligibility for programs and service.
- Based on data assessed by a team of professionals and the child's parents, an IEP is prepared for eligible students, which establishes the framework for the provision of a FAPE.
- An educational placement is chosen by a team of parents and professionals in which to carry out the IEP. The placement must be the LRE appropriate to meet the child's educational needs. Schools must have a continuum of placements available to meet the needs of all eligible children with disabilities.
- Parents are entitled to an extensive system of procedural safeguards, including attendance at meetings, notice of school actions, due process hearings, and confidentiality of education records.

A major component of all three federal statutes related to the education of children with disabilities is the requirement that children with disabilities must be educated, to the maximum extent appropriate, with children who do not have disabilities. This concept is known as the "least restrictive environment." Only in the last 15 to 20 years has it become recognized that for most children with disabilities, the least restrictive school environment is the regular classroom. Only when regular class placements are not appropriate due to the child's disruption of the regular class environment or lack of educational benefit accruing to the child, may the child with disabilities be served in a special education setting. Educators must consider the use of supplementary aids and services and accommodations and modifications in establishing an appropriate educational environment where the child will benefit and not be disruptive.

Approaches

A review of student enrollment data over the last decade establishes that greater numbers of children are being identified as having disabilities and needing special education than ever before. The data also show that significantly greater numbers of children are being educated in regular class settings. Knowledgeable and understanding educational leaders are essential to the success of including students with disabilities in regular class settings. They contribute greatly through their leadership by role modeling acceptance of students with disabilities, establishing a positive, accepting school climate, and by assigning equally desirable space, schedules, and school duties to both regular and special education staff. Leadership involves facilitating cooperation and collaboration among staff and parents, acceptance among students, and maintaining good relations within the community.

Some efforts at implementing inclusive programs are part of larger school reform projects that affect the improved learning of all students. Whereas the final impact of state and national accountability for student achievement growth efforts, such as "No Child Left Behind" (NCLB) legislation, is unclear, accountability legislation almost certainly has the potential for both positive and negative implications for the education of children with disabilities.

SPECIAL EDUCATION AND CONSIDERATIONS OF INCLUSION

Every abrupt change catches a certain percentage of the population unaware, or at least insufficiently prepared. That certainly is true of the sweeping changes in the education of children with disabilities enacted into law in the United States in the mid-1970s. Although parents of children with disabilities had been aware of problems for their children within the public education system and struggled toward solutions for agonizing years—sometimes decades—most people involved in the education system remained unaffected by these struggles.

In the mid-1970s most educators were not trained to work with students with disabilities and did not expect to do so. In 1977 the situation changed dramatically with the implementation of the Education for All Handicapped Children Act, originally enacted in 1975 (Public Law 94–142), and the mandate to teach children with disabilities in the LRE. Regular class teachers found students with disabilities assigned to their classrooms, special class teachers had to relinquish ownership of "their" students and routines, new systems had to be implemented, parents' doubts, of both regular and special education, had to be allayed, and a myriad of smaller changes had to be made. Principals, it often seemed, were responsible for making it all happen.

As with other significant changes in education, placing children with disabilities appropriately in regular education classes and activities has not been, and will not be, accomplished overnight. Passage of the IDEA legislation has in many ways marked the beginning, not the end, of the process of change. Much has been learned since the late 1970s, and it is clear that more changes are forthcoming. A good example of a recent change in interpretation and perspective involved the concept of "inclusion" of students with disabilities in regular classrooms and activity settings. Although the concept of "least restrictive environment" has been legally mandated for 30 years, its actual implementation in regular education settings primarily occurred in the 1990s.

The term *inclusion* is not found anywhere in the law and is used inconsistently in the education literature. For the purposes of this book "inclusion" does not mean that all children with disabilities will be educated in the regular classroom. Instead, it refers to that aspect of the LRE legal requirement that mandates that *all* considerations of the educational placement of a child with disabilities begin with placement in the regular classroom and in regular student activities. Inclusive settings in regular classrooms, with the provision of appropriate supplementary aids and services, represent the least restrictive environment setting on the required "continuum" of alternative settings. Each public school must have a range of appropriate settings available for the educational placement of children with disabilities needing special education and related services.

There is a legal presumption that a child with disabilities will be educated in the regular classroom. It is only when that presumption is overcome by data and the professional judgment of the placement team members that the child may be placed in settings other than a regular education setting. The child may be placed in special education settings for programs and services only when the team determines that the child will not receive more benefit, or that the child will be significantly disruptive in the regular education placement. A full array of supplementary aids and services must be available and considered by the placement team to support the student and teacher in the regular education setting. The level and quality of support for students and staff is the key to successful efforts at inclusion. Only when the cost of needed supplementary aids and services to allow the child to benefit and not be disruptive is excessive may the team decide to not provide special education programs and services in the regular classroom environment. This concept of "supported inclusion" has been frequently overlooked by school districts and their educational placement teams.

Early History

Throughout much of human history, individuals with disabilities have been treated with superstition and fear. Infanticide, shunning, attributions of witchcraft or divine punishment, and even awed respect have all been socially sanctioned. With the rise of scientific understanding and democratic values in the late 1700s (the Age of Enlightenment), attitudes began to change. Persons with disabilities began to be seen as capable of learning, and the earliest special schools were founded for children who were deaf and blind. In institutions for the mentally ill and retarded (then grouped together indiscriminately), people were literally freed from their chains and conditions became somewhat more humane.

During the 19th century, reformers in the United States campaigned for new and more humane institutions, which generally were based on earlier European residential models, each one accommodating a different categorical population (e.g., blind, deaf, retarded). Some facilities were state operated and some private with some obviously better than others. Their overall capacity was limited, programs were methodologically experimental, and many children, especially those with severe or multiple disabilities, were not served. Even though much of the United States later experienced the enactment of compulsory attendance laws for most children, those with disabilities, especially those with noticeable disabilities, were often excluded and even expelled from school (Yell, 2006).

The early 20th century saw the beginning of community-based programs and the first university training programs for teachers of students with disabilities. However, progress was slow. In most cases, the public attitude was "at best . . . bare tolerance of exceptional children" (Reynolds & Birch, 1977, p. 17). Programs still tended to be segregated along categorical lines and separate from regular classes and schools. Some students attended classes for only a minimal number of hours each day, and many others were not served at all. Students with mild disabilities who did attend the public schools often were held back and forced to repeat grade after grade.

In the decades since World War II, however, there has been growing momentum for profound and rapid change marked by great increases in student enrollments, teacher training programs, and state support for special programs—even before the federal government became fully involved. Spurred in part by the response of wounded war veterans who were unwilling to accept a segregated, unproductive life, a national change in philosophy was underway. Whereas earlier reformers had argued for segregated schools as the most humane and receptive environment for educating students with disabilities, the new trend was toward integration and "normalization" of individuals' lives.

This trend was supported by the fusion of two important social elements pressuring for change: (a) the civil rights movement of the 1950s and 1960s and (b) the development of organizations of parents and supporters of students with disabilities. Many other 20th-century developments also contributed to the advancement of special education, including

- the development of the first standardized intelligence tests and other types of reliable educational assessment;
- the development of new professional fields such as psychiatry, speech pathology, and educational psychology;
- advances in medical understanding and treatment of previously mysterious diseases, such as epilepsy and polio;
- technological developments in such diverse and important areas as public transportation, artificial limbs and braces, and electronic communication aids for the heard of hearing and visually impaired.

By the mid-1970s, these combined forces and developments had resulted in a legalized commitment to educate all the nation's young people with disabilities and to do it in the most typical school setting appropriate for the child.

To put this in reasonable perspective, it must be understood that public education itself is a relatively recent institution. Not until 1918

did all states in the United States have compulsory education laws. Child labor, which had
involved a large percentage of school-age children, was not effectively banned on a national
level until 1938. Federal government involvement with the special rights and needs of children also began in the 20th century with the
first White House Conference on Children and
Youth in 1909.

The concept of universal public education
won wide acceptance in this country only after
the tremendous influx of immigrants during
the late 19th and early 20th centuries prompted
concerns that the U.S. population be "Ameri-
canized." Even then, large numbers of children
and youth were seriously underserved (as in
the case of many students with disabilities,
racial minorities, and Engish as a second language immigrants) or given no education at all
(as many as one million children with disabilities in the early 1970s). Government attention
to the educational needs of all children was a
necessary prerequisite to the development of
special education.

Legal History

All of the aforementioned 20th-century
developments—educational, governmental, theoretical, technological, medical, and organizational—formed the roots of the powerful
movement for educational change in the 1960s
and 1970s. The organizations lobbying for improvements in education for students with disabilities were in many ways inspired and
influenced by the successes of the civil rights
movement. For example, the Supreme Court
ruling in *Brown v. Board of Education* (1954)
against racially "separate but equal" schooling
and its affirmation of the importance of education to all Americans was also viewed as relevant to students with disabilities. Over
the following 20 years, advocacy groups led an
active, and ultimately successful, campaign to
win legal guarantees for the education of students with disabilities.

The efforts to raise public awareness
received an important boost from President
John F. Kennedy, whose sister was mentally

disabled. In 1961, he initiated a Presidential
Panel on Mental Retardation and in the ensuing
decade, Congress passed several laws that began to address the issue of education for students with disabilities. The Elementary and
Secondary Education Act (ESEA) of 1965 (P. L.
89–10) provided funding to meet the needs of
educationally deprived students, and later ESEA
amendments provided state agencies with special funds to evaluate and educate students with
disabilities (and later gifted students as well).
The federal Bureau for Education of the Handicapped was created in 1966 and state grant
programs were established. The Handicapped
Children's Early Education Act of 1968 (P. L.
90–247) provided funds to establish model
demonstration programs for young children
with disabilities.

Just as the court decision in *Brown* preceded major congressional acts in the civil
rights arena, key court decisions also helped set
the stage for passage of Section 504 (P. L.
93–112, 1973), the Education for All Handicapped Children Act (EAHCA; P. L. 94–142,
1975), and the Americans with Disabilities Act
(ADA; P. L. 101–336, 1990). The two cases
most often cited as influential are *Pennsylvania
Association for Retarded Citizens (PARC) v.
Pennsylvania* (1971/1972) and *Mills v. Board of
Education* (1972). The rulings in *PARC* and
Mills included many of the principles that were
later incorporated into federal statute, including
the right of all children with disabilities to a free
appropriate public education and provision of
parent procedural safeguards.

Section 504, the EAHCA (now IDEA), and
the ADA are the three most important statutes
governing special education in the United
States and form the basis for legal discussions in
this book. Section 504 and the ADA are essentially civil-rights statutes, whereas the EAHCA
specifically defined and authorized funding for
special education programs. Over the years,
Congress has regularly reviewed and amended
(reauthorized) the original special education
laws found in the EAHCA. In 1986, the law was
amended to allow the awarding of attorney fees
for parents who prevail in due process proceedings and litigation, and a new voluntary

Part H (now Part C) was added to assist states with early intervention services for infants and toddlers (birth through age 2).

It was also in 1986 that the movement to include special education students in regular education settings started in earnest. Although a number of educators and researchers had previously argued for integrating students with disabilities into regular classrooms, it was then that Madeline Will, an assistant secretary of education, spoke and wrote about the "shared responsibility" of regular and special education programs toward students with disabilities. Will (1986) envisioned that the educational needs of all students be met through teams of regular and special teachers and support staff working toward that goal. Initially the movement toward inclusion was often referred to as the regular education initiative (REI). Its goal was to find ways to serve students with mild and moderate disabilities by encouraging partnerships between regular and special education (Stainback & Stainback, 1995). At various times, the concept has taken on slightly different meanings and been referred to as integrated education, normalization, and mainstreaming.

From 1989 through 1994, the inclusion movement gained significant momentum as a result of a series of important rulings by federal circuit courts of appeal interpreting the concept of "least restrictive environment" (see *Chapter 5* for details).

In 1990, Congress changed the name of the EAHCA to the Individuals with Disabilities Education Act (IDEA). Furthermore, in response to public demands for greater school safety, the 1990 Amendments authorized greater flexibility for schools in dealing with students bringing firearms to school. Amendments in 1994 allowed greater coordination between ESEA Chapter I remedial programs in reading and mathematics and special education programs for children with disabilities. In 1997, after a 2-year heated debate in Congress, extensive amendments were written into law that greatly clarified understanding on a number of controversial and complex legal issues, including discipline of students with disabilities. With the 1997 Amendments, congressional focus began to shift from

implementation of educational programs and services to a greater emphasis on assuring quality public education programs and improving and evaluating student performance (House Report 105–95 , 1997, pp. 83–84). The emphasis on quality programming, the opportunity of access to the regular curriculum, and accountablity of schools was continued and amplified in the 2004 Amendments to the IDEA.

One of the express findings of Congress in the 2004 Amendments was that "research and experience have demonstrated that the education of children with disabilities can be more effective by having high expectations . . . and ensuring their access to the general educational curriculum in the regular classroom, to the maximum extent possible, . . . " [*20 U.S.C. §1401(c) (5)*].

Comparison of Section 504, ADA, and IDEA

Section 504 is a broad civil rights provision protecting persons with disabilities or who are regarded as being disabled (e.g., an abnormal, although not disabling, appearance) of all ages who are impacted by a public or private agency that receives federal contracts or grants. Public schools do not receive any specific additional funds for its implementation. Educators come into contact with Section 504 provisions most frequently when parents of children with disabilities are unable to establish that their children are eligible for special education programs and services under the IDEA. Thus, Section 504 presents concerns primarily for regular education programs in the identification of "reasonable accommodations" for students with disabilities and is not considered special education programming. Accommodations under Section 504 must be based on the student's educational needs and be reasonable in nature (Hehir, 2003).

Section 504 has potentially broader application than the IDEA for those children with physical or mental disabilities that substantially "affect one of the major life activities" (walking, seeing, breathing) but do not necessarily significantly impact the child's ability to learn. An example might be a child with severe arthritis, who under Section 504 is allowed extra passing time between classes, or a child being treated for cancer who is allowed an adjusted attendance policy. For such students, a team of parents and educators conducts an evaluation and determines eligibility for Section 504 services. Although schools must "conduct an evaluation" of the student, most Section 504 evaluations are completed only through the gathering and consideration of existing data, including previous medical records and educational testing (Copenhaver, 2001).

Under Section 504, an accommodation plan must be developed for an eligible student by a group of persons knowledgeable about the student. The plan must document modifications or accommodations to be made by the school and its staff that will allow the child to benefit from the school's education services in both academic and nonacademic activities. The administration of physician-prescribed medications, alternative passing time between classes to eliminate being jostled by other students, and additional time to complete class assignments or tests may be accommodations considered for some students. The list of potential accommodations is limited only by students' needs and team imagination. Copenhaver (2001) compiled a list of 100 examples of accommodations, including having a student orally repeat directions given by the teacher, use of verbal and physical cues by the teacher, peer tutoring, color-coded materials, and study carrels in the classroom. The accommodation plan is not required to be in writing, but best practice indicates that a written plan is the ideal safeguard for all concerned. Sometimes, an accommodation plan merely documents a team's consideration of a student's needs and a team determination that no accommodations are justified under the circumstances.

Although not as detailed or extensive as the IDEA, Section 504 requires that schools must implement procedural safeguards for students and parents. These include a notice of rights, parent consent for the initial evaluation, an opportunity to review student records, an opportunity for due process hearing, and an opportunity for further review of local hearing decisions. Schools may use existing grievance procedures (e.g., equity or sexual harassment) when those procedures comply with Section 504 requirements. Local hearings must allow the parents an opportunity to challenge school decisions regarding identification; evaluation; provision of accommodations, modifications, and services; and changes in services. Hearings should be conducted by an impartial hearing officer at no cost to the parents, and parents may have legal representation if they wish. As an alternative to hearings, parents may file a complaint with the Office of Civil Rights (OCR) in the U.S. Department of Education, and an investigation will be conducted (Zirkel, 2003). Schools should have written policies that incorporate these procedures and comply with other 504 requirements, such as school designation of a Section 504 coordinator.

The ADA is also a civil rights statute, but it prohibits discrimination on the basis of disability in employment, services, and accommodations in both the public and private sectors. Thus, its impact on education is indirect. The ADA is based on the language and interpretations of Section 504 and includes many of the issues covered by Section 504. The OCR, which interprets and enforces both Section 504 and the ADA, has determined that discrimination issues in education will be interpreted identically under both statutes. It is unlikely that students in public schools gained any more rights under the ADA than they already had under the IDEA and Section 504 requirements (Osborne, 1995).

To better understand how the IDEA, Section 504, and the ADA impact each other in the educational setting, one can use an analogy of three inverted kitchen mixing bowls, each one a little larger than the previous one. Likewise, each law encompasses the previous smaller one and is somewhat greater in coverage. The smallest mixing bowl represents the IDEA, which requires that special education and related services be provided to children with disabilities who need special education. The legal provisions of the IDEA are interpreted and monitored by the Office of Special Education Programs (OSEP) in the U.S. Department of Education.

The second largest bowl represents Section 504, which makes it illegal for recipients of federal funds, including public schools and many private schools, to discriminate against persons with disabilities. Section 504 regulations contain many IDEA concepts, such as free appropriate public education (FAPE) and least restrictive environment (LRE), and compliance with the IDEA requirements of FAPE and LRE usually signifies compliance with Section 504 requirements in the same areas.

Some areas of potential discrimination exist under Section 504 which are outside the IDEA. A student with a specific learning disability, for instance, may be receiving a special education program under the IDEA, but obtaining low grades in courses and thus be ineligible to participate in athletics. The question under the IDEA would be whether the provided program was appropriate, an educational question. But, under Section 504 and the ADA, the question would be whether ineligibility due to low grades was a result of the student's disability, which could be prohibited discrimination and thus a question of law (Sullivan, Lantz, & Zirkel, 2000). Also, under Section 504 a school's refusal to administer needed physician-prescribed medication during school hours to a child with disabilities, regardless of whether she or he receives special education, may establish a claim of discrimination. As the inverted mixing bowl analogy reveals, all students eligible for special education are also protected against discrimination under Section 504, but not all students eligible for Section 504 nondiscrimination protections are eligible for special education programs and services under the IDEA (Letter to Veir, 1993).

The ADA, in our analogy, is represented by the largest mixing bowl. In addition to prohibiting discrimination on the basis of disability by recipients of federal grants and contracts (i.e., public schools), the ADA also prohibits discrimination in the private sector, including public accommodations. That is why public accommodations, such as movie theaters, must accommodate patrons who use wheelchairs and department stores must have disability-accessible restrooms and elevators. Both Section 504 and the ADA have been applied to private schools that receive federal funds.

General Principles of the IDEA

In addition to providing partial funding and establishing a system to monitor and evaluate state and local programs, the IDEA contains a number of provisions designed to ensure that all eligible students receive the education programs to which they are entitled. The IDEA Part B contains the following major principles:

- *Child Find* requirements mandate that public school staff locate, evaluate, and identify children who potentially meet the eligibility requirements of the IDEA, including homeless children, wards of the state, and children attending private school (see *Chapter 3*).
- *Children with disabilities* are those children between the ages of 3 and 21 who have been evaluated and found to have at least 1 of 13 disabilities, and who because of that disability need special education and related services (see *Chapters 12* and *13*).
- *Free appropriate public education* (FAPE) is special education and related services determined through the IEP development process (see *Chapter 4*).
- *Special education* is defined in the IDEA as "specially designed instruction, at no cost to parents, to meet the unique needs of a child with a disability" (see *Chapter 4*).
- *Related services* are those services necessary to assist the child with disabilities to benefit from special education (see *Chapters 4* and *5*).
- *Individualized education program* (IEP) is a written statement of an educational plan and program based on education data for a child with a disability that is developed, reviewed, and revised in accordance with federal law. IEPs must contain prescribed components, such as annual goals containing progress-monitoring criteria, participation in state- and school-wide testing, and transition plans for leaving high school (see *Chapter 4*).
- *Least restrictive environment* (LRE) requires that children with disabilities be educated with nondisabled children to the maximum extent appropriate. Special classes or settings

may be used only when the nature of the disability is such that "education in the regular classes with the use of supplementary aids and services cannot be achieved satisfactorily" (*34 C.F.R. § 300.114*). Schools must ensure that a *continuum* of alternative placements are available (see *Chapter 5*).

- *Supplementary aids and sevices* are those aids, services, modifications, and other supports required by law to be provided in the regular class, or regular education-related settings, "to enable the child with disabilities to be educated with nondisabled children to the maximum extent appropriate . . . " (*34 C.F.R. § 300.41*). The phrase differs from "related services" in that related services support special education programming usually provided in special education environments (see *Chapter 5*).

- *Assistive technology* is any device, piece of equipment, or product system that is used to increase, maintain, or improve the functional capabilities of a child; and *assistive technology service* is any service that directly helps a child select, acquire, or use an assistive technology device, including evaluation, purchasing, customizing, and training.

- *Identification and evaluation* must be individually planned and conducted with multiple valid and nondiscriminatory assessment instruments and procedures to evaluate a child suspected of being eligible for special education (see *Chapter 3*).

- *Regular education interventions* are scientifically proven methodologies, practices, and educational tools identified and recommended by an interdisciplinary team of regular and special educators to a regular class teacher. These interventions are to be used in assisting an individual student who is not succeeding in the regular class learning activities, does not exhibit an obvious need for a formal special education evaluation, and who has not been identified as needing special education. Under the 2004 Amendments to the IDEA, the intervention team must carefully measure and monitor the child's response to interventions (RTI) to determine whether the child suspected of having a

specific learning disability should eventually be referred for special education evaluation and services (see *Chapter 3*).

- *Procedural safeguards* are provided to parents in an extensive and detailed system of notices, processes, and practices in order to assure meaningful parent participation in decision making and allowing parents to advocate for their child (see *Chapter 2*).

- *Confidentiality of student information* must be maintained through specified education record disclosure procedures, and parents must be provided access to the educational records of their children (see *Chapter 2*).

Overview of the Process of Special Education

Once a child is referred for IDEA eligibility consideration, a chain of activities is set in motion, with three basic steps prescribed by law:

1. *Eligibility is identified and determined.* A full, thorough, nondiscriminatory (e.g., not biased by race, language, gender) evaluation must assess all areas of possible disability, and a team of qualified professionals and the student's parents determine the child's eligibility (see *Chapter 3*). Eligibility is determined using a two-pronged approach: (a) establish that the student has a disability, and (b) establish that as a result of the disability the child needs special education.

2. *An IEP is prepared.* This document is based on the evaluation data and formulated in a meeting involving the student's parent(s), a specified team of educators, and other individuals. The IEP documents the student's current levels of educational functioning, including how the disability impacts the student's progress in the general curriculum, and a specified list of content items. The IEP must be completed before special education programs and services can be provided (see *Chapter 4*).

3. *The Educational placement is determined.* Placement must be in an educational setting in which the IEP programs and services can

be carried out and which meets other legal requirements. The school district must have a continuum of placements available and provide related and supplementary services, whether by the district itself or under contract or other arrangements through outside agencies. Placement decisions must be made by a group of persons knowledgeable about the child, including the parents, and placement must be in the LRE appropriate for the child (see *Chapter 5*).

All three steps may be accomplished by the same core group of parents and specified educator team members (IEP team), with additional professional and support persons being involved when appropriate. Specific state, district, and school practices have been developed to help each step proceed smoothly.

Each chapter in this book contains relevant information on legal requirements and trends at the federal level. However, state laws and school district policies are not covered here and, because they often affect the options available to local education leaders, should be consulted.

The IDEA is essentially a contract between the federal government and each state, whereby the state agrees to follow certain regulations in exchange for federal funds. To qualify for these funds, each state must submit a program plan, including assurances that the basic principles of the federal law will be followed, copies of relevant state laws and regulations, counts of children with disabilities in the state and where they are served, monitoring and evaluation activities, proposed use of funds and accounting systems, facilities available, and other information. The state, in turn, makes funds available to intermediate educational agencies and local school districts upon receipt of their applications. Local applications must include descriptions of facilities, personnel, and services available; guarantees that federal guidelines are being followed; plans for parent participation; accounting systems; and agreement to furnish data required by the state for its reports.

Thus, each state is responsible for fulfilling the terms of its agreement with the federal gov-

ernment. Each school district is held accountable by the state department of education, which itself is monitored by the federal government. To ensure contract compliance, program data and planning information must be collected and delivered to the federal government each year. This, in brief, is the legal and financial reality behind many of the paperwork requirements that go along with special education.

CHILDREN ENROLLED IN SPECIAL EDUCATION

According to the data in the U.S. Department of Education's *2004 Digest of Education Statistics* (2005) on the implementation of the IDEA, in the 2003–04 school year about 13.8% of all children ages 3 to 21 enrolled in public schools were enrolled in special education. That is higher than the 1993–94 school year, when about 12% of students ages 3 to 21 enrolled in public schools were identified as needing special education. According to the data, the approximate breakdown of children ages 3 to 21 receiving special education in 2003–04 by disability category was as follows:

Specific Learning Disability	42.7%
Speech or Language Impairment	21.7%
Mental Disability	8.9%
Emotional Disturbance	7.4%
Other Health Impairments	7.0%
Multiple Disabilities	2.1%
Autism and Traumatic Brain Injury	2.8%
Developmental Delay	4.6%
Other	2.8%

Data have established that even though national figures for overall student enrollment between the ages of 3 and 21 have increased slowly over recent years (about an 11% increase between the 1993–94 and 2003–04 school years), the number of identified students with disabilities has increased at more than twice that rate (27%). The data also establish that since the early 1990s, the percentage of students with disabilities who are educated in regular classrooms increased between the 1992–93

TABLE 1-1   *Trend toward inclusion: The percentage of students with disabilities (ages 6 to 21) in the regular class setting[a]*

Category	1992–1993 (%)	1997–1998 (%)	2002–2003 (%)
All types of disabilities	39.8	46.4	46.9
Specific learning disabilities	34.8	43.8	48.2
Emotional disturbance	19.6	24.9	28.8
Mental disabilities	7.1	12.6	11.0
Speech language impairments	81.7	87.8	87.0
Orthopedic impairments	35.1	46.6	45.8
Multiple disabilities	7.5	10.0	11.6
Visual impairments	45.4	48.1	52.5
Hearing impairments	29.5	38.8	43.0
Deaf–blindness	12.5	13.6	17.6
Other health impairments	40.0	41.4	49.5
Autism	[b]	18.3	24.7
Traumatic brain injury	[b]	29.8	28.5
Developmental delay	[b]	[b]	46.3

[a]Regular class setting in federal government data means outside the regular class for services less than 21% of the school day.
[b]Not a category in 1992–93 and 1997–98.
(United States Department of Education, 2005, Table 53; United States Department of Education, 2000, Table 54; United States Department of Education, 1996, Table 52).

and 2002–03 school years (from 39.8% to 46.9%). During that same decade, the percentage of students educated in resource rooms increased (31.7% to 38.6%) and separate classes declined (23.5% to 13.5%) (U.S. Department of Education, 2005, Tables 52 & 53; U.S. Department of Education, 1996, Table 52).

The current trend toward moving students with disabilities to less restrictive settings has involved all disability categories. Not surprising, the greatest movement toward inclusion involved students with the mildest cognitive disabilities (e.g., specific learning disabilities and speech/language impairments). Categories of students with more challenging behaviors and substantial disabilities (e.g., multiple disabilities and mental disabilities) are experiencing less progress. Whereas the available data demonstrates substantial progress is being made

toward inclusion, the trends vary dramatically between states and among the various disabilities. *Table 1-1* shows the percentage of children by categories of disabilities in the regular class setting in the 1992–93, 1997–98, and 2002–03 school years. Notice that in the last five years for which we have data, some categories of disabilities have slowed in the growth of students in regular class settings, and a few have experienced slight regression.

NEW CHALLENGES AND THOUGHTS

Many past difficulties in the education of students with disabilities might be summarized as the failure to individualize. Despite educational and legal progress, today's schools are not immune from the impulse to act on prejudice or stereotype rather than provide supportive understanding of individual students' strengths and needs. To help combat that impulse, principals and teachers alike should remember that students' performance problems can result from many interacting factors, including inappropriate behaviors and practices on the part of schools.

School Reform and Inclusion

Schools that implement inclusive programs are often simultaneously engaged in other school reform efforts. Commentators have observed that there may be a relationship between school reform and a school's commitment to the inclusion concept. They have found that schools engaged in reform efforts often focus on the education and preparation of *all* children for productive and satisfying lives (First & Curcio, 1993).

A number of researchers have identified positive relationships resulting from simultaneous joint school-wide improvement efforts and the implementation of inclusion programs. Salisbury and McGreger (2002) found a commonality of characteristics among five elementary principals of exemplary schools that promoted quality instructional and inclusive practices. They concluded that all of the principals exhibited collaborative and supportive prospectives toward change, shared decision-making with staff, actively promoted the core values of inclusion and high-quality instruction, promoted learning communities, and encouraged and participated in reflective staff inquiry regarding school improvement.

Positive side effects of the inclusion effort have also been observed in Vermont, which has been a leader in the nation in the percentage of children with disabilities in regular classrooms. Thousand and Villa (1995) reported the following observations from Vermont's inclusion efforts:

- The number of students identified for special education and related services had decreased.
- Student performance, behavior, and social engagement had not diminished.

- Other education improvement initiatives were linked with inclusion to their mutual strengthening.
- Both regular and special educators had come to believe, through experience, that inclusion results in positive and rewarding changes in job roles for educators.

In an examination of schools engaged in varied levels of school reform activities, Duchnowski, Kutash, and Oliveira (2004) determined that schools actively engaged in school improvement activities included special education programs in their change efforts more than the less-active schools. They concluded that schools actively engaged in school improvement efforts felt the need to include special education teachers and staff in long-range planning and decision-making roles.

The Inclusion Debate

Whereas some educators and parents call for an approach that would require all children with disabilities to be placed in the regular class setting all the time (full inclusion), others continue to defend the value of separateness for special education students. Parents of children with severe disabilities are especially divided on the issue of placing all children with disabilities in the regular education classroom (Palmer, Fuller, Arora, and Nelson, 2001). Many of the most experienced educators and notable researchers do not call for an all-or-nothing approach, but see value in the maintenance of the currently required variety of available instructional settings (continuum). They recognize that inclusion in the regular class setting may not be appropriate or desirable for *all* children with disabilities (Hehir, 2003; Zigmond, Jenkins, Fuchs, Deno, & Fuchs, 1998). It is critical to keep in mind that one solution does not fit all, and that educators and parents need to protect students from a single-mold mentality. Educators have been known to become overzealous with a good idea.

The realization that courts will no longer ignore the portion of the LRE concept that requires consideration of regular class placement for students with disabilities, as well as greatly increased coverage of the benefits of inclusion in the education literature, resulted in confusion among educators regarding their changing professional roles and responsibilities. The National Education Association (NEA) sought to resolve the confusion over a decade ago through the creation of an ad hoc committee to study the issue and attempt to establish a national policy statement that represented best practice for inclusion in the school setting. Here is the result of that effort, which in 1994 became the "National Education Association Policy Statement on Appropriate Inclusion":*

> The National Education Association is committed to equal educational opportunity, the highest quality education, and a safe learning environment for all students. The association supports and encourages *appropriate* inclusion. *Appropriate* inclusion is characterized by practices and programs that provide for the following on a sustained basis:
> - A full continuum of placement options and services within each option. Placement and services must be determined for each student by a team that includes all stakeholders and must be specified in the individualized education program (IEP).
> - *Appropriate* professional development, as part of normal work activity, of all educators and support staff associated with such programs. *Appropriate* training must also be provided for administrators, parents, and other stakeholders.
> - *Adequate* time, as part of the normal school day, to engage in coordinated and collaborative planning on behalf of all students.
> - Class sizes that are responsive to student needs.
> - Staff and technical assistance that is specifically *appropriate* to student and teacher needs.
> - Inclusion practices and programs that lack these fundamental characteristics are *inappropriate* and must end. (NEA, 2005)

---

*Emphasis added. From "National Education Association Policy Statement on Appropriate Inclusion." Available at: http://www.nea.org/specialed/inclusionpolicy.html. Reprinted by permission.

Notice the importance and emphasis of the adjectives "appropriate" and "adequate" in the NEA statement. This statement recognizes that in the creation of inclusive programs, there is a "right way" and a "wrong way." It is the former, not the latter, that this book was envisioned to encourage. When inclusion practices are thoughtfully planned and implemented, mutual benefits accrue to all students, both those in regular and special education, and staff (Summers, Gavin, Purnell-Hall, & Nelsen, 2003).

Accountability—No Child Left Behind

The 2004 Amendments to the IDEA merged components of the IDEA and NCLB in several important areas. Congress wanted to assure high academic expectations and greater access to the general education curriculum in preparation for productive and independent lives as adults (Yell, 2006). The requirement of "highly qualified teachers" in special education programs (see *Chapter 10*), encouragement of inclusive practices to allow students with disabilities greater access to the general curriculum (see Chapter 5), and greater IEP emphasis on academic achievement evidenced through standardized testing (see *Chapter 4*) are examples of that merger.

The concept of holding public education accountable for student academic achievement and progress has been a source of controversy in this country's education circles for at least the last four decades. However, before the enactment of NCLB legislation most suggestions for holding schools accountable did not come to fruition. In NCLB many political forces and agendas came together and crafted a challenging, if not threatening, legalized future of accountability in the lives of public school children, including those with disabilities.

The laudatory stated purpose of NCLB is the creation of a fair and equal opportunity for all students to obtain a high-quality education and be at least minimally proficient on challenging state academic achievement standards. The evaluation of state success in the creation of the opportunity for a good education will be through mandated annual state assessments for students in grades 3 through 8, including those with disabilites, in reading/language arts, mathematics, and science (by 2007).

Assessment results must be reported in a disaggregated manner by poverty, race and ethnicity, limited English proficiency, and disabilty. Congress was concerned that if students with disabilities were not part of the accountability system, they might be ignored and not receive the appropriate academic attention they deserve and need (Yell, Katsiyannas, & Shiner, 2006). The NCLB legislation provides for sanctions for schools failing to make adequate yearly progress (AYP) by students as a whole, and by disaggregate subgroups, in meeting "challenging" state standards. The AYP goal is set progressively higher each year in order to establish upward progress toward the goal for the school year 2013–14. In that year all students, including those with disabilites, must meet their state's self-determined profiency level of academic achievement. Sanctions include parent choice to transfer their child to a "successful" school when the school of attendance fails to met AYP goals for 2 consecutive years, mandated provision of special services and programs for some students for failure over 3 consecutive years, replacement of school staff or implementation of a new institutional structure after 4 consecutive years of failure, and eventually the state or a contracted private agency taking over management of the school.

The National Assessment of Education Progress (NAEP) must be administered by states every other year in grades 4 and 8 in reading, math, and science as a way of determining the rigor and effectiveness of state annual assessments. Yet, many questions regarding the appropriateness of the use of the NAEP for evaluating state assessment exams are not resolved (Bracey, 2003; Hombo, 2003).

Ysseldyke et al. (2004) have conducted a review of available knowledge about the consequences of high-stakes testing for students with disabilities. They concluded that raising academic expectations for students with disabilities through high-stakes assessments can have positive results in the number of students who receive improved instruction, the improved use of data in making ajustments to students' IEPs, and improved communication with parents about their children. They raise concerns, however, about the lack of empirical data on the impact of testing on student and parent anxiety, dropout rates, curriculum narrowing, teaching for the test, and the placement of struggling students into lower-track classes with negative results. Ysseldyke et al. conclude that educators, politicians, and policy makers do not yet know enough about the consequences of implementing high-stakes testing on a large scale to reasonably assume that holding schools responsible will lead to increased instructional effort and better outcomes for students. They emphasize that quality of schooling is not the only factor that impacts student learning and test results.

Many special educators anticipate that the overall impact of NCLB on programs for students with disabilities will be negative and lead to a corresponding negative impact on students whose individual needs are currently being served in special education programs (McGrath, Johns, & Mathur, 2004).

It is natural that such an all-encompassing legislative act as NCLB will impact the educational lives of students with disabilities as well as those without disabilites. For that reason many chapters of this book will discuss the challenges that NCLB presents to educators attempting to provide quality educational programs for all children.

CONCLUSION

Effective implementation of the special education procedures and concepts outlined in the IDEA will require new understanding and awareness, new roles for educators, and new flexibility in schools. It calls for active and informed leadership. School principals and other educational leaders are essential to the success of inclusion through their climate-building activities and practices, modeling acceptance, and meeting challenges in a spirit of togetherness.

16   PART I: LEGAL AND POLICY ISSUES

Meeting these challenges requires a sharing of information, cooperation, and an understanding that all the efforts are worth it. The experience in thousands of classrooms across the country has shown that the inclusion experience, when done correctly, can be successful and productive, not only for students with disabilities but for all students and staff involved.

VIEW FROM THE COURTS

Board of Education of Hendrick Hudson Central School District v. Rowley (1982)(the meaning and determination of "appropriate"). The parents of Amy Rowley, a student with a hearing impairment, requested that the school provide their daughter with a sign-language interpreter for academic class settings. When the school determined that Amy did not need a sign-language interpreter, the parents sought a due process hearing and subsequent court review. The Supreme Court considered two questions of law: What did the IDEA mean by "free appropriate public education," and what was the proper role of the courts in reviewing special education "appropriateness" issues?

The Court ruled that the requirement of FAPE did not mean that schools were required to "maximize" the potential of students with disabilities or provide the "best" program possible. Schools are required to provide access to specialized instruction and related services that are individually designed through the IEP process to provide educational benefit to the student.

Under the IDEA the courts were relegated the task of determining the meaning of technical legal terms and whether parent procedural safeguards have been provided. Courts were directed to enter the issue of determining "appropriateness" with great hesitation and reluctance, and most subsequent lower court rulings have followed that directive. When disputed, the question of appropriateness of educational methodology for a specific child was primarily left with state and local education officials.

Timothy W. v. Rochester, New Hampshire School District, (1989) (zero reject). The parent of a severely disabled child appealed a lower court ruling that held the school was not obligated to provide special education to a child who was so severely disabled that he was not capable of benefiting from special education. The appellate court ruled that children with disabilities who need special education are entitled to special education, and Timothy W. did not have to establish that he would benefit from special education in order to receive services.

RECOMMENDED READINGS

deBettencourt, L. U. (2002). Understanding the differences between IDEA and Section 504. *Teaching Exceptional Children, 34*(3), 16–23. This article discusses the distinctions between the IDEA and Section 504 and provides helpful ideas regarding the implementation of both.

Kohn, A. (2004). Test today, privatize tomorrow: Using accountability to "reform" public schools to death. *Phi Delta Kappan, 85,* 148–164. This article, by one of America's greatest minds in education, raises concerns regarding the political motivation behind "No Child Left Behind."

Yell, M. L., Katsiyannas, A., & Shiner, S. G. (2006). The No Child Left Behind Act, adequate yearly progress, and students with disabilities. *Teaching Exceptional Children, 38*(4) 32–39. This excellent article provides an overview of the impact of NCLB on students with disabilities and offers excellent suggestions for implementation of the law.

Relevant Federal Regulations

34 C.F.R. Part 104 (2005) Nondiscrimination on the basis of disability in programs and activities receiving federal financial assistance–Section 504 regulations.

34 C.F.R. Part 300 Assistance to States for the Education of Children with Disabilities [70 Fed. Reg., 35,833–35,880 (June 21, 2005)].

300.8	Child with a disability.
300.17	Free appropriate public education.
300.22	Individualized education programs.
300.23	Individualized education program team.
300.34	Related services.

300.38	Special education.
300.41	Supplementary aids and services.
300.114	General LRE requirements.
300.115	Continuum of alternative placements.

SELECTED WEBSITES

Code of Federal Regulations–Government Printing Office–National Archives and Record Administration
http://www.gpoaccess.gov/cfr/index.html

Council for Exceptional Children
http://www.cec.sped.org

U.S. Department of Education–Office of Special Education and Rehabilitative Services
http://www.ed.gov/about/offices/list/osers/index.html

Individuals with Disabilities Education Act Data
http://www.ideadata.org

National Center for Educational Statistics
http://nces.ed.gov/programs/digest

Internet Resources for Special Children
http://www.irsc.org

National Dissemination Center for Children with Disabilities
http://www.nichcy.org

QUESTIONS FOR THOUGHT

1. Would the education of children with disabilities be better today if Congress had directed in 1975 that children with disabilities not be provided "special" education, but that all children be educated appropriately in the regular classroom?
2. From a legal perspective, are the IDEA, Section 504, and the ADA all needed, or are they so similar that they should be combined into one law?
3. What one or two changes in the law in the last 30 years, including court interpretations of the IDEA, will have the most meaningful impact on the lives of children with disabilities when they become adults?
4. What would be the likely causes of slowdown and reversal of the rate of regular class placement for some disability categories in *Table 1-1*?

REFERENCES

Americans with Disabilities Act. (1990). P. L. 101–336, 42 U.S.C. §§ 12101–12213.

Assistance to States for the Education of Children with Disabilities 70 Fed. Reg. 35,833–35,880 (June 21, 2005).

Board of Education of Hendrick Hudson Central School District v. Rowley, 458 U.S. 176, 102 S. Ct. 3034 (1982).

Bracey, G. W. (2003). The condition of public education. *Phi Delta Kappan, 85*, 148–164.

Brown v. Board of Education, 347 U.S. 483, 74 S. Ct. 686 (1954).

Copenhaver, J. (2001). *Section 504 primer for parents, educators and administrators.* Logan, UT: Author.

Duchnowski, A. J., Kutash, K., & Oliveira, B. (2004). A systematic examination of school improvement activities that include special education. *Remedial and Special Education, 25*, 117–129.

First, P. F., & Curcio, J. L. (1993). Implementing the disabilities acts: Implications for educators. Bloomington, IN: Phi Delta Kappa Educational Foundation, Fastback No. 360.

Hehir, J. (2003). Beyond inclusion. *School Administrator, 60*(3), 36–39.

Hombo, C. H. (2003). NAEP and No Child Left Behind: Technical challenges and practical solutions. *Theory into Practice, 42*(1), 59–65.

House Report 105–95 (1997). The Committee on Education and Workforce to Accompany Individuals With Disabilities Education Act Amendments of 1997, 2, *United States Code Congressional and Administrative News*, 78–146.

Individuals with Disabilities Education Act, 20 U.S.C. §§ 1,401–1,487.

Letter to Veir, 20 IDELR 864 (OCR, 1993).

McGrath, M. Z., Johns, B. H., & Mathur, S. R. (2004). Is history repeating itself—services for children with disabilities endangered. *Teaching Exceptional Children, 37*(1), 70–71.

Mills v. Board of Education, 348 F. Supp. 866 (D.D.C. 1972).

National Education Association. (2005). *NEA Policy Statement on Appropriate Inclusion.* Retrieved April 6, 2005, from http://www.nea.org/specialed/inclusionpolicy.html

"No Child Left Behind." (2002). P. L. 107–110, 20 U.S.C. §§ 6,301–7,941.

Osborne, A. G. (1995). Court interpretations of the Americans with Disabilities Act and their effect on school districts. *Education Law Reporter, 95,* 489–497.

Palmer, D. S., Fuller, K., Arora, T., & Nelson, M. (2001). Taking sides: Parent views on inclusion for their children with severe disabilities. *Exceptional Children, 67,* 467–484.

Pennsylvania Association for Retarded Citizens v. Pennsylvania, 334 F. Supp. 1257 (E.D. Pa. 1971); 343, F. Supp. 279 (E.D. PA. 1972).

Reynolds, M. C., & Birch, J. N. (1977). *Teaching exceptional children in all of America's schools.* Reston, VA: Council for Exceptional Children.

Salisbury, C. L., & McGreger, G. (2002). The administrative climate and context of inclusive elementary schools. *Exceptional Children, 68,* 259–274.

Section 504, Rehabilitation Act of 1973, 29 U.S.C. § 794.

Stainback, W., & Stainback, S. (1995). Contemplating inclusive education from a historical perspective. In R. A. Villa, & J. S. Thousand (Eds.), *Creating an inclusive school* (pp. 16–27). Alexandria, VA: Association for Supervision and Curriculum Development.

Sullivan, K. A., Lantz, P. J., & Zirkel, P. A. (2000). Leveling the playing field or leveling the players? Section 504, the Americans with Disabilities Act and interscholastic sports. *The Journal of Special Education, 33,* 258–267.

Summers, J. A., Gavin, K., Purnell-Hall, T., & Nelsen, J. (2003). Family and school partnerships: Building bridges in general and special education. *Effective Education for Learners with Exceptionalities, 15,* 417–444.

Thousand, J. S., & Villa, R. A. (1995). Inclusion: Alive and well in the green mountain state. *Phi Delta Kappan, 77,* 288–291.

Timothy W. v. Rochester, New Hampshire, School District, 875 F.2d 954 (1st Cir. 1989).

U.S. Department of Education. (2005). Digest of Education Statistics, 2004. Retrieved November 21, 2005, from http://nces.ed.gov/programs/digest

U.S. Department of Education. (1996). Retrieved November 21, 2005, from National Center for Educational Statistics http://nces.ed.gov/programs/digest/

Will, M. C. (1986). Educating children with learning problems: A shared responsibility. *Exceptional Children, 52,* 411–415.

Yell, M. L. (2006). *The law and special education* (2nd ed.). Upper Saddle River, NJ: Prentice Hall.

Yell, M. L., Katsiyannas, A., & Shiner, J. G. (2006). The No Child Left Behind Act, adequate yearly progress, and students with disabilities. *Teaching Exceptional Children, 38*(4) 32–39.

Ysseldyke, J., Nelson, J. R., Christenson, S., Johnson, D. R., Dennison, A., Trieznberg, H., Sharpe, M., & Hawes, M. (2004). What we know and need to know about the consequences of high-stakes testing for students with disabilities. *Exceptional Children, 71,* 75–94.

Zigmond, N., Jenkins, J., Fuchs, D., Deno, S., & Fuchs, L. S. (1998). When students fail to achieve satisfactorily. *Phi Delta Kappan, 77*(4), 303–306.

Zirkel, P. A. (2003). Conducting legally defensible §504/ADA eligibility determinations. *Education Law Reporter, 176,* 1–11.

CHAPTER 2

PARENTS AS PARTNERS

CHAPTER PREVIEW

Focus

The IDEA requires that schools optimize parents' opportunity for participation in several aspects of their child's education. Conventional wisdom and best practice also suggest that the education of all children is more effective when teachers and parents work together to help the student achieve her or his learning and behavioral goals. A number of factors can impact the parent-school relationship. Among these factors are the previous experiences that parents have had with schools, teacher comfort and knowledge levels in working with parents, the amount of emphasis that the school places on fostering effective parent-teacher relationships, and the willingness of the school and parents to communicate frequently and honestly.

Rationale

Because parents have the greatest overall responsibility for their children, they are automatically involved in and concerned with their child's education. Their special knowledge of the child and commitment to his or her future make them valuable partners in providing successful education programs.

Legal Issues

The IDEA assures several rights to parents of children with disabilities, including that the parents

- must provide informed written consent before an initial evaluation and a reevaluation, before initial placement can take place, and before student education records are released to others;

- can expect to participate in team decisions involving their child's evaluation and determination of eligibility, the preparation of the child's IEP, and in the determination of the appropriate educational placement for their child;
- can expect that special education and related services contained in the IEP will be provided at no cost to the family;
- must be notified in advance (in their native language or mode of communication) each time the school proposes (or refuses) to initiate or change the child's identification, evaluation, program placement, or provision of a free appropriate public education;
- must be provided access to, and assured the confidentiality of, education records created and maintained by the school regarding their child;
- may contest any school decision they feel inappropriate or not in keeping with the law through mediation or an impartial due process hearing;
- can expect that the school district will notify them of their rights.

Approaches

Parent-school relationships can be positively impacted by a thorough knowledge of parent rights, best practices in working with parents, and sensitivity to the challenges often faced by parents of children with disabilities. Education leaders should make certain that they, as well as the teachers and staff in their schools, accept parents as equal partners in the education of their child. Educators should request information from parents that may be helpful, listen nonjudgmentally, and ask how the school can be of help to them. Frequent positive communication about school events, the student's progress, and other topics of common interest and concern should be maintained on a regular basis. School staff should be proactive and avoid waiting until a problem arises to initiate communication with parents. It is easier to deal with school problems when positive and nonthreatening communication has already taken place.

Educators must be sensitive to the subtleties of language, racial, cultural, and other diversity experienced in schools. Special school services to parents, such as discussion groups, workshops, and forums, can be beneficial.

Various school choice programs, such as charter schools, vouchers, and those inherent in some aspects of "No Child Left Behind" legislation present important, but manageable, challenges to educators in traditional school settings. Educators must be willing to listen and respond to family concerns in an appropriate and professional manner.

THE ROLE OF PARENTS

Giving birth to and raising a child with disabilities can be an extremely stressful experience replete with grief, guilt, fears, family disruptions, financial strains, and relentless hard work. The families of students with disabilities, just as surely as the students themselves, need help and support. Yet, it is striking how seldom they receive it.

Educators must be proactive in their work with parents. By the time the parents of children with disabilities have attended their first or second or tenth school conference, they may have good cause to be suspicious or defensive. In particular, educators should be sensitive to parents'

- stresses in raising a child with disabilities;
- previous negative experiences with professionals of various kinds;
- fears about school, based either on their own negative experiences or on the expectation that the schools as they knew them will be unable to accommodate their child (e.g., fears that the child will be teased and rejected, that the teacher will set unfair expectations and scold the child for not living up to them, or that the child will not be understood and appreciated).

Whether their child's disability is mild or severe, parents often experience emotions that are difficult to relate to immediately. Parents may have an emotional history of attempting to work unsuccessfully within systems, such as schools, human services, Medicaid, and social security. These parents have one or two particular events they return to time and time again as examples of service agency callousness and the cause of their frustration. For example, while one of the authors was serving as a child advocate for a high school student with a specific learning disability in reading and attention deficit/hyperactivity disorder, the boy's mother shared several photographs of her son's sixth-grade classroom desk. It had been placed in a back corner of the room and surrounded by large cardboard boxes to isolate the boy and prevent him from communicating with or even seeing anyone in the class. The painful memory of that one teacher's unprofessional actions toward her son would always be with that mother while advocating for him.

A frequently overlooked factor in educators working with parents of children with disabilities is the uniqueness that each family brings to the school. They exhibit differing levels of resiliency in the form of strength, determination, endurance, and persistence. Research indicates that family resiliency differences can be related to such matters as the severity of the disability, family structure, family income, and the presence or absence of challenging student behaviors (Ferguson, 2002).

A study conducted by Turnbull and Ruef (1997) is helpful in understanding the emotion and complexity of the family perspective. They found that siblings are often resentful, frustrated, and embarrassed by the challenge of a brother or sister with a disability. Extended family members did not feel connected to or comfortable around the child with a disability. Over half of the parents in the study expressed frustration and disappointment in attempting to participate in common family pursuits, such as religious activities, as a family. Over two-thirds of the families of children with problem behavior could not identify a single friend of their child's.

The same study also sought to learn about family members' perceptions of the teachers and administrators working with their child. A majority of the families in the study expressed concern and frustration over teacher participation because the teachers were considered unable to deal with important student issues. Parents considered teachers to be unwilling to change, defensive at suggestions posed by parents, too quick to give in to students with disabilities as a way of dealing with behavior problems, not forthcoming with concrete answers to parent questions, willing to give up too early on efforts with difficult students, and intimidated by students with serious behavior problems.

Four specific concerns with school administrators were expressed by families in the study: (a) inability to identify available resources, (b) constant "pushing" for a more restrictive placement, (c) failure to implement the IDEA properly, and (d) using the wrong administrative criteria for student placement (i.e., how many students are already in the class instead of which teacher will most likely succeed in helping the student). Only one family in the study praised the school administration because it had set the tone for an accepting school environment.

It cannot be denied that some educators contribute to parent anxieties and stresses. For a variety of reasons, some educators exhibit a

- lack of commitment to the least restrictive environment (especially inclusion);
- lack of knowledge, training, or experience;
- resistance to sharing education decision-making responsibility with parents.

Any of these factors can be perceived by parents. When they are detected, the result is a negative impact on the family's relations with the school.

In a review of results from several studies, Epstein (1995) concluded that good school-family relationships can be created where they did not previously exist. This is true because nearly all families, students, and teachers were found to believe that good school-family relationships are important in benefiting all students. Epstein concluded that nearly all

- families care about their children, want them to succeed, and are eager to obtain better information from schools and communities in order to remain good partners in their children's education;
- teachers and administrators would like to involve families, but many do not know how to build positive and productive programs and consequently are fearful about trying. Thus, educators are stuck in a "rhetoric rut," expressing support for partnerships without taking any action;
- students at all levels—elementary, middle, and high school—want their families to be more knowledgeable partners about schooling and are willing to take active roles in

maintaining good communication between home and school.

In a very important sense, the majority of parents of children with disabilities are strong supporters of school efforts on behalf of their children. This should not be overlooked by schools when reaching out to the community for support for programs or when conducting assessments of parent satisfaction. In a national survey, 84% of parents of children with disabilities responded in agreement with the statement, "My child's teachers really care about him/her as a person," and 77% responded in agreement with the statement, "My child's special ed team treats me like I'm part of the team" (Johnson & Duffett, 2002).

LEGAL ISSUES IN WORKING WITH PARENTS

As noted throughout this book, parents must be provided the opportunity to be involved in decision making in every major phase of the education of a child with a disability. As a result, it is important to identify a "parent" for each and every child with a disability. The 2004 Amendments to the IDEA define parent as "a natural, adoptive, or foster parent of a child (unless a foster parent is prohibited by state law from serving as a parent); a guardian; an individual acting in the place of a natural or adoptive parent with whom the child lives; an individual who is legally responsible for the child's welfare; or . . . an individual assigned . . . to be a surrogate parent" [20 U.S.C. § 1402(23)].

Persons Acting as Parents

When natural parents or legal guardians are not available, persons acting as parents of the child (e.g., grandparent, stepparent, or other responsible person with whom the child lives) or a person legally responsible for the child's welfare can carry out the rights and responsibilities given to "parents" under the IDEA. The exception is when the state or the state's appointed representative is the guardian. When the child is a ward of the state and not residing with a parent, the state must make reasonable efforts to obtain involvement from the parent. When parental rights have been terminated under state law or the parents cannot be located after a reasonable search, a surrogate parent must be appointed to participate in educational decision making (*34 C.F.R. § 300.519*). Foster parents may make educational decisions for the child without being appointed a surrogate, so long as state law does not prohibit foster parents from doing so.

When the wishes of persons acting as parents conflict with those of the natural parents whose rights have not been extinguished under law, the federal regulations are of little help. The position of OSEP is that state law should be consulted for the answer.

Surrogate Parents

Surrogate parents must be appointed for students with disabilities when no "parent" can be identified or located after a reasonable effort to discover the whereabouts of the parents, the child is a ward of the state under state law, or the child is a homeless youth not accompanied by the child's parent. A surrogate parent is a person appointed to represent the best interests of the child in matters related only to the identification, evaluation, placement, and provision of a free appropriate public education when the child needs special education. All other legal rights and duties remain with parents, guardians, or other legal custodians. A person appointed as a surrogate parent may not be an employee of the state education agency, the local school district, or any public agency that is involved in the education or care of the child. A surrogate may be an employee of a nonpublic agency that provides only non-educational care for the child when the person meets the other criteria for being a surrogate parent. The surrogate parent may not have any interests that conflict with the child's interests and must have adequate knowledge and skills to appropriately represent the child. The means of appointing, monitoring, training, and setting the terms of surrogate par-

ent appointments are determined by state law. When the child is a ward of the state, the judge overseeing the child's care may appoint a surrogate parent. Surrogate parents should be appointed within 30 days of the determination that a child needs a surrogate parent [*20 U.S.C. § 1415 (b) (2)*].

Parental Procedural Safeguards

Informed Written Consent The school must obtain the informed written consent of a parent prior to conducting an initial evaluation, a reevaluation, the initial provision of special education and related services (placement), and the release of confidential student education records. Parental consent is not required for administering a test that is given to all children, or before staff reviews of existing data.

The concept of "informed" written consent denotes a great deal of communicated information before the parent is requested to give consent. The parent must be fully informed, in the parent's native language when necessary, and understand all information relevant to the proposed activity. The notice and request for written consent sent to the parent must contain the seven content requirements found on pages 26–27 as well as an explanation of parent procedural safeguards found on page 29.

The parent must agree in writing to the school's carrying out of the activity proposed. A parent's mere signature without an affirmative statement of agreement consistent with actually giving consent does not imply consent.

Parents should understand that their consent may be revoked at any time; however, revocation of consent cannot be retroactive. Revocation of consent does not negate school action that has occurred following proper consent being given and before consent was revoked. For instance, revocation of consent is not effective for a change in educational placement already begun, does not require the return of education records previously transferred, and does not require that partially completed evaluations be discarded or ignored.

When parents refuse to give schools informed consent for an initial evaluation or reevaluation, the school has three options; it may: (a) acquiesce to the parent's refusal, (b) continue to work to gain the parent's confidence and consent while attempting modifications and accommodations in the regular classroom, or (c) file a request for mediation or due process hearing. School requests for mediation or due process hearing are made in the same manner in which parents begin the mediation or hearing process. After an opportunity for a hearing, a hearing officer may affirm or override parental objections to providing initial consent for evaluation or reevaluation.

With regard to reevaluations only, when the parent fails to respond to a school request for consent, without actually refusing to give consent, written consent for the reevaluation is not necessary. The school must, however, document that it has taken reasonable measures to obtain consent and the parent has failed to respond.

Parental refusal of written consent for initial provision of special education and related services (placement) cannot be challenged through a due process hearing, but the school may offer to mediate the issue. When the parent of a child with disabilities refuses to give consent for the initial provision of services to the child, the school is not required by law to provide the child special education and related services and is not required to develop an IEP for the child [*20 U.S.C. § 414 (a) (1) (D) (ii)*]. Those students should be treated as "general education" students for all purposes, including discipline (Letter to Grantwerk, 2003). Good faith efforts to meet the child's educational needs in the regular education classroom must continue.

Parental Participation in Meetings Parents must be provided a meaningful opportunity to participate in all formal school meetings regarding the identification, evaluation, and educational placement of their child, and the provision of FAPE. The meetings to which parent participation applies do not necessarily include school staff preparatory activities or informal conversations involving school personnel on issues such as daily teaching methodology, lesson plans, and coordination of services that are not specified in the IEP. Parents need not be invited to

school staff activities in the preparation of school proposals, or school responses to parent proposals, that will be discussed with parents at subsequent meetings.

Parents must be notified (orally or in writing) of formal meetings regarding the evaluation, identification, educational placement, and the provision of FAPE early enough to ensure their opportunity to attend. Although written notice of meetings is not required by law, written notice provides documentation of the invitation to parents and helps ensure meaningful parent participation. At a minimum, notice must indicate the purpose of the meeting, the time, the location, who will be in attendance (at least by title), and the potential participation of other persons with knowledge or special expertise regarding the child. All team meetings must be scheduled at a mutually agreed upon time and place.

Although the IDEA is very much a "procedural" law, the courts have not usually placed the importance of process higher than that of substance (Osborne, 2004). Courts have historically given schools a great deal of latitude in the implementation of the detailed procedural rights of parents required under the IDEA. However, school violations of parent procedural rights that result in the parent being deprived of meaningful participation in team decisions have been dealt with harshly.

Federal law expressly requires educators to do in meetings with parents what professional educators have done consistently over the years; they must listen to parents. Concerns and information provided by parents must be considered in all decision making. Educational evaluations obtained by the parents must receive a full and fair consideration by team members.

Generally, team decisions regarding evaluation, identification, the IEP, and placement may be made in the absence of parent participation, but only when the other appropriate team members are present and the school can document its reasonable effort to ensure parental involvement. Documentation could include school offers of telephone conference calls, home visits, or video conferencing (Osborne, 2004).

The school has the right to determine the extent of use of recording devices at meetings. However, the school may not prohibit the parent use of recording devices when a parent, for a variety of reasons, is unable to understand what occurs at IEP meetings (e.g., nervousness, personal disability). An audio or videotape recording should be allowed in those situations to ensure that the parents understand the decision-making process and their rights.

Prior Notice Requirement—Proposed Change

Throughout the initial evaluation, identification, IEP development, and placement processes, parents exercise control of their child's education status. Once a child has been identified, planned for, and placed in special education with parent consent, the school can exercise greater control over the child's education. This occurs through the school's initiation of changes, and school refusal of parent-requested changes.

Once the initial evaluation has been completed and the initial provision of services has begun with parental-informed written consent, additional parental consent is no longer required under federal law for subsequent decisions or changes involving the student's educational program. (State law may be different, and should be consulted.) The necessity of parent consent for reevaluations and release of student records remains.

Following initial placement in special education programs and services, federal law requires only that schools provide parents with a full, detailed written notice, in easily understandable language, regarding any school proposed change or refusal of a parent request for change. This required notice is similar in content to that required for the school's initial evaluation and initial placement request for written parent consent found later on this page. Following notice to parents, whether the parents are in full agreement or not, the school may proceed with the proposed change after waiting a reasonable amount of time. This brief delay in making changes allows parents the opportunity to consider the proposed change (or refusal) and to weigh requesting mediation or a due process hearing involving the proposed school action.

When a request for due process hearing is made by parents, the child's then current educational program cannot be changed until the issue is resolved, except with the mutual agreement of the parents and school. See "stay put" in *Chapter 11*.

The requirement of prior notice to parents applies each time the school proposes, or refuses a parent request, to initiate or change the identification, evaluation, educational placement, or the provision of FAPE to the child. For example, consider the situation where a 10th-grade student with a specific learning disability in reading is being provided an inclusive program in the regular classroom. Even with appropriate supplementary aids and services the child continues to struggle to the point of frustration in specific subjects, such as history and literature. During an annual IEP review, a suggestion may arise that the student's placement be changed to a special education or resource class for assistance with reading skills, especially as they apply to history and literature classes.

Even with unanimous agreement of the IEP team, including the parents, written notice of the proposed change should be provided to the child's parents within a reasonable amount of time prior to the change. The reasonableness of the amount of time would depend on all the circumstances involved (i.e., urgency owing to rapidly changing circumstances).

Notice Contents

The content requirements of the written notice to parents deserve careful attention because they are more detailed and lengthy than any other type of notice that schools typically provide parents. This notice must include:

1. A description of the action proposed or refused
2. An explanation of why the action is proposed or refused
3. A description of the other options considered and the reasons they were rejected
4. A description of each evaluation procedure, test, or observation used as a basis for the proposed or refused action

5. A description of any other factors relevant to the proposal or refusal

6. A reminder that parents have protections under procedural safeguards and a statement of where a copy of a description of the safeguards can be obtained. When notice is for initial referral for evaluation or initial provision of services, a copy of the parent safeguards must be provided

7. A list of sources from which parents can obtain assistance in understanding their rights (see *Parent Training and Information Centers and Community Parent Resource Centers* on page 36)

Education Records The confidentiality and accuracy of student information kept by the school is protected by the Family Educational Rights and Privacy Act [*FERPA; 34 C.F.R. Part 99, (2005)*] as well as by provisions of the IDEA. FERPA regulations apply to the education records of all students, not just those with disabilities.

Parent Access. Each school must allow parents, and their representatives, to inspect and review any education record relating to their child. Schools must comply with a parental request for access without unnecessary delay, especially prior to IEP meetings and hearings, but in no instance more than 45 days after a request has been made. The school must expect to provide explanations and interpretations of records when necessary, and provide copies when necessary to allow the parent to have full access to and inspection of the records. Reasonable fees for copying may be charged, except when charging a fee prevents reasonable access. Parents are presumed to have the right of access to their child's education records unless the school has received evidence of legal reasons to the contrary, such as a court order ending parental rights.

When a parent believes that information in a record is inaccurate, misleading, or in violation of privacy or other rights of a child, the parent may request that the record be amended. If the school refuses the request, it must advise the parent of the right to a hearing under local school policy. If, after a hearing, the school continues to refuse to amend the records, the parent must be advised of the right to place a written statement in the records giving their reasons for the disagreement. The parent statement must be kept in the student's records as long as the contested record is kept and must be disclosed to other persons each time the contested record is disclosed.

Confidentiality of Records. Each school must assure the confidentiality of education records and have policies and procedures for doing so. Parents must regularly be provided notice of such policies and procedures. With several exceptions similar to other education records, the school must be provided with informed written parental consent prior to the release of special education records to other persons.

Each school must keep a record (log) of all persons and agencies having access to the student's education records, except access by the parent, a party having written parent consent, and school employees having a legitimate educational interest in the student. School employees accessing a student's record without a legitimate educational interest must make a record of their access and have the parent's written consent. The log must show the name of the person, date, and the purpose of the access to the records. Only the parent and persons responsible for maintaining the record of access may see the log containing the names of persons who have previously reviewed the student's education records.

Although parent rights with regard to education records not used for special education are transferred to students upon turning age 18 or on the student's attendance at a postsecondary educational institution, under the IDEA special education records are treated differently. Only when state law provides for the transfer of IDEA parent rights to the student at the age of majority, may students exercise former parental rights over their own special education records.

Documents regarding a student's disciplinary records may be transmitted to the same extent discipline records of nondisabled students are transmitted in the state, especially when they are relevant to the safety of the student or other persons. If a state requires the transmission of disciplinary records between schools, then the student's records must also include both the current IEP and any statement regarding disciplinary action taken against the child.

State law may allow or require the release of education records necessary for the juvenile justice system to effectively provide services to a student under its jurisdiction prior to adjudication. Officials receiving the education record must provide assurances that information will not be disclosed to third parties, except as authorized under state law.

Some confusion has arisen over the release of education records that may include health or medically related matters. These could include immunization records, records of occupational or physical therapy, student health plans attached to IEPs, and some Section 504 accommodation plans. The confusion arose over interpretations that the exceedingly complex and restrictive Health Insurance Portability and Accountability Act of 1996 (HIPAA) applies to school education records containing medically related information. The Family Policy Compliance Office, the agency that interprets FERPA, has issued an interpretative letter which states that HIPAA's restrictive regulations do not apply to student education records kept by schools (Letter to Holloway, 2004).

Directory Information. Directory information includes education record data that generally would not be considered harmful or invasion of privacy if disclosed. It includes, but is not limited to: name; address; telephone listing; electronic mail address; photograph; date and place of birth; major field of study; participation in officially recognized activities and sports; weight and height of members of athletic teams; dates of attendance; grade level; enrollment status; degrees; honors and awards received; and the most recent previous school attended. Schools may release "directory information" regarding students without the written consent of the parents when two conditions are met: The school must annually advise all parents that it may

release directory information regarding students, and it must allow parents a reasonable time to object in writing to the release of directory information regarding their child. Schools need not include all directory items in their local policy if they do not wish to release them.

A school that has not adopted a directory information policy must obtain the written consent of parents to release what otherwise would be directory information.

Different Treatment of Records. Under the IDEA and FERPA, schools must generally treat student education records of students both with and without disabilities the same. However, the IDEA requires a few differences in the handling of student education records that are additional to FERPA requirements. Under the IDEA, the school

- must provide parents, on request, a list of the types and locations of education records collected, maintained, or used by the school;
- must designate a person to assume responsibility for ensuring education record confidentiality;
- must maintain for public inspection a current listing of the names and positions of employees who may have access to student education records;
- must inform parents when special education records on a student are no longer needed to provide services to the student;
- must destroy special education records when requested by the parents following receipt of the school's notice that records are no longer needed;
- may maintain indefinitely information necessary to identify the student's record while at that school (permanent record);
- must comply in a timely manner with a parent's request to see their child's records prior to any IEP meeting or due process hearing;
- must provide training to all persons collecting or using education records on IDEA students;
- must transfer, to the extent permitted by FERPA, copies of a student's special education and disciplinary records to appropriate authorities when reporting a crime committed by a child with a disability.

Public Notice Schools must provide parents with a published annual notice of a description of the students on whom personally identifiable information is maintained in school records, the types of information kept, the methods of gaining information, and the uses to be made of the information. Schools must also provide a summary of school policies and procedures regarding disclosure to third parties, storage, retention, and destruction of personally identifiable student information. Parents must receive a description of all parental rights regarding education records.

Procedural Safeguards Notice

A written notice of all procedural safeguards must be provided to parents in a language or manner understood by the parents. The notice need be provided parents only once a year. However, a copy must also be provided when the school requests written consent for the initial evaluation (even at parent request), upon the first occurrence of the filing of a request for due process hearing by either the parent or the school, and upon a parent request for a copy. Schools may also place a current copy of parent procedural safeguards on its internet website, if one exists [*20 U.S.C. § 1415 (d)*]. When notice of procedural safeguards to parents is required, it must contain a full explanation of each of the following procedural safeguards:

1. Independent educational evaluation (*Chapter 3*)
2. Prior written notice (pp. 26–27)
3. Parental consent (pp. 24–25)
4. Access to education records (p. 27)
5. Opportunity to initiate due process hearings, including the time limitation in which to make a complaint, the opportunity for the school to resolve the complaint, and the availability of mediation; and state complaint procedures, including the difference between them and due process complaints (*Chapter 11*)
6. The availability of mediation (*Chapter 11*)
7. Student's placement during due process hearings (*Chapter 11*)

8. Interim alternative education setting procedures (*Chapter 9*)
9. Requirements for parent unilateral placement in private schools at public expense (*Chapter 5*)
10. Due process hearing procedures (*Chapter 11*)
11. State-level appeals, if applicable (*Chapter 11*)
12. Civil actions (*Chapter 11*)
13. Attorney's fees (*Chapter 11*)

THE IMPORTANCE OF GOOD COMMUNICATION WITH PARENTS

Parents of children with disabilities must be considered equal partners in the educational process. Parents who appear disinterested in their child's educational programming cannot, for the sake of the child, be disregarded by educators. Positive working relationships between parents and educators are vital to the child's success in school. The key to productive school-parent relationships is good two-way communication. Parents should never be "talked down to" or made to feel that they are less than equals in the educational planning for their child. Instead, parents must be consulted regularly about their expectations and goals for the future as well as their child's educational needs.

Researchers at the University of Kansas have identified six indicators of professional behavior that contribute to successful collaborative partnerships with parents: engaging in frequent, open and honest communication in a sensitive manner; demonstrating commitment and dedication to the child's best interest; working from a position of equality of persons; exercising skills to make things happen for the child; creating a sense of trust; and maintaining a sense of mutual respect (Blue-Banning, Summers, Frankland, Nelson, & Beegle, 2004).

Methods and Frequency

Parents of exceptional children need to know that their involvement is welcomed by the school, just as their youngsters are welcome. A good school climate is established when communication with parents occurs frequently and stresses positive, as well as troublesome, aspects of the child's school experience. It is easier to deal with problems when positive communication, or at least nonthreatening communication that does not elicit negative emotions from parents, has already taken place. A teacher whose communication goes no further than necessary paperwork and crisis calls to discuss misbehavior should expect parents to build up negative associations with school contact. Such negative associations are not conducive to a good cooperative relationship.

Educators should seek out opportunities to introduce themselves to parents and listen to the goals and expectations that parents have for their children. Some examples include:

• A letter of introduction to parents before the school year begins and a handbook of school class policies and practices sent home the first week or even before school starts
• Contact with parents early in the year to see whether they have any skills they would like to share or ways they would like to help (a questionnaire is useful)
• Daily or weekly report cards under certain conditions (sociability, behavior, or academics)
• Awards or acknowledgments of positive behavior and achievements
• Periodic newsletters for all parents and students (each student must be recognized at some point during the school year)
• Telephone calls, e-mails, or conferences to share positive information about the student
• A stated time when parents are especially welcome
• Invitations to parents to come see new or special projects
• Notifications to local news media about school activities of special interest
• School programs and workshops scheduled at times when all parents could be invited to attend
• A practice of sending all school communications home with students each Monday; this provides time until Friday for parents to return necessary papers and offers the school an opportunity to send home positive news each week
• Workshops on parenting skills, such as how to help with homework

Grande (2004) has reported on a succesful parent involvement project in the primary grades. First-, second-, and third-grade students were provided bookbags of literacy materials and library games and activities for use by the parents in working with their children at home. The results indicated that the planned activities and materials aided parent understanding of the school's expectations of student growth for specific age and grade levels and brought the parents, students, and school closer together. The home learning activities were considered enjoyable by both parents and their children.

Dardig (2005) has identified 15 activities to establish better school-parent relationships, including workshops, individual student progress reports, and recommending resources, such as internet website addresses. But, she emphasizes that the beginning place for an individual educator wanting to improve and maintain good teacher-parent communication is the development of a personal philosoply statement. The statement should document their understanding of the role of parents of children with disabilities and how the educator will relate to and assist parents.

Pogoloff (2004) has stressed the importance of building a positive and trusting relationship between parents and staff. Among other specific suggestions, she suggests that every parent conversation begin with a positive statement and a special effort be made to communicate good news on a regular basis. Parents will thus look forward to speaking with school staff and engaging in problem-solving activities, and negative information will be easier for all concerned. Pogoloff also recommends interacting with families in multiple environments as much as possible and demonstrating an interest and respect for the child as a person, not merely as a school student. Families and students have interests much broader than school and they respect school staff with similar broad interests. One especially good Pogoloff suggestion is never to send a formal notice home without first consulting with the parents and informing them of the background and purpose of the notice. Formal communication from school can be intimidating and add to already complex and confusing situations.

Davern (2004) strongly recommends the use of a notebook that the student carries between home and school for improved communication. Both the parents and teacher can send messages about how the child is progressing, events that are taking place at home or school, health concerns, homework assignments, and the child's day or evening. She recommends that teachers guard against communicating excessive trivia or a preponderance of bad news and problems. She believes that parents desire a balanced approach to good news and areas of concern. Parent communication through notebooks is most effective when parents are asked beforehand how they wish to communicate, what types of information are most meaningful, and how often they wish to communicate.

Some educators have provided parents with videotapes of their children in the context of classroom activities. The videotapes allow parent participation in observing and monitoring their child's progress on IEP goals. As a result of videotapes, parents were better able to observe their child outside the family setting, understand discussions at parent-teacher conferences, and participate more fully in IEP reviews (Hundt, 2002).

Recognizing that the support of family members is important to successful inclusive programs, Salend (2006) recommends that schools provide families with education sessions that provide understanding of the purposes and local practices involved in inclusive programs. Such programs need to be well planned, implemented with the needs of families in mind, evaluated, and the evaluations used to improve the programs for regular use.

Educators' Attitudes and Communication Skills

To be effective in communicating with parents, educators must be attentive to and honest about their own attitudes toward the students and their families. Successful cooperation requires attitudes of mutual trust, respect, acceptance, and sharing. Positive school-parent relationships are not reinforced when educators view parents as clients or patients, the cause of the child's disability, adversaries, or intellectual inferiors. Educators who view the parent conference solely as an opportunity to deliver information—rather than sharing with equals—can expect problems.

In a review of theory and research articles related to parental involvement in their children's education, Hoover-Dempsey and Sandler (1997) concluded that effective school parental involvement programs are positively related to strong parental support both for their children's schools and for student achievement. Schools must take parental contributions and involvement seriously before any school program to increase parental involvement will be successful.

For parents of secondary school children, researchers recommend hiring someone professionally prepared to facilitate increased communication about teachers' learning goals, activities, and specific suggestions for parental help at school and at home. Efforts at improving high-level involvement of parents are most effective when directed at all segments of the school community, regardless of socioeconomic level (Summers, Gavan, Purnell-Hall, & Nelson, 2003).

In their work, Bennett, DeLuca, and Bruns (1997) learned that inclusion planning by teams of parents and educators presents especially difficult challenges to cooperation. They found that although many parents of children with disabilities had positive attitudes toward inclusion and voiced strong opinions, many teachers, especially those with many years of teaching experience, were found to have significantly less positive attitudes toward inclusion. They also found that teachers tended to express preference for limited parent involvement, parents not questioning teachers' expertise, and parents not becoming active advocates for their children. The researchers also found that as parents became greater advocates for their children, the natural, if not preventable, result was a decline in parent/educator working relationships. This poses the question of how much introspection educators need to use when efforts to work cooperatively with parents break down and go badly.

Bennett, DeLuca, and Bruns suggest the following useful techniques and school staff behaviors in planning for successful inclusion (p. 129):

- Start where the parent is and realize that this may not be the same place as the teacher is in terms of goals for the student.
- Listen for common understandings with the parents.
- Bring up concerns in an honest way in order to problem-solve together.
- Respond to parent concerns by working with the parents to see how these concerns may be approached at both home and school.
- Communicate an attitude of acceptance of the child and a genuine desire and commitment to make inclusion work.
- Focus on the child's strengths.
- Realize that social concerns are very important to parents.
- Access resources needed to make inclusion work.
- Demonstrate the personal qualities of flexibility and open-mindedness.
- Be determined and committed to make inclusion work.

Educators frequently take for granted that parents are in the same place they are in terms of thinking and planning. Then, without taking parent considerations into account in working for specific solutions, educators push on ahead without parent understanding or support. Imagine the disastrous results of using sometimes expensive assistive technology devices with children when family attitudes, interests, and values are not taken into account. In situations where events are changing, both parents and educators need a regular exchange of reliable information in order to prevent the waste of scarce educational resources (Parette & McMahon, 2002).

One obvious way to establish sensitivity of school staff members in parent perspectives is to conduct formal surveys of parents' attitudes and perceptions regarding school programs. Sharing survey results with staff and parents, jointly analyzing concerns, planning possible solutions, and identifying resources can begin to build a lasting understanding of each others' perspectives (Salend & Duhaney, 2002). Student homework also appears to be a good focus for parent-school collaboration. Parents and teachers can communicate their expectations and individual needs and jointly determine how to monitor successful homework plans (Bos, Nahmias, & Urban, 1999). Regular planned written communication regarding homework assignments, accommodations, responsibilities, and conferences is highly recommended by regular education teachers (Hall, Wolfe, & Bollig, 2003).

An area of specialized focus for communication concerns might be with parents of students experiencing especially troublesome behaviors. The developers of a model project for increasing school involvement for families of students with emotional and behavioral disabilities developed the following suggestions for improving parent-teacher communication:*

- Maintain a positive and cheery demeanor when working with parents.
- Meet in a comfortable room with furniture that fits adults while recognizing that school may be an uncomfortable setting for parents.
- Provide snacks whenever possible. Feed the mind and body.
- Provide everyone an opportunity to speak.
- Facilitate meetings; don't monopolize or preach to one another.
- Don't interpret behavior as attacking; consider behavior of all involved as that of concern for the student.
- Encourage parents to share their expertise with the group. Ask them to bring background material about their child to the group.
- Build on individual strengths and develop plans based on these strengths.
- Try not to dwell on problems. Use problem-solving to generate solutions.
- Use lots of praise and encouragement, and stay optimistic in meetings.

- Listen, listen, listen and engage parents as equal partners.

Cultural Considerations

Special care and attention must be given to working with parents of culturally and linguistically diverse students (See *Chapter 14*). Their needs may sometimes differ from other parents for a variety of reasons, and a concerted effort may be needed to understand their perceptions and preferred method of communication with the school. Cultural differences vary widely regarding values, beliefs, and expectations. Schools must be assured that their goals and actions are not at cross purposes with family cultural differences (Summers et al., 2003).

Using data from a nationally representative database, Neely-Barnes and Marcenko (2004) have determined that the impact of a childhood disability in families is variable among different racial and ethnic groups. As a result, they recommend that educators remember that racial groups differ in their needs, and flexibility must be maintained in the provision of services.

Native American values especially contrast with those of mainstream American schools. Their view of the importance of tribe and extended family events may conflict with regular school attendance. A child residing with many different relatives over time may not be understood, and sharing with others being more prized than competition may be considered abnormal. Time is considered in the present and long-term goals and timed tests do not hold meaning for many Native American students. The failure to give appropriate attention to Native American values can quickly bring about negative educational results (Garrett, Bellon-Harn, Torres-Rivera, Garrett, & Roberts, 2003).

Immigrant parents may have difficulty with language, and educators need to be sensitive to IDEA procedures, forms, and educational jargon that cannot be resolved by good translation (Al-Hassan & Gardner, 2002). As a first step, teachers and administrators should work with parents in an effort to better develop commonality of understanding in important areas. These would include an understanding of and knowl-

edge about the child's disability, alternatives for dealing with the child's disability and the preferred manner in which to do so, and the preferred method and frequency of communication between school and home (Linan-Thompson & Jean, 1997). Educators should also attempt to improve their knowledge of and sensitivity toward cultural diversity and recognize many parents' lack of understanding of American school systems, special education, and written materials (Craig, Hull, Haggart, & Perez-Selles, 2000).

The understanding of cultural differences often can be used to improve appropriate family communication and planning. Acceptance and understanding of parents' beliefs can lessen parents' feeling that they need to hide their traditional beliefs for educators (Lamorey, 2002). The cultural patterns of South and Southeast Asian Americans are a good example. Their showing of respect for persons in authority, avoidance of freely expressing their thoughts and feelings, and respect for family members' privacy may be misinterpreted and have potential impact on their particpation in school matters, including special education.

In some cultures it may be desirable for the school to enlist the help and support of a well-respected community leader to serve as liaison and facilitator until trust and understanding are strengthened between home and school. When extended family is a cultural characteristic, those persons who often care for the child should be involved along with parents in school conferences and planning (Parette & Petch-Hogan, 2000).

Good decisions for children require educators who are aware of and sensitive to cultural patterns differing from their own. Recognizing the diversity of cultural traits and making appropriate adjustments will lead to better educational programming for the child (Mathews, 2000).

PARENT SERVICES

Many parents of children with disabilities are likely to look to schools as an important—perhaps the most important—source of help in raising their children. Parents often cannot, however, be equal partners in the education of their children without schools considering the parental need for preparation and support (Summers et al., 2003). In addition to scheduling conferences to discuss individual student needs, many schools offer more intensive services and structured parent activities, including family counseling and referrals, parent advisory committees, parent-to-parent support groups, and parent training programs and workshops (Bailey & Smith, 2000).

Student IEPs may, when desired, expressly provide for parent counseling and training as a related service and thereby assist parents in becoming empowered through knowledge, understanding, and skill building. This, in turn, will help parents support school efforts while the child is in the home environment.

Other types of services that can provide family support have been recommended by Sussell, Carr, and Hartman (1996):*

- Parent Advisory Committee newsletter
- List of community resources (e.g., human resources, advocacy, and self-help)
- Lists of state and national organizations of interest to families with special needs
- Information folders on different disabilities for distribution to, or reference by, parents and staff
- A file containing articles of special interest to parents
- Parent access to instructional materials
- Parent invitation to participate in staff development activities
- Staff development programs regarding the "changing role of parents"
- Establishment of parent support groups
- Regular education students educated regarding persons with disabilities
- Establishment of respite care opportunities

School-planned meetings with parents may take many forms, including informal sessions

planned and run by parents in their home, school-wide conferences organized by administration to inform parents of policies or solicit their help in developing school policies, Parent-Teacher Association (PTA) events, and special interest groups small enough to encourage parents to speak and share. The two general topics of most importance to parents are how to help their children successfully progress in school and how to be more effective parents. These two universally important topics can be used as the central focus for providing supporting activities to parents.

Donley and Williams (1997) have reported on a family education program in a school that involves family members observing their children regularly in school, developing data sets on their own child's progress, and then creating a poster presentation for sharing the year's activities and growth with other parents as an end-of-the-year group activity.

Some educators suggest regular monthly telephone calls to parents. The goal is to seek parents' questions and concerns and give parents a regular opportunity to talk about their child without being encumbered by negative messages from school. Some schools have experimented with telephone voice messaging systems where teachers and principals can leave either general or child-specific messages for parents. Parents, in turn, can leave questions and comments in teacher and principal voice mail. Programs using voice mail can be established on a district-wide basis, or tailor-made for improving communication between the school and specific families. Researchers have found that parents of children in special education programs have made greater use of messaging systems than other groups of parents (Morris, Kay, Fitzgerald, & Miller, 1997).

An indirect service to parents might include planned activities with and for the siblings of students with disabilities. Siblings have many questions that deserve answers, needs that should be met, and perspectives that need understanding. A variety of sibling activities and workshops can be undertaken that will result in a stronger school-family partnership (Cramer et al., 1997).

---

*From "Families R Us: Building a Parent/School Partnership," by A. Sussel, S. Carr, & A. Hartman, 1996, *Teaching Exceptional Children, 28*(4), p. 55. Copyright 1996 by the Council for Exceptional Children. Adapted by permission.

For parents of students in culturally or linguistically diverse schools, the schools can provide many programs that have multiple benefits for the school and community. Parent education programs can be established that are designed to teach English as a second language, basic reading, mathematics, and reasoning skills to improve parents' functional skills and sense of self-worth. Such programs can be developed to ensure that parents and schools become equal partners in problem-solving discussions about students.

Awareness training programs that utilize role playing and simulations can be used to build parent confidence and understanding in their relationship with school personnel. Employment opportunities for parents, such as paraeducators, can help ensure a bond between schools and their culturally and linguistically diverse communities (Craig et al., 2000; Sileo, Sileo, & Prater, 1996).

The negative impact of poverty on the quality of family life cannot be underestimated. About one quarter of children with disabilities live in families where the total family income is below the poverty level as defined by the federal government. Those families deserve to receive services from various agencies to meet their many advanced needs. No one agency can expect to meet them alone. Schools are in a unique position to create agency partnerships for providing services to meet the needs of poor children, with and without disabilites, and their families (Park, Turnbull, & Turnbull, 2002).

Bernheimer, Weisner, and Lowe (2003) have determined that families living in poverty with at least one child with significant problems (achievement and/or behavior problems and/or disabilities) deserve special consideration from a service agency perspective. The family's daily lives are made difficult from the cumulative and interactive effects of few resources, the altered ability to be regularly gainfully employed, health concerns and expenses due to the lack of insurance, and the various stresses and strains resulting from one or more children with significant problems. Their level of adaptation and resiliency is lower than the middle class and deserve an adequate variety of benefits and services from schools and other agencies in order to mitigate other family problems.

Fox and colleagues (2002) have recommended that due to the broad and pervasive role that a child's behavior can have on the entire family, that families of children with serious behavior problems be given special attention. Family interventions need to involve a family-centered partnership of schools and other community agencies taking into account the needs of all family members. Lessenberry and Rehfeldt (2004) have concluded from their review of research that parental stress levels resulting from their child's disabilities have a significant influence on the child's development. They recommend the regular assessment of parent stress levels during a child's education. This is to provide individualized parent support services to assist in lowering their stress level and allowing the parent to play a more productive role in the overall development of the child at home and at school.

Parents must be respected as individuals. Educators cannot expect all parents to want to participate equally or to take advantage of all the services the school has arranged, particularly if such arrangements are made without asking parents what help they feel they need. Until parents perceive a need for advice or assistance, they may not listen. Furthermore, too many offers of help can be overwhelming and a burden in themselves.

Some schools and intermediate educational agencies feel so strongly about the importance of the school relationship with parents that programs of assistance and cooperation have become formalized and made part of the agency structure. The Parent Education Partnership (PEP) Program at one intermediate educational service agency maintains a local parent support group list of over 35 area parent, parent-educator, and disability-specific support groups and their primary contact persons so that agency staff can help parents locate parent peer-support.

The PEP Program provides a resource library and staff of trained parents and educators who are willing to assist other parents and educators in their efforts to communicate and understand each other. Some local school districts that make up the agency also have appointed "Parent Partners" to assist parents and local groups in identifying additional information resources and support (Grant Wood Area Education Agency, 1997).

PARENT TRAINING AND INFORMATION CENTERS AND COMMUNITY PARENT RESOURCE CENTERS

Every state has a federally funded parent training and information center, and many communities have federally funded parent resource centers to provide information and training to parents of children with disabilities at no cost. The centers ensure that children with disabilities and their parents receive training and information designed to assist the children in meeting developmental and functional goals, including academic achievement goals, and to assist them in leading productive independent adult lives. The centers provide children and their parents training on their rights and responsibilities under the law and the development of skills desirable to effectively participate in planning and decision making. The centers help ensure that parents, educators, and school staff have appropriate technology and technical assistance and information to help improve the educational results for children with disabilitles and their families (*20 U.S.C. § 1470*). The information centers are nonprofit and run by boards of directors with a majority of the directors being parents of children with disabilities. Other board members are people working in special education and related fields and people with disabilities. The centers view parents as full partners in the educational process and provide parents with information on disabilities, their legal rights, and practical strategies for advocating for their child. By stressing working cooperatively with educators, centers help parents become a source of assistance and support to other parents. In many states, training and information centers contract with the state educational agency to provide individuals to meet with parents to explain the mediation process as a viable method of dispute resolution. In cooperation with other private and public agencies, parent training and information centers generate and distribute informational materials. (Visit the Technical Assistance Alliance for Parent Centers' Web site at http://www.taalliance.org/centers/index.htm)

Community parent resource centers provide similar functions to those of the information centers but are more focused on networking with community agencies. In that way, they ensure that underserved low income, limited English proficient parents, and parents with disabilities have the training and knowledge to help their children with disabilities develop and meet academic and functional goals leading to productive and independent adult lives (*20 U.S.C. § 1472*). The resource centers are expected to establish partnerships with information centers, but focus their activities on families in the community that are significantly isolated from traditional sources of information and supports.

SCHOOL CHOICE AND ITS IMPLICATIONS

School choice (e.g., open enrollment, charter schools, vouchers) has gained popularity as a "school reform" issue, especially among politicians, while little solid research has been completed to help verify its validity. When parents exercise choice options, local public schools lose in numerous ways that extend beyond reduction in local school revenues. When children with disabilities transfer, schools lose the opportunity to have strong school support in the community from parents who are often the most concerned for their children and the most loyal to those who understand their children's needs. Schools whose staff members are committed to listening to parent concerns and working collaboratively with parents in an effort to meet the needs of their students will build a strong foundation of community support for the local schools.

A group of researchers at the University of Minnesota has studied the "open enrollment" form of school choice and its impact on students with disabilities. The study was conducted with the primary purpose of gaining a better understanding of parent motivations for transferring their children with disabilities through the Minnesota open enrollment choice program (Lang, Ysseldyke, & Lehr, 1997). A total of 12% of the 19,000 Minnesota students transferring to another school district in the 1995–96 school year were students with disabilities. The resulting data and analysis say a great deal about how some local schools are failing to meet the needs of students with disabilities and the expectations of parents. Researchers learned that Minnesota parents who made the difficult choice to open enroll their children with disabilities outside the district of residence expressed unmet needs of their children in the local resident district as justification for their decision to take their children elsewhere for their education. Those expressed unmet needs included:

- Access to education programs in an inclusive setting with appropriate accommodations and adaptations to provide real access
- Opportunities for personal and social adjustment among role-modeling peers where friendships and sense of belonging is fostered
- A warm, positive, supportive environment that values every child
- Good two-way, respectful communication between home and school

The researchers recommended that each school district determine the reasons for local parental decisions to transfer their children and communicate those findings to all school personnel. With that knowledge, school staff can examine and improve home-school communications and improve the provision of student accommodations and modifications. School leaders should regularly evaluate school climate and attempt to establish a more positive learning environment, determine whether all students are being challenged, and help school personnel to be more sensitive to the needs of children with disabilities and their families.

Another type of parent choice will require similar close attention and sensitivity to the needs of families of children with disabilities. Under "No Child Left Behind" (NCLB) legislation, schools must make adequate yearly progress (AYP) in student academic performance. When a school, previously determined to be in need of improvement, fails to make AYP in the second year, parents must be notified that they have the option of transferring their child to another public school not indentified as being in need of improvement. For students receiving programs and services under the IDEA, the public school choice option of the parent must continue to provide FAPE to the student. When a school fails to make AYP for three or more years, the school must make supplemental services available to enable students to attain proficiency in meeting state academic standards. Failure to make AYP for five years can result in the school being reorganized and staff employment terminated.

CONCLUSION

From its inception over 30 years ago, the IDEA has placed the importance of parent involvement front and center in special education programming for children with disabilities. The 1997 Amendments to the IDEA greatly strengthened the philosophy of collaboration, rather than independent unilateral school action, by providing for increased parental participation in the decision-making processes, especially evaluation and placement. Even more important is the knowledge and experience of educators regarding how the successful education of children, both with and without disabilities, is a cooperative effort between home, school, and community. When any one of those factors is diminished, omitted, overlooked, or ignored, education efforts are much less likely to be successful.

By setting a tone of empathy, cooperation, and respect for parents, and providing committed leadership in meeting the practical and philosophical goals of the IDEA, educational leaders can establish strong and significant community support for schools through their thoughtful and professional delivery of education programs and services.

Educators must treat parents and families of children with disabilities as they themselves wish to be treated. Anything less diminishes us all.

VIEW FROM THE COURTS

Amanda S. v. Webster City Community School District, (1998) (notice is important for meaningful parent participation in meetings). After observing Amanda S. act in an inappropriate and disruptive manner in a middle-school classroom, school officials orally asked the parents to attend an IEP meeting the next day. At the meeting, the team, including the parents, agreed to change Amanda's IEP and her educational placement to a more restrictive environment in another school district. Later that day, the parents telephoned school officials and advised them that they had changed their minds and did not want a change in Amanda's IEP or placement. The school proceeded to make the changes, and the parents challenged the school's action in federal court.

The court ruled that the school's lack of express notice to the parents that the purpose of the meeting was to consider a change in the IEP and to change placement to a more restrictive placement setting in another school district, and the lack of express notice to the parents regarding who would be present at the meeting, deprived the parents of meaningful participation in the decision. The team decision was reversed.

Taylor v. Vermont Department of Education (2002) (effect of legal loss of parental rights). The natural mother of a student with disabilities brought suit against a school and the State Department of Education as a noncustodial parent under a state court divorce and custody decree. The decree had awarded the father custody and sole educational decision-making authority. The mother alleged that the school and state agency had illegally denied her request for an independent educational evaluation for her daughter under the IDEA, and denied her the right to request a due process hearing to challenge that decision. The father opposed the due process hearing. The Court of Appeals for the Second Circuit found that the natural mother's right to make educational decisions for her daughter was based in state law. Because the mother's educational decision-making rights had been removed under state law, she did not qualify as a "parent" under the IDEA. As a result, the mother had no legal standing to challenge the local school or state department's decisions refusing to grant her a due process hearing under the IDEA.

RECOMMENDED READINGS

Al-Hussan, S., & Gardner, R. (2002). Involving immigrant parents of students with disabilities in the educational process. *Teaching Exceptional Children, 34*(5), 52–58. This article provides specific recommendations for involving immigrant parents in the education of their children.

Brandes, J. (2005). Partner with parents. *Intervention in School and Clinic, 41*, 52–54. This article provides 20 specific suggestions on ways to partner with parents.

Dabkowski, D. M. (2004). Encouraging active parent participation in IEP team meetings. *Teaching Exceptional Children, 36*(3), 34–39. This article provides specific recommendations on assessing and improving the particpation of parents in IEP team meetings.

Evans, A. (2003). Empowering families, supporting students. *Educational Leadership, 61*(2), 35–37. This article provides suggestions on the improvement and maintenance of parent participation in their child's education.

Garrett, M. T., Bellen-Hern, M. L., Torres-Rivera, E., Garrett, J. T., & Roberts, L. C. (2003). Open hands, open hearts: Working with native youth in the schools. *Intervention in School and Clinic, 38*, 225–235. This article provides excellent advice on working with families of Native American students.

Hundt, T. A. (2002). Videotaping young children in the classroom: Parents as partners. *Teaching*

Exceptional Children, 34(3), 38–43. The article suggests an excellent strategy for improvement of parent participation in their child's education.

Lamorey, S. (2002). The effects of culture on special education services: Evil eyes, prayer meetings, and IEP. *Teaching Exceptional Children, 34*(5), 67–71. This article discusses the many implications that cultural diversity has on the delivery of special education programs.

Mathews, R. (2000). Cultural patterns of South Asian and Southeast Asian Americans. *Intervention in School and Clinic, 36*, 101–104. This article identifies cultural differences of many Asian-American families and their implications for educators.

Relevant Federal Regulations

34 C. F. R. Part 99 (2005) Student records (FERPA).

34 C. F. R. Part 300 Assistance to States for the Education of Children with Disabilities [70 Fed. Reg., 35,833–35,880 (June 21, 2005)].

§ 300.30	Parent.
.132	Provision of services for parentally placed private school children with disabilities—basic requirement.
.148	Placement of children by parents if FAPE is at issue.
.229	Disciplinary information.
.300	Parental consent.
.322	Parent participation.
.500	Responsibility of State Education Agency (SEA) and other public agencies.
.501	Opportunity to examine records; parent participation in meetings.
.502	Independent educational evaluation.
.504	Procedural safeguards notice.
.519	Surrogate parents.
.613	Access rights.
.614	Record of access.
.615	Records on more than one child.
.616	List of types and locations of information.
.617	Fees.
.618	Amendment of records at parent's request.
.619	Opportunity for a hearing.
.620	Result of hearing.
.621	Hearing procedures.
.622	Consent.
.623	Safeguards.
.624	Destruction of information.
.625	Children's rights.
.626	Enforcement.

SELECTED WEBSITES

Code of Federal Regulations–Government Printing Office
http://www.gpoaccess.gov/cfr/index.html

The Parent Advocacy Coalition of Educational Rights (PACER)
http://www.pacer.org

The Technical Assistance Alliance for Parent Centers (The Alliance)
http://www.taalliance.org/centers/index.htm

Families and Advocates Partnership for Education (FAPE)
http://www.fape.org

Citizen's Alliance to Uphold Special Education
http://www.causeonline.org

Disability Rights Education and Defense Fund
http://www.dredf.org

Special Needs Advocate for Parents (SNAP)
http://www.snapinfo.org

Reed Martin J.D.
http://www.reedmartin.com

Center for Law and Education
http://www.cleweb.org/issues/rights.htm

Office of English Language Acquistion–U.S. Department of Education
http://www.ed.gov/about/offices/list/oela/index.html

U.S. Department of Education—Office of Special Education and Rehabilitative Service
http://www.ed.gov/about/offices/list/osers/index.html

Internet Resources for Special Education
http://www.irsc.org

Alta Vista's Translation
http://www.world.altavista.com

Council for Exceptional Children
http://www.cec.sped.org

QUESTIONS FOR THOUGHT

1. Why have some educators denied parents full and equal decision-making participation regarding students?
2. Why does the IDEA provide so many procedural safeguards for parents and so few for schools?
3. Should surrogate parents be appointed for children with disabilities whose parents show little or no interest in their child's education?
4. Why do educators need to be sensitive to the parents' "history" of working with various agencies?
5. Why are good school and parent partnerships a concern in special education when research has long established that parents, students, and educators appreciate and value good working relationships between home and school?
6. What do parents of children with disabilities really want from public schools?

REFERENCES

Al-Hassan, S., & Gardner, R. (2002). Involving immigrant parents of students with disabilities in the educational process. *Teaching Exceptional Children, 34*(5), 52–58.

Amanda S. v. Webster City Community School District, *27* IDELR 698 (N.D. IA. 1998).

Assistance to states for the education of children with disabilities, 34 C.F.R. Part 300, 70 Fed. Reg., 35, 833–35, 880 (June 21, 2005).

Bailey, A. B., & Smith, S. W. (2000). Providing effective coping strategies and supports for families with children with disabilities. *Intervention in School and Clinic, 35,* 294.

Bennett, T., DeLuca, D., & Bruns, D. (1997). Putting inclusion into practice: Perspectives of teachers and parents. *Exceptional Children, 64,* 115–131.

Bernheimer, L. P., Weisner, T. S., & Lowe, E. D. (2003). Impacts of children with troubles on working poor families: Mixed-method and experimental evidence. *Mental Retardation, 41,* 403–419.

Blue-Banning, M., Summers, J. A., Frankland, H. C., Nelson, L. L., & Beegle, G. (2004). Dimensions of family and professional partnerships: Constructive

guidelines for collaboration. *Exceptional Children, 70,* 167–184.

Bos, C. S., Nahmias, M. L., & Urban, M. A. (1999). Targeting home-school collaboration for students with ADHD. *Teaching Exceptional Children, 31*(6), 4–9.

Craig, S., Hull, K., Haggert, A. G., & Perez-Selles, M. (2000). Promoting cultural competence through teacher assistance teams. *Teaching Exceptional Children, 32*(3), 6–12.

Cramer, S., Erzkus, A., Mayweather, K., Pope, J., Roeder, J., & Tone, T. (1997). Connecting with siblings. *Teaching Exceptional Children, 30*(1), 46–51.

Dardig, J. C. (2005). The McGlurg monthly magazine and 14 more practical ways to involve parents. *Teaching Exceptional Children, 38*(2), 46–51.

Davern, L. (2004). School-to-home notebooks: What parents have to say. *Teaching Exceptional Children, 36*(5), 22–27.

Donley, C. R., & Williams, G. (1997). Parents exhibit children's progress at a poster session. *Teaching Exceptional Children, 29*(4), 46–51.

Epstein, J. L. (1995). School/family/community partnerships: Caring for the children we share. *Phi Delta Kappan, 76,* 701–717.

Ferguson, P. M. (2002). A place in the family: An historical interpretation of research on parental reactions to having a child with a disability. *The Journal of Special Education, 36,* 124–130.

Fox, L., Vaughn, B. J., Wyattem M. L., & Dunlap, G. (2002). We can't expect other people to understand: Family perspectives on problem behavior. *Exceptional Children, 68,* 437–450.

Garrett, M. T., Bellon-Harn, M. L., Torres-Rivera, E., Garrett, J. T., & Roberts, L. C. (2003). Open hands, open hearts: Working with native youth in the schools. *Intervention in School and Clinic, 38,* 225–235.

Grande, M. (2004). Increasing parent participation and knowledge using home literacy bags. *Intervention in School and Clinic, 40,* 120–126.

Grant Wood Area Education Agency. (1997). *A solution-focused process for addressing student needs.* Cedar Rapids, IA: Author.

Hall, T. E., Wolfe, P. S., & Bollig, A. A. (2003). The home-to-school notebook: An effective communication strategy for students with severe disabilities. *Teaching Exceptional Children, 36*(2), 68–73.

Hoover-Dempsey, K. V., & Sandler, H. M. (1997). Why do parents become involved in their children's education? *Review of Educational Research, 67,* 3–42.

Hundt, T. A. (2002). Videotaping young children in the classroom. *Teaching Exceptional Children, 34*(3), 38–43.

Johnson, J., & Duffett, J. (2002). *When it's your own child: A report on special education from the families who use it.* New York: Public Agenda.

Lamorey, S. (2002). The effects of culture on special education services: Evil eyes, prayer meetings, and IEPs. *Teaching Exceptional Children, 34*(5), 67–71.

Lang, C. M., Ysseldyke, J. E., & Lehr, C. A. (1997). Parents' perspectives on school choice. *Teaching Exceptional Children, 30*(1), 14–19.

Lessenberry, B. M., & Rehfeldt, R. A. (2004). Evaluating stress levels of parents of children with disabilities. *Exceptional Children, 70,* 231–244.

Letter to Grantwerk, 39 IDELR 215 (OSEP, 2003).

Letter to Holloway, 7 FAB 17, 104 LRP 8867 (FPCO, 2004).

Linan-Thompson, S., & Jean, R. E. (1997). Completing the parent participation puzzle: Accepting diversity. *Teaching Exceptional Children, 30*(2), 46–50.

Mathews, R. (2000). Cultural patterns of South Asian and Southeast Asian Americans. *Intervention in School and Clinic, 36,* 101–104.

Morris, J. L., Kay, P. J., Fitzgerald, M. D., & Miller, C. T. (1997). Home/school communication: The use of a computerized voice message system by families of children with disabilities. *Case In Point, 10*(2), 42–53.

Neely-Barnes, S., & Marcenko, M. (2004). Predicting impact of childhood disability on families: Results from the 1995 National Health Interview Survey Disability Supplement. *Mental Retardation, 42,* 284–293.

Osborne, A. G. (2004). To what extent can procedural violations of the IDEA render an IEP invalid? *Education Law Reporter, 185,* 15–29.

Parette, H. P., & Petch-Hogan, B. (2000). Approaching families: Facilitating culturally/linguistically diverse family involvement. *Teaching Exceptional Children, 33*(2), 4–10.

Parette, P., & McMahon, G. A. (2002). What should we expect of assistive technology? Being sensitive to family goals. *Teaching Exceptional Children, 35*(1), 56–61.

Park, J., Turnbull, A. P., & Turnbull, H. R. (2002). Impacts of poverty on quality of life in families of children with disabilities. *Exceptional Children, 68,* 151–170.

Pogoloff, S. M. (2004). Facilitate positive relationships between parents and professionals. *Intervention in School and Clinic, 40,* 116–119.

Salend, S. J. (2006). Explaining your inclusion program to families. *Teaching Exceptional Children, 38*(4), 6–11.

Salend, S. J., & Duhaney, L. M. (2002). What do families have to say about inclusion? How to pay attention and get results. *Teaching Exceptional Children, 35*(1), 62–66.

Sileo, T. W., Sileo, A. P., & Prater, M. A. (1996). Parent and professional partnerships in special education: Multicultural considerations. *Intervention in School and Clinic, 31,* 145–153.

Summers, J. A., Gavan, K., Purnell-Hall, T., & Nelson. J. (2003). Family and school partnerships: Building bridges in general and special education. *Effective Education for Learners With Exceptionalities, 15,* 417–444.

Taylor v. Vermont Department of Education, 313 F.3d 768 (2nd Cir. 2002).

Turnbull, A. P., & Ruef, M. (1997). Family perspectives on inclusive lifestyle issues for people with problem behaviors. *Exceptional Children, 63,* 211–227.

CHAPTER 3

IDENTIFICATION AND EVALUATION OF STUDENTS

CHAPTER PREVIEW

Focus

A child's need for special education and related services must be established by an evaluation of eligibility. The evaluation confirms that the child has a disability affecting progress in the general curriculum. The evaluation also helps the Individualized Education Program (IEP) team determine the services the child will need, which are specified in the content of the IEP.

Legal Issues

The 2004 Amendments to the Individuals with Disabilities Education Act (IDEA) spell out several protections regarding the evaluation of students with disabilities, including:

- A variety of technically sound assessment tools must be used to gather data.
- No single procedure may be used as the sole criterion for determining eligibility.
- Materials and procedures used may not be discriminatory on a racial or cultural basis.
- The evaluation must be administered in the language and form most likely to yield accurate information on what the child knows and can do and by trained and knowledgeable personnel according to assessment instructions.
- Evaluations must be used for the purposes for which the assessments are valid and reliable.

    The evaluation and determination of eligibility for special education services must be made by a team of qualified professionals and the parents. Parents must receive prior notice of the types of identification and evaluation activities proposed by the school and of their rights in the process. They also must give informed written consent before the initial evaluation or any reevaluation can take place. Should parents not provide consent or fail to respond to requests for consent, the school may request mediation or a due process hearing. However, if parents refuse to consent, the school is not obligated to provide a free appropriate public education nor develop an IEP for the child. If dissatisfied with the evaluation results, parents may obtain their own independent evaluation, or request and attempt to receive an independent evaluation at public expense. All independent evaluation results must be considered in decisions regarding the child's educational program.

Schools must guard against the overidentification and disproportionate representation of minority and limited English proficiency children in special education. Prereferral approaches must be developed in school districts reporting an disproportionate representation.

Rationale

A child's educational program must be based on an accurate picture of that child's abilities and needs. An appropriate evaluation must meet the requirements of the 2004 Amendments to IDEA, assess the student in all areas of suspected disability, and be of use to IEP teams in designing the child's educational program.

Approaches

Referral for an evaluation of eligibility for special education or related services should occur if academic or behavioral concerns cannot be addressed with support services in general education classrooms. Many school districts are working both to improve the effectiveness of their screening and referral systems, and to institute assistance team interventions that can identify and resolve many learning problems without the provision of formal special education services.

CHILD FIND

The law under both the IDEA and Section 504 requires that "child find" efforts be conducted. When the IDEA was reauthorized in 2004, the provision requiring each state to develop a plan for locating, identifying, and evaluating all children with disabilities in need of special education and related services was retained. States must find students requiring special education and related services, including those who attend private schools, are highly mobile (such as migrant and homeless children) or wards of the state, and who might otherwise be overlooked because they are successfully advancing from grade to grade. Also called *child search,* the identification step includes public awareness programs, such as medical outreach, mailings to parents, television advertisements, and coordination with hospitals, clinics, and service agencies, as well as periodic and continuing school screening and referral systems. In addition to the general child find requirements under Part B (special education between the ages of 3 and 21) of the 2004 Amendments to IDEA, Part C (special services from birth to 2 years) also makes participating states responsible for identifying, locating, and evaluating infants and toddlers from birth through 2 years of age who are disabled or suspected of being disabled.

The responsibilities of child find extend to various school professionals, including counselors, school administrators, and regular education teachers. School personnel should be aware of child find duties and of the school's referral process. Regular educators must be familiar with indicators that suggest a child may have a disability adversely affecting his or her educational performance. Possible indicators are listed in Figure 3-1.

EDUCATIONAL EVALUATIONS

An evaluation determines whether a child has a disability and the educational needs of the child. Appropriate evaluations must meet the technical requirements of the IDEA, assess the child in all areas of suspected disability, and be of use to IEP teams in designing educational programs (Etscheidt, 2003). The evaluation must provide relevant data useful to the IEP team in determining what special education or related services the child needs.

The school must obtain written parental consent prior to conducting an evaluation. Within 60 days of receiving parental consent, the school must complete the evaluation. If the parent does not provide consent or fails to respond to the request for consent, the school may—but is not required to—use mediation or due process procedures to initiate an evaluation. Evaluations, reevaluations, and eligibility determinations are to be conducted by teams of persons consistent with those persons on IEP teams (see Chapter 5), including the child's parents and other qualified professionals with the knowledge and skills necessary to interpret the evaluation data collected. The evaluation data should assist the IEP team in developing appropriate goals for the child.

Reevaluations must be conducted if the school determines that the educational or related

---

FIGURE 3-1   *Possible indicators of children who may have a disability adversely affecting educational performance and who may require special education or related services*

- The child's rate of progress is not what is expected.
- The child's level of performance is significantly discrepant from peers.
- The child has a physical or health condition affecting educational performance.
- The child's behavior or interpersonal interactions are adversely affecting educational performance.
- The child's response to classroom accommodations and modifications has not been successful.

services needs of the child warrant a reevaluation or if the child's parents or teacher requests a reevaluation. A reevaluation must occur not more than once a year unless the parent or school agree otherwise, and not less than every three years unless the parent and school agree that a reevaluation is unnecessary [20 U.S.C. § 1414 (a) (2)]. Parental consent must be obtained for reevaluations unless reasonable measures to obtain consent were taken and the parent has failed to respond.

As part of an initial evaluation or reevaluation, the IEP team must review existing evaluation data, including information provided by the parents, classroom-based local or state assessments, and classroom-based observations by teachers and related service providers. Parental consent is not required for this review. Based on the review, the IEP team determines what, if any, additional data are necessary to establish (a) the child's eligibility, (b) the present levels of academic achievement and related developmental needs of the child, (c) whether the child needs or continues to need special education and related services, and (d) whether any modifications to the child's IEP are needed to enable the child to meet the goals of the IEP. If no additional data are needed for the evaluation, parents are notified of that determination and their right to request additional evaluations.

The team's review of existing data is an effort to reduce school time and expense associated with evaluations and reevaluations. If the team can determine a child's continuing eligibility, his or her educational needs, and necessary modifications to the IEP without additional testing and evaluation, unnecessary additional assessments should not be conducted (House Report No. 105–95, 1997, p. 97).

Evaluations for Eligibility Determination

The 2004 Amendments to the IDEA require that a full and individual initial evaluation be conducted prior to the initial provision of special education and related services. The evaluation determines whether a child has a disability, how the child's learning is impacted by the disability, and the educational needs of such child.

In conducting the evaluation, several requirements must be followed. The IEP team must use a variety of assessment tools and strategies to gather relevant functional and developmental information, including information provided by the parent, that may assist in determining whether the child has a disability and the content of the child's individualized education program. The data must include information related to enabling the child to be involved in and progress in the general curriculum or, for preschool children, to participate in appropriate activities. The evaluation may not use any single procedure as the sole criterion for determining whether a child has a disability or determining an appropriate educational program. The evaluation must also use technically sound instruments that can assess the relative contribution of cognitive and behavioral factors, in addition to physical or developmental factors. The tests and other evaluations must not be discriminatory on a racial or cultural basis. They must also be provided and administered in the child's native language or other mode of communication most likely to yield accurate information on what the child knows and can do academically, developmentally, and functionally. The evaluation may include standardized tests only if they have been validated for the specific purpose for which they are used, are administered by trained and knowledgeable personnel, and are administered in accordance with any instructions provided by the producer of such tests. The child must be assessed in all areas of suspected disability, and assessment tools and strategies must provide relevant information to directly assist people in determining the educational needs of the child [20 U.S.C. § 1414 (b) (2 & 3)]. The evaluation is the basis for making eligibility determinations.

Following the administration of tests and the consideration of other evaluation material, the IEP team—including the parents of the child—determines whether the child is eligible for special education and related services. Currently, the 2004 Amendments to the IDEA specify 13 disability categories of eligibility. Although the 2004 Amendments do not require that children be classified by their disability, the child must have one of the disabilities listed and require special education and related services [20 U.S.C. 1412 (a) (3) (B)]. The 13 categories are listed in Figure 3-2 and are described in Chapters 13 and 14. Administrators and other members of the IEP team must be aware of the variety of disabilities that may qualify a child for services under the IDEA.

The determination of whether a child suspected of having a specific learning disability has a disability is made by the child's parents and a group collectively qualified to

- conduct individual diagnostic assessments in the areas of speech and language, academic achievement, intellectual development, and social-emotional development;
- interpret assessment and intervention data, and apply critical analysis to those data;
- develop appropriate educational and transitional recommendations based on the assessment data;
- deliver and monitor specifically designed instruction and services to meet the needs of a child with a specific learning disability.

The team must include a special education and general education teacher, and other professionals as appropriate.

Federal regulations require that a group may determine that a child has a specific learning disability if

- the child does not achieve commensurate with the child's age in oral and written expression, listening comprehension, reading, or mathematics when provided with appropriate learning experiences;
- the child fails to achieve a rate of learning to make sufficient progress to meet state-approved standards when assessed with a response to a scientific, research-based intervention process;
- the child exhibits a pattern of strengths and weaknesses in performance, achievement, or both relative to intellectual development;
- the group confirms that the child was provided appropriate high-quality, research-based instruction in regular education settings and that parents were provided data-based documentation of repeated assessments.

FIGURE 3-2   *Definitions for the 13 disability categories are provided in the federal regulations [34 C.F.R. § 300.8 (1-13)].*

- Autism means a developmental disability significantly affecting verbal and nonverbal communication and social interaction, generally evident before age 3, that adversely affects a child's educational performance. Other characteristics often associated with autism are engagement in repetitive activities and stereotyped movements, resistance to environmental change or change in daily routines, and unusual responses to sensory experiences.

- Deaf-blindness means concomitant hearing and visual impairments, the combination of which causes such severe communication and other developmental and educational problems that they cannot be accommodated in special education programs solely for children with deafness or children with blindness.

- Deafness means a hearing impairment that is so severe that the child is impaired in processing linguistic information through hearing, with or without amplification that adversely affects a child's educational performance.

- Emotional disturbance means a condition exhibiting one or more of the following characteristics over a long period of time and to a marked degree that adversely affects a child's educational performance: (a) an inability to learn that cannot be explained by intellectual, sensory, or health factors; (b) an inability to build or maintain satisfactory interpersonal relationships with peers and teachers; (c) inappropriate types of behavior or feelings under normal circumstances; (d) a general pervasive mood of unhappiness or depression; and (e) a tendency to develop physical symptoms or fears associated with personal or school problems. The term includes schizophrenia. The term does not apply to children who are socially maladjusted, unless it is determined that they have an emotional disturbance.

- Hearing impairment means impairment in hearing, whether permanent or fluctuating, that adversely affects a child's educational performance but that is not included under the definition of deafness in this section.

- Mental retardation means significantly subaverage general intellectual functioning, existing concurrently with deficits in adaptive behavior and manifested during the developmental period that adversely affects a child's educational performance.

- Multiple disability means concomitant impairments (such as mental retardation-blindness, mental retardation-orthopedic impairment, etc.), the combination of which causes such severe educational problems that the problems cannot be accommodated in special education programs solely for one of the impairments. The term does not include deaf-blindness.

- Orthopedic impairment means a severe orthopedic impairment that adversely affects a child's educational performance. The term includes impairments caused by congenital anomaly, impairments caused by disease (e.g., poliomyelitis, bone tuberculosis), and impairments from other causes (e.g., cerebral palsy, amputations, and fractures or burns that cause contractures).

- Other health impairment means having limited strength, vitality, or alertness, including a heightened alertness to environmental stimuli, that results in limited alertness with respect to the educational environment; that is due to chronic or acute health problems such as asthma, attention deficit disorder or attention deficit hyperactivity disorder, diabetes, epilepsy, a heart condition, hemophilia, lead poisoning, leukemia, nephritis, rheumatic fever, and sickle cell anemia; and that adversely affects a child's educational performance.

- Specific learning disability means a disorder in one or more of the basic psychological processes involved in understanding or in using language, spoken or written, that may manifest itself in an imperfect ability to listen, think, speak, read, write, spell, or to do mathematical calculations, including such conditions as perceptual disabilities, brain injury, minimal brain dysfunction, dyslexia, and developmental aphasia. The term does not include learning problems that are primarily the result of visual, hearing, or motor disabilities; of mental retardation; of emotional disturbance; or of environmental, cultural, or economic disadvantage.

- Speech or language impairment means a communication disorder, such as stuttering, impaired articulation, a language impairment, or a voice impairment, that adversely affects a child's educational performance.

- Traumatic brain injury means an acquired injury to the brain caused by an external physical force, resulting in total or partial functional disability or psychosocial impairment, or both, that adversely affects a child's educational performance. Traumatic brain injury applies to open or closed head injuries resulting in impairments in one or more areas, such as cognitive; language; memory; attention; reasoning; abstract thinking; judgment; problem-solving; sensory, perceptual, and motor abilities; psychosocial behavior; physical functions; information processing; and speech. Traumatic brain injury does not apply to brain injuries that are congenital or degenerative, or to brain injuries induced by birth trauma.

- Visual impairment including blindness means an impairment in vision that, even with corrections, adversely affects a child's educational performance. The term includes both partial sight and blindness.

If the team determines that the child has not made adequate progress under conditions of high-quality instruction delivered by qualified personnel, the child must be referred for evaluation.

When evaluating a child for a specific learning disability, the 2004 Amendments to the IDEA specify that the school is not required to establish a discrepancy between achievement and intellectual ability in a variety of areas including reading, math, and written or oral expression. Rather, the IEP team may use a process that examines the child's response to scientific, research-based intervention as part of the evaluation procedures.

The removal of the discrepancy requirement for establishing a learning disability that requires special education services is a consequence of much dialogue and debate concerning the potential bias of IQ tests and the undesirability of a "wait to fail" eligibility approach. Although the 2004 Amendments permit such a "response to scientific, research-based intervention" as part of the process in determining whether a child has a specific learning disability [20 U.S.C. § 1414 (b) (6)], many schools are adopting a noncategorical, response to intervention (RTI) approach for all students with academic and behavioral needs.

The RTI approach is the practice of obtaining student outcome data in response to providing high-quality interventions to assist multidisciplinary teams in making eligibility decisions (Batsche et al., 2005). A child's learning rate and level of performance are monitored as indices of a child's needs for special education or related services. The RTI approach emerged due to problems in the traditional eligibility process, including the potential for bias in standardized assessment instruments and requiring a specified discrepancy between potential and achievement prior to eligibility determination. For example, a documented discrepancy between a measure of potential and a measure of achievement was required for children with learning disabilities to receive special education or related services. The 2004 Amendments to the IDEA discourages discrepancy-based identification and encourages the inclusion of RTI in the eligibility process.

Noncategorical Evaluation and Eligibility Determination

The fallibility of labels and disability categories in explaining poor achievement or in planning instruction has been consistently demonstrated (McLaughlin & Nolet, 2004). A relatively recent approach to eligibility determination is the use of functional classification criteria to guide eligibility decisions. Rather than using disability categories or traditional measures (Tilly, Reschly, & Grimes, 1998), the noncategorical approach establishes a child's need for special education services based on that child's RTI. Many IEP teams establish a child's need for special education services based on evidence of resistance to reasonable general education intervention efforts and evidence of a severe discrepancy from peers' performance levels in the areas of concern. The team provides a data-based description of the resources necessary to improve and maintain the individual's rate of learning at an acceptable level and the data-based evidence supporting the teams' eligibility decision. The advantages of noncategorical eligibility approaches by examining RTI have been described by Shinn, Good, and Parker (1998) and Prasse and Schrag (1998).

Eligibility Determination

Following completion of initial testing and the gathering of other data, including parent input, the team of qualified professionals and the parents must determine whether a student is eligible for special education services. A copy of the evaluation report and documentation of the determination of eligibility must be provided to the parents. If a child's educational needs are determined to be due to a lack of instruction in reading or math or to limitations in English proficiency, then the child cannot be determined eligible for special education services.

If, after careful review of all available data, a determination is made that a child has a disability and needs special education and related services, then an IEP must be developed. The first IEP team meeting must be held within

30 days of the eligibility determination. In many situations, an eligibility determination meeting may be phased into an IEP team meeting when the appropriate notice has been provided to the parents and the appropriate people for an IEP team are present. Special education and related services are expected to begin as soon as feasible following completion of the IEP and obtaining informed written parent consent for the initial provision of special education services. However, if parents refuse to consent to the provision of special education or related services, the school may not use mediation or due process proceedings to obtain an agreement or ruling that services may be provided. If the parent refuses services offered, the school district is not obligated to provide a free appropriate public education or to develop an IEP for the child [*20 U.S.C. § 1414 (a) (1) (D) (ii)*].

In the event a student who has been evaluated for special education services transfers to another school across state lines before an IEP is completed, the receiving school district must determine whether it will accept the student's most current evaluation and disability determination conducted in the other state. After all, the former evaluation may not meet the receiving state's education standards for evaluations. If the receiving school district accepts the evaluation and determination of disability, it must so notify the child's parents and begin the IEP development process. If the receiving school district refuses to adopt the former school district's evaluation, the receiving district must provide appropriate notice to the parents and then conduct its own evaluation without unnecessary delay. In the latter situation, the child may be placed into an interim IEP placement, unless the receiving school and parents cannot agree on an interim placement, in which case the student should be placed in the regular school program. If the receiving school's evaluation indicates a disability and a need for special education services, the school must convene an eligibility determination meeting and IEP meeting within 30 days of the determination (OSEP Memorandum 96–5, 1995).

Medical Evaluations

For some children with suspected disabilities, it will be desirable or necessary to have medical professionals on the evaluation team, or at least available to conduct medical evaluations. The 2004 Amendments to IDEA define "related services" to include "school health services" provided by a school nurse or other qualified person and "medical services for diagnostic or evaluation purposes." This latter phrase specifically refers to services provided by a licensed physician to determine a child's medically related disability that may result in his or her need for special education and related services.

Special education and related services must be provided at no cost to parents. Parents of children with disabilities who are covered by public insurance, such as Medicaid, may be asked to use those benefits for medical and other services so long as several conditions are met: The school cannot require the parents to enroll the child in a public insurance program as a condition of receiving FAPE, incur out-of-pocket expenses, (e.g., deductibles, copayments), or suffer any detriment, such as a decrease in the lifetime benefit or increased premiums.

A school may access parents' private insurance only so long as there is no cost to the parents, including the lowering of lifetime coverage, increased premiums, or deductibles or copayments. Each time a school proposes to access parents' private insurance, it must obtain informed prior written consent (see Chapter 2) and advise the parents that refusal will not jeopardize services to the child. Federal special education funds may be used to pay private insurance copayments and deductions in order to provide services at no cost to parents.

LEGAL ISSUES

Several legal issues have emerged concerning the evaluation and identification of students. First, the adequacy of the school's evaluation and the parent's right to an independent educational evaluation (IEE) have been the issue of several administrative decisions and judicial cases. The potential for racial and cultural bias in the evaluation process has also received considerable attention and discussion.

The Right to an Independent Educational Evaluation

When parents consent to an evaluation by the school, but are not satisfied (disagree) with its results, they have the right to obtain an IEE. The evaluation must be conducted by a qualified examiner who is not employed by the school nor an agent of the school. In such instances, the school must provide information about where an independent evaluation can be obtained. The parents may obtain an independent evaluation at their own expense or request an independent evaluation at public expense. In the latter situation, the school must provide parents with its criteria (i.e., qualifications of the examiner) for such examinations and pay the full cost of the evaluation, or otherwise ensure that it is provided at no cost to the parents. Medicaid can be used to pay for all or part of an IEE for students entitled to Medicaid services. The parent's insurance, however, can be used to pay for all or part of an IEE only so long as it does not cost the parents anything, such as through increased premiums or reduced claim coverage, and the parents voluntarily consent in writing to claims being filed. Schools are required to pay for only one independent evaluation for each school evaluation, and then only when parents actually disagree with an evaluation conducted by the school (Hudson v. Wilson, 1987).

However, when a parent requests that the school pay for the independent evaluation, and the school feels strongly that the evaluation it conducted was adequate and appropriate, it may, without unnecessary delay, contest the parents' request for an independent evaluation at public expense by filing a request for a due process hearing. If the hearing officer decides in favor of the school, then the parents must pay the cost of the independent evaluation.

The results of any independent evaluation—whether paid for by parents or a public agency—must be considered in planning the child's educational program and may be offered as evidence at a subsequent hearing. When a hearing officer requests an independent evaluation as part of a due process hearing, it must be provided at no cost to the parents.

Etscheidt (2004) reviewed 50 state-level administrative due process hearing or court decisions published between 1997 and 2001 that addressed the need to conduct or reimburse parents for the cost of IEEs. Compliance with IDEA procedural requirements was used to gauge the appropriateness of district evaluations. When evaluations met those requirements, requests or reimbursement for IEEs were denied. Further, if the evaluation did not assess the student in all areas of suspected disability (i.e., the scope of the evaluation), IEEs were ordered or reimbursed. The failure to assess the student in all areas of suspected disability or a limited selection of assessment tools resulted in reimbursement of parentally arranged IEEs and/or tuition reimbursement of parentally arranged school programs. Another result was the court awarding compensatory education for the months or years the child had been in a program that was selected or based on inadequate evaluations. Finally, if an IEE identified specific needs that a district's evaluation failed to discover or offered new information, recommendations, or accommodations to address educational needs, requests for reimbursements were awarded. Conversely, when an IEE did not provide any new or significantly distinguishing information, courts determined that parents were not entitled to publicly funded IEEs. The district's evaluation must have been of use to the IEP team in planning educational programs; otherwise, reimbursement of parentally arranged IEEs or an order for an additional IEE resulted.

Schoolwide or districtwide staff development sessions for personnel who routinely serve on evaluation teams should be conducted to review IEE regulations and guidelines for practice (Imber & Radcliff, 2003). Such efforts may help schools avoid the costs of an IEE obtained by parents dissatisfied with the district's own evaluation.

Bias in the Identification Process

Certainly the most controversial issue surrounding student evaluations for eligibility has involved alleged racial and cultural bias. A 1975 study conducted by the federal government found that although only 15% of the nation's students were African American, 38% of students identified as mentally disabled were African American (U.S. Department of Education, 1996).

A 1999 study conducted on a nationally representative sample of data compiled in 1992 indicated that the issue had not abated. African American students were about 2.4 times more likely than their non-African American peers to be identified as mentally disabled and 1.5 times more likely to be identified as having emotional disabilities (Oswald, Coutinho, Best, & Singh, 1999). These data led researchers to examine the representation of minority students in special education (Katzman, 2003).

Disproportionate representation is problematic when the program in question is ineffective or stigmatizing or if the process of identification and placement is not applied equally to different groups of students (Heller, Holtzman, & Messick, 1982). From Finn's (1982) first examination of national disproportionate representation trends, data from the Office of Civil Rights (OCR) Compliance Reports have been used in subsequent studies to verify patterns of minority overrepresentation in special education (see Reschly, 1997; MacMillan & Reschly, 1998; and Oswald, Coutinho, Best, & Singh, 1999). In a recent meta-analysis of studies examining overrepresentation, Hosp and Reschly (2003) used a mean risk ratio to find that evaluation referral rates for African Americans were significantly higher than for Caucasians.

Much of the blame for overrepresentation of minorities in special education has been attributed to current referral and evaluation practices, surprisingly due in part to IDEA's emphasis on nondiscriminatory assessment (Overton, 2003, p. 72). In attempting to meet IDEA's nondiscriminatory mandates, a variety of tests have been used, yet those tests often contribute to assessment bias. Possible sources of bias in assessment include inappropriate content, inappropriate standardization samples, unqualified examiners, or invalid predictive validity (Reynolds, Lowe, & Saenz, 1999). Increasing awareness of potential sources of the bias at the preservice level may assist in decreasing overrepresentation (Valles, 1998).

In the 1970s and 1980s, the courts responded to a rash of lawsuits charging that culturally biased tests had led to the misclassification of large numbers of minority students. The resulting disproportionality of minority and non-English-speaking students receiving special education services, especially when the decision was made based on a single IQ test score, was not easily defended. The primary focus of the criticisms was that the tests had been developed for the white, middle-class socioeconomic majority of students in the United States, and the questions on many standardized tests had no validity when asked of minority and non-English-speaking students. Judicial rulings included orders to dismantle certain programs for mentally disabled students in which minority children were overrepresented. Courts also prohibited the future use of IQ tests to place children in some types of ability tracks or in classes for the mentally retarded when the tests had brought about improper racial imbalance in those classes (Turnbull & Turnbull, 1998, p. 105).

Test bias may also be due to differences in socioeconomic status, community culture, accepted speech styles, transient status, self-concepts, and stereotypes, among other things (Obiakor, 1999).

Poverty

Additional reasons offered for disproportionate representation include cultural bias influencing teacher referrals for special educational services and poverty. Yet Donovan and Cross (2002) concluded the evidence available is insufficient to give bias or discrimination a significant role in overrepresentation. Further, a study examining the association between poverty and risk of disability concluded that the link between childhood poverty and services needed under the IDEA was still an assumption (Fujiura & Yamaki, 2000, p. 194), although findings were "highly suggestive" of an increased risk for disability among constituencies defined by poverty. Future research must search beyond placement pattern data and limited findings of placement studies (e.g., bias and poverty) to examine social and cultural explanations to the overrepresentation issue. As Artiles (2003) concluded, "the problem will not be solved with quotas and it is an oversimplification to blame it on either massive bias or child poverty . . . part of the problem is whether we are adequately addressing students' educational problems and needs" (p. 176).

Limited English Proficiency

The issue of cultural bias in testing, with its associated problem of appropriateness for limited English proficiency (LEP) students, is rapidly enlarging, especially in certain parts of the country. The number of LEP students in California increased from 524,000 in 1985 to over 1,300,000 in 1996, and helped fuel a state-wide political debate over bilingual education (Wenkart, 1998). Rather than targeting placement rates for minority and LEP students, the presence of disproportionality figures should be viewed as an opportunity to examine more complex issues such as administrator and teacher attitudes about diversity and the availability of academic and social support services (Artiles, Rueda, Salazar, & Higareda, 2005).

The 2004 Amendments to the IDEA attempt to address the problems of cultural and language bias in assessment by requiring that: (a) all testing and evaluation materials and procedures "be selected and administered so as not to be discriminatory on a racial or cultural basis" (although these terms are not further defined), (b) they be administered in the child's native language or other mode of communication, and (c) a variety of assessment tools and strategies are used, including information provided by the parents. The concern regarding language proficiency is apparently directed at misidentification only, because the IDEA does not speak to bilingual education or the provision of special

education services in native languages (Wenkart, 1998). The 2004 Amendments to the IDEA note the discrepancies in the levels of referral and services to both minority and limited English proficient children, and calls for greater efforts to prevent the "intensification of problems connected with mislabeling" [20 U.S.C. § 1401 (c) (12) (A)]. The law also requires that personnel development include the "effective teaching strategies, classroom-based techniques, and interventions to ensure appropriate identification of students who may be eligible for special education services, and to prevent the misidentification, inappropriate overidentification, or underidentification of children having a disability, especially minority and limited English proficient children" [20 U.S.C. § 1462 (b) (2) (A) (iii)]. Figure 3-3 highlights the current protections in evaluation procedures under the 2004 Amendments to the IDEA.

EXPANDING PREREFERRAL APPROACHES

Problem-Solving and General Education Interventions

Once a child is referred for a formal preplacement evaluation, a series of assessment activities is initiated that are required by law and generally result in substantial investments of time and school resources. Prior to the reauthorization of IDEA in 2004, the commission charged with recommending changes in the law concluded that the "wait to fail" approach to eligibility must be replaced with a preventive, prereferral process to address the academic and behavioral needs of children (President's Commission on Excellence in Special Education, 2002). Consequently, the current law permits states to use up to 15% of federal funds to support prereferral activities.

School districts are adopting policies and procedures that attempt to solve individual student learning problems before the legal process of the IDEA evaluation is set in motion. These services generally involve informal interventions

FIGURE 3-3   *IDEA protections in evaluation procedures*

- Tests are provided and administered in the child's native language or mode of communication.
- Standardized tests must have been validated for the specific purpose for which they are intended.
- Standardized tests are administered by trained personnel in conformity with the publisher's instructions.
- The evaluation will be tailored to assess the child's specific areas of educational need, including information provided by the parent that may assist in determining disability and the content of the IEP.
- The evaluation must be designed to reflect the student's aptitude or achievement level rather than reflecting the student's disability.
- No single procedure is used as the sole criterion for determining the presence of a disability, the student's program, or placement.
- Decisions are made by a multidisciplinary team, including one person knowledeable in the child's suspected area of disability.
- The child is assessed in all areas related to the suspected disability.

From *The Law and Special Education* by Mitchell L.Yell, © 2006. Adapted with permission of Prentice Hall, Inc. Upper Saddle River, NJ.

with students or teachers in the regular classroom and have largely been found to be highly successful. Before children are referred for an evaluation to establish the need for special education services, a concerted effort is made in regular education to remediate the child's learning needs.

These efforts to address students' school performance problems prior to a referral to establish the need for special education services have been described as problem-solving methods. These methods include the delivery of interventions prior to referral for special education eligibility, a practice described as "prereferral intervention" (Graden, Casey, & Christenson, 1985). The 2004 Amendments to the IDEA encourage such efforts as "the education of children with disabilities can be made more effective by . . . providing incentives for whole-school approaches and prereferral intervention to reduce the need to label children as disabled in order to address their learning needs" [*20 U.S.C. § 1400 (c) (5) (F)*]. Problem-solving methods were developed to provide effective services to students who are at educational risk (McNamara & Hollinger, 2003) and to successfully resolve performance problems without the

need for more intensive special education services. Research has shown that problem-solving approaches have increased services to at-risk students in general education settings and reduced special education referral rates (Fuchs, Fuchs, Harris, & Roberts, 1996; Pugach & Johnson, 1989). Prereferral practices involve teachers effectively differentiating instruction and intervening at the "first sign of trouble . . . to prevent or ameliorate a wide variety of learning or behavioral problems prior to formal special education identification" (Del'Homme, Kasari, & Forness, 1996). For example, early intervention in reading and literacy has been shown to reduce the number of referrals for special education evaluation (O'Connor & Simic, 2002; Manset-Williamson, St. John, Hu, & Gordon, 2002).

Many schools now have some kind of intervention assistance team that meets regularly for a short time each week. The name of the teams vary from district to district (e.g., Child Study Team, Child Assistance Team, Teacher Assistance Team), as do their composition, specific activities, and structure. Team members often include special and regular education teachers, the school principal, counselor, or nurse, and possibly other specialists as well. An individual child's parents may be involved in meetings involving their child, but at all times parents are informed of school concerns and informal efforts to resolve those concerns. Communication with parents must always be open and be designed to go both ways.

Although there are many variations among intervention assistance teams, the procedure generally is as follows: Teachers (and sometimes parents) refer students directly to the intervention team, rather than referring the child for formal special education identification procedures. Team members then share information on those students gleaned from student files, interviews with the teacher and parents, and observation of the child in the classroom. They discuss (brainstorm) possible modifications in the curriculum, classroom environment, or mode of instruction and make recommendations for intervention. In some cases, committee members may offer direct assistance to students or classroom teachers. The goal of intervention assistance teams is to help regular teachers meet the needs of as many students as possible in the regular classroom and to limit the number of referrals for special education services. Many state educational agencies recognize the effective and efficient nature of this approach and now require the implementation of intervention teams.

A study of intervention teams conducted in three states concluded that teams generally operate in a positive and effective manner, experienced members strongly endorse their use, and members value the team collaboration as an important aspect of the process. A major concern identified by team members was inadequate assessment of the success of strategies used with students. Researchers recommended that specific indicators of student change, such as graphing results, using pre- and post-intervention measures, and using systematic classroom observation, be included in the assessment of the various interventions. They recommend that states develop a policy of establishing intervention teams and providing staff training funds for consistent implementation (Bahr, Whitten, Dieker, Kocarek, & Manson, 1999).

The effectiveness of intervention activities depends on adequate and appropriate professional development. Logan, Hansen, Neimireh and Wright (2001) found that elementary teachers were not using student support teams as designed. The teachers believed the primary purpose of the student support team was to test and determine students who required special education services, and that the evaluation process was covert. Ongoing staff development will be essential to the success of problem-solving teams.

Bias may also affect the problem-solving process. Knotek (2003) found that problem solving became more subjective, especially in problem identification and intervention, for African American children flagged as poor or troublemakers by problem-solving teams. These students were more quickly referred for special education evaluation. Problem-solving teams must strive for unbiased discussions and recommendations.

At least one state has established by administrative rule a Systematic Problem Solving Process. This process is designed to examine educationally related problems for students to determine whether the child will benefit from general education interventions or require referral to determine the need for special education services. Schools first attempt to resolve problems in the general education environment, and in doing so may use special education support and instructional personnel working collaboratively with regular education staff. "Active parent participation" is mandated. The team has the option of proceeding immediately to referral for special education evaluation when deemed appropriate. Intervention teams cannot be used to deny or slow access to evaluation and programs for children who need them.

The Systematic Problem Solving Process, sometimes referred to as a solutions-focused approach, contains the following elements:

1. The presenting problem or behavior is described in objective and measurable terms.
2. Collection of the data on the presenting problem or behavior is conducted in a variety of settings and through a variety of sources.

FIGURE 3-4   *Activities to support intervention teams*

Training Activities

• Provide in-service for team members in effective communication, the collaboration process, and intervention strategies.

• Arrange team visitations to schools with intervention teams in order to exchange ideas.

• Provide in-service for every building staff member on the intervention team's goals, purpose, and process.

Team Development

• Include a variety of professionals as team members.

• Encourage parent involvement in a collaborative relationship (and notification).

• Emphasize equal status of principal and others as team members.

• Assign team roles at each meeting to ensure full participation (brainstormer, recorder, facilitator, follow-up).

Team Support

• Schedule regular weekly meetings.

• Schedule time for the collaborative process.

• Use a collaboration log (documentation) of the problem, intervention, evaluation, and follow-up.

• Ensure team follow-up.

• Support intervention assistance teams district-wide.

From E. Whitten (1995). Intervention assistive teams: The principal's role identified. *Case in Point, IX,* (2), 25. Published by the Council of Administrators of Special Education, a Division of the Council for Exceptional Children. Reprinted by permission.

3. Interventions are designed based on the defined problem and data collected as determined by the combined judgments of the group and a plan is developed for implementing the intervention, progress monitoring, and persons responsible.

4. Systematic Progress Monitoring is conducted through the use of regular and frequent data collection and analysis and interventions are modified as necessary.

5. Evaluations of the intervention effects are analyzed and decisions regarding effectiveness made (*Special Education, 281 I.A.C. § 41.47, 41.48, 2000*).

A number of authors have identified the importance of intervention assistance teams and have highlighted the important role played by educational leaders. For example, Whitten (1995–96) has identified three activities principals can initiate to support intervention assistance teams. These activities are listed in Figure 3-4.

Prereferral approaches have been successful in designing interventions that improved academic and behavioral performance before special education or related services were warranted. For example, Fuch, Fuchs, and Speece (2002) used a treatment validity model that examined student response to regular class instruction and adaptation, which delayed referrals to special education services.

Some schools also use systematic problem-solving intervention teams as Section 504 terms to consider reasonable the accommodations for students in the regular education setting. Problem-solving approaches make efficient and effective use of the expertise and collaborative skills of the team members. However, once a child meets Section 504 requirements and acquires an accommodation plan, the parents must be helped to recognize that the procedural safeguards afforded parents under the 2004 Amendments to the IDEA are not available under Section 504.

Some schools use a preevaluation conference to inform parents of their rights and the formal special education and Section 504 procedures available. At that point, parents can agree to the proposed program of informal interventions or request a formal evaluation and subsequent special education procedures. Intervention strategies should never be allowed or used to slow access to evaluation and special education services for children who appear to need them. When parent agreement for the informal program is received, the school staff can proceed to assist the classroom teacher by providing materials; demonstrating materials and methods in class; providing direct, short-term instruction to the student in class; or observing student behavior and activities in class. In each case, all interventions must be documented and recorded in student files.

When intervention assistance efforts to meet the student's needs in the regular class setting have not been successful, the next step is to proceed to referral for special education or 504 evaluations. When not previously conducted, a preevaluation conference may serve to share information and perspectives or help to open lines of communication and develop trust.

General Educators' Involvement

Because the identification of children's educational needs is the linchpin of the referral process and provision of special education and related services, input from general education teachers is vital in the referral process. The role of the general education teacher in the referral process is impacted by several factors including: (a) dissatisfaction with the referral process, (b) racial or gender bias, and (c) tolerance levels.

Over the years, surveys of regular education teachers have reported general, but only lukewarm, satisfaction with the existing special education referral process. In addition to the common complaints about too much paperwork involved in referrals, many regular educators have reported that the referral process moved too slowly. They have also complained that the opinions of regular educators were not given enough weight in determinations of eligibility (Chalmers, Ortega, & Hoover, 1996).

Chalmers, Ortega, and Hoover have recommended a number of approaches for increasing regular education teacher involvement and satisfaction with the referral process. They recommend that staff-development programs and coursework be used to improve regular educator knowledge of the referral process so they can better understand the process. Also, the rationale for attempts at remediation of student's educational needs prior to formal evaluation for special education services should be made known to teachers and ingrained in each school's philosophy. Regular educator's important role in the referral process should be recognized and supported by special educators and administrators. Both regular and special educators should regularly review the entire referral process with a view toward improving its efficiency and effectiveness.

As discussed earlier, racial and cultural bias may affect both referral rates for special education evaluation and the determination that a child requires special education services. The concern for overrepresentation of minorities receiving special education services has prompted a careful monitoring at both federal and state levels. In addition to the potential for cultural bias, researchers have investigated additional sources of bias in special education referral and services. Wehmeyer and Schwartz (2001) examined the possibility of gender bias in special education referrals, and concluded that females who could benefit from special education services are underrepresented, possibly due to gender bias. Taylor, Gunter, and Slate (2001) found that male teachers rated African American female students as having more behavioral difficulties than did female teachers and concluded that "the gender of the teacher and the gender of the students appeared to have the most influence on teachers' perception of behavior" (p. 150). Cultural awareness needs to be an important factor in intervention team considerations, when appropriate. Expectations related to behavior, student-adult exchanges, responses to adult questions, asking for help when needed, and various other school situations common among white, middle-class students may not be commonplace among children and families new to the traditional majority culture. When identifying educational problems and potential solutions involving students from diverse cultures, intervention teams need to be comfortable with their cultural awareness (Craig, Hull, Haggart & Perez-Selles, 2000). Awareness of the potential influence of gender bias may assist general education teachers in the referral process.

Differences in teacher expectation and tolerance for behavior may also affect referral rates of general education teachers. According to Shinn and colleagues (1987), teachers vary in their tolerance of student behaviors, and the different degree of teacher tolerance for behaviors resulted in bias in referral and assessment. Research has consistently supported the conclusion that teachers value academic productivity and may not tolerate noncompliance and inadequate self-control (e.g., Safran & Safran, 1988; Landon & Mesinger, 1989). Teachers view effective learning environments as characterized by compliant, controlled behavior, and may more quickly refer students whose behaviors are difficult to tolerate.

No Child Left Behind and Special Education Eligibility

President Bush signed the "No Child Left Behind" (NCLB) Act of 2001 into law on January 8, 2002. This legislation amends the Elementary and Secondary Education Act (ESEA) and extends the standards-based reform measures instituted in the 1994 Amendments to the ESEA. Individual state plans are submitted to the Department of Education and must be coordinated with the 2004 Amendments to the IDEA.

NCLB and Students with Disabilities

Each state must establish measurable annual objectives for continuous and substantial improvement of all students, as well as separate objectives for four specific populations: economically disadvantaged students, students from major racial and ethnic groups, students with disabilities, and students with limited English proficiency. Schools must show that 95% of all students and 95% of students in each subgroup were included in the assessment results. The results of state assessments for students with disabilities must be included in each state's determination of adequate yearly progress (AYP) and also disaggregated for analysis. Each of the four specific populations must make AYP if the school as a whole is to achieve AYP. However, if any of the identified groups does not meet AYP proficiency, but the group decreased its failure rate by 10% or more, and has made progress on one or more of the other academic indicators the state had identified, the school would still be considered to have achieved AYP. This exception is known as the "safe harbor" provision of NCLB.

The NCLB Act specifies that the four specific populations are to take the assessment "with accommodations, guidelines, and alternative assessments provided in the same manner as those provided under . . . the Individuals with Disabilities Education Act" [20 U.S.C. § 6311 (b) (2) (I) (ii)]. The 2004 Amendments to the IDEA require students with disabilities to be included in state and districtwide assessments, and for IEP teams to consider individual modifications in the administration of assessments that are needed in order for the child to participate in such assessments. An IEP team may also determine that participation in state or districtwide assessment is not appropriate for a child, and propose an alternative assessment to measure student achievement [20 U.S.C. § 1414 (d) (1) (A) (v)]. NCLB that would limits the percent of students who could be considered proficient against alternative achievement standards to 1% of the district's or state's school-age population in the grades tested. This will ensure that only truly significantly cognitively impaired students are held to different standards. Although any number of students could take an alternative assessment, only 1% could be used in calculating the AYP. Therefore, the IEP team must carefully determine assessment participation for students with disabilities "because the decision is likely to have an effect on school accountability" (National Center on Educational Outcomes, 2003, p. 5).

The accountability and assessment requirements of NCLB may impact the identification and evaluation requirements of the 2004 Amendments to the IDEA in several ways. Many students are identified for special education services due to lack of proficiency in reading or math. For many students, the need for special education services is based on that lack of proficiency: "If [special education students] were able to meet 100% proficiency, they would be, by definition, ineligible for special education and related services" (Nealis, 2003, citing Hueschel, 2003).

Caruso (2003) suggested that the NCLB "may turn into an eligibility and referral tidal wave" for both the 2004 Amendments to the IDEA and Section 504. Because both the IDEA and Section 504 permit the use of accommodations on state and districtwide assessments, administrators may forward more referrals to secure "every advantage to help them improve scores"(¶4). School teams may seek to obtain test exemptions for students who are deemed eligible under the IDEA and test modifications for students referred and served under Section 504. As standards-based reform measures are implemented, the impact on historically marginalized racial and linguistically diverse groups must be carefully monitored. Artiles (2003) cautions that minority students are predicted to be most affected by standard-based reforms, and referral rates for special education services may increase.

The state-selected assessment methods will be included in the "variety of assessment tools and strategies" used to determine eligibility for special education services. They will also be used to develop the "content of the child's individualized education program, including information related to enabling the child to be involved in and progress in the general curriculum" [20 U.S.C. § 1414 (b) (2) (A)]. The yearly assessment data may be helpful in establishing annual goals

"related to meeting the child's needs that result from the child's disability to enable the child to be involved in and progress in the general curriculum" [20 U.S.C. § 1414 (d) (1) (A) (ii) (I)].

CONCLUSION

The first step toward the provision of appropriate education programs and services to children who have disabilities affecting educational performance is identification based on an eligibility evaluation. This evaluation should reveal how the disability impacts educational performance and assist in ascertaining the child's educational needs. Using this information, IEP teams can develop appropriate educational programs. Prereferral, problem-solving approaches have replaced disability-specific, "wait-to-fail" models of eligibility. Teachers, counselors, administrators, and other school personnel must be aware of child find duties, including a familiarity with problem-solving interventions prior to referral.

The evaluation conducted to determine eligibility for special education and related services must meet the procedural requirements of the IDEA, assess the child in all areas of suspected disability, and be useful in planning educational programs. Based on the evaluation, a group of qualified professionals and parents must determine whether a child is eligible for services. If parents disagree with the district's evaluation, they may seek an independent educational evaluation.

Issues in evaluation and eligibility determination include bias in evaluation instruments or processes and overrepresentation of minority groups receiving special education services. The 2004 Amendments to the IDEA include protections in evaluation to reduce the potential for bias, and also requires states and districts to conduct a self-study of overrepresentation issues.

Prereferral approaches to problem-solving show great promise in addressing academic and behavioral concerns in the general education classroom. Before children are referred for special education evaluation, general education interventions are designed to improve academic and behavioral performance in general education classrooms. Not only do these prereferral approaches reduce the number of children referred for special education evaluation, these problem-solving interventions provide an array of services to students at risk.

VIEW FROM THE COURTS

Larry P. v. Riles (1979) (bias in identification). The *Larry P.* case began in 1971 as a class action lawsuit filed on behalf of African American students in the San Francisco public schools who had been placed in special education programs for children with mental disabilities. Although African American students comprised only 28.5% of the district's overall enrollment, they constituted over 66% of all students in the special education mental disability programs. Judge Robert Peckham ruled in 1972 that the disparate treatment of African American students in placement decisions did exist and issued a preliminary injunction forbidding the use of IQ tests in San Francisco. The court concluded that IQ tests were racially and culturally biased, and discriminated against African American students. The misidentification and placement of African American students to "an inferior and 'dead-end' education" was discriminatory and violated the students' fourteenth amendment rights. The U.S. Court of Appeals for the Ninth Circuit affirmed the decision in 1984. In 1986 the ban on IQ testing was expanded to all special education placement decisions involving African American students in California.

RECOMMENDED READINGS

Batsche, G., Elliott, J., Graden, J. L., Grimes, J., Kovaleski, J. F., Prasse, D., Reschly, D. J., Schrage, J., & Tilly, W. D. (2004). *Response to intervention: Policy considerations and implementation.* Alexandria, VA: National Association of State Directors of Special Education.

Craig, S., Hull, K., Haggart, A.G., & Perez-Sellers, M. (2000). Promoting cultural competence through teacher assistance teams. *Teaching Exceptional Children, 32*(3), 6–12. This article includes a number of specific helpful ideas to assist intervention teams in developing cultural awareness.

deBettencourt, L. U. (2002). Understanding the differences between IDEA and Section 504. *Teaching Exceptional Children, 34*(3), 16–23. This article discusses differences in the identification process for IDEA and Section 504.

Falk, C. L. (1997). How to PINPOINT and solve day-to-day problems. *Teaching Exceptional Children, 29*(3), 78–81. This article provides a practical step-by-step review of one example of a systematic problem-solving approach.

Landrum, T. J. (2001). Assessment for eligibility: Issues in identifying students with emotional or behavioral disorders. *Assessment for Effective Intervention, 26*(1), 1–49. This article discusses some difficulties in identifying students with emotional and behavioral disorders (E/BD) and the potential for overrepresentation of this group in special education programs.

La Paro, K. M., Olsen, K., & Pianta, R. C. (2002). Special education eligibility: Developmental precursors over the first three years of life. *Exceptional Children, 69*(1), 55–66. This article discusses the early screening of young children who may benefit from special education services.

Scruggs, T. E., & Mastropieri, M. A. (2002). On babies and bathwater: Addressing the problems of identification of learning disabilities. *Learning Disability Quarterly, 25*(3), 155–168. This article discusses the continuing controversy concerning the reliable assessment of learning disabilities, and suggested alternative approaches that to not radically change current conceptualizations of learning disabilities.

Wehmeyer, M. L., & Schwartz, M. (2001). Disproportionate representation of males in special education services: Biology, behavior, or bias? *Education and Treatment of Children, 24*(1), 28–45. This article examines the possibility of gender bias in referral and admission to special education services.

Wolery, M, & Bailey, D. B. (2002). Early childhood special education research. *Journal of Early Intervention, 25*(2), 88–99. This article identifies assessment and eligibility as one of five areas needed in early childhood research.

Relevant Federal Regulations

34 C.F.R. Part 104 (2005). Nondiscrimination on the basis of disability in programs and activities receiving federal financial assistance–Section 504 regulations.

    34 C.F.R. Part 300 Assistance to states for the education of children with disabilities [70 Fed. Reg., 35833–35880 (June 21, 2005)].

300.111(a)	Child find.
300.301	Initial evaluations.
300.308	Child with a disability (definitions).
300.303	Reevaluations.
300.306	Eligibility determination team.
300.300	Consent (definition).
300.502	Independent educational evaluation.
300.122	Initial evaluations.
300.304	Evaluation procedure.
300.305	Determination of needed evaluation data.
300.306	Determination of eligibility.
300.308	Additional team members—specific learning disabilities.
300.309	Criteria for determining the existence of a specific learning disability.
300.310	Observation—specific learning disability.
300.311	Written report—specific learning disability.

SELECTED WEBSITES

Council for Exceptional Children: Council for Educational and Diagnostic Services (CEDS)
http://www.unr.edu/educ/ceds/

Internet Special Education Resources: Special Education Assessment
http://www.iser.com/

LD Online: Special Education Evaluation
http://www.ldonline.org/

National Association of School Psychologists
http://www.nasponline.org/

National Center for Research on Evaluation, Standards, and Student Testing
http://cresst96.cse.ucla.edu/

National Center on Educational Outcomes.
http://education.umn.edu/nceo/

NICHCY
http://www.kidsource.com/NICHCY/special_ed.html

Reed Martin: Evaluation Articles and Resources
http://www.reedmartin.com/

QUESTIONS FOR THOUGHT

1. Discuss the advantages and disadvantages of eligibility labels (e.g., learning disabled, behavioral disordered).
2. Could prereferral approaches deny students a FAPE? Why or why not?
3. Many scholars have concluded that intelligence tests cannot be free of bias. Do you agree?
4. What obstacles would a school district encounter by seeking due process to evaluate a child when unable to obtain parental consent?

REFERENCES

Artiles, A. J. (2003). Special education's changing identity: Paradoxes and dilemmas in view of culture and space. *Harvard Educational Review, 73*(2), 164–202.

Artiles, A. J., Rueda, R., Salazar, J. J., & Higareda, I. (2005). Within-group diversity in minority disproportionate representation: English language learners in urban school districts. *Exceptional Children, 71*(3), 283–300.

Assistance to states for the education of children with disabilities (2000), 34 Code of Federal Regulations, Part 300.

Bahr, M. W., Whitten, E., Dieker, L., Kocarek, C. E., & Manson, D. (1999). A comparison of school-based intervention teams: Implications for educational and legal reform. *Exceptional Children, 66*(1), 67–83.

Caruso, B. (2003). Will NCLB impact referrals, accommodations? Retrieved January 23, 2004 from http://www.specialedconnection.com.

Chalmers, L., Ortega, J. C., & Hoover, J. H. (1996). Attitudes of rural and small-town educators toward special education referral. *Case in Point, 10*(1), 21–28.

Craig, S., Hull, K., Haggart, A. G., & Perez-Selles, M. (2000). Promoting cultural competence through teacher assistance teams. *Teaching Exceptional Children, 32*(3), 6–12.

Del'Homme, M., Kasari, C., & Forness, S. (1996). Pre-referral intervention and students at-risk for emotional or behavioral disorders. *Education and Treatment of Children, 19*, 272–285.

Donovan, S., & Cross, C. (2002). *Minority students in special and gifted education.* Washington, DC: National Academy Press. Retrieved January 28, 2004 from http://www.nas.edu/nrc/

Etscheidt, S. (2003). Ascertaining the adequacy, scope, and utility of district evaluations. *Exceptional Children, 69*(2), 227–247.

Finn, J. D. (1982). Patterns in special education placement as revealed by the OCR survey. In K. A. Heller, W. Holtzman, & S. Messick (Eds.), *Placing children in special education: A strategy for equity* (pp. 322–381). Washington, DC: National Academy Press.

Fuchs, D., Fuchs, L., Harris, A., & Roberts, P. H. (1996). Bridging the research-to-practice gap with mainstreaming assistance teams: A cautionary tale. *School Psychology Quarterly, 11*, 244–266.

Fuchs, L., Fuchs, D., & Speece, D. L. (2002). Treatment validity as a unifying construct for identifying learning disabilities. *Learning Disabilities Quarterly, 25*(1), 33–45.

Fujiura, G. T., & Yamaki, K. (2000). Trends in demography of childhood poverty and disability. *Exceptional Children, 66*(2), 187–199.

Graden, J. L., Casey, A., & Christenson, S. L. (1985). Implementing a prereferral intervention system: Part I: The model. *Exceptional Children, 51*, 337–384.

Heller, K. A., Holtzman, W. H., & Messick, S. (Eds.) (1982). *Placing children in special education: A strategy for equity.* Washington, DC: National Academy Press.

Hosp, J. S., & Reschly, D. J. (2003). Referral rates for intervention and assessment: A meta-analysis of racial differences. *The Journal of Special Education, 37*(2), 67–80.

House Report No. 105-95. (1997). *U.S.C. Congressional and Administrative News, 78*–146.

Hudson v. Wilson, 828 F.2d 1059 (4th Cir. 1987).

Individuals With Disabilities Education Act, 20 U.S.C. §§ 1401–1487.

Imber, S. C., & Radcliff, D. (2003). Independent educational evaluations under IDEA '97: It's a testy matter. *Exceptional Children, 70*(1), 27–44.

Katzman, L. (2003). Editor's review: Minority students in special and gifted education. *Harvard Educational Review, 73*(2), 225–239.

Knotek, S. (2003). Bias in problem solving and the social process of student study teams. *The Journal of Special Education, 37*(1), 2–14.

Landon, T., & Mesinger, J. F. (1989). Teacher tolerance ratings on problem behaviors. *Behavioral Disorders, 14*, 236–249.

Larry P. v. Riles, 495 F. Supp. 926 (N.D. Cal. 1979), *aff'd in part, rev'd in part*, 793 F.2d 969 (9th Cir. 1986).

Logan, K., Hansen, C. D., Nieminen, P. K., & Wright, E. H. (2001). Student support teams: Helping students succeed in general education classrooms or working to place students in special education? *Education and Training in Mental Retardation and Developmental Disabilities, 36*(3), 280–292.

MacMillan, D. L., & Reschly, D. J. (1998). Overrepresentation of minority students: The case for greater specificity of the variables examined. *The Journal of Special Education, 32*, 15–24.

McLaughlin, M. J., & Nolet, V. (2004). *What every principal needs to know about special education.* Thousand Oaks, CA: Corwin Press.

McNamara, K., & Hollinger, C. (2003). Intervention-based assessment: Evaluation rates and eligibility findings. *Exceptional Children, 69*(2), 181–193.

Manset-Williamson, G., St. John, E., Hu, S., & Gordon, D. (2002). Early literacy practices as predictors of reading related outcomes: Test scores, testing passing rates, retention, and special education referral. *Exceptionality, 10*(1), 11–28.

National Center on Educational Outcomes (2003). *Accountability for assessment results in the No Child Left Behind Act: What it means for children with disabilities.* Minneapolis: University of Minnesota, National Center on Educational Outcomes. Retrieved January 23, 2004 from http://education.umn.edu/NCEO/OnlinePubs/NCLBdisability.html

Nealis, L. K. (2003). AYP and students with disabilities. *NASP Communique, 32*(4). Retrieved January 23, 2004, from http://www.nasponline.org

Obiakor, F. E. (1999). Teacher expectations of minority exceptional learners: Impact of "accuracy" of self-concepts. *Exceptional Children, 66*(1), 39–53.

O'Connor, E. A., & Simic, O. (2002). The effect of reading recovery on special education referrals and placements. *Psychology in the Schools, 39*(6), 635–646.

OSEP Memorandum 96-5 (Hehir), 24 I.D.E.L.R. 320 (OSEP, 1995).

Oswald, D. P., Coutinho, M. J., Best, A. M., & Singh, N. N. (1999). Ethnic representation in special education: The influence of school-related economic and demographic variables. *The Journal of Special Education, 32*(4), 194–206.

Overton, T. (2003). *Assessing learners with special needs: An applied approach* (4th ed.). Upper Saddle River, NJ: Merrill/Prentice Hall.

Prasse, D. P., & Schrag, J. A. (1998). Providing non-categorical, functional, classroom-based supports for students with disabilities: Legal parameters. In D. J. Reschly, W. D. Tilly, and J. P. Grimes (Eds.), *Functional and non-categorical identification and intervention in special education.* Des Moines: Iowa Department of Education.

President's Commission on Excellence in Special Education (2001). *A new era: Revitalizing special education for children and their families.* Washington, DC: United States Department of Education.

Pugach, M., & Johnson, L. (1989). Pre-referral interventions: Progress, problems, and challenges. *Exceptional Children, 56*, 217–226.

Reschly, D. J. (1997). *Disproportionate minority representation in general and special education: Patterns, issues and alternatives.* Des Moines: Iowa Department of Education.

Reynolds, C. R., Lowe, P. A., & Saenz, A. L. (1999). The problems of bias in psychological assessment. In C. R. Reynolds & T. Gutkin (Eds.), *The handbook of school psychology* (3rd ed.), pp. 556–557. New York: Wiley.

Safran, S. P., & Safran, J. S. (1988). Perceptions of problem behaviors: A review and analysis of research. In R. B. Rutherford, C. M., Nelson, and S. R. Forness (Eds.), *Severe behavior disorders in children and youth* (pp. 39–50). Boston: College Hill Press.

Shinn, M. R., Good, R. H., & Parker, C. (1998). Non-categorical special education services with students with severe achievement deficits. In D. J. Reschly, W. D. Tilly, and J. P. Grimes (Eds.), *Functional and non-categorical identification and intervention in special education.* Des Moines: Iowa Department of Education.

Shinn, M. R., Tindal, G. A., & Spira, D. A. (1987). Special education referrals as an index of teacher tolerance: Are teachers imperfect tests? *Exceptional Children, 54*, 32–40.

Taylor, P. B., Gunter, P. L., & Slate, J. R. (2001). Teachers' perceptions of inappropriate student behavior as a function of teachers' and student's gender and ethnic background. *Behavioral Disorders, 26*(2), 146–151.

Tilly, W. D., Reschly, D., & Grimes, J. (1998). Disability determination in problem solving systems: Conceptual foundations and critical components. In D. J. Reschly, W. D. Tilly, and J. P. Grimes (Eds.), *Functional and non-categorical identification and intervention in special education.* Des Moines: Iowa Department of Education.

Turnbull, H. R., & Turnbull, A. (1998). Free appropriate public education: *The law and children with disabilities.* Denver: Love Publishing.

U.S. Department of Education (1996). *Profile assessment and resolution reviews.* Washington, DC: Author.

Valles, E. C. (1998). The disproportionate representation of minority students in special education: Responding to the problem. *The Journal of Special Education, 32*, 52–54.

Wehmeyer, M., & Schwartz, M. (2001). Disproportionate representation of males in special education services: Biology, behavior, or bias? *Education and Treatment of Children, 24*(1), 28–45.

Wenkart, R. D. (1998). Native language instruction and the special education student: Who decides the instructional methodology? *Education Law Reporter, 125*, 581–594.

Whitten, E. (1995–96). Intervention assistance teams: The principal's role identified. *Case in Point, 9*(2), 21–32.

Yell, M. L. (2006). *The law and special education* (2nd ed.). Upper Saddle River, NJ: Merrill/Prentice Hall.

CHAPTER 4

INDIVIDUALIZED EDUCATION PROGRAM (IEP)

CHAPTER PREVIEW

Focus

The school administrator's role in the area of IEP development and implementation includes devising efficient, effective, and appropriate professional implementation systems; improving communication and cooperation among staff members involved with parents; and meeting student needs through responsible use of school resources. IEPs are the documentation of team planning necessary to provide students with disabilities appropriate educational programs. An appropriate program allows a student with disabilities to access education and obtain meaningful benefit from it. Schools do not have to provide a program that is the best or one that maximizes educational opportunity for the child.

IEPs must be completed before providing services to eligible students. The content of IEPs must be reviewed by the IEP team when the student's progress is in doubt and at least annually.

Legal Issues

The law addresses two aspects of the IEP: the IEP meetings and the education program itself. The meetings should be

- initiated by the school no later than 30 days after determining a child is eligible for special education;
- held at least annually to review and update each student's program progress;
- attended by the parent(s), a regular education teacher, a special education teacher, a school district representative, the child (when appropriate), and others at the discretion of parents or school (at least one team member must be familiar with student assessment);
- followed as soon as possible by implementation of the agreed-upon program.

The IEP document itself must include

- a statement regarding the child's present levels of academic achievement and functional performance, including how the disability impacts participation and progress in the general curriculum;
- a statement of annual goals, including measurable criteria in order to monitor progress;
- a statement of the specific special education, related services, assistive technology, supplementary aids and services to be provided the child or on behalf of the child, and modifications and supports for school personnel to be provided;
- an explanation of the extent, if any, to which the child will not participate in regular education programs and nonacademic activities;
- projected dates, frequency, location, and duration of services;
- a statement of how the student's progress will be communicated to parents;
- a statement of participation in district-wide assessments;
- transition planning and services for older children;
- behavioral interventions when the child's behavior interferes with the education of the child or others.

Decision-making in the IEP process is accomplished through consensus building and not by majority vote. When consensus cannot be achieved, the school is to complete the IEP and provide parents with offical notice of its contents. The parents can decide whether to accept the IEP as written, or request mediation or a due process hearing to challenge the IEP.

The school district is legally bound to provide all programs and services listed in the IEP and to make a good faith effort to assist the child to achieve the IEP's goals.

Rationale

The requirement of an IEP for each student with a disability is a response to (a) the reality that students with disabilities differ significantly from each other as well as from the student who is developing typically, and (b) past abuses, in which students with disabilities frequently suffered from inappropriate educational placements based on categorical labels alone. Furthermore, the practices of IEP process individualization, goal-oriented planning, and periodic evaluation embodied in the law have proved educationally sound practices for all students.

Approaches

The best aid to efficient and successful IEP meetings is advance preparation, good communication, and the development of trust among the participants. Meaningful participation by parents and other team members is a necessary element of the program's success. Although school staff members should not arrive at the meeting with a completed IEP, they should be well prepared. People attending the IEP meeting should be familiar with the student, the evaluation data, and the school's programs and services, and be ready to offer realistic proposals to meet the child's educational needs.

Parents, and students when appropriate, should be encouraged to prepare for and participate in IEP meetings. Regular school staff communications with parents can help to build trust and understanding which, in turn, can make it easier to reach agreement.

When needed, changes can and should be made in the IEP after implementation has begun, but there should be an effort to do the best possible planning the first time. Changes in the IEP may be made through IEP team meetings, or more informally through mutual school and parent agreement, but all changes must be documented.

THE IEP: KEY TO THE IDEA

The IEP is critical to the educational philosophy embodied in the IDEA. The law requires that each student with a disability be treated as an individual and educated according to the child's unique needs and capabilities. Students with disabilities are no longer expected to adapt to the school services available; schools are expected to adapt and devise some means of providing the services that students as individuals require (Keyes & Owens-Johnson, 2003). The success of schools in meeting the needs of the students they serve often depends on ensuring that school staff members understand this basic paradigm shift and are prepared to implement it. The IEP also represents a dramatic change in public school orientation from the general to the specific, and from the convenience of the programs available in the school district to programs that meet the needs of the child.

In recent decades, schools have come a long way from the rigid homogeneity of serving certain students in certain classrooms based on disability label to much more flexibly arranged and fluid programs and classrooms. The inclusion of students with disabilities into regular classrooms and activities can be seen as simply another step in an already well-established direction. Similarly, the process of writing and implementing IEPs can be seen as a training tool for educators in the continuing process of individualization of instruction for all students.

Writing an IEP for each student is time consuming, meeting scheduling problems may be substantial, and disagreements common. However, a well-designed school process that values, respects, and rewards professionalism can alleviate many potential problems. An understanding of the educational value of the IEP process builds tolerance. With this understanding in mind, the IEP fulfills several important purposes:

1. It is a management tool to ensure provision of appropriate special education and related services. Important in this respect are the ongoing evaluation components that are designed to continuously measure a student's progress.
2. It is a communication vehicle between/among all participants involved in programming for the student with disabilities. As such, it inherently provides an opportunity for problem solving and resolving differences of opinion.
3. It is a written commitment of resources.
4. It is an extension of procedural protections guaranteed to parents and students.
5. It is a compliance monitoring device to determine whether a student with disabilities is receiving a free appropriate public education.

IEP DEVELOPMENT

When the IEP Is Required

The first IEP team meeting must be held within 30 days of the evaluation team's determination that the student is eligible for special education. Additional meetings may be held as often as necessary. The initial completed IEP must be implemented as soon as possible following the meetings, and the IEP must be in place before the start of special education programs and services. Programs and services must be provided to a student within a reasonable time following receipt of initial parent consent to evaluate a child. There can be no undue delay. For most children it can be expected that services offered under an IEP would begin within about 60 days of the school's receipt of parental consent for the initial evaluation.

The IDEA requires that IEPs be reviewed by the IEP team periodically as needed, but at least annually. The intent of the law is that school districts and parents, based on assessment/ evaluation findings and student progress, regularly review all of the IEP components and review the continuum of placement options to determine that the program, services, and placement remain appropriate. Changes in the IEP that relate to appropriate programming, including annual goals, related services, accommodations, and supplementary aids and services can be made only through the IEP team review process. Acceptable unilateral changes made by the school are very limited (i.e., day-to-day adjustments in curriculum materials used to meet an objective).

Parents and schools may request IEP reviews more frequently than annually. It is anticipated that whenever a student is not making meaningful progress under an IEP, the school will reconvene the IEP team to review the student's progress and make necessary adjustments. When a school believes a review is unnecessary and refuses parent requests, it must provide parents the full detailed written notice discussed in Chapter 2. This allows the parents an opportunity to request mediation or a due process hearing to resolve the issue.

Each student's IEP must be accessible to each regular and special education teacher and to each related service or other service provider responsible for its implementation. Each teacher, service provider, and their temporary substitutes must be personally informed of his or her specific responsibilities regarding implementation of the IEP and specific accommodations, modifications, and supports that must be provided for the student. Education leaders are responsible for establishing and maintaining these important communication procedures.

Appropriate Programming

Every child with a disability who is entitled to special education under the IDEA must be provided a free public education (FAPE). Although that phrase conveys some specific meaning (e.g., *free* means at no additional cost to parents above what other public school parents pay for their children), the word *appropriate* has no precise meaning in statute or regulation. That is why IEP teams often struggle with their role.

After more than 30 years of implementation, the IDEA itself still does not provide much direction. Naturally, the courts have been called on to fill that void. The first Supreme Court ruling interpreting the IDEA had as the primary legal issue the interpretation of the word *appropriate*. The Court ruled that, in providing appropriate programs, schools are required to provide access to educational programs for children with disabilities that are individually designed, through the IEP process, to provide educational benefit to the child. Schools are not required to maximize student potential or provide the best programs possible (*Board of Education v. Rowley,* 1982).

Subsequent lower court rulings have made it clear that minimal or trivial educational benefit will not be considered appropriate (e.g., *Drew P. v. Clarke County School District,* 1989). Several court rulings have required the application of a meaningful educational benefit standard in determining whether a school's IEP met the minimal standard of appropriateness. Some have ruled that a determination of benefit for an individual student must be flexible enough to take the student's potential into consideration (e.g., *Deal v. Hamilton County Board of Education,* 2004).

Several courts have used automobiles as an analogy to appropriate programming. They have stated that students with disabilities are entitled under the IDEA to at least a "Chevrolet" of a program, but not necessarily a "Cadillac" of a program (e,g., *Doe v. Board of Education,* 1993).

Neither the law contained in statute, regulations, nor court interpretations clearly establishes an exact standard of *appropriate,* applicable to educational programming developed by IEP teams. That determination is left to the IEP teams, people who best know the child's educational needs and available resources. The IEP must be designed, at a minimum, to provide an educational benefit for the child that is meaningful in terms of the child's educational progress and overall potential (e.g., *Deal v. Hamilton County Board of Education,* 2004).

Participants in the IEP Meeting

Parents as Partners Educators must make a conscious effort to ensure that parents have the opportunity to meaningfully participate in the IEP process. Parents are full and equal team participants. Teams must consider parent concerns and the information they provide in both developing and reviewing IEPs (Bateman & Linden, 2006).

Parents can provide critical information about the child that cannot be easily obtained elsewhere, such as health history, interests, behavior outside school settings, and special abilities. Educators should encourage parents and their child to think about what the family sees as the child's future. Some sources recommend that families be assisted in developing a vision of the child's future on which the IEP team can focus its attention (see the model IEP form in Appendix E).

Maintenance of a good parent/school relationship is of great practical importance. Parent support for the education program in the home will increase the likelihood of successful results at school. Even though parents are not legally required to carry out the terms of IEPs in the home, they will normally cooperate in an effort to support their child and the school. Johnson and Duffett (2002) report that 77% of parents state that their child's IEP team treats them like they are fully part of the team and 84% state that their child's teachers really care about their child as a person.

School District Representative The person designated in the school's procedures to represent the district at the IEP meeting must be qualified to provide or supervise the provision of specially designed instruction, be knowledgeable about and have the authority to commit school resources, ensure that IEP services will be delivered, and be knowledgeable about the general education curriculum (the curriculum content adopted for all children). Due to the No Child Left Behind (NCLB) emphasis on student academic achievement, access to the general curriculum for appropriate programming for a student with disabilities is more important than ever.

The school representative is frequently the school principal, but it also may be a special education administrator or specialist, such as a speech therapist. The school may designate another of the school's IEP team members to serve as the school's representative, so long as all the qualification criteria are met.

Services agreed on at the IEP meeting will, in fact, be provided and may not be altered or vetoed at a higher administrative, or even school board, level.

Special Education Teacher At least one of the student's special education teachers or special education providers must be on the IEP team. When considering which special education teacher or provider should be involved, consideration should be given first to people responsible or likely to be responsible for implementing the student's IEP.

In a three-year study of secondary IEP meetings, researchers confirmed that special education teachers usually lead the IEP meeting process. They were found to be more knowledgeable about, and participative in, the IEP process than all other groups participating in the study, including administrators (Martin, Marshall, & Sale, 2004).

The school must ensure that the child's actual special education teacher receives a copy of the finalized IEP before beginning work with the child.

Regular Education Teacher At least one of the child's regular education teachers must attend when the child is, or may be, participating in the regular education environment. Due to the IDEA's strong preference for inclusion of students in the regular classroom, the vast majority of IEP teams will include at least one regular education teacher. In the case of a child whose behavior impedes the learning of himself or others, a regular education teacher of the child knowledgeable about "appropriate positive behavioral interventions and supports, and other strategies" should be invited to attend. [20 U.S.C. § 1414(d)(3)(C)].

When the child has more than one regular education teacher, the school may designate which teacher will participate. It is recommended that the participant be a teacher who will be responsible for implementing the IEP. Other regular education teachers may attend when their attendance would be appropriate.

The primary purpose of having a regular education teacher on the IEP team is to help facilitate, through her or his expertise regarding the general curriculum and regular classroom environment, the successful placement of the child in the regular classroom (inclusion). The implementation of NCLB legislation makes the presence of regular education academic teachers even more important than before. The focus of NCLB is the academic achievement of all students, and regular class teachers will have a good understanding of the teaching and testing accommodations needed by individual students (Baird, 2003; Washburn-Moses, 2003).

Regular education teachers are also important in helping determine supplementary aids and services, program modifications, classroom accommodations, and supports for the school staff working with the child. Participation on the team presents an opportunity for regular educators to exercise influence in obtaining the supports they need to provide effective programming to special education students (e.g., advance training, time for collaboration) (Huefner, 2006). Baird (2003) has compared this arrangement with medical model problem-solving teams. The expert specialists work hand-in-hand with the generalists as a collaborative team. She believes that this collaborative effort in developing IEPs helps break down the *two box* model involving *our* students vs. *your* students in the school setting.

The importance of the regular class teacher in the IEP development process is underscored by several federal court decisions. The Court of Appeals for the Ninth Circuit has ruled that the failure of a school to ensure participation of a regular class teacher on the IEP team was a fatal flaw in the integrity of the IEP process (*M. L. v. Federal Way School District,* 2004). The Sixth Circuit has ruled that the school's failure to have a regular class teacher involved in IEP planning resulted in substantial detriment to the child's education program (*Deal v. Hamilton County Board of Education,* 2004).

Unfortunately, regular education teachers who have so much to add to IEP teams are often the professionals least comfortable in, and knowledgeable about, their roles on IEP teams (Martin, Marshall, & Sale, 2004). Preservice

teaching program components and professional development opportunities must be provided to regular class teachers to help them become better accustomed to and knowledgable about the IEP process and to ensure that their team participation will be meaningful.

Attendance by too many teachers and other staff members can make an IEP meeting unwieldy and sometimes intimidating to parents. It is advisable to solicit opinions from the student's other teachers before a meeting without requiring their attendance.

All teachers of a particular child should be informed about the results of the meeting and have easy access to a copy of the IEP. Educational leaders are responsible for ensuring that relevant IEP content is made known and available to those staff members who must carry out its provisions.

All school staff members should be reminded from time to time about the confidentiality of education records. Without the written consent of parents, information from education records, including IEPs, should not be disclosed to school employees or volunteers who do not have a legitimate educational interest in the child.

Others When appropriate, as determined largely by the parents, the child may attend IEP meetings, in whole or in part. Parents should be advised before each IEP meeting that they may invite their child to participate, and the appropriateness of their decision may be discussed by the team beforehand. The primary questions for consideration on child involvement are whether the child will be helpful in developing an IEP, whether the child will benefit from attendance and participation, or both.

When part of the purpose of the IEP meeting is planning transition services for the student who will turn 16 years of age, the school must invite the student and the parents must be informed that their child will be invited. If the child does not attend meetings where transition is considered, the school must attempt to ensure that the student's preferences and interests are known to the team and are considered.

Students should be prepared in advance for fulfilling their role in IEP team meetings. Research indicates that students participate in their own IEP meetings much less than all other team members and need to be supported in their team leadership and involvement skills (Martin et al., 2006). The IEP concept and process should be explained or modeled in ways that students understand their importance. They should be helped to prepare in advance of the meetings and develop their own personal meeting objectives. Participation provides students the opportunity to take ownership in the process that is so important to their lives and their futures (Lee et al., 2006; Van Dycke, Martin, & Lovett, 2006). For more details regarding student participation in the IEP development process, see Chapter 8.

In order for the IEP to be in effect when the child turns 16 years of age, the IEP must contain transition planning. This requires the consideration of inviting additional people to the IEP meetings who represent community agencies who are knowledgeable about and provide community transition services. This would include post-secondary vocational training, adult education, independent living, leisure activities, and community mobility. Chapter 8 provides more detail on transition programming.

At the discretion of the parents or the school, other individuals who have knowledge or special expertise regarding the child may attend as appropriate. Attendance at meetings by related services staff members, such as physical and occupational therapists, therapeutic recreation specialists, and adaptive physical education teachers can help resolve many inclusion concerns, ranging from mobility to pain relief (Shapiro & Sayers, 2003). The determination of whether the invited person has adequate knowledge or expertise to participate is delegated to the parents or school who invite the person to be a member of the IEP team.

The presence of attorneys has long been discouraged at IEP meetings, especially when their participation would create an adversarial atmosphere not in the best interest of the child (Letter to Diehl, 1993). Developments over the years indicate that there may be a continuing trend toward reducing attorney participation in order to remove the legalistic atmosphere from some IEP meetings (Rosenfeld, 2000).

At least one person on the IEP team must be able to interpret the instructional implications of evaluation results. This requirement is an effort to connect evaluation findings on the needs of the child and the specific programs and services to be provided the child (Bateman & Linden, 2006). This person may also play another role on the team (e.g., special education teacher).

Attendance of Team Members at IEP meetings

Generally, all IEP team members will be present for both the initial development and annual reviews of a student's IEP. The 2004 Amendments, however, recognized the difficulty inherent in planning for the attendance of all IEP team members. They allow individual team members to be absent from meetings, in whole or in part, when the member's area of curriculum or related services is not being discussed or modified. When a team meeting does involve a member's area of curriculum or related services, the member may still be excused, in whole or in part, when he or she submits written input to the IEP development prior to the meeting. In both instances, the school and the parent must agree that the team member may be absent, and this agreement must be documented in writing [20 U.S.C. § 1414(d)(1)(C)]. This modified form of meeting attendance will take some time for adjustment. In the meantime, Beekman (2005) suggests that schools consider several issues and devise the following operational procedures in advance of incidents arising:

- Determine who will have the authority to enter into agreements on behalf of the school.
- Develop a form.
- Make contingency plans for assuring that written input by the excused member is available and how to handle questions for excused IEP members.

Amendments to an IEP, after an annual IEP review for a school year, may be made without a formal meeting of the IEP team when the parents and the school agree. Such amendments must be documented in writing and attached to the IEP [*20 U.S.C. § 1414(d)(3)(D)*]. Thus, noncontroversial changes to an IEP may be agreed to over the telephone or by e-mail. Although alternative means of amending an IEP provide efficiency to the participants, Beekman (2005) recommends that schools establish operational procedures that address several important issues:

- Who has the authority to commit the school to an amended IEP?
- What specific form would the IEP addendum take?
- Should the parents (and other parties) be provided written notice of the amendment(s)?

The 2004 Amendments also expressly allow for alternative means of meeting participation, such as video conferencing and telephone conference calls. The parents and school must agree to the use of alternative means of participation [*20 U.S.C. 1414(f)*].

IEP Team Decision Making

Consensus   The IEP team decision-making process is accomplished through consensus, not by majority vote. Consensus is a type of group decision making based upon general agreement. Consensus does not require unanimity. It does not necessarily represent each member's first choice, but is a decision that each team member can accept and support. Consensus is reached when all group members are willing to accept an idea as the best choice for the group; and each team member is willing to accept the decision as a decision for the group and will not attempt to later sabotage the decision. Team members who cannot accept and live with a particular decision have an obligation to make their position known.

The process of IEP team decision making is the epitome of the concept of team empowerment. Student IEPs may not be unilaterally changed by any one person or group of persons in the school district, except the IEP team. Team decisions involving appropriate programs and services, when made in conformance with the law, can be changed only through a subsequent IEP team decision or a

due process hearing decision rendered by a hearing officer.

When School and Parents Disagree   The ultimate responsibility to ensure that an appropriate IEP is timely developed remains with the school. When disagreements over IEP terms arise, the school and parents should attempt first to resolve differences through negotiation. They may jointly agree to an interim IEP (e.g., one to nine weeks), with appropriate monitoring, and then meet again to formally determine whether the interim IEP should be continued or modified. Specific conditions and interim IEP terms should be developed in the usual IEP format, and parents should be fully involved. When achievement of consensus on IEP terms is not likely on even an interim basis, the school staff should proceed to complete the development of the IEP and provide copies to the parents. Because written consent of the parents is required only before the initial IEP can be implemented, subsequent IEPs can be implemented without parent consent, so long as parents are provided proper notice (See Chapter 2).

When parents receive written notice of a proposed change in an IEP, they may initiate mediation or a due process hearing to challenge the appropriateness of the proposed change in program. If, after a reasonable amount of time no hearing has been initiated by the parents, the school may implement the proposed change. Some states require a specific waiting time (e.g., 10 days) between parent receipt of the notice and implementation of the proposed change.

When a request for a due process hearing is made, the most current educational program in which the child had been previously placed remains in effect until differences are resolved by mutual agreement or through a due process hearing (See *stay-put* provisions in Chapter 11).

When Educators Disagree   The give and take of consensus building will normally achieve agreement among educators, albeit it may not always be strong support. Rarely will educators remain strongly divided and resistant to attempt at least trial programs and approaches for a student under an interim IEP. The IDEA does not address the possibility that educators on an IEP team (and evaluation and placement teams) may remain divided. Thus, although some state laws provide for dissenting opinions to team decisions, the school must carry out its duty and implement a team decision. A dissenting group of educators has no clear status under federal law (Letter to Anonymous, 1996).

Elements of an IEP

IEP Format   The format and length of the IEP are not prescribed or determined by the law, and historically the length of the IEP document has continued to grow. Even after Congress publicly prided itself in reducing the paperwork required in the 1997 Amendments to the IDEA, Huefner (2000, p. 203) stated that "the IEP paperwork implications are daunting."

A model IEP form, which is comprehensive and seven pages in length, is included in Appendix E. Although it may be possible to develop shorter IEP forms, additional brevity may result in important IEP content or other considerations being overlooked by IEP teams.

IEP Content   *Child's Present Levels of Educational Performance (PLEP).* The IEP must describe the child's present levels of academic achievement and functional performance, including the effects of the child's disability on any relevant educational area—academic, personal-social, living skills, physical education, or vocational education. It must include a description of how the disability affects the child's participation and progress in the same curriculum available and provided to children who are not disabled (general curriculum). It should also reflect the IEP team's considerations of the child's strengths and the results of evaluations. For preschool children, as appropriate, the PLEP should identify how the disability affects the child's participation in age-appropriate activities. The information should be accurate, stated in measurable terms as much as possible, and explained in language that is easily understood.

The importance of the PLEP in the development of IEPs should not be underestimated by the team. It is the foundational basis for the appropriate educational program and services identified in the IEP. There must be a direct identifiable link between the PLEP and the goals and services provided in the IEP. The reporting of mere test score results in the PLEP does not provide sufficient data for the rest of the IEP process. (See Appendix A for sample PLEP statements.)

The 2004 Amendments to the IDEA added greater emphasis to academic achievement than was previously present. However, the book's authors think that the term Present Levels of Educational Performance (PLEP) used previously in the law remains a better description of the purpose and intent of this introductory statement. Some authors have used other phrasing, such as "present levels of academic achievement and functional performance" (PLAAFP) (Yell, 2006) and "present levels of performance" (PLOP) (Bateman, & Linden, 2006).

Annual Goals.   Annual goals, both academic and functional, written in response to the PLEP statement, must be based on assessment results and parent input when it is provided. Goals should be designed to meet the child's needs that will enable the child to be involved in and make progress in the general educational curriculum and meet the child's other educational needs. Annual goal statements should be specific and indicate (a) the direction of change (e.g., increase or decrease), and (b) the desired or expected levels of change in specific skill areas. These goals should be the team's best estimate of what the student will be able to accomplish within one year. Generally, one to three goals should be provided for each affected disability area identified in the PLEP statement. Educators often look for the following four characteristics of well-written goals:

- Meaningful
- Measurable
- Monitored (able to be)
- Making decisions (enhanced)

Educators sometimes apply the *stranger test* to goal writing; can a stranger to the IEP process understand and implement the goal as written? (See Appendix B for sample goal statements.)

The IEP team must also make an individualized determination of which educational needs will not be addressed in the general curriculum and how those needs will be met. For preschool children (ages three to five), goals should be designed to allow the child to participate in age-appropriate activities. IEP goals should not be written for a child's progress in the general curriculum when the child's disability does not require more support than accommodations and modifications in the regular education classroom.

In order to assist a student to achieve the goals, regular or special education teachers may make day-to-day adjustments in instructional methods, approaches, and materials, which are not fundamental elements of the student's special education. These minor adjustments can usually be made without obtaining agreement and approval from the IEP team.

Although the 2004 Amendments have removed the legal requirement that IEPs for most students must identify short-term objectives or benchmarks for annual goals, it may be desirable for individual students to include objectives or benchmarks. The team will need to consider the monitoring of the student's progress on annual goals and regularly report that assessment of progress to parents. Essentially, much of the same progress monitoring that was previously required under the IDEA continues to be required, only they are no longer referred to as short-term objectives or benchmarks.

For the few students taking alternative district or state assessments based on alternative standards, the IEP must identify short-term objectives or benchmarks associated with annual goals.

Evaluation Criteria—Monitoring. Each annual goal must include specific evaluation criteria which informs the IEP team whether the child is progressing on the goal and how much progress has been made (Bateman & Linden, 2006). Such criteria should be realistic and not exceed the standards expected of regular students. Evaluation procedures might include examinations, teacher observations, frequency counts, or other types of continuing data collection, such as anecdotal records and student self-evaluation. A

report on progress in meeting the annual goals must be provided parents on a regular basis; not less frequently than the issuance of report cards to nondisabled students in the school.

The performance criteria should not be listed as a separate section but integrated into student goals (see Appendix C for examples). The evaluation criteria serves to objectively assess the child's progress toward the stated goals. Evaluation criteria (a) provide a continuous progress monitoring capability for individual students on individual goals, (b) assist the teacher with information in making better instructional decisions, (c) provide students with motivation, and (d) help parents understand their child's current performance level (Pemberton, 2003). Attention must be given to assigning staff responsibility in the monitoring process. Improved monitoring of progress will ensure that education programs will be meaningful and beneficial for students (Etscheidt, 2006). Evaluation criteria also serve as aids in assessing the effectiveness of the IEP so that the IEP can be revised, when desirable, in order to meet the child's instructional needs. IEP teams are expected to address unsatisfactory progress on goals. Failure to do so is difficult to justify. Without continuous progress monitoring, determining the appropriateness of a student's IEP would be difficult. (For examples of how progress monitoring can be incorporated within IEP forms, see Appendix E.)

Gunter, Miller, Venn, Thomas, and House 2002 propose student maintenance, wherein students graph and chart their own data using individually appropriate computer software packages. They believe that students taking responsibility for graphing their own performance data empowers the students in a way that makes change more personal and motivating to the students.

Integrated PLEP and Goals. The interdependent relationship of the PLEP and progress monitoring criteria in the IEP is very important. Care and attention given to the successive drafting of each results in an integrated educational program.

In their book on IEP development, Bateman and Linden (1998) provided excellent advice about IEP formation, content, and development. Following are two brief examples of their perspective of the important integration of the PLEP, goal, and services provided students:*

1. PLEP: Reads first grade material at 20–30 words per minute with 5–10 errors, guesses at all unknown words.

   Annual Goal: Will read third-grade material at 80–100 words per minute with 0–2 errors.

   Progress monitoring #1: By December 15, will read second-grade material at 40–60 words per minute with 0–5 errors.

   Progress monitoring #2: By March 15, will read third-grade material at 50 words per minute with 0–4 errors.

   Services provided: One-to-one tutoring in a highly structured reading program; five lessons weekly, 45 minutes each, provided in private, quiet area of resource room.

2. PLEP: Several times (five to ten) daily, student draws or talks inappropriately about bodily functions.

   Annual goal: No inappropriate talk or drawings about bodily functions.

   Progress monitoring #1: By February 1, fewer than two such inappropriate drawings or vocalizations per week.

   Progress monitoring #2: By April 15, fewer than two such inappropriate drawings or vocalizations per month.

   Services provided: Behavioral contingency plan with student-selected reward and response cost.

Other examples of integrated IEP components can be found in Appendix D.

Special Education, Related Services, and Other Services. Special education is defined under the IDEA as specially designed instruction to meet the unique needs of a child with a disability, regardless of educational setting. Specially designed instruction includes a broad

range of adjustments, including the adaptation of content, methodology, or delivery of instruction to address the child's unique needs that result from the disability. The objective is to ensure the child's access to the general curriculum adopted by the school to be applicable for all children and specifically general curriculum content. The effort at a clear distinction between special education and the general curriculum for many children may be illusory. This is because the IEP considerations and support for achievement in the general curriculum (i.e., accommodations, supplementary aids and services) are driven by the IDEA's strong preference for the inclusion element of LRE. Although special education may sometimes include different content or different delivery of content, the IDEA aims to help the child meet the educational achievement standards expected to apply to all children and to ensure that children with disabilities have the opportunity to achieve those standards.

Related services are those services necessary to help the student benefit from special education. (A sample list can be found in Chapter 5.) The IEP must include a statement of all education services needed by the student, not just those readily available in the school district. The IEP must identify who will provide the services, even when an agency other than the school provides them. Services must be delivered at no additional cost to the student's family above the cost of fees normally charged to the parents of students without disabilities.

The IEP must contain a statement about supplementary aids and services to be provided to the child or on behalf of the child in the regular class or regular activity setting. These would include program modifications, accommodations, and school personnel supports that will be provided for the child in the regular education setting.

Support for school staff could include such items as specific training in behavior strategies, classroom management, collaboration skills, and effective models for the integration of children with disabilities into regular school settings. These staff development activities normally would be expressly provided in an IEP to help staff meet the needs of a specific child.

---

*From *Better IEPs: How to Develop Legally Correct and Educationally Useful Programs* (3rd ed.) (pp. 104–105), by B. D. Bateman and M. A. Linden, 1998, Longmont, CO: Sopris West. Copyright 1992–1998 by Bateman and Linden. Adapted by permission.

The IDEA requires that assistive technology devices and services be made available to students with disabilities, when required, as part of students' special education, related services, or supplementary aids and services. Generally, the phrase *assistive technology device* refers to equipment used to aid the functional capabilities of children with disabilities (e.g., calculator in mathematics, word processor for writing), and *assistive technology service* refers to the services of a technician or trainer required to assist a child with a disability use and benefit from an assistive technology device. By express exclusion in the law, assistive technology device and technology service does not include surgically implanted medical devices and services related to them.

Assistive technology devices are not usually considered to include personalized devices such as eyeglasses, hearing aids, or leg braces that children will require regardless of whether or not they attend school. However, if an IEP team determines that a personal device is required for a child in order to ensure that the child receives FAPE, then it must be provided at no cost to the child's parents.

Assistive technology includes both technology related to a child's individual needs (e.g., electronic notetakers, cassette recorders) as well as general technology devices used by all students. The school must assure that necessary accommodations are provided to allow the child to use technology devices commonly used by all students. The use of assistive technology devices in a child's home, and training for the student and parents, are to be determined by the IEP team based on curricular expectations (i.e., homework). Parents cannot be charged for normal use and wear and tear on the devices. Subject to state law, however, parents may be responsible for loss, theft, or damage of assistive technology equipment due to negligence or misuse.

The 2004 Amendments state that education programs and services be "based on peer reviewed research to the extent practicable." Beekman (2005) recognized that research is lacking in many areas of special education programs and services. Beekman therefore recommends that schools identify the extent of existing research to support its various programs and services, and where necessary, be prepared to take the position that it is not practicable to base a particular program or services on peer reviewed research. He also recommends that parents requesting specific programs and services for their children be asked about their knowledge of relevent peer reviewed research on those programs and services.

Once special education, related services, supplementary aids and services, assistive technology, and modifications and accommodations are included in an IEP, any subsequent significant changes, deletions, and amendments require review and approval by the IEP team.

Duration of Services. To ensure that the school's resource commitment is clear to parents and other IEP team members, the projected date for the beginning of services, and the anticipated frequency, location, and duration of services, must be expressly stated in the IEP. Some general standard of time for services (e.g., minutes per day or week) must be indicated that is appropriate to the specific service to be provided and clear to all participants.

Behavioral Interventions. When the behavior of a student with disabilities interferes with the student's learning or that of other students, the IEP team must formally develop positive behavioral interventions, strategies, and supports for the student or school personnel. Failure to address a student's disruptive behavior in the development and implementation of the IEP would result in denying the child FAPE. Multiple suspensions of the child from school for terms of a few days each cannot be substituted for the IEP team's addressing the child's behavior in the IEP (Appendix A to 34 C.F.R. Part 300, question No. 38, 2004). A federal district court in Maine concluded that FAPE was not provided a student with attendance problems related to his diagnosed emotional disabilities. The school was aware of the boy's attendance issues, but did not provide any behavioral supports in his IEP (*Lamoine School Committee v. Ms. Z.,* 2005). The team can decide to plan and conduct a functional behavioral assessment (FBA) and use those results in developing a behavioral intervention plan (BIP), which becomes part of an IEP. See Chapter 9 for a detailed discussion of the FBA and BIP.

The rationale behind these extra considerations for disruptive behavior is to foster increased participation of the student with disabilities in an inclusive educational setting or other LRE (Appendix A to 34 C.F.R. Part 300, question No. 39, 2004).

Transition Planning. No later than development of the IEP, which will be in effect when the student turns age 16, the IEP team must begin formal planning for transition from high school to adult life. It must identify and annually update appropriate measurable postsecondary goals based on age-appropriate transition assessments related to training, education, employment, and independent living skills where appropriate.

The IEP must contain statements regarding needed transition services and identify participating community agencies that will be responsible for providing those services before the student leaves school. If any community agency fails to provide a planned transition service while the child is still in school, the school must initiate a new IEP meeting as soon as possible to identify alternative agencies and services to meet the transition objectives provided in the student's IEP. Secondary education and transition planning details can be found in Chapter 8. For examples of transition planning, see Appendix F.

District-Wide Assessments. Under NCLB legislation, students with disabilities are required to participate in state and district-wide achievement tests to determine their growth in "general curriculum" content areas. When modifications and accommodations are desirable in the administration of the tests, the IEP must document that need and the modifications and accommodations must be provided to the student. Accommodations are meant to make the testing experience fair, not to give students with disabilities a special advantage. Reasonable accommodations do not change the substance of what is tested and should not impact test validity.

They merely help assure valid test results for individual students with disabilities (Edgeman, Jablonski, & Lloyd, 2006). Modifications and accommodations in testing could involve time (i.e., length, breaks), directions (i.e., highlighting, simplifying), presentation of questions (i.e., large print, fewer per page), response (i.e., oral, word processor), and setting (i.e., lighting, noise).

Test-taking accommodations similar to those provided a student in the classroom under an IEP may be determined appropriate for the state-wide exams (Yell, Katsiyannas, & Shiner, 2006). However, accommodations for state-wide tests under NCLB are limited only to changes in testing materials and procedures that ensure that testing results are not invalidated by a child's disability. For instance, out-of-level testing in reading that might be used as a classroom testing accommodation under an IEP is not available under NCLB guidelines. Bolt and Thurlow (2004) have reported that very little definitive research has been conducted that demonstrate the validity and reliability effects of accommodations on assessments. State policies and practices are evolving and being used with greater numbers of students (Thurlow, Lazarus, Thompson, & Morse, 2005). Various concerns have been expressed regarding the effect of NCLB's testing implementations on students with disabilities by national organizations, including the Council for Exceptional Children (Allbritten, Mainzer, & Ziegler, 2004).

Parents of students with disabilities tend to approve of the trend toward a greater emphasis on academics in their childrens' education program. Johnson and Duffett (2002) report that nearly 80% of parents surveyed, both those with and without children with disabilities, agreed that schools should be paying more attention to the academic progress of children.

When the IEP team determines that a child's participation in general assessments is not appropriate, the IEP must indicate why that assessment is not appropriate for the child. The IEP of each student with disabilities not participating in state- and district-wide assessment must contain a description of the individualized means of assessment that will be used with that student. Most children in this category will be in alternative curricular programs and not be expected to meet the school's general curriculum goals.

The alternative assessments aim to determine a student's needs in areas other than the core curriculum content standards of traditional assessments. Testing methodology may well include a variety of tests, portfolio reviews, student record reviews, observations, and interviews gathered from persons, both adults and students, who know the student (Ysseldyke & Olsen, 1999). Some initial teacher reactions to the early alternative assessment effort have raised issues regarding how IEP teams decide who receives alternative assessments, the amount of staff time required, increased documentation, reduced time for teaching, and the reliability of scoring inherent in alternative assessment strategies (Kleinert, Kennedy, & Kearns, 1999).

Alternative assessment use is greatly limited. Use of alternative means to determine student academic growth in place of state-wide tests, even with accommodations, cannot be used by more than 1% of all students in grades assessed, and then only for students with significant cognitive disabilities. To qualify for alternative assessment status under NCLB, the student must be performing at three or more standard deviations below the mean on intellectual functioning measures (measured IQ of 55 or below). The regulation requiring this (34 C.F.R. 200.6, 2005) is in apparent conflict with two primary concepts of the IDEA: (a) That no one test or assessment can be used to make decisions regarding students with disabilities, and (b) it is the IEP team that makes individualized determinations of appropriate alternative testing and provides justification. Schools can seek an exemption from the 1% limitation when the district can prove that more than 1% of its students have significant cognitive disabilities. There is evidence that the states have made good progress in the alignment of alternative assessment and state academic standards (Roach, Elliott, & Webb, 2005). There is also evidence and that teacher training in instruc-

tional pratices use of alternate assessments results in better student growth on both IEP goals and state standards (Browder, Karfanen, Davis, Fallin, & Courtade-Little, 2005).

Many issues regarding alternative assessment remain in a state of flux. In response to expressed concerns of federal limits on students allowed to take alternative assessments, the U.S. Secretary of Education announced in 2005 the creation of a new category of students who will be allowed to be assessed against modified academic standards in limited situations (U.S. Department of Education, 2005). When a school does not achieve AYP under NCLB criteria solely on the basis of the scores of the students with disabilities subgroup, the school may, for the short-term and in limited circumstances, allow up to 2% of all students tested to be labeled *persistently academically disabled*. The new subgroup includes students who are unable to test at grade level despite the school's best efforts to provide good instruction.

Reports to Parents.   Each child's IEP must contain a statement of how the child's progress toward annual goals will be measured and how and when the child's parents will be regularly informed. Parents of students with disabilities must be periodically informed of their child's progress on annual goals. This may consist of regular reports provided at the same time report cards are issued. However, this requirement is in addition to the regular school reports of academic progress in curricular areas that many parents of children with disabilities will receive. For an example of how this report of progress can be made an integral part of the IEP, see the model IEP in Appendix E.

Health Plans.   Some states require that student health plans be made part of the IEP for those students needing special health services. This is especially important when the health services are related to educational goals, placement in an inclusive setting, or otherwise referenced in the IEP. In those situations, the school nurse will likely be an indispensable member of the IEP team. The nurse's knowledge of the medical needs of students and the nurse's specialized training and experience in providing direct services or training to others is an important related service component of the IEP (Bigby, 2004). Whether or not health concerns are made part of an IEP, they should be kept confidential on a need-to-know basis.

Other IEP Content. A presumption has been created in the law that the student with disabilities will participate in education programs and activities along with children without disabilities (LRE), unless a written IEP statement is provided explaining why the child will not participate in regular class or regular activities. It is likely that Congress intended to make an IEP team's decision to exclude the child from regular classes and activities more difficult by requiring it to justify its decision in writing.

When a child with disabilities has limited English proficiency, the IEP team must consider the language needs of the child as they relate to the child's IEP.

Physical education and vocational education are given special status in IEP development. This is in part a recognition of the connection between physical activity and human growth and development (Etzel-Wise & Mears, 2004) and the lifelong importance of skills associated with gainful employment. When the IEP does not mention physical or vocational education, it is expected that the child will participate in the same physical and vocational education programs as children without disabilities. When special or adaptive physical education or specially designed vocational education programs are to be provided, the child's IEP must expressly describe those programs.

When state law provides for the transfer of parental rights under the IDEA to the child at the age of majority, usually age 18, the IEP must provide evidence that the child has been provided notice of the impending change. At least one year before the student reaches the age of majority, the IEP must include a statement that the student has been informed of the student's rights that will transfer at the age of majority. For details on the transfer of parent rights to the student, see Chapter 8.

IEP Development in a Nutshell

Contrary to expressed congressional goals, the IEP development process and paperwork have not become less burdensome and can at times seem formidable, if not impossible. Be assured, however, thousands of educators and parents have survived the process, and in reality have gotten better at it each time. In keeping with their user-friendly approach to providing advice on IEP development, Bateman and Linden (2006) summarized the process nicely in a list of IEP "Do's" and "Don'ts":[*]

Do's: Program Planning

1. Do individualize the child's program. The IEP must reflect the child's unique needs.
2. Do base the IEP on the individual child's needs, not on the present availability of services in the district.
3. Do figure out what supports the child might need to participate in the general curriculum. If there is no need for modifications or supplementary aids and services in the regular classroom, there is reason to question a child's eligibility.
4. Do consider the child's strengths and parents' concerns for enhancing the child's education.
5. Do specify and describe (not just name or list) all necessary special education, related services, supplementary aids and services, program modifications, and supports for school personnel.
6. Do include positive behavioral interventions and discipline strategies (a behavior intervention plan) when there is reason to believe that behavior is or may be an issue.
7. Do meticulously observe all procedural requirements for IEP development and content.
8. Do ensure full equal and meaningful parent participation.

*From *Better IEPs: How to Develop Legally Correct and Educationally Useful Programs* (4th ed.) (pp. 24–25), by B. D. Bateman and M. A. Linden, 2006, Verona, WI: Attainment Corporation Inc. Copyright 2006 by Bateman and Linden. Reprinted by permission.

9. Do include objectives or other progress markers for each goal, even though the IDEA no longer requires them on all IEPs.

Don'ts: Program Planning

1. Don't worry about "opening floodgates." Providing certain services to one child does not set a precedent for other children. IEPs address the unique needs of individual children, so what one child's needs has no implications for what the district must provide to others.
2. Don't clutter IEPs with detailed goals and objectives for all the content standards in the general curriculum. Instead, focus on the accommodations and adjustments an individual child needs for appropriate access to and participation in the general curriculum. Goals should be prioritized and deal with large, important areas.
3. Don't include more than three or four objectives or progress markers for each annual goal. Progress markers should describe "how far, by when" the child should progress toward achievement of each annual goal and ordinarily should coincide with grading periods.
4. Don't use lack of funds or staff as an excuse for failure to provide a FAPE.
5. Don't ever provide services categorically! For example, don't say that only emotionally disturbed students may have behavioral components in their IEPs or that only students with learning disabilities may be allowed extra time on tests. All services must be based upon the individual child's needs without regard to disability category.

OTHER IEP ISSUES

Inclusion Inherent in IEP Process

The word *inclusion* is not found anywhere in the IDEA statutes or regulations, but its presence is unmistakable. Regular education teachers must be included on IEP teams to help determine appropriate supplementary aids and services, class modifications, and accommodations and supports for school staff for use with the child while in the regular classroom. The IEP must specify supplementary aids and services, modifications, accommodations, and support for school staff. School staff responsible for those services must be advised of their required duties by school officials. The IEP must include in the PLEP how the child's disability affects the child's participation and progress in the general school curriculum. It must also specify that special instruction be provided that will ensure the child's success in the general curriculum.

A legal presumption has been established within the IDEA that the child will be educated in the regular classroom and participate in regular nonacademic activities. That presumption may be overcome only through a written statement in the IEP justifying why the child will not participate in regular classes or activities.

Cost of FAPE

Because school budgets have declined relative to an expanding public school mission, many school staff members consciously attempt to keep expenditures low. Generally, there is no reason why members of IEP teams cannot attempt to be conscientious about expenses involved in providing special education programs and services. They should not, however, allow the costs associated with programming to dictate what is, or is not, appropriate for a specific child's needs. Except for general phrases like "at no cost to parents," "at public expense," and "free appropriate public education," the IDEA has no language regarding the expense or cost of programming. The legal result is that for IEP team considerations of program appropriateness, cost usually is not relevant to the team's deliberations (Bartlett, 1992; Bartlett & Rosenfeld, 1993). However, the cost of providing supplementary aids and services in appropriate inclusion settings may be relevant when the cost is significant (See Chapter 5).

In its decision in *Clevenger v. Oakridge School Board* (1984), the Court of Appeals for the Sixth Circuit ruled on the issue of whether it was appropriate to consider the $33,000 annual cost difference between the school-proposed program ($55,000) and a parent-proposed program ($88,000). The court ruled that any cost differences between proposed programs may be considered by the IEP team only when both programs are appropriate. When only one program under consideration is appropriate, the cost of providing that program should not become involved in IEP team consideration. Because the parents' proposed placement was determined by the court to be the student's only appropriate placement option, the court ruled that the school could not insist on providing its recommended program on the ground it could be provided at less cost.

Schools have found that they cannot refuse to place children with disabilities in appropriate programs with the argument of "difficult budget constraints." Several federal courts have held that financial "constraints do not provide sufficient grounds for refusing to comply with the Hearing Officer's decision" on placement. The courts ordered the schools to immediately comply with the hearing decisions (e.g., *Grace B. v. Lexington School Committee*, 1991).

In the 1980s, the Oregon state legislature attempted to limit its financial responsibility for the IEPs of children in certain institutional settings by capping its financial responsibility to the state's availability of funds. When the legislature subsequently appropriated less funds than were needed to carry out the IEPs of the children in the institutional settings, their educational programs were curtailed, and parents brought suit. The Court of Appeals for the Ninth Circuit ruled that Oregon had illegally failed to provide the children with disabilities with a FAPE and ordered the state to ensure that the FAPE of children with disabilities in the institutional settings would be sufficiently funded (*Kerr Center Parents Association v. Charles*, 1988).

School efforts to cut costs in special education programs and services for individual students can backfire. If the cost cutting results in a child not receiving an appropriate program, the parents may unilaterally place the child in a private, often more expensive, program and seek reimbursement from the public school. (See private school placements by parents in Chapter 5.)

School District Responsibility and Accountability

When a student receives programs and services under a resident district contract with another district or a private agency, the district in which the child resides remains responsible for initiating and conducting IEP meetings, covering costs, and ensuring that the student's program complies with the law. If a child's placement is out-of-state, the sending state often, through the local resident school district, remains responsible for ensuring that the child receives FAPE through the development, support for, and implementation of an IEP. Once a child is placed in a private facility by the public school, the private facility staff, at the discretion of the school district, may initiate meetings to review and revise the IEP. The public agency must ensure that one of its representatives and the child's parents attend those private facility IEP meetings and approve any program changes.

The IEP documents the school's commitment to provide the programs and services identified, and acts in a quasi-contract capacity in that its terms are enforceable. However, IEP goals and objectives do not impose a liability on the school staff when a student does not meet IEP goals, so long as school staff makes good faith efforts to carry out the IEP provisions (Yell, 2006).

Transfer Students

When a student receives special education and services from one school district and unilaterally transfers to another school district (i.e., family moves), the new district of residence is responsible for providing education and services in conformity with an IEP. An IEP must be in effect before programs and services may begin. The new school, if in the same state, may in consultation with the parents provide services comparable to those in the previously held IEP until the school adopts the previously held IEP or develops and adopts a new IEP. When the former school was in another state, the school must consult with the parents and provide the student with comparable services until a new evaluation may be conducted, if necessary, and a new IEP can be developed, if necessary [34 C.F.R. § 300.323 (e)(1)].

To facilitate the transition for a child moving to another school district, the new school must promptly take reasonable steps to obtain the student's education records. The previous school of attendance must take reasonable steps to promptly respond to such request [34 C.F.R. § 300.323 (e)(2)]. When the parents disagree with the receiving school's new IEP, they may file a request for mediation or due process hearing.

IEP Development Through Technology

Many computer software packages are available to assist teams with IEP development. They often provide standardized alternatives for meeting the individual needs of students. As a result, teams using software must be diligent in remembering that the "I" in IEP means individualized, and not become complacent and hurried so that individualization is lost.

One of the authors, while serving as a hearing officer, asked a principal during a hearing why page six of a student's IEP goals had another student's name on the top. The principal's explanation that the IEP team had been sloppy in using a computer program in the development of IEP goals was very embarrassing to the team, which had not noticed. The explanation did not result in a favorable impression on the hearing officer.

Some software packages allow the IEP forms to be projected on a screen or wall for all IEP team participants to see. Although only one member uses the keyboard to enter the IEP elements, each team member sees what is being entered and can immediately make suggestions for improvement. All team members, including parents, can more easily participate and a nearly complete IEP is ready for

distribution when the meeting concludes. No one person is responsible for later synthesizing and documenting all that was decided at an IEP meeting.

IEP Pilot Programs

During congressional negotiations on the 2004 IDEA Amendments, attention was given to reduction of staff time spent serving on IEP teams and associated paperwork. One proposed response to these issues was the use of multi-year IEPs. Unable to reach agreement on multi-year IEPs, Congress determined that as a pilot program, up to 15 states would be allowed to experiment with multi-year IEPs, gather data, and report the data back to Congress.

The conditions established in the pilot program may be so burdensome that few states will be tempted to implement the multi-year IEPs. The IEPs must last a maximum of three years; have parent consent; have measurable goals that coincide with student transition points, such as moving from middle school to high school; and have an annual review of progress.

IMPROVING COMMUNICATION IN IEP DEVELOPMENT

There are no typical IEP meetings; each is unique unto itself, and each has varying degrees of success. Rosenfeld (1998) has outlined a number of excellent suggestions for improving the likelihood of a successful IEP meeting. As a whole, they represent a relatively complete package of planning and preparation for a successful IEP meeting:*

- *Begin Planning Well in Advance*—Inadequate planning and preparation results in too much time being taken explaining common

---

*These excellent suggestions were adapted from "Ten Ways to Have More Productive IEP Meetings," by S. J. Rosenfeld, 1998, EDLAW Briefing Papers, VIII (2), pp. 2–7, Copyright 1998 by EDLAW, Inc. Adapted by permission.

procedures and unfamiliar terms. Informal preliminary informational meetings, especially for first IEPs with parents, can greatly enhance understanding and cooperation and help parents and educators become comfortable working with each other.

- *Give or Send Information Well Before Meeting*—Parents need to have a fundamental understanding of the IEP process and what is expected of them. They will have great difficulty participating in a meaningful way if they are absorbed in attempting to understand related services, LRE, and recent evaluation results. Give parents a blank IEP in advance of the meeting and explain the content and structure of the form. Provide recent evaluation results and a list of resources that may help their understanding. Provide a listing of some of the ideas school staff members are considering so the parents may give the ideas consideration and ask others about them.
- *Beware the Draft IEP*—Draft IEPs can give parents the impression that all decision making has previously been completed or that the burden is on them to challenge existing language. It is no wonder that parents may become defensive.
- *Offer to Answer Questions Before Meetings*—Provide the names, professional responsibilities, and telephone numbers of staff members who will be involved in the IEP meeting. Encourage parents to contact staff and ask questions. Help parents understand the options available.
- *Ask About Meeting Preferences*—Times and places of IEP meetings must be mutually convenient to both parents and staff. Ask for and attempt to accommodate parent preferences as much as possible. Parent time and participation are also important.
- *Be Flexible in Setting Times for Meetings*—When parents indicate problems meeting at times available to school staff, offer to meet early or late in the day so that disruption to the parents' schedules can be minimized.
- *Allow Adequate Time for IEP Meeting*—Parents will quickly recognize and resent school staff who do not give them adequate time to address their child's needs. Meetings should not have hard and fast times for ending, especially those with the next parents waiting to begin their IEP meeting. Time estimates may be given to parents, but staff should also advise parents that if the time is not adequate, the meeting will be reconvened so that more time will be available. IEP meetings cannot be limited to predetermined, fixed amounts of time.
- *Keep Meeting Size Reasonable*—Only school staff required by law or the child's needs should attend IEP meetings. The opinions and views of other staff members should be solicited and reported on, preferably in writing, and made available if needed. Everyone's time is equally valuable and should not be wasted. Unnecessary staff member presence may result in the parents being intimidated or frightened, neither of which adds to meaningful parent participation.
- *Choose Adequate and Comfortable Facilities*—Child-sized seats may be counter-productive for adult meetings. So, too, are cramped quarters or rooms with poor lighting and ventilation. It may be desirable to provide a folder with all materials in advance of the meeting and something with which to write. Modest refreshments, especially beverages, are appreciated. The room should reflect the importance of the meeting.
- *Agree to Disagree*—Although agreement is the recognized goal of the IEP meetings, disagreement is not unhealthy or unwanted. Emphasize areas of agreement and attempt to resolve areas of disagreement, but always move forward. In early communication with parents and staff, it may be desirable to remind participants of this important point. It provides everyone with a license to take an active part in the decision-making process.

Rosenfeld concluded his recommendations with the following sage advice: "taking the extra steps to have a calm and cordial meeting is a sign of strength, not weakness, and is likely to return benefits far beyond the effort" (p. 7).

CONCLUSION

The importance of the IEP cannot be overestimated. Even when done correctly, there is no guarantee that all will go well with a student's education. But, when done incorrectly, a poor IEP will almost guarantee that a student's educational program will not succeed. The IEP is derived from the assessment of the child's educational needs and is the driving force behind the student's educational placement.

The IEP process and IEP document presents one of the strongest and most effective tools educators have in their arsenal of strategies and methodologies. It is a process that allows the child's educational needs to be identified and met. Experienced professional educators, service providers, and parents together plan and implement an individualized education plan for a child who is unlike any other.

The IEP, of necessity, is built upon a trusting relationship between schools and parents. Its focus is joint problem solving to meet a child's needs. There are many IEP elements to consider and to determine their value to an individual child. IEPs are subject to adjustment by the IEP team, as needed, and are now more easily adjusted than ever before to meet the changing needs of the child.

VIEW FROM THE COURTS

Deal v. Hamilton County Board of Education (2004) (school's unilateral determination of an IEP). Parents of a child with autism challenged a school's determination that it would provide an educational program to the child that was opposed by the parents. The evidence established that the school had predetermined the type of program available to all students identified with autism in the district and refused to consider any alternative program regardless of evidence of the child's

needs to the contrary. The Court of Appeals for the Sixth Circuit ruled that the school's predetermination effectively deprived the parents of meaningful participation in the IEP process that resulted in substantive harm and deprived the child of his right to FAPE. The court concluded that parent "participation must be more than mere form; it must be meaningful" (p. 858).

The court also ruled that failure to have a regular education teacher present at the various IEP meetings resulted in the student being deprived of FAPE.

Neosho R-V School District v. Clark (2003) (student behavior issues must be addressed in IEPs). A school district appealed a district court ruling which upheld a state hearing decision that the school had failed to provide FAPE to a student when it did not properly address his problem behaviors in a behavior improvement plan. The Court of Appeals for the Eighth Circuit found that the boy's need for a behavior improvement plan had existed for a long time before the school attempted to address the behaviors, and as a result the boy had not adequately benefited from his education. The Eighth Circuit upheld the hearing officer and district court's decision that the boy had not received FAPE as a result of the school's failure to address his behavior issues. The court also concluded that the parents were prevailing parties and entitled to attorney fees to be paid by the school.

Gerstmyer v. Howard County Public Schools (1994) (the IEP must be individualized). The school held an IEP meeting in October and presented the parents with an IEP in November, six months after the parents had first requested an evaluation for their son. The IEP was not individualized to meet the boy's special needs and was nothing more than a collection of general goals that had been prepared for other students. The parents withdrew their son from school, placed him in a private school and sought reimbursement for their expenses, including tuition. The court found that the school had not timely evaluated the student and had not provided him an appropriate individualized IEP. The result was ruled a school denial of FAPE to which the student was entitled.

RECOMMENDED READINGS

Allbritten, D., Mainzer, R., & Ziegler, D. (2004). Will students with disabilities be scapegoats for school failures? *Teaching Exceptional Children, 36*(3), 74–75. This two-page article summarizes the Council for Exceptional Children's concerns with NCLB legislation.

Bateman, B. D., & Linden, M. A. (2006). *Better IEPs: How to develop legally correct and educationally useful programs* (4th ed.). Verona, WI: Attainment Company, Inc. This practical, easy-to-use book is a "must have" for learning how to develop good IEPs.

Byrnes, M. A. (2004). Alternate assessment FAQs (and answers). *Teaching Exceptional Children, 36*(6), 58–63. This article describes the current circumstance of alternate assessments under NCLB and provides suggestions on developing appropriate alternate assessments.

Cheney, C. O. (2000). Ensuring IEP accountability in inclusive settings. *Intervention in School and Clinic, 35,* 185–189. This article discusses a model form to be used in monitoring student progress on IEP objectives in both regular and special education classrooms.

Edgeman, E. A., Jablonski, B. R., & Lloyd, J. W. (2006). Large-scale assessments: A teacher's guide to making decisions about accommodations. *Teaching Exceptional Children, 38*(3), 6–11. This article provides suggestions on how to develop and evaluate testing accommodations.

Gunter, P. L., Miller, K. A., Venn, M. L., Thomas, K., & House, S. (2003). Self-graphing to success: Computerized data management. *Teaching Exceptional Children, 35*(2), 30–34. This article describes how students can play an important role in monitoring their own IEP using computer software.

Keyes, M. W., & Owens-Johnson, L. (2003). Developing person-centered IEPs. *Intervention in School and Clinic, 38,* 145–152. This article describes a student-centered IEP development process that focuses on a broad range of student needs rather than on more traditional school procedures.

Van Dycke, J. L., Martin, J. E. & Lovett, D. L. (2006). Why is this cake on fire: Inviting students into the IEP process. *Teaching Exceptional Children, 38*(3) 42–47. This article provides the rationale behind and a process for involving student in their own IEP meetings.

Zirkel, P. (2001). High stakes testing accommodations and modifications for students with disabilities. *Education Law Reporter, 155,* 13–19. This article, written by a recognized national expert in education law, organizes and briefly summarizes dozens of state and federal court decisions on testing accommodations.

Relevant Federal Regulations

Assistance to States for the Education of Children with Disabilities (70 Fed. Reg., 35,833-35,880 (June 21, 2005)).

34 CFR § 300.17   Free appropriate public education.

.22   Individualized education program.

.23   Individualized education team.

.24   Individualized family service plan.

.132   Provision of services for parentally placed private school children with disabilities—basic requirement.

.320   Definition of individualized education program.

.321   IEP team.

.322   Parent participation.

.323   When IEPs must be in effect.

.324   Development, review, and revision of IEP.

.325   Private school placements by public.

.328   Alternative means of meeting participation.

SELECTED WEBSITES

Code of Federal Regulations–Government Printing Office–National Archives and Record Administration *http://www.gpoaccess.gov/cfr/index.html*

Council for Exceptional Children
  http://www.cec.sped.org

United States Department of Education–Office of Special Education and Rehabilitation Services
  http://www.ed.gov/about/offices/list/osers/index.htm

IDEA Practices–IDEA Law and Resources
  http://www.ideapractices.org

Individuals with Disabilites Education Act Data
  http://www.ideadata.org

Internet Resources for Special Education
  http://www.irsc.org

National Dissemination Center for Children and Youth with Disabilities
  http://www.nichcy.org/pubs1.htm

Families and Advocates Partnership for Education (FAPE)
  http://www.fape.org/idea/index.htm

Individualized Education Program–Learning Disability
  http://www.ldonline.org/ld_indepth/special_education/index.html

National Center on Educational Outcomes–Alternate Assessment Policies and Practices
  http://www.education.umn.edu/NCEO (click on Alternate Assessments)

QUESTIONS FOR THOUGHT

1. What strategies can schools use for making efficient use of time in developing IEPs without interfering with parents' right to meaningful participation?

2. Which of the five purposes served by the IEP is most important to the educators involved? To the parents? To the student's progress? Why?

3. How knowledgeable and understanding are school boards, superintendents, and principals of the IEP team empowerment concept? How does this result in decision-making issues at the local level?

4. Is consensus decision-making on IEP teams better than majority vote?

5. Is it better for model IEPs to be long and detailed, or brief with only the most important decision-making elements presented?

REFERENCES

Allbritten, D., Mainzer, R., & Ziegler, D. (2004). Will students with disabilities be scapegoats for school failures? *Teaching Exceptional Children, 36*(3), 74–75.

Assistance to States for the Education of Children with Disabilities. 34 C.F.R. Part 300 (2004).

Assistance to States for the Education of Children with Disabilities. 70 Fed. Reg., 35,833–35,880 (June 21, 2005).

Baird, M. (2003). *Keeping general educators out of special education purgatory.* LRP Conference Virtual Seminar, October 22, 2003.

Bartlett, L. D. (1992). The cost of FAPE: Can LRE make a difference? *Ed Law Briefing Paper, 1*(9), 1–7. Hollywood, FL: EDLAW Inc.

Bartlett, L., & Rosenfeld, S. J. (1993). Economic cost factors in providing a free appropriate public education: The legal perspective. *The Journal of Law and Education, 22*, 27–60.

Bateman, B. D., & Linden, M. A. (2006). *Better IEPs: How to develop legally correct and educationally useful programs* (4th ed.) Verona, WI: Attainment Company, Inc.

Bateman, B. D., & Linden, M. A. (1998). *Better IEPs: How to develop legally correct and educationally useful programs* (3rd ed.). Longmont, CO: Sopris West.

Beekman, L. (2005). *Avoiding litigation under the new IDEA.* LRP Publications Audio Conference (April 20, 2005).

Bigby, L. M. (2004). Medical and health-related services: More than treating boo-boos and ouchies. *Intervention in School and Clinic, 39*, 233–235.

Board of Education of Hendrick Hudson Central School District v. Rowley, 458 U.S. 176, 102 S.Ct. 3034 (1982).

Bolt, S. E., & Thurlow, M. L. (2004). Five of the most frequently allowed testing accommodations in state policy. *Remedial and Special Education, 25*, 141–152.

Browder, D. M., Karvonen, M., Davis, S., Fallin, K., & Courtade-Little, G. (2005). The impact of teacher training on state alternate assessment scores. *Exceptional Children, 71*, 267–282.

Clevenger v. Oak Ridge School Board, 744 F.2d 514 (6th Cir. 1984).

Deal v. Hamiton County Board of Education, 392 F.3d 840 (6th Cir. 2004).

Doe v. Board of Education, 9 F.3d 455 (6th Cir. 1993).

Drew P. v. Clarke County School District, 887 F.2d 927 (11th Cir. 1989).

Edgeman, E. A., Jablonski, B. R., & Lloyd, J. W. Large-scale Assessments: A teacher's guide to making decisions about accommodations. *Teaching Exceptional Children, 38*(3), 6–11.

Etscheidt, S. K. (2006). Progress monitoring: Legal issues, and recommenations for IEP teams. *Teaching Exceptional Children, 38*(3), 56–60.

Etzel-Wise, D., & Mears, B. (2004). Adapted physical education and therapeutic recreation in schools. *Intervention in School and Clinic, 39*, 223–332.

Gagnon, J. C., & McLaughlin, M. S. (2004). Curriculum, assessment, and accountability in day treatment and residential schools. *Exceptional Children, 70*, 263–283.

Gerstmyer v. Howard County Public Schools, 850 F. Supp. 361 (D. Md. 1994).

Grace B. v. Lexington School Committee, 762 F. Supp. 416 (D. Mass. 1991).

Gunter, P. L., Miller, K. A., Venn, M. L., Thomas, K., & House, S. (2003). Self-graphing to success: Computerized data management. *Teaching Exceptional Children, 35*(2), 30–34.

Huefner, D.S. (2006). *Getting comfortable with special education law: A framework for working with childen with disabilities* (2nd ed.). Norwood, MA: Christopher-Gordon.

Huefner, D. S. (2000). The risks and opportunities of the IEP requirements under IDEA '97. *The Journal of Special Education, 33*, 195–205.

Improving the Academic Achievement of the Disadvantaged. 34 C.F.R. Part 200 (2005).

Individuals with Disabilities Education Act, 20 U.S.C. §§ 1,400–1,487.

Johnson, J., & Duffett, A. (2002). *When it's your own child: A report on special education from the families who use it.* New York: Public Agenda.

Kerr Center Parents Association v. Charles, 842 F.2d 1052 (9th Cir. 1988).

Keyes, M. W., & Owens-Johnson, L. (2003). Developing person-centered IEPS. *Intervention in School and Clinic, 38*, 145–152.

Kleinert, H. L., Kennedy, S., & Kearns, J. F. (1999). The impact of alternate assessments: A statewide teacher survey. *The Journal of Special Education, 33*, 93–102.

Lamoine School Committee v. Ms. Z., 353 F. Supp. 2d 18 (D. Me. 2005).

Lee, S., Palmer, S. B., Turnbull, A. P., & Wehmeyer, M.L. (2006). A model for parent-teacher collaboration to promote self-determination in young children with disabilities. *Teaching Exceptional Children, 38*(3), 36–41.

Letter to Anonymous, 25 IDELR 529 (OSEP, 1996).

Letter to Diehl, 22 IDELR 734 (OSEP, 1993).

Martin, J. E., Marshall, L. H., & Sale, P. (2004). A 3-year study of middle, junior high, and high school IEP meetings. *Exceptional Children, 70*, 285–297.

Martin, J. E., Van Dycke, J. L., Greene, B. A., Gardner, J. E., Christensen, W. P., Woods, L. L., Lovet, D. L. (2006). Direct observation of teacher-directed IEP meetings: Establishing the need for student IEP meeting instruction. *Exceptional Children, 72*, 187–200.

M. L. v. Federal Way School District, 394 F.3d 634 (9th Cir. 2004).

Neosho R-V School District v. Clark, 315 F.3d 1022 (8th Cir. 2003).

Pemberton, J. B. (2003). Communicating academic progress as an integral part of assessment. *Teaching Exceptional Children, 35*(4), 16–20.

Roach, A. T., Elliott, S. N., & Webb, N. L. (2005). Alignment of an alternate assessment with state academic standards: Evidence for the content validity of the Wisconsin Alternate Assessment. *The Journal of Special Education, 38*, 218–231.

Rosenfeld, S. J. (2000). Should attorneys be in IEP meetings? *EDLAW Briefing Paper, 10*(3), 1–7.

Rosenfeld, S. J. (1998). Ten ways to have a more productive IEP meeting. *EDLAW Briefing Paper, 8*(2), 1–7.

Shapiro, D. R., & Sayers, L. K. (2003). Who does what on the interdisciplinary team regarding physical education for students with disabilities? *Teaching Exceptional Children, 35*(6), 32–38.

Thurlow, M. L., Lazarus, S. S., Thompson, S. J., & Morse, A. B. (2005). State policies on assessment participation and accommodations for students with disabilities. *The Journal of Special Education, 38*, 232–240.

U.S. Department of Education (2005). Secretary Spellings announces new flexibility for states raising achievement for students with disabilities. Retrieved February 16, 2006, from www.ed.gov/print/news/newsletters/extracredit/2005/05/index.html

Wasburn-Moses, L. (2003). What every special educator should know about high-stakes testing. *Teaching Exceptional Children, 35*(4), 12–15.

VanDycke, J. L., Martin, J. E., & Lovett, D. L. (2006). Why is the cake on fire. *Teaching Exceptional Children, 38*(3), 42–47.

Yell, M. L. (2006), *The Law and Special Education*. Upper Saddle River, NJ: Merrill/Prentice Hall.

Yell, M. L., Katsiyannas, A., & Shiner, J. G. (2006). The No Child Left Behind Act, adequate yearly progress, and students with disabilities. *Teaching Exceptional Children, 38*(4), 32–39.

Ysseldyke, J., & Olsen, K. (1999). Putting alternate assessments into practice: What to measure and possible sources of data. *Exceptional Children, 65*, 175–185.

CHAPTER 5

PLACEMENT

CHAPTER PREVIEW

Focus

The placement decision is frequently the most important factor affecting the success of the education of a student with disabilities. It is inherently controversial because it must balance the often conflicting demands and desires of a number of individuals and groups. Although the law requires placement in a program appropriate to the student's needs and educational growth, the school's actual ability to meet those needs often is limited by a lack of available trained personnel, variety of program options, support service options, and adequate funding.

Legal Issues

The law requires that educational placement decisions be

- made by a group that includes the parents and other people familiar with the child, the evaluation data, and the placement options;
- reviewed at least annually;
- based on the student's IEP;
- made to provide a placement located as close as feasible to the child's home;
- provided in the most typical school setting feasible that allows contact as much as reasonably possible with nondisabled peers;
- based on documented information from a variety of sources.

Inherent in the educational placement of some students is the physical accessibility of programs and services. Section 504 requires that all programs and activities must be readily accessible to students and their parents and provides guidelines for accomplishing appropriate accessibility.

The educational placement of a child with disabilities is presumed to be in the regular class setting and in regular student activities. Special education placements may be considered only when, compared with a regular class placement, the placement team determines that the child will benefit significantly more from a special class placement, or be significantly disruptive in the regular class. The team must consider the provision of the whole range of supplementary aids and services in the regular school setting to provide educational benefit to the student and to lessen disruption. The student may be placed in special education programs when the cost of supplementary aids and services necessary to allow the child to benefit and not be disruptive in the regular class is excessive.

The school district must ensure that a continuum of alternative placements is available to meet the needs of children with disabilities for special education and related services. Educational program and support services prescribed in the IEP must be provided at public expense, under public supervision and direction, and without charge. Placement settings must meet the state's minimal standards and licensure requirements for public education.

Support services for students include those required to assist a child with a disability to benefit from special education (related services), those provided in regular education classes or activities (supplementary aids and services), and modifications and accommodations in curriculum, instructional methodology, and assessment.

In order to receive appropriate education programs, some students with disabilities will be provided extended school year (ESY) programs. These programs extend portions of their IEPs to the summer months and other traditional school vacation periods.

Public school placement of a student in a private school carries with it continued responsibility for provision of the student's IEP terms and parent rights under the IDEA. A parent's unilateral placement of her or his child in a private school changes the public school responsibility to provision of more general and limited public school services.

Rationale

Historically, children with disabilities have often been placed inappropriately or denied public education altogether. A strong public commitment has become necessary to correct this problem. Given appropriate opportunities and support, all children can learn. Research has established that both children with disabilities and those without disabilities benefit from an integrated educational environment.

Approaches

Educational placement decisions account for a significant number of the formal due process hearings requested by parents. It is unlikely that serious disputes in this area can be avoided entirely. The best preventive strategy lies in attending to the procedural requirements of the law and in developing relationships of mutual trust and respect between all involved including teachers, parents, special education staff, and community members.

In order to assure student success in educational placements, educators have a variety of appropriate methodologies, technologies, and strategies at their disposal. The essential principle is that the educators working closely with parents in providing the student a meaningful education must be cognizant of the various available alternatives through professional development activities and regular review of professional literature.

PLACEMENT ISSUES

The identification of, and placement in, an appropriate educational program is, quite simply, the most controversial point in the process of educating children with disabilities. Even when all parties agree on the goals and services identified in a child's IEP, the means of carrying out a child's IEP (which is essentially the meaning of placement) may generate heated disputes. In the early years of special education, a 1980 survey of due process hearings in special education showed that fully 89% involved placement disputes (Smith, 1981). A more recent study of due process hearings experienced in one midwestern state in a 12-year period found that placement was involved in 50% of the hearings and was the most common area of dispute (Rickey, 2003).

From the student's perspective, placement is often the main factor in determining whether the educational experience will be rewarding or frustrating, enjoyable or humiliating. All the effort that goes into good student assessment and good IEP development can be lost when the placement decision is not attended to by the placement team. Educators see the placement decision as key to the child's educational progress in behavioral and social as well as academic areas. Parents bring to the decision a host of other concerns, doubts, and desires. From the perspective of the school district, the chief question unfortunately often becomes how to maximize resources to students without overtaxing an already inadequate budget.

School administrators occupy a particularly precarious position at the center of the controversy with their simultaneous focus in four directions: the needs of students and parents, the staff, the budget, and the law. And what about the law? Does it offer guidelines explicit enough to stand behind? Don't the federal regulations point out clear resolutions to these controversies?

Not really. The laws and regulations governing placements are both intentionally and distressingly vague. They tend not to spell out, but only to imply, the basis on how educational decisions must be made and evaluated. This vagueness allows the placement team a great deal of discretionary latitude in considering placement options, but a side effect is that placement decisions can often be inherently contentious.

LEGAL ISSUES

What Is Placement?

Educational placement is the last in a series of three important formal steps required in planning and carrying out FAPE under the IDEA. Beginning with the initial evaluation and identification, each step influences, but does not strictly determine, the next. Each step relies on the satisfactory completion of the previous step. Thus, the evaluation process helps to determine IEP content, which in turn forms the basis for the placement decision.

The IEP identifies the student's educational goals and related services. It must include the special education the child is to receive and an explanation of the extent (if any) the student will be placed in special education settings rather than in regular education settings. The IEP for a student must be completed prior to consideration of placement.

What then does *placement* mean? The law is not entirely specific on the meaning of placement: It does not offer a closed and concise definition. Certainly, it means an arrangement in which it is possible to meet the goals and provide services included in the IEP and in which the student can learn and make educational progress (Yell & Katsiyannis, 2004). The physical location or type of program itself is not nearly as important as the effective teaching and service strategies that are provided (Zigmond, 2003). Placement must be in the least restrictive environment (LRE), based on a broad range of information, located as close as feasible to the child's home, and reviewed at least annually.

As difficult as it may seem at first, "placement" under the IDEA is not a place. It is an overall educational setting where the student's IEP terms can be implemented. The courts have ruled that mere changes of physical location of programs provided students do not constitute changes in placement, so long as the provision of IEP terms and services are not altered as a result of the program relocation. In this context "placement" refers to the educational program setting, not the particular site where the program is implemented (e.g., *Veazey v. Ascension Parish School Board,* 2005).

An IEP can be appropriately carried out in several very different educational settings, and the various parties on the placement team can have very different criteria for deciding which is appropriate. When it is determined that two or more placement options are equally appropriate, the assignment to a particular school or classroom can be an administrative determination, provided that it is consistent with the placement team's determinations (Letter to Veazey, 2001).

The key legal and procedural requirements for the placement decision-making stage are listed in greater detail on pages 95–102. Immediately following are details on specific topics that may prove helpful in the overall understanding and implementation of the concept of placement.

Related Services

Related services are an important part of the placement decision. They are support services required to assist a child with a disability to benefit from special education. The related services expressly identified in the law are: transportation, speech-language pathology and audiology services, interpreting services, psychological services, physical and occupational therapy, recreation (including therapeutic recreation), social work services in the schools, school health services, school nurse services as described in the student's IEP, counseling services (including rehabilitation counseling), orientation and mobility services, parent counseling and training, and medical services for diagnostic and evaluation purposes only (early identification and assessment of disabling conditions). This list of related services should not be considered an exhaustive list. Related services may include other supportive services (e.g., music

therapy, independent living services) when such services are required to assist a child with a disability to benefit from special education. The only two areas of potential related services that a school clearly does not have to provide as related services are medical treatment by a physician and medical devices (including maintenance and replacement) that are surgically implanted, such as cochlear implants.

Some related services have special considerations involved and the team should carefully review each for appropriate application. For instance, transportation includes travel to and from school and between schools, but also includes travel in and around school buildings and specialized equipment, when required to provide special transportation for a particular child. Transportation arrangements must be based on a child's needs, not on preexisting arrangements or concepts, such as existing school bus routes or schedules. Unless a child's IEP provides otherwise, most children with disabilities will be assumed to receive transportation on the same basis as nondisabled students. Integrated transportation services are preferred when appropriate for the child.

Desirable related services may include assisting parents in understanding their child's special needs, providing parents with information about child development, and helping parents acquire the necessary skills that will allow them to support the implementation of their child's IEP in the home setting.

Paraeducators (sometimes referred to as teacher aides or teacher associates) are a commonly provided related service. They can provide a variety of services to students and staff, and the IEP should specify as clearly as possible the exact nature of the service(s) to be provided.

The provision of "medical services" and "school nurse services" as related services have resulted in considerable controversy and litigation. The Supreme Court has issued interpretations related to those phrases in two decisions. In *Irving Independent School District v. Tatro* (1984), the Court ruled that clean intermittent catheterization services provided by a school nurse or other qualified person was a related service that the school had to provide in order for the child to benefit from special education. The Court drew a distinction between medical treatment provided by a physician and health services performed by other health professionals, such as school nurses. Services that required the attention of a licensed physician, except for diagnostic and evaluation purposes, were determined to be properly excluded from the list of required related services under the IDEA.

A series of lower court rulings subsequent to *Irving Independent School District v. Tatro* (1984) were not faithful to the *bright line* physician treatment test, and involved decisions based on issues related to the complexity and expense of the health services needed. As a result, the issue of nonphysician health services, as a related service, became muddied. The Supreme Court agreed to again hear the issue of health services as a related service in the case of *Cedar Rapids Community School District v. Garret F.* (1999).

The question presented in *Cedar Rapids Community School District v. Garret F.* (1999) was whether schools may refuse to provide health services to children at school because the services are unduly burdensome owing to excessive cost or medical complexity. In a brief and succinct opinion, a majority of seven justices ruled that the appropriate distinction on required health services as a related service under the IDEA was whether those services required the attention of a trained and licensed physician. School nursing services are required as a related service, regardless of cost or complexity, so that children with health problems may receive an education in the LRE. The *Cedar Rapids Community School District v. Garret F.* (1999) decision has had important implications in the delivery of special education programs and services (Bartlett, 2000). Some people fear that one result will be extensive increases in medical expenses for services provided by schools. Rebore and Zirkel (1999) have concluded, however, that the relatively small number of students requiring such services and the availability of alternative funding sources (e.g., Medicaid) will

not result in an enduring financial impact on school district resources. For more information, see the section on third-party payers on pages 94–95.

The IDEA does not require all related services personnel to regularly attend IEP meetings. However, their input into IEPs and placements is important and their written recommendations should be available to the team when the related services staff person is not present (Downing, 2004).

Assistive Technology Devices and Services

Congressional findings in the 2004 Amendments to the IDEA concluded that 30 years of research and experience in the education of children with disabilities support the development and use of technology to maximize the accessibility and effectiveness of education for children with disabilities [20 U.S.C. § 1401 (c) (5) (H)].

Assistive technology devices and technology services can be related services. When used to support a student in the regular class setting, they can also be considered supplementary aids and services. Assistive technology and services merely refers to the use, selection, coordination, and training regarding items, equipment, or product systems used to increase, maintain, or improve the functional capabilities of a child with disabilities.

In developing each IEP, the team should consider the student's potential need for technology and the desirability of an assessment of needs. When indicated, comprehensive assistive technology assessments must be conducted by someone knowledgeable in the field (Day & Huefner, 2003).

Decisions on specific technology devices should be made through a systematic process involving the various perspectives and expertise of the IEP team members and other expertise as needed (Lankutis, 2004). Technology presents a wide range of new educational tools that can help make learning easier for students both with and without disabilities. Electronic books (e.g., eBook), available online, at bookstores, and sometimes through common forms of text readers, present a lightweight alternative to books (Cavanaugh, 2002). Most eBook readers have built-in adaptable accommodations, such as adjustable text size, adjustable reading speed, colored highlights, a word dictionary, and even reading-aloud features (Boyle et al., 2002).

Students with limited organizational and management skills may benefit from handheld computers, such as Palm Pilots, in inclusion settings (Bauer & Ulrich, 2002). Students can record and organize their assignments, access spelling lists, check mathematics solutions, be provided prompts, and obtain helpful information from their classmates and teachers.

When planning assistive technolgy devices and services, the child's family must be actively involved in making decisions. Parents will be able to bring valuable input to the decision process regarding the child's experience and comfort level with technologies (Lankutis, 2004). Using devices that limit the child's independence and acceptance by other children, establishing reasonable expections of immediate results, and determining family resource commitments jointly, all impact the successful use of technology by students. Sensitivity to family needs will help to ensure that appropiate decisions are made (Parette & McMahan, 2002).

Medication Administration An important service that schools commonly provide as a service to children with disabilities is the administration of physician-prescribed medications during school hours. Students who have accommodation plans under Section 504, as well as some students without disabilities, may also require school staff assistance with medications (Huefner, 2006). Many states require local schools to have medication administration policies for children receiving special education services and require that they contain a number of important provisions. Those comprehensive provisions can apply to policies covering the administration of medications for all students. Each policy should include statements on the training and other requirements necessary for persons administering medication, as well as the following:

1. A requirement that the parent provide a signed and dated written statement requesting medication administration at school
2. A statement that medication shall be in the original labeled container, either as dispensed or in the manufacturer's container
3. A written medication administration record shall be on file at school including:
   a. Date
   b. Individual's name
   c. Prescriber or person authorizing administration
   d. medication
   e. medication dosage
   f. administration time
   g. administration method
   h. signature and title of the person administering medication
   i. any unusual circumstances, actions, or omissions
4. A statement that medication shall be stored in a secured area unless an alternate provision is documented
5. A requirement for a written statement by the parent or guardian requesting individual student administration of medication, when competency is demonstrated
6. A requirement for emergency protocols for medication-related reactions
7. A statement regarding confidentiality of information. (Iowa Department of Education, 2005)

The 2004 Amendments to the IDEA addressed a concern sometimes expressed by parents that the school required them to obtain medication for their child while in school. The law now expressly prohibits any school from requiring a child to obtain a medical prescription as a condition of attending school, receiving an evaluation, or receiving services [20 U.S.C. § 1412 (a) (25)]. This prohibition does not preclude IEP teams, including parents, from considering and discussing the desirability of medication for a child, but it does prohibit the team from prescribing a medication. The responsibility for the decision to obtain medication for a student rests solely with the family and its physician.

Extended School Year Services

Arrangements must be made through the IEP and placement processes to see that each child receives an appropriate education program. Some students with disabilities may need school services at times of the year in which schools do not traditionally provide services (e.g., summer months, long holidays, breaks between sessions) (Etscheidt, 2002). The main difference between these extended school year (ESY) programs and other types of summer or vacation school programs is that ESY programs must be expressly provided for in the IEP and the placement decision must be related to at least one of the IEP goals. Unlike summer school, ESY must be provided at no cost to parents.

The courts have provided a much better understanding of the ESY concept and criteria than have federal statutes or regulations. That may be because the concept was first identified by the courts as an extension of consideration of FAPE. Those early court decisions made it clear that considerations of ESY were to be individualized to the child and no arbitrary or standard criteria could be used. Early court reliance on student regression (education loss) or time for recoupment (education recovery) as the sole criterion for determining ESY eligibility has given way to additional criteria. The best criterion for IEP placement team decisions on ESY is whether the benefits gained by the student under the IEP during the regular school year will be "significantly jeopardized" when the student is not provided an educational program during breaks in schooling (e.g., *J. H. v. Henrico County School Board*, 2003).

IEP teams making decisions on ESY will have no magic formula to assist them. Using their best professional and parental judgment, IEP teams must review and consider existing empirical and qualitative data, as well as predictive data and the reasoned opinions of team members. For some students, it may be determined that only a limited portion of IEP goals, or only one related service, is needed during breaks in schooling.

One of the authors served as a member of an IEP/placement team that considered ESY for a high-functioning 9-year-old boy with autistic tendencies. In reviewing the boy's goals, the team determined that progress only in goals related to social skills was in jeopardy of being significantly diminished over the summer months. As a response, the team determined that the boy should attend a YMCA summer daycamp, accompanied by a paraeducator. The camp staff was advised of the boy's existing behavior plan and social skills needs. It was also determined that the paraeducator and the boy would spend one hour, two days a week, visiting his regular school classroom so that he would remain accustomed to the school environment when the fall term started. All components of the summer program, including transportation and camp fees, were provided under IEP provisions at no cost to the parents. The summer was determined to be very successful by all, except perhaps for the paraeducator who was exhausted attempting to keep up with the boy's socialization activities.

Costs and Parental Responsibilities

The IDEA requires that each child with a disability be provided an appropriate education "at public expense, under public supervision and direction and without charge...." [34 C.F.R. § 300.17 (a)]. Specifically, this includes special education and related services called for in an IEP that meet state standards and are provided in conjunction with regular education programs. Parents, however, may be responsible for "incidental fees which are normally charged to nondisabled students or their parents as part of the regular education program" [34 C.F.R. § 300.38 (b) (1)], such as book and locker fees.

Third-Party Payers When related services are of a medical nature (i.e., occupational and physical therapy), schools may want to attempt to recover the cost of some services from Medicaid or the family's private medical insurance. Medicaid is publicly funded and provides insurance-type coverage for children and families who meet specific qualification guidelines, primarily income. Schools cannot require the family to apply for Medicaid or withhold educational services conditioned upon Medicaid coverage.

The regulations under the IDEA provide that private parent insurance may be requested to pay for student medical services when the parents provide informed written consent each time. In order for consent to be informed, parents must be advised that claims filed by the school may result in increased premiums, lowered payment limits, or other potential future financial costs. Parents should be advised to check with their private insurance carrier before giving consent. Parents must also be informed that their refusal to provide consent will not alter the school's responsibility to provide the services to the student at no cost to the parent (34 C.F.R. § 300.154).

Even though the federal rules imply that parent's private insurance, with consent, may be used to pay for some medical expenses, an unresolved legal inconsistency remains. The courts have been consistent in interpreting IDEA requirements of FAPE to be at no expense to parents above normal student fee expenses charged to families of all students. This definition of "free" is found elsewhere in federal regulations (34 C.F.R. § 300.17).

The 2004 Amendments to the IDEA reinforced the concept that states cannot establish maximum dollar limits that may be spent on a child with a disability [20 U.S.C. § 1411 (e) (3)]. For a single child with multiple or complex disabilities, the annual cost of appropriate programming may be tens of thousands of dollars, and greatly reduce the amount of money available for the education programs of other students. The 2004 Amendments provided, for the first time, a system of support to local schools to meet the expense of providing programs and services to "high need children." Those are children for which the provision of programs and services exceed three times the average per pupil expenditure in the state. States are authorized to set aside a portion of the federal funds they receive under the IDEA to assist local schools, and consortiums of local schools, to establish innovative and effective cost sharing of expenses of providing programs and services to

"high need children" with disabilities. The law also provides that a portion of the funds received may be used to fund local school "risk pools" or "high cost funds." The state, in cooperation with local schools, must define "high need" children with disabilities and establish a state plan to address and reduce the financial impact a "high need" child with a disability has on a local school district budget.

PLACEMENT IN THE LEAST RESTRICTIVE ENVIRONMENT

Under the LRE principle, as defined in the regulations implementing the IDEA, each school must ensure that:

1. To the maximum extent appropriate, children with disabilities, including children in public or private institutions or other care facilities, are educated with children who are not disabled.
2. Special classes, separate schooling, or other removal of children with disabilities from the regular educational environment occurs only when the nature or severity of the disability is such that education in regular classes with the use of supplementary aids and services cannot be achieved satisfactorily.
3. Each child with a disability participates with nondisabled children in nonacademic and extracurricular services and activities to the maximum extent appropriate to the needs of the child (34 C.F.R. § 300.117).

Each school must also ensure that a continuum of alternative placements is available to meet the needs of children with disabilities for special education and related services. This continuum must include instruction in regular classes, special classes, special schools, home instruction, and instruction in hospitals and institutions. Figure 5-1 puts the LRE continuum concept in a student-need visual context.

From the available continuum of placements, choices must be made, and the role of making those decisions belongs to the placement team. The placement team must consist of

FIGURE 5-1 *Continuum of educational
services*

Severe	Special education services in a non-school environment	Most Restrictive
	Special education services in a special school environment	
	Special education services in a school other than school of usual attendance	
Educational Needs	Special education services in a school of usual attendance	Restrictiveness
	Mix of general education and special education services in a school of usual attendance	
	Mix of general education with part-time special education services in a school of usual attendance	
	Mix of general education with special education support in school of usual attendance	Least Restrictive
Mild	General education in school of usual attendance	

From *The Least Restrictive Environment (LRE) and The
Individualized Education Program (IEP): Legal Educa-
tional and Practical Guidelines for Educators and Families*
(p. 7), Iowa Department of Education, 1996, Des Moines,
IA: Mountain Plains Regional Resource Center, Drake
University. Reprinted by permission.

a group of people, including the parents and
other people who are knowledgeable about the
child, the evaluation data, and the placement
options. The IEP team may also serve as the
placement team and make the placement determination. In some states, such as South Dakota,
the IEP team has served for many years in multiple roles as the placement and evaluation
teams.

The placement decision must be made on
an individual student basis as opposed to a
group or label basis. The placement must be
consistent with the LRE concept, based on the
IEP, reviewed at least annually, and provided in
an appropriate program as close as possible to

the child's home, particularly the school the
child would attend if not disabled. Parents may
successfully challenge placement in distant
schools when it is apparent that an appropriate
program is available closer to home.

In considering the LRE, the placement team
must consider the potential harmful effects of
the placement on the child or on the quality of
services the child receives. This allows school
districts latitude for grouping students with
unique needs. For example, visually impaired
students in similar grade levels in a district
can be assigned to the same regular education
attendance center for efficiency purposes in
providing a mobility training specialist and
equipment for producing materials in Braille
(See *White v. Ascension Parish School Board*,
2003). Such students may not, of course, be
segregated owing to their disability and must be
provided programming with peers without disabilities in the LRE.

Some educators have been unnecessarily
concerned that the LRE requires the placement
of disruptive students in regular and special settings. This is not so. For nearly 30 years, the
federal regulations accompanying both Section
504 and the IDEA have clarified the LRE and
student disruption:

> . . . it should be stressed that where a handi-
> capped [sic] child is so disruptive in a regular
> classroom that the education of other students
> is significantly impaired, the needs of the
> handicapped [sic] child cannot be met in that
> environment. Therefore, regular placement
> would not be appropriate to his or her needs.
> (34 C.F.R. Part 104—Appendix, Paragraph 24;
> quoted in 34 C.F.R. 300.552, note 2, 1997)

Under the current IDEA, regular class
teachers must be provided assistance when students in inclusive programs present potential
problems of class disruption. The IEP team is
expressly required to consider positive behavioral interventions, supplementary aids and
services, and accommodations and modifications that are designed to reduce or eliminate
the likelihood of disruption resulting from a
student's placement in the regular class.

Home instruction, sometimes called *homebound* instruction, should be considered among the last placement options used with disruptive students and should never be used when the school staff is seeking respite rather than appropriate placement. Home instruction for school-aged children has been considered by some courts to be the most restrictive placement because it does not permit education to take place with other children. Even residential and hospital education settings often have several children present, whereas home instruction does not. Home instruction is usually appropriate on a long-term basis (more than 30 days) for only a small number of children who are medically fragile or for some other reason are unable to participate with other children in an educational environment (e.g., *Thomas v. Cincinnati Board of Education*, 1990).

Meaning of Inclusion

Some of the most important educational terminology involved in providing the LRE is not found in statutes or regulations and, as a result, is frequently confusing to parents, educators, and judges alike. *Mainstreaming, inclusion,* and *full inclusion* are such terms. In the vast arena of published articles and court rulings, these terms are often used interchangeably. For the purpose of this book, the authors have adopted and used the terms as defined in the well-thought-out article in the *Phi Delta Kappa Research Bulletin* entitled "The Inclusion Revolution":*

> Mainstreaming: This term has generally been used to refer to the selective placement of special education students in one or more "regular" education classes. Mainstreaming proponents generally assume that a student must "earn" his or her opportunity to be mainstreamed through the ability to "keep up" with the work assigned by the teacher to the other students in the class. This concept is closely linked to traditional forms of special education service delivery.

> Inclusion: This term is used to refer to the commitment to educate each child, to the maximum extent appropriate, in the school and classroom he or she would otherwise attend. It involves bringing the support services to the child (rather than moving the child to the services) and requires only that the child will benefit from being in the class (rather than having to keep up with the other students). Proponents of inclusion generally favor newer forms of education service delivery ..., i.e., heterogeneous grouping, peer tutoring, multi-age classes, and cooperative learning.

> Full Inclusion: This term is primarily used to refer to the belief that instructional practices and technological supports are presently available to accommodate all students in the schools and classrooms they would otherwise attend if not disabled. Proponents of full inclusion tend to encourage that special education services generally be delivered in the form of training and technical assistance to "regular" classroom teachers.

The concept of "mainstreaming" that was once prevalent in the provision of special education instructional programs is now clearly inappropriate (Huefner, 2006). A series of federal court decisions between 1989 and 1994, as well as the 1997 and 2004 Amendments, provide a clear understanding that students with disabilities are not required to earn the opportunity to be in a regular class placement. Students with disabilities cannot be required to demonstrate achievement of a specific level of performance as a prerequisite for placement into a regular class setting. A legal presumption exists that a child with disabilities will be in a regular class placement. Only when placement in a regular class (or regular nonacademic setting or extracurricular activity) cannot be satisfactorily achieved, even with the use of supplementary aids and services, may the child be placed in a special education class.

Many educators and parents support the attempt to provide *full inclusion* experiences for children with disabilities. However, the reality for

---

*From "The Inclusion Revolution," by J. Rogers, (1993), *Phi Delta Kappa Research Bulletin, 11,* 4–5. Reprinted by permission.

some children with disabilities is that they would not benefit from the experience (Hehir, 2003), their needs would overtax the school's resources, or the situation would cause significant disruption to the learning of other students. The authors applaud voluntary efforts at full inclusion, but the law clearly does not require full inclusion efforts (Howard, 2004; OSEP Memorandum 95–9, 1994; Letter to Goodling, 1991), and it is not likely to do so in the immediate future.

Nonacademic LRE Settings

The concept of LRE goes beyond the classroom setting and includes nonacademic settings, such as meals, recess, transportation, health services, and employment, both in and out of school, when arranged by the school. Also included in LRE considerations are such extracurricular activities as athletics, recreational activities, and clubs. The IEP must contain a statement of services and modifications to be "provided to the child, or on behalf of the child" to allow the child to participate in desired nonacademic settings and activities with children who are not disabled. When a child who wants to participate in activities does not, an explanation of why the child will not participate in activities with children without disabilities must be placed in the IEP (34 C.F.R. § 300.320 (a) (5)). The restrictiveness of the appropriate placement for a child, including residential settings, does not alter the school's responsibility to provide opportunities for participation with children who are not disabled.

Opportunities for interaction, including the bringing of students without disabilities into the segregated environment of children with disabilities, must be created. The same concepts of LRE apply when a child is placed in a private or public institution by a public school in order to provide educational programming, and each state is expected to make arrangements with private schools for the provision of LRE.

The Philosophy of Inclusion

A variety of information and suggestions are offered in this and later chapters on building better relationships among special and regular education students and among staff members.

Because these relationships are rooted in a commitment to the concept of LRE and inclusion, it becomes imperative to explore and understand inclusion in a broad philosophical sense. A good understanding of the philosophical underpinnings of inclusion is found in the book *Creating an Inclusive School*, published by the Association for Supervision and Curriculum Development:*

Pragmatic Definition of Inclusive Education
So what is inclusion or inclusive education? First, it is an attitude—a value and belief system—not an action or set of actions. Once adopted by a school or school district, it should drive all decisions and actions by those who have adopted it. The word include implies being a part of something, being embraced into the whole. Exclude, the antonym of include, means to keep out, to bar, or to expel. These definitions begin to frame the growing movement of building inclusive schools. The very meaning of the terms inclusion and exclusion helps us to understand inclusive education.

Inclusive education is about embracing all, making a commitment to do whatever it takes to provide each student in the community—and each citizen in a democracy—an inalienable right to belong, not to be excluded. Inclusion assumes that living and learning together is a better way that benefits everyone, not just children who are labeled as having a difference (e.g., gifted, non-English proficient, or disability).

An inclusive school values interdependence as well as independence. It values its students, staff, faculty, and parents as a community of learners. An inclusive school views each child as gifted. An inclusive

*From "What Is an Inclusive School?" (pp. 6–11), by M. A. Falvey, C. C. Givner, and G. Kimm, 1995, R. A. Villa and J. S. Thousands (Eds.), *Creating an inclusive school*. Alexandria, VA: Association for Supervision and Curriculum Development. Copyright © 1995 by the Association for Supervision and Curriculum Development. Reprinted by permission. All rights reserved.

school cherishes and honors all kinds of diversity as an opportunity for learning about what makes us human. Inclusion focuses on how to support the special gifts and needs of each and every student in the school community to feel welcomed and secure and to become successful. Another assumption underlying inclusive schooling is that good teaching is good teaching, that each child can learn, given the appropriate environment, encouragement, and meaningful activities. Inclusive schools base curriculum and daily learning activities on everything known about good teaching and learning.

Implications of Inclusive Education

Inclusion is the opposite of segregation and isolation. Segregated specialized education creates a permanent underclass of students, with a strong message to these students that they do not "cut the mustard," and that they do not fit or belong. Segregation assumes that the right to belong is earned rather than an unconditional human right.

The growing diversity of our student population is a topic of great debate and concern. Diversity differences may include language, culture, religion, gender, disability, sexual preference, socioeconomic status, geographic setting, and more. Diversity often is spoken about as if it were a plight rather than a wonderful opportunity for learning, that is, learning about the rich variety of each others' lives and also learning about what it is to be human—to be included, to be valued and respected for just who we are in a naturally diverse world.

Inclusion is not just for students with disabilities, but rather for all the students, educators, parents, and community members. Experience tells us that as communities and schools embrace the true meaning of inclusion, they will be better equipped to learn about and acquire strategies to change a segregated special education system to an inclusive service delivery system, with meaningful, child-centered learning. In the

process, a society and world intolerant and fearful of difference may change to one that embraces and celebrates its natural diversity.

Even after it is operationally defined, inclusion is still an elusive term. Part of the confusion arises from the varying assumptions that people associate with inclusive education—for example, that it is a "program" or that it is a research-devised strategy. The underlying assumption, however, is that inclusion is a way of life, a way of living together, based on a belief that each individual is valued and does belong.

The educational philosophy of each student being valued and belonging has also become part of the legal understanding of inclusion. The notable federal court decision in *Oberti v. Board of Education* (1992) expressed the concept in terms easily understandable by educators and parents:

> The IDEA incorporates a vision of our educational system in which, whenever possible, children with disabilities become fully integrated members of the educational community. The goal of the IDEA is realized when a child with a disability can become included, accepted, and respected as a full member of a regular class, and is no longer seen as an outsider. (p. 1329)

Decision Making for Inclusive Programming

The primary legal and educational issues involved with inclusion are *who* decides whether regular class placement can be achieved satisfactorily for an individual student and *how* is it determined. It has long been understood that the placement team must determine each child's appropriate placement. Team determinations of placement are the product of consensus on the part of team members, not majority vote and not solely by educators on the team.

A series of important court rulings, exemplified in *Greer v. Rome City School District* (1992), have taken much of the guesswork out of the placement team's role in *how* to plan for the inclusion of a child with a disability

(Bartlett, 1992). Beginning in 1989, those rulings have held that the IDEA created a strong preference favoring inclusion. Thus, a court reviewing a placement team decision regarding LRE must first review the evidence to determine whether the school has taken meaningful steps to include children with disabilities in the regular classroom. When a school has no history of successful inclusion, the court need look no further in its review; the school loses. However, if a school can demonstrate that it has previously taken meaningful steps to include students with disabilities in regular classrooms, the court review will turn its attention to the placement team's decision regarding a specific child.

In making its decision, the placement team must first give consideration to the placement of the child with disabilities in the regular school environment, in whole or in part, as appropriate for the individual child. Only when the child will receive greater benefit, either academically or from role modeling (e.g., language, behavior, social skills) in a special class setting or when the child, through behavior or excessive demands on teacher time and attention, is disruptive so that the learning opportunity of other students is significantly impaired, may the child be placed in a setting other than regular education. Meaningful consideration must always be given to the provision of supplementary aids and services and necessary modifications and accommodations that will allow the child to benefit from regular class placement and reduce disruption resulting from the child's presence. As the court in *Greer v. Rome City School District* (1992) said, the IEP team, as part of its process, must consider provision of "the whole range of supplemental aids and services" available that

FIGURE 5-2 *IEP and placement team planning*

Determination of Least Restrictive Environment

Decisions by the IEP/placement team should be based on data collected throughout the assessment and IEP process. Because there is an educational and legal preference for placement in the regular class setting, that is where consideration must begin. The team members, including the parents, should honestly address a series of questions that will lead them to a proper conclusion.

1. Has the school taken meaningful steps to support and maintain students with disabilities in the regular classroom?

    What supplementary aids and services have been considered? Which have been used? What accommodations and modifications have been considered? Which have been used? What interventions have been considered? Which have been used?

    Note: Only if the answer to question 1 is "yes" may the team proceed to questions 2, 3, and 4. If the answer is "no," much more work needs to be done.

2. Will the benefits of a special education placement for this student significantly outweigh the benefits of placement in regular education, even with the provision of supplementary aids and services?

    Academic benefits?

    Nonacademic benefits (e.g., role modeling of social skills, behavior, communication)?

3. Will the education of other students be significantly disrupted as a result of this student's presence in the regular class, even with the provision of supplementary aids and services?

    Due to the student's behavior?

    Due to the inordinate amount of teacher attention diverted from other students?

4. Will the financial cost of supplemental aids and services be substantial when compared with the total special education budget?

will allow the regular class placement to be successful (p. 696). Only when the extra cost of supplemental aids and services necessary to allow the student with disabilities to benefit from, and not be disruptive in, the regular class is excessive can financial cost be a factor in denying regular class placement.

Figure 5-2 presents a detailed, highly formalized, step-by-step approach for an IEP placement team analyzing the question of inclusion for a particular child. This approach synthesizes the holdings in major court decisions on the issue of court review of inclusion decisions. As teams become more experienced at applying the concept, their considerations will likely become less formal.

The application of the benefit, disruption, and cost of supplemental aids and services analysis by the placement team can be quite effective,

and will result in legally defensible decisions. A number of courts reviewing placement team decisions have applied the criteria and upheld the placement team findings that one or more of the analysis factors weighed against regular class placement for a specific child. (Examples include *T. W. v. Unified School District No. 259*, 2005, where in a low-functioning first-grader with Down Syndrome experienced a highly unsuccessful trial placement in kindergarten; *Clyde K. v. Puyallup School District*, 1994, a secondary student with Tourette Syndrome and Attention Deficit Hyperactivity Disorder (ADHD); and *Hudson v. Bloomfield Hills*, 1995, a seventh-grade student with a measured IQ of 42 and other disabilities).

Some educators have placed students in inclusive settings, even though they knew the student was likely to fail. This was likely under

---

Note: If the answer to questions 2, 3, and 4 is "no," the student must be placed in the regular class placement. You may not proceed to a special education placement. Only if the answer to question 2, 3, or 4 is "yes," can you go to the next question.

5. Has full consideration been given to the previous three questions (Nos. 2, 3, 4) with regard to the student's placement in regular academic settings, at least part-time?

   In which specific academic settings, with provision of supplemental aids and services, will the student benefit and not be disruptive?

   Note: If the answer to question No. 5 is "no," do not proceed. More work is needed.

6. Has full consideration been given to questions 2, 3, and 4 with regard to placement in nonacademic settings and activities, at least part-time?

   In what nonacademic settings and activities, with appropriate supplementary aids and services, will the student benefit from and not be significantly disruptive?

   Note: If the answer to question No. 6 is "no," do not proceed. More work is needed.

7. If the student is being educated in a setting other than the regular classroom, is the student provided the opportunity to interact with nondisabled peers to the maximum extent appropriate?

   In what academic settings is the child integrated with peers without disabilities? In what nonacademic settings is the child integrated with peers without disabilities?

8. What are the reasons that the student cannot be provided all or part of his or her program in a regular school setting? (The answer to this question must be included in the student's IEP.)

9. What related services are needed to support the student in a special education program? Why can't the child be served in a regular class environment with provision of those related services?

the misguided notion that students need to experience failure in the regular classroom setting before a special education placement can be justified. That is not a good practice from either an educational or a legal perspective (34 C.F.R. Part 300, Appendix A, Question No. 1, 2005).

Accessibility

Inherent in the placement of some students is the issue of accessibility of programs for both students and parents. Accessibility issues are directly covered in the nondiscrimination regulation provisions of Section 504 (34 C.F.R. § 104.21–23, 2005). In summary, those regulations require:

1. Each program and activity must be readily accessible to people with disabilities.
2. Not all existing school facilities must be made accessible, so long as all programs and activities are accessible to people with disabilities.
3. Accessibility may be accomplished through the reassignment of classes, services, or activities to accessible facilities or parts of facilities; the provision of accommodations, alteration of existing facilities, and construction of new facilities; or any other method that results in the program or activity being accessible.
4. Structural changes in existing buildings are required only when other efforts are not effective in making programs accessible.
5. Alternative methods of accessibility must give priority consideration to providing programs in the most integrated setting appropriate.
6. New facility construction, in whole or in part, must be designed so that the new facility is readily accessible to persons with disabilities.
7. When existing facilities are altered, the alteration must be conducted in such a way as to allow accessibility to the maximum extent feasible.
8. The above does not apply to agencies employing fewer than 15 persons when no reasonable method of accessibility can be determined.
9. Schools must ensure that interested persons, including those with impaired vision or hearing, can obtain information regarding accessibility of programs and services.

APPROACHES TO RESOLVING PLACEMENT CONCERNS

Controversies surrounding placement can never be entirely prevented. A more realistic goal is to avoid unfavorable hearing and court decisions by following the specific requirements of the law, minimizing disagreements by building a foundation of trust with parents, and increasing the educational options available to students through openness to new opportunities and new ways of doing things.

Some educational leaders mistakenly attempt to use inclusion as a budget-stretching device, often to the detriment of the students, both with and without disabilities, and to the staff (Baines, Baines, & Masterson, 1994; Rogers, 1993). Although the final word is not yet in on the overall cost of inclusion, it is unlikely, if done correctly, to be much greater than the cost of pull-out programs and services. In response to one school district's argument that inclusion of a particular student was too expensive, a federal district court rejected the school's conclusion. It noted that the costs per child between placement in a regular class with support services were comparable to placement in a special class with more support and fewer students (*Board of Education v. Holland,* 1992).

It is a serious professional mistake, with legal implications, to attempt to implement inclusive programs without proper planning and provision of appropriate support services. When appropriate planning and support are provided, all students in an inclusive school environment can benefit from the experience, without academic detriment to any group of students (OSEP, Memorandum, 95–9, 1994, research cited; Rogers, 1993; Stevens & Slavin, 1995).

Inclusive Classroom Considerations

Successful inclusion begins in the regular classroom; thus the regular class teacher must be properly prepared. Because many changes occur in the regular classroom with the introduction of students with special needs, consideration must be given to supplementary aids and services, instructional materials, class content, instructional methodology, and student assessment.

Supplementary Aids and Services

Many answers to the questions of accommodating students with disabilities in inclusive programs lie in determining appropriate modifications and accommodations and the provision of supplementary aids and services as support for the staff or student. The phrase "supplementary aids and services" means "aids, services and other supports that are provided in regular education classes or other education related settings to enable children with disabilities to be educated with nondisabled children to the maximum extent appropriate . . . " [emphasis added; 20 U.S.C. § 1402 (33)]. Supplementary aids and services and modifications must be provided to enable the child to benefit from his or her instructional program in the regular class or nonacademic setting without becoming a significant disruption. IEP teams should develop a clear process for determining the specific accommodations, modifications, and supplementary aids and services to be provided to, or on behalf of, a student. The following division of IEP team consideration into four separate classroom dimensions of physical, social-behavioral, collaborative, and instructional consideration presents but one appropriate organizational approach to the IEP team consideration.*

> *Physical Environment.* Modifications in the physical environment are the most straightforward. Special environmental considerations related to each disability (covered in Part III) include accessibility, adequate lighting, pre-enrollment

*Summarized from "The IDEA Amendments: A Four-Step Approach for Determining Supplementary Aids and Services," by S. K. Etscheidt and L. Bartlett, 1999, *Exceptional Children, 65,* pp. 169–72. Copyright 1999 by Council for Exceptional Children. Adapted by permission.

classroom orientation, and appropriate seating.

> *Social-Behavioral.* This dimension includes factors related to the student's behavior. The 1997 Amendments to the IDEA require that the IEP team consider a child's behavior when the behavior impedes the student's learning or the learning of others, and to consider appropriate positive behavioral interventions, strategies, and supports to address that behavior. Students experiencing frequent behavior problems may have a behavior plan attached as part of their IEP.

> *Collaborative.* This area pertains to personnel factors, and includes the establishment of periods of time for joint planning and a means of regular communication about the student between regular and special educators, support staff, consultants, and others providing programs and services. It may also include specialized skill development or special training for staff in working with students with special needs. The regular class teacher may need regular conferencing times with behavior specialists or curriculum modification consultants. The paraeducator may need training in discipline, instructional models, parent communication, or health procedures. Staff members may require staff development in sign language, autism, or functional behavioral assessment.

> *Instructional Strategies, Content, and Assessment.* In inclusion settings, educators must assure the availability of appropriate modifications in teaching strategies both in the materials used and the means of presenting information. Some of these modifications are obvious. If a student with a visual impairment is present in the classroom, for example, it will not be possible to rely exclusively on visual communication. Assignments may have to be tape recorded, visual and spatial concepts

may have to be explained, and appropriate tools and materials, such as large print books, word processors, or Braille writers, may be needed.

Other, less obvious, modifications will be required with many exceptional students. These may include the use of concrete examples in explaining new concepts, extra opportunities for rehearsal and repetition, consistent daily schedules, cooperative small group structures, special reinforcers, and so on.

The two most important supplementary aids and services identified in the research to enhance the likelihood of successful inclusive programs, are specialized training for the staff, including the regular class teacher (i.e., behavior management, communication, collaboration skills), and planned times for staff to collaborate (i.e., plan strategies, communicate, coordinate activities). Figure 5-3 lists examples of commonly used supplementary aids and services.

Instructional Materials Familiarity with materials analysis procedures will be helpful during the initial selection of the materials to be used in each class and in locating or preparing materials appropriate for specific students. Specialists such as physical therapists, special education consultants, and resource room staff should be able to provide assistance to the regular class teacher in this process.

Factors to analyze when choosing materials include reading level (probably the most critical), concept level, graphic presentation (e.g., dark print, print size, use of colored film filters), skills development, and adaptability (e.g., high lighting, study guide, variable assignments).

Methodologies Curriculum content modifications are most likely to be required for students with mental disabilities but may also be appropriate for others who for some reason (e.g., lack of prerequisites, poor reading skills) cannot master the normal curriculum. The need for such modifications should never be assumed by disability label, but rather based on individ-

FIGURE 5-3 *Examples of supplementary aids and services*

- Modifications to the classroom curriculum
- Assistive technology
- Peer tutors
- Use of tape recorder
- Read exam orally
- Take-home exams
- Open-book exams
- Use of paraeducators
- Collaboration with special education teacher
- More time allowed to complete assignments or exams
- Shortened assignments
- Cooperative learning
- Carbon copy of class notes
- Teacher presentation of outlines
- Large print materials
- Peer in-service
- Staff in-service
- A highlight marker to identify key vocabulary and concepts

From *Least Restrictive Environment: Supplementary Aids and Services* (p. 12). Developed by the Mountain Plains Regional Resource Center, 1997, Logan: Utah State University. Reprinted by permission.

ualized assessments that pinpoint each student's specific needs. Examples of differing approaches include mastery teaching/learning, teaching only essentials, concept-based instruction, parallel (or dual) curriculum, providing supplements (e.g., study skills, opportunities for practice), and modifying class expectations.

Curriculum Mapping Almost all current modifications, accommodations, and alternative techniques in curriculum require staff time and planning, which is why they are seldom accomplished by only one teacher working alone. Successful inclusion requires the collaboration of teams of staff members working together to effectuate modifications and adaptations to meet the unique needs of individual students, whether or not they are disabled.

Team collaboration and communication can be greatly enhanced through the process of curriculum mapping. The regular class teacher can identify class content coverage, align content with expected student skill and performance outcomes, and identify various methods of assessment. Koppang (2004) has provided an example of a life science teacher first identifying planned unit content regarding plants (i.e., characteristics, reproduction, location). The second step identifies the student skills needed (i.e., list, compare . . ., describe . . .). The final step identifies the assessment methods (i.e., drawings, oral presentation, essay).

An electronic spreadsheet identifying these factors can be shared with special education and media resource staff. Staff then identify and add materials available at differing ability levels and additional instructional methodologies to the spreadsheet. Special education staff can use the information on the spreadsheet to identify materials and activities to assist individual students' learning the content being used in the regular classroom. The sharing of maps of curriculum content, skills, assessment, and materials across areas of staff specialization provides an understanding of what each other is doing, what gaps exist in the curriculum, and where repetition might occur. Staff can thus discuss and plan any areas of needed revision or additional planning. Curriculum mapping places decisions about curriculum in the hands of teachers and staff who actually deliver the instruction. This collaborative effort to vary classroom content and presentation to meet the needs of individual students goes a long way in meeting student achievement goals and school goals involved with No Child Left Behind.

Univeral Design—The Future of Materials and Methodology

In enacting the 1997 and 2004 Amendments to the IDEA, Congress made it clear that it wanted a greater emphasis on improving the academic performance of students with disabilities and greater assurance of their receipt of quality public education. At the same time, Congress recognized that each child with a disability would not be able to learn at the same level, at the same rate, or through the same methodology or modality. Congress anticipated that regular education staff, with the help and support of special education staff, will meet the educational needs of the vast majority of special education students in the regular classroom using the general curriculum with all students.

Many teams of local educators have done an excellent job of making more materials and knowledge available to a greater number of children. Unfortunately, most teachers cannot easily meet all the educational needs of the linguistically, culturally, cognitively, sensorily, and physically diverse student populations sometimes found in a single classroom. Current written materials and texts and most audiovisual materials are very limited in the flexibility of their use in an inclusive classroom (Cawley, Foley, & Miller, 2003). Multiple and varied pathways are needed to meet various student needs and support their learning (Hitchcock, Meyer, Rose, & Jackson, 2002).

Many advanced thinkers searching for that flexibility of approaches and accommodations to meet a greater number of individual student learning needs are looking to digital resources for a solution (CAST, 2004). Computer software has been created through which students with diverse needs can read stories and participate in activities related to the readings because the text can be enlarged, changed in color, highlighted, or made audible in several languages as needed for individual students.

These early digital successes have encouraged a number of professional, corporate, and governmental entities to work together and separately to create and promote a new curricular concept called *universal design curriculum*. Universal design curriculum is the concept of diversifying instruction in the regular education classroom to meet the needs of nearly every student, regardless of their individual specific educational need and learning style. It provides multiple means of presentation style, multiple and flexible means of student engagement and participation, and multiple means of student response (CAST, 2004; Pisha & Stahl, 2005). Students who are disabled, nondisabled, gifted, and immigrant can learn using the same software materials and equipment. Through the use of technology, curriculum can be developed with built-in adaptations and inclusive accommodations to meet students' needs by accounting for differences in ability to see, hear, speak, move, read, write, understand English, pay attention, organize, interact, and remember (Hitchcock & Stahl, 2003). Teachers would seldom need to create other new methods and materials to meet diverse individual student needs. Accommodations for wide disparities in student educational needs would be built into the system (CAST, 2004; Universal design, 1996).

As this revolution in curriculum occurs, the need for committed educational leaders will be as great as ever. Because this is a regular education and not a special education innovation, all students and all teachers will be involved, not just a few. Teaching staff will need a great deal of professional support, assistance in bringing about the change, professional development opportunities, and innovation in securing needed resources (Curry, 2004). The local community will need to be educated in what for many citizens will be a giant leap ahead of what they personally experienced as students. Business and community leaders must be kept informed and their support solicited for innovations that will significantly affect the learning of all students.

Assessment

Grading. Suppose that the previously discussed modifications, accommodations, and changes in methodology have been made and the regular classroom is accessible. Appropriate texts, materials, and technology have been selected and the curriculum altered to match each student's abilities. What happens when grading time comes around? What evaluation system can be fair to both the students with disabilities, who may be putting forth tremendous effort and still not meeting the usual course goals and expectations, and those in the nondisabled majority, who may question a grading system they perceive as unequal and unfair?

This is one of the most difficult issues facing educators in an inclusive setting, and it has generated persistent and difficult questions among parents, teachers, and students. Teachers have been known to refuse to take exceptional students in their classes because of the awkwardness of developing an evaluation system that is fair to all students; one that reinforces effort but also realistically reports performance.

In grading tests and other class activities, the key issues are fairness and a firm grip on what is being evaluated and what is not. It would be important, for example, that teachers not downgrade a student because of poor handwriting or poor grammar if a test is designed to assess knowledge of social studies concepts. This is true especially if writing is a skill that is directly affected by the student's disability.

The same may be true of timed tests. Several disabilities may have an adverse affect on students' ability to demonstrate skills and knowledge accurately under time pressure. These may include physiological impairments that make writing slower and emotional problems that exaggerate stress when time is not a critical part of the performance being measured. It would be inappropriate to penalize such students' scores because of the length of time it took to complete the test. The goal, after all, is to measure students' acquired skills and achievements, not skills extraneous to the content being taught.

An obvious solution to many of these problems is to assign multiple grades for each task or subject. For example, principals could recommend that teachers grade work separately on content and form, individual student effort, and/or amount of time spent. Students might receive one grade for individual achievement or improvement and another on their relation to the achievement level of peers. Another possibility is to give a grade that reflects fulfillment of the central intent of the lesson, regardless of specific issues of quality.

Munk and Bursuck (2003) have conducted research on student grading generally and with regard to students with disabilities in particular. They recommend that teams composed of the student, parents, and both special and regular educators identify specific expectations of the regular classroom, clarify what purpose grades serve (e.g., content mastery, effort, growth, skills acquisition), consider specific grading adaptations in light of the student's IEP and individualized needs, and develop a written plan for individualized grading adaptations and monitoring the student's achievement.

Such a Personalized Grading Plan could take into account any variety of the five types of grading adaptations identified by researchers that can be used to assign students with disabilities grades, both in class and on report cards. The five types of grading adaptations are (a) progress on IEP objectives, (b) improvement over previous performances, (c) performance on only identified and prioritized content, (d) emphasis on correct process and effort, and (e) modifying the weight given for specific performances and modifying the grade scale (Silva, Munk, & Bursuck, 2005).

It is possible to develop individualized, fair, accurate, and justifiable evaluation systems for students in inclusive settings. Clearly, because so many potential problems can be avoided by doing so it is to the educational leader's advantage to be aware of these strategies and to assist teachers in implementing them.

Modifying Assessments. The vast majority of parents of students with disabilities (75%), as with parents of students without disabilities, agree that schools should pay more attention to and place more emphasis on student academic performance and growth. Both groups of parents oppose social promotion, the act of passing students on to the next grade level before they have learned the appropriate material. About one third of parents of children with disabilities (34%) prefer to have their child take the same assessments as students who are nondisabled and half (50%) prefer that their child take the same assessment, but with accommodations. Only about 15% of parents

of children with disabilities prefer that their child take an alternate assessment or be excused all together from achievement testing (Johnson & Duffett, 2002).

The same tests that are quite adequate for the majority of students may not yield fair and accurate results for some students with special needs. It would obviously be inappropriate to give an exam to a hearing-impaired student in which all instructions and questions were given orally, or to give a student with visual impairment or blindness a written test without providing a Braille version or a reader.

The following list is a variety of testing accommodations that teachers may decide are desirable to meet the needs of individual students. Obviously, not all modifications will be appropriate or necessary for all students.

- *Visual Presentation:* Teachers must be sure that the test is clearly printed and easy to read. Small flaws in print may be extremely distracting and frustrating to some students. Teachers should type rather than handwrite tests whenever possible, print on only one side of the page, be sure the duplicating or copy machine works properly, use dark ink on white paper, and avoid presenting too much material on each page. Some students benefit from the use of colored film (plastic) overlays.
- *Organization:* Teachers should number all pages, ask questions in sequential order, group questions of the same format together (e.g., multiple choice), and print all instructions on the page and review these instructions orally before testing begins. Teachers should allow plenty of space for the students' responses and provide lines for them to write on, and group questions (e.g., matching questions) into small sets, rather than long lists.
- *Minimizing Stress:* Teachers must minimize distracting noise and activity levels, place the students in a quiet location, try not to give oral instructions while students are taking the test, and be available to answer individual questions quietly. It is preferable to give several short tests rather than one long one. Timed

tests should be avoided, except where speed is an essential element of the skill. Bonus questions or other options for improving grades could be provided for those who perform poorly in exam situations. Bonus points should not be allowed to mask minimum mastery. Point values should be assigned to each part of the test and noted on the page. Teachers should help students prioritize their time in testing situations. Many teachers ease student stress by teaching test-taking skills and providing the opportunity for practice exams.

- *Communication Mode:* Students should be allowed to take a test orally when needed, or the exam should be structured to minimize writing (e.g., they could mark an X beside the correct response, rather than writing in the entire word). Teachers should give both oral and written instructions, as needed; assign another student to write down responses; tape record the test; or have the student indicate correct answers by pointing to them, as needed.
- *Clarity:* Teachers should provide simple, clear instructions and questions and avoid asking questions with many multi-part answers. They should walk around the room during the tests, checking the students' work to be sure they are all following the directions accurately.
- *Format:* Teachers who discern that a student responds much better to one type of test (e.g., multiple choice) than another should consider preparing tests for that student in the format that assures the most accurate performance. Tests can be offered with a balanced selection of formats and point values (e.g., 25% essay, 25% matching). Students may also be allowed to demonstrate knowledge or ability using assessment techniques other than tests.
- *Extraneous Material:* Material unrelated to student mastery and trivial questions should be eliminated whenever possible.

A student's grade in a class should not be altered or modified when reasonable testing accommodations have been made, and the teacher's content or skill expectations have not been altered. However, when accommodations substantially change or lower the teacher's expectations or standards, an alternative grading system can be considered. A student with disabilities enrolled in a general education class for reasons other than learning class content, such as learning social skills, should be evaluated based on specific IEP objectives rather than class content.

The following alternatives to traditional testing can be used with testing, or in place of testing, for obtaining reasonable evaluation results of student performance.

- *Continuous Assessment:* Although summative and standardized assessments have value in determining student learning, many teachers are involved in continuous constructive evaluations of students. It is important in today's classrooms of diverse learners that teachers recognize the importance of documented teacher observations of students while engaged in learning activities in order to have "snapshots" of student learning over time (Alexandrin, 2003). Curriculum-based measurement (CBM) is a viable approach to accurately monitoring the continuous progress of student learning that has been validated by several decades of research (Fuchs, 2004). CBM is a series of small, intermittent measurements of current student learning, at least weekly, that focuses on the desired year-end performance. Data collection and management are efficient and may be maintained or graphed electronically. The CBM approach especially lends itself to monitoring student progress in light of the No Child Left Behind legislation and the 2004 Amendments to the IDEA. As a result of the 2004 Amendments, regular monitoring of progress, especially on student achievement goals, is required, and using CBM is a resourceful way to assess student progress toward annual achievement goals.
- *Alternative Assessment:* Many schools are turning to the alternative assessment models, such as portfolios, to aid in assessing student progress. As a collection of student work

samples that serves to integrate academic learning activities, portfolio assessment presents a number of advantages. Portfolios document individual performance and progress, including the documentation of both affective and cognitive skills. Specific skills can be targeted for remedial attention, and progress can be monitored over time. This approach is very helpful in carrying out an IEP. Asking students to evaluate their own work encourages students' reflection on their own work and increases student-teacher collaboration in the classroom. Content will vary with subject matter and overall purpose, but creative and flexible approaches will even involve academic areas thought by some to not be suited for portfolios, such as mathematics (Kleinert, Green, Hurte, Clayton, & Oetinger, 2002; Prestidge & Glaser, 2000).

- *Contracts:* The teacher and student may sit down together and negotiate a specific grade for a specific amount of work at an agreed-upon level of functioning. For example, the agreement might be that over the course of the grading period, the student will earn a B for completing two spelling lists per week with an average of 90% accuracy. The contracted educational goals must be positive (what the student will do, not won't do), measurable, clearly stated, honest, and reasonable, given the student's current ability levels. Student and teacher must understand and agree on each part of the contract, then each must sign it and retain a copy. Progress toward stated goals should be evaluated periodically.

- *Differing Requirements:* The teacher can allow the student to respond in a different communication mode, require different amounts or kinds of work, or allow a longer period of time for completion of an assignment. For example, a one-page rather than a two-page essay can be required, or one chemical experiment rather than two, and so forth. Care must be exercised in using this option for a variety of reasons. Sometimes students with disabilities need more practice, rather than less, to master a skill. Social factors are important considerations, especially

for adolescents who do not want to be perceived as different from their peers. Inappropriately low expectations may hinder chances of reaching true potential.

- *Small Group Assignments:* The teacher can divide the class into small, heterogeneous groups and assign a task to the whole group. Students with disabilities can be assigned specific, appropriate roles in a cooperative learning structure. All group members receive the same grade for work completed, or one group grade and one for individual effort. This structure can generate extra benefits in terms of the sharing of skills and understanding and acceptance of the classmate with disabilities. (See Chapter 6 for more details.)

OTHER INCLUSION CONSIDERATIONS

Staff Readiness and Understanding

U.S. educators are as good as any found in the entire world. Yet many are not ready, or do not think they are ready, for the opportunity and challenge of implementing inclusive educational practices. There seems to exist a general feeling of inadequacy and lack of preparation for what lies ahead.

In a review of 28 research studies conducted between 1958 and 1995, Scruggs and Mastropieri (1996) found that regular education teachers felt that they had not been provided sufficient time to successfully plan and provide services to children with disabilities included in regular education. The vast majority of those teachers felt that they had been provided inadequate training and preparation for including students with disabilities in the regular classroom and that adequate resources were not readily available. Those teacher perspectives from the various research studies were consistent over several decades. Neither did the perceptions of teachers change significantly over time when identifying professional needs to help facilitate successful inclusion. Their "want list" included time for planning, training, and working with consultants and colleagues; personnel resources in the form of paraeducators and regular contact with special education teachers; materials and equipment resources appropriate for the student needs; and greater consideration of the severity of the disability—the more severe the disability, the more time and resources must be made available.

Teachers over the years have often been justified in feeling alone and unsupported when faced with the challenges of mainstreaming and inclusion. Educational leaders must do a better job of allaying concerns and supporting teachers who are involved with inclusion efforts. Long gone is the day when the principal escorted the student with a disability to the classroom, opened the door, gently nudged the child into the room, closed the door, and walked away. Both good educational practice and the law dictate that meaningful support and necessary resources accompany that child into the regular classroom. Successful inclusion does not just happen as the result of merely placing students with disabilities in regular education classrooms.

Community Readiness

The primary goal of this book is to provide educators with the knowledge, basic skills, and incentive to enable them and their colleagues to provide good and meaningful educational experiences for all the children in the United States. The trend across all disability categories, but especially the mildest, has been toward moving students to less restrictive placements (See Figure 1-1 in Chapter 1).

However, not all the attention needs to be focused internally. Although there is strong support among families of children with disabilities for inclusion (Johnson & Duffett, 2002), the general public appears to lag in its support for, or knowledge of, the inclusion concept. The annual Phi Delta Kappa/Gallup Poll of Public Attitudes Toward Education provides evidence that the general public lacks a great deal of understanding and support for inclusion. In

the last two polls soliciting opinions about inclusion in 1995 and again in 1998, participants were asked whether children with learning problems should be placed in the same classroom with other students, or in special classes of their own. For both years, only 26% of those polled favored students with learning problems being placed in the regular classroom, and nearly two-thirds of those polled favored placement in special classes (Rose & Gallup, 1998).

Local education leaders must make a conscious effort to meet with local community leaders, civic organizations, and news media to present the community with an understanding of inclusion and education for all students.

PRIVATE SCHOOL PLACEMENT

By Public Schools

Children with disabilities may be placed in private schools by the public school or by their parents. When the public school is responsible for the placement or referral to a private school, the public school must conduct an IEP meeting. The public school must also ensure that representatives of the private school attend, or in some other way participate in, the IEP meeting (e.g., *Shapiro v. Paradise Valley Unified School District*, 2003). The private school may conduct annual reviews of IEPs, but the parents and a representative of the public school must be involved in IEP decisions and agree to any changes before they are implemented. The responsibility for compliance with the IEP, LRE, parent safeguards, and other provisions of the IDEA remain with the public school.

By Parents

When a child's parents unilaterally decide that the child's placement should be in a private school, the public school plays a very different role. The public school is not responsible for the cost of the education at the private school, so long as the public school has a FAPE available for the student and the parents choose the private school placement anyway. Disagreements over the availability of FAPE at the public school are subject to mediation and due process hearing, as discussed in Chapter 11. When the parents of a child with disabilities had previously enrolled the child in the public school, and subsequently enrolled the child in the private school, they may recover their education expenses when they can establish (a) that the public school did not have a FAPE available to the child in a timely manner, and (b) their private school placement of the child is educationally appropriate. Recovery of education costs by parents may be reduced when the parents have not informed the public school of their education concerns and their intent to change enrollment. Public schools must be notified by parents no later than the most recent IEP meeting attended by the parents, or in a written notice to the public school at least 10 days prior to their removal of the child from the public school. The requirement of parent advance notice to the school provides the school an opportunity to fully consider parent concerns prior to the parents actually changing the child's placement.

Public school officials must be involved in the education of private school children with disabilities placed by their parents for other than an appropriate education in ways that will at times seem confusing. For instance, the public school must spend on parentally placed resident private school children attending a private school located in its jurisdiction an amount of money proportional to what it receives from the federal government under the IDEA.

For parentally placed children with disabilities in private schools, when FAPE is not an issue, there is no individual student right to special education and related services under federal law. The private schools will not receive any federal funds to support the special education needs of students, and private schools are not required to evaluate students for IDEA eligibility (Letter to Barr, 1998). Public school officials are required to engage in timely and meaningful consultation with representatives of private schools and representatives of parentally placed children. Together they determine a thorough and complete child find process to determine the number of parentally placed children with

disabilities attending private schools. They then decide what services, if any, will be provided to which categories of children and how the services will be provided.

Service plans, rather than IEPs, must be developed for each private school child served and address only the services the public school has determined it will make available. In those limited situations where some services are available at the private school, the public school is responsible for the service plan development, review, and implementation and must ensure that a private school representative participates. Service plans, to the extent appropriate, must meet the general development, review, and revision requirements of IEPs. Services may be provided on the private school site, including religious schools, to the extent consistent with law. However, special education and related services provided private school students, including materials, must be secular, religiously neutral, and nonideological [20 U.S.C. § 1412 (a) (10) (A) (vi) (II)]. The school district must maintain records of children determined to be disabled attending private school and the number of children served by the public school.

When the local public school disagrees with the service provision perspective of the private school officials, the public school must provide a written explanation of the reasons for its decision to the private school officials. When a timely and meaningful consultation has occurred, the public school must document the consultation with a written affirmation from the private school officials or documentation of its own. Private school officials may submit a complaint to the state, or request mediation or a due process hearing, when they believe the local public school does not engage in timely and meaningful consultation or appropriately consider the views of the private school officials (Yell, 2006).

Some states have enacted laws that require selected special education services be provided to children enrolled in private schools. Thus, caution dictates that state law should be consulted.

Some parents who unilaterally place their child in a private school may be willing to dually enroll their child in a public school at the same time in order to take advantage of special education programs and services at the public school. Public schools must provide programs and services for dually enrolled children who are otherwise entitled to them.

CONCLUSION

The determination of appropriate educational placement of a child with disabilities is an important and complex task for parents and educators. A successful placement is not something that just happens. Advance preparation of the school staff, school environment, and teacher and student support systems will aid greatly in achieving a successful placement. So will a trusting relationship between parents and educators. Placement of the child in the appropriate LRE setting is most achievable when all of the people involved, including parents, are provided the opportunity to adequately participate in the planning and preparation for implementation of the placement. Improperly implemented placements have a significant potential for student failure, administrative challenges, poor staff morale, and losing legal battles. School leaders have a duty to see that the school's resources, creative staff, and parent wishes result in a successful and meaningful educational placement for children with disabilities.

VIEW FROM THE COURTS

Florence County School District Four v. Carter (1993) (parent unilateral placement). The parents of a child with specific learning disabilities objected to an IEP that established goals in reading and mathematics of only four months' progress for the entire year. They unilaterally placed the child in an unapproved private school. The girl experienced three years' academic growth in her three years at the private school. The parents then requested, and were refused, reimbursement for their private school expenses from the public school. The issue before the Supreme Court was whether parents

could recover their expenses for a unilateral placement in a private school that did not meet state approval requirements.

The Supreme Court ruled in favor of the parents, highlighting the fact that appropriate placement was the issue and not whether the private school met state approval standards. In response to the public school's complaint that it would be unfairly required to pay the high tuition rate for the private school, the Court said that public schools could avoid high tuition rates for private schools either by providing children with FAPE itself or placing children in appropriate settings of the public school's choosing.

Greenland School District v. Amy N. and Robert N. (2004) (parent unilateral private school placement without notice to the school). Parents unilaterally transferred their fifth-grade daughter to a private school and subsequently, after determining that the girl had a disability, to a second private school that specialized in providing services to students with specific learning disabilities and attention deficit/hyperactivity disorder. The parents sought tuition and expense reimbursement from the public school.

The court noted that the student had not been identified as needing special education at the time the parents transferred their daughter. The court also noted that the parents had not initiated the original transfer for purposes of obtaining FAPE under the IDEA, and the parents failed to provide the public school with the required notice of their intent to transfer their daughter to a private school.

The court ruled that because the parents were not originally transferring their daughter out of the public school as a result of their daughter not receiving FAPE and did not provide the school with notice, they were not entitled to have the public school reimburse their tuition and other expenses.

Oberti v. Board of Education (1993) (inclusion). Rafael was an eight-year-old boy with Down's syndrome who was removed from a regular kindergarten classroom by the school and placed in a segregated special education class. Rafael had experienced a number of serious disruptive behavioral problems in the regular classroom, including temper tantrums, crawling and hiding under furniture, hitting, spitting, and toileting accidents. His IEP did not address behavior problems or provide for special education staff consultation and communication for the kindergarten teacher. Rafael's parents argued that the school had not provided adequate support for the regular class teacher.

The court determined that the IDEA had created a "strong presumption" in favor of inclusion and applied the benefit and disruption tests from previous decisions in other states. The court ruled that had Rafael and his teacher been provided appropriate supplementary aids and services, Rafael would have benefited in, and not have been disruptive of, the regular class. Because Rafael's school had not provided an appropriate level of supplementary aids and services to meet his behavior needs, it could not properly justify his exclusion from regular class based on those same behavior problems.

Renollet v. Independent School District 11 (2005) (reduced inclusion). The parents of a 17-year-old student with disabilities challenged a placement team decision to reduce the boy's inclusion from two to one regular class. The court noted that the student recognized his difference from other students in inclusive class settings and engaged in aggressive behavior as a result of frustration when asked to complete tasks beyond his ability. It also noted that the provided supplementary aids and services had met with only limited success. The placement team decision to reduce the amount of time in the regular classroom was upheld.

RECOMMENDED READINGS

Acrey, C., Johnstone, C., & Milligan, C. (2005). Using universal design to unlock the potential for academic achievement of at-risk learners. *Teaching Exceptional Children, 38*(2), 22–31. This article explains universal design and provides examples of teacher-made universal design materials.

Etscheidt, S. K., & Bartlett, L. (1999). The IDEA Amendments: A four-step approach for determin-

ing supplementary aids and services. *Exceptional Children, 65,* 163–174. This article explains the legal importance of supplementary aids and services under the IDEA and suggests an approach to more effectively determine appropriate supplementary aids and services for children.

Hitchcock, C., Meyer, A., Rose, D., & Jackson, R. (2002). Providing new access to the general curriculum: Universal design for learning. *Teaching Exceptional Children, 35*(2), 8–17. This article discusses and provides examples of the concept of universal design in meeting the individual needs of students in the regular curriculum.

Koppang, A. (2004). Curriculum mapping: Building collaboration and communication. *Intervention in School and Clinic, 39,* 154–161. This excellent article describes the use of curriculum mapping across general and special education as a tool in meeting students' instructional needs.

Prater, M. A. (2003). She will succeed! Strategies for success in inclusive classrooms. *Teaching Exceptional Children, 35*(5), 58–64. This article provides a number of specific examples in preparing the teacher to help modify the regular education class to accommodate students with disabilities.

Scott, V. G., & Weishaar, M. K. (2003). Curriculum-based measurement for reading progress. *Intervention in School and Clinic, 38,* 153–159. This article provides detailed steps desirable in helping teachers implement a reading progress measurement and instructional change program for students.

Silva, M., Munk, D. D., & Bursuck, W. D. (2005). Grading adaptations for students with disabilities. *Intervention in School and Clinic, 41,* 87–98. This excellent article provides advice and examples on the implementation of grading adaptations for students.

Thomas D. D. (2004). Use transportation as a related service. *Intervention in School and Clinic, 39,* 240–245. The author explores 20 ways in which transportation is used as a related service.

Voelz, D. L., Brazil, N., & Ford, A. (2001). What matters most in inclusive education: A practical guide for moving forward. *Intervention in School and Clinic, 37,* 23–30. This article provides practical strategies for helping educators create educational environments conducive to inclusive practices.

Relevant Federal Regulations

34 C.R.F. Part 104 (2005) Nondiscrimination on the basis of disability in programs and activities receiving federal financial assistance—Section 504 regulations.

34 CFR § 104.21   Discrimination prohibited.
           .22   Existing facilities.
           .23   New construction.

34 C.F.R. Part 300 Assistance to States for the Education of Children with Disabilities [70 Fed. Reg., 35, 833–35,880 (June 21, 2005)].

300.5	Assistive technology device.
.6	Assistive technology service.
.17	Free appropriate public education
.34	Related services.
.38	Special education.
.41	Supplementary aids and services.
.105	Assistive technology; proper functioning of hearing aids.
.106	Extended school year services.
.114	Least restrictive environment requirements.
.115	Continuum of alternative placements.
.116	Placements.
.117	Nonacademic settings.
.130–.144	Private school placement by parents.
.145–.147	Private school placement by public schools.
.148	Placement of children by parents if FAPE is at issue.
.209	Treatment of charter schools and their students.
.320	Definition of individualized education program.

SELECTED WEBSITES

Code of Federal Regulations–Government Printing Office–National Archives and Record Administration
www.gpoaccess.gov/cfr/index.html

Council for Exceptional Children Technology and Media Division
www.tamcec.org

U.S. Department of Education Office of Technology
www.ed.gov/about/offices/list/os/technology/index.html

National Center on Accessing the General Curriculum
www.cast.org

Recording for the Blind & Dyslexic
www.rfbd.org

Project Personalized Grading Plans Accommodations–Model
www.cedu.niu.edu/projectpgp

National Center on Educational Outcomes–Standards–Assessment–University of Minnesota
www.education.umn.edu/nceo

FairTest–National Center for Fair & Open Testing
www.fairtest.org

Association for The Advancement of Computing in Education
www.aace.org

Association for Educational Communications and Technology
www.aect.org

Frontline: Testing Our Schools Public Broadcasting Corporation
www.pbs.org/wgbh/pages/frontline/shows/schools

Center for Applied Special Technology (CAST)
http://www.cast.org/teachingeverystudent

The Center for Universal Design–North Carolina State University
http://www.design.ncsu.edu/cud

Policy Maker Partnership at the National Association of State Directors of Special Education
http://www.ideapolicy.org

Internet Resources for Special Education
http://www.irsc.org

Apple's Disability Site (search disabilities)
http://www.apple.com/education/k12/disability

Rehabilitation Engineering & Assistive Technology Society of North America
http://www.resna.org

Behavioral Research and Teaching–University of Oregon
http://brt.uoregon.edu/techreports

QUESTIONS FOR THOUGHT

1. Can you identify and rank order six ways that school leaders can provide support for teachers in preparing for inclusion?
2. What skills and characteristics are imperative for school leaders to have in the successful implementation of inclusive programs?
3. What skills and characteristics are imperative for school leaders to have in order to maintian an existing successful school inclusive program?
4. If a student with disabilities meets the mainstreaming qualification of having adequate skills and abilities to participate in a regular class setting, why would he or she be identified as needing special education?
5. An expert witness in a hearing, who was a specialist on including children with autism into regular class settings, testified "whenever inclusion fails, it is not because the child has in some way failed, it is because the adults have failed." Is that an accurate statement?

REFERENCES

Alexandrin, J. R. (2003). Using continuous, constructive, classroom evaluations. *Teaching Exceptional Children, 36*(1), 52–57.

Assistance to the States for the Education of Children with Disabilities. 34 C.F.R. Part 300 (1997).

Assistance to the States for the Education of Children with Disabilities, 34 C.F.R., Part 300, 70 Fed. Reg., 35,833–35,880 (June 21, 2005).

Baines, L., Baines, C., & Masterson, C. (1994). Mainstreaming: One school's reality. *Phi Delta Kappan, 76*(1), 39–40, 57–64.

Bartlett, L. D. (1992). Mainstreaming: On the road to clarification. *Education Law Reporter, 76,* 17–25.

Bartlett, L. D. (2000). Medical services: The disputed related service. *The Journal of Special Education, 33,* 215–223.

Bauer, A. M., & Ulrich, M. E. (2002). "I've got a palm in my pocket." Using handheld computers in an inclusive classroom. *Teaching Exceptional Children, 35*(1), 18–22.

Board of Education v. Holland, 786 F.Supp. 874 (E.D. Cal. 1992).

Boyle, E. A., Washburn, S. G., Rosenberg, M. S. K., Connelly, V. J., Brinckerhoff, L. C., & Banergee, M. (2002). Reading's slick with new audio texts and strategies. *Teaching Exceptional Children, 35*(2), 50–55.

CAST (2004). *Universal design for learning: Frequently asked questions.* National Center on Accessing the General Curriculum. Retrieved February 21, 2004, from http://www.cast.org/ncac/FrequentlyAskedQuestions2120.cfm.

Cavanaugh, T. (2002). E Books and accommodations: Is this the future of print accommodation? *Teaching Exceptional Children, 35*(2), 56–61.

Cawley, J. F., Foley, T. E., & Miller, J. (2003). Science and students with mild disabilities: Principles of universal design. *Intervention in School and Clinic, 38,* 160–171.

Cedar Rapids Community School District v. Garret F., 24 IDELR 648 (N.D. Ia. 1996); *aff'd.*, 106 F.3d 822 (8th Cir. 1997), *aff'd.*, 526 U.S. 66, 119 S.Ct. 992 (1999).

Clyde K. v. Puyallup School District, 35 F.3d 1396 (9th Cir. 1994).

Curry, C. (2004). Universal design: Accessibility for all learners. *Educational Leadership, 61*(2), 55–60.

Day, J. N., & Huefner, D. S. (2003). Assistive technology: Legal issues for students with disabilities and their schools. *Journal of Special Education Technology, 18*(2), 23–34.

Downing, J. D. (2004). Related services for students with disabilities. *Intervention in School and Clinic, 39,* 195–208.

Etscheidt, S. (2002). Extended school year services: A review of eligibility criteria and program appropriateness. *Research and Practices for Persons with Severe Disabilities, 27,* 188–203.

Etscheidt, S., & Bartlett, L. D. (1999). The IDEA Amendments: A four-step approach for determining supplementary aids and services. *Exceptional Children, 65*(2), 163–174.

Falvey, M. A., Givner, C. C., & Kimm, C. (1995). What is an inclusive school? In R. A. Villa & J. S. Thousand (Eds.), *Creating an inclusive school* (pp. 1–12). Alexandria, VA: Association for Supervision and Curriculum Development.

Florence County School District Four v. Carter, 510 U.S. 7, 114 S. Ct. 361 (1993).

Fuchs, L. S. (2004). The past, present and future of Curriculum-Based Measurement research. *School Psychology Review, 33,* 188–192.

Greer v. Rome City School District, 950 F.2d 688 (11th Cir. 1991); withdrawn and remanded 956 F.2d 1025 (11th Cir. 1992); reinstated 967 F.2d 470 (11th Cir. 1992).

Greenland School District v. Amy N. and Robert N., 358 F.3d 150 (1st Cir. 2004).

Hehir, T. (2003). Beyond inclusion. *School Administrator, 60*(3), 36–39.

Hitchcock, C., Meyer, A., Rose, D. K., & Jackson, R. (2002). Providing new access to the general curriculum. *Teaching Exceptional Children, 35*(2), 8–17.

Hitchcock, C., & Stahl, S. (2003). Assistive technology, universal design, universal design for learning: Improved learning opportunities. *Journal of Special Education Technology, 18*(4), 45–52.

Howard, P. (2004). The least restrictive environment: How to tell? *Journal of Law and Education, 33,* 167–180.

Hudson v. Bloomfield Hills Public Schools, 910 F. Supp. 1291 (E.D. Mich. 1995); *aff'd* 108 F.3d (6th Cir. 1997).

Huefner, D.S., (2006). *Getting comfortable with special education law: A framework for working with children with disabilities* (2nd ed.). Norwood, MA: Christopher Gorden Publishers, Inc. Individuals with Disabilities Education Act. 20 U.S.C. §§ 1,400–1,487.

Iowa Department of Education. (1996). *The least restrictive environment (LRE) and the individualized education program (IEP): Legal educational and practical guidelines for educators and families.* Des Moines, IA: Mountain Plains Regional Resource Center, Drake University.

Iowa Department of Education. (2005). *Administrative rules of special education.* Iowa Administrative Code, 281–41.

Irving Independent School District v. Tatro, 468 U.S. 883, 104 S. Ct. 3371 (1984).

J. H. v. Henrico County School Board, 326 F.3d 560, (4th Cir. 2003).

Johnson, J., & Duffett, A. (2002). *When it's your own child: A report on special education from the families who use it.* New York: Public Agenda.

Kleinert, H., Green, P., Hurte, M., Clayton, J., & Oetinger, C. (2002). Creating and using a meaningful alternate. *Teaching Exceptional Children, 34*(4), 40–47.

Koppang, A. (2004). Curriculum mapping building collaboration and communication. *Intervention in School and Clinic, 39,* 154–161.

Lankutis, T. (2004). Special needs technologies: An administrator's guide. *Technology and Learning, 25*(2), 30–35.

Letter to Barr, 30 IDELR 146 (OSEP, 1998).

Letter to Goodling, 18 IDELR 213 (OSEP 1991).

Letter to Veazey, 37 IDELR 10 (OSEP, 2001).

Mountain Plains Regional Resource Center. (1997). *Least restrictive environment: Supplementary aids and services.* Logan: Utah State University.

Munk, D. D., & Bursuck, W. D. (2003). Grading students with disabilities. *Educational Leadership, 61*(2), 39–43.

Nondiscrimination on the basis of handicap in programs and activities receiving federal financial assistance. 34 C.F.R. Part 104. (2004).

Oberti v. Board of Education, 789 F. Supp. 1322 (D.N.J., 1992); *aff'd* 995 F.2D 1204 (3rd Cir., 1993).

OSEP Memorandum 95–9, 21 IDELR 1152 (OSEP, 1994).

Parette, P., & McMahan, G. A. (2002). What should we expect of assistive technology? *Teaching Exceptional Children, 35*(1), 56–61.

Pisha, B., & Stahl, S. (2005). The promise of new learning environments for students with disabilities. *Intervention in School and Clinic, 41,* 67–75.

Prestidge, L. K., & Glaser, C. H. W. (2000). Authentic assessment: Employing appropriate tools for evaluating students' work in 21st century classrooms. *Intervention in School and Clinic, 35,* 178–182.

Rebore, D., & Zirkel, P. A. (1999). The Supreme Court's latest special education ruling: A costly decision? *Education Law Reporter, 135,* 331–141.

Renollet v. Independent School District No. 11, 42 IDELR 201 (D. Minn. 2005).

Rickey, K. (2003). Special education due process hearings. *Journal of Disability Studies, 14,* 46–53.

Rogers, J. (1993). The inclusion revolution. Research Bulletin No. 11, *Phi Delta Kappan,* May 1993, 4–9.

Rose, L. C., & Gallup, A. M. (1998). Public's attitudes toward the public schools: The 30th annual Phi Delta Kappa/Gallup Poll. *Phi Delta Kappan, 80,* 41–58.

Scruggs, T. E., & Mastropieri, M. A. (1996). Teacher perceptions of mainstream/inclusion, 1958–1995: A research synthesis. *Exceptional Children, 63,* 59–74.

Shapiro v. Paradise Valley Unified School District, 317 F.3d *1072* (9th Cir. 2003).

Silva, M., Munk, D. D., & Bursuck, W. D. (2005). Grading adaptations for students with disabilities. *Intervention in School and Clinic, 41,* 87–98.

Smith, T. C. (1981). Status of due process hearings. *Exceptional Children, 48,* 232–236.

Stevens, R., & Slavin, R. (1995). The cooperative elementary school. *American Educational Research Journal, 32,* 321–351.

Thomas v. Cincinnati Board of Education, 918 F.2d 618 (6th Cir. 1990).

T. W. v. Unified School District No. 259, 43 IDELR 187 (10th Cir. 2005).

Universal design: Ensuring access to general education curriculum. (1996). Research Connections in Special Education (5); ERIC Clearinghouse No. EC307411; Available at http://www.ericec.org.

Veazey v. Ascension Parish School Board, 42 IDELR 140 121 Fed, Appx. 552 (5th Cir. 2005) (per Curiam).

White v. Ascension Parish School Board, 343 F.3d 373 (5th Cir. 2003).

Yell, M.L. (2006). *The law and special education* (2nd ed.). Upper Saddle River, NJ: Merrill/Prentice Hall.

Yell, M. L., & Katsiyannis, A. (2004). Placing students with disabilities in inclusive settings: Legal guidelines and preferred practices. *Preventing School Failure, 49,* 28–35.

Zigmond, N. (2003). Where should students with disabilities receive special education services? Is one place better than another? *The Journal of Special Education, 37,* 193–199.

CHAPTER 6

STUDENT RELATIONSHIPS

CHAPTER PREVIEW

Focus

The IDEA and Section 504 require that students with disabilities be educated and participate in nonacademic activities to the maximum extent appropriate in the company of their peers who are not disabled. Placing the two groups in physical proximity can be successfully achieved through planning, advance preparation, and the use of research-based and proven best-practices strategies. Proper planning can ensure a learning environment that is beneficial to both students with disabilities and those without disabilities, and serves to help break down learned negative stereotypes.

Educators have a legal and ethical responsibility to plan and support school environments that carry out the spirit, as well as the letter, of the law. For many students, both disabled and nondisabled, the school years are the beginning of long-lasting relationships that add greatly to the quality of life. Educational leaders are responsible for providing and supporting educational programming that will serve the needs of all students for the "long haul," not only during the school years.

Rationale

Individuals with disabilities deserve to experience as normal a life as possible. To this end, schools have a responsibility to provide children with disabilities appropriate life experiences as well as educational programming. In support of this goal, educators must combat negative attitudes and foster an atmosphere of acceptance, understanding, and appreciation in which students with disabilities, and those without, can form a variety of positive relationships and associations.

Social factors are as important as academic ones in preparing students for an active and satisfying role in the adult community. This means that educators must develop and provide all students with as representative a lifestyle and personal experiences as is feasible. The future will be one of acceptance of, and accommodation for, individuality and all students should begin experiencing the future now.

Approaches

Educators must be aware that successful inclusion requires active efforts on their part to create appropriate educational environments and the nurturing of receptive attitudes by students without disabilities and their parents. School leaders should begin by modeling positive, accepting, and nonjudgmental attitudes toward special education students and their teachers. That starts by providing equal opportunities for status within the school to all students. The importance of positive peer relationships should be stressed, and principals should encourage teachers to establish research-proven structured learning experiences that provide academic, emotional, and social benefit to all students. When inclusion programs are implemented properly, students with disabilities, under reasonable expectations for their performance, can successfully work interdependently with peers who are not disabled. In properly implemented inclusion settings, all students can succeed.

PEER INTERACTIONS

Most school leaders recognize that federal law, both the IDEA as amended in 2004 and Section 504, contain provisions which require that the education of children with disabilities be provided in the least restrictive environment (LRE) to "the maximum extent appropriate." Considerations of educational placement must begin in the regular education classroom and nonacademic activity environment. Some inexperienced administrators without a background in special education programming, however, do not fully understand the public policy behind those legal mandates. That understanding will come with time, experience, and reflection. Most educational leaders eventually become able to "walk in the shoes" of those children with disabilities and their parents and gain a clearer understanding of the lifelong importance of inclusive practices in schools.

Much educational theory and research in the past has focused on child-adult (teacher, parent) relationships. When educators referred to peer interaction at all, they were likely to approach it as a problem of off-task behavior and classroom disruption. Parents, for their part, also were likely to have a negative understanding of peer interaction, worrying about peer influences in areas such as drugs, disobedience, and sexuality. But those concerns, however important, are only part of the complex and vital role that peer relationships play in a child's development and growth. It is through interactions with their friends and classmates at school that children practice and learn socialized values, control of aggressive impulses, empathy for others, personal identity, and social skills.

Because of the importance that peer environment has on the effect on regular students, it is not surprising that the consistent separation of students with disabilities from their typically developing peer group would have some negative impact. One study compared the social networking of elementary students with emotional and behavioral disabilities placed in segregated classrooms to that of nondisabled peers in regular classrooms and found considerable differences in the social lives of the two groups (Panacek & Dunlap, 2003). Nondisabled students placed in regular classrooms established strong networking with friends in both their home neighborhood and school settings. The students with disabilities in segregated classrooms, however, became dependent on friends near their home and not at school. The researchers concluded that placing students with disabilities in segregated settings greatly restricted their establishment of supportive social networks.

Another study reported that students with disabilities who are placed in segregated classrooms for most academic subjects, and in general education for only nonacademic subjects, such as art, gym, and music, do not have the same level of social development as do students with typical educational needs (Wenz-Gross & Siperstein, 1997). The students who were segregated tended to seek social support from their peers much less than children without disabilities, and they even looked less to family members for help in solving problems. As children with disabilities advance through adolescence, this lessening of both family support and peer social networking may place them at greater risk for not succeeding in life as adults.

Educators need to make an effort to develop a favorable social as well as academic classroom environment and continue to role model acceptance of students with disabilities for the benefit of their nondisabled peers. The absence of a conscious effort by professional staff members to assist students with disabilities in their development of positive social support and peer relationships may cause a lifelong negative effect in this important area of human development.

Controversy

Many educators would claim that a greater opportunity for interaction with students without disabilities is an argument favoring the practice of inclusion. Other people, especially some parents of students with severe disabilities, would say that greater opportunities for interaction is an argument against inclusion. The latter group claims that in a special school or special classroom setting their children are not judged inferior by able-bodied classmates and are not as susceptible to teasing and exclusion as they are in an integrated setting with nondisabled students. In addition to the academic advantages of smaller, more homogeneous special classes, the partisans say, there are social advantages. In a school where all children are disabled, some parents believe there is widespread understanding, acceptance, and lack of prejudice (Palmer, Fuller, Arora, & Nelson, 2001). There are similar modes of communication (e.g., signing among deaf students) and similar constraints and student needs—all of which foster an experience of equality and make the development of friendships less difficult. The parents and advocates of some groups of children with disabilities (e.g., aural/oral philosophy involving students with hearing impairments) argue that segregation for specialized training in the early years will allow a greater likelihood of later integration into society as adults.

Proponents of inclusion emphasize the necessity not of evading situations laden with potential problems and prejudices, but of confronting them and working for change and understanding. They argue that stereotyping and prejudice will never disappear if people without disabilities do not have an opportunity to regularly interact with people with disabilities and to exchange those one-dimensional stereotypes for the richer experiences of personal contact. If the information and attitudes gleaned from personal experiences are to be received clearly, the contacts must begin in childhood.

A report of a poll of families of children with disabilities conducted by Public Agenda, an organization dedicated to aiding in a better understanding of the public point of view on national policy issues, has indicated that parent concerns with inclusion may be lessening. Parents of children with disabilities report that most of their child's school day is spent in regular classrooms with almost three-fourths (73%) reporting regular class placement and only 14%

reporting placement in a self-contained classroom. The majority of those parents polled (69%) believe that their child experiences much less stigma in school today than would have been present in the past (Johnson & Duffett, 2002).

It is unlikely that adults will ever completely eliminate teasing and ridicule among children. Educators can, however, make a conscious effort to teach all students about the value of differences and showing mutual respect, but it is a never-ending responsibility. Sandra Lawrence, a former president of the National Elementary School Principals' Association, once told one of the authors how constant a job it is: "You work hard for months, thinking that you are making an important difference, then you hear one child on the playground call another a 'retard,' and you start all over again."

Villa and colleagues (1995) have concluded that the real solution to teasing is teacher and administrator role modeling. Students observe and imitate adult behaviors toward others and practice adult actions in dealing with conflict. From their joint perspective spanning many years of experience, the seven author researchers and educators observed that less ridicule and teasing occurs in appropriately planned inclusive schools.

The problem does not lie with having students who are not disabled in an inclusive classroom. Most students understand and accept reasonable accommodations used in meeting the needs of individuals. In a synthesis of 20 studies investigating the perceptions of thousands of students in all grade levels, Klingner and Vaughn (1999) found that both students with and without learning disabilities appreciated classroom adaptations and accommodations that facilitated learning for all students. All student groups in the studies expressed appreciation for class instruction about learning strategies and a combination of text learning and activity-based learning. They valued teachers who slowed down instruction when needed, explained concepts, and taught material in different ways so that all students can learn. Good teaching stands as good teaching for all students.

Current Realities

While inclusion practices have been controversial among some groups, the current status of inclusion appears to be one of watchful optimism. That is to say:

- It is no longer a question of whether to integrate and include; the laws have clearly mandated such a change, and it is being carried out.
- On a social level there have been successes, cases in which inclusion has resulted in greater respect and understanding among people of different groups.
- Integrated and inclusive education per se, and more specifically, the means of bringing them about, are still controversial, but have become much less so.
- There also have been failures. Inadequately planned educational inclusion of the disabled, as with different racial/ethnic populations, has been known to increase existing prejudices and antagonism, rather than to dissipate them. When implemented *improperly,* inclusion can contribute negatively to the self-image of students with disabilities.
- Working in proximity to students without disabilities provides exposure to appropriate social cues and behavior modeling, leading to recognition of appropriate responses to situations.
- Exposure of students without disabilities to persons with disabilities and the opportunity to relate to and help others are important concepts in a society that values each individual.
- When done properly, integration and inclusion of children with disabilities are successful for students and for staff.

In short, the need for positive social interactions in childhood is great and is sometimes difficult to achieve in today's heterogeneous classrooms. Principals and other educational leaders have an obligation to recognize both the benefits and the challenges associated with interactions between students with disabilities and those without, and to work attentively to foster positive educational environments for all students.

THE INCLUSIVE MODEL

The concerns of educators and parents that students with exceptionalities would become social outcasts when placed in inclusive school settings have not been supported by research findings. One study examined three inclusive elementary classrooms, and found that existing social relationships were normal for students identified as being in three categories of exceptionality: those who are academically gifted, those with learning disabilities, and those with emotional and behavioral disorders. The researchers concluded that all three groups of exceptional students had been well integrated into the classroom social structure (Farmer & Farmer, 1996).

A study of middle-school and high-school students conducted in Illinois, Iowa, and Florida has supported other findings which establish that students without disabilities are willing to form friendships with school peers with severe disabilities (Hendrickson, Shokoohi-Yekta, Hamre-Nietupski, & Gable, 1996). The reasons most often given by nondisabled students for their friendships were "They need friends, too," "I like to help people," "I would feel good about myself," and "It would be fun."

When the students in the multistate study were asked how to best arrange situations for social interactions, they advised researchers that friendships among students should be facilitated by adults. The best method identified by the nondisabled students to improve social interactions was through the placement of students with disabilities in the regular classroom setting for all or part of the school day. The youngsters theorized that all the students would learn better together and many would also learn more about disabilities.

In a study conducted in the Midwest, researchers attempted to determine whether 37 middle-school students (grades six through eight) with mild disabilities attending classes with nondisabled students had different feelings about themselves and their school than did their peers without disabilities (Hansen & Boody, 1998). The school, with a total enrollment of about 500 students, had been committed to placing students with disabilities in regular class environments for several years. The researchers hypothesized that if the school's effort at placing students with mild disabilities in regular classes had been accomplished successfully, the students with disabilities would express similar feelings about themselves and the school as did their peers without disabilities.

The Midwest study found that the students with disabilities did not express feelings of being unwelcome or being put down by the other students in the school. They rated their positive school and classroom experiences slightly higher (but not statistically significant) than did the students without disabilities. The specific student perceptions looked at by the researchers included many of those characteristics associated with a good school climate:

- The degree of friendship students feel for each other
- The degree of help and friendship the teacher has given the students
- The degree of emphasis on completing planned activities and staying on task
- The degree to which students compete with each other for grades and recognition and how hard it is to achieve good grades
- The degree to which students behave in an orderly and polite manner, and the overall quality of the organization of assignments and classroom activities
- The degree of emphasis on establishing and following a clear set of rules
- The strictness of the teacher in enforcing the rules
- The degree to which students contribute to planning classroom activities, and the extent to which the teacher uses new techniques and encourages creative thinking
- Being attentive and interested in, as well as participating in, class activities and doing additional work on one's own.

The researchers concluded that their finding of no significant differences existing between students with and without disabilities in perceptions regarding school and classroom environments provided evidence that the school's commitment and effort to provide good educational experiences to all students had been successful.

The development of social networking for students with severe disabilities in the regular school environment has great significance. Other than school, children with severe disabilities have few avenues in which to develop friendships. Studies have established that students with severe disabilities, when supported appropriately, can benefit socially from placement in regular education classes.

Fisher and Meyer (2002) determined from a 2-year study of 40 students with severe disabilities across all school age groups, that the students placed in inclusive settings made greater significant developmental and social competence gains than a comparison group in self-contained settings. Kennedy, Shukla, and Fryxell (1997) found that students with severe disabilities who were placed and properly supported in intermediate grade classes interacted more frequently, had more social contacts outside the classroom, and had reciprocity of higher levels of social support than did their counterparts who were educated in self-contained special education classes. They also established larger friendship networks and had more durable relationships with peers without disabilities.

Proper adult support is a key element in the success of inclusive programs. Mere placement of students in the same proximity without adequate planning, coordination, and monitoring by a wide range of professionals would likely have had less positive results as was found in these studies. Findings of substantive social benefits for students with severe disabilities who participate in inclusive educational arrangements provide additional incentive to educators and parents to consider inclusion efforts for a broader range of students with disabilities.

The lack of friendships is one of the most serious problems confronting persons with disabilities, especially in adolescence. It can have dire effects on the individuals' self-image, psychological adjustment, and even vocational skills. If individuals with disabilities are to lead productive and satisfying adult lives, they must experience a variety of interactive social situations and they must find acceptance and bonds of friendship among the acquaintances of childhood. Obviously, this cannot occur naturally when children are segregated based on artificial criteria, such as disabilities.

Another issue at the heart of the inclusion debate is the question of its effect on academic achievement. Generally, studies do not indicate a decline in academic performance of students with disabilities or their nondisabled classmates in inclusive classrooms (OSEP memorandum 95–9, 1994; Sharpe, York, & Knight, 1994). Rea, McLaughlin, and Walther-Thomas (2002) conducted a comparison study of eighth-grade students with specific learning disabilities in inclusive and pull-out special education delivery models. The researchers concluded that students with disabilities in the regular education classes demonstrated as good or better achievement outcomes in language arts, social studies, mathematics, and science as the students in special education only programs. On the Iowa Tests of Basic Skills, the students with learning disabilities in the inclusive program achieved higher scores on language arts and mathematics subtests and comparable scores in other areas. On a state proficiency test, the students with learning disabilities in the inclusive setting demonstrated scores comparable to those of students in pull-out programs. The successful inclusive school had provided its staff with common planning time and regular team meetings that facilitated communication and collaborative problem solving, and the development of appropriate support services.

Research findings exemplify the point that appropriately supported standard school curriculum is not beyond the ability of students with learning disabilities. These findings have vastly important ramifications for state and federal testing mandates, especially No Child Left Behind (NCLB). For all students, the curriculum needs to be challenging. When content is not challenging enough, less is learned than is possible. When content is too difficult, students may become frustrated and learning will be impeded. Close monitoring of student response to content expectations will provide needed feedback data for individualized adjustments.

In a larger comparison study of the effects of inclusive school settings in six different geographic regions of Indiana, researchers determined that students with mild learning disabilities and mild mental disabilities benefited academically from inclusive classroom instruction in reading and mathematics. Interestingly, study results established that the students without disabilities in the inclusive classrooms also made significant gains in reading and mathematics achievement compared to their peers in classrooms where students with disabilities were pulled out from regular class instruction (Cole, Waldron, & Majd, 2004). Presumably, the additional supports that were available to the students with disabilities in the inclusive classrooms benefited all students in the classes.

In the context of the inclusion class and pull-out model debate, educators are realizing that the place, location, or type of environment is not necessarily the key to successfully educating children with disabilities. In a review of 35 years of research on the relative efficacy of one type of placement over another, Zigmond (2003) concluded that no clear superiority of one type of placement over another has been established. She concluded that the physical setting of a child's education is much less important than what is available to students in effective teaching strategies and individualization of approaches. Rather than asking whether an individual child should be in a resource room or self-contained class, the more appropriate question is what placement option would provide appropriate support for the effective teaching and service practices necessary for the child to meet the child's educational goals and objectives. Chapter 10 discusses the beneficial elements of desirable staff organizational arrangements for successful inclusion programs in greater detail.

Setting the Tone

Principals and other educational leaders are in a unique position to greatly influence the quality of student attitudes and relationships in inclusive schools. Enthusiasm and commitment on the part of administrators will be conveyed through teachers and staff to the students served. To model and communicate a positive attitude, principals should:

- Ensure that special students have the same access to status activities as other students (e.g., working in the office, carrying messages, names appearing in school newsletters and on bulletin boards, participation in assemblies).
- Get to know the students, call them by name, and model acceptance and interest.
- Encourage a variety of activities in which special students can participate and play prominent roles (i.e., provide support for students when necessary).
- Encourage awareness and efforts to foster productive social relationships among students during school and after-school activities.
- Make sure that separate special classes and resource rooms and separate special education staff members, if they exist, have equal access to the same pleasant physical accommodations and desirable schedules (e.g., lunchtime) as do other classes and staff.
- Provide the fullest support possible (e.g., clerical and logistical help, materials, planning time, in-service classes) needed to make special education programs successful.
- Remove stigmas from special programs through techniques such as renaming a resource room the activity room, stocking it with interesting resources and activities, and setting hours each day when it is open to all students and faculty members for browsing and exploring; also, invite gifted students to the room for occasional special activities.

Questions of Fairness

School leaders and teachers must be prepared for expressed student and parent concerns about students being treated unfairly as a result of some students receiving accommodations, modifications, and supplementary aids and services. Such concerns can be dealt with most

effectively by teaching and reinforcing an understanding of the differences between equality, equity, and need as they apply to fairness among students and staff (Welch, 2000). Fairness, from a standpoint of equality, implies that every student is treated the same; equity implies that students receive assistance proportionate to their contribution; and need implies that students receive assistance as determined by individual necessity. Special education, related services, modifications, and accommodations are provided based on need and are not provided to everyone (equality) or on the basis of merit (equity) in all situations. School leaders must be able to explain or demonstrate that differing student needs require different applications of fairness.

Welch (2000) recommends that teachers respond to student concerns about fairness. Students will more likely respond favorably to individualization when they have a better understanding of the meaning of basic fairness. Some potential issues of equality in the delivery of accommodations for one or a few students can be precluded by providing classroom adaptions and accommodations to all students in a class. All student groups have been determined to express appreciation for teachers who use a variety of teaching styles, a combination of text learning and activity-based learning, and who provide instruction in various learning and test taking strategies (Klingner & Vaughn, 1999).

PEER TUTORING

Traditional Peer Tutoring

Peer and cross-age tutoring are other constructive organized student activities that can promote friendships and understanding among students with and without disabilities, and also can help principals and teachers meet the demanding and challenging need for individualizing instruction. Properly structured student tutorials have proved as effective as tutoring by adult paraeducators with potential benefits for all categories of students involved (Brewer, Reid, & Rhine, 2003).

Ryan, Reid, and Epstein (2004) reviewed 14 studies using a variety of peer tutoring strategies (same age peers, cross-age peers, and class-wide peer tutoring) with students with emotional disturbance/behavioral disorders (E/BD). The studies indicated the successful use of peer interventions across academic subject areas (mathematics, reading, spelling, and history) and grade levels in consistently producing effective academic and social gains for students. The reviewers emphasized the desirability of teachers and principals becoming more knowledgeable and experienced in the implementation of peer-assisted teaching methods. They noted that incorporation of such empirically based teaching methods is encouraged by both NCLB and IDEA legislation.

For student tutors, benefits of peer tutoring include increased academic and social maturity, self-confidence, improved behavior, improved attitudes toward school, and improved attitudes toward individuals who are different from themselves (Brewer, Reid, & Rhine, 2003). All students in a class frequently receive indirect benefit from peer tutoring as a peripheral effect of the classroom teacher's work in performing task analysis and individually designed curricular programming.

Good peer tutors should be dependable, responsible, caring students, or those likely to develop those traits. Generally, they must have the required academic competence and the time to spare. It is important, however, to be cautious about possibly exacerbating existing social gender and racial tensions. For example, principals or teachers should not consistently choose able-bodied white boys as tutors for members of all other groups. Girls may respond better to female tutors and minority students to tutors of their same racial and ethnic group. Many students have an easier time accepting tutors who are at least somewhat older than they are. This will not be true in every case, of course, but the choices demand sensitivity on the part of the staff involved. It should also be possible to find appropriate tutoring roles for many students with disabilities.

Some students have participated as committed tutors for two or three years. To combat potential boredom or loss of motivation in long-term tutorial arrangements, teachers occasionally can change tutor-tutee pairs, providing reinforcing events for both members of the dyad (such as parties or celebrations), and help make tutoring a prestigious activity in the school.

Peer-Assisted Learning Strategies (PALS)

Several faculty members at Peabody College of Vanderbilt University, the University of Minnesota, and a number of other institutions of higher education have been working with classroom teachers and faculty of other institutions in the development of a successful instructional program for use in diverse elementary, middle, and high school reading, spelling, history, and mathematics classes. Their Peer-Assisted Learning Strategies (PALS) accommodates a wide range of student diversity through the decentralization of the learning process. For only a part of the school week (two or three 30- or 40-minute sessions), students in the entire class are paired to work on loosely structured activities related to reading, spelling, history, or mathematics. This results in 13 to 15 unique instructional experiences occurring simultaneously in a classroom instead of a single incidence of teacher-directed learning. The teacher circulates about the class providing support and individualized remediation where needed. Although tutoring pairs are selected based on needs, each session is reciprocal so that each student assumes both the coach and player role. At the end of each 2 weeks, students change partners. Fuchs and Fuchs (2005) have established that the PALS is an especially important instructional strategy when differentiated instruction is called for because the teacher can oversee many different levels of curricula and instructional procedures simultaneously.

Fulk and King (2001) recommend beginning with simple drill and practice activities, such as spelling words or math facts. This allows the students to become familiar with the process before moving on to more challenging content, concepts, or higher-order thinking skills. Fuchs and Fuchs (2005) have established PALS as an important strategy for promoting word recognition, fluency, and reading comprehension in young children, including those in kindergarten and first grade.

Learning activities are structured, planned, and sometimes use a reward system for success based on multiple criteria. PALS reading, spelling, history, and mathematics programs have repeatedly established greater academic progress than that resulting in typically structured classrooms. This includes progress among various and diverse student groupings, including inclusion students, low-performing students, average-achieving students, and high-achieving students (Calhoon & Fuchs, 2003; Fuchs & Fuchs, 2005; Fuchs, Fuchs, Mathes, & Simmons, 1997). Unlike some self-professed modern educational panaceas that require nearly full-time emersion of students into planned activities, PALS requires only 60 to 120 minutes per week and the rest of the class time can be used in other teaching methodologies and activities. Educators who are concerned that NCLB testing and preparation activities dominate today's school curriculum to the exclusion of other important areas, such as the arts and development of non-test taking skills, should strongly consider implementing the PALS approach.

When combined with curriculum-based measurement (CBM) strategies, PALS has become an economical and impressive teaching tool with built-in procedures to detect those individual students with whom the PALS procedures are not attaining the desired effect. Simply stated, CBM is a weekly or biweekly administration of short probes sampling the expected curricular skills or knowledge attained by students. Individual student performance is graphed or charted and thus illustrates past, present, and probable future growth. Research indicates that student motivation is positively related to their involvement in CBM graphing and creation of other nonverbal representations of their own progress (Calhoon & Fuchs, 2003). Teachers can quickly identify when one student, a group, or an entire class is not making

adequate progress. A remedial instructional program for a few or all may then be indicated. There has been extensive research, including over 140 empirical studies, confirming the technical adequacy, instructional utility, and the logistics of implementations of the use of CBM in monitoring progress in general education of both students with and without disabilities (Fuchs, 2004). Teachers, paraeducators, or the students themselves with even limited technical skills can computerize these monitoring operations and greatly enhance teacher decision making and student learning (Mathes, Fuchs, & Fuchs, 1995).

The use of the PALS approach, sometimes referred to as Class-Wide Peer Tutoring (CWPT), with or without CBM, provides one way in which teachers can accommodate a greater range of instructional needs in their classrooms while providing critical learning strategies and increased practice time for individual students. CWPT has proven effective across grade levels, disabilities, English as a second language classes, and in classrooms in urban, suburban, and rural settings. Burks (2004) determined that CWPT, coupled with motivation strategies, was an effective method for teaching spelling to elementary students with specific learning disabilities in reading and writing. CWPT can be combined with other teaching strategies to provide increased communication skills, time-on-task, practice, feedback, and continual correction unavailable in many other classroom settings (Keller, 2002). One group of experienced and knowledgeable educators suggested that CWPT is especially useful for teaching the subjects of health and safety (e.g., guns, drugs, fire) where peer tutors exercise a greater than usual amount of influence (Reddy et al., 1999).

Saenz, Fuchs, and Fuchs (2005) have demonstrated the power of PALS with Spanish-speaking English language learners (ELL). The ELL study involved 132 native Spanish-speaking students with specific learning disabilities and low-, average-, and high-achieving peers in grades 3 through 6. Twelve teachers were randomly assigned to PALS groups and non-PALS control groups of students. PALS sessions were conducted 3 times a week for 15 weeks. Students were assessed with pretreatment and posttreatment tests. The students with specific learning disabilities using the PALS methodology significantly outgrew the contrast students on reading comprehension, and the other student categories (low-, average-, and high-achieving) involved in the PALS group had strong positve results. Study findings established that PALS improved the reading comprehension of Spanish-speaking students, with and without specific learning disabilities (SLD), in bilingual education classrooms. The researchers noted that their findings were of special significance due to the importance of reading success in elementary school and the greatly increasing need for improved learning methodologies for non-English language students. As an extra benefit, the researchers noted that teachers considered PALS easy to implement and students enjoyed the interaction of working in paired groups.

A Secondary Peer-Tutoring Example

Longwill and Kleinert (1998) have reported on a high school peer tutoring program in Kentucky. Students without disabilities enrolled voluntarily in courses for which they received grades and credit toward graduation. Part of their course requirements was to engage in a self-study of beliefs and attitudes toward disabilities and the rights of persons with disabilities. Students were provided a range of opportunities, both in school and in the community setting, to engage in cooperative learning and peer-tutoring activities with students with disabilities. Students met course requirements through various reflective writing assignments.

A natural project for the peer-tutoring program was the development of individual student portfolios that was an outgrowth of Kentucky education reforms. As nondisabled students helped their peers with disabilities prepare their portfolios, they in turn simultaneously completed materials for their own portfolios.

The Kentucky peer-tutoring program became a natural part of regular education programs. One of the peer-tutor assignments involved the identification of regular class adaptations for students with disabilities across a variety of classes. The following are a few examples of the school accommodations devised with the help of peer tutors:

- Instead of drawing pictures in art class, Richard, who has severe disabilities, pasted pictures cut from magazines.
- Instead of completing research papers, Tony worked with picture symbols on the topic or theme of his choice. He used pictures arranged or copied from his communication system to make a research report.
- Instead of a large reading assignment for Karla, peers wrote summaries of each reading. This helped the students who developed the summary learn the material and helped Karla understand the basic themes or ideas.
- Instead of long assignments in typing class, Tom typed what he did in the community that day.
- Instead of writing in yearbook class, Lauren classified photographs into activity categories, such as school classes, clubs, and sports.
- Instead of an oral research presentation in biology, Derrick developed a collage of local fruits and vegetables and the best places to purchase the seeds for each of those plants.

Peer tutors in the Kentucky program also became a natural link to the community. They introduced the students with disabilities to their own part-time jobs and co-workers, and provided support to students with disabilities in their respective job searches. Both peer tutors and students with disabilities helped each other develop job resumés. They went shopping together and practiced budgeting, banking, and nutrition skills. Some relationships continued into leisure time activities of movies, pizza, and bowling. All participants in the Kentucky program, including regular class teachers, thought they profited by the experiences.

COOPERATIVE LEARNING ACTIVITIES

What, exactly, can educational leaders do to ensure that teachers help promote positive peer interactions? Several researchers, including Johnson and Johnson (1986, 1992) and Stevens and Slavin (1995), have proposed that the most effective means is through structured cooperative student learning activities. Educational leadership efforts should be directed toward structuring cooperative, rather than competitive (spelling bees, grading on a curve) or individual student activities (giving the special student an alternative lesson to sit and work on alone).

According to proponents of cooperative learning, competitive or individualistic learning pits students against one another. They seek outcomes that are personally beneficial, and as such are detrimental to others in the class. Individual learning goals are unrelated to the other students and other students' goals are irrelevant. When a few students in a competitive environment win, the others lose (Johnson & Johnson, 1992).

Hundreds of studies have been conducted and reported on cooperative learning as an instructional approach. According to Johnson and Johnson (1992), we "know more about cooperative learning than we do about lecturing, age grouping, departmentalization, starting reading, the 50-minute period, or almost any other aspect of education" (p. 175).

The cooperative learning concept broadly encompasses a variety of instructional strategies that encourages student-to-student interaction regarding curricular content in a supportive and cooperative environment. Commonly, students must work in small groups, explicitly assist each other in learning, and share in the evaluation of the learning experience. Students help each other clarify the nature of assignments, help make instructions clear, share ideas, and share responsibility. The students are empowered to take responsibility for both their own learning and that of all the other students in

their group. Students are rewarded for fulfilling their expressed responsibility in seeing that all members of the group have learned the material. The teacher's role is transformed into that of facilitator rather than provider of information, or into a combination of the two.

Many studies have demonstrated the benefits of substituting structured cooperative formats for traditional competitive or isolated individualistic approaches to learning for all categories of students. Such benefits include greater self-esteem, higher academic achievement, increased motivation, greater liking for other students and school personnel, greater seeking and exchanging of information, and generally improved classroom climate (Gillies & Ashman, 2000; Slavin, 1991). Most research results, however, have involved studies of moderate length (1 to 6 months), and few have looked at the long-term effect of cooperative learning. Stevens and Slavin (1995), however, have reported the results from a 2-year study of several elementary schools that used cooperative learning as a school-wide philosophy across content areas. The teachers planned cooperatively, used peer coaching (see Chapter 10), and actively sought parent involvement. Students with learning disabilities were included in cooperative learning activities, with special education teacher support on a team teaching basis.

The results at the end of the second year established that the cooperative schools experienced great successes. All student grouping categories experienced significantly higher achievement in reading vocabulary, reading comprehension, language expression, and math computation. The students with learning disabilities also had significantly higher achievement results in math application. Results from gifted students showed that those with cooperative learning classes had significantly higher achievement than their peers in other schools who were provided enrichment programs without cooperative learning. It was determined, in the study, that social relations were better in the cooperative learning schools and that students with disabilities were more accepted than students with disabilities in schools with traditional pull-out programs.

Jenkins, Antil, Wayne, and Vadasy (2003) found that regular education teachers using cooperative learning reported that students receive a broad range of benefits from cooperative learning. Identified benefits include improved student self-esteem, an emotionally safe environment in which to learn, better learning products from the experience, and greater participation in classsroom activities. Nearly all the teachers in the study expressed the belief that cooperative learning was an effective strategy for regular, special, and remedial education students.

Antil, Jenkins, Wayne, and Vadasy (1998) have identified factors that have contributed to the popularity of cooperative learning. It is obvious from their descriptions why the cooperative learning concept so neatly fits the individualization desirable in inclusive settings:

- It has great potential for accommodating individual student differences; in fact, individual differences are used to promote learning.
- It can achieve multiple educational goals and improve academic performance, social development, interpersonal skills, and communication development.

Goor and Schwenn (1993) have highlighted the fact that multiple learning activities and strategies exist within the cooperative learning umbrella. Some examples are:

- Student Teams—Achievement Divisions require students to complete common work in groups of four to five, but to take individualized tests. A team's score is based on individual student's improvement over previous performance.
- Think-Pair-Share involves students first attempting to answer a question individually, then discussing their thoughts with a partner, and then the partners share with a small group or the class.
- Jigsaw uses teams wherein each member is given (or researches) a piece of information and is asked to teach it to the others.

- Team Accelerated Instruction provides for student assignment of materials at their level (four seventh-graders received 20 on-grade-level spelling words; one received an additional five; and one received 10 words from the third-grade level) and peer-assisted practice. Group points are awarded on improvement on individual tests.
- Group Investigation is where the group decides what to investigate and what each member will contribute.
- Learning Together uses teams working on one assignment to start, and stresses self-analysis of the team success in, working together.

The most common example of cooperative learning student teams normally involves assigning a research topic to a small, heterogeneous group. Each student is responsible for checking a particular source or for contributing one element of the group's report. The essential characteristics of effective cooperative learning experiences that distinguish it from other student group work are that:

- Students in the learning group are interdependent and must work together in order to reach a goal. Students must interact in order to promote each other's success.
- Roles are clear and each individual is accountable for fulfilling an assigned task or for mastering the information in the lesson.
- Work is evaluated based on the whole group's performance and each group member gets the same grade, but each member is individually accountable for the group success.

Adjustments in cooperative learning for students with disabilities can be made in the type of role assigned, the portion of the group work for which they are held responsible, and the grading of their work. It is essential to set reasonable expectations for students so that they are challenged but not frustrated and so that other group members are not penalized for their willingness to cooperate and work with their peers with disabilities. Special educators can be consulted for assistance in making these adjustments. They also can help by training all students in cooperative social skills. The role of the regular teacher in setting up these activities includes:

- Specifying, as far as possible, the instructional objectives
- Selecting the group size most appropriate for the lesson
- Assigning students to groups (common practice is to maximize heterogeneity)
- Setting up an appropriate physical arrangement of the classroom
- Providing appropriate materials
- Explaining the task and cooperative group support
- Observing the student-student interaction
- Intervening, as a consultant, to help students solve problems and learn interpersonal skills and ensure that all members are learning
- Evaluating group products (Johnson & Johnson, 1992)

Depending on the activity, multiple grades may be awarded, one for achievement, one for improvement, and one for contribution.

Research indicates that some students with disabilities, especially those with behavioral disorders and mental disabilities, may require advance training or preparation in group processes, social skills, and cooperation in order to make cooperative learning successful for all participants (Goodwin, 1999; Pomplun, 1997). Some educators have advocated the use of ongoing strategy reminders (cue cards) for use by secondary special education students in group work in any setting (Goor et al., 1996).

In interdependent classroom and activity settings, students not only develop positive attitudes about themselves and their peers, they also become more realistically aware of the nature of disabilities and their effects on the individual. The disability then takes on a dynamic, rather than a static, or stereotyped meaning and students become better able to perceive persons with disabilities as unique and worthy individuals (Slavin, 1991). Whether cooperative learning activities are used for advanced training, ongoing memory joggers,

or continuing training, when used as an educational methodology, cooperative learning appears to be well worth the effort to make it work.

COLLABORATIVE PROBLEM-SOLVING

Salisbury, Evans, and Palombaro (1997) have reported a successful and logical extension of the cooperative learning concept, the collaborative problem-solving (CPS) process. It was undertaken over a 2-year period in an elementary school where both teachers and students were trained in CPS strategy. They then used it to identify and solve problems related to the physical, social, and instructional inclusion of students with mild to profound disabilities.

CPS involved shared authority and responsibility among participants for idea generation, accountability, and the sharing of resources and rewards. Teachers modeled the process as relevant situations arose, and supported a climate of shared responsibility and decision making with each other and with students. As a constant reminder, each classroom posted a chart of the steps in the CPS process.*

- Identify the issue: "What's happening here?" To identify an issue, state the desired outcomes.
- Generate all possible solutions: "What can we do?" Brainstorm potential solutions.
- Screen solutions for feasibility: "What would really work?" Review for feasibility and match solutions to the group's value base. Predict possible benefits and detriments.

---

*From "Collaborative Problem-Solving to Promote the Inclusion of Young Children with Significant Disabilities in Primary Grades," by C. L. Salisbury, I. M. Evans, and M. M. Palombaro, 1997, *Exceptional Children, 63,* p. 199. Copyright 1997 by the Council for Exceptional Children. Adapted with permission.

- Choose a solution to implement: "Take Action." Create stakeholders and thus provide support and commitment throughout the consensus process.
- Evaluate the solution: "How did we do? Did we change things?"

Evaluate the effects of the solution and determine whether concerns remain, how the group feels about the result, and what has been learned.

In a relatively short time, CPS became the routine problem-solving mechanism for many issues; for example, a child in a wheelchair in the cafeteria being unable to sit with classmates, a student being excluded from playground activities owing to potential head injury, lack of participation on field trips, planning classroom game modifications, planning a Mother's Day card for a child who cannot speak or hear, planning participation in physical education activities, and involvement in class academic activities. Within 2 years, the process of CPS became intuitive among the children. In addition to being involved in successfully removing barriers to physical, social, and instructional inclusion in the classroom and building, all the students involved achieved important personal outcomes:

- Developed concern for others
- Developed acceptance and value of diversity
- Empowered to create change
- Worked with others to solve problems
- Developed meaningful ways to include everyone
- Fostered understanding and friendship

The CPS process resolved many barrier problems for inclusion students, and also fostered growth in numerous ways for their typically developing peers. It mobilized the creativity of peers while working on participative solutions; promoted positive social, cognitive, and communicative outcomes; and resulted in the use of advocacy, creative thinking, communication, and assessment skills in meaningful situations.

Informal peer problem solving has implications far broader than inclusive settings. Students gain a deeper understanding and confidence of their own problem-solving capabilities that are applied in various task and social situations (Kolb & Stuart, 2005). When nondisabled students in inclusive settings learn to ask about and solve questions regarding their peers with disabilities participating in school events, they become more sophisticated and comfortable dealing with diversity in a broader sense and beyond the walls of the school. They recognize their own role in solving other community concerns related to diversity, such as racism, homophobia, and English-language-only proponents (Sapon-Shevin, 2003).

UNIVERSAL DESIGN MATERIALS

One of the major difficulties of aligning IDEA requirements with NCLB legislation is the historical reliance of the general curriculum on print materials (i.e., textbooks, worksheets) for dissimination of content. Print materials often present significant barriers to the successful presentation of general curriculum content to learners with diverse educational needs. That is why many searchers for solutions to the problem have turned to a digital answer in the form of universally designed curriculum materials. These materials are designed to meet a wide range of student sensory, cognitive, linguistic, motor, and affective abilities and disabilities. Universal design for learning is not a curriculum; it is a digitalized flexible media presentation of curriculum content that can be devised through the use of computer software to meet a wide range of individual student needs in the same classroom setting (Hitchcock & Stahl, 2003). As a result, diverse learners using universal design media for content acquisition can work together more easily in the same environment. See Chapter 5 for more discussion of Universal Design for learning.

ATTITUDE CHANGE PROGRAMS

Should inclusion-class teachers devise and present special curriculum units on disabilities as a means of changing student attitudes? The research suggests a cautious affirmative response. Some program components that appear effective with inclusive classes include:

- Opportunities to interact with adults with disabilities
- Adequate information to dispel fears and promote understanding
- Sanctioned opportunities for staring (either at individuals or at media representations)
- Opportunities to discuss feelings and beliefs
- Simulations (e.g., blindfolds, one hand behind back, wheelchairs) and an opportunity to explore and experiment with assistive aids and devices, such as crutches and hearing aids

Technology-based strategies, including Internet Web sites, videos, and CDs can offer rich, varied, and informative opportunities for learning about disabilities. (See the Selected Web Sites section at the end of this chapter.)

Three Canadian researchers working with students with mobility limitations and their parents identified several factors influencing inclusion. These factors include intentional attitudinal (e.g., bullying, teasing) and unintentional attitudinal (e.g., lack of knowledge, understanding) barriers that existed in schools, in addition to expected physical barriers (e.g., inaccessible restrooms) and personal physical limitations (e.g., lack of strength, dexterity) (Pivik, McComas, & LaFlamme, 2002). The attitudinal barriers were perceived by the students with disabilities as the most hurtful in their school experiences. The researchers concluded that schools need to institute disability awareness, sensitivity, and social program opportunities for students without disabilities. Panels of students with mobility concerns, and their parents, should be invited to describe, from their personal experiences, mobility limitations to the staffs in individual schools.

At times, it may be appropriate to provide special training for the nondisabled peers of students with disabilities (Chadsey & Han, 2005). Kamps et al. (2002) conducted a 3-year study involving the improvement of social interactions between elementary students with autism and their nondisabled peers. Impaired social interaction and failure to develop peer relationships are common characteristics of children with autism. The researchers provided the nondisabled peers with special training in social skills and peer interactions. The result was greatly improved social interaction by the students with disabilities with both trained and untrained peers with whom they were familiar. In some situations, the level of interaction was on a level similar to that observed between and among nondisabled students.

Some educators suggest that school counselors are especially sensitive to the issues of peer acceptance and should make a conscious effort to provide information and understanding to the peers of students with disabilities. Methods, such as the use of disability simulations and role playing, were considered especially appropiate (Bruce, Shade, & Cossairt, 1996).

One study, noting that young, typically developing, kindergarten-age children have low levels of acceptance for children with disabilities, provided participants in the study with a 6-week structured intervention. This intervention consisted of stories and guided discussion about children with disabilities, structured play experiences with children with disabilities, and a home reading activity with their own parents. The study found that the children participating in the intervention were much more open to the integration, acceptance, and belonging of children with disabilities than children who did not participate (Favazza, Phillipsen, & Kumar, 2000).

Although family members play an important role in modeling acceptance of individual differences among people, in many families there is a reluctance to address disabilities with their nondisabled children. Whether the reluctance is based in lack of knowledge or personal experience with persons with disabilities, family members of young children can be encouraged by school staff to model acceptance of persons with disabilities and foster inclusive values in their children. School staff can provide families of students without disabilities general information about individual disabilities and accommodations provided to meet the needs of students with disabilities. Often, parents of students with disabilities will give written permission to school staff to share specific information related to their child's needs so that the child's peers will better understand and relate to their child (Salend, 2004).

Friendship Circles

The concept of Circle of Friends is a structured group project that has been established as having a positive effect on the social acceptance of a student with disabilities by classmates (Fredrickson & Turner, 2003). It emphasizes the importance of social interaction compared to mere physical presence of a student with disabilities in inclusion settings. The goal is for the group to identify ways to foster reciprocal and meaningful relationships with the student with disabilities.

Selected peers of a student with disabilities are first led in discussions about peoples' need for friendship and the various roles friends play. Students are then asked if they would like to befriend a student with disabilities. Those students interested are encouraged to think of ideas of what it means to be friends at school and in a variety of situations. The focus child is discussed, with parental consent, first on the child's strengths and then how friendships might impact the child's difficulties. The better alternatives are narrowed down and six to eight students volunteer to participate in regular planned friendly activities. The activities occur in school, and sometimes outside of school, with the student with a disability. Activities and regular meetings are managed so that all students feel that the experience is supportive and positive. A group assessment of the achievement of goals since the previous meeting, and joint planning of what should be done next takes place regularly (Frederickson & Turner, 2003).

In a study of the impact of friendship circles on three elementary students with mild disabilities, Miller, Cooke, Test, and White (2003) found that interactions between the students with disabilities and their peer networks increased during lunch, recess times, and in the classrooms. Classroom interactions were often of an academic supportive nature and resulted in improved academic progress. Students with disabilities who were the focus of the study and their peers in the network continued their level of social interaction even after the regular meetings and planned interaction activities ended. Moreover, the students with disabilities sought out and engaged in social activities with students outside the original planned network of peers.

Some students may drop out of the circle and others may choose to continue or even expand their relationships. Sometimes parents of the students get to know each other through the circle, and that leads naturally to joint family activities outside school.

Peer-Support Programs

Copeland et al. (2004) have reported on a study of nondisabled high school students who provided ongoing support for their peers with moderate or severe disabilities in general education. Support was provided on a paired basis in social and academic areas through a service-learning program entitled the Peer Buddy Program.

The Program was voluntary and participating students received course credit toward graduation. Participants received a manual and orientation to disabilities, communication strategies, suggestions for social interaction, and strategies for dealing with inappropriate behavior. Peer Buddies were paired and interacted with their peers on a daily basis and engaged in a variety of activities in a variety of settings, including community-based sites.

Participating students acknowledged the challenges inhibiting the integration and socialization of students with moderate and severe disabilities into the modern high school. They indicated widespread agreement, however, that the Peer Buddy Program effectively addressed many of the challenges and promoted access to general education for students with disabilities.

Friendship-Facilitation Strategies Several interesting studies of middle school students who had friendships with students with disabilities were conducted in an effort to synthesize their recommendations for friendship facilitation (Chadsey & Han, 2005). Most of the students with friendships with peers with disabilities had met their friends in classes at school. The majority stressed the desirability of inclusive classroom practices and stressed that segregation was unfair.

The peer suggestions for friendship-facilitation strategies reinforce much of the foregoing material on educator-assisted relationship building. They also provide an excellent window into the perspective and insights of peers without disabilities who have befriended students with disabilities.

- Students with disabilities should be placed in regular classrooms more often and be provided extra help when needed; don't put students with disabilities in separate classes.
- Teachers should talk to students without disabilities to discuss specific characteristics, differences (e.g., behavior), and learning needs of peers with disabilities; similarities between the two groups need to be emphasized.
- Don't let students make fun of students with disabilities.
- Create informal nonacademic programs where students with and without disabilities can spend time together and get to know each other.
- Use volunteer peer partners or buddy programs.
- Group students with disabilities into groups of other students, not only with just one buddy.
- Have students with disabilities explain their disabilities to students who are not disabled.
- Students with disabilities should be included in after-school activities and clubs.
- Students with disabilities should take the same school bus as peers without disabilities.

From "Friendship-Facilitation Strategies: What Do Students in Middle School Tell Us?" by J. Chadsey and K. G. Han, 2005, *Teaching Exceptional Children, 38*(2), p. 53. Copyright 2005 by the Council for Exceptional Children. Adapted with permission.

CONCLUSION

Whether a school uses peer tutoring, cooperative learning, collaborative problem solving, traditional teacher-directed learning, or a combination of these and other methodologies is not important. The important thing to remember is that all students can benefit socially and emotionally, as well as academically, from experiences in appropriately planned and supported inclusive settings. America's public schools were created for just such a purpose. Society provides schools, teachers, and staff so that a broad range of student and societal needs will be met through the education of children. That means meeting the needs of all children, not just a few. Although curriculum content learning is enhanced for all students through appropriate inclusive practices, America's schools were intended for much more. When students with disabilities learn in inclusive settings, so do their peers without disabilities.

Principals, and other educational leaders, must set the tone and establish the vision of a broadly conceived appropriate education for all children. We truly are all in this together.

VIEW FROM THE COURTS

T. W. v. Unified School District No. 259 (2005) (student's disruptive behavior in the regular classroom warranted placement in a self-contained class). The parents of a first-grade student with Down's syndrome challenged the placement of their son in a self-contained special education class. They argued that the boy had experienced some academic and behavioral progress in a regular kindergarten class, and other students learned tolerance for persons with disabilities from the experience.

The court agreed with the parents' argument, as far as it went. The court concluded, however, that the boy's need for a modified curriculum was so extreme that it could not be adequately met by the regular class teacher. His behavior in the regular class was so disruptive to the other students that it overcame any positive influence his presence in class had on the other students. The court ruled in favor of the school's placement of the student in special education.

Brillon v. Klein Independent School District (2004) (modification of general curriculum was unduly burdensome to regular class teacher and other students). Parents of a second-grade student challenged the school's proposal to teach the boy science and social studies in a special education class. The regular class teacher testified that the curriculum would have changed beyond recognition and that she would have to teach a classroom within a class in order to accommodate the boy's needs. The court ruled in favor of the school's proposed special education placement. Curriculum revisions needed to be made by the regular class teacher would be "unduly burdensome modifications" resulting in detriment to the other students in the regular classroom setting.

RECOMMENDED READINGS

Brewer, R. D., Reid, M. S., & Rhine, B. G. (2003). Peer coaching: Students teaching to learn. *Intervention in School and Clinic 39*, 113–126. This excellent article provides step-by-step directions and model forms to use in the establishment of a peer-tutoring program.

Fulk, B. M., & King, K. (2001). Classwide peer tutoring at work. *Teaching Exceptional Children, 34*(2), 49–53. This brief article provides recommendations on the implementation of a Peer-Assisted Learning Strategies (PALS) program.

Goodwin, M. W. (1999). Cooperative learning and social skills: What skills to teach and how to teach them. *Intervention in School and Clinic, 35*, 29–33. This article highlights the teaching of social skills desirable for cooperative learning, describes several cooperative learning strategies, and provides advice for beginning cooperative learning.

Keller, C. L. (2002). A new twist on spelling instruction for elementary school teachers. *Intervention*

in School and Clinic, 38, 3–7. This brief article provides detailed instruction on the implementation of a combined Class-Wide Peer Tutoring and Spelling Strategies Program.

Prater, M. A. (2000). Using juvenile literature with portrayals of disabilities in your classroom. *Intervention in School and Clinic, 35*, 167–176. This article lists and describes 46 books that portray characters with disabilities and provides suggestions for classroom use.

Relevant Federal Regulations

34 C.F.R. Part 300 Assistance to States for the Education of Children with Disabilities [70 Fed. Reg. 35,833-35,880 (June 21, 2005)].

34 C.F.R. § 300.114	LRE requirements.
.115	Continuum of alternative placements.
.116	Placements.
.117	Nonacademic settings.
.119	Technical assistance and training activities.
.120	Monitoring activities.
.320	Definition of individualized education program.
.321	IEP team.
.324	Development, review, and revision of IEP.

SELECTED WEBSITES

Code of Federal Regulations–Government Printing Office
http://www.gpoaccess.gov/cfr/index.html

The National Dissemination Center for Children with Disabilities
http://www.irsc.org

Council for Exceptional Children
http://www.cec.sped.org

The Office of Special Education and Rehabilitation Services
http://www.ed.gov/about/offices/list/osers/index.html

Center for Applied Special Technology (CAST)
  http://www.cast.org/teachingeverystudent

Peer-Assisted Learning Strategies (PALS)—Vanderbilt University
  http://www.kc.vanderbilt.edu/kennedy/pals

Peer-Assisted Learning Strategies in Reading
  http://www.ldonline.org/ld_indepth/reading/peer_assisted.html

Disability Awareness Web Sites

CeDIR's Disability Awareness Site for Youth
  http://www.iidc.indiana.edu/cedir/kidsweb

Disability Awareness Kit
  http://www.openroad.net.au/access/dakit/welcome.htm

Special Needs—Special Kids (Disability Awareness)
  http://www.members.tripod.com/~imaware

Disability-Related Virtual Museums

Disability Rights Movement Virtual Museum (Smithsonian)
  http://www.americanhistory.si.edu/disabilityrights/welcome.html

Disability History Museum
  http://www.disabilitymuseum.org

United States Holocaust Museum (Nazi treatment of individuals with disabilities)
  http://www.holocaust-trc.org/hndcp.htm

Disability Simulation Web Sites

Misunderstood Minds
  http://www.pbs.org/wgbh/misunderstoodminds

Pediatric Neurology.Com
  http://www.pediatricneurology.com/adhd2.htm

National Coalition of Auditory Processing Disorders
  http://www.ncapd.org

Mrs. Karen Lake's Home Page
  http://www.nacs.k12.in.us/staff/lake/lake.html

QUESTIONS FOR THOUGHT

1. Who has more difficulty accepting students with disabilities into the regular classroom, peers (other students) or adults (teachers, principals)? Why?

2. What is the greatest challenge for successful inclusion in a regular class from the perspective of peer acceptance, mental disability, reading disability, emotional disability, or behavior disability?

3. Why don't more teachers use peer tutoring, cooperative learning, and collaborative problem-solving methodologies in their classrooms?

4. How are school activities related to "No Child Left Behind" affected by peer tutoring and cooperative learning strategies?

REFERENCES

Antil, L. R., Jenkins, J. R., Wayne, S. K., & Vadasy, P. F. (1998). Cooperative learning: Prevalence, conceptualizations, and the relation between research and practice. *American Educational Research Journal, 35,* 419–454.

Brewer, R. D., Reid, M. S., & Rhine, B. G. (2003). Peer coaching: Students teaching to learn. *Intervention in School and Clinic, 39,* 113–126.

Brillon v. Klein Independent School District, 41 IDELR 121, 100 Fed. Appx. 309 (5th Cir. 2004) (per carium).

Bruce, M. A., Shade, R. A., & Cossairt, A. (1996). Classroom-tested guidance activities for promoting inclusion. *The School Counselor, 43,* 224–230.

Burks, M. (2004). Effects of classwide peer tutoring on the number of words spelled correctly by students with LD. *Intervention in School and Clinic, 39,* 301–304.

Calhoon, M. B., & Fuchs, L. S. (2003). The effects of peer-assisted learning strategies and curriculum-based measurement on the mathematics performance of secondary students with disabilities. *Remedial and Special Education, 24,* 235–245.

Chadsey, J., & Han, K. G. (2005). Friendship-facilitation strategies: What do students in middle school tell us? *Teaching Exceptional Children, 38*(2), 52–57.

Cole, C. M., Waldron, N., & Majd, M. (2004). Academic progress of students across inclusive and traditional settings. *Mental Retardation, 42,* 136–144.

Copeland, S. R., Hughes, C., Carter, E. W., Guth, C., Presley, J. A., Williams, C. R., & Fowler, S. E.

(2004). Increasing access to general education: Perspectives of participants in a high school peer support program. *Remedial and Special Education, 25*, 342–352.

Farmer, T. W., & Farmer, E. M. (1996). Social relationships of students with exceptionalities in mainstream classrooms: Social networks and homophily. *Exceptional Children, 62,* 431–450.

Favazza, P. C., Phillipsen, L., & Kumar, P. (2000). Measuring and promoting acceptance of young children with disabilities. *Exceptional Children, 66,* 491–508.

Fisher, M., & Meyer, L. H., (2002). Development and social competence after two years for students enrolled in inclusive and self-contained educational programs. *Research and Practice for Persons with Severe Disabilities, 27,* 165–174.

Frederickson, N., & Turner, J. (2003). Utilizing the classroom peer group to address children's social needs: An evaluation of the Circle of Friends intervention approach. *The Journal of Special Education, 36,* 234–245.

Fuchs, D., & Fuchs, L. S. (2005). Peer-assisted learning strategies: Promoting word recognition, fluency, and reading comprehension in young children. *The Journal of Special Education, 39,* 34–44.

Fuchs, D., Fuchs, L. S., Mathes, P. G., & Simmons, D. C. (1997). Peer-assisted learning strategies: Making classrooms more responsive to diversity. *American Educational Research Journal, 34,* 174–206.

Fuchs, L. S. (2004). The past, present, and future of curriculum-based measurement research. *School Psychology Review, 33,* 188–192.

Fulk, B. M., & King, K. (2001). Classwide peer tutoring at work. *Teaching Exceptional Children, 34*(2), 49–53.

Gillies, R. M., & Ashman, A. F. (2000). The effects of cooperative learning on students with learning difficulties in the lower elementary school. *The Journal of Special Education, 34,* 19–27.

Goodwin, M. W. (1999). Cooperative learning and social skills: What skills to teach and how to teach them. *Intervention in School and Clinic, 35,* 29–33.

Goor, D., & Schwenn, J. O. (1993). Accommodating diversity and disability with cooperative learning. *Intervention in School and Clinic, 29,* 6–16.

Goor, M., Schwenn, J., Eldridge, A., Mallein, D., & Stauffer, J. (1996). Using strategy cards to enhance cooperative learning for students with learning disabilities. *Teaching Exceptional Children, 29*(1) 66–68.

Hansen, L. L., & Boody, R. M. (1998). Special education students' perceptions of their mainstreamed classes. *Education, 118,* 610–615.

Hendrickson, J. M., Shokoohi-Yekta, M., Hamre-Nietupski, S., & Gable, R. A. (1996). Middle and high school students' perceptions on being friends with peers with severe disabilities. *Exceptional Children, 63,* 19–28.

Hitchcock, C., & Stahl, S. (2003). Assistive technology, universal design, universal design for learning: Improved learning opportunities. *Journal of Special Education Technology, 18*(4), 45–52.

Jenkins, J. R., Antil, L. R., Wayne, S. K., & Vadasy, P. F. (2003). How cooperative learning works for special education and remedial students. *Exceptional Children, 69,* 279–292.

Johnson, D. W., & Johnson, R. T. (1986). Mainstreaming and cooperative learning strategies. *Exceptional Children, 52,* 553–561.

Johnson, D. W., & Johnson, R. T. (1992). Implementing cooperative learning. *Contemporary Education, 63,* 173–180.

Johnson, J., & Duffett, A. (2002). *When it's your own child.* New York: Public Agenda.

Kamps, D., Royer, J., Dugan, E., Kravits, T., Gonzalez-Lopez, A., Garcia, J., Carnazzo, K., Morrison, L., & Kane, L. G. (2002). Peer training to facilitate social interaction for elementary students with autism and their peers. *Exceptional Children, 68,* 173–187.

Keller, C. L. (2002). A new twist on spelling instruction for elementary school teachers. *Intervention in School and Clinic, 38,* 3–7.

Kennedy, C. H., Shukla, S., & Fryxell, D. (1997). Comparing the effects of educational placement on the social relationships of intermediate school students with severe disabilities. *Exceptional Children, 64,* 31–47.

Klingner, J. K., & Vaughn, S. (1999). Students' perceptions of instruction in inclusion classrooms: Implications for students with learning disabilities. *Exceptional Children, 66,* 23–37.

Kolb, S. M., & Stuart, S. K. (2005). Active problem solving: A model for empowerment. *Teaching Exceptional Children, 38*(2), 14–20.

Longwill, A. W., & Kleinert, H. L. (1998). The unexpected benefits of high school peer tutoring. *Teaching Exceptional Children, 30*(4), 60–65.

Mathes, P. G., Fuchs, D., & Fuchs, L. S. (1995). Accommodating diversity through Peabody classwide peer tutoring. *Intervention in School and Clinic, 31,* 46–50.

Miller, M. C., Cooke, N. L., Test, D. W., & White, R. (2003). Effects of friendship circles on the social interactions of elementary age students with mild disabilities. *Journal of Behavioral Education, 12,* 167–184.

Office of Special Education Memorandum Programs 95–9, 21 IDELR 1152 (1994) (research cited).

Palmer, D. S., Fuller, K., Arora, T., & Nelson, M. (2001). Taking sides: Parent views on inclusions for their children with severe disabilities. *Exceptional Children, 67,* 467–484.

Panacek, L. J., Dunlap, G. (2003). The social lives of children with emotional and behavorial disorders in self-contained classrooms: A descriptive analysis. *Exceptional Children, 69,* 333–348.

Pivik, J., McComas, J., & LaFlamme, M. (2002). Barriers and facilitators to inclusive education. *Exceptional Children, 69,* 97–107.

Pomplun, M. (1997). When students with disabilities participate in cooperative groups. *Exceptional Children, 64,* 49–58.

Rea, P. J., McLaughlin, V. L., & Walther-Thomas, C. (2002). Outcomes for students with learning disabilities in inclusive and pullout programs. *Exceptional Children, 68,* 203–222.

Reddy, S. S., Utley, C. A., Delquadri, J. C., Mortweet, S. L., Greenwood, C. R., & Bowman, V. (1999). Peer tutoring for health and safety. *Teaching Exceptional Children, 31*(3), 44–52.

Ryan, J. B., Reid, R., & Epstein, M. H. (2004). Peer-mediated intervention studies on academic achievement for students with EBD. *Remedial and Special Education, 25,* 330–341.

Saenz, L. M., Fuchs, L. S., & Fuchs, D. (2005) Peer-assisted learning strategies for English language learners with learning disabilities. *Exceptional Children, 74,* 231–247.

Salend, S. J. (2004). Fostering inclusive values in children: What families can do. *Teaching Exceptional Children, 37*(1), 64–69.

Salisbury, C. L., Evans, I. M., & Palombaro, M. M. (1997). Collaborative problem-solving to promote the inclusion of young children with significant disabilities in primary grades. *Exceptional Children, 63,* 195–209.

Sapon-Shevin, M. (2003). Inclusion: A matter of social justice. *Educational Leadership, 61*(2), 25–28.

Sharpe, M. N., York, J. L., & Knight, J. (1994). Effects of inclusion on the academic performance of classmates without disabilities. *Remedial and Special Education, 15,* 281–287.

Slavin, R. E. (1991). Synthesis of research on cooperative learning. *Educational Leadership,* 48(5), 71–81.

Stevens, R. J., & Slavin, R. E. (1995). The cooperative elementary school: Effects on students' achievement, attitudes, and social relations. *American Educational Research Journal, 32,* 321–351.

T. W. v. Unified School District No. 259, 43 IDELR 187 (10th Cir. 2005).

Villa, R. A., Vander Klift, E., Udis, J., Thousand, J. S., Nevin, A. I., Kunc, N., & Chapple, J. W. (1995). Questions, concerns, beliefs, and practical advice about inclusive education. In R. A. Villa, & J. S. Thousand (Eds.), *Creating an inclusive school* (pp. 136–161). Alexandria, VA: Association for Supervision and Curriculum Development.

Welch, A. B. (2000). Responding to student concerns about fairness. *Teaching Exceptional Children, 33*(2), 36–40.

Wenz-Gross, M., & Siperstein, G. N. (1997). Importance of social support in the adjustment of children with learning problems. *Exceptional Children, 63,* 183–193.

Zigmond, N. (2003). Where should students with disabilities receive special education services? Is one place better than another? *The Journal of Special Education, 37,* 193–199.

CHAPTER 7

INFANT AND TODDLER AND PRESCHOOL PROGRAMS

CHAPTER PREVIEW

Focus

Because federal legislation and some states mandate educational programs for children with disabilities younger than age five, educational leaders without training or experience in prekindergarten education programs may become involved in preschool administration or programming. Some components of infant and toddler programs (birth through age 2) and preschool programs (age 3 through 5) may also be housed in elementary school buildings, thereby adding to administrator responsibilities.

Legal History

Two key Congressional actions are related to the education of young children with disabilities from birth through age five. They include:

- Education for All Handicapped Children Act (EAHCA, 1975) (later IDEA), at first gave states the option of providing education for children with disabilities ages three through five, but was amended in 1986 to make services to preschool children a requirement.
- Part C, added to IDEA in 1986, provided for voluntary state programs for infants and toddlers with disabilities under age three years.

Part B

The IDEA Part B program and services requirements, including Child Find, parental safeguards, the evaluation of students for eligibility, IEP development and appropriate educational placement apply to all children with disabilities who need special education from age 3 to graduation from high school (or age 21 when appropriate).

Part C

Part C is a voluntary state program for infants and toddlers (under age 3) with disabilities that uses a comprehensive multi-service agency approach for resolving the needs of all members of the family, not just the child with disabilities. Each child served must have an individualized family service plan (IFSP) to meet both family and child needs, and each plan must have a person designated as coordinator of services. States may also independently choose to serve "at-risk" children in the under 3-year-old age group. Between the ages of 3 and 5, a smooth plan for transition of the child to education services under Part B and an IEP are to be completed. Schools, with parent consent, may continue an IFSP until the child enters or is eligible for kindergarten.

Rationale

Research suggests that early intervention improves the potential for educational growth for all children. It increases the likelihood of children with disabilities remaining in school, keeping up with nondisabled peers, and maximizing their educational potential.

Approaches

Infant and toddler and early childhood education options for children with disabilities are comprised of a great variety of programs. Included are interventions provided in the child's home, classes at schools or other centers, parent training, infant stimulation programs, and traditional preschool programs. Some programs have highly structured curricula focusing on the development of pre-academic skills, and others have structured, but child-directed, curricula for homogeneous groups (e.g., hearing-impaired). Preschool programs, for children ages 3 through 5, are more likely than early childhood programs to be provided in a center-based or school setting.

Many approaches have proven beneficial for young children with disabilities in both early childhood and preschool programs when the programs emphasize:

- collaborative staff teaming processes;
- strong parent participation;
- well-designed and adaptive learning environments;
- social growth;
- positive disciplinary techniques; and
- age appropriate and individualized learning activities.

EMERGING EARLY CHILDHOOD AND PRESCHOOL PROGRAMS

Few children are identified as having disabilities at birth. Mild disabilities and specific learning disabilities often are not identified or confirmed until the school years. Even rather severe cognitive or sensory impairments may not be correctly identified until the child is 2 years of age or older. Yet many states attempt to begin educational programming for identified children with disabilities from the first days of life. Who, exactly, are the children served by these programs, and what do educators hope to accomplish?

The answers to these questions can be summarized under the headings of prevention and compensation. The latter, compensatory programming, is the older approach and the easiest to comprehend. A child who is disabled cannot always be expected to make normal developmental progress with the same type of informal parental guidance that is adequate for most preschoolers. Such children can greatly benefit from special training in speech, mobility, and other skills. Parenting skills development, assisted by educator consultation, is one way to provide that help. In addition, many young children with disabilities will need time, training, and special equipment to help them compensate for their disabilities. The advantages of beginning such training as early as possible include maximizing the children's potential to keep up with peers in later schooling and allowing them and their families more positive family experiences in the early years. Research, including longitudinal studies, has demonstrated the general effectiveness of developmentally appropriate early education programs for at-risk children, those with special needs, and those with normal development (Hibbert & Sprinthall, 1995).

The notion of prevention in the context of early childhood education is a relatively new one. It evolved from a complex set of developments during the 1950s and 1960s, including research on the effects of early stimulation; the child development theories of Piaget, Erikson, and others; and mounting statistical evidence from actual program evaluations. Emerging themes, such as the critical importance of early childhood development and the effect of the child's environment on intelligence, were picked up and promoted by contemporary social movements. The result was a widespread belief that gaps in educational achievement among different socioeconomic groups could be mitigated or prevented through early educational intervention (Scarborough et al., 2004).

The Head Start Program for preschool-age children, begun in 1965, was one response. Head Start was amended in 1972 to set aside 10% of enrollment opportunities for children with disabilities, to establish a number of programs with the goal of limiting the effects of disabilities at an early age, and to provide extra monies for preschool demonstration projects.

In the following decades, as new attitudes toward education of the disabled developed, it was natural that the principle of preventive early intervention should be extended to the young disabled population. Early childhood education was advocated as a means of preventing or limiting the effects of disabilities on children's school experience. This is what some authors have referred to as the "downward escalation of educational services" (Ysseldyke, Algozzine, & Thurlow, 2000). Initially, preschool services under the IDEA were extended for the 3- through 5-year-olds, and then expanded downward to the early childhood years for infants and toddlers, ages birth through 2 years. Even pre-birth services to the mother and child are provided in some areas of the country as preventative measures against future potential problems of an at-risk nature. Colorado, for instance, has provided extensive medical and counseling services for expectant mothers who receive public assistance for a number of years, and Vermont attempts to identify the needs of individual children immediately after birth.

In 1996 the federal government began the Early Head Start (EHS) program as an extensive response to meeting the needs of very young children living in poverty. Over 700 EHS programs currently serve about 62,000 children (Peterson et al. 2004). Designed as a service provider to families, beginning as early as a woman's pregnancy and continuing until her child reaches the age of three years, EHS is designed to enhance early intervention supports available to families through home-based and center-based options. Like Head Start, EHS programs must make 10% of their enrollments available to children with disabilities. It is expressly designed to collaborate and cooordinate with IDEA Early Intervention Programs (Part C) serving infants and toddlers with disabilities and their families.

There is a national trend to provide greater educational opportunities at an earlier age to more children. A study by the National Institute of Child Health and Human Development (NICHD, 2002) determined, in the early years of a longitudinal study of over 1,000 young children, that the quality of early child care provided to children was associated positively with the academic and language performance skills before the child started formal schooling. High quality child care was also positively associated with better language, cognitive, and pre-academic skills in children entering kindergarten.

This view is consistent with a study of national data conducted by Magnuson, Meyers, Ruhm, and Waldfogel (2004). They concluded that children attending center-based preschool programs for the year prior to kindergarten generally have better reading and math skills in kindergarten and first grade, and are less likely to repeat kindergarten than their peers who did not attend a preschool program. The researchers determined that the greatest positive academic effect for children attending preschool programs was among children from economically disadvantaged families. Although race and ethnicity have been discarded by researchers as independent at-risk factors for children, when combined with factors such as poverty and single-parent families, they continue to represent a significant source of the acknowledged increase in rates of childhood disability (Fujiura & Yamaki, 2000).

Children at Risk

Children living in poverty is a growing phenomenon in the United States with significant implications for schools and society. Qi and Kaiser (2003) reviewed 30 studies conducted between 1991 and 2002 and concluded that children from low socioeconomic backgrounds had a higher likelihood of problem behavior in later years when compared to children in the general population. They strongly recommended that interventions and supports be provided to preschool children living in poverty and identified as being at increased risk for behavior problems later in life. Other at-risk groups have also been identified, including children born prematurely, those of low birth weight or stressful births, those born with the HIV infection that causes AIDS, and those born to mothers exposed to toxic drugs or infections during pregnancy. Unfortunately, little is being done to deal with these new social issues, and the task to ameliorate their effect will likely fall on the public schools (Ysseldyke, Algozzine, & Thurlow, 2000).

In many cases, "at risk" is a more useful and accurate term than "disabled" when referring to very young children. Some early childhood educators prefer it exclusively, fearing that the early application of labels (e.g., mentally retarded) may result in stereotypes that negatively affect adults' attitudes and expectations of a child and result in lifelong damage. In partial recognition of concerns of labeling children at an early age, and the recognition of the difficulty of assessment in the early years, the federal government now allows the use of the phrase "developmental delay" to identify children ages 3 through 9 who are appropriately diagnosed with special educational needs [34 C.F.R. § 300.111 (b)].

Because early educational opportunities have an important effect on the future needs of children at risk of developing educational problems, their need for early identification and provision of services is obvious. Yet, America's record in identifying and serving those in society who are least able to fend for themselves is not stellar.

It is estimated that during the 1991–92 school year approximately 593,000 American children under six years of age were served in IDEA programs. One researcher has estimated, however, that the number of children eligible for programs was actually 851,000 (Bowe, 1995). That means that public schools were reaching only about 70% of the eligible preschool population. Bowe's research further determined that most of the unserved or underserved children were from low socioeconomic or minority families, societal groups that could least afford to be left out of educational opportunities.

By the 2004–05 school year, 279,154 children were participating in Part C (2.3% of that age group population) and 693,245 were participating in Part B preschool programs (ages 3 through 5, 5.87% of that age group population). The infant and toddler and early childhood programs combined were serving 972,400 children in the United States (IDEA data, Tables 1–2, 1–11, 6–1, 2005).

Homeless Children

Research focusing on the level of need for special education services for homeless children living in emergency homeless shelters has identified a dual problem. Those children are at risk for learning problems, and they do not have regular and consistent access to special education programs. In one study, nearly one half (46%) of the homeless children involved screened positive for at least one disability requiring special education programs and services (Zima, Farness, Bussing, & Benjamin, 1998).

Families with children, mostly single-parent families, are the fastest growing group of homeless persons in America. Attendance at school is especially important for the children of such families. The effects of homelessness present significant health and nutrition issues as well as developmental, psychological, social growth, and academic progress issues. Students with disabilities who are homeless present significant and unique challenges to schools in the form of identification and continuity of special education services (Jackson, 2004).

School policies and practices should not contribute to the problem. School staffs must make conscious efforts to not make life more difficult for homeless children. They can help homeless children by establishing a stable, safe, and nonthreatening educational environment and by establishing as typical a school experience as possible. Schools may, after all, provide the only opportunity for stability in a life otherwise filled with uncertainty (Yamaguchi, Strawser, & Higgins, 1997).

In 1987, Congress enacted the McKinney Homeless Assistance Act. It was subsequently amended several times and in 2001 was amended to become the McKinney-Vento Homeless Assistance Act as part of the No Child Left Behind (NCLB) legislation. It was enacted in an effort to remove numerous barriers to obtaining an education and to provide access to the general school curriculum for homeless children that would allow them to be successful on state standardized achievement exams. The law was further amended to take into account barriers to special education programs and services encountered by homeless children and was incorporated into the 2004 Amendments to the IDEA. The law now requires public schools be a help, rather than a hindrance, in the life of homeless children, including those with disabilities. Child find requirements of the IDEA expressly require the identification and evaluation of highly mobile children with disabilities, including migrant and homeless children. Figure 7-1 summarizes the provisions of the McKinney-Vento Act that impact public schools.

Is Early Intervention Education Effective?

Although still a relatively new and rapidly changing field, especially with the birth-to-age-three population, early childhood and preschool education have been around long enough to generate follow-up data. A determination of effectiveness depends on the expectations and on the definition of success.

Early education does not seem to be preventive in the sense, say, that the Salk vaccine prevents polio. One or two years of special education services—no matter how early—cannot be expected to counteract all the effects of most risk factors or disabilities. On the other hand,

FIGURE 7-1 *Provisions of the McKinney-Vento Homeless Assistance Act—local school requirements*

The local education agency shall, according to the child's best interest:

- continue the child in the school of origin (in which last enrolled) for the duration of homelessness to the extent feasible, except when opposed by the parent; or enroll the child in the school where the child is actually living;
- enroll the child immediately even when documents such as school records, medical and immunization records, and proof of residency are not immediately available;
- provide transportation services to and from the school of origin;
- provide educational services for which the child qualifies, such as Title I, special education, section 504, limited English proficiency, talented and gifted, and school nutrition programs;
- coordinate services with other agencies poviding services to homeless children.

Additionally, local schools must:

- regularly review and revise school policies that act as barriers to the enrollment and retention of homeless children in school;
- designate a local staff person as liaison for homeless children to identify homeless children, ensure equal educational opportunity for homeless children, make referral to other appropriate services, such as health and dental services;
- assure parents meaningful opportunities to participate in the education of their children;
- ensure that homeless children will attend schools and programs available to all resident children and will not be segregated;
- ensure that homeless children are given the opportunity to meet all challenging state standards that all students are expected to meet. Source: 42 U.S.C. § 11432 (g).

at-risk children who have experienced early intervention do fare better in measures of educational achievement later in life than those at-risk children who have not experienced early intervention (Hibbert & Sprinthall, 1995).

The first five years of life are of extreme importance in the growth of a variety of life's important competencies, such as linguistic, social, and cognitive. There is a positive connection between good educational experiences in the years before school and later learning outcomes (U.S. Department of Education, 2000).

Gains can be sustained when students with disabilities continue to receive special education services during their school years. A number of studies have identified early childhood and preschool education for at-risk students as a cost-effective strategy for future savings in

education, welfare, and crime prevention (Turnbull & Turnbull, 1998).

One well-known longitudinal study of 123 three- and four-year olds has been reported in the media by Kirp (2004). Beginning in the early 1960s, 58 of the 123 children were randomly selected to attend a preschool program that emphasized cognitive development. Other than that early educational experience, the two groups were virtually identical. They were all youngsters raised in poverty in a low socioeconomic neighborhood in Michigan. The neighborhood had run-down public housing and a high crime rate. All the youngsters attended the Perry Elementary School.

Children in the program attended 3 hours a day, 5 days a week for 2 years. The curriculum emphasized development of problem-solving skills and viewed young children as active learners. Teachers were well trained and there was a low teacher to student ratio (1 to 5). Teachers made weekly home visits to encourage and help parents to teach their own children at home. For the study, data was collected every year from ages 3 through 11, 14, 15, 19, 27, and most recently, age 40. An amazing 97% of the original group who lived to age 40 remained part of the study.

Early study results indicated little difference in student achievement scores and measured scores of intelligence between the two groups. However, telling differences between the two groups became clearer during continuation of the study. The preschool participant group members were less likely to be identified later as mentally disabled and provided special education services, their attitude toward school was better, their average high school grade point was higher, and a substantially higher percentage graduated from high school (66% to 45%). Nearly twice as many earned college degrees, and more were employed and owned their own homes. They were less likely to have been on welfare and earned more money annually. Fewer of the preschool group had been arrested for violent drug-related crimes or crimes against property. About half as many had been sentenced to prison or jail. Economists attaching a monetary value to the preschool experience calculated the return to society on its initial investment to be 17 dollars for every dollar spent on the early childhood program.

Not everyone in either group experienced the fate of the average person in the group. Some of the people who did not attend preschool did well, and some that did attend did not fare well. What the study suggests is that a timely intervention of a quality preschool exerience has the potential of positive impact that lasts for a lifetime (Kirp, 2004).

Legal History

In 1964, the Economic Opportunity Act provided funding for preschool education programs designed to compensate for the negative effects of poverty. By the following year, 550,000 children were enrolled in preschool programs as part of Head Start. Early research studies indicated that most anticipated academic gains for those children disappeared by the end of second grade. More recent controlled studies, however, have identified lasting gains for Head Start students (Udell, Peters, & Templeman, 1998; Ysseldyke, Algozzine, & Thurlow, 2000).

Several efforts through the late 1960s provided funding for model programs, including children with disabilities in preschool programs, and for early child find efforts. In 1975, the forerunner of the IDEA (P. L. 94-142) included funding for preschool programs serving children ages 3 through 5. In 1986, the special education statutes were amended to make preschool (ages 3 through 5) a requirement of Part B. Part H was designed to provide early intervention services for infants and toddlers with disabilities from birth through age 2. Part H, changed to Part C in 1997, was a voluntary program whereby states could receive federal funds when they agreed to provide services to children with disabilities under age 3 and their families. All states and territories currently participate. Part C was initially written to provide a 5-year phase-in period for states. This extended lead-in time was primarily to allow for possible difficulties in incorporating a number of new approaches to dealing with children with disabilities and their families. This was especially true for its requirement of inter-agency cooperation at the state and local levels. For most states, the 5-year preparation period had to be extended an additional 3 years, and many states continue to find full compliance difficult.

Congress has agreed with research and experience that establish that the educational needs of many children can be more effectively met at an early stage through provision of scientifically based educational methodologies than only providing special education programs and services later in life. In the 2004 Amendments to the IDEA, Congressional findings expressly included the need for "early intervening services to reduce the need to label children as disabled" [20 U.S.C. § 1401 (c) (5) (F)]. Under a new provision in the IDEA, schools may use up to 15% of the federal funds received under the IDEA to develop and coordinate "early intervening services in grades kindergarten through grade 12 with special emphasis on kindergarten through grade 3" [20 U.S.C. § 1413 (f) (1)].

LEGAL ASPECTS OF FEDERAL PROGRAMS

Part C of the IDEA

Federal grants are available under Part C of the IDEA to states which adopt a policy of early intervention services to all infants and toddlers with disabilities and their families, including homeless children and wards of the state [20 U.S.C. § 1435 (a) (7)].

Child find provisions of federal law (discussed in Chapter 3) require that states must have procedures in place to ensure that all children with disabilities (birth through age 21) residing in the state and who need special education services are identified and evaluated, whether or not the state participates in Part C. All participating states must have an IEP, or comparable individualized family service plan (IFSP), in place for each identified child by the child's third birthday. At parent request, the IFSP may be continued until the child is eligible for kindergarten.

Under Part C, parents, educators, and appropriate staff members from health, job services, human services, mental health, and other service agencies are expected to work in a coordinated interdisciplinary effort. Together, they are to meet the unique needs of the family of an infant or toddler with disabilities and to identify funding for necessary services. The focal point of these services is the IFSP, which serves a function similar to an IEP. The IFSP represents an important paradigm shift in the evaluation of needs and delivery of services not only to the child, but also to the entire family. The extent of family resources, priorities, and goals are important parts of the IFSP concept.

The IFSP must be developed within a reasonable time after the child and family's needs

have been determined. The contents of the IFSP must be fully explained to the parents and generally may not be implemented without the informed written consent of the parents. When the parents do not provide written consent with regard to a particular intervention service, only the services to which consent has been given may be provided. Some early intervention services may begin prior to actual completion of evaluations, with parent consent. The IFSP must be evaluated at least once a year, and the family must be provided a review of the plan's status at least every six months. Someone must be designated as IFSP case manager in the organization of service delivery and follow-up and in maintaining important communication networks. Parents have the right to access mediation and due process hearings as dispute resolution options when the parents and Part C program providers cannot agree on services (20 U.S.C. § 1435).

An interesting aspect of the Part C process is that it is based, in part, on the current school reform philosophy: Schools must work cooperatively with other agencies that serve children in order to bring about a stronger and unified effort to the issues of the at-risk child (Turnbull & Turnbull, 1998).

States participating in the Part C Program may voluntarily agree to serve children who are at-risk in areas other than disabilities. This is largely due to the difficulty of diagnosing disabilities in young children, and in the recognition of the role environmental and socioeconomic factors play in identifying children with special education needs. An at-risk infant or toddler is defined as a child under 3 years of age who is at risk for experiencing a "substantial developmental delay" if intervention services are not provided [20 U.S.C. § 1432 (1)].

The five goals for Part C, as expressly identified by Congress, are preventative in nature and are broader and more comprehensive than those of Part B:

1. To enhance the development of infants and toddlers and minimize their potential for developmental delays, and to recognize the significant brain development that occurs during a child's first 3 years of life

2. To reduce the costs to our society, including that of special education to schools
3. To maximize the child's potential for independent living
4. To enhance the capabilities of families in meeting the needs of their children
5. To enhance the capacity of state and local agencies and service providers to identify, evaluate, and meet the needs of historically underrepresented populations [20 U.S.C. § 1431 (a)]

Inherent in the early childhood inclusion movement is the belief that children with disabilities in such settings will make positive gains in their social and communication skills. This has been verified through research findings (Lillie & Vakil, 2002). By law, children with disabilities are to be provided early childhood services in natural environments to the maximum extent appropriate, including settings in which children without disabilities participate [20 U.S.C. § 1435 (a) (16)]. The most common approach is through the use of community-based early childhood programs and child-care centers. Many private child-care centers make a concerted effort to enroll children with various disabilities, sometimes numbering up to 50% of their clients.

The first comprehensive national review of children enrolled in Part C early intervention systems established that participants exhibited greatly diverse and varied characteristics. The study found that 38% of all children in Part C programs are identified as being eligible during the first year of life. Disproportionally high members of the infants and toddlers are male (60%), African American (21% vs 14% in the general population), living in poverty (32% vs 24%), receiving foster care (7% vs 1%), and were born with low birth weights (32% vs 8% of the general population) (Scarborough et al., 2004).

Vital Concepts Many educators believe that the specific preschool curriculum used for programming is not as important for a successful educational experience as other program characteristics. The U.S. Department of Education (2000) has identified seven Vital Concepts to guide planning for effective early childhood programs:

1. *Intensity of Participation Matters.* The amount and length of time a child participates in individualized high-quality experiences each day with experienced adults and in small group settings is important.
2. *Teacher Expertise is a Crucial Ingredient.* Daily interactions between children and adults experienced in listening, observing, and asking good questions is key.
3. *Family Links are Essential.* The years of early childhood education set the pattern for the family's future contact with school systems. Educators must reach out to parents and help them understand their responsibility in supporting their children's educational growth.
4. *Children's Pace of Development is not Uniform.* The needs of individual children must guide the learning situation.
5. *Early Childhood Education Can Benefit all Children.* All children, including those with disabilities, benefit from high-quality preschool experiences. It is especially important that children from lower socioeconomic backgrounds have access to early childhood education.
6. *Continuity Sustains Positive Effects.* Staff turnover should be kept to a minimum and transitions must be carefully planned.
7. *Quality Requires Resources.* Early childhood programs that economize do so to the potential detriment of their student's promise of future school success.

IFSP Contents The IFSP must be in writing and contain (a) a statement of the child's present levels of physical, cognitive, communication, social or emotional, and adaptive development based on objective criteria; (b) a statement of the family's resources, priorities, and concerns with regard to the child; (c) a statement of measurable results or outcomes expected to be achieved for the child and family, including preliteracy and language skills, and the criteria to be used to determine the degree of progress toward the outcomes; (d) a statement of early intervention services based on peer-reviewed research, to the extent practicable; (e) a statement of the natural environments (settings in which children without disabilities participate) in which services will be provided, including justification for any service not provided in a natural environment (Letter to Morris, 2005); (f) the projected dates, frequency, and duration of services; (g) the identification of the service coordinator who will be responsible for the implementation and coordination of the plan, including transition services; and (h) the necessary steps to support the transition to preschool or other services [20 U.S.C. § 1436 (d)]. For a sample IFSP form, see Appendix G. Under the 2004 Amendments to the IDEA, the U.S. Secretary of Education is to develop and disseminate a model IFSP form.

The IFSP process is accompanied by procedural safeguards. A process must exist for the timely resolution of parent complaints and when necessary, an appeal into court; confidentiality of information, including the written notice of and written consent to agency exchange of information and limited outsider access to information; parents right to reject any proposed services; appointment of a surrogate parent whenever the parents are not known, cannot be located, or the child is a ward of the state; written notice of proposed service changes (or refusals to change); and parent access to records used in the development of the IFSP.

When an IFSP is developed in accordance with the provisions and terms of IEP development (i.e., appropriate team and content), the IFSP may serve as the IEP when the child transitions from an early intervention program to a preschool program at age 3. The school must provide the parents a detailed explanation of the differences between an IFSP and an IEP, and the parents must express their consent in writing. One alternative is to hold a transition meeting no later than age 3, and develop an IEP that conforms to the IEP requirements of Part B (See Chapter 4).

The 2004 Amendments allow individual states to establish a policy whereby parents of a child served under Part C may choose to continue the early intervention services under Part C until the child enters or is eligible for kindergarten [20 U.S.C. § 1435 (c)]. Parents in those states must be given notice of their right to elect a continuation of Part C services. When parents elect to continue Part C services past the age of 3 years, schools are relieved from formally beginning services under Part B until the services under Part C end.

The state-wide organizational requirements of Part C are somewhat unique. Part C envisions an inter-agency approach to family needs, not just the child's educational needs. Therefore, the governor of each participating state must designate one state agency, usually education or health, as the lead agency for carrying out the administration and supervision of the program in that state. This includes the identification and coordination of all available resources, a resolution process for intra-agency and inter-agency disputes, and the assignment of agency financial responsibility. The governor must appoint the members of an interagency coordinating council to plan, coordinate, and assist the state's lead agency in resolving infant and toddler programs service issues. Coordinating council membership must include a variety of stakeholders including at least 20% parents, 20% public or private service providers, and at least seven members who meet specific criteria, such as a representative from the state's health insurance agency and a member of the state legislature.

Transition Transition is an issue of concern for any significant change in a child's formal learning experience, even between grade levels or between attendance centers. This is especially true of the transition from an infant and toddler program (often provided in the home setting) to a preschool program (often a center-based program). That is why federal law requires that educators pay special attention to the planning entailed in the transfer of responsibility for a child's learning between Part C and Part B. Transitioning must be smooth and effective. The 2004 Amendments provide two options for transition between Parts C and B. The first is the development of an IEP, or a comparable IFSP, to be in place no later than the child's third birthday. The alternative is to maintain the IFSP as the basis for educational programming under Part B from ages 3 to kindergarten eligibility, when the parent agrees that the IFSP be continued. When an IEP team plans the transition from an IFSP to an IEP, the team members must be familiar with and consider the IFSP content, and the IFSP case manager may attend meetings when invited by the parents.

Education leaders cannot expect to transition young children into new environments with new expectations without a good deal of advance preparation and planning (Lillie & Vakil, 2002). One year for planning, with regularly planned meetings, may be desirable in many situations. The family, the sending teacher, the receiving teacher, and relevant staff members need to be fully informed and prepared for the coming changes (Udell, Peters, & Templeman, 1998).

The planning for transition must be centered around the family's needs and expectations. Educators must recognize that at this stage in child development the family plays a dominant and vital role in the child's future. Patience must be shown in creating family awareness of available options through discussions of favorable and unfavorable component options (Lillie & Vakil, 2002).

Le Ager and Shapiro (1995) found that a child's successful integration is aided when school staff members formally anticipate the demands and expectations that the child with disabilities is likely to experience at the next level and teach the child the necessary skills prior to entrance into that next level. O'Shea (1994) has recommended preparing for transition by sharing with the child and family the descriptions of the future site, curricula and materials, teaching methodologies, expected child behaviors and responsibilities, assessment methods, and overall expectations. LaCava (2005) has recommended the use of videos, photographs, maps, and social stories to help explain the expectations of the new environment. Especially helpful are opportunities for visitation and conversation

wherein the child and family can meet and become familiar with the new program staff members and surroundings.

Hadden and Fowler (1997) have emphasized the need for improved communication with the family about the inherent differences between infant and toddler and preschool programs. The services for infants and toddlers are usually home based, which allows frequent opportunities for open communication with parents each time the service provider visits the home.

Part B of IDEA

Under the early versions of the IDEA, public schools were responsible for education services beginning at age 5 or 6, depending on each state's laws regarding school entrance. The IDEA was amended in 1986 to require that FAPE be provided to all children age 3 through 21 (or graduation) who were entitled to special education, unless the requirement was inconsistent with state law.

By 1987, nearly 261,000 children ages 3 to 5 were receiving preschool special education services, and 2 years later the number had increased to 362,443. This extraordinary growth highlighted many of the difficulties in identifying disabilities and determining appropriate programming for children of such young age, and increasing concerns about early age labeling of children (Ysseldyke, Algozzine, & Thurlow, 2000).

For children ages 3 through 5, and for some 2-year-olds who will turn 3 during the school year, states may obtain federal grants for preschool programs. Provisions of the law for Part B preschoolers are identical to those for school-aged children with disabilities (e.g., FAPE, parent safeguards, IEP, LRE).

Preschool Programs and Families   Even when families of children in center-based programs are encouraged to participate in activities with service providers, the logistics of center-based preschool programs often work against family-school interaction. School-provided transportation schedules and a more hectic atmosphere of children simultaneously arriving and leaving center-based programs are not conducive to quality school-family interaction.

Because so many interruptions to good communication are present, Hadden and Fowler (1997) recommend a continuous and concerted school effort to encourage communication between the program staff and families throughout the transition phase. In addition to informal exchanges, they specifically recommend the formal exchange of school questionnaires and family responses that may be kept by the school staff for future reference, discussions, and conferences. Figures 7-2, 7-3, and 7-4 provide good examples of easy ways to secure information needed by school staff and that are likely to facilitate good communication.

Although all three sample questionnaires to families present good ideas for opening lines of communication, they should not be abused or used indiscriminately. Not all questions are relevant to all situations. Also, schools should not file and then forget the information. Parents will rightly expect that if the school took the time to ask the question, and they, the parents, took time to answer the question, the school will know and remember the answers.

Rump (2002) has written about the importance of involving both parents in transitioning and other important decisions involving preschool youngsters. She reminds us that the majority of early childhood intervention professionals are female and sometimes the importance of the male role model in a child's life is overlooked. She recommends involving the fathers as much as possible and being sure to seek out their perspectives. Rump has also recommended regular review of policies and practices with the goal of encouraging participation of noncustodial parents (mothers or fathers).

Curriculum and Instruction Preschool programs have a number of alternative educational philosophies—each one giving rise to different approaches. A few of these alternative philosophies are as follows:

- *Child Development Model.* This traditional approach to preschool emphasizes age-appropriate skills and social-emotional development. Many activities are made available for the children to explore as they choose. The teacher's role is a relatively informal one.
- *Montessori Model.* Children are provided with a carefully sequenced and structured series of activities to explore at their own pace. The program emphasizes individual

FIGURE 7-2 *Worksheet for sharing information about your child*

1. What types of things does your child enjoy learning?
2. What things are the most difficult for your child to learn?
3. What are your child's favorite toys?
4. How does your child get along with other children?
5. What types of rewards work best for you child (e.g., hugs, praise, stickers)?
6. What types of discipline work best with your child?
7. What kind of support or help, if any, does your child need during routines such as eating, dressing, toileting, and napping?
8. What was your child working on in the last program that you would like to see continued in the new program?
9. What other goals would you like to see for your child in the new program?
10. What other information would you like to share about your child?

From "Preschool: A New Beginning for Children and Parents," by S. Hadden and S. A. Fowler, 1997, *Teaching Exceptional Children, 30*(1), pp. 37–38. Copyright 1997 by the Council for Exceptional Children. Adapted by permission.

FIGURE 7-3 *Items for teacher questionnaire for families of new students*

1. How does your child communicate?

2. What words does your child use?

3. What gestures does your child use?

4. What words does your child understand?

5. What are your child's most and least favorite foods?

6. Are there activities that your child really likes or dislikes?

7. How does your child ask to go to the bathroom?

8. Does your child like to be hugged or touched?

9. Are there certain textures that your child dislikes?

10. What directions does you child follow easily?

11. How does your child indicate displeasure?

12. Does your child need to nap?

13. Does your child take medication?

14. What do you see as your child's strengths?

15. How does your child ask for help?

16. What other information would you like to share?

From "Preschool: A New Beginning for Children and Parents," by S. Hadden and S. A. Fowler, 1997, *Teaching Exceptional Children, 30*(1), pp. 37–38. Copyright 1997 by the Council for Exceptional Children. Adapted by permission.

autonomy and the development of sensory, motor, and language skills.

- *Cognitive Development Model.* This approach is based on the theories of Piaget and others who conceive of development as the product of maturation through a sequence of distinctive stages and through interaction with the environment. Emphasis is on integrated cognitive development and children are encouraged to invent, explore, play, question, observe, and experiment.

- *Behavioral Model.* This is the most controlled of the approaches and emphasizes the acquisition of defined, measurable skills. These skills are divided into their component parts (task analysis) and taught sequentially. As each skill is mastered, the next is introduced. Desired behavior is rewarded and continuous data collection guides the child's program planning.

- *Direct Instruction.* A highly defined and specific method that includes essential behavioral elements, this approach was developed

for use with children of low-income families who are at risk for educational failure. It has six distinguishing elements: a movement from simplified to complex contexts, practice, prompting and fading of cues, teacher feedback, a transition from overt to covert problem-solving strategies, and a shift from teacher to learner as a source of information.

- *Combinations.* New curricula are being developed that combine cognitive developmental theories with measurable behavioral objectives and useful techniques from multiple approaches.

The greatest and most lasting achievements come from programs for individual children that last 2 to 4 years, involve individual and age-appropriate activities, and are followed by appropriate special programming in elementary schools.

Location and Population One major difference among preschool programs is whether

FIGURE 7-4 *Communication schedule*

Child		
How will we communicate:	**How often will we communicate?**	**Best times to communicate?**
telephone	daily	
notes	weekly	
conferences	monthly	
notebook	other	
pickup or drop off		
talks		
other		

From "Preschool: A New Beginning for Children and Parents," by S. Hadden and S. A. Fowler, 1997, *Teaching Exceptional Children, 30*(1), pp. 37–38. Copyright 1997 by the Council for Exceptional Children. Adapted by permission.

they are home-based (program staff members go to the children's homes), center-based (the children go to a school or other location), or a combination of the two. Center-based programming may be difficult or impractical in rural areas, and for some programs that are directed toward a single type of low-incidence disability, such as hearing impairment. In many areas, limited funds and other restrictions generally dictate that preschool programs be designed to accommodate children with a variety of disabilities and individual needs.

Least Restrictive Environment The least restrictive environment provisions of the IDEA apply to preschool children just as they do to all other children covered by Part B (34 C.F.R. § 300.116). This means that considerations for inclusion under the IDEA are required for preschoolers and should not be overlooked when considering appropriate placement options (34 C.F.R. § 300.116). This requirement has resulted in an increasing educational interest in inclusion at both the preschool and primary-school-age levels and is sometimes referred to as "naturalistic" environments (Correa & Jones, 2003). The Council for Exceptional Children supports the position that services for young children with disabilities be provided, whenever appropriate, in a context that includes children without disabilities. One rationale for its

position is that effective inclusion experiences "can form the roots of respect for diversity in all children" (2004).

A study conducted by Rafferty, Piscitelli, and Boettcher (2003) found that young children with disabilities who were higher functioning were more likely than others to be placed in inclusion settings, and children with more severe disabilities were more evenly distributed between inclusion and segregated settings. Students with severe disabilities in inclusion settings were determined to experience greater language and social skill development than their peers in segregated settings. Jenkins, Odom, and Speltz (1989) found that even the mere placement of preschool children with disabilities in the same classroom with typically developing children, without special supports, resulted in positive impacts (albeit minimal) on their fine motor, language, pre-academic, and social skills. An effort at planned and organized social interaction between advanced and less competent peers was found to result in significantly greater interactive and social play, improved social competence, and improved language development.

Additional studies have found that planned inclusive efforts are needed for the best educational results. One group of researchers found that by using rotating trained stay-play-talk peers (buddies) with children with disabilities in a preschool setting, social and communication interactions of children with disabilities were greatly improved (English, Goldstein, Shafer, & Kaczmarek, 1997). The researchers concluded that results might improve further in relationship development if the trained peers remained consistent and were not regularly rotated.

Hibbert and Sprinthall (1995) found that even in a classroom where nearly half of the preschool children had special needs, all the children with disabilities made important positive growth gains in social, emotional, and cognitive areas. Collaborative staff interaction, planning, and ongoing assessment and program revision have been found to be important keys to successful inclusive preschool programs (Correa & Jones, 2003).

A group of researchers working with kindergarten-age children determined that a good way to develop positive student attitudes toward their peers with disabilities was through a planned promotional program of acceptance. The researchers developed and implemented a program that involved the use of children's books depicting persons with disabilities, guided adult discussions with the children about disabilities, provision of appropriate materials to parents, and structured play between young children with and without disabilities (Favazza & Odom, 1997).

Staffing Issues   Staffing models for the integrated preschool vary greatly. At one extreme is the *pull-out* model, wherein a student is removed periodically from class for work with a specialist who may or may not coordinate directly with the preschool classroom teacher. At the other extreme are fully cooperative models where all staff members are considered to have joint responsibilities for all the students and there is extensive collegial sharing of skills and expertise.

Inclusion of young children can sometimes result in unexpected staffing difficulties. Many teachers who have general early childhood education backgrounds may have little training in disabilities. Problems may arise among professionals from different disciplines regarding coordination, turf protection, and the sharing of skills and responsibilities. These issues, however, should not pose insurmountable problems. Programming at this age level allows for a great variation in developmentally appropriate activities, and inherently allows for the inclusion of children with disabilities with a minimum of advanced planning or adaptation (Udell, Peters, & Templeman, 1998).

The single most important influence on the successful implementation of inclusion practices in preschool programs is the attitude and support of educational leaders toward the concept of inclusion. Strong leadership enhances the infrastructure, practices, and policies that make inclusion successful for all students (Hanson et al., 2001). Other important factors are whether the staff has a shared vision that holds the inclusion concept in high regard, and whether state and local practices and policy support inclusion (Lieber et al., 2000).

The more cooperative and integrated early childhood and preschool models require more time for staff members to plan and collaborate with their co-workers. Meaningful and continuing staff development opportunities must be available to all. It is critical that schools create working conditions that support and reward continuous learning and updating of skills. This is true especially for paraeducators who may not have the skills or positive experiences to adequately support inclusive practices (Stoiber, Gettinger, & Goetz, 1998). Paraeducators assigned to early childhood and preschool programs need to exhibit competencies that may be additional to those exhibited by paraeducators in other educational settings. Paraeducators in early childhood and preschool settings need to be able to prepare and use developmentally appropriate materials and to use developmentally appropriate instructional interventions in the cognitive, motor, self-help, social play, and language areas for curricular activites.

Elementary Centers

Early childhood and preschool education programs have not historically been located in school buildings, but that is changing (Marvin,

LaCost, Grady, & Mooney, 2003). Preschool education programs and child-care centers, even those privately owned, are now frequently housed in local elementary schools. Many of these programs provide services for children with disabilities, and many school principals may be unfamiliar with the philosophy and management of programs for infants and toddlers and preschoolers. When early childhood and preschool education programs, public and private, are located in public schools, it is important that:

- the school principal maintains a committed leadership role and helps create channels for communication, interaction, and input between the two systems;
- early childhood, preschool, and regular school staff members have an opportunity to meet with each other before the school year begins and on a regular basis;
- regular class teachers understand the early childhood and preschool programs and the rationale behind them;
- the principal facilitates maximum inclusion opportunities for preschool program and public school students.

A study conducted of early childhood teachers and school administrators in a midwestern state found a broad range of knowledge, experience, and support on the part of elementary school principals (Marvin, LaCost, Grady, & Mooney, 2003). Many of the elementary principals were found to depend heavily upon the early childhood teachers for their expertise and knowledge in the management of the programs. The study concluded that school leaders need to develop a better understanding of early childhood programming. The study also expressed the need for more collaboration and interdependence between early childhood staff and principals in successfully meeting the needs of young children and their families, especially those at risk of school failure.

Educational leaders should always be open to expanding the inclusion opportunities of children in early childhood and preschool programs as well as institutional segregated or home-bound settings. It may be appropriate to establish a type of *reverse integration* programming, wherein typically developing children are encouraged (and assisted) to interact with children with disabilities in otherwise isolated settings. Many activities, such as playing and reading aloud, readily adapt to such situations and benefit both the children with and without disabilities.

Although early childhood and preschool special education programs are generally the responsibility of the school principal, expressly or implied, clear legal responsibilities may not always be obvious. The additional consideration of early childhood programming, with the involvement of a variety of service agencies, may also result in confusion of responsibility and authority. It is hoped that the inter-agency coordinating councils in various states under Part C will resolve confusion regarding the responsibilities of school principals.

CONCLUSION

The value and need for planned quality educational experiences for children with disabilities from birth forward have been established through research and experience. Along with other children at risk of not having successful educational and life experiences due to poverty, health issues, and environment, young children with disabilities can be provided early educational programming to assist in meeting their needs. Although those needs are being met on a professional and consistent basis in some localities, in others they are ignored or provided haphazardly.

The law requires that public schools engage in a concerted effort to identify children with disabilities as early as possible through the activities of "child find." It provides financial incentives and processes to provide children with appropriate services and educational programs. The children initially served under Part C are later transitioned into more traditional school regular and special education programming under Part B.

Educational leaders, working with a variety of community professionals from other fields, play an important part in ensuring that children with disabilities and their families receive timely needed assistance and support. Future special education programming and parent-school relationships will both likely be more effective when educators pay adequate attention to this important time in a child's life.

VIEW FROM THE COURTS

L. B. & J. B. v. Nebo School District, (2002/2004) (inclusion for a preschooler). A preschool child diagnosed with an autistic spectrum disorder was placed by the school's placement team in a special education preschool that had some typically developing children attend along with children with disabilities. The parents desired placement in a program with predominantly typically developing children, and requested a due process hearing. The hearing officer upheld the school district's placement and the federal district court affirmed the hearing officer's decision. The district court ruled that placement in a school with a minority of typically developing peers was adequate inclusion programming.

The Court of Appeals for the Tenth Circuit, however, reversed the district court's decision. The court found that placement in a private school, with a majority of typically developing students, provided the girl with appropriate role model peers that were desirable for her academic, behavioral, and social needs. It also found that the regular private school provided her with academic benefits that she would not have received in the public special education school.

RECOMMENDED READINGS

Beck, J. (2002). Emerging literacy through assistive technology. *Teaching Exceptional Children,* *35*(2), 44–48. This article provides specific exam-

ples of ways to assist young children with emergent literacy through the use of technology.

Justice, L. M. (2004). Creating language-rich preschool classroom environments. *Teaching Exceptional Children,* *37*(2), 36–44. This article provides specific suggestions for building language-rich preschool classroom environments.

LaCava, P. G. (2005). 20 ways to facilitate transitions. *Intervention in School and Clinic, 41,* 46–48. This brief article provides 20 excellent considerations when student is transitioning between school programs.

Smith, J., Brewer, D. M., & Heffner, T. (2003). Using portfolio assessments with young children who are at risk for school failure. *Preventing School Failure, 48,* 38–40. This brief article discusses the role and benefits of portfolio assessment use with young children.

Visoky, A. M., & Poe, B. D. (2000). Can preschoolers be effective peer models? An action research project. *Teaching Exceptional Children, 33*(2), 68–73. This article provides specific examples of naturalistic interventions for facilitating social interaction between children with special needs.

Relevant Federal Regulations

34 C.F.R. Part 300 Assistance to States for the Education of Children with Disabilities (70 Fed. Reg. 35,833–35,880 (June 21, 2005.)

34 C.F.R. Part 300.24	Individualized family service plan.
.101	Free appropriate public education (FAPE).
.102	Limitation-Exception to FAPE for certain ages.
.109	Full educational opportunity goal (FEOG).
.111	Child find.
.124	Transition of children from Part C to preschool programs.
.323	When IEPs must be in effect.
34 C.F.R. Part 303	Early intervention programs for infants and toddlers with disabilities.

SELECTED WEBSITES

Code of Federal Regulations–Government Printing Office–National Archives and Record Administration
http://www.gpoaccess.gov/cfr/index.html

Council for Exceptional Children
http://www.cec.sped.org

U.S. Department of Education
http://www.ed.gov

Individuals With Disabilities Education Act Data–Office of Special Education Programs
http://www.ideadata.org

National Center for Educational Statistics
http://nces.ed.gov/programs/digest

ERIC Clearinghouse on Elementary and Early Childhood Education
http://www.eric.ed.gov

National Center for Early Development and Learning
http://www.fpg.unc.edu/~ncedl

National Institute on Early Childhood Development and Education, Early Childhood Institute
http://www.ed.gov/offices/OERI/ECI

National Association of the State Directors of Special Education
http://www.nasdse.org

National Center for Homeless Education
http://www.serve.org/nche

National Association for the Education of Homeless Children and Youth
http://www.naehcy.org

Circle of Inclusion
http://www.circleofinclusion.org

Culturally and Linguistically Appropriate Services (CLAS), Early Childhood Research Institute
http://www.clas.uiuc.edu

Early Childhood Research Institute on Inclusion
http://www.fpg.unc.edu/~ECRII/

Family and Child Transitions into Least Restrictive Environments
http://facts.crc.uiuc.edu

QUESTIONS FOR THOUGHT

1. How does the policy premise of "pay some now or pay more later" apply to infant and toddler and early childhood education programs?
2. Should the IFSP concept of addressing family needs be included in IEP considerations for older children with disabilities?
3. Would infant and toddler and preschool programs and community services be better coordinated for community service agencies if they were all provided at public elementary school attendance centers?
4. How can public school services and programs to parents of young at risk children benefit the community and the school?

REFERENCES

Bowe, F. G. (1995). Population estimates: Birth-to-5 children with disabilities. *The Journal of Special Education, 28,* 461–471.

Correa, V. I., & Jones, H. (2003). Early childhood special education: Effective education for learners with exceptionalities. *Advances in Special Education, 15,* 351–372.

Council for Exceptional Children (2004). Policies for delivery of services: Early childhood. Retrieved March 18, 2004, http://www.cec.sped.org/pp/polec.html

English, K., Goldstein, H., Shafer, K., & Kaczmarek, L. (1997). Promoting interactions among preschoolers with and without disabilities: Effects of a buddy skills-training program. *Exceptional Children, 63,* 229–243.

Favazza, P. C., & Odom, S. L. (1997). Promoting positive attitudes of kindergarten-age children toward people with disabilities. *Exceptional Children, 63,* 405–418.

Fujiura, G. T., & Yamaki, K. (2000). Trends in demography of childhood poverty and disability. *Exceptional Children, 66,* 187–199.

Hadden, S., & Fowler, S. A. (1997). Preschool: A new beginning for children and parents. *Teaching Exceptional Children, 30*(1), 36–39.

Hanson, M. J., Horn, E., Sandall, S., Beckman, P., Morgan, M., Marquart, J., Barnwell, D., & Chou, H. Y. (2001). After preschool inclusion: Children's educational pathways over the early school years. *Exceptional Children, 68,* 65–83.

Hibbert, M. T., & Sprinthall, N. A. (1995). Promoting social and emotional development of preschoolers: Inclusion and mainstreaming for children with special needs. *Elementary School Guidance and Counseling, 30,* 131–142.

IDEA data (2004). Individuals With Disabilities Education Act Data–Office of Special Education Programs, U.S. Department of Education. Retrieved November 29, 2005, from http://www.ideadata.org

Jackson, T. L. (2004). Homelessness and students with disabilities: Educational rights and challenges. A Project Forum paper of the National Association of State Directors of Special Education. Retrieved December 6, 2004, from http://www.nasdse.org

Jenkins, J. R., Odom, S. L., & Speltz, M. L. (1989). Effects of social integration of preschool children with handicaps. *Exceptional Children, 55,* 420–428.

Justice, L. M. (2004). Creating language-rich preschool classroom environments. *Teaching Exceptional Children, 37*(2), 36–44.

Kimball, J. W., Kinney, E. M., Taylor, B. A, & Stromer, R. (2003). Lights, camera, action: Using engaging computer-card activity schedules. *Teaching Exceptional Children, 36*(1), 40–45.

Kirp, D. L. (2004, November 24). Life way after Head Start: A new study turns up some surprising midlife benefits of preschooling for poor children. *New York Times Magazine, 32,* 34, 35, 36.

L. B. and J. B. v. Nebo School District, 214 F. Supp. 2d 1172 (D. Utah 2002); reversed, 379 F. 3d 966 (10th Cir. 2004).

Le Ager, C., & Shapiro, E. S. (1995). Template matching as a strategy for assessment of and intervention for preschool students with disabilities. *Topics in Early Childhood Special Education, 15*(2), 187–218.

Letter to Morris, 44 IDELR 97 (OSEP, 2005).

Lieber, J., Hanson, M. J., Beckman, P. J., Odem, S. L., Sandall, S. R., Schwartz, I. S., Horn, E., & Wolery, R. (2000). Key influences on the initiation and implementation of inclusive preschool programs. *Exceptional Children, 67,* 83–98.

Lillie, T., & Vakil, S. (2002). Transitions in early childhood for students with disabilities: Law and best practice. *Early Childhood Education Journal, 30,* 53–58.

Magnuson, K. A., Meyers, M. K., Ruhm, C. J., & Waldfogel, J. (2004). Inequality in preschool education and school readiness. *American Educational Research Journal, 41,* 115–157.

Marvin, C., LaCost, B., Grady, M., & Mooney, P. (2003). Administrative support and challenges in Nebraska public school early childhood programs: Preliminary study. *Topics in Early Childhood Special Education, 23,* 217–228.

National Institute of Child Health and Human Development (NICHD) (2002). Early child care and children's development prior to school entry: Results from the NICHD study of early child care. *American Educational Research Journal, 39,* 133–164.

O'Shea, D. J. (1994). Modifying daily practices to bridge transitions. *Teaching Exceptional Children, 26*(4), 29–34.

Peterson, C. A., Wall, S., Raikes, H. A., Kisker, E. E., Swanson, M. E., Jerald, J., Atwater, J. B., & Qiuo, W. (2004). Early Head Start: Identifying and serving children with disabilities. *Topics in Early Childhood Special Education, 24,* 76–88.

Qi, C. H., & Kaiser, A. P. (2003). Behavior problems of preschool children from low-income families: Review of the literature. *Topics in Early Childhood Special Education, 23,* 188–216.

Rafferty, Y., Piscitelli, V., & Boettcher, C. (2003). The impact of inclusion on language development and social competence among preschoolers with disabilities. *Exceptional Children, 69,* 467–479.

Rump, M. L. (2002). Involving fathers of young children with special needs. *Young Children, 57*(6), 18–20.

Scarborough, A. A., Spiker, D., Mallik, S., Hebbler, K. M., Bailey, D. B., Jr., & Simeonsson, R.J. (2004). A national look at children and families entering early intervention. *Exceptional Children, 70,* 469–483.

Stoiber, K. C., Gettinger, M., & Goetz, D. (1998). Exploring factors influencing parents' and early childhood practitioners' beliefs about inclusion. *Early Childhood Research Quarterly, 13,* 107–124.

Turnbull, H. R., & Turnbull, A. P. (1998). *Free appropriate public education.* Denver: Love.

Udell, T., Peters, J., & Templeman, T. P. (1998). From philosophy to practice in inclusive early childhood programs. *Teaching Exceptional Children, 30*(3), 44–49.

U.S. Department of Education (2000). *Building strong foundations for early learning: Guide to high-quality early childhood education programs.* Washington, DC: Author.

Visoky, A. M., & Poe, B. D. (2000). Can preschoolers be effective peer models? *Teaching Exceptional Children, 33*(2), 68–73.

Yamaguchi, B. J., Strawser, S., & Higgins, K. (1997). Children who are homeless: Implications for educators. *Intervention in School and Clinic, 33*(2), 90–97.

Ysseldyke, E., Algozzine, B., & Thurlow, M. L. (2000). *Critical issues in special education* (3rd ed.). Boston: Houghton Mifflin.

Zima, B. T., Farness, S. R., Bussing, R., & Benjamin, B. (1998). Homeless children in emergency shelters: Need for prereferral intervention and potential eligibility for special education. *Behavioral Disorders, 23*(2), 98–110.

CHAPTER 8

SECONDARY SCHOOL CONSIDERATIONS

CHAPTER PREVIEW

Focus

Special education programming at the secondary level must take into account a variety of factors. These include diploma and graduation requirements, the coordination of class schedules, social and behavioral issues associated with adolescence, the cumulative effects of past schooling, vocational education, post-secondary education, and preparation for adult life. Yet the great majority of existing special education models are elementary-age oriented, and few regular or special secondary teachers have adequate preparation in secondary special education pregramming and service. Consequently, many secondary students with disabilities, especially those with mild and moderate disabilities, are inadequately served.

Legal Issues

Consideration of graduation requirements for individual students in special education programs must be flexible and based on the individual student's educational needs. Some students remain in secondary school through age 21 and are provided opportunities for additional education and training, often designed largely for preparation for life as adults. The planning for transition to adult life must consider the student's various future needs, interests, and abilities. These include skills in decision making, employment, mobility, continuing education, leisure activities, and daily living. Students should be encouraged and assisted in developing self-determination skills so that they can act as the primary decision maker in those matters, large and small, that are important to the students' future quality of life.

The need for development of decision making skills is exemplified by the legal requirement that parental safeguards, including the right to request mediation or a due process hearing, may transfer to the student at the age of majority (18 years under most state laws) if the student is capable of making important decisions.

Participation in inclusive programs, when appropriate for secondary students, is vitally important to the likelihood of future success of students with disabilities as adults. Inclusion programs also assist students who develop typically to better understand and relate to the diverse society they are about to enter.

Rationale

Appropriate educational programming and activities provided at the secondary level greatly increases the chances of success for individuals with disabilities in finding and maintaining employment and leading independent adult lives. These benefits extend beyond individuals with disabilities to society as a whole. Effective programs that prepare students for transition to adult lives capture otherwise lost human potential, reduce the costs of social programs, and relieve the fear and anxiety experienced by family members who are concerned about their child's future.

Types of Secondary Programs

Generally, the secondary program for students with special needs will fall into one of four categories:

- Regular college preparatory programs, with support for student and teachers
- Regular vocational programs with appropriate support services that meet standard graduation requirements
- Special vocational and community living preparation programs that emphasize practical skills, with part-time placement in regular classes as appropriate
- Special individualized programs for students with severe disabilities

Approaches

The overall goal of secondary special education is to maximize all students' potential for independent, productive, and satisfying lives in the adult community. For students with disabilities, this should be reflected in IEPs, which in turn may take precedence over standard graduation requirements as the guideline for programming. For many students, the focus of the high school curriculum will shift from academics to practical skills, including self-help, social skills, and vocational education. Educators should plan ahead to prepare students with the necessary prerequisite skills for each course and experience and for transition from school to the post-school environment.

In order to promote the provision of secondary students with disabilities the opportunity for successful growth and development, education leaders should

- model acceptance and understanding of the students, acknowledge individual differences, and encourage flexibility in accommodations of school schedules and programs to meet individual needs;
- promote cooperation and regular communication among regular, special, and vocational educators, and ensure that teachers are provided with needed information, training, and support;
- guarantee that students with disabilities have appropriate access to vocational education programs;
- assign a faculty adviser to each student (one individual with responsibility for overall coordination and advocacy for that student);
- give all of the student's teachers an opportunity to participate in program planning; and
- use community resources for transition services and vocational education.

COPING WITH SECONDARY SCHOOL

Adolescence can be a rough time for almost everyone. The complex and mysterious process of movement from childhood and dependence to adulthood and independence is full of familiar perils from acne to awkwardness, social and family pressures, and emotions that sometimes seem to race out of control. As every adult who works with adolescents knows, it is a time of testing authority (often rebelliousness) as well as optimism as emerging identities are explored and plans for the future begin to take form.

Young people with disabilities experience the same physical changes, quest for independence, and feelings of hope and doubt, joy and disappointment that other adolescents must confront. But, in addition to the challenges faced by all young people as they mature, these youths have the added challenge of learning to manage a disability. It can make the difficult transition of adolescence even more stressful when a young person is faced with the problems of

- coping with a frustrating learning difficulty at a time when there is a strong desire to feel competent and in control;
- looking visibly different from one's peers when there is so much emphasis on achieving a common style, on fitting in; and
- managing behavior problems in a period of life when peers and personal stresses often encourage acting out.

Some disabilities may not be deemed serious enough to warrant special programming as an eligible student at a younger age (e.g., certain behavior disorders or health impairments), but would identify a student for special education in secondary school. Discrepancies between actual performance and academic or social expectations may also tend to increase as the student moves into the upper grade levels. Although certain learning problems, such as some speech disorders, may be solved effectively through temporary interventions at an early age, many more will require lifetime accommodations.

Because the teen years pose special challenges for young people with disabilities, they also bring special problems for educators. The size, diversity, and complexity of the secondary curriculum make individualized instruction difficult to plan and carry out. The stress on Carnegie Units (a year-long course of study of approximately 50 minutes each day, 5 days per week) and other graduation requirements also contribute to the relative inflexibility of traditional secondary, as opposed to elementary, programming. A secondary teacher who sees 130 to 150 students per day cannot be expected to assume the same level of knowledge and responsibility for an individual student's educational program as can the elementary school teacher who has the same 25 to 30 students in class throughout the school day. The traditional stereotype of a regular secondary teacher is one who primarily works individually in a lockstep, grade-by-grade curriculum with an emphasis on course content and competition for grades. Students are tracked by ability, with learning occurring only within the four walls of the classroom. The teacher would seldom have contact with, much less responsibility for, special education students.

The teachers in junior and senior high schools are not as likely to have received the preservice experience necessary to prepare them for the task of accommodating exceptional learners in the secondary classroom. Indeed, few teacher training institutions in the country offer programs of study in secondary special education and many states lack special licensure for those who work with secondary students. The entire field of secondary special education remains relatively undeveloped. Most special education instruction is still based on an elementary model, although clearly the approaches, strategies, and materials are sometimes inappropriate for secondary students and unsuited to the secondary school environment.

The importance of the IEP in individualizing this process cannot be overemphasized. Secondary students, like elementary students, who qualify for special education and related services represent a full range of intelligence, skill levels, and abilities. Some will be able to complete a college preparatory curriculum and go on to postsecondary and even graduate study. For others, the focus on secondary programming will be on mastery of basic social, self-help, and vocational skills. It is as harmful to deprive an able student of the opportunity to achieve as it is to force another student through a standard high school curriculum at the expense of needed training in survival skills. Students who, with appropriate programming, can complete mandated Carnegie Units for graduation along with their peers should be assisted in doing so. For other secondary students with special needs, the IEP goals and objectives (not standard graduation requirements) must be the ultimate guide to educational programming and graduation.

It should also be acknowledged, however, that traditional high school academic programming will not be appropriate for all youths. Some simply will need too much of their limited school time to master practical skills. For many students, the overriding goal of secondary education is to maximize their potential for independent adult functioning and not necessarily to earn a diploma, although this should be attempted when possible. The focus should be on applied skills and related academic course work. For a secondary student with low cognitive ability, it may be much more critical to learn how to make change for a dollar or how to use the local transportation system, rather than to struggle through algebra. It may be essential to learn how to vote, but it may not be possible—within the time remaining after classes in vocational and daily living skills—to study more abstract social studies concepts such as the Constitution and the structure of American democracy. Ideally, the school will be flexible enough to acknowledge this and to arrange, in some cases, for a student to attend a class, such as civics, when content is appropriate for the individual student.

For many years, the effectiveness of secondary schools meeting the needs of adolescents with disabilities was taken for granted. Then, follow-up studies conducted in the 1980s and 1990s established that following high school, many of these students were ill-equipped for adult life. Many were found to be dependent on their families, unemployed, underemployed, and lacking in the ability to become successfully involved in their own community. Such studies paint a bleak picture that can be greatly modified only through improved educational opportunities for students with disabilities.

These are but some of the inherent difficulties in the implementation of any special education program at the secondary level. Thus, it is not surprising that inclusive special education programs at the secondary level have developed more slowly compared with the elementary level. Cole and McLesky (1997) have identified eight general barriers to inclusive education programs at the secondary level that in some ways overlap the issues previously discussed regarding special education generally:*

1. Secondary teachers emphasize complex curricular material, whereas elementary teachers focus on basic academic and social skills.
2. Secondary students with disabilities exhibit larger gaps between skill level and classroom demands and expectations.
3. Secondary curricular content is much broader in range than elementary curriculum.
4. Secondary classrooms are teacher-centered, and instruction is usually didactic and infrequently differentiated for varying student needs.
5. Secondary teachers are trained as content specialists, and sometimes are not inclined to make individual adaptations for students with disabilities.
6. Secondary students are going through a complex, frustrating time called adolescence, which impacts them in every conceivable way.
7. Secondary schools are subject to greater pressure from outside agencies, such as

*From "Secondary Inclusion Programs for Students with Mild Disabilities," by C. M. Cole and J. McLesky, 1997, *Focus on Exceptional Children, 29*(6), pp. 1–2. Copyright 1997 by Love Publishing Company. Adapted by permission.

businesses, state government, and colleges and universities, to provide students with specific skills and knowledge.

8. Secondary teachers have a significant autonomy in the development and delivery of curriculum.

LEGAL ISSUES

All the legal protections of the IDEA for nondiscriminatory evaluation, individualized programming, LRE, and procedural safeguards apply to students in secondary-level educational programs, whether academic or vocational. For example, youths with disabilities should be placed into regular vocational programs, with appropriate support for the student and teacher, when that is the LRE in which to meet the goals of the IEP. Vocational education refers to those educational programs related to preparation for a career not requiring a college degree.

The term *special education* is specifically defined in federal law to include vocational education when it consists of specially designed instruction. The obvious inference is that a child with disabilities will be in regular vocational programs unless special vocational programs and services are required to meet the child's needs. Any special vocational programming must be provided for in the IEP and provided the student at no cost to the student or the family.

Age of Majority

States may provide that a child with disabilities reaching the age of majority under state law (age 18 in many states) will be granted the procedural safeguard rights previously reserved under the IDEA to the child's parents. When states do transfer parent rights to the child at age of majority, schools, through the IEP development process, must notify both the parents and the child of the transfer of rights at least one year beforehand. (See Chapter 4.) In the event the student does not have the ability to provide informed consent and make decisions, and has not been the subject of a state legal proceeding to establish incompetency, other persons, in-

cluding parents, may be appointed under state procedures to make educational decisions for the student.

Even when procedural safeguard rights are transferred to the student at majority age, both the parents and student must be provided notices required by the law that formerly had to be given only to parents (i.e., IEP meetings, change in FAPE).

Extended Opportunities

Unless students have graduated from high school, the IDEA requires most states to provide special education and related services through the end of the school year in which students with disabilities turn 21. This requirement gives students who need more time extended opportunities for vocational training or additional courses for which they may not previously have had the necessary prerequisites or maturity. It gives schools the opportunity to develop special programs in vocational training, work experience, cooperative placements with business and industry, and life skills. This time is not intended as a time to recycle students through academic courses they may have already completed. Planning for these extra school years, as for others, should be appropriate and individualized.

Extended programs and services for 18- through 21-year-olds need not be provided to all students with disabilities, but only to those whose IEP calls for them. Such an IEP may contain goals related to readiness for jobs, postsecondary education programs, or related life-skill objectives. Students who complete standard graduation requirements and receive a regular diploma are no longer eligible for continued education services under the IDEA. However, it is not legal, or ethical, for schools to award diplomas inappropriately or to force graduation on students as a means of removing the students from the school system and thus ending the student's special education program. The school's responsibility to provide special education to students with disabilities ends upon graduation, but only when the student is awarded a regular high school diploma. When the school awards an alternative document to the student (i.e., certificate of attendance), the student remains entitled to special education services until the student is later awarded a regular diploma, or attains the age of 21 [34 C.F.R. § 300.102 (a) (3)]. In consideration of social and family needs, it is common for schools to permit students to participate in graduation ceremonies with their peers without having actually earned or received a diploma until they later complete their planned additional years of study.

Because graduation with a regular diploma ends the student's eligibility for FAPE, graduation is considered a change in placement. Chapter 2 highlighted parental safeguards, including the requirement that changes in educational placement must be preceded by a detailed written notice of the proposed change and a reminder about procedural safeguards. These safeguards include the right to challenge the proposed change through mediation or a due process hearing. This notice requirement and right to challenge graduation is especially important when the student or parents do not believe that appropriate graduation requirements have been met. Re-evaluations normally required for other student changes in placement, however, are not required when a student graduates with a regular diploma or exceeds eligibility for special education as determined by state law (usually 21).

The 2004 Amendments have added a new school responsibility to those students who are terminated from special education due to graduation with a regular diploma or who exceed age eligibility for FAPE. For those students, the school must provide them with a "summary of the child's academic achievements and functional performance" and recommendations on how to assist the student in meeting the student's postsecondary goals [34 C.F.R. § 300.305 (e)].

Transition in the IEP

In recent years, more attention has been paid to the period of transition of students with disabilities from school to adult work, post high school education, and life activities. The federal Office of Special Education and Rehabilitation Services (OSERS) explained the term in its early usage as follows:

> Transition is a period that includes high school, the point of graduation, additional postsecondary education or adult services, and the initial years of employment. Transition is a bridge between the security and structure offered by the school and the opportunities and risks of adult life. Any bridge requires both a solid span and a secure foundation at either end. The transition from school to work and adult life requires sound preparation in the secondary school, adequate support at the point of school leaving, and secure opportunities and services, if needed, in adult situations.

> Since the services and experiences that lead to employment vary widely across individuals and communities, the traditional view of transition as a special linking service between school and adult opportunities is insufficient. The present definition emphasizes the shared responsibility of all involved parties for transition success, and extends beyond traditional notions of service coordination to address the quality and appropriateness of each service area. (Will, 1984, p. 2)

Transition Planning Both common sense and contemporary research suggest that planning for the successful transition from school to adult life should be a continuous process, beginning in the very early grades and gaining increased emphasis through the advanced grades. The most successful transition programs provide for the coordinated development of transition competencies from elementary school through high school.

The development of personal, social and self-help skills critical to successful adult living can often be most effectively taught in the early grades (Van-Belle, Marks, Martin, & Chun, 2006). Remediation of inappropriate behaviors becomes increasingly difficult over time when such behaviors are practiced without question or consequence.

The primary goal of secondary school transition planning is to coordinate the resources of the school and the community to create the greatest opportunity reasonably possible for a young adult with disabilities to experience an adult life as normal as possible. This is made possible through provision of special education as identified in the IEP (Kohler & Field, 2003).

Two researchers have analogized transition as a vehicle that takes a student from one place to another, fueled by IEP planning, and finally arriving at a destination (Nuehring & Sitlington, 2003).

The significance of formal planning for the important step from school to adult life is obvious, and that is the reason the law requires that special consideration be given to this important time in a student's life. One of the express purposes of the 2004 Amendments was to "ensure that all children with disabilities have available to them . . . special education and related services designed to . . . prepare them for further education, employment and independent living" [20 U.S.C. § 1401 (d) (1) (A)].

No later than the IEP which is in effect when the student turns age 16 (or younger, when appropriate), IEPs must contain measurable postsecondary goals based on appropriate transition assessments related to education, training, employment, and where appropriate, independent living skills. IEPs must also include needed transition services, including courses of study, needed to reach those goals [20 U.S.C. § 1414 (d) (1) (A) (i) (VII)]. The increased emphasis on assessment of transition needs and transition planning in the 2004 Amendments appears to be a congressional attempt to force students, parents, schools, and postsecondary service providers to meet the student's future needs. These are to be met through the provision of supports and self-determination and self-advocacy skills early enough to make transition implementation successful (Beekman, 2005). Schools must be assured their staff members understand and can implement the new transition assessment requirements.

For samples of transition services statements in IEP planning, see Appendix F. In many states the individualized transition plan (ITP) is a separate document attached to the IEP. In others the ITP is a part of the IEP form.

The course of study required for transitioning identifies the direction and focus of the student's course work while in school. The following are examples of course of study statements for students with differing needs:*

- Math through Algebra II, all industrial arts classes that focus on engineering and technology, path to construction fields, job shadowing, and community work experience
- Functional classes to develop skills for working on a team collaboratively, work experience in a sheltered workshop, and functional life skills
- As many family and consumer science classes as possible to acquire adult living skills, functional math, and community-based work experience in the health and food service area
- Health occupation path to include courses in science through Physics, math through Algebra II, college preparation core classes, and work based on learning experiences in medical settings

Sensitivity Needed   Although parents of students without disabilities share similar concerns for their children's future with parents of students with disabilities, the latter group experiences a much greater sense of discomfort and concern about what the future holds. Educators need to be aware of the parent's sense of helplessness and vulnerability at this important juncture and be ready to help assist families in preparing for life after schooling (Whitney-Thomas & Hanley-Maxwell, 1996).

More than 4 out of 10 parents of students with disabilities (45%) say that their child's special education program is failing or needs improvement in preparing their child for adult life after high school (Johnson & Duffett, 2002). Although that figure represents some success on the part of educators in meeting the parent-perceived needs of their children, it

*From "Their Future . . . Our Guidance," (p. 29), by the Iowa Department of Education, 1998, Des Moines. Iowa Department of Education. Adapted by permission.

also establishes that a significant number of parents remain unsatisfied with their child's transition planning.

Working with parents of culturally diverse students in the transition process calls for conscious educator sensitivity and understanding. In a study of culturally and linguistically diverse parent involvement in transition planning, Geenen, Powers, and Lopez-Vasquez (2001) determined that educator perceptions of diverse parent involvement in transition planning were different than the parent perceptions. Although the educators and parents expressed similar recognition of the needed elements of transition, educators involved in the study expressed dissatisfaction with the level of parent participation. The parents, on the other hand, viewed themselves as active participants in the transition process.

The researchers determined that the differences in perception resulted from the differing foci of educators and parents. The educators focused on parent involvement in school-directed transition planning, whereas the parents' focus was much broader and involved extended family and community in the planning. To parents of culturally and linguistically diverse students, school presents many barriers to successful joint planning (i.e., language, lack of cultural or racial understanding). The researchers concluded that because the parents understand the importance of the time of transition and believe that their participation is important, educators should adjust their narrow thinking of school-only focused transition to incorporate the parents' broader-based family and community perspective. That would mean planning school-based transition support for the students that complemented and supported the parents in home and community transition activities.

Vision Strategy No later than the beginning of junior high school, a comprehensive assessment of student and family desires, intentions, and plans should be conducted and updated regularly (McAfee & Greenawalt, 2001). Miner and Bates (1997) have described a process for transition planning they call "person-centered

transition planning," which incorporates elements of self-determination and family involvement. Sometime prior to the scheduled transition planning session, one or two educators meet with the student and family members to explore the needs and resources of the family. They identify the student's preferences and dislikes, strengths and needs, and especially, what the family and student foresee as a desirable future lifestyle. The educators should be especially interested in ascertaining the family's perspectives and use open-ended inquiries in their quest:

> Where will Carla live? What will Carla do during the day? What will Carla do for fun and recreation?

Focusing on the student's strengths, the educators, the student, and the family develop a vision statement about what the student's daily life will look like in the future. From that perspective they can draw on resources available to aid the student in achieving the vision (See Chapter 4 on IEP development). Oftentimes, changes are made in the service delivery system and planned steps are altered as a result of taking the time to involve the student and family from a personalized perspective. Many family members who are involved in the vision strategy have expressed strong support for this method of transition planning.

Secondary IEP Planning Issues

It usually is not feasible, or desirable, for all of a secondary student's teachers to attend IEP and placement meetings. However, all teachers should have the opportunity to provide input into the process, and all must be familiar with the contents of the completed IEP. At a minimum, each teacher should contribute essential information about courses taught, including initial student competencies required and teacher expectations of students, so that a reasonable match between students and classes can be made. Students should not be placed in classes unless they have the skills and supplementary aids and services (for both student and teacher) reasonably necessary for success in meeting IEP goals. Education leaders must accept the primary responsibility of ensuring that IEPs are available to staff and appropriate IEP information is shared with staff, including substitutes, support staff, custodial staff, bus drivers, and secretarial staff, on a need-to-know basis.

As part of the transition process, some educators recommend creation of a formalized document called a *transition profile* (Neubert & Moon, 2000). These documents contain relevant personal information, such as medical history, personal goals, and strengths and needs, as well as skills, characteristics, and service eligibility status. The profile provides service providers and counselors current and accurate information about the young adult preparing to leave the school system. It also serves a variety of purposes, including documentation of progress, program eligibility determinations, employment, and reminders of unmet needs.

The use of a transition case manager or transition coordinator to help students stay in school and to make transitions to adult vocational service providers is a growing practice in many parts of the country (Nuehring & Sitlington, 2003). Its growth is based largely in the IDEA emphasis on transitioning and the general historical lack of success of transition programs. In Virginia, where the practice is well-established, a group of transition coordinators have attempted to clarify, and even define, their job descriptions (Asselin, Todd-Allen, & deFur, 1998). The group was able to identify 71 specific job tasks for transition coordinators and organized them into nine general categories:

• Intra-school, intra-agency linkages
• Inter-agency linkages
• Assessment and career counseling
• Transition planning
• Education and community training
• Family support
• Public relations
• Program development
• Program evaluation

Although elementary educators enter the IEP conference with a focus on basic skills and the current school year, at the secondary level the focus may be more on applied skills and long-term planning. The most important consideration at the secondary level is the student's future as an adult. For many individuals with special needs, high school is the last opportunity for formal education before entering the adult world. The drafters of an adolescent's IEP must ask themselves: "When that transition comes, will the student be ready for it? What skills must this student master before the end of schooling in order to achieve a maximum level of independent adult functioning? Which of these skills—or their prerequisites—should be taught this year to enable the student to meet those long-term goals?"

Over the years, a number of authors have compiled lists of the recommended and necessary competencies that should be mastered by a student for independent functioning in adult life. Those lists have differed in form more than substance. To assist planners in assessment and transition planning from a holistic perspective, a contemporary list of critical areas of student need has been identified by a state educational agency as follows:*

> *Self-Determination*—Competencies needed to understand one's abilities, needs, and rights; to speak for one's self; and to act as one's own advocate. Competencies needed for problem solving and decision-making.
>
> *Mobility*—Academic and functional competencies to interact and travel within and outside the community.
>
> *Health and Physical Care*—Academic and functional competencies needed to maintain the full range of physical, emotional, and mental well-being of an individual, such as selecting health care professionals, determining whom to contact in the case of emergency, obtaining assistive devices, and using personal hygiene skills.

---

*From "Infusing Transition Into Individual Education Programs" (p. 23), by the Iowa Department of Education, 1996, Des Moines, IA: Iowa Department of Education. Reprinted by permission.

Money Management—Academic and functional competencies such as budgeting, balancing a checkbook, and doing insurance planning.

Social Interaction—Competencies needed to participate and interact in a variety of settings in society.

Workplace Readiness—Academic and functional competencies and basic work behaviors, such as staying on task as expected, responding appropriately to instructions, and working under pressure. Knowledge of occupational alternatives and self-awareness of needs, preferences, and abilities related to occupational alternatives.

Occupationally Specific Skills—Academic and functional competencies required in specific occupations or clusters of occupations.

Academic and Lifelong Learning—Academic and functional competencies needed to pursue and benefit from future educational and learning opportunities.

Leisure—Academic and functional competencies, interests, and self-expression of the individual that can lead to enjoyable and constructive use of leisure time.

IEP goals and objectives based on these young adult need areas may seem a mystery to educators involved in transition planning for the first time. But the task is not as difficult as it may seem at first. Examples of transition goals and objectives are found in Appendix F.

SELF-DETERMINATION

Traditionally, young adults with disabilities have had parents and teachers make decisions for them. It has become evident to many people working with secondary school students that allowing others to make decisions for students is detrimental to student development of skills associated with self-determination that are critical to the success of the transition process. Stated in its simplest terms, *self-determination*

is the student acting as a primary choice maker in the decisions that are important to the student's future quality of lifestyle. Researchers have found that students who exhibit higher measures of self-determination at graduation are more likely to live elsewhere other than with parents or family, maintain a bank account, and be employed one year after leaving high school than those who score low on measures of self-determination (Wehmeyer & Schwartz, 1997).

Educators should encourage self-determination (decision-making) activities for students through the use of role playing, simulation, modeling, and brainstorming. Lee, Palmer, Turnbull, and Wehmeyer (2006) recommend that self-determination begin at an earlier age than the high school years, and that self-determination will be most effective when parents and teachers collaborate and are consistent. They believe that the promotion of self-determination in younger children may improve the child's quality of life, and also that of the entire family. Students should be encouraged to make choices, express priorities and preferences and, most important, actually be allowed to experience and assess the outcomes of good and poor choices (King, 2000; VanDycke, Martin, & Lovett, 2006; Van-Belle, Marks, Martin, & Chun, 2006). All of this includes learning how to access resources and information and playing an active role in the planning, implementation, and assessment of their own education program as soon as practicable (Torgerson, Miner, & Shen, 2004). Through self-advocacy training, students with disabilities learn how to let others know what they need and to what they are entitled (Van-Belle et al., 2006). Over 60 curricula have been developed to promote self-determination skills in students, and help to assess the appropriate program for specific students is available (Test et al., 2000).

A group of researchers at the University of North Carolina at Charlotte, in an effort to determine conditions that support and inhibit a successful implementation, examined six programs with a major emphasis on promoting self-determination with students with disabilities (Karvonen, Test, Wood, Browder, & Algozzine, 2004). They determined that successful self-determination programs frequently had at least one staff member that modeled self-determinination behaviors, exhibited high expectations for student potential, and assummed roles as mentor, teacher, counselor, and case manager. Parents of students in the successful programs also assumed multiple roles of supporter, coach, role model, and advocate that paralleled the school's program. Both teachers and parents learned to adapt as students matured and became able to assume more responsibility for their own decision making.

The researchers found several barriers to successful self-determination programs. The most common, which had been overcome eventually at most program sites, was weak administrator support or understanding of the concept. Another barrier came from some students who did not at first like the self-determination program due to previously being taken care of by others. They had learned to be helpless and had difficulty adjusting. A third barrier involved some professionals clinging to old roles. They had difficulty adjusting to greater student planning participation and students running their own IEP meetings.

Mason, Field, and Sawilowsky (2004) have determined from a survey of teachers, administrators, and related services staff that a significant need exists for training and technical assistance support for all school staff related to student self-determination and student involvement in the IEP process. Survey respondents were highly supportive of both self-determination skills training for students and their involvement in their own IEP process. However, only 8% were satisfied with the approach they were using to teach self-determination, and only 34% expressed satisfaction with the level of student involvement in the IEP process.

As the student enters secondary school, IEP planning should increasingly be the responsibility of the student (McAffee & Greenwalt, 2001). Student involvement in the IEP process is at the heart of self-determination and self-advocacy, yet most special education students are seldom expected to be personally involved in planning their own IEP. This lack of student participation is not, however, because students are not capable of being involved. One review of the literature involving a synopsis of 16 research studies established that all interventions directed at greater student involvement in their own IEP development resulted in either greater increases in student participation in the IEP process or increased scores on a self-determination assessment (Test et al., 2004). The study concluded that students with widely varied disabilities can be successfully involved on their own IEP teams. Interventions commonly used in the studies included role playing, simulation, and the use of verbal, visual, or physical prompts. A study by Carter, Lane, Pierson, and Glaeser (2006) determined that adolescents with emotional disturbance (ED) were in especially great need of help in being prepared for self-determination assistance and training.

Students should be prepared in advance for fulfilling their role in IEP team meetings. In a 3-year study of middle, junior, and senior high IEP meetings, researchers found that although 70% of the students attended their own IEP meetings, of the various team participants, the students knew and understood less about the process than any other group of team participants (Martin, Marshall, & Sale, 2004). Only a few of the students had instruction about IEP meetings beforehand.

A recent study involving 109 IEP meetings found that special education teachers talked 51 percent of the time, family members 15 percent, general educators and administrators 9 percent, support staff 6 percent, and students 3 percent (Martin et al., 2006). Another part of that study established that with IEP leadership instruction the number of students who exhibited the skills taught was greatly enhanced, including student participation time and activity in IEP meetings (VanDycke et al., 2006). The study concluded that educators need to place more emphasis on teaching students how to participate in transition activities, and research establishes that such approaches are successful (Martin, Van Dycks, Christensen et al., 2006).

Students often need to be encouraged and supported to increase their levels of development in their own IEPs (Keyes & Owens-Johnson, 2003; Martin, et al., 2006). Participation provides the opportunity for students to take ownership in the process and to have more to say about their lives and their futures (Mason, McGahee-Kovac, & Johnson, 2004; Myers & Eisenman, 2005).

Students should have the IEP concept and process explained, modeled, or role-played in ways that ensure understanding. They should be helped to organize and prepare their thoughts in advance of IEP meetings, coached by staff during meetings as necessary, and be debriefed following the meeting as a follow-up to aid in their understanding. Many special education teachers provide classroom activities designed to assist students' understanding of participation in the IEP process. They ask their students to identify their own vision of their future, they go over a written meeting agenda, and students develop their own list of personal IEP meeting objectives.

CAREER AND VOCATIONAL EDUCATION

Employment Data

Employment statistics for the nation's citizens with disabilities are poor. Studies have documented the difficulty that graduates of special education programming have making the transition into the adult world of work.

A large longitudinal study of former high school students for up to 5 years after leaving school showed an improved competitive employment rate for youth with disabilities in the late 1980s over previous years (Blackorby & Wagner, 1996). However, it showed a continued significantly lower young adult employment rate for those with disabilities compared to youth generally, 2 years (46% compared with 59%) and 3 to 5 years (57% compared with 69%) after leaving school. Only 17% of youth with multiple disabilities reported being competitively employed 5 years after secondary school. Females with disabilities continued to be employed 5 years after high school at a lower rate and at lower pay than their male counterparts.

Attendance in all types of postsecondary education after 5 years showed a much higher rate for youth in the general population compared with those with disabilities (68% com-

pared with 27%). Independent living became more common the longer youth with disabilities were out of high school, but after 5 years still lagged behind young adults in the general population (37% compared with 60%) (Blackorby & Wagner, 1996).

Vocational Assessment and Planning

Appropriate career and vocational goals, like all goals written into the IEP, should be based on accurate and appropriate assessments. Vocational assessments, as envisioned in the 2004 Amendments, should address students' academic, perceptual, and social skills, and should include assessments of interests, attitudes, aptitudes, and achievement levels in areas related to work. They may include pencil-and-paper tests, apparatus tests, situational assessments, and job tryouts. Smaller school districts that cannot afford work sample tests will find that they can work out an adequate combination of other types of assessments.

Three levels of vocational assessment should be carried out in the schools:

1. Screening, including a limited number of tests, often general ones
2. Partial vocational assessments, including only tests selected to answer specific questions
3. Comprehensive vocational assessments, including a full range of tests of interests, aptitudes, and abilities

Before completing a vocational assessment, an individual vocational evaluation plan should be developed that lists the questions to be answered by the assessment, provides background information on the student, and identifies the tests and situations to be used. It is essential to personalize the vocational evaluation; otherwise it will be too time consuming and expensive and will not yield useful information essential for planning.

At any level, the assessment process will yield a report that must be interpreted and used by the student's teachers. Therefore, the information must be clearly presented and easily understood. It is recommended that the vocational evaluator who prepares the report participate in the ensuing IEP meeting.

For students with special needs in vocational education, four basic types of educational placement are generally available:

1. Regular vocational program with minor adjustments and/or consultative assistance to the teacher
2. Regular vocational program with more substantial direct assistance and support to the student
3. Special vocational programs that emphasize practical skills, with part-time placement in regular vocational classes as appropriate
4. Specially designed vocational programs for students with severe disabilities

Although vocational educators' participation in IEP meetings is not required, it can be beneficial. Instructors can contribute important information, such as expected course entry skills, physical and intellectual requirements of course activities, materials and equipment used and possible adaptations, supplemental materials and instruction required for attainment of vocational objectives, prerequisite courses, existing job opportunities and postsecondary training opportunities in the vocational area, work study and on-the-job training available, and courses available within each vocational area.

In turn, IEP participation can provide non-special education vocational staff with information about

- the student's learning style and achievement levels (in academic, personal and social, and daily living skills);
- special teaching techniques;
- classroom accommodations;
- assistance available from other staff members;
- the most effective reinforcers for the student;
- special education vocational options; and
- a system for monitoring student progress.

Improving Vocational Programs

A study involving several hundred students, both with and without disabilities, in Oregon and Nevada one year after school completion has helped identify valuable components of good vocational programming (Benz, Yovanoff, & Doren, 1997). The findings support a common need for students with and without disabilities to be involved in combined school-based and work-based programs and continued vocational support for a time following school. To be successful, students must have a work-based learning program that integrates related academic skills, communication skills, and social skills. Work-based learning can include service learning, job shadowing, internships, apprenticeships, school-based enterprises, and paid work experience.

The concept of integrating academic and vocational program components is neither new nor unique. The educational concept of Tech Prep incorporates a curriculum designed as a parallel to college preparatory curricula. It combines mathematics, science, communications, and social sciences in an applied academic mode and competency-based curriculum. The curriculum is based around a career cluster of occupations and is designed to build a strong foundation for later advanced course work. It is generally believed that the integration of academic content and the "world of work" across disciplines will reduce student drop-out rates and raise overall student academic achievement (Razeghi, 1998).

All of this preparation must be well founded in effective career guidance and planning by competent staff. Support services, remedial assistance, and counseling should not end with the traditional conclusion of secondary school. Networking between and among various agencies and support services is a goal of a modern transition plan. Special educators can provide expertise in the integration of academics through curricular design, instruction techniques, accommodation strategies, the use of technology, and individualization of support services.

There are several actions that educational leaders can take to improve the appropriate vocational education programming and services to special education students. For instance, vocational instructors, like other regular education teachers, often lack training and experience in working with students with disabilities and may have specific concerns about safety, behavior management, extra time requirements, ultimate employability of the student, and other similar issues. Such concerns are understandable and deserve serious consideration and response.

To win instructors' support for including students with disabilities in regular and vocational education programs, IEP teams and educational leaders should take the following steps:

1. Assign student appropriately, based on an honest and reasonable assessment of his or her abilities and of the course requirements (with reasonable adaptations and assistance).
2. Provide adequate support to the instructor(s).
3. Involve the regular educator(s) in program planning and establish open lines of communication with special education staff.
4. Inform instructors about requirements of the law.
5. Counter stereotypes and misconceptions with the reality of the record of job success for employees with disabilities.
6. Take advantage of available community resources.
7. Encourage flexibility in scheduling to accommodate such possibilities as 8-hour job placements 1 or 2 days a week, attending regular classes for some units of study and not others, and so on.
8. Acquaint the instructors with the disability and what can reasonably be expected from the student.
9. Offer to obtain a substitute for the vocational teacher for a few days so that the teacher can visit other schools with successful inclusion vocational programs.

Additional strategies for facilitating students' successful integration into regular vocational classes can be effective. A trial period in which the student is exposed to several class sessions one semester before placement is finalized may be helpful. An orientation to the classroom that is sensitive to the student's needs may also be beneficial. For example, a student with visual impairment should be intro-

duced to the location of all desks and equipment, and should have an opportunity to get accustomed to the room when no other students are present. A student with cognitive disabilities may simply need extra orientation to equipment use and safety strategies. Before a course starts, the vocational instructor should meet the student and learn about the disability. In class, it is important that the instructor

- accept the student as an individual;
- avoid overprotection;
- encourage independence;
- adapt the task and environment as necessary;
- provide ample time for completion;
- work ahead to avoid problems (e.g., introduce vocabulary before the lesson);
- use resource personnel within and outside the school;
- be sensitive to the student's endurance/attention span;
- provide simple, concise instructions;
- change a strategy that does not work and try another.

Some researchers in career development and employment for students with disabilities stress career development in a broad, general sense. They emphasize that few young adults will leave school with realistic career goals and stick with them for life. Instead of teaching skills for a specific job or career, focus should be on lifelong career development. Morningstar (1997) has made several recommendations to educators for nonspecific career development:

- Consider developing skills and values across an entire lifespan and for career maturity and change.
- Establish an understanding of self, the world of work, decision making, implementing decisions, and adapting and advising.
- Provide meaningful community-based work experience.
- Involve the student's family in career development.
- Support student participation and involvement in career development.

Secondary students with emotional and behavioral disorders (E/BD) present especially difficult vocational transition challenges. Many drop out of high school and do not attend post-secondary educational programs. They experience great difficulty in obtaining, and especially in maintaining, gainful employment. In studying the situation, Carter and Wehby (2003) concluded that a significant discrepancy existed between what young adults with E/BD thought were important work behaviors and what their employment supervisers thought were important work behaviors. The young adults with E/BD rated their own job performance much higher than their supervisors. There clearly was a disconnect between work behavior expectations of supervisors and fulfillment of expectations by students.

The researchers concluded that transition vocational services must do a better job of identifying important work behaviors for different employment environments. Vocational programs must provide students with E/BD opportunities to develop those work behaviors and assist in their self-assessment strategies. They noted the difficulty of providing support services for young adults with E/BD in actual work environments due to the need to prevent social stigmatizing because many of their supervisors are likely not aware that the young adults have a disability.

Recognizing the need to help students identified as E/BD make more realistic connections to adult work life, Owens-Johnson and Johnson (1999) have reported on a successful school-to-work curriculum for middle and high school students. The program involves students planning and implementing a local employer survey through advance research and interviews with local employers regarding job qualifications, duties, and performance expectations. The project integrates many academic skills, including writing, reading, mathematics, word processing, oral communication, and social skills. The result is a project that connects students with E/BD and the real world of work and community by increasing their awareness of various local employment opportunities and improving their realistic self-impressions of employablility.

Sources of Help with Career and Vocational Needs

Vocational Rehabilitation   Some schools are less prepared than others to meet the career and vocational needs of students with disabilities. Consequently, they must look to outside agencies and providers of these unique services. Representatives of Vocational Rehabilitation Services are frequent participants on the IEP teams of secondary students. Vocational Rehabilitation is a federally funded program designed to help persons of all ages with disabilities reach their employment potential and goals. Each eligible student (or adult) works with a trained counselor to develop a plan designed to lead to appropriate vocational assessment, training and experience, and successful employment. Employment goals are individualized depending on abilities, needs, and preferences. Options available include working for wages, sheltered work, supported employment, and self-employment.

In order to be eligible, a person must have a physical, mental, or emotional disability that presents problems preparing for, obtaining, or keeping employment. Vocational Rehabilitation Services must be needed for a person to get and keep a job. Disability is defined similarly to that for Section 504: An ongoing condition that limits any major life activity, including walking, learning, working, or caring for oneself. A disability must be related to a diagnosis by a physician, psychoanalyst, or similar health professional.

Vocational Rehabilitation assesses the career interests and employment needs of individuals with disabilities, as well as trains and counsels people on employment and job placement. Vocational Rehabilitation also helps with supported employment services, such as providing special training, equipment, or a job coach, as well as independent living training services.

Inter-agency Cooperation   Many school special vocational education programs have agreements with multiple public agencies with overlapping responsibilities for vocational training. Typically, these involve money-saving arrangements in which specialists from various fields combine their expertise, resources, and facilities to meet the needs of a varied client population.

Secondary vocational education programs provide especially good examples of educational needs that have drawn together resources from the local school district, community colleges, state departments of vocational rehabilitation and developmental disabilities, charitable organizations, professional organizations, and private businesses. The authors have observed many examples of success in the effort to link schools with other agencies to provide services for children with disabilities. The greatest successes are found where the needs have been the greatest and the staff members have been determined to overcome obstacles. The following is a brief synthesis of several similar cooperative secondary transition programs observed by the authors that serve as an example of one area of successful inter-agency cooperation.

It is common for school districts to approach community colleges, which have long experience in vocational training, for help. However, community colleges and technical schools have little experience working with students who have a wide variety of skill deficits that require differentiated training and support services.

Given time, effort, planning, and flexibility, school districts, area community colleges, and vocational schools are able to work out the details of high quality programs. Thousands of young adults with disabilities have transitioned from school to varying degrees of gainful employment and independence in community living through such programs (Pearman, Elliott, & Aborn, 2004).

Community college staff members often attend transition planning IEP meetings to obtain an individualized picture of the students' strengths and needs. Staff members from state vocational rehabilitation programs may perform vocational assessments, and vocational rehabilitation funding is sometimes available. The high school staff works with the individual student

to develop basic skills and a knowledge base and with the parents to prepare them for their child's next step into the future.

In order to assure adequate funding, the student's enrollment in high school is often continued beyond the traditional age of graduation. This allows the school to continue receiving state aid revenues for support of the young adult's continued education. However, it also means the student cannot officially graduate and receive a regular diploma. Graduation would end the student's entitlement to special education programs under federal law and the laws of most states. Because an IEP documents the student's continued need to learn more vocational and life skills, it is not illegal or inappropriate to continue the student's enrollment in school past the traditional graduation age of 18 or 19. In fact, for some students with disabilities, it may be illegal to end their secondary school experience before they have met their IEP transition goals and have not yet reached 21 years of age.

Many families want their child to participate in graduation ceremonies at the traditional age of 17 or 18. Different arrangements can be worked out locally so the student can participate in the graduation ceremony but not actually graduate with a regular diploma until completion of the program.

Having not graduated from high school, in the official sense, the student may attend a community college transition program under the terms of her or his IEP. The local resident school district continues to receive state and sometimes federal funds to pay to the community college for the continued education program in the form of tuition. The student receives vocational education and readiness training as called for in the IEP. Many students who need life-skills education (e.g., social skills, hygiene, nutrition, personal purchases, self-determination) live in supervised dormitories or group homes with nearly continuous opportunities for education provided by trained staff.

Schools and community colleges in such programs have proved that together they can be more effective in providing needed community services than either can be individually.

Given unlimited resources, either could provide an excellent vocational transition program, but in the reality of limited resources, neither could do an adequate job alone. Pearman, Elliot, and Aborn (2004) have reported on the implementation of another transition services model in the Los Angeles area involving 12 local school districts and a local community college. The program served 1,500 students with disabilities, ages 18 to 22 years old. Students are exposed to post-secondary education, a variety of social and life skills, and social and recreation opportunities. The program supported students with academic advising, career counseling, liason with faculty, needed accommodations, self-determination skills, and life skills. The authors concluded that the transition services model can be adapted for use by other community colleges and school districts. This is but one example of inter-agency cooperation where the whole can be greater than the sum of its parts.

POST-HIGH SCHOOL EDUCATION PLANNING

A significant number of students with disabilities will attend college, community college, trade school, or some other form of specialized training school. This is a shift in emphasis of post-secondary opportunities for students. The change is often credited to the IDEA requirement that IEP teams give careful consideration to a high school student's program of studies, including college preparation as part of individualized transition programming. Also thought to be related to this shift is the increase in self-determination programs that help students develop their own self-advocacy skills and plans for the future. Self-advocacy experience can make a great difference between success and failure for students with disabilities transitioning to post-secondary education programs (Lock & Layton, 2001).

Mull, Sitlington, and Alper (2001) reviewed research articles published over a 15-year period that reported on postsecondary education services for students with specific learning dis-

abilities. They identified several implications for educators working with the transitioning of secondary students to postsecondary institutions. Their recommendations include

- preparation in areas of self-determination that help the student determine which accommodations and supports used at the secondary level will be appropriate for use at the postsecondary level, and the advocacy skills to acquire these accommodations and supports under Section 504 and the ADA;
- training in the use of assistive technology devices;
- training in the acquisition of various skills, supports, and accommodations necessary for the social recreation, leisure, and academic demands of postsecondary educational environments; and
- assistance in documentation of disability for Section 504 and ADA eligibility. This is important because many secondary schools have eliminated the use of disability labels.

For students with disabilities in high schools served under an IEP or a Section 504 accommodation plan, going to college or any post-secondary educational institution may present quite a shock. Where the IDEA requires schools to identify children with disabilities eligible for special education and related services (child find), Section 504 reverses the burden of identification of students with need. Students attending a post-secondary institution must self-identify and establish disability status and the need for accommodations (Sahlen & Lehmann, 2006). The fact that a student had an IEP or Section 504 accommodation plan in high school does not in themselves establish the right to accommodations in post-secondary institutions (Madaus, 2005).

Neither are post-secondary institutions required to provide evaluations and reevaluations of changing student needs, specially designed instruction, related services, or to provide students with placement assistance (Madaus & Shaw, 2004). An understanding of the differences by the high school student's IEP team, and a recognition that incorporating the knowledge of these differences and how the student can best respond, are important components in transition planning and developing self-determination and advocacy skills (Sahlen & Lehmann, 2006).

Although certain aspects and opinions expressed in educational literature suggest that schools should assist students transitioning to secondary education through creation of appropriate documentation of disability (Sahlen & Lehmann, 2006), it is not a requirement under the IDEA. OSEP has stated that evaluations and reevaluations conducted under the IDEA are not intended to be used by postsecondary institutions to determine eligibility status under Section 504 and the ADA. Nor are they intended to determine reasonable accommodations for students after completion of high school requirements (Letter to Moore, 2002).

The role and use of assistive technology by students in post-secondary educational settings is important. Mull and Sitlington (2003) have reviewed the literature on the use of technology by students with specific learning disabilities. They recommend that the student's secondary IEP team planning for the transition of the students to post-secondary education lay the ground work for the successful use of technology devices in the post-secondary setting. Mull and Sitlington specifically recommend that the IEP team

1. identify funding sources for the anticipated technology needs of the student in post-secondary education;
2. assess the student's anticipated needs in light of the demands of the particular post-secondary environment;
3. provide appropriate training in the proper use of the technology device before the student transitions to postsecondary education; and
4. carefully consider any proposed changes in special education status that might affect eligibility to receive reasonable accommodations at the postsecondary level.

The importance of technology skills in enhancing the academic and career success of post-secondary students with disabilities has been established. Kim-Rupnow and Bargstahler (2004) have reported on an exemplary program for college-bound high school students with dis-

abilities that provides a technology-enriched summer component, year-round computer and Internet activities, and work experiences involving the use of computers. The program incorporated integrated self-determination, advocacy, and social skills. Participants reported significant growth in their level of preparation for college and skills needed for employment.

Post-secondary foreign language requirements, both entrance and exit, present difficulty of a unique nature for many students with a specific learning disability (Madaus, 2003). Some learning disabilities significantly affect the ability to learn and retain skills in foreign languages. One of the authors of this book worked with a student attempting to attend a university without the required language prerequisite. The student excelled in foreign language courses that focused on the written language, but failed miserably in spoken and conversational language courses. A psychologist's assessment was obtained which stated that the student had a specific learning disability that resulted in his being "functionally deaf" when attempting to learn spoken foreign languages. The university identified alternative criteria for entrance that met its foreign language requirement and the young man was accepted to the university.

SEX EDUCATION

An important aspect of any young adult's health and physical care are those issues related to sex education. Children with disabilities experience the same biological changes and intensified sexual feelings as adolescents without disabilities. The result is that many teenagers with disabilities need access to sex education, and the issue has largely remained ignored. Despite the fact that many adolescents and young adults are sexually active, in most schools sex education remains controversial. The result is exposure of students with disabilities to greater risk of abuse, exploitation, and to sexually related health problems (Hingsburger & Tough, 2002; Lumley & Scotti, 2001).

A number of educators recognize the desirability of sex education for students with disabilities and believe that most curriculums dealing with sex can be modified to meet the needs of students with disabilities. Wolfe and Blanchett (2003) acknowledge the need for sex education for students with disabilities, but are concerned that existing curriculum must be a good match for both student and family needs. As a result, they developed a Sexuality Education Protocol (SEP) assessment to evaluate various sexuality education curricula in a systematic manner. After gathering the data required on the SEP, educators involved in program planning are able to answer the following questions:

1. Does the curriculum reflect the attitudes and values of the families of the students?
2. Does the curriculum match student's age and ability level?
3. Are goals and objectives on the IEP written in a manner that will facilitate learning?
4. Does the curriculum meet the needs of the student?
5. Does the curriculum allow for a variety of instructional methods?
6. Does the curriculum allow for individualized student adaptations?
7. Is the cost of the curriculum reasonable relative to its uses?

Hingsburger and Tough (2002) are strong advocates for people with disabilities developing healthy and safe sex lives in the context of relationships. Their main concerns are for those adolescents with disabilities in the care of families or service systems that forbid any recognition of sexual expression. Instead, well-meaning persons often attempt to instill fear in the adolescents in the hope that sex will never become an issue. Hingsburger and Tough recommend the establishment of a safe and wholesome sexual environment where individuals with severe disabilities can become whole persons. They recommend such environments have four essential components:

1. A clear policy related to the expression of sexuality and appropriate parent or staff responses. The policy should include what is allowed as well as what is forbidden. Young adults with disabilities sometimes need protection from their "protectors."

2. Parents and staff participate in sexuality awareness seminars. They need to recognize that sexuality is a part of who we are as human beings. There are realistic concerns with sexual activity and they must be addressed openly.
3. Young adults with disabilities should be encouraged to be self-advocates. In the absence of the person's voice, parents and staff can fall back on well-meaning but inadvisable protectionist approaches.
4. Young adults should receive training in relationship building and appropriate expression of sexuality. Deliberate efforts to instill fear of sexual encounters through misinformation must be stopped.

Lumley and Scotti (2001) raise issues similar to those raised by Hingsburger and Tough and support many of their solutions. Lumley and Scotti, however, have focused on a long-term approach through a person-centered planning process similar to IEP development. It involves a thorough individualized assessment of sexuality orientation status, identifying areas of concern, and team development and implemention of a planned approach.

Studies have reported that significantly less than half of the students with disabilities have received sex education. This may in part owe to the fact that less than half of the people in special education teacher programs have had preservice preparation for teaching sex education.

In replicating a 1980 study, May and Kundert (1996) found that little change had occurred in sex education training in the preparation of special education teachers. Only about 40% of the special education teacher preparation programs they studied offered any sex education course work, and the amount of time spent in courses on sex education had actually decreased since the initial study in 1980. In some cases, only a few minutes in preservice special education teacher programs were spent on sex education coverage.

IEP teams need to recognize that some parents may look unfavorably on sex education programs because of family beliefs or unspoken fears related to risks of adult sexuality (e.g., pregnancy, disease). Even though this topic is controversial, teams should give greater consideration to this issue, and for some students it should be considered as a transition planning requirement.

DRIVER EDUCATION

Although much of the focus of transition planning is directed at increasing mobility, independence, access to employment, and leisure and social activities, the importance of driver education in helping many students reach their potential is often overlooked. Many students may not be good prospects for driver education due to the type or severity of disability they experience. Others with mild to moderate physical disabilities make good candidates for driver education with the appropriate adaptive equipment and properly trained instructors. McGill and Vogtle (2001) conducted a study of high school students with physical disabilities in Alabama. They found that the students held strong feelings about the importance of driving in their lives. They believed that learning to drive would provide them with more freedom, independence, and greater self-esteem. Yet, most of the students were denied access to both driver training and classroom preparation for driving. The few students who did take driver training were delayed while the schools made adjustments in the form of materials and adaptive equipment, finding willing instructors, or referral to outside providers.

The researchers concluded that due to the great importance of learning to drive in the transition to adult life, and the anti-discrimination provision of Section 504 and the ADA, educators and parents need to be proactive in IEP planning. They need to assure that students with physical disabilities receive predriving assessments, and when individually appropriate, driver education while in high school.

DROP-OUT REDUCTION

The primary reason the law expressly allows for transition planning and services in an IEP earlier than age 16 is the recognized need to increase schools' commitment to potential drop-outs. An Arizona study conducted by Malian and Love (1998) found that students with disabilities who complete high school special education programs were more likely to have favorable post-high school outcomes in terms of maintaining gainful employment, fewer criminal arrests, and fewer drug-related problems than those who dropped out. The researchers also determined that a greater percentage of young people with disabilities who completed high school had spent large amounts of time included in the regular classroom. As a result, they recommended that greater attention be given to regular class support, adaptations, and accommodations for those students with disabilities identified as potential drop-outs.

During the 2002–2003 school year, nearly 82,000 students with disabilities between the ages of 14 and 21 years dropped out of school in America (N.C.E.S., 2004). The problem is one of obvious concern. Yet, research indicates that schools can, and do, make a difference in reducing the dropout rate among students with disabilities.

Dunn, Chambers, and Rabren (2004) conducted a study of 228 students with specific learning disabilities (SLD) or mental disabilities (MD) who had dropped out of school and 228 students with SLD or MD who had not dropped out of school. They found several factors in student drop-out rates over which schools can exercise or influence in promoting students' staying in school. Students who perceived that their high school experience had meaning in preparing their future lives as adults, who could identify at least one helpful class, and who developed positive helpful relationships with at least one school staff member were more likely to remain in school.

The researchers recommended that teachers assess student interests and perceptions and highlight the portions of the curriculum that address students' vision of life as an adult. They further recommended that teachers gain a recognition and understanding that positive and respectful relationships contribute to a sense of attachment with school that are related to success and school retention. Students with disabilities who recognize the advantages of staying in school and improving prospects of future employment, have access to classes considered by them as helpful preparation for the future, and who develop relationships at school with caring persons are not as likely to end their education precipitously.

As a result of a study of nearly 300 school drop-outs, both with and without disabilities, Scanlon and Mellard (2002) determined that many school policies and practices designed to prevent drop-outs actually result in increased drop-out rates. Education leaders need to regularly review drop-out data and school practices and policies related to student drop-out rates. Data should be maintained to determine whether school practices impact races, ethnic groups, and gender differently. Policies on regular attendance especially need a collective review and response from educators, mentors, and peer support programs for students. Supportive programs need to be established to encourage students' continued school attendance. Scanlon and Mellard also recommend that school transition practices be reviewed and strengthened. For those students on the verge of dropping out, a concerted effort needs to be made to connect the students with other community resources, such as vocational rehabilitation, community colleges, and support groups and to strengthen student self-advocacy skills.

THE QUESTION OF DIPLOMAS, GRADES, HONOR ROLLS, AND TRANSCRIPTS

Diplomas

The inclusion of students with disabilities into the traditional secondary school environment raises some difficult policy issues. Should a student who completes the IEP, but not the required Carnegie Units, be included in graduation ceremonies with classmates? Should a diploma be awarded? Should the diploma be the same as that earned by other students or should it take the form of a special certificate instead? How does the nondiscriminatory requirement of Section 504 of the Rehabilitation Act apply? What about the current push for competency tests for graduating seniors and for so-called excellence in education? Underlying all of these issues is the expectation of students and parents. One survey of parents found that 82% of parents of children with disabilities in high school expected their child to receive a standard diploma (Johnson & Duffett, 2002).

Advocates of competency testing and excellence would add more academic courses to those already required for graduation, thereby making it more difficult for even regular vocational students to complete both school diploma requirements and important vocational training. The demand for pregraduation competency testing would also jeopardize the ability of students with disabilities to earn regular diplomas (Benz, Lindstrom, & Yovanoff, 2000). The problem is controversial. On one side is the popular complaint that a high school diploma does not mean anything anymore. If students cannot meet reasonable levels of competency in reading, mathematics, and other basic skills and general knowledge, they should not receive a standard diploma. Perhaps a certificate of attendance or some other alternative would be appropriate. Others argue that exceptional students should not be penalized or stigmatized by receiving an alternative diploma or certificate. Some suggest that this would, in fact, be an illegal denial of equal benefits under the law.

The issues are complex and solutions vary from state to state and locality to locality. School leaders must understand the nature of the dispute and the range of alternatives that are in place around the country. Some states recommend awarding a standard diploma for completion of the IEP; others issue certificates of attendance instead. Some states administer competency tests but have special guidelines or accommodations for students with disabilities; others simply stress the responsibility of outsiders reviewing a student's transcripts to determine what the diploma really means. In some states, the policies apply statewide; other states allow local district discretion. Although several statutes seem to apply, federal law does not explicitly address exit policy for high school students. Many of the issues of testing, graduation, and diplomas for students with disabilities are in the process of interpretation through litigation (O'Neill, 2001).

The Office of Civil Rights (OCR) has issued a ruling interpreting the application of Section 504 and the ADA to graduation and diploma issues (Letter to Runkel, 1996). Under the ruling, Section 504 and the ADA do not require parent procedural safeguards be provided for graduation, even though the IDEA does. Students with disabilities may participate in the school's graduation ceremony if a student wishes to do so. When a separate graduation is preferred, comparable facilities must be used.

The OCR ruling also stated that special education students are entitled to a diploma when they complete a school's criteria for graduation. Objective criteria must be used for differing diplomas, and all students must have an opportunity to complete the requirements for and be awarded any diploma on a nondiscriminatory basis. Diplomas should be similar in all significant aspects. Variations in wording should not be based on disability as a category of students. Diplomas may refer to individual transcripts for exact courses completed. Schools, through the IEP team, may modify or adjust local graduation requirements in order to be consistent with the student's IEP (Lanford & Cary, 2000).

In some instances where the IEP planning has not addressed the issue, a student may complete a school's minimum graduation requirements, but may not have completed all of the goals in the IEP. The student's potential eligibility for FAPE does not end until the student has graduated or reached age 21.

Upon graduation with a regular diploma or exceeding the age of eligibility for FAPE, the local school must provide the student with a summary of the student's academic achievement and functional performance. The summary must include recommendations on how to assist the student in meeting the student's postsecondary goals [20 U.S.C. § 414(c)(5)].

Grades

Grades may not be modified or determined based on the student's disability status or status as a student eligible for special education services. Alternate grading systems are appropriate only when they are also used for students without disabilities. It is desirable to discuss alternative grading systems in the IEP, especially with respect to classes taken in the regular education setting. As a general rule, students in inclusive settings with reasonable accommodations and modifications should not receive altered grades owing merely to altered teaching or testing methods (Salend, 2005). Accommodations and modifications are usually changes only in the way things are done and are not changes in a school's expectations or standards for a course.

Whenever a course's content standards or expectations are substantially changed for an individual student, however, the student may be awarded an alternate grade for that course. Changes from the norm in curricular expectations for a student and the alternative grading should be included in the student's IEP. When a student is placed in a regular education course for other than content purposes (e.g., social skills), the IEP should outline the planned criteria for grading. In many situations, it may be appropriate for the regular and special education teachers to collaborate on grades. In some situations, it may be desirable to use a pass/fail grading system. However, to eliminate justified claims of discrimination, participation should be voluntary and available to all students.

Education leaders and teachers must be conscious of the relative purpose of a grade; whether it is to relay the quality of the work, readiness for future learning, level of mastery, or progress and effort. Whatever the grading system used, it should be communicated to students, family, and staff, and opportunities for understanding and implementation training sessions should be provided (Salend & Duhaney, 2002).

Munk and Bursuck (2001b) have determined in a study that parents of students both with and without disabilities did not believe that report card grades were very effective in meeting ten specific acknowledged purposes. Participants in the study generally had negative reactions to the grading practices of schools and many suggested greater individualization was desirable in the grading system and report card grades.

Both groups of parents responded that report card grades are important for the purpose of communication of general achievement, effort and work habits, strengths and needs, and feedback on how to improve. However, they responded that grades are only somewhat effective at meeting those purposes. This is a little disturbing because report card grades typically become transcript grades depended upon for making decisions important to a student's future.

Munk and Bursuck (2001a) have reported on the success of a personalized grading plan (PGP) model for determining report card grades for middle-school students with learning disabilities included in regular classrooms. The PGPs are developed by students, parents, and regular and special education teachers in five stages:

Stage 1   Participants identified, by ranking a list of ten purposes of grading, what purpose they believed grades should meet.

Stage 2   Participants reviewed their school's grading policy, compared it to their preferred purpose, and reviewed a menu of potential grading adaptations.

Stage 3   Participants met to review their perceived purposes for a grade for report cards and identified one or more mutually agreed upon purposes to be used in determining specific adaptations for individual students.

Stage 4   The group collaborated to implement the PGP.

Stage 5   Assessment of students', parents', and teachers' satisfaction with the accuracy of the PGP took place.

The researchers reported that teachers and parents were generally pleased with the outcomes of the PGP process. The students reported that they tried harder and were more satisfied with their grades (even though all did not receive a higher grade). There was enhanced collaboration between regular and special education. The researchers warned that while the PGP process enhanced satisfaction regarding individualized adaptations for particular students, no specific type of grading adaptation was proven more effective than others.

Honor Rolls

Honor rolls and grade point averages used for scholarships and class ranking present a special problem. Grades received in regular education classes by students with disabilities, with support from special education services, should never be arbitrarily discounted or excluded. Schools should never arbitrarily assign lower weights or values to all special education classes. Such systems would prevent special education students from ever being recognized for their accomplishments. However, an objective weighting system may be established that assesses actual differences in content or difficulty compared with regular education courses. A list of core courses open to all students may be designated as the only courses eligible for honors consideration.

Transcripts

Student transcripts should be careful to not designate courses as *special education* or *resource room.* By doing so they identify the student as having a disability. Permissible labeling might include *"modified curriculum," "basic level,"* or *"practical,"* so long as such terms are also used with courses for students without disabilities, such as those in remedial and at-risk programs.

Identification symbols should not be used to identify courses taken only by students with disabilities. Asterisks or other symbols on transcripts may be used to designate modified curricula only so long as they are also used for modified curriculum for students without disabilities, such as for accelerated course work or remedial course work. Special symbols or asterisks should never be used to identify completion of course work where only accommodations and modifications were provided. Students and parents should be notified regarding transcript content before it is released to third persons.

NONACADEMIC CONSIDERATIONS

Socialization

Secondary students have a variety of educational needs, not all of which are strictly vocational or academic. School personnel should be sensitive to students' social needs, an area that has implications for classroom management as well as student growth.

All adolescents are affected by a strong student culture and a need to experience acceptance by their peers. Students with disabilities may be especially vulnerable to peer pressures that result in negative or socially unacceptable behaviors. When making placement decisions, it is important that school personnel safeguard against negative influences by assigning students to classes where they will encounter positive, not detrimental, role models. The conscious development of social skills and self-esteem contribute to positive in-school behaviors and preparation for adult life. Many excellent social and interpersonal curricula for students with exceptionalities are now available.

Within secondary school settings there are programs that have social benefits for typical students and students with disabilities, such as popular service-learning programs (Frey, 2003; Kleinert, et al., 2004). Service learning is a program, voluntary or required, where students are provided an opportunity to take part in group community service projects (e.g., working with the elderly, environmental projects) in an effort to make the students more aware of their community and themselves. One report of a service learning project involving a diverse group of students concluded that the students with special needs learned a great deal about themselves and greatly increased their self-esteem through working with and helping younger children and the elderly in the community (Yoder, Retish, & Wade, 1996).

Frey (2003) has reported on a successful service-learning project for students with emotional and behavior disorders. The well-planned and implemented grounds beautification project at a senior citizens' apartment complex increased student positive opinions about school, self-concept, and working with others. Student attendance and behaviors at school improved, which in turn resulted in an improved learning environment. Similar findings of student growth were observed by Abernathy and Obenchian (2001) in a service-learning project that actively engaged students with mild and moderate specific learning disabilities in a community improvement project. They found that student ownership of and dedication to the project were related to the degree of planning and decision making experienced by the students. They also noted the importance of a reciprocal community relationship that allowed community members to have the opportunity to observe and work with meaningfully engaged students with disabilities. School principals can promote such programs through facilitation, support, and even participation.

Copeland et al. (2004) have reported on a service-learning peer support program for high school students without disabilities. The Peer Buddy Program was designed to have high school peers provide social and academic support for students with moderate and severe disabilities. The study focused on the perspectives of students without disabilities who had extensive interactions with students with severe disabilities in six high schools. The students reported that generally unsupportive academic and social environments were greatly improved in the high schools involved in the program. Inherent barriers to high school inclusion, such as differing teacher expectations, lack of accommodations and supports, and the physical and social isolation of special education students in regular education classes, were largely mitigated by the nondisabled students providing their peer buddies with support, communication, and help with class work. The training and support received by the students who were not disabled were found to result in better skills and attitudes on their part and a greater willingness to interact with peers with disabilities. As a result of the isolation breakdown, students without disabilities not directly involved with the program took advantage of the provided opportunities interacted with students with disabilities.

Extracurricular Activities

Students' participation in extracurricular activities may help promote social development and self-esteem. This often does not occur without conscious effort from the school staff, including the principal. Students with exceptionalities are sometimes excluded formally or informally from clubs, organizations, and athletics through stereotyped negative attitudes, lack of recruitment efforts, lack of needed support, low social status, and lack of a role to play that matches their abilities and needs. Consequently, these students are deprived of important opportunities to develop self-confidence, mix socially with their peers, and gain a sense of ownership and belonging to the school. This sense of belonging, in turn, is instrumental in improving students' attitudes toward school and in reducing the likelihood of their dropping out.

In a large 3-year study of high school transitioning in Arizona, Malian and Love (1998) observed that extracurricular activities ranked high on both student and parent indicators of quality of life. They also learned that 70% of special education students who dropped out of high school before graduation had not been involved in extracurricular activities. Strategies suggested by Malian and Love for increasing exceptional students' participation in extracurricular activities include

- actively recruiting the students (this can be done by teachers, special educators, club advisers, or other students)
- identifying or designing roles in the club or activity that the students can fulfill
- considering setting up a buddy system with a respected peer or group involved in that club or activity

- providing positive role models (faculty advisers should demonstrate acceptance of the exceptional students and respect for their contributions)

In recognition of the importance of nonacademic activities in a child's life, the law now requires that student IEPs contain a statement of supplementary aids and services to be provided, and supports for school personnel, so the child may participate in extracurricular and nonacademic activities with other children. When a student with disabilities wants to, but cannot, participate with nondisabled children in activities, the IEP must provide a statement of justification.

Eligibility for Activities

Academic eligibility for school activities, including athletics, presents issues of fairness and potential discrimination. When a student's low grades may be the result of a disability, the school should make a conscious determination of whether a relationship exists. When a relationship does exist, and other reasons (e.g., lack of motivation) cannot be established, the academic eligibility criteria may need to be waived or based on other criteria, such as progress on the IEP. IEP teams of struggling students should also revisit the accommodations, modifications, and support services being provided for the student and the student's teachers in order to determine whether the school is appropriately meeting the student's academic needs.

Competitive Athletics

Some students with special needs have the potential to become good athletes but are prevented from participation in varsity sports for a number of reasons:

- The attitude that winning is the only goal often prohibits consideration of athletes with special needs. Some coaches and some schools are more open to the importance of other values, such as teaching cooperation and teamwork, developing self-confidence, and rewarding excellence of effort.

- The lack of time can pose problems. Although clearly talented, students with exceptionalities may require much more individual coaching and supervised practice to achieve their athletic potential.
- Some states have health and safety requirements that legally prevent participation by students with some disabilities. This should be researched in every case.

Some possible strategies and solutions for the school to increase participation of athletes include

- encouraging students to try out and coaches to be open-minded;
- setting up extra coaching assistance provided by aides, adult volunteers, or other students;
- making minor adaptations as needed; for example, a student with visual impairment can compete in varsity wrestling if competitors are required to be in physical contact at the beginning of the match.

One of the authors attended a high school homecoming football celebration where returning athletic letter winners were introduced during the half-time ceremony. The crowd gave a standing ovation to a returning alumni football letter winner with Down's syndrome. Compare that to another author's observed situation where a highly talented athlete was denied an opportunity to play varsity football because of a coaching staff's concern that "he might do something to embarrass the team." Given these two scenarios, it is not difficult to choose which one most contemporary school leaders would like to foster among staff.

Educators should be aware that alternative sports opportunities exist outside the school for students with disabilities. Those with cognitive disabilities can participate in Special Olympics, which is relatively noncompetitive and emphasizes self-concept. For those with physical and sensory disabilities, other organizations provide competitive athletics such as wheelchair sports and athletics for the visually impaired, including skiing. Students may be encouraged to participate in community leagues and recreational

teams. However, these alternatives alone should not be considered sufficient for students who, with a little assistance, really are capable of participating in varsity activities.

IMPORTANCE OF INCLUSION IN PLACEMENT

Inclusion does not mean that teenagers with mild disabilities should be dumped into regular secondary classrooms without special assistance for the students or their teachers. Neither does it mean that they should be directed automatically through a standard or remedial curriculum that is not attentive to their individual needs. When educators and parents merely place a student with disabilities in regular education settings with no consideration of actively involving the student in the curriculum or the activity, the outcome can be detrimental to the student, teacher, and classmates. IEP teams must have expectations of progress for the student, and they must provide appropriate supports to achieve progress.

Successful inclusion for secondary students is essential for several reasons:

- Continued association with nondisabled peers in a variety of environments provides needed role models and socialization experiences and helps prepare students to function in the world as adults.
- Placement in segregated settings, after successful integration experiences in elementary schools, may be traumatic and harmful to students' self-esteem.
- Students without disabilities learn that people with disabilities have many of the same fears, interests, and hopes about the future that they experience, and both are better prepared for integrated life situations as adults, including in the workplace.
- Education in the least restrictive environment appropriate is required by law.

In a study of four high schools in different states that were identified as successful in including students with disabilities in regular education classes, researchers at the University of Minnesota identified several favorable results of secondary inclusive programs (Wallace, Anderson, Bartholomay, & Hupp, 2002). They determined that all students, both those with disabilities and those without, exhibited high levels of engagement in academics and low levels of inappropriate behavior in inclusive settings. There were no significant differences found in a comparison of the behavior of students with and without disabilities. Teachers were found to be actively engaged in instruction and interaction with students 75% of the time. The researchers noted that the high schools involved in their study were successfully engaging all students in learning activities and not merely placing students with disabilities in regular classrooms in compliance with legal mandates.

Secondary Inclusion Considerations

Successful integration of exceptional students at the secondary school level can be enhanced in several ways. One is to assign responsibility for each student to one staff member, much as each college student has a faculty adviser. Students with disabilities need a personal relationship with a trusted adult who will be available to support and encourage them when needed. Research has established that such relationships are related to successful completion of high school (Benz, Lindstrom, & Yovanoff, 2000). Professionals such as therapists, consultants, special educators, and willing regular class teachers can be assigned a limited number of special needs students for whom they will serve as advocates, advisers, and coordinators of overall educational plans.

School principals must accept responsibility for seeing that staff members are regularly and fully informed. No matter how the responsibilities are divided, it is always essential in secondary school settings to keep lines of communication open among the various professionals involved. For example, if a resource room model is being used, the resource teacher might send a weekly or biweekly note to each instructor asking how a student is progress-

ing and whether any particular assistance is needed. Technology, such as use of e-mail and list-serv, may ease the burdens of regular communication. Regular communication will help build beneficial relationships of trust and cooperation.

Behavior is often a priority issue for teachers of secondary students. Discipline and a good educational environment are not the sole domain of special education. All staff, including support staff, have a role to play in maintaining a school climate of safety, support, acceptance, and cooperation. It is the educational leader's responsibility—through facilitation of training and services, keeping communication channels open, and role modeling—to develop and maintain a proper climate of school discipline. Chapter 9 offers a variety of suggestions to promote positive behavior within the complex restrictions of special education law.

A Secondary Inclusion Reform Model

A flexible, but complex, collaborative secondary school instructional model is recommended by Gable et al. (1997) and involves the use of teams of staff to support regular education teachers. A secondary student instructional support team (ASSIST) is made up of two or more supportive teachers of various subject content areas along with specialists, special education teachers, and service providers. This mixture of staffing for collaboration affords a mix of direct and indirect and large and small group instruction. A wide range of class arrangements can be devised depending on student needs. Although the focus is on a regular individualized supervised curriculum, student instructional needs can be met through one-on-one, small group, parallel teaching, and large group activities. Thus, this arrangement is sometimes called a class-within-a-class. The team can address wide range of student needs and issues (e.g., failing grades, absences, lack of assignment completion).

ASSIST members work in a variety of configurations, share their knowledge of students, methodologies, and content, and plan accordingly. Having several different adults moving in and out of student activities aids in sharing each other's strengths through student praise and student motivation and lessens the impact of individual staff weaknesses. Teachers who observe and interact with their peers also grow in their own teaching skills, to the benefit of all students. New instructional arrangements such as ASSIST represent a paradigm shift for which many secondary teachers are ill-prepared. It takes a wise and energetic educational leader to plant the seeds, create the climate, and support the growth of such innovations.

THE PRINCIPAL'S ROLE

Education leaders at the secondary level, like those in the elementary level, should model acceptance and understanding of individual student differences. They should also support flexibility and individualization of schedules and programs, promote cooperation and communication among all segments of the school staff, and support all staff with information and professional development opportunities as needed.

A study conducted by Jung (1998) involving 12 high schools with successful inclusion programs found several consistent themes. She concluded that knowledge and understanding educational leaders are crucial to successful secondary inclusive programs. Each school in the study had a principal who was committed to the concept of inclusion, helped establish a positive school climate through decision making and practices, helped locate resources, and rewarded participating staff through praise and evaluations. As with any educational reform, the path to inclusive programs is a lengthy process and teachers must be properly supported and rewarded for their courage, persistence, and optimism. Most programs in the study involved co-teaching between one regular education and one special education teacher, and most experienced a continuous struggle with coordination and collaboration (e.g., lack of adequate planning time) and classroom man-

agement issues. Owing to the stresses of the new teaching style for all teachers, participants were usually limited to volunteers, actual course content was not greatly altered, and teachers focused on using multiple teaching styles. More class time was used to teach study skills and more accommodations were provided students.

Cole and McLesky (1997) drew similar conclusions regarding the importance of voluntary teacher participation and administrative support in secondary co-teaching efforts. Teachers have a legitimate need to know that the necessary administrative support will be available. This includes creating time for communication, collaboration, and planning, the facilitation of meaningful professional development programs, and emotional support for the tough times. Chapter 10 contains more detailed information on co-teaching and other collaborative teaching methodologies.

CONCLUSION

The concept of educational leadership, as opposed to mere management, finds a significant challenge in the secondary school setting. It is there that ingrained traditions and values are the most difficult to alter, and some people may speculate whether a feather or a sledgehammer will achieve the most successful results. Whichever it is, climate improvement is a necessity in many secondary schools. Too many students, both with and without disabilities, are harmed by content-driven curriculum, prevailing lecture methodology, and apprehension of anything smacking of change. Calls for secondary school reform are becoming a call to action for change in the interest of all students. Educational leaders play the key role in the continued and progressive evolution of secondary schools, including special education.

The reasonability for transitioning secondary school students into their lives as young adults in the community is foreign to many schools. Students vary greatly in their successes and failures in making the transition to adult life after high school. The law requires only that students with disabilities have a transition period with assessment of individual needs, and a transition program planned and implemented prior to graduation. That perspective of transitioning may be beneficial to a great number of students, including many without disabilities.

The law and good education require that students with disabilities be educated with students without disabilities to the maximum extent appropriate. An inability to do this successfully at the secondary level would tell us a great deal about our current education system and its leadership. Challenges help us all to grow. The challenges of legally mandated special education and the necessary accompanying inclusion teamwork and collaboration provide us all with the opportunity to grow together.

VIEW FROM THE COURTS

Susquehanna Township School District v. Frances J. (2003) (failure of school to carry out a transition plan). An IEP stated that the student would be provided, as a transition service, one year's education at a college preparatory school. This was for the purpose of developing confidence and assuredness in the boy. The next year, the IEP was amended so that learning support, in place of attendance at the college prep school, would be provided the boy as a transitional service. The change in transitional services was made without parent involvement, consultation, or consent. The court ruled that the school did not provide the planned transition services in the form of a college preparation program for one year as provided in the IEP transition plan and ordered the school to do so.

East Penn School District v. Scott B. (1999) (a transition plan must consider much more than vocational issues). The parents of a 20-year-old student with multiple disabilities challenged the adequacy of the school's transition assessment, plan, and services for their son. The hearing officer ruled in favor of the school and the parents

appealed the decision to a State Appeals Panel. The Appeals Panel upheld portions of the school's position, but found that the school's transition planning in the IEP process had been inappropriate for a period of 3 school years. The Panel ordered the school to provide 3 years of compensatory education in the form of transition services to the soon to be 21-year-old.

The school appealed the Panel decision into the federal district court challenging its ruling on transition. The court agreed with the Appeal Panel and ruled that 3 years of compensatory transition services was the appropriate remedy for the situation. The court found that the school had evaluated the boy for vocational education needs and provided vocational training, but igorned the full panoply of services that transition envisions. Specifically, the school IEP was found deficient in failing to identify any transition goals for the boy after he leaves school, and thus, was not really a transition plan for the future; for not covering the multi-year period prior to graduation; and in failing to address the boy's individual and unique needs by placing him in generic transition programs. The transition plan had not addressed community mobility issues or community recreation opportunities he could use. The court noted that although the school had completed and provided a vocational plan and training, a vocational plan was not the same thing as a transition plan, which is much broader and more inclusive. The court upheld the Appeals Panel award of 3 years compensory transition planning and services.

RECOMMENDED READINGS

Abernathy, T. V., & Obenchain, K. M. (2001). Student ownership of service-learning projects: Including ourselves in our community. *Intervention in School and Clinic, 37*(2), 86–95. This article provides detailed information about a successful service-learning project designed so that students have a sense of ownership in the project.

Babbitt, B. C., & White, C. M. (2002). "R U READY ?" Helping students assess their readiness for postsecondary education. *Teaching Exceptional Children, 35*(2), 62–66. The article provides specific recommendations and forms for assessing the postsecondary educational readiness of students with disabilities.

Conderman, G., Ikan, P. A., & Hatcher, R. E. (2000). Student-led conferences in inclusive settings. *Intervention in School and Clinic, 36*(1), 22–25. The article provides specific strategies for the meaningful implementation of student–led IEP meetings.

Copeland, S. R., McCall, J., Williams, C. R., Guth, C., Carter, E. W., Fowler, S. E., Presley, J. A., & Hughes, C. (2002). High school peer buddies: A win-win situation. *Teaching Exceptional Children, 35*(1), 16–21. The article describes a secondary school planned program of pairing students with disabilities and students without disabilities to provide peer support for secondary students with disabilities.

Frey, L. M. (2003). Abundant beautification: An effective service-learning project for students with emotional or behavioral disorders. *Teaching Exceptional Children, 35*(5), 66–75. This article explains in detail the planning and implementation of a highly successful service-learning project.

Kleinert, H., McGregor, V., Durbin, M., Blandford, T., Jones, K., Owens, J., & Miracle, S. (2004). Service-learning opportunities that include students with moderate and severe disabilities. *Teaching Exceptional Children, 37*(2), 28–34. This article provides an 11-step planning strategy for developing a service-learning program and several examples of successful community programs.

Lock, R. H. & Layton, C. A. (2001). Succeeding in postsecondary ed through self-advocacy. *Teaching Exceptional Children, 34*(2), 66–71. The article contains detailed suggestions on preparing students for self-advocacy in the post-secondary educational setting.

Madaus, J. W. (2005). Navigating the college transition maze: A guide for students with disabilities. *Teaching Exceptional Children, 37*(3), 32–37. This article compares secondary school and post-secondary school programs' educational support for students with disabilities.

Mason, C. Y., McGahee-Kovac, M., & Johnson, L. (2004). How to help students lead IEP meetings. *Teaching Exceptional Children, 36*(3), 18–25. This article provides excellent detailed advice on how to help students with disabilities lead their IEP meetings.

Munk, D. D., & Bursuck, W. D. (2003). Grading students with disabilities. *Educational Leadership, 61*(2), 38–43. This article by leading experts discusses fair and meaningful grading adaptations.

Myers, A., & Eisenman, L. (2005). Student-led IEPs: Take the first step. *Teaching Exceptional Children, 37*(4), 52–58. This article provides suggestions regarding the implementation of student-led IEP programs.

Pearman, E., Elliott, T., & Aborn, L. (2004). Transition services model: Partnership for student success. *Education and Training in Developmental Disabilities, 39*(1), 26–34. This excellent article describes a cooperative arrangement between schools and a community college in the provision of transition services.

Prater, M. A. (2003). She will succeed! Strategies for success in inclusive classrooms. *Teaching Exceptional Children, 35*(5), 58–64. The article presents a 14-step process for teachers to assess their classrooms' readiness for perspective inclusion students.

Saland, S. J. (2005). Report card models that support communication and differentiation of instruction. *Teaching Exceptional Children, 37*(4), 28–34. This excellent article provides a detailed discussion of grading alternatives for students with disabilities.

Test, D. W., Browder, D. M., Karvonen, M., Wood, W., & Algozzine, B. (2002). Writing lesson plans for promoting self-determination. *Teaching Exceptional Children, 35*(1), 8–14. This article provides sample lesson plans and resources for promoting student self-determination.

Torgerson, C. W., Miner, C. A., & Shen, H. (2004). Developing student competence in self-directed IEPs. *Intervention in School and Clinic, 39*(3), 162–167. The article provides excellent information regarding the contents of a good self-determination curriculum.

Wolfe, P. S., & Blanchett, W. J. (2003). Sex education for students with disabilities. *Teaching Exceptional Children, 36*(1), 46–51. This article provides assessment information and tools for selecting an effective sex education curriculum for students with disabilities.

Wood, W. M., Karvonen, M., Test, D. W., Browder, D., & Algozzine, B. (2004). Promoting student self-determination skills in IEP planning. *Teaching Exceptional Children, 36* (3), 8–16. This article explains how student planning participation results in greater transition results.

Relevant Federal Regulations

34 C.R.F. Part 300 Assistance to States for the Education of Children With Disabilities (70 Fed. Reg. 35,833-35,880 [June 21, 2005]).

34 C.F.R. 300.35	Secondary school.
.42	Transition services.
.102	Limitation-exceptions to FAPE for certain ages.
.107	Nonacademic services.
.117	Nonacademic settings.
.170	Suspension and expulsion rates.
.320	Definition of Individualized Education Program.
.321	IEP team.
.324(c)	Development, review, and revision of IEP.
.520	Transfer of parental rights at age of majority.

SELECTED WEBSITES

Code of Federal Regulations–Government Printing Office
http://www.gpoaccess.gov/cfr/index.html

Western Regional Resource Center
http://www.internetwork.org.wrrc

Individuals With Disabilities Act Data
http://www.ideadata.org

U.S. Department of Education
http://www.ed.gov

Project Personal Grading Plan
http://www.cedu.niu.edu/projectpgp

Self-Determination Lesson Plans
http://www.uncc.edu/sdsp

National Dissemination Center for Children with Disabilities (NICHCY)
http://www.nichcy.org

"A student's guide to the IEP" (2nd ed.)
http://www.nichcy.org/pubs/stuguide/stlbook.htm

"Helping students develop their IEPs" (2nd ed.)
http://www.nichcy.org/pubs/stuguide/ta2book.htm

National Service-Learning Clearinghouse
http://www.servicelearning.org

Learn and Serve America
http://www.learnandserve.org

Learning In Deed
http://www.learningindeed.org

Public Agenda (survey research)
http://www.publicagenda.org

Self-Determination Synthesis Project: Lesson Plans for Promoting Self-Determination
http://www.uncc.edu/sdsp/sd_curricula.asp

Heath Resource Center–George Washington University–National Resource Center on Post-Secondary Education for Individuals With Disabilities
http://www.heath.gwu.edu

Students in Service to America–Service Learning
http://www.studentsinservicetoamerica.org

QUESTIONS FOR THOUGHT

1. Should transition planning for students with disabilities be available to all secondary students regardless of disability?
2. A number of decades ago, American education replaced specialized high schools (i.e., technical, vocational) with the comprehensive high school; one to meet the educational needs of all students. Who do the current comprehensive high schools serve?
3. What impact will high school reform efforts aimed at increasing rigor in academic course work have on high school students with disabilities?

REFERENCES

Abernathy, T. V., & Obenchain, K. M. (2001). Student ownership of service-learning projects: Including ourselves in our community. *Intervention in School and Clinic, 37*(2), 86–95.

Asselin, S. B., Todd-Allen, M., & deFur, S. (1998). Transition coordinators. *Teaching Exceptional Children, 30*(3), 11–15.

Beekman, L. (2005). Avoiding litigation under the new IDEA. LRP Publications Audio Conference, April 20, 2005.

Benz, M. R., Lindstrom, L., & Yovanoff, P. (2000). Improving graduation and employment outcomes of students with disabilities: Predictive factors and student perspectives. *Exceptional Children, 66,* 509–529.

Benz, M. R., Yovanoff, P., & Doren, B. (1997). School-to-work components that predict post-school success for students with and without disabilities. *Exceptional Children, 63,* 151–165.

Blackorby, J., & Wagner, M. (1996). Longitudinal post school outcomes of youth with disabilities: Findings from the National Longitudinal Transition Study. *Exceptional Children, 62*(5), 399–413.

Carter, E. W., Lane, K. L., Pierson, M. R., & Glaeser, B. (2006). Self-determination skills and opportunities of transition age youth with emotional disturbance and learning disabilities. *Exceptional Children, 72,* 333–346.

Carter, E. W., & Wehby, J. H. (2003). Job performance of transition-age youth with emotional and behavioral disorders. *Exceptional Children, 69,* 449–465.

Cole, C. M., & McLesky, J. (1997). Secondary inclusion programs for students with mild disabilities. *Focus on Exceptional Children, 29*(6), 1–15.

Copeland, S. R., Hughes, C., Carter, E. W., Guth, C., Presley, J. A., Williams, C. R., & Fowler, S. E. (2004). Increasing access to general education: Perspectives of participants in a high school peer support program. *Remedial and Special Education, 25*(6), 342–352.

Dunn, C., Chambers, D., & Rabren, K. (2004). Variables affecting students' decisions to drop out of school. *Remedial and Special Education, 25*(5), 314–323.

East Penn School District v. Scott B., 29 IDELR 1058 (E. D. Penn. 1999).

Frey, L. M. (2003). Abundant beautification: An effective service-learning project for students with emotional or behavioral disorders. *Teaching Exceptional Children, 35*(5), 66–75.

Gable, R. A., Manning, M. L., Hendrickson, J. M., & Rogan, J. P. (1997). A secondary student instructional support team (ASSIST): Teachers face the challenge of student diversity. *The High School Journal, 81,* 22–27.

Geenen, S., Powers, L. E., & Lopez-Vasquez, A. (2001). Multicultural aspects of parent involvement in transition planning. *Exceptional Children, 67*(2), 265–282.

Hingsburger, D., & Tough, S. (2002). Healthy sexuality: Attitudes, systems and policies. *Research and Practice for Persons with Severe Disabilities, 27*(1), 8–17.

Iowa Department of Education. (1996). *Infusing transition into individualized education programs.* Des Moines, IA: Author.

Johnson, J., & Duffett, A. (2002). When it's your own child: A report on special education from the families who use it. Public Agenda, New York.

Jung, B. (1998). Mainstreaming and fixing things: Secondary teachers and inclusion. *The Educational Forum, 62,* 131–138.

Karvonen, M., Test, D. W., Wood, W. M., Browder, D., & Algozzine, B. (2004). Putting self-determination into practice. *Exceptional Children, 71*(1), 23–41.

Keyes, M. W., & Owens-Johnson, L. (2003). Developing person-centered IEPs. *Intervention in School and Clinic, 38,* 145–152.

Kim-Rupnow, W. S., & Bargstahler, S. (2004). Perceptions of students with disabilities regarding the value of technology based support activities in post-secondary education and employment. *The Journal of Special Education Technology, 19*(2), 43–55.

King, B. (2000). ASSERT yourself: Helping students of all ages develop self-advocacy skills. *Teaching Exceptional Children, 32*(3), 66–70.

Kleinert, H., McGregor, V., Durbin, M., Blandford, T., Jones, K., Owens, J., & Miracle, S. (2004). Service-learning opportunities that include students with moderate and severe disabilities. *Teaching Exceptional Children, 37*(2), 28–34.

Kohler, P. D., & Field. S. (2003). Transition-focused education: Foundation for the future. *The Journal of Special Education, 37*(3), 174–183.

Lanford, A. D., & Cary, L. G. (2000). Graduation requirements for students with disabilities. *Remedial and Special Education, 21*(3), 152–160.

Lee, S., Palmer, S. B., Turnbull, A. P., & Wehmeyer, M. L. (2006). A model for parent-teacher collaboration to promote self-determination in young children with disabilities. *Teaching Exceptional Children, 38*(3), 36–41.

Letter to Moore, 39 IDELR 189 (OSEP 2002).

Letter to Runkel, 25 IDELR 387 (OCR 1996).

Lock, R. H., & Layton, C. A. (2001). Succeeding in postsecondary ed through self-advocacy. *Teaching Exceptional Children, 34*(2), 66–71.

Lumley, V. A., & Scotti, J. R. (2001). Supporting the sexuality of adults with mental retardation: Current status and future direction. *Journal of Positive Behavior Interventions, 3*, 109–119.

Madaus, J. W. (2003). What high school students with learning disabilities need to know about college foreign language requirements. *Teaching Exceptional Children, 36*(2), 62–66.

Madaus, J. W. (2005). Navigating the college transition maze: A guide for students with learning disabilities. *Teaching Exceptional Children, 37*(3), 32–37.

Madaus, J. W., & Shaw, S. F. (2004). Section 504: Differences in the classroom for secondary and postsecondary education. *Intervention in School and Clinic, 40*(2), 81–87.

Malian, I. M., & Love, L. L. (1998). Leaving high school: An ongoing transition study. *Teaching Exceptional Children, 30*(3), 4–10.

Martin, J. E., Marshall, L. H., & Sale, P. (2004). A 3-year study of middle, junior high, and high school IEP meetings. *Exceptional Children, 70*, 285–297.

Martin, J. E., Van Dycke, J. L., Christensen, W. R., Greene, B. A., Gardner, J. E., & Lovett, D. L. (2006). Increasing student participation in IEP meetings: Establishing the self-directed IEP as an evidence based practice. *Exceptional Children, 72,* 299–316.

Martin, J. E., Van Dycke, J. L., Greene, B. A., Gardner, J. E., Christensen, W. R., Woods, L. L., & Lovett, D. L. (2006). Direct observation of teacher directed IEP meetings: Establishing the need for student directed IEP meeting instruction. *Exceptional Children, 72,* 187–200.

Mason, C., Field, S., & Sawilowsky, S. (2004). Implementation of self-determination activities and student participation in IEPs. *Exceptional Children, 70*(4), 441–451.

Mason, C. Y., McGahee-Kovac, M., & Johnson, L. (2004). How to help students lead their IEP meetings. Exceptional Children, *36*(3), 18–25.

May, D. C., & Kundert, D. K., (1996). Are special educators prepared to meet the sex education needs of their students? A progress report. *The Journal of Special Education, 29*(4), 433–441.

McAfee, J. K., & Greenawalt, C. (2001). IDEA, the courts, and the law of transition. *Preventing School Failure, 45*(3), 102–107.

McGill, T., & Vogtle, L. K. (2001). Driver's education for students with physical disabilities. *Exceptional Children, 67*(4), 455–466.

Miner, C. A., & Bates, P. A. (1997). Person-centered transition planning. *Teaching Exceptional Children, 30*(1), 66–69.

Morningstar, M. E. (1997). Critical issues in career development and employment preparation for adolescents with disabilities. *Remedial and Special Education, 18*, 307–320.

Mull, C. A., & Sitlington, P. L. (2003). The role of technology in the transition to postsecondary education of students with learning disabilities: A review of the literature. *The Journal of Special Education, 37*(1), 26–32.

Mull, C., Sitlington, P. L., & Alper, S. (2001). Postsecondary education for students with learning disabilities: A synthesis of the literature. *Exceptional Children, 68*(1), 97–118.

Munk, D. D., & Bursuck, W. D. (2001a). Preliminary findings on personalized grading plans for middle-school students with learning disabilities. *Exceptional Children, 67*(2), 211–234.

Munk, D. D., & Bursuck, W. D. (2001b). What report card grades should and do communicate. *Remedial and Special Education, 22*(5), 280–287.

Myers, A., & Eisenman, L. (2005). Student-led IEPs: Take the first step. *Teaching Exceptional Children, 37*(4), 52–58.

National Center for Education Statistics (N.C.E.S.). (2004). Retrieved December 4, 2005, from nces.ed.gov/programs/digest/04/tables, table 109.

Neubert, D. A., & Moon, M. S. (2000). How a transition profile helps students prepare for life in the community. *Teaching Exceptional Children, 33*(2), 20–25.

Nuehring, M. L., & Sitlington, P. L. (2003). Transition as a vehicle: Moving from high school to an adult vocational service provider. *Journal of Disability Policy Studies, 14,* 23–35.

O'Neill, P. T. (2001). Special education and high stakes testing for high school graduation: An analysis of current law and policy. *Journal of Law and Education, 30*, 185–222.

Owens-Johnson, L., & Johnson, J. (1999). The local employer survey project: An effective school-to-work curriculum. *Teaching Exceptional Children,* *31*(5), 18–23.

Pearman, E., Elliott, T., & Aborn, L. (2004). Transition services model: Partnership for student success. *Education and Training in Developmental Disabilities, 39,* 26–34.

Razeghi, J. A. (1998). A first step toward solving the problem of special education dropouts: Infusing career education into the curriculum. *Intervention in School and Clinic, 33,* 148–156.

Salend, S. J. (2005). Report card models that support communication and differentiation of instruction. *Teaching Exceptional Children, 37*(4), 28–34.

Salend, S. J. & Duhaney, L. M. G. (2002). Grading students in inclusive settings. *Teaching Exceptional Children, 34*(3), 8–15.

Scanlon, D., & Mellard, D. F. (2002). Academic and participation profiles of school-age dropouts with and without disabilities. *Exceptional Children, 68*(2), 239–258.

Shalen, C. A. H., & Lehmann, J. P. (2006). Requesting accommodations in higher education. *Teaching Exceptional Children, 38*(3), 28–34.

Susquehanna Township School District v. Frances, J., 39 IDELR 5, 823 A.2d 249 (PA. Comm. Ct. 2003).

Test, D. W., Karvonen, M., Wood, W. M., Browder, D., & Algozzine, B. (2000). Choosing a self-determination curriculum: Plan for the future. *Teaching Exceptional Children, 33*(2), 48–53.

Test, D. W., Mason, C., Hughes, C., Konrad, M., Neale, M., & Wood, W. M. (2004). Student involvement in individualized education program meetings. *Exceptional Children, 70*(4), 391–412.

Torgerson, C. W., Miner, C. A., & Shen, H. (2004). Developing student competence in self-directed IEPs. *Intervention in School and Clinic, 39*(3), 162–167.

U.S. Department of Education (2003). Annual Report to Congress on the Implementation of the Individuals with Disabilities Education Act. Retrieved 2004, from http://nces.ed.gov/pubs2003/digest02/tables.

Van-Belle, J., Marks, S., Martin, R., & Chun, M. (2006). Voicing one's high school students with developmental disabilities learn about self-advocacy. *Teaching Exceptional Children, 38*(4), 40–46.

Van Dycke, J. L., Martin, J. E., & Lovett, D. L. (2006). Why is this cake on fire? Inviting students into the IEP process. *Teaching Exceptional Children, 38*(3), 42–47.

Wallace, T., Anderson, A. R., Bartholomay, T., & Hupp, S. (2002). The ecobehavioral examination of high school classrooms that include students with disabilities. *Exceptional Children, 68*(3), 345–359.

Wehmeyer, M., & Schwartz, M. (1997). Self-determination and positive adult outcomes: A follow-up study of youth with mental retardation or learning disabilities. *Exceptional Children, 63*(2), 245–255.

Whitney-Thomas, J., & Hanley-Maxwell, C. (1996). Packing the parachute: Parents' experiences as their children prepare to leave high school. *Exceptional Children, 63,* 75–87.

Will, M. (1984). *OSERS programming for the transition of youth with disabilities: Bridges from school to working life.* Washington, DC: Office of Special Education and Rehabilitation Services, pp. 1–2.

Wolfe, P. S., & Blanchett, W. J. (2003). Sex education for students with disabilities. *Teaching Exceptional Children, 36*(1), 46–51.

Yoder, D. I., Retish, E., & Wade, R. (1996). Service learning: Meeting student and community needs. *Teaching Exceptional Children, 28*(4), 14–18.

CHAPTER 9

DISCIPLINE

CHAPTER PREVIEW

Focus

Schools are prohibited by law, in some situations, from applying the same disciplinary procedures to students with special needs as have been traditionally applied with regular education students. This problem is compounded by the fact that a small percentage of students with special needs exhibit unusually difficult and disruptive behavior problems.

Legal Issues

The 2004 Amendments to the IDEA include several provisions that address disciplinary sanctions for students with disabilities.
The major points are as follows:

- School officials may not change a student's placement in response to misconduct without certain procedural safeguards. A change in placement would include suspending students for more than 10 consecutive or cumulative days or expelling a student.
- When school officials consider disciplinary sanctions that constitutes a change in placement, the local education agency, the parent, and relevant members of the IEP team must determine whether the misconduct was caused by or had a direct and substantial relationship to the child's disability or if the conduct was the direct result of a failure to implement the child's IEP.
- When a student's misconduct is determined to be related to the student's disability, the IEP team must conduct a functional behavioral assessment and implement a behavioral intervention plan if such assessment and planning had not been conducted prior to the misconduct.

- Parents must be provided notice of IEP meetings to discuss discipline issues as well as written prior notice to implementing a change in placement resulting from disciplinary action.
- A student with a disability who is excluded from school for more than 10 school days in a school year for disciplinary reasons, consecutive or not, must be provided FAPE with services that enable the student to progress in the general curriculum and advance toward IEP goals.
- School officials may unilaterally place a student with disabilities in an interim alternative educational setting for up to 45 school days when the misconduct involves weapons, drugs, or inflicting serious bodily injury.
- School officials may seek a hearing officer's order for a student's placement in an interim alternative educational setting for up to 45 school days when the school can establish or prove that student's current placement is substantially likely to result in injury to the child or to others.
- Parents may challenge decisions regarding manifestation determinations and placement for disciplinary reasons through an expedited due process hearing procedure.
- Student "stay put" requirements differ from the norm for parent appeals regarding placement in interim alternative educational settings.
- School officials must consider extending the discipline procedural safeguards to students not yet identified as IDEA-eligible when they have knowledge that the child may have been a child with a disability before the misconduct occurred.
- Students involved in minor disciplinary infractions may be disciplined as other students are disciplined, so long as the discipline does not result in a change in placement or the deprivation of FAPE, and students without disabilities are treated in the same manner.

In general, the application of certain disciplinary sanctions to students with disabilities that would be viewed as a change of educational placement must be preceded by several procedural safeguards, including a manifestation determination, parental notice, and opportunity for a due process hearing. The burden of proof, or justification, for unilateral long-term exclusion from school for disciplinary reasons is on the school. Even for properly expelled students (i.e., provided procedural safeguards prior to a decision to change placement with long-term suspension or expulsion), access to an educational services must be continued.

Rationale

Denial of an education to students because of their disability-related behavior may violate several aspects of the IDEA and the principles behind the right to (a) an appropriate public education, (b) an education in the LRE, and (c) prescribed procedures for changes in placement. It is neither legal nor logical to remove a student from special education services for the same behavioral characteristics and disability that entitled the student to such programs in the first place.

Approaches

Although disciplinary sanctions may be applied to students with disabilities when procedural safeguards have been provided, school officials should consider preventive approaches to address behavior problems and misconduct. Alternatives to reactive, punitive responses such as suspension and expulsion should be explored for all students, including students with disabilities. Such alternatives may include prosocial responses to anger and

aggression, home-school collaboration, self-control techniques, conflict resolution, school counseling, vocational education, and social skill instruction.

LEGAL HISTORY UNDER THE ACT

The original legislation that became the IDEA did not address student discipline. That void in the statute was partially filled through numerous court decisions that resulted from expensive litigation. Schools were required to rely on the outcome of the litigation to develop and implement their disciplinary practices with students with disabilities. Those lawsuits, beginning at least as early as 1978, cost schools and parents a great deal of time, money, and effort. Finally, when Congress reviewed the IDEA for the 1997 revisions, those amendments included discipline provisions. These provisions attempted to balance the need for school safety with the need to provide appropriate programs to student with disabilities, including behavioral disabilities. Much of the debate concerning the discipline provisions centered on the perception that a double standard would exist in school, whereby students with disabilities were disciplined in a different manner from students without disabilities. In the end, the 1997 amendments attempted to strike a careful balance between the school's duty to ensure a safe environment conducive to learning and the school's obligation to ensure that children with disabilities receive a FAPE (House Report No. 105–95, 1997, p. 106).

In order to bring consistency to what it considered the chaotic state of court and administrative interpretations on the discipline of students with disabilities, Congress determined to place nearly all legal guidance on discipline in one location, the IDEA. The result was expected to be a better understanding of the protections available to children with disabilities by educators and parents. Congress also required that states gather, analyze, and report data regarding long-term suspensions and expulsions of children with disabilities. If discrepancies in the disciplinary treatment of children with disabilities occur within a state, the state must

ensure that policies and practices are reviewed and necessary changes are implemented.

In 2004, the IDEA was again reauthorized and additional revisions to the discipline provisions were included in the IDEA. The new provisions extend the unilateral authority of school officials for misconduct involving serious bodily injury upon another person at school and clarify when a functional behavioral assessment must be conducted.

LEGAL REQUIREMENTS

IEP Process Alternative

The most effective approach to addressing the behavior problems of students with disabilities is to develop and provide appropriate education programs. The IEP for a student with behavioral needs should include a behavior intervention plan (BIP) that includes goals for improving behavior and strategies to achieve those goals. The IEP may also include related services necessary to address behavior needs, such as counseling services, psychological services, and social work services. Supplemental aids and services necessary to support the child's educational program may be provided to the child, to his or her teachers or support staff, or to peers.

Behavioral Intervention Plans

Educators must remember that any time a student's behavior impedes the student's learning or the learning of others, IEP teams must consider appropriate strategies, including positive behavioral interventions and supports, to address student behaviors. The failure to do so is considered by OSEP to constitute a denial of FAPE to the child. Prior to the application of long-term suspension or expulsion for behaviors that are not a manifestation of the child's disability, the IEP team must develop or review the student's behavioral intervention plan. During the last decade, the results of significant research efforts establishing the efficacy of positive behavior interventions have been published regularly in the education literature (Lane et al., 2003;

Lewis, Hudson, Richter, & Johnson, 2004; Turn-bull, Wilcox, Stowe, Raper, & Hedges, 2000). Short-term suspensions and denial of some privileges for infraction of school rules could be part of a behavioral intervention plan, so long as they do not result in the student being denied a FAPE. Short-term suspensions of students should not be used as a substitute for appropriately considering and addressing a student's behavior problems with positive supports.

Short Fixed-Term Suspensions

Short, fixed-term suspensions are available as disciplinary sanctions for students with disabilities. Congress intended, and the regulations of the U.S. Department of Education provide, that students with disabilities may be unilaterally removed from their current educational placement (i.e., suspension) for up to 10 consecutive school days by school authorities, without IDEA implications, so long as children without disabilities are subject to the same discipline.

School officials are allowed a reasonable degree of flexibility when dealing with violations of school rules by children with disabilities, and a student's loss of educational programming for 10 consecutive school days or less is not considered to impose an unreasonable educational burden on a child with disabilities. Prior to the reauthorization, the specific language of 20 U.S. C. 1415(k) (4) (A) appeared to treat suspension of 10 days or less similarly to long-term suspensions (Huefner, 1998; Mead, 1998), which caused considerable concern for school administrators. Case law and administrative decisions interpreted the language to mean that short-term suspensions amounting to 10 school days or less do not implicate the IDEA (e.g., *Northeast Indep. Sch. Dist.*, 1998; *Smith County Sch. Sys.*, 1998). The 2004 Amendments to the IDEA clarified that only sanctions exceeding 10 school days would require additional procedural safeguards.

Suspensions of indefinite length can result in special problems. Although it may be desirable in some situations to make a student's return to school following a suspension conditional upon some occurrence (e.g., until parents come to

school to visit with the principal, until completion of additional assessment), it remains the duty of the school to see that the legal requirements of the IDEA are met. Suspension or expulsion from school for more than 10 consecutive school days cannot be permitted, even when conditions for the student's return have not been met.

Unilateral removal from school for periods of time will also require the provision of constitutional procedural due process. (See the discussion of *Goss v. Lopez* (1975) at the end of this chapter.) Although not as elaborate as those protections for long-term suspensions or expulsion, the student must be provided basic due process for even short (e.g., 1 to 3 day) suspensions. These procedures involve informing the student of the evidence and permitting the student to respond to the evidence prior to implementing short-term suspensions.

Accumulated Suspensions

The IDEA statute clearly identifies a consecutive 10 school day limit to the use of suspension for students with disabilities. Suspensions of 10 days or less do not require IDEA procedural safeguards. Justifying the use of suspensions exceeding a total of 10 days has been difficult for school districts. Parents have been able to establish that such action constitutes a change in placement and denial of the right to a free, appropriate public education (e.g., *Manchester School District v. Charles M. F.*, 1994; *Boston Public Schools*, 2002). When accumulated suspensions exceed 10 school days, the result is considered a change in educational placement and, as explained in Chapter 2, the IDEA requires a placement team decision and parental procedural safeguards, including notice to parents and re-evaluation for changes in placement. This provision is consistent with OSEP's long-standing administrative interpretations involving accumulated short-term suspensions.

Partial Day and In-School Suspensions

When suspension from school is for only part of a school day, the partial day is applied to the

10-day consecutive and cumulative limitations. An in-school suspension is not normally considered a part of the 10-day suspension limitation (either consecutive or accumulated) so long as the student is afforded the opportunity to appropriately progress in the general curriculum, continue to receive services under the IEP, and continue to participate with students without disabilities. The U.S. Department of Education has consistently drawn distinctions between in-school suspensions that deprive a student of an IEP program and services and those that do not.

In-school suspensions that deprive students of IEP programs and services will probably count toward the 10-day suspension limitation provisions, both consecutive and accumulated. These suspensions will also trigger the procedural safeguards of a manifestation determination, functional behavioral assessment and BIP requirements, as well as the continuation of FAPE. In-school suspensions that allow access to licensed special education teachers, IEP services, and accommodations may not count toward the 10-day exclusion limit, especially when they also allow for appropriate interactions with peers without disabilities. The determinative issue is whether in-school suspension deprived the student of FAPE.

Suspension from school transportation must be treated as a suspension from school when transportation is identified as a related service on a student's IEP. In some situations, suspension from transportation for more than 10 days must be preceded by the procedural safeguards of notice, a manifestation determination, functional behavioral assessment, and BIP examination or development. When transportation is not part of an IEP, OSEP does not consider removal from transportation itself to be a suspension. It is expected that the child's parents will be responsible for transportation on the same basis as parents of children without disabilities. However, some state laws treat transportation as an integral part of special education services and should be consulted. Student misbehavior occurring during transportation can be addressed in the IEP and behavioral intervention plan of the child, and should be addressed when misbehavior on the school bus is similar to that experienced in the classroom.

Because exclusions from school will have a significant negative impact on a student's ability to succeed in school, FAPE must be provided for all removals exceeding 10 school days in the same school year. Whether or not the misconduct was a manifestation of the child's disability, the child must continue to receive educational services, to participate in the general education curriculum, and to progress toward meeting the goals set out in the child's IEP. The child must receive, as appropriate, a functional behavioral assessment, behavioral intervention services, and modifications that are designed to address the behavior violation so that it does not recur.

Expulsion and Long-Term Suspensions

The IDEA allows for the expulsion, long-term suspension (more than 10 consecutive school days), and accumulated suspensions exceeding 10 school days in a school year that result in a change in placement for students with disabilities when procedural safeguards are followed. A manifestation determination must be conducted by the local education agency, the parent, and relevant members of the IEP team, as determined by the parents and local education agency. If this group determines that no relationship exists between a student's disability and the misconduct, the student may be excluded from school in the same manner as students without disabilities (see later discussion). Most important, under all circumstances, a student with disabilities properly expelled from school must continue to receive a FAPE. If the IEP team determined the misconduct was a manifestation of the child's disability, expulsion or long-term suspension are not options as disciplinary sanctions. Instead, a functional behavioral assessment must be conducted or reviewed, and a behavioral intervention plan must be developed or modified. The child is then returned to the placement from which she or he was removed, unless the parent and school personnel agree to a change of placement as part of the modifications of the behavior intervention plan (20 U.S.C. § 1415 (k) (1) (F)).

The services a child must continue to receive when removed from his or her current placement for misconduct must enable the child to continue to participate in the general education curriculum and to progress toward meeting the goals set out in the IEP. The child must receive, as appropriate, a functional behavioral assessment, behavioral intervention services, and modifications that are designed to address the behavior violation so that it does not recur.

When parents file a request for a due process hearing regarding either a change in placement resulting from the proposed exclusion exceeding 10 days or a manifestation determination, the school cannot change the student's educational placement until the hearing has concluded and the school has prevailed. The exception to this rule involved placement in an Interim Alternative Educational Setting (IAES), discussed below.

In summary, students with disabilities can be excluded from school for less than 10 consecutive school days in a school year, and accumulated suspensions exceeding 10 school days that result in a change in placement can occur only when IDEA procedural safeguards are provided. If relevant IEP team personnel determine the misconduct was not a manifestation of the student's disability and receives no appeal from the parents notified of the intended disciplinary action, a student with disabilities can be excluded from school for more than 10 days. During the exclusion period, the student must continue to provide FAPE. If the IEP group determines the misconduct was a manifestation of the student's disability, a functional behavioral assessment must be conducted or reviewed, a behavioral intervention plan must be developed or modified, and the child must be returned to the placement from which she or he was removed.

Interim Alternative Educational Setting

In three student disciplinary situations, school personnel (e.g., principals) have limited unilateral authority to remove a child with disabilities from the child's current educational placement and to place the child in an appropriate interim alternative educational setting (IAES) for up to 45 days. These 45 days are school days, and do not include weekends and school vacations. The three situations for which school personnel may unilaterally remove a child to an IAES include when:

- a student with a disability carries or possesses a weapon to school, on school premises. Weapon means a "weapon, device, instrument, material, or substance, animate or inanimate, that is used for, or is readily capable of, causing death or serious bodily injury," except a pocket knife with a blade less than 2 1/2 inches in length (18 U.S.C. § 930). Included are guns, acids, and poisons, but questions will arise about many items. For example, a pencil might be a weapon depending on its intended use;
- a student with a disability possesses or uses illegal drugs, or sells or solicits the sale of a controlled substance, while at school, on school premises, or at a school function;
- a student has inflicted serious bodily injury on another person while at school, on school premises, or at a school function. Serious bodily injury involves a substantial risk of death, extreme physical pain, protracted and obvious disfigurement, or protracted loss of body function (18 U.S.C. § 1365 (h) (3)).

During the placement in the IAES, relevant members of the IEP team must conduct a manifestation determination to determine whether the misconduct was caused or related to the child's disability. If not, the child may be expelled from school with educational services continuing. If a relationship between the misconduct and the disability is found, a functional behavioral assessment must be conducted or reviewed, and a behavioral intervention plan must be developed or modified. Unless the parents and school personnel agree to a change in placement, the child must be returned to the educational placement the child was assigned prior to the IEAS placement.

While temporarily placed in the IAES and in subsequent long-term suspension or expulsion settings, the student must be provided services to enable the child to continue to participate in the general education curriculum and to progress toward meeting the goals set out in the IEP. The child must receive, as appropriate, a functional behavioral assessment, behavioral intervention services, and modifications that are designed to address the behavior violation so that it does not recur.

Unilateral placements in an IAES may be repeated for separate offenses during the school year so long as necessary legal requirements (i.e., manifestation determination and functional behavioral assessments) are met. Placements in an IAES may also be administered in conjunction with other disciplinary removal. For instance, the school may suspend a child for up to 10 consecutive school days while convening the IEP team to determine an appropriate IAES. In such situations, the student should be placed in the AES no later than the end of the 10th day of suspension.

Congress created the IAES placement to enable schools to ensure learning environments that are safe and conducive to learning for all, and to give schools the opportunity to determine appropriate future placement for the student. Placement in an IAES by school officials is an exception to the "stay-put" requirement and may continue even when the student's behavior is determined to be related to the student's disability, or when the parent requests a due process hearing to challenge the IAES placement. Placements in an IAES can be for periods of time shorter than 45 school days. Also, IAES placements may be shortened by events, such as when the IEP team (including parents) and school officials mutually agree to a change in placement to another educational setting.

Placement in the IAES by a Hearing Officer or Administrative Law Judge (ALJ) for Disruptive Behavior

If a child engages in dangerous or disruptive misbehavior that does not involve weapons, drugs, or serious bodily harm, school officials may request that an expedited due process hearing be held. A hearing officer may order the child placed in an IAES for not more than 45 school days. An expedited hearing must be held within 20 school days of the request for hearing and a decision must be issued 10 days after the hearing. Specific procedures for expedited hearings may be determined by states.

A hearing officer may order placement in an IAES for students who are alleged to pose a threat to themselves or others. In doing so, the school district must show that maintaining the current placement of the child is substantially likely to result in injury to the child or to others. The hearing officer must review the appropriateness of the proposed IAES setting and direct appropriate modifications if necessary. The criteria for an interim alternative educational setting are highlighted in Figure 9-1.

When the school has not previously removed the student from school through suspensions of 10 consecutive school days or less in a manner that resulted in a change of placement for the student, the school may remove the student through a short-term suspension so long as a change in placement does not result. During the time of the removal, arrangements may be made for an expedited due process hearing to determine whether an IAES is appropriate. Obviously, there are few appropriate school settings currently available that will meet the IAES criteria. How will schools comply? Are

FIGURE 9-1   *Criteria for an interim alternative eduation setting*

- The setting must enable the child to continue receiving educational services in order to participate in the general education curriculum;

- permit the child to progress toward meeting the goals in the IEP; and

- permit the child to receive, as appropriate, a functional behavioral assessment and behavioral intervention services and modifications, so that the misconduct does not recur.

alternative schools with appropriately licensed staff an answer? These questions will be presented in the Questions for Thought section at the end of this chapter.

Court Injunction

In *Honig v. Doe* (1988), the Supreme Court stated that when the actions of the student were hazardous to the student or to others, schools could attempt to obtain court orders that would allow schools to remove students from education placements on a temporary basis. A very heavy burden of proof was assigned to schools in their effort to obtain such court orders. The 1997 Amendments now provide that schools may request that a hearing officer order the child to be placed in an IAES for behavior that presents a danger to the student or to others. It is not clear whether Congress intended to deprive schools of the right to continue to also go to court to obtain court-ordered approval of their actions to temporarily remove violent students (Mead, 1998, p. 526). OSEP has taken the position that schools may either seek a court injunction or an order from a hearing officer to obtain an alternative placement for dangerous or disruptive students (OSEP, 1995).

Home-Bound

Many educators considering IAES options may consider some form of home-bound education program (sometimes called home-study). Home-study placements are not conducive to appropriate educational programming for the vast majority of students, are among the most segregated of placements, and are not favored by parents or courts. When used as an IAES, home-bound instruction must ensure that the child continues to receive services that enable the child to participate in the general education curriculum and to progress toward meeting the goals set out in the IEP. The child must receive, as appropriate, a functional behavioral assessment, behavioral intervention services, and modifications that are designed to address the behavior violation so that it does not recur. As such, attempts to use home-bound as an IAES

will be difficult to defend (Huefner, 1998), and OSEP has expressed concern regarding the use of home-bound instruction as an IAES.

Manifestation Determination

When expulsion or long-term suspension (more than 10 consecutive school days) is considered for student disciplinary infractions, when a student is placed in an IAES, or when a student's accumulated suspensions of over 10 school days result in a change of placement, the school must determine whether the student's misconduct was a manifestation (result) of the student's disability. A review of the potential relationship between the student's disability and misbehavior must be conducted no later than 10 school days after a decision by school officials to take disciplinary action is made, and sooner when possible. There is a legal presumption that a relationship exists between the disability and the misconduct, which must be overcome during the review. If the legal presumption of the existence of a relationship is not overcome during the manifestation determination review, then the child may not be expelled or otherwise unilaterally removed from school for more than 10 days during a school year. The review is to be conducted by members of the IEP team, including parents, and other relevant school personnel (which are not specified in the law but determined by the parent and local education agency). The team must consider all relevant information in the student's file, including the child's IEP, any teacher observations, and any relevant information provided by the parents. If a determination is challenged, the burden of proof falls on the school to prove that no manifestation existed. The relevant IEP team members must determine whether the conduct in question was

- caused by, or had a direct and substantial relationship to, the child's disability; or
- the direct result of the local educational agency's failure to implement the IEP.

If a direct and substantial relationship is found to exist between the misbehavior and disability, or if the school did not provide or properly implement an appropriate program and services through an IEP, then the team must conclude that a manifestation existed and immediate steps must be taken to remedy deficiencies in the existing IEP or placement. The student may not be punished by unilateral long-term exclusion. Instead, when a student's misbehavior is related to the disability, the IEP team must take the disciplinary needs of the student and the needs of the school into account, and identify and implement a revised appropriate education program and, possibly, placement. If the student has been excluded for more than 10 consecutive school days from school and it is determined that a relationship between the disability and the misconduct existed, then the student must be returned to the setting where IEP educational programming was offered. If the student has been placed in an IAES, then the school must return the student to the former setting for IEP programming. Only when the behavior was not a manifestation of the student's disability may the student be disciplined in the same manner as students without disabilities, including possible expulsion. No detailed explanation of the manifestation determination process or application of the standards is provided in law, and IEP teams will be on their own in determining what these standards mean. It is clear from previous court and administrative interpretations that this decision is one of team consensus and may not be made unilaterally by administrators or other school officials. In the final analysis, taking all the data into account, it will be up to sound professional judgment (with parental participation) to determine whether the misconduct was, or was not, a manifestation of the disability: "There is no cookbook criterion" (Osborne, 1997, p. 330).

A review of administrative decisions and case law reveals several important points concerning the manifestation determination. First, relevant members of the IEP team must be included in the manifestation review (Tehachapi Unified School District, 2006). The manifestation review must be based on current assessment data (*Anahuac Independent School District*, 1994) and include a functional behavioral assessment (*Russell Farrin v. Maine*

School Administrative District No. 59, 2001). In conducting the manifestation review, the IEP team must consider all relevant data (*Dallas School District*, 1998). A sample manifestation determination form is provided in Appendix H-4.

Only when there is no finding of a relationship between the misconduct and the student's disability may school officials choose to treat the student as they would a student without disabilities, including long-term suspension or expulsion when appropriate. Because both long-term suspension and expulsion would result in a change of placement, additional procedural safeguards of notice and right to request mediation or a due process hearing must be followed. A change in placement triggers the right of parents to receive a detailed written notice of the proposed change and procedural safeguards such as the right to file an appeal. When an appeal is filed, parents have the right to have the child's status quo maintained until the dispute is resolved, attorney fees if the parents prevail, an independent educational evaluation, and so forth. In *Honig v. Doe* (1988), the Supreme Court ruled that when parents request a due process hearing, schools must maintain students' educational placement and cannot unilaterally exclude students, even those with violent tendencies. In extreme situations, schools may seek court intervention to remove disruptive students.

When students needing special education services are unilaterally disciplined for behavior that is a manifestation of their disability, and that discipline results in a change of placement, the disciplinary action would violate both the IDEA and Section 504.

Notice and Parent Requests for Due Process Hearing

School officials must notify parents no later than the date on which a decision is made to exclude a student from school for more than 10 consecutive school days, to suspend a student for less than 10 school days in a series of suspensions that constitute a pattern of exclusion, to place a child in an IAES, or to seek hearing officer approval for an IAES placement, and provide them with notice of the general procedural safeguards available to them. A parent may request a hearing regarding any decision regarding disciplinary placement, including those involving a change in placement, a manifestation determination, or placement in an IAES. Parent requests for due process hearings regarding school disciplinary decisions are handled differently than those involved in other due process hearings. When a parent requests a hearing on a decision regarding discipline, the school must arrange for an expedited due process hearing. Expedited hearings must meet the requirements of standard due process hearings, except that the hearing must be scheduled within 20 school days of the request for a hearing and a decision rendered within 10 school days after the hearing. Individual states may establish different procedural rules for expedited hearings. Decisions resulting from expedited hearings may be appealed the same as nonexpedited due process hearing decisions. Mediation remains available as an alternative dispute resolution process.

"Stay-Put" (Status Quo) and IAES

Unlike the typical due process hearing requested by parents, a parent request for a hearing regarding disciplinary placements in an IAES and related manifestation determinations do not result in the child remaining in the current educational placement ("stay-put"). Instead, the child remains in the IAES until the hearing officer renders a decision, or until the time of placement in IAES expires, whichever occurs first. Of course, the parent and school may mutually agree on a placement alternative to IAES. Normally, following the expiration of the time of placement in IAES, the student will be returned to the previous educational placement. When the school proposes to change the student's educational placement through the IEP change-in-placement process following an IAES placement, the parent may challenge the school's proposed change in placement. In these situations, the student will

normally be returned to the previous educational placement.

When, during the pending due process proceeding on the proposed change-in-placement, school personnel consider a return to the student's previous educational placement to be dangerous for the child or others, the school may seek an expedited due process hearing on the issue. In an expedited proceeding, the school may seek a hearing officer's ruling allowing an additional alternative placement by the school for up to 45 school days. School officials may request subsequent additional expedited hearings if deemed necessary.

If the parent due process hearing request is to challenge disciplinary decisions other than those regarding placements in IAES and related manifestation determinations, such as an expulsion and related manifestation decisions, then the general "stay-put" rule applies. Thus, when parents appeal the proposed expulsion of a student or the school's determination that no manifestation existed regarding that situation, the school would be required to maintain the student in his current educational setting until the dispute was resolved.

Non-eligible Student Discipline Protections

School officials must consider extending the procedural safeguards for disciplinary action to students who are not currently IDEA-eligible when the school had knowledge that the student was a student with a disability prior to the behavior that precipitated the disciplinary action. If the school did not have knowledge that the student had a disability and was entitled to special education services prior to the misconduct, then the student may be subjected to the same disciplinary procedures as students without disabilities.

Much of the philosophy or policy inherent in the knowledge provision is based in the school's duty to continuously carry out its child find function. School staff members are expected to refer students for evaluation when their behavior or performance indicates they may have a disability covered by the IDEA, even when they are advancing from grade to grade (34 C.F.R. § 300.121 (e), 2000).

A school is considered to have "knowledge" of a student's disability when

- the parent has expressed concern in writing to supervisory or administrative personnel of the appropriate educational agency, or a teacher of the child, that the child is in need of special education and related services;
- the parent has requested an evaluation of the student to determine eligibility for special education services;
- the student's teacher, or other school personnel, has expressed specific concerns about a pattern of behavior demonstrated by the child directly to the director of special education or other supervisory personnel.

A school is deemed to not have "knowledge" when

- the parents of the child had not allowed an evaluation of the child or refused services; or
- the school had conducted an evaluation and determined that the child was not eligible.

Either of these reasons for not extending the procedural safeguards must be provided to parents asserting IDEA protection from disciplinary sanctions.

If a parent request for evaluation for a non-identified student is made during the time the student is being disciplined, then an evaluation and determination of eligibility must be expedited. Until the requested evaluation is completed, the student will remain in the educational placement determined by the school. If the child is subsequently determined to be a child with a disability and is eligible for special education services, then the school must provide the child with special education and related services, including those required under the disciplinary procedures of the IDEA, if appropriate.

Referral to Law Enforcement

Schools may report crimes committed by students with disabilities to appropriate authorities, if it would also do so regarding students without disabilities. However, schools may not use this process to circumvent their IDEA

responsibilities, such as IEP review and revision and manifestation determinations. Law enforcement and judicial authorities may exercise their regular jurisdiction over children with disabilities who commit crimes.

A school reporting a crime committed by a child with a disability must ensure that copies of the child's special education and disciplinary records are transmitted for consideration by the appropriate authorities to whom it reports the crime, but only to the extent that education record transmission is permitted under the Family Educational Rights and Privacy Act (FERPA). The transfer of such records is permitted under FERPA only when state statute allows or requires such record transfer to the juvenile justice system for the purpose of effectively serving the needs of the student prior to adjudication. Law enforcement authorities must verify in writing that the transferred records will not be disclosed to third parties, except as provided under state law.

The FERPA also allows the transfer of student records when a school complies with a court order or subpoena and attempts to notify the parents in advance of compliance, and when student record disclosure is made in connection with a health or safety emergency (Bartlett, 2004).

Functional Behavioral Assessment and Behavior Intervention Plans

If the relevant members of the IEP team determine that the behavior was a manifestation of the child's disability, the school must convene the IEP team and develop a functional behavioral assessment plan, if one has not been previously conducted. Behavioral assessment plans that require new individualized student assessment and are not merely a review of existing data may require written parental consent for evaluation (see Chapter 3).

As soon as is practicable after an assessment plan is developed and assessments are completed, the IEP team must meet to develop appropriate behavioral interventions and then implement those interventions. The functional behavioral assessment planning and behavioral intervention planning meetings may be held in conjunction with a manifestation determination review (as discussed later in this chapter) when desired. If a behavioral intervention plan already exists for a student, then the team must review the plan and its implementation and make modifications as necessary.

Functional Behavioral Assessment   Federal law does not define or explain the phrase "functional behavioral assessment." A perhaps oversimplified understanding of functional behavioral assessment provides that it is an effort to determine the purpose of the student's behavior. Taking the context of the situation into account (What events occurred prior to the event? What misbehavior occurred? What happened to the student?), the educators attempt to determine the reason for the student's behavior. The focus is on the *function* or purpose of the behavior from the perspective of the student. When the function is determined, educators can then develop and teach an appropriate alternative behavior for the student to attain what the student wants without having to resort to improper behavior. Inappropriate behavior will no longer be necessary for the student in order to obtain the result wanted (i.e., peer attention, adult attention, or escape from the situation or environment). For example, if a student hits another student in order to escape the embarrassment of doing long-division problems at the board, being sent to the principal's office would not be appropriate. It would reinforce the student's reason for the misbehavior. An acceptable way for the student to communicate the need to avoid doing division at the board, and thereby escape embarrassment, can be identified and taught (such as express permission to request excusal), and thereby replace the inappropriate behavior.

McConnel, Hilvitz, and Cox (1998) note the functional behavioral assessment process was originally developed to help provide an understanding of behaviors exhibited by students who were limited in verbalizing the function of their behavior. For instance, it has been determined that for some self-injurious behavior in students with severe disabilities, the behavior serves the child as a function for obtaining attention from adults. As an appropriate alternative, the child might be taught to use an electric switch that activates a colorful light or music to draw adult attention to the student's needs. Thus, the student no longer needs the self-injurious behavior in order to obtain attention. Once the possible reason for problem behavior is discovered, interventions to teach replacement behaviors can be planned (Neel & Cessna, 1993). Replacement behaviors achieve the same intent as that achieved by the problem behavior, but these behaviors are socially acceptable. For example, if the intent of the problem behavior is to gain peer attention, the intervention may be focused on socially appropriate ways to provide the student with peer attention (e.g., peer tutoring, cooperative activities, class buddies). Drasgow and Yell (2001) outlined procedures for conducting legally correct and educationally appropriate FBAs. The authors suggested that (a) the people conducting the FBA are qualified; (b) the parents are notified about the FBA early enough to ensure they have opportunity to provide input; (c) the FBAs include interviews, multiple direct observations, and summaries of the variables and functions influencing the problem behavior; and (d) the FBAs are conducted in a timely manner. Etscheidt (2002) proposed that the discipline provision of the IDEA would serve as tacit reform initiatives to change disciplinary practices and improve services to students: "The FBA provisions will assist school personnel in examining misconduct and planning supportive program for students within local schools" (p. 415). Although all authors may not be in agreement (Smith, 2000), initial research has established that regular classroom teachers are able to perform FBAs with minimal specialized training (Ellingson, Miltenberger, Stricker, Galensky, & Garlinghouse, 2000).

Behavior Intervention Plans (BIPs)   A BIP must be discussed and developed at an IEP meeting for a child whose behavior impedes his or her learning or that of others. The IEP team must consider the use of positive behavioral interventions and supports and other strategies to address problem behavior.

The components of the BIP are not specified in either statute or regulation. Yell (1998) suggested that such plans consist of planned behavior goals and objectives and strategies, as well as positive behavioral interventions to meet behavioral goals.

The regular education teacher's participation on the IEP team is required, in part, to help determine appropriate positive interventions and strategies for the child. The regular education teacher also helps identify supplementary aids and services, program modifications, and supports for school personnel to assist the child's successful inclusion into the regular class. A functional behavioral assessment guides the development of a BIP. If neither a FBA nor BIP was in place prior to the misconduct, IEP teams are required to conduct a FBA and develop or review a BIP prior to applying disciplinary sanctions that would result in a change of placement.

Each subsequent disciplinary removal of the student from school will result in IEP team member reviews of the BIP. A formal team meeting will be required only whenever one or more team members determine that modifications to the existing plan are desirable. When a student's IEP includes strategies to address a particular behavior, the appropriate school response to student misbehavior would almost always be to use the behavioral strategies in the IEP, rather than the implementation of school punishment, especially removal from school. For this reason, it is imperative that educational leaders be aware of individual student BIPs.

Developing Behavioral Intervention Plans

Prior to the emergence of functional assessment, intervention plans for challenging behaviors were based primarily on professional opinion. Functional assessment leads IEP teams to a behavioral intervention plan based on an understanding of environmental events associated with the problem behavior. Following a functional assessment, school personnel have completed the necessary foundation for writing behavioral intervention plans (Buck, Polloway, Kirkpatrick, Patton, & Fad, 2000). Functional assessment helps IEP teams select interventions to address problem behavior (Ellingson et al., 1998).

The behavioral intervention plan is based on the results of the functional assessment. If the functional assessment revealed that certain elements in the instructional environment were contributing to the problem behavior, those elements are modified or reduced so that future problem behavior is prevented. These modifications will

reduce the occurrence of disruptive behavior (Cessna, 1993). Curricular modifications and adaptations alter an academic task or environment with the intent to increase the student's success rate while decreasing inappropriate behavior. Functional assessment guided and informed intervention plans address variables such as task difficulty, shortened assignment length, student interest and preference, and student choice. If skill deficits were suspected as influencing problem behavior, the behavior intervention plan might include intensive, one-on-one instruction in content areas such as reading, math, or written expression. The input of the general education teacher regarding instructional modifications will be of critical importance.

The functional assessment may reveal that factors in the social environment contribute to the occurrence of problem behavior. Behavioral intervention plans may be targeted at modifying the social environment (e.g., changing seating arrangements, alternate aide) and/or improving social skills. (See Walker, Ramsey, and Gresham, 2004, for a thorough discussion of selected approaches to social skill instruction.) Students may need social isolation (e.g., "think time") or social interaction (e.g., a crisis interventionist) as part of the BIP.

If non-school factors may be influencing problem behavior, collaboration with support personnel and/or agencies may be a helpful component of a behavioral intervention plan. For example, the IEP team may decide to provide the student with counseling or psychological services in an attempt to address the problem behavior. Recently, several authors have suggested that language problems have both a direct and indirect impact on behavior (Rinaldi, 2003; Rogers-Adkinson, 2003) and recommended interventions such as self-talk, parallel talk, and social stories to address problem behavior (Hyter, 2003; Rogers-Adkinson & Hooper, 2003). A speech/language pathologist might assist in conducting a functional assessment and in designing a behavioral intervention plan.

The IEP team may also want to include motivational strategies in the BIP. To increase academic, social, or replacement skills, the team may decide to include a reinforcement plan. Reinforcement plans may include a token economy, behavioral contracts, or group-oriented contingencies (see Maag, 2004, for a discussion of reinforcement techniques). Another motivational strategy is self-monitoring. Students monitor their own behavior, which has resulted in improved academic productivity and social skills. The student, in conjunction with the teacher, sets a goal for the occurrence of the academic, social, or replacement skill. A self-monitoring device is designed, and the time period for monitoring the skill occurrence is set. Each time the student displays the skill target, she or he records the occurrence on the self-monitoring device. The student regularly evaluates the monitored behavior against the established goal. Both teachers and students view self-monitoring as an attractive behavioral intervention (Maag, Reid, & DiGangi, 1993).

The behavioral intervention plans should include (a) the results of the functional assessment, (b) goals and interventions selected to achieve the goals, and (c) progress monitoring. The BIP, like the IEP, must be reviewed at least annually. However, the IEP team may want to establish procedures for frequent data collection to evaluate the effectiveness of the plan. One of the authors, while serving as a hearing officer, rendered the decision *Mason City Community School District and Northern Trails Area Education Agency 2* (2001), which identified the legal criteria for a behavioral intervention plan. Based on a review of case law, the legal criteria for an appropriate BIP include: (a) the BIP must be based on assessment data, (b) the BIP must be individualized to meet the child's unique needs, (c) the BIP must include positive behavior change strategies, and (d) the BIP must be consistently implemented as planned and its effects monitored.

McConnel, Hilvitz, and Cox (1998) have developed a 10-step FBA and behavior plan process that is appropriate for use by regular and special educators in most school situations. The plan is presented in Figure 9-2.

FIGURE 9-2 *Functional behavioral assessment plan*

1. Identify the student's behavior.
2. Describe the problem behavior. Use clear, specific, and detailed terms.
3. Collect the behavior baseline data and academic information. Document frequency, duration, and intensity.
4. Describe the environment and setting of the behaviors—when, where, who, what.
5. Complete the functional assessment interview form. The IEP team will attempt to identify the context of the behavior.
6. Develop a hypothesis. The team will look at the factors surrounding the behavior and develop a theory about the purpose or function of the student's behavior.
7. Write a behavioral intervention plan (BIP) or review the existing plan. Include a description of the specific interventions to use in the classroom.
8. Implement the behavioral intervention plan or review the existing plan. The classroom teacher will have the primary responsibility.
9. Collect the behavioral data.
10. Conduct an assessment meeting. The IEP team will review and assess the data results. Modifications and adaptations to the plan will be made, if successful. If not successful, a new hypothesis will be developed and a new behavioral plan constructed.

From "Functional Assessment: A Systematic Process for Assessment and Intervention in General and Special Education Classrooms," by M. E. McConnel, D. B. Hilvitz, and C. J. Cox, 1988, *Intervention in School and Clinic, 34*(1), pp. 11–16. Copyright 1998 by PRO-ED, Inc. Adapted with permission.

Although numerous approaches to an FBA and behavioral intervention planning have been proposed (e.g., Drasgow, Yell, Bradley, & Shrirer, 1999; Fesmire, Lisner, Forrest, & Evans, 2003; Packenham, Shute, & Reid, 2004; Shippen, Simpson, & Crites, 2003; Skiba, Waldrom, Bahamonde, & Michalek, 1998), most models will include interviews, behavior observation, goals, interventions, and progress monitoring components. Sample interview and observation forms are provided in Appendices H-1 and H-2. A sample behavior intervention plan is provided in Appendix H-3.

THE CONTINUING DILEMMA

The courts have, in numerous decisions, limited the traditional unilateral discretionary authority of school officials in disciplining students with disabilities. These rulings have prevented schools from expelling students with disabilities when the misconduct was related to the disability, no matter how serious the behavioral infraction, and they have forced the readmission of some students to previous educational placements. Moreover, many court decisions have been based on what seem to be technical or procedural issues rather than on substantive ones. The result was the appearance of a dual system of discipline that required schools to discipline students with disabilities differently from students without disabilities. This resulted in a concern that the rights of violent students with disabilities took precedence over the need for a safe school environment. By creating IAES placements and requiring functional behavioral assessment plans and manifestation determination in both the IDEA and 2004 Amendments, Congress attempted to strike a balance between the two interests. However, not all observers believe that the appearance of a dual system of discipline is likely to lessen under the current student discipline provisions of the IDEA (Turnbull & Turnbull, 1998, p. 60).

THE NEW POSITIVE, PREVENTIVE APPROACH

Zurkowski, Kelly, and Griswold (1998) highlight the importance of balancing the rights of students with disabilities with the need for safe schools with a protected learning environment. They note that the long-term removal of students from school has had little value as a therapeutic behavioral intervention, and some students who act inappropriately actually want to be removed from school. They conclude that removing misbehaving students from the school environment may make schools safer for short periods, but the net effect is to make society less safe. Zurkowski and colleagues commend the shift in focus from punishment of students to one of addressing positive behavior change in students. The use of functional behavior assessment to identify the reason for the misbehavior and development of behavioral intervention plans to provide educators with the tools and resources to teach students new behaviors are viewed as the means for addressing student behavior problems in proactive, positive ways rather than from a reactive, punitive perspective. The requirement that schools continue to address behavioral problems of students, even in IAES placements as appropriate, is viewed favorably because it requires schools to address student behavior problems through education, rather than allowing schools to exclude students with disabilities.

When traditional disciplinary practices based on punishment are examined closely, research does not validate their continued use. Glennon (1993) has made a compelling argument that educators must create a new disciplinary paradigm that views misbehaving students as learners and behavioral education as an integral part of a general education program. According to Glennon, educators must set aside their traditional belief system that student misbehavior is the result of evil intent (justifying punishment) or illness (requiring medication) and focus on what educators do best: evaluate, diagnose, plan, and prescribe learning experiences, including those designed to improve behavior. Educators need to assume greater responsibility for focusing on the nature and causes of student misbehavior. They need to design programs and services that minimize, control, and perhaps even overcome students' previously learned inappropriate reactions to situations. Etscheidt (2002) summarized that the discipline provisions of the IDEA would force school officials to examine alternatives to suspension and expulsion for all students. With greater accountability for all students, no student will be deprived the benefits of an education.

APPROACHES TO RESOLVING PROBLEMS

The discipline provisions of the 2004 Amendments to the IDEA attempt to strike a balance between the rights of students with disabilities to a FAPE and the need to maintain a safe school environment. The traditional sanctions of suspension and expulsion were limited for students with disabilities, requiring prior procedural safeguards and the continuation of FAPE for properly expelled students. By requiring school officials to possibly expand the protections from suspension and expulsion to students not currently eligible for IDEA services, the statute has limited those traditional sanctions for an even larger portion of the school population. Given the possibility that suspension and expulsion will be significantly restricted for all students, educational professionals must explore alternatives to resolve discipline problems.

The professional literature is replete with evidence-based interventions for addressing the behavioral needs of students. These recommendations can be categorized in preventive, supportive, and corrective dimensions.

Preventive Measures

Preventing discipline problems begins with creating positive school environments. Both school-wide and classwide programs may assist in promoting appropriate interactions and preventing discipline problems.

School-Wide Prevention Instruction on appropriate behavior school-wide is increasing in its implementation and is not used solely with students exhibiting undesirable behavior (Kern & Manz, 2004; Horner & Sugai, 2000). Sugai et. al. (2000) developed a comprehensive model of positive behavioral support (PBS) with three levels of systemic prevention: (a) universal systems—prevention strategies applied school-wide for all students, (b) targeted systems—school-wide and individualized prevention and response strategies aimed at the 10% of the school population for whom universal systems were not effective, and (c) intensive systems—individualized prevention and response strategies aimed at the 1 to 3% of students for whom universal or targeted systems had been ineffective. An example of a universal preventive strategy would be positive student discipline, whereas a targeted system intervention would include small group social skills instruction. An intensive system intervention might include arrangements with mental health agencies outside of the school to provide services to a student. Researchers examining the effects of seven school-wide positive behavioral support programs concluded PBS programs offered positive, effective, data-driven, and collaborative alternatives to traditional punitive discipline (Safran & Oswald, 2003).

Martella, Nelson, and Marchand-Martella (2003) describe a School-wide Positive Behavioral Intervention and Support (SEPBIS) model to achieve socially important behavior change across all school environments. Six organization systems are included in SEPBIS: (a) leadership (e.g., administrator, parental, and staff support); (b) school-wide organization (e.g., clearly defined discipline roles and responsibilities with a clearly defined crisis response plan); (c) non-classroom organization (e.g., identification of times or places where supervision is emphasized such as hallways or playground); (d) classroom organization (e.g., consistent discipline procedures, staff developing activities, teacher access to assistance and resources for behavioral problems); (e) individual organization (e.g., evidence-based interventions for students at-risk for school failure, established behavioral support team, solution-focused intervention); and (f) academic support system (e.g., evidence-based academic intervention in reading, language, and mathematics).

Nelson, Crabtree, Marchand-Martella, and Martella (1998) described an elementary school that implemented a school-wide comprehensive discipline plan designed to help prevent disruptive behavior. The basis for the program was a lively, engaging curriculum and effective teaching practices. Students were taught the behavioral expectations of the school. Regular supervision of common school areas associated with student misbehavior was conducted primarily by trained, unlicensed staff. The teachers used a simple but effective shared system of working with student classroom problems that minimized disruptive negative classroom exchanges and power struggles, and provided a structure for change. When a student's behavior disrupted a class, the teacher sent the child with a note to a colleague's classroom. As soon as practical, the receiving teacher questioned the student privately about the situation and asked if there might have been a better way for the student to have dealt with the situation. After a brief period of reflection and cooling down, the student was returned to the original classroom with a minimum of disruption to the learning environment of both classrooms. Individual students exhibiting severe disruptive behavior patterns were identified and provided intensive, multi-agency positive interventions (i.e., wraparound interventions). The program was effective in decreasing behavior problems and in increasing academic performance (i.e., an increase of 20% on standardized tests). This performance growth was attributed to teachers and students spending more time on instruction and learning and less time on disciplinary disruptions.

A study of the use of school-based prevention programs focusing on conflict resolution and peer mediation in three middle schools showed a decline in overall office referrals for disruptive and aggressive behavior (Daunic, Smith, Robinson, Miller, & Landry, 2000). It was determined that middle school students can learn and implement the skills necessary for establishing an alternative dispute resolution program, especially when committed teachers and educational leaders were involved.

Walker, Ramsey, and Gresham (2004) describe school-wide interventions to help reduce or eliminate anti-social behavior. These include study skills to improve academic performance, social skills training to improve teacher-, peer-, and self-related forms of adjustment, and health awareness to identify the consequences of a high-risk lifestyle. In their book, *Techniques for Managing a Safe School*, Johns and Keenan (1997) discuss the use of peer and adult mediators in conflict resolution: "We firmly believe that all schools should have a system in place for resolving student-student and staff-staff conflicts" (p. 22). The authors recommend the Teaching Students to be Peacemakers Program (Johnson & Johnson, 1996) as a research-based, K–12 approach to teaching students negotiation and mediation procedures. Jones and Jones (1995) identified additional components for effective schoolwide management, which included: (a) determining the roles and responsibilities of all parties involved in managing student behavior (e.g., students, parents, teacher, administrators, counselors); (b) using a problem-solving model that is taught to staff and students; (c) establishing several forms of communication between teachers, administrators, and parents, and (d) organizing a school-wide student management committee. Other authors have advocated the use of peer-tutoring strategies to teach social interaction skills and facilitate positive mental health and social competence in the general student population (Strayhorn, Strain, & Walker, 1993). Other school-wide discipline programs address bully prevention (Barton, 2003), democratic discipline (Hoover & Kindsvatter, 1997), school-wide character education (Lickona, 2000), and school civility (Scott, 1998). Administrators may assess the effectiveness of school-wide positive behavioral supports with a variety of measures (Horner et al., 2004).

Classroom-Wide Prevention   Several authors have offered suggestions for establishing effective class-wide discipline programs. Some suggestions concern the general classroom environment. Martella, Nelson, and Marchand-Martella (2003) describe several features of a class-wide preventive program. These include effective classroom and seating arrangements, classroom rules and routines, on-going social skill development, high levels of student engagement, successful lesson and curriculum pacing, and effective instructional methods. Essential elements of a synergetic classroom with gentle discipline were offered by Charles, 2000. These include ethics (e.g., teacher fairness, kindness, helpfulness, and honesty), trust, charisma (e.g., sharing special skills or knowledge, sharing personal experiences), communication (e.g., listening, understanding, reacting helpfully, encouraging), student interest (e.g., identify students' needs and preferences, facilitating student selection of topics and activities), class agreements, coopetition (building on the best of aspects of cooperation and competition), human relations (reacting positively to others, showing respect), and problem resolution (soliciting solutions from students). Glasser (1997) offered his Choice Theory as a guide for classroom management. This theory suggests that when teachers fail to meet students' psychological needs for survival, belonging, power, freedom, and fun, misbehavior results. Glasser recommends that classrooms help students satisfy those psychological needs.

Abrams and Segal (1998) have determined that student aggression in school is often directly related to teacher behaviors, and great reductions in student aggression can occur when teachers modify their classroom environments. Abrams and Segal offer an outline of the elements of such an environment (p. 12):

- Order, structure, and consistency
- Well-organized and predictable environment
- Clear and realistic expectations
- Evidence of student success, academically and socially
- Student choice, input, and expression of feeling
- High levels of social interaction

- Attention to students' psychological needs (belonging, safety, competence, and self-esteem
- Positive teacher-student relationships

Other models for class-wide management offer more specific strategies. Alper, Schloss, Etscheidt, and Macfarlane (1995) describe a model for classroom management. The program includes preventive, supportive, and corrective strategies for establishing and maintaining effective classroom environments.

Other class-wide models involve reinforcement systems. Canter and Canter's (1992) Assertive Discipline model features rewards and consequences built into everyday classroom life, as well as interventions to correct misbehavior, such as limit setting. Students receive tokens for appropriate behaviors, which are later exchanged for enjoyable class activities. A Level System is a class-wide management strategy that establishes a hierarchy of increasing expectations for behavior improvement with increasing student reinforcement and decreasing behavioral structure (Kerr & Nelson, 2002). Typically, the program involves four or five levels of increasingly higher expectations for academic performance and social behavior. Students are rewarded and advanced through each level based on progress against specific criteria for social and academic behavior. Other class-wide models include Discipline with Dignity (Curwin & Mendler, 1997), Positive Classroom Discipline (Jones, 1987), Consistency Management and Cooperative Discipline (Freiberg, 1999), and Judicious Discipline (Gathercoal, 1997).

Some class-wide models use corrective interventions for more serious forms of misconduct. These corrective interventions work most effectively when combined with preventive and supportive measures (Rutherford & Nelson, 1995).

Response cost involves the removal of a reinforcer following misconduct. Therefore, response cost programs are used in conjunction with preventive reinforcement systems such as Level Systems or Assertive Discipline. Inappropriate behaviors that will result in "fines" are identified. If a student displays the inappropriate behavior, a certain amount of the reinforcer or reinforcing activity is removed. For example, if a student is earning minutes for free computer time as a reinforcing activity, a certain number of minutes would be removed following the occurrence of inappropriate behavior. Although easy to implement and effective (Maag, 2004), response cost systems can be overused and result in a negative classroom atmosphere.

Time-out serves to decrease inappropriate behavior by denying a student access or opportunity to receive reinforcement. Before considering time-out, teachers must be sure that reinforcing consequences for appropriate behavior are available in the classroom or time away from that environment will not deter misbehavior. Many variations of time-out may be used. Students can be denied access to reinforcement within the classroom for a period of time following misconduct (i.e., nonseclusionary time-out) or be taken outside the classroom for more serious disruptive behavior (i.e., exclusionary time-out). If a time-out room is used, the procedure is called seclusionary time-out (Alberto & Troutman, 2003). As with response cost, time-out can be overused and result in students spending considerable time away from the learning environment.

Isolation is a corrective measure designed to provide an immediate response to serious misconduct and to assist a student in improving future behavior. Following the misconduct, the student is removed to an isolated area outside of the classroom. A teacher (e.g., interventionist) accompanies the students and helps the student reestablish self-control. The interventionist then helps the student identify the cause of the misconduct and develop a plan to replace the inappropriate behavior with an alternative, appropriate response.

A number of court decisions, including the Supreme Court in *Honig v. Doe* (1988), have stated that minor disciplinary punishments of students with disabilities, such as time-out, detention, or restriction of privileges, do not implicate the IDEA so long as they do not result in a change in placement or a change in FAPE and are also used with children without disabilities.

Although corrective measures are permitted under the IDEA, some authors call for a new perspective on school discipline that substitutes a variety of prevention components for corrective measures. Skiba and Peterson (2000) suggest a comprehensive combination of preventive approaches (called an *early response model* of discipline). Included are conflict resolution, social instruction, classroom strategies to prepare teachers on how to respond to situations without escalation, parent involvement, early warning signs training, crisis planning, school-wide discipline plans, and functional assessment and behavior plans for a variety of students, not just those receiving special education services.

CULTURAL AWARENESS

In an increasingly multicultural society, understanding cultural influences on behavior becomes especially important to educational settings (Zirpoli, 1995). A teacher's lack of understanding regarding students' cultural, social, and linguistic characteristics may lead to mischaracterization of problem behavior (Kea & Utley, 1998). Teachers' perceptions of and responses to student behavior must reflect cultural awareness and sensitivity (Jones, Dohrn, & Dunn, 2004). Teachers must consider student diversity when developing classroom management programs or individual student BIP's: "No longer can educators plan classroom management procedures just for the majority culture (whatever the majority culture is) and their perspectives of appropriate behavior" (Manning & Bucher, 2003, p. 8). For example, the disproportionate rate of suspensions and expulsions for African-American students may decrease as teachers and administrators become more aware of African-American students' cultural styles (Townsend, 2000) and implement management strategies to meet students' social needs.

Grossman (1995) provided several considerations that educators must address in developing individual and class-wide discipline plans:

- *Disciplinary style:* Students from different ethnic backgrounds may have unique responses to positive or negative consequences, group consequences, or may have unique perceptions of authority figures (e.g., male vs female). Educators must carefully consider an appropriate disciplinary style to meet the needs of all students.

- *Relationship style:* A teacher's classroom management efforts may be enhanced by understanding the different relationship styles that can exist among different ethnic groups (e.g., individual versus group rights, giving and sharing, relationships with the opposite sex). Teachers should take these differences into consideration when establishing rules, procedures, and expectations.

- *Communication style:* Educators should keep in mind the differences in communication styles as they manage their classrooms. Mismatches between communication styles (e.g., formal vs informal communication, emotional vs subdued communication, direct vs indirect communication) may lead to misunderstanding or misperception.

Educators may end up with counterproductive results when they do not take cultural differences into account when disciplining students. McIntyre (1992) suggests a greater awareness of how culture impacts student and parent behavior. Better student management can often be achieved through the recognition of cultural differences. He also recommended an approach that transcends cultural differences—a positive, helpful approach to discipline, rather than a negative, confrontational one. He concluded that when educators are knowledgeable about culturally-based student behavior, students will be less likely to create much of the behavior about which educators complain.

WHAT THE FUTURE HOLDS

Experience has shown that it pays for schools to develop clear and consistent policies based on the requirements of the law. But the law is not always as straightforward as it sounds. It is not fixed; it is continually being modified by court decisions, administrative interpretations,

and new legislation. The information provided in this book, because it has been simplified, is a guideline for use in many situations, but it cannot be guaranteed to predict the legal outcome of every situation. It is a good practice for educational leaders to update themselves periodically through professional publications, professional development programs, and by requesting opinions from the school district's attorney.

When relevant procedures under the IDEA are followed, the student's IEP may be modified or the student can be transferred to a different educational program. Educators frequently overlook this approach, even though it is obvious. The IEP process can be used for a variety of behavior solutions, including a change to a more restrictive placement, special training for the regular class teacher, assignment of a teacher associate, and the implementation of a behavior improvement plan (Jensen, 1996).

When the IEP process is used to deal with problems of discipline, none of the limitations about days of exclusion will come into play, manifestation determinations will not be needed, and the various situations involving the provision of FAPE to excluded students will not have to be defended.

The IEP Process

The IEP process continues to provide educators with more than adequate tools to evaluate student behavior needs, determine solutions, and marshal the resources, both inside and outside the school, necessary to provide all children with disabilities an appropriate educational program behavior plan component. The law even allows for educational programming in institutionalized and residential settings when appropriate for an individual student. Only when parents are so strongly opposed to the proposed educational solution that they will challenge the IEP team decision through due process hearings will the effective, efficient, and solution-oriented IEP process be disrupted. Compared with the near certainty of disruptions inherent in unilateral school actions, such as proposed unilateral expulsions and IAES placements, and the opportunity for parent challenges to school decisions they present, the IEP process stands out as an empowering tool for educators and parents working together to resolve student behavior concerns to all in the school environment. With the discipline provisions of IDEA 1997 came great concerns and critical commentary. Parents of student without disabilities and school officials complained about a dual system that limited the school's authority to discipline disruptive and dangerous students. Legal scholars argued that the discipline provision represented misguided policy and uninvited federal intrusion into the daily operation of schools. For example, Bryant (1998) suggested that the manifestation determination was illusory and "a black hole, totally capable of sucking all misbehavior by disabled students into the protected class of conduct" (p. 527). Rachelson (1997) suggested that the consideration of discipline protections for students not yet eligible for IDEA protections would be easily abused, and Bryant concluded that the discipline provisions "signal the death knell of expulsion" (p. 492).

Yet other authors proposed that the discipline provisions represented tacit reform initiatives to revise school disciplinary policies and restrict the use of suspension and expulsion (Etscheidt, 2002). Such a revision is warranted, given the ineffectiveness of suspension and expulsion as disciplinary tools: (a) suspensions do not deter future misconduct as evidenced in a level of recidivism of 50% (Bock, Savner, & Taspcott, 1998; Johns, Carr, & Hoots, 1997); (b) students who have been suspended experience serious academic problems upon return to school; (c) removing students from school displaces the problem to the community, which may lead to delinquent behavior, violence, and crime (Nichols, Ludwin, & Iadicola, 1999); (d) suspensions fail to address the underlying reasons for problem behavior; and (e) suspensions do not support or assist students with behavioral needs (Hartwig, Robertshaw, & Ruesch, 1991). As Etscheidt observed: "The discipline protections will challenge schools and communities to explore innovative initiatives to educate all students . . . so that no student is deprived of the benefits of an education" (p. 419).

CONCLUSION

This chapter is not intended to be comprehensive in providing educational leaders with ideas for approaches to resolving problems of discipline and creating a school climate conducive to the pursuit of education. Dozens of good books, hundreds of articles in professional publications, and great staff-development opportunities are available to serve that end. The authors are truly pleased at the great variety of quality resources currently available. A list of websites for positive behavioral supports follows this section.

VIEW FROM THE COURTS

Goss v. Lopez (1975) (student suspensions and due process) The well-known case, *Goss v. Lopez*, set the standard for constitutional due process in student suspensions from school. The Supreme Court ruled that the degree of due process afforded to students in the event of a suspension of 10 days or fewer need not be as extensive as the due process required if the suspension were to be for a longer period. In the case of a suspension of 10 days or fewer, the minimum due process that was required included a statement (written or oral) to the student of the charges or allegations against the student; if the student denied the charges, a statement explaining the evidence available; and, most important, an opportunity for the student to explain the student's version of what happened. (Although few, if any, courts have ruled on the issue, parents or advocates may need to be involved in situations of students unable to understand or comprehend what is occurring.) The right to a more formal hearing, the right to have counsel present, and so forth, may be required in situations where a more serious loss of rights is a possible outcome (i.e., long-term suspension, expulsion).

As with any student, in the event that a child with disabilities is excluded from a public school for even short periods of time, or expelled or excluded for more than 10 school days, school officials must provide appropriate constitutional procedural due process. *Honig v. Doe* (1988) ("stay-put" and dangerous students) In 1988, the Supreme Court reviewed a lower court ruling that held that students with special needs could not be unilaterally kept out of school by school officials even when the student's conduct was disruptive and potentially dangerous. The case involved students whose parents had filed appeals of their impending expulsions and argued that the "stay-put" provisions of the IDEA prohibited exclusion of the students from school while the appeal was pending. The Supreme Court agreed with the lower court. It said that in enacting the IDEA, Congress clearly meant to strip schools of their unilateral authority to exclude students with disabilities pending the outcome of appeals filed to challenge the proposed change in placement that results from expulsion. The Court concluded that schools can suspend for up to 10 days those students with disabilities who are dangerous or who severely disrupt the school environment. The 10-day period provides school officials with time to seek additional student evaluation and an alternative placement. When 10 days is not sufficient to find an alternative placement with which the parent agrees, the school must seek a court injunction to keep the student out of school for more than 10 days. In such situations, a heavy burden falls on the school to establish a safety need to keep the student out of school.

RECOMMENDED READINGS

Abrams, B. J., & Segal, A. (1998). How to prevent aggressive behavior. *Teaching Exceptional Children, 30*(4), 10–15. This excellent article reviews a great deal of the research on the causes and prevention of student aggression.

Anderson, C., & Katsiyannis, A. (1997). By what token economy? A classroom learning tool for inclusive settings. *Teaching Exceptional Children, 29*(4), 65–67. This article details a complex token economy used in an entire fifth-grade classroom.

Buggey, T. (1999). "Look I'm on TV." Using videotaped self-modeling to change behavior. *Teaching Exceptional Children, 31*(4), 27–30. This article reviews the research on various uses of videotaping students' behavior and provides practical uses of such videotapes to bring about changes in student behavior.

Egnor, D. (2003). *IDEA Reauthorization and the student discipline controversy.* Denver, CO: Love Publishing. This book examines why the IDEA specifically addressed discipline provisions in the 1997 reauthoriziation and the resulting controversy concerning a possible double standard.

Horner R. H., & Sugai, G. (2000). School-wide behavior support: An emerging initiative. *Journal of Positive Behavior Interventions, 2*(4), 231–232. This is the introductory article to articles that describe seven different implementations of school-wide behavior support systems.

Iverson, A. M. (2003). *Building competence in classroom management and discipline* (4th ed.). Upper Saddle River, NJ: Merrill/Prentice Hall. This textbook identifies various competencies for discipline, including home-school collaboration, school-wide discipline, communication, instruction, and positive behavior management.

McConnel, M. E., Hilvitz, D. B., & Cox, C. (1998). Functional assessment: A systematic process for assessment and intervention in general and special education classrooms. *Intervention in School and Clinic, 34*(1), 10–20. This excellent article makes functional assessment understandable and functional for educators.

McIntyre, T. (1992). The culturally sensitive disciplinarian. *Severe Behavior Disorders Monograph, 15,* 107–115. Reston, VA: Council for Exceptional Children. This brief article presents an excellent summary of the issue of cultural considerations to be taken into account when disciplining students.

Nelson, J. R., Crabtree, M., Marchand-Martella, N., & Martella, R. (1998). Teaching good behavior in the whole school. *Teaching Exceptional Children,*

30(4), 4–9. This article details a school-wide discipline plan, including a classroom management strategy that has the potential for wide application.

Martin, G., & Pear, J. (2003). *Behavior modification: What it is and how to do it.* Upper Saddle River, NJ: Prentice Hall. This textbook provides numerous examples of behavior modification including positive reinforcement, shaping, extinction, and generalizing behavior change.

Saren, D. (1999). The decision tree: A tool for achieving behavioral change. *Teaching Exceptional Children, 31*(4), 36–40. This article presents a methodology to help IEP teams determine what is behaviorally important for a child and what is not.

Scanlon, D., & Mellard, D. (2002). Academic and participation profile of school-age dropouts with and without disabilities. *Exceptional Children, 68*(2), 239–258. This interesting article interviewed 277 young adults with and without learning disabilities or E/BD regarding their school and post-drop-out experiences.

Turnbull, A., Edmonson, H., Griggs, P., Wickham, D., Sailor, W., Freeman, R., et al., (2002). A blueprint for schoolwide positive behavior support: Implementation of three components. *Exceptional Children, 68*(3), 377–402. This article describes universal, group, and individual positive behavioral supports and provides examples of positive behavioral support plans.

Zimmerman, B. F. (2000). *On our best behavior: Positive behavior-management strategies for the classroom.* Horsham, PA: LRP Publications. This text provides classroom-based examples of positive behavioral supports.

Relevant Federal Regulations

34 C.F.R. Part 104 (2005). Nondiscrimination on the basis of disability in programs and activities receiving federal financial assistance–Section 504 regulations.

34 C.F.R. Part 300 Assistance to states for the education of children with disabilities [70 Fed. Reg., 35,833–35,880 (June 21, 2005)].

300.101	Free appropriate public education (including that for suspended and expelled students).
300.170	Suspension and expulsion rates.
300.324	Development, revision, and review of IEP (behavior).
300.530	Authority of school personnel (discipline).
300.530(e)	Manifestation determination.
300.530(c)	Determination that behavior was not manifestation of disability.
300.531	Determination of setting.
300.532	Parent appeal.
300.532(b)	Authority of hearing officer—(discipline).
300.532(c)	Expedited due process hearings (disciplinary).
300.533	Placement during appeals (discipline).
300.534	Protections for children not yet eligible for special education and related services.
300.535	Referral to and action by law enforcement and judicial authorities.
300.536	Change of placement for disciplinary removals.

SELECTED WEBSITES

OSEP Technical Assistance Center on Positive Behavioral Interventions and Supports
http://www.pbis.org/

Rehabilitation Research & Training Center on Positive Behavior Support
http://rrtcpbs.fmhi.usf.edu/

Center for Effective Collaboration and Practice
http://cecp.air.org/
http://www.taalliance.org/

The IDEA Local Implementation by Local Administrators (ILIAD) and the Associations of Service Providers

ERIC Digest resources for Positive Behavior Support
http://www.ericfacility.net/

National Dissemination Center for Children with Disabilities.
http://www.nichcy.org/

National Association of School Psychologists
http://www.nasponline.org/

Council for Exceptional Children Step by Step Program: Positive Behavioral Supports
http://www.cec.sped.org/

Learning Disabilities OnLine: Positive Behavior Support
http://www.ldonline.org/

QUESTIONS FOR THOUGHT

1. How have the discipline provisions of the IDEA impacted general education teachers? Educational administrators? Special education teachers and support staff?

2. The availability of interim alternative educational settings is limited, particularly in rural areas. Why would home settings not be recommended as an IAES? What settings could serve as IAES in your school district? Are alternative schools a possible setting?

3. Despite the evidence of ineffectiveness, in-school and out-of-school suspensions continue to be used by school officials. To what do you attribute this continuation?

4. Glennon (1993) argues that misbehaving students are viewed through either a punitive lens (i.e., students are bad and need punishment) or a medical lens (i.e., students are sick and need to be diverted from school to mental health facilities). She recommends that a new disciplinary lens be created. What might that be?

5. Some authors (e.g., Fennimore, 1995) have argued that discipline problems are due to a curriculum that is not child-centered nor meaningful or relevant to learners. Do you agree?

REFERENCES

Abrams, B. J., & Segal, A. (1998). How to prevent aggressive behavior. *Teaching Exceptional Children, 30*(4), 10–15.

Alberto, P. A., & Troutman, A. C. (2003). *Applied behavior analysis for teachers* (6th ed.). Upper Saddle River, NJ: Merrill/Prentice Hall.

Alper, S., Schloss, P. J., Etscheidt, S. K., & Macfarlane, C. A. (1995). *Inclusion: Are we abandoning or helping students?* Thousand Oaks, CA: Corwin Press.

Anahuac Independent School District, 21 IDELR 411 (SEA TX 1994).

Analysis of Comments and Changes, 1999. Fed. Reg., *64*(48), 12,537–12,668.

Assistance to States for the Education of Children with Disabilities and the Early Intervention Program for Infants and Toddlers with Disabilities, 34 C.F.R. Part 300 (2000).

Bartlett, L. D. (2004). Special education students and the police: Many questions unanswered. *Education Law Reporter, 185,* 1–14.

Barton, E. A. (2003). *Bully prevention: Tip and strategies for school leaders and classroom teachers.* Glenview, IL: SkyLight Professional Development.

Bock, S. J., Savner, J. L., & Tapscott, K. E. (1998). Suspension and expulsions: Effective management for students? *Intervention in School and Clinic, 34*(1). 50–52.

Boston Public Schools, 102 LRP 35377 (SEA MA 2002).

Bryant, T. J. (1998). The death knell for school expulsion: The 1997 amendments to the Individuals with Disabilities Education Act. *The American University Law Review, 47,* 487–555. Retrieved January 14, 2002, from http://web.lexis-nexis.com/universe.

Buck, G. H., Polloway, E. A., Kirkpatrick, M. A., Patton, J. R., & Fad, K. M. (2000). Developing behavioral intervention plans: A sequential approach. *Intervention in School and Clinic, 36*(1), 3–9.

Canter, L., & Canter, M. (1992). *Assertive discipline: Positive behavior management for today's classrooms.* Santa Monica, CA: Lee Canter & Associates.

Cessna, K. K. (1993). *Instructionally differentiated programming: A needs-based approach for students with behavior disorders.* Denver: Colorado Department of Education.

Charles, C. M. (2000). *The synergetic classroom: Joyful teaching and gentle discipline.* New York: Longman.

Curwin, R. L., & Mendler, A. N. (1997). Discipline with dignity: Beyond obedience. *The Education Digest, 63*(4), 11–14.

Dallas School District, 28 IDELR 1225 (SEA OR 1998).

Daunic, A. P., Smith, S. W., Robinson, T. R., Miller, M. D., & Landry, K. L. (2000). School-wide conflict resolution and peer mediation programs: Experiences in three middle schools. *Intervention in School and Clinic, 36*(2), 94–100.

Drasgow, E., & Yell, M. L. (2001). Functional behavioral assessments: Legal requirements and challenges. *School Psychology Review, 30*(2), 239–251.

Drasgow, E., Yell, M. L., Bradley, R., & Shrirer, J. G. (1999). The IDEA Amendments of 1997: A schoolwide model for conducting functional behavioral assessments and developing behavioral intervention plans. *Education and Treatment of Children, 22*(3), 244–266.

Ellingson, S. A., Miltenberger, R. G., Stricker, J., Ervin, R. A., DuPaul, G. J., Kern, L., et. al. (1998). Classroombased functional and adjunctive assessments: Proactive approaches to intervention selection for adolescents with attention deficit hyperactivity disorders. *Journal of Applied Behavior Analysis, 31,* 65–78.

Ellingson, S. A., Miltenberger, R. G., Stricker, J., Galensky, T. L., & Garlinghouse, M. (2000). Functional assessment and intervention for challenging behaviors in the classroom by general classroom teachers. *Journal of Positive Behavior Interventions, 2*(2), 85–97.

Etscheidt, S. (2002). Discipline provision of IDEA: Misguided policy or tacit reform initiatives? *Behavioral Disorders, 27*(4), 408–422.

Fennimore, B. S. (1995). *Student-centered classroom management.* Albany, NY: Delmar.

Fesmire, M., Lisner, M. C. P., Forrest, P. R., & Evans, W. H. (2003). Concept maps: A practical solution for completing functional behavioral assessments. *Education and Treatment of Children, 26*(1), 89–103.

Freiberg, H. J. (1999). Consistency management and cooperative discipline: From tourists to citizens in the classroom. In H. J. Freiberg (Ed.), *Beyond behaviorism: Changing the classroom management* paradigm. Boston: Allyn & Bacon.

Gathercoal, F. (1997). *Judicious discipline* (4th ed.). San Francisco: Caddo Gap Press.

Glasser, W. (1997). *The quality school teacher.* New York: Harper Perennial.

Glennon, T. (1993). Disability ambiguities: Confronting barriers to the education of students with emotional disabilities. *Tennessee Law Review, 60,* 295–369.

Goss v. Lopez, 419 U.S. 565, 95 S. Ct. 729 (1975).

Grossman, H. (1995). *Classroom behavior management in a diverse society* (2nd ed.). Mountain View, CA: Mayfield Publishing.

Hartwig, E. P., Robertshaw, C. S., & Ruesch, G. M. (1991). Disciplining children with disabilities. *Individuals with Disabilities Education Law Report* (Special Rep. No. 5). Horsham, PA: LRP Publications.

Honig v. Doe, 484 U.S. 305, 108 S. Ct. 592 (1988).

Hoover, R. L., & Kindsvatter, R. (1997). *Democratic discipline: Foundation & practice.* Upper Saddle River, NJ: Merrill/Prentice Hall.

Horner, R. H., & Sugai, G. (2000). School-wide behavior support: An emerging initiative. *Journal of Positive Behavior Interventions, 2*(4), 231–232.

Horner, R., Todd, A., Lewis-Palmer, T., Irvin, L., Sugai, G., & Borland, J. (2004). The school-wide evaluation tool (SET): A research instrument for assessing school-wide positive behavior support. *Journal of Positive Behavior Interventions, 6*(1), 3–12.

House Report No. 105–95 (1997). U.S.C. Congressional and Administrative News, West, 78–146.

Huefner D. S. (1998). The Individuals With Disabilities Education Act Amendments of 1997. *Education Law Reporter, 122,* 1,103–1,122.

Hyter, Y. D. (2003). Language intervention for children with emotional or behavioral disorders. *Behavioral Disorders, 29*(1), 65–76.

Individuals with Disabilities Education Act, 20 U.S.C. §§ 1,401–1,487.

Jensen, G. (Spring 1996). Disciplining students with disabilities: Problems under the Individuals With Disabilities Education Act. *B.Y.U. Education and Law Journal,* 34–54.

Johns, B. H., Carr, V. G., & Hoots, C. W. (1997). *Reduction of school violence: Alternatives to suspension.* Horsham, PA: LRP Publications.

Johns, B. H., & Keenan, J. P. (1997). *Techniques for managing a safe school.* Denver, CO: Love Publishing Company.

Johnson, D., & Johnson, R. (1996). Peacemakers: Teaching students to resolve their own and schoolmates' conflicts. *Focus on Exceptional Children, 28*(6), 1–12.

Johnson, L. R., & Johnson, E. E. (1999). Teaching students to regulate their own behavior. *Teaching Exceptional Children, 31*(4), 6–10.

Jones, F. H. (1987). *Positive classroom instruction.* New York: McGraw-Hill.

Jones, V., Dohrn, E., & Dunn, C. (2004). *Creating effective programs for students with emotional and* behavior disorders: Interdisciplinary approaches for adding meaning and hope to behavior change interventions. Boston: Allyn & Bacon/Pearson.

Jones, V. F., & Jones, L. S. (1995). Comprehensive classroom management: Creating positive learning environments for all students (4th ed.). Boston: Allyn & Bacon.

Kea, C., & Utley, C. (1998). To teach me is to know me. The Journal of Special Education, 32, 44–47.

Kern, L., & Manz, P. (2004). A look at current validity issues of school-wide behavior support. Behavioral Disorders, 30(1), 47–59.

Kerr, M. M., & Nelson, C. M. (2002). Strategies for addressing behavior problems in the classroom (4th ed.). Upper Saddle River, NJ: Merrill/Prentice Hall.

Lane, K. L., Wehby, J., Menzies, H. M., Doukas, G. L., Munton, S. M., & Gregg, R. M. (2003). Social skills instruction for students at risk for antisocial behavior: The effects of small-group instruction. Behavioral Disorders, 28(3), 229–248.

Lewis, T. J., Hudson, S., Richter, M., & Johnson, N. (2004). Scientifically supported practices in emotional and behavioral disorders: A proposed approach and brief review of current practices. Behavioral Disorders, 29(3), 247–259.

Lickona, T., (2000). Sticks and stones may break my bones and names will hurt me: Thirteen ways to prevent peer cruelty. Our Children, 26(1), 12–14.

Maag, J. W. (2004). Behavior Management: From theoretical implications to practical applications (2nd ed.). Belmont, CA: Wadsworth.

Maag, J. W., Reid, R., & DiGangi, S. A. (1993). Differential effects of self-monitoring attention, accuracy, and productivity. Journal of Applied Behavior Analysis, 26, 329–344.

Manchester School District v. Charles M. F., 21 IDELR 732 (D.C. NH 1994).

Manning, M. L., and Bucher, K. (2003) Classroom management: Models, applications, and cases. Upper Saddle River, NJ: Merrill/Prentice Hall.

Martella, R. C., Nelson, J. R., & Marchand-Martella, N. E. (2003). Managing disruptive behaviors in the schools: A schoolwide, classroom, and individualized social learning approach. New York: Pearson Education, Inc.

Mason City Community School District and Northern Trails Area Education Agency 2, 36 IDELR 50 (SEA IA 2001).

McConnel, M. E., Hilvitz, D. B., & Cox, C. J. (1998). Functional assessment: A systematic process for assessment and intervention in general and special education classrooms. Intervention in School and Clinic, 34(1), 10–20.

McIntyre, T. (1992). The culturally sensitive disciplinarian. Severe Behavior Disorders Monograph, (15), 107–115. Reston, VA: Council for Exceptional Children.

Mead, J. F. (1998). Expressions of congressional intent: Examining the 1997 Amendments to the IDEA. Education Law Reporter, 126, 511–531.

Neel, R. S., & Cessna, K. K. (1993). Behavioral intent: Instructional content for students with behavior disorders. In K. Cessna (Ed.), Instructionally differentiated programming: A needs-based approach for students with behavior disorders. Denver: Colorado Department of Education.

Nelson, J.R., Crabtree, M., Marchand-Martella, N., & Martella, R. (1998). Teaching behavior in the whole school. Teaching Exceptional Children, 30(4), 4–9.

Nichols, J. D., Ludwin, W. G., & Iadicola, P. (1999). A darker shade of gray: A year-end analysis of discipline and suspension data. Equity and Excellence in Education, 32(1), 43–54.

Northeast Indep. Sch. Dist., 28 IDELR 1004 (SEA TX 1998). Office of Special Education Programs (OSEP) (1995). OSEP memorandum as 16.22 MELR531.

Osborne, A. G. (1997). Making the manifestation—determination when disciplining a special education student. Education Law Reporter, 119, 323–330.

Packenham, M., Shute, R., & Reid, R. (2004). A truncated functional behavioral assessment procedure for children with disruptive classroom behavior. Education and Treatment of Children, 27(1), 9–25.

Rachelson, A. D. (1997). Expelling students who claim to be disabled: Escaping the Individual with Disabilities Education Act's "stay-put" provision. Michigan Law and Policy Review, 2. Retrieved January 14, 2002, from http://web.lexis-nexis.com/universe.

Rinaldi, C. (2003). Language competence and social behavior of students with emotional or behavioral disorders. Behavioral Disorders, 29(1), 34–42.

Rogers-Adkinson, D. L. (2003). Language processing in children with emotional disorders. Behavioral Disorders, 29(1), 43–47.

Rogers-Adkinson, D. L., & Hooper, S. R. (2003). The relationship of language and behavior: Introduction to the special issue. *Behavioral Disorders, 29*(1), 5–9.

Russell Farrin v. Maine School Administrative District No. 59, 35 IDELR 189 (D.C. ME 2001).

Rutherford, R. B., & Nelson, C. M. (1995). Management of aggression and violent behavior in schools. *Focus on Exceptional Children, 27*(6), 1–15.

Safran, S. P., & Oswald, K. (2003). Positive behavior supports: Can schools reshape disciplinary practices? *Exceptional Children, 69*(3), 361–373.

Scott, V. (1998). Breaking the cycle of incivility. *The High School Magazine, 6*(1), 4–7.

Shippen, M. E., Simpson, R. G., & Crites, S. A. (2003). A practical guide to functional behavioral assessment. *Teaching Exceptional Children, 35*(5), 36–44.

Skiba, R., Waldron, N., Bahamonde, D., & Machalek, D. (1998). A 4-step model for functional behavioral assessment. *NASP Communique, 26*(7). Retrieved August 2, 2005, from http://www.nasponline.org.

Skiba, R. J., & Peterson, R. L. (2000). School discipline at a cross-roads: From zero tolerance to early response. *Exceptional Children, 66*(3), 335–347.

Smith, C. R. (2000). Behavioral and discipline provisions of IDEA '97: Implicit competencies yet to be confirmed. *Exceptional Children, 66*(3), 403–412.

Smith County Sch. Sys., 27 IDELR 764 (SEA TN 1998).

Strayhorn, J., Strain, P. S., & Walker, H. M. (1993). The case for interaction skills training in the context of tutoring as a preventative mental health intervention in the schools. *Behavioral Disorders, 19*(1), 11–26.

Sugai, G., Horner, R. H., Dunlap, G., Hieneman, M., Lewis, T. J., Nelson, C. M., et. al. (2000). Applying positive behavior support and functional behavioral assessment in schools. *Journal of Positive Behavior Interventions, 2*, 131–143.

Tehachapi Unified School District, 106 CRP 22450 (SEA CA 2006).

Townsend, B. L. (2000). The disproportionate discipline of African American learners: Reducing school suspensions and expulsions. *Exceptional Children, 66*(33), 381–391.

Turnbull, H. R., & Turnbull, A. P. (1998). *Free appropriate public education: The law and children with disabilities* (5th ed.). Denver, CO: Love Publishing.

Turnbull, H. R. III, Wilcox, B. L., Stowe, M., Raper, C., & Hedges, L. P. (2000). Public policy foundations for positive behavioral interventions, strategies, and supports. *Journal of Positive Behavior Interventions, 2*(4), 218–230.

Walker, H. M., Ramsey, E., & Gresham, F. M. (2004). *Antisocial behavior in school: Evidence-based practices.* Belmont, CA: Wadsworth.

Yell, M. L. (1998). *The law and special education.* Upper Saddle River, NJ: Merrill/Prentice Hall.

Zirpoli, T. J. (1995). *Understanding and affecting the behavior of young children.* Upper Saddle River, NJ: Merrill/Prentice Hall.

Zurkowski, J. K., Kelly, P. S., & Griswold, D. E. (1998). Discipline and IDEA 1997: Instituting a new balance. *Intervention in School and Clinic, 34*(1), 3–9.

CHAPTER 10

STAFF RELATIONSHIPS AND STAFFING PATTERNS

CHAPTER PREVIEW

Focus

Meeting the needs of students with disabilities in inclusive classrooms and other school settings demands cooperative efforts among regular and special educators and support professionals. Such cooperation often is made difficult, however, by the traditional separation of these professional disciplines and by associated attitudes of suspicion, competition, and exclusivity. Research has established that such barriers can be broken down through staff participation in positive inclusion experiences.

Rationale

Collaborative professional arrangements, such as co-teaching and peer coaching, are often the most efficient and child-centered means of delivering appropriate instruction to all students. Unlike the completely separate educational environments of parallel regular and special education programs from the past, they allow students with disabilities to learn in the most typical environment appropriate. The planned opportunity for students with disabilities to be included in the regular classroom and general curriculum has obvious benefits for school districts attempting to meet the student achievement mandates of "No Child Left Behind" legislation. Professional commitment to pursue what is best for all children should engender a commitment to collaboration.

Approaches

Educational leaders must encourage and model a positive approach toward the presence of students with special needs in the school. School facilities, resources, and time schedules, as well as nonacademic tasks and responsibilities, should be distributed equitably among staff members. All staff should be provided adequate time for planning and coordination. Regular class teachers and specialists should be encouraged to be flexible, tolerant of teaching differences, and nondogmatic. Both should be encouraged to readily use the knowledge and experience of each other as resources.

The principal should consider collaboration and communication skills when hiring new staff members. They should be a priority for staff development opportunities, when needed. The duties of special educators and regular teachers should overlap and both should have responsibilities for all students (e.g., consultation on materials and curriculum modification for all students).

The necessity of proper staff preparation and professional development is inherent in a systematic planning and delivery process. Persons employed as teachers must meet the "highly qualified" criteria of "No Child Left Behind." Relevant research findings and best practices must be made accessible to all staff members.

STAFFING CONCERNS INHERENT IN THE IDEA

By its very nature, the implementation of the IDEA requires the coordination, communication, and cooperation of a number of professionals. How those persons are selected, organized, supervised, and trained is an important factor in the quality of programming received by all students. The expectations of a professional collaborative environment must be communicated and maintained. It cannot be left to chance.

The IDEA expressly requires interdisciplinary input at several points in the special education process. The evaluation-diagnostic team can include persons who will be part of the IEP team, and must include parents and other qualified professionals, as appropriate. The team assembled for IEP development must include the parents of the child, one school representative, at least one regular education teacher and one special education teacher, an individual who can interpret evaluation results, and others as desired. Interdisciplinary co-operation is also implicit in the requirement to provide related services, and supplementary aids and services, such as physical therapy, audiological and psychological services, and transportation, which are necessary for the child to be able to benefit from the special education programs and inclusive settings. The list of covered services is so broad that a great number of specialists may potentially be involved in any given school setting. Decisions regarding placement for educational programming must be made by a group of people, including the parents and other people knowledgeable about the child, the meaning of the evaluation data, and the placement options, and may include members of the IEP team. Special education, properly conceived, is truly an interdisciplinary program.

Challenges in Staffing Relationships

In schools where special and regular educators are not accustomed to working together, complaints such as the following may be all too familiar to administrators:

"I have 28 students in my class already. Why should I have to take in their students,

especially when they have to deal with only five or six at a time?"

"If regular class teachers had better attitudes toward kids with disabilities, if they individualized their teaching in the first place instead of expecting all students to learn in the same way . . . if they just had more commitment, there wouldn't be so many special students."

"I'm tired of so-called experts coming in and telling me how to run my class. Half the things they tell you don't work anyway."

"In a regular class, my students don't get the acceptance and understanding they need. It's a continual experience of failure, instead of a chance to find out what they really can do."

Attitudes inherent in expressions such as these tend to make cooperation difficult, if not impossible. Such complaints and prejudices are not always verbalized. Instead, they may emerge as avoidance (e.g., failure to contact a specialist for advice), as subtle assertions of power (e.g., use of professional jargon that others do not understand, refusal to acknowledge the opinion of a colleague from a profession of less status), the waste of valuable meeting time on petty disputes, and so on.

Although frustrating and obstructive, such attitudes do have understandable historic origins. After all, educators' training has historically been oriented toward producing autonomous experts, individuals in control of their own classroom, office, or clinical setting. There has also been pronounced separation between the disciplines of regular and special education—different training, different educational philosophies, different working conditions, and different populations of students. Yet, the educational philosophy embodied in the IDEA, especially the LRE concept, depends on cooperation between regular classroom teachers, special education teachers, and a variety of specialists.

Therein lies an important challenge for educational leaders. Whether a school plans to meet the legal requirements of inclusion for students where appropriate or go beyond to full inclusion, the challenge will be present. This chapter emphasizes the issue from an inclusion perspective, but most of the issues discussed are also present in school efforts at full inclusion.

Although we have moved closer in this country to breaking down barriers between regular and special education, much more is left to be done. In a survey conducted of graduate and undergraduate students in both regular and special education preparation programs, there was strong agreement with the philosophical basis of inclusion and with the position that the teaching of students with disabilities should be a responsibility shared by both regular and special education staff members. Those surveyed also agreed that regular class structure, curriculum, and teaching methodologies would have to be reevaluated with a view toward possible revision in order to meet the needs of a broader range of students that would result from implementing inclusive programs. However, regular educators differed from special educators in their belief that students with mental or behavioral disabilities should not be in inclusive settings. The researchers concluded that teacher preparation programs need to better reflect an understanding of an individual student's needs, which are both behind and beyond the special labels, and provide good information about modifying regular class structure, curriculum, and pedagogy (Taylor, Richards, Goldstein, & Schilit, 1997).

The result of many years of special education pull-out programs, where the child leaves the regular classroom in order to receive special education programs and services, has been an educational environment based on a notion of "our" students versus "their" students and accompanying attitudes of suspicion, defensiveness, and intimidation. Despite the demand for cooperative efforts imposed by the IDEA, clear collaborative roles and structures have been slow to evolve.

What Research Shows

Resources in education remain scarce and expectations have multiplied. To some extent, educational conflicts over special education are really outlets for broader-based educator frustrations. The disparity in attitude between some regular and special educators over the concept of inclusion may be as much a personal relationship to experience and practice as anything else. In a study involving teams of regular and special educators working with children with severe disabilities in an inclusive setting, Wood (1998) found that attitudes and behavior changed. During the early stages of a new inclusion experience, the teachers maintained traditional discrete role differences. However, those roles became less rigid and education became a more collaborative effort as the school year progressed.

In addition, Phillips, Sapona, and Lubic (1995) found that for first-year inclusion teams, high anxiety levels at the beginning of the school year were typical. There was general concern expressed over the lack of role clarity and constantly having other adults observe them in the work setting. Like Wood, these researchers found that the teachers' anxiety largely vanished by year's end. They indicated that all the teachers in their study had their belief systems altered by experience, and had become supporters of and focused on cooperative inclusive settings for students.

These findings are almost universal. Similar results were identified by Giangreco, Dennis, Cloninger, Edelman, and Schattman (1993) in a study of 19 regular education teachers having at least one student with a severe disability in class. At the beginning of their inclusion experience all the teachers shared serious apprehensions, initially experienced minimal involvement with the students with disabilities in their classes, and had expectations that someone else would be responsible for the students' education. By the end of the first school year, 17 of the 19 teachers described personally transforming experiences occurring during the year. The 17 were able to identify many benefits of the inclusion experience to the students with disabilities, to their classmates, and to themselves professionally as teachers. The two teachers who had not expressed a change in professional perspective had not become as professionally involved with the students with disabilities as had their colleagues. One of the teachers who did not find the experience beneficial to herself, or the student, disagreed with two other teachers who had previously had the same student included in their classes. Interestingly, none of the 19 teachers had any significant training to prepare them for their inclusion experience, yet almost all had successful experiences when shedding their initial apprehensions.

In another study involving almost 700 educators at 32 school sites judged as providing heterogeneous educational opportunities for all children, Villa, Thousand, Meyers, and Nevin (1996) found that experience with inclusion over time increased approval toward inclusion for both regular and special education educators. Increased support for inclusion among regular educators was found to be positively correlated to

- the amount of related in-service training and technical assistance that was provided;
- the higher degree of administrative support;
- the extent to which regular and special educators collaborated;
- the amount of time structured for collaboration;
- accompanying organizational restructuring and reform initiatives begun within the school.

The expressed belief structure of both experienced regular and special educators involved in inclusive programming in the study supported the following concepts:

- Regular and special educators share a responsibility for meeting the needs of all children.
- Regular and special educators are able to work together as co-equal partners.
- The achievement level of students with disabilities does not decrease in the regular classroom.
- Team teaching enhances the feelings of competency for all teachers.
- Inclusion practices promote participatory decision-making, collaborative practices, and mutual support.

The researchers concluded that appropriate amounts of time for staff collaboration and planning must be an important part of any school's consideration of general restructuring of school-time parameters, such as changing from traditional to block scheduling. They also

recommended that the concept of shared decision making must be supported by administrators.

Principal's Role

Principals alone, with a wave of the hand, cannot be expected to work miracles to erase decades of teacher isolation, suspicion, and turf protection. They can, however, make an important difference. Principals can model interest in and acceptance of all students, staff, and programs in the school. They can distribute space, schedules, and resources in a way that minimizes conflict and structure new roles and formats in which staff members can work together supportively (C.E.C. & N.A.E.P., 2001). One study has indicated that the most important type of leadership support perceived by both special and regular educators is the emotional support that can be provided by principals. Because teachers generally receive little recognition for their efforts, they are appreciative of principals who seek teachers' input into important school decisions, exhibit trust in their judgment, show concern for all students and programs, and promote a sense of importance to teachers' efforts on behalf of students (Littrell, Billingsley, & Cross, 1994). Even when options are severely limited by such factors as the availability of resources, staff personalities, and lack of maneuvering room within district policies, the principal is in a better position to improve staff relationships than any other individual in the school.

Nowhere is that leadership function so closely tied to successful programming as it is in the area of staff collaboration in the implementation of inclusive programs. Nearly every study and report published on successful inclusive collaboration programs has emphasized the necessity of administrative support through

- joint problem-solving;
- maintaining and analyzing data;
- facilitating and participating in staff development programs;
- providing emotional support during tough times;
- modeling collaborative traits and communication;

- providing resources and helping establish priorities for their use;
- providing advocacy;
- ensuring that research-based interventions are planned and implemented;
- providing time for staff to engage in collaboration;
- assessing program efforts (Cole & McLesky, 1997; Cook & Friend, 1995; Mainzer, Deshler, Coleman, Kozleski, & Rodriguez-Walling, 2003).

Goor, Schwenn, and Boyer (1997) have identified five essential core beliefs that education leaders, particularly school principals, must have in order to establish or maintain successful school inclusive programs (pp. 134–135):

- Believe all children can learn.
- Accept all children as part of their school community.
- Believe teachers can teach a wide range of students.
- Believe teachers are responsible for all students.
- Believe that principals are responsible for the education of all children in their school.

In a study of school climate in inclusive schools, Salisbury and McGregor (2002) found that principals of successful inclusive schools shared several common characteristics: innovativeness, commitment to diversity, and an interest in school improvement. Other common chacteristics involved shared decision-making with staff members, leading by example (role modeling), promoting learning communities, and extending the core values of inclusion and quality to new innovations throughout the school.

Although no one support activity of educational leaders is more important than others, the one most mentioned by researchers is the scheduling of time for collaborative planning, communication, and problem-solving. Education leaders need to be creative and flexible in finding that crucial time. It may be through overtime pay before or after school, paid summer planning, planned use of paraeducators or volunteers, early release days for students, days set aside from instruction and devoted to consultation, combining classes temporarily, or the principal covering a classroom.

One of the authors has observed a successful inclusion program where in the school district assured each participating staff member up to 2 full days of "floating substitute" time each school year for collaboration as scheduled by inclusive group staff members. The program had been working successfully district-wide for over 15 years. At the secondary level, a well-planned block scheduling approach holds possibilities for greater staff communication and collaboration (Santos & Rettig, 1999).

Some authors suggest a greater use of technology to improve efficiency of planning and communication among inclusion team members. Robertson, Haines, Sanche, and Biffart (1997) have described the use of specialized computer software to enhance collaborative relationships in a Canadian school district. The use of technology allows faster, more frequent communication and joint problem-solving (e.g., e-mail), better record-keeping, and immediate access to data, checklists, student assessments, forms, and notes. Principals can initiate such programs where more traditional collaboration efforts are less feasible.

The Educational Leader as Agent of Change

Unfortunately, many educational leadership preparation programs ignore the special education component of many modern school settings and do not adequately provide preparation for the challenges ahead (Praisner, 2003; Sirotnik & Kimball, 1994). Praisner has established that exposure to special education concepts through coursework and professional development are correlated to a more positive attitude toward and success with inclusion in schools. The desired response is at least twofold: First, leadership preparation programs need to better integrate special education issues into their curricula, and second, individual educators need to make personal assessments of their own performance as educational leaders for all students.

Salisbury and McGregor (2002) have determined from their study of successful principals that inclusive practices were brought about through incremental steps and were not hurried. The slow, deliberate approach allowed for supports for students and staff to be identified and implemented. Important in bringing about this change was a reflective inquiry approach, an ongoing dialogue among staff and administrators about the implications of diversity, inclusion, collaboration, and new instructional practices on their specific school and classroom setting.

Because educational leaders are the chief agents of change in schools, new conceptions of the school administrator's role must be developed and understood by all. In the area of improving staff relationships, a principal might, for instance, begin the process with a self-evaluation along these lines:

1. Have I really accepted students with disabilities here?
2. Have I demonstrated that acceptance before all faculty members (in meetings, newsletters, special programs, etc.)?
3. Have I shown unfairness or favoritism in the treatment of either group of teachers (regarding room assignments, time schedules, other indications of status, etc.)?
4. Have I ensured that students with special needs have had access to status roles and activities?
5. Have I provided the support necessary to make it possible for inclusion to succeed (planning time, in-service training, teacher associates, etc.)?
6. Are both regular and special educators convinced that I understand their problems (and their contributions) and that I am committed to the best possible use of school resources to bring needed improvements?

PERSONNEL FUNCTIONS AND CHANGE

A principal newly assigned to a school is greatly limited in what she or he can accomplish in a short time with regard to staff and climate. Assessment of needs can be made and plans for future staff can be thought out. However, important and lasting change will come only through long-range decisions involving staff, including attracting and hiring persons who can implement the vision and philosophy of the school.

In the latest revision of their book on the human resources function in education, Young and Castetter (2004) have continued Castetter's earlier development of distinct personnel system functions, and now identify six major human resource processes. All six designations are relevant to obtaining and maintaining a good personnel resource pool. Whether a school is seeking regular education and special education teachers or support staff to fill roles involving students with disabilities, all six of these personnel functions need to be attended to, with obvious adjustments made depending on the anticipated role:

- In the area of *recruitment,* all advertisements and announcements should include expected job-related behaviors, responsibilities, and philosophies that impact an inclusion program. Therefore, it is very important to specify the school's needs, which mirror the intended results. Neither side wants any surprises when key personnel are recruited for important roles. For instance, advertisements for teaching staff might read "applicants are expected to role model behaviors that encourage acceptance of differences in others; demonstrate effective management of the learning environment; cooperate with colleagues in problem-solving; use multimodality for instruction, evaluation, and planning learning experiences; use a variety of student assessment and information-gathering techniques; maintain good professional relationships with parents; and maintain a familiarity with issues in special education and inclusion."

- In the area of *selection*, the same principles apply. Look for resumé items that provide experiences with inclusion or willingness to learn. During interviews, be sure to ask "how to" questions and perhaps engage in simulation or role playing to ensure that the person has the listening, communication, collaboration, problem-solving, and other skills required to be a successful inclusion team member. Ask about specific experiences, course work, and workshops attended on specific relevent topics.

- *Induction* programs provide knowledge of the school and its culture, emotional and professional support, and assistance with improving the quality of instruction (Boyer, 2005). Induction to the school environment and to an inclusion team is a crucial component of the successful integration of staff. New staff members need to be brought up-to-date on the history and philosophy of the school's inclusion program, rules, practices, and expectations. They need to be assigned to a successful experienced mentor and at the beginning of new employment, there should be time provided for many planned opportunities for debriefing and feedback (Lloyd, Wood, & Moreno, 2000). Effective mentoring is positively associated with educators' plans to stay in the profession (Boyer, 2005; Whitaker, 2000). Mentors should be rewarded for their important work. Rewards can take many forms, including professional development opportunities though attendance at state and national conferences of interest to the mentor, arranging for selected mentors to conduct demonstrations and workshops for other teachers, and recognition dinners sponsored by local community organizations supportive of local schools.

- *Professional development* opportunities can be used to meet a variety of staff needs, both individual and group. They can reinforce good behaviors; assist in strengthening planning, communication, and problem-solving skills; bring in new knowledge; and set the tone for program assessment and changes. A meaningful development program must include staff members in the needs assessment, planning, and delivery of their own staff development programs. Individual staff development opportunities should be developed and made available on an as-needed basis, rather than on previously scheduled dates only. Visitation to other classrooms and nearby successful programs should be available as needed. Supported attendance at state or national conferences enhances the recognition of professionalism while allowing the educators to remain current in their practices.

- *Appraisal*, or *evaluation*, must take into account whether the staff member is meeting the expectations that were made clear in the recruitment, selection, and induction processes. Staff evaluation can help to bring about or reinforce change, no matter what appraisal approach is used. There should be no surprises for either the school or staff member. Expectations should have been made clear all through the various personnel processes. The evaluation process merely measures individual performance against inclusion goals and school expectations in those areas. Areas of weakness, of both individuals and groups, can be identified and bolstered through professional development activities.

- *Compensation policy* and *practice* must be fair and equitable so that prospective staff will not be asked to financially sacrifice and so that current effective staff will not be seeking "greener" pastures elsewhere.

Although the foregoing discussion of personnel functions speaks directly to teaching and support staff, it also has important applications for volunteers, substitutes, and future professionals participating in student teaching and practicum experiences.

Celebrate Success

Educators do not celebrate their successes enough. Celebration should become an inherent part of personnel functions. In their detailed guide for people seeking to implement inclusion programs, Kochhar and West (1996) outlined the steps to successful inclusion programs. The tenth step is to "plan for a reward system to renew the staff and celebrate success." Kochhar and West recognized that celebration and recognition of both individual staff member and program successes are important to the development and reinforcement of the spirit of collaboration and coordination. This is the one step in bringing about change that is most frequently overlooked by many school leaders.

INTERSTATE SCHOOL LEADERS LICENSURE CONSORTIUM (ISLLC)

Educational leadership, both now and in the future, will require both the strengthening of existing skills and the building of new ones. A number of national groups have therefore studied the desirable and necessary elements exhibited by educational leaders that should be inherent in all educational leadership preparation programs.

The Council of Chief State School Officers has spearheaded a consortium of state educational agencies and various professional associations to establish a proposed set of guidelines for the preparation of educational leaders. The goal has been to stimulate debate about the necessary quality of educational leadership and to provide specific ideas that will enhance effective leadership of America's schools. The published report of the Interstate School Leaders Licensure Consortium (ISLLC) (Council of Chief State School Officers, 1996) provides six general, but informative, standards for principal licensure programs and professional development. Each standard is accompanied by more specific knowledge, disposition, and performance criteria indicators. A significant number of states have adopted the ISLLC standards as their state's philosopical foundation for school leader licensure preparation and professional development programs.

The guidelines aim to promote a quality education for all students. The six standard statements focus on teaching and learning and the creation of powerful learning environments. As you review the guidelines, think about how they parallel the rest of the material in this chapter and this book's expressed philosophy.

A school administrator is an educational leader who promotes the success of *all* students by

1. facilitating the development, articulation, implementation, and stewardship of a vision of learning that is shared and supported by the school community;
2. advocating, nurturing, and sustaining a school culture and institutional program conducive to student learning and staff professional growth;
3. ensuring management of the organization, operations, and resources for a safe, efficient, and effective learning environment;
4. collaborating with families and community members, responding to diverse community interests and needs, and mobilizing community resources;
5. acting with integrity, fairness, and in an ethical manner; and
6. understanding, responding to, and influencing the larger political, social, economic, legal, and cultural context. (pp. 10-20)

The inside back cover of this book list the chapters strongly identified with these six ISLLC standards.

COLLABORATIVE ROLES

The historical approach to education of students with disabilities has often been called the "two-box" model; students and staff were assigned to either regular or special education, without overlap (Reynolds & Birch, 1977). Staff members in one "box" had no particular reason to consult with those in the other. Today's schools are required to discard that historical delivery approach and design a continuum of educational placements to ensure that all students with disabilities are served in the most typical educational environment appropriate in the company of peers who are not disabled (see Chapter 5).

Although the level of services for each child varies, each type of arrangement in the placement continuum requires some measure of cooperation among special educators and other professionals. At a minimum, there is a need to coordinate schedules. Beyond that, almost limitless opportunities exist for sharing knowledge and experience in ways that directly benefit students with disabilities and also result in increased acceptance and understanding on the part of others. For example, through joint planning, a resource teacher can schedule remediation or skills development work to complement lessons in the regular class. Regular class teachers can learn to monitor and reinforce students' progress on these skills in the regular classroom. A special educator in a consulting role might offer help in anything from individualizing lessons or identifying appropriate materials to creating an accepting social environment among classmates without disabilities.

Collaboration has no established model; it has no boundaries beyond the imagination of the people arranging the program and organizing to meet the needs of students. By definition, collaboration means joint planning, decision-making, and problem-solving directed at a common, agreed-upon goal. This definition leaves a great deal of room for group initiative, experimentation, and problem-solving. About the only certainty to collaborative structure is that one person does not do it alone. Stanovich (1996) has listed six general characteristics of successful collaboration. Collaboration

- is voluntary;
- requires parity among participants;
- is based on mutual goals;
- depends on shared responsibility for participation;
- involves individuals who share their resources and decision-making;
- involves individuals who share accountability for outcomes.

Hunt, Soto, Maier, and Doering (2003) have developed and evaluated a process of collaboration between regular education staff, special education staff, and parents. This collaboration process proved successful in providing consistent and needed instruction to both at-risk students and students with severe disabilities. The researchers determined that their collaborative teaming process was successful because of the shared expertise, knowledge, and responsibility of the individual team members. Regularly scheduled opportunities for collaboration provided ample time for sharing and group reflection and was supported by school leadership who encouraged collaborative teams. Collaborative teams can sometimes be quite large, such as a middle school language arts team, and managing a mutually ageeable meeting time for everyone can be a great difficulty. It may be desirable to establish a smaller "working" team to ensure regular and effective planning and problem-solving.

An important key to successful collaboration directed at inclusion is the regular education teacher who volunteers to be part of these efforts. Many educators experienced in inclusive programs recommend not forcing regular education teachers into inclusion efforts (Chalmers & Faliede, 1996). Only willing teachers should be involved. Many resistant teachers will be willing to join the effort later as success is observed. Regular education teachers commonly underestimate their ability to meet the needs of a diverse student population. They must be helped to understand that successful teachers of students without disabilities have the necessary skills to teach those with disabilities (Giangreco, 1996). Small steps at the beginning of the implementation of inclusion programs will lessen frustration for the reluctant teacher and aid the inclusion effort in the long run.

Barriers to Collaboration

A number of authors have identified common barriers to successful collaboration. Principals need to pay special attention to these barriers because as education leaders they play a key role in their removal. Bondy and Brownell (1997) have identified the following barriers as important inhibitors of collaboration:

Belief System

- Teachers view their roles in narrow, specialized terms (e.g., secondary mathematics, gifted, elementary education).
- Teachers view other people's students as being the responsibility of the other person (i.e., ours and theirs, the two-box model).

- Teachers have preconceived perceptions of others that may discourage approaching other teachers as partners.
- Teachers view parents from distant and threatening perspectives.

Professional Isolation

- Limited opportunity to correct distorted perceptions.

Collaboration Skills

- Weak social and communication skills.
- Not used to working with other adults.
- Unpracticed in problem-solving skills.

Bondy and Brownell recommend that principals resolve collaboration deficiencies among staff by: (a) honestly assessing their own collaboration skills, (b) assessing their own interpersonal skills, (c) observing strong collaborators as role models and reflecting on what makes them successful, (d) listening carefully, (e) withholding judgment; (f) respecting others' worth and opinions; (g) attempting to find common ground, and most important, (h) focusing on the needs of students. Bondy and Brownell conclude their remarks with a reminder of the underlying philosophy of collaboration, "it takes a village to raise a child" (p. 114–115).

Examples of Collaboration

Co-Teaching One regular education teacher and one special education teacher teach the same class of students with diverse needs. The goal is to offer their combined expertise to all students in a coordinated fashion. Both teachers usually become more effective in meeting a wide range of students' needs. The specific mix of responsibilities is worked out between the partners and may change as classroom needs change. Implementation is varied:

> *Grazing*—one teacher provides direct class instruction; the other moves among the students to assist individuals.
>
> *Teaching on Purpose*—one teacher provides direct class instruction. The other gives short (5 minutes or less) direct

instruction to small groups of students as review, follow-up, or mini-lessons.

> *Tag-Team Teaching*—teachers take turns providing direct instruction; often used early in collaboration as teachers get to know each other.
>
> *Small-Group Teaching*—class is divided into two groups to allow for more interaction, often a follow-up or wrap-up to whole group instruction (sometimes called parallel teaching).
>
> *Flexible Heterogeneous*—grouping by skill or need level—groups change as subject or activity changes.
>
> *Multiple Groups*—similar to cooperative learning or learning centers, with two teachers actively circulating to respond to student group requests for assistance, or circulating presenting mini-lessons to small groups (sometimes called station learning).
>
> *Simultaneous Alternative Teaching*—teachers teach the same lesson to the same class, only they take turns. One teacher will follow the other's lesson with examples, review, or extensions of concepts (Vaughn, Schumm, & Arguelles, 1997).

Bauwens and Hourcade (1997) have described and diagrammed 17 different variations of co-teaching.

Co-teaching has many beneficial outcomes for staff and students. Cook and Friend (1995) found that co-teaching increases instructional options, improves program intensity and continuity among staff, reduces the stigma of individual attention for many students, and increases professional support where it counts the most, in the classroom. This can be especially beneficial at the secondary level where content is crucial and students with specific learning disabilities are in the classroom (Dieker & Little, 2005).

Cole and McLeskey (1997, p. 11) summarized their perspective of the benefits of co-teaching as follows:

1. Administrative duties, often disruptive to student learning (e.g., attendance, record-keeping), are shared.

2. Two adults in the classroom allows for problem intervention with minimal disruption.
3. Students receive more individualized attention.
4. Collegial feedback and evaluation enhance instructional quality.
5. Regular contact enhances opportunities for problem-solving and creativity.
6. Offers renewal and reinforcement from observing each other.
7. Provides students with model for collaboration and cooperation.
8. Teacher strengths balance against each others' weaknesses.

In his review of 10 studies conducted on co-teaching, Reinhiller (1996) found that both students with disabilities and those without benefited from greater specialized and more individualized instruction. As a side benefit, the school staff members involved in the 10 studies reported personal and professional growth benefits resulting from their shared classroom experiences.

One drawback to team teaching between high school regular class teachers and special education teachers is the shortage of available licensed special education teachers. This shortage has resulted in the development of hybrid cooperative learning models such as those developed in a county school district in Maryland. In one model, a special education teacher divides time between two classes on a relatively equal basis. In a different version of the same concept, the special education teacher maintains a collaborative scheduling with two regular class teachers and the three decide when the special educator will be in each class and what activity the special education teacher will provide. A third variation of the collaborative teaching model occurs when the special education teacher is part of an interdisciplinary team of teachers and the team determines the needed services and schedule of the special educator on a weekly basis. A fourth variation involves a more extensive use of paraeducators who team closely with the special educator to support students with disabilities in the regular classrooms. Each of these models have their own positives and negatives, but the

variety of approaches provides greater flexibility for teams of regular and special educators to serve the needs of all students (Walsh & Jones, 2004).

Having more than one adult in the secondary school classroom means that more time will be spent in active student engagement in academic learning with better achievement results (Wallace, Anderson, Bartholomay, & Hupp, 2002). But, it also means that regular educators, special educators, and paraeducators need to learn how to work together cooperatively and need additional time for planning. The absence of time for planning and appropriate training in collaboration skills and can seriously impact the quality and quantity of instruction received by students. It can also lead to wasted expertise on the part of a special education teacher with a master's degree performing the work of a paraeducator (Mastropieri et al., 2005; Weiss & Lloyd, 2002).

Mastropieri et al. (2005) conducted a series of case studies of co-teaching in science and social studies classes. They found that although the specific academic content itself had no influence on the degree of success of co-teaching, the special education teacher's level of mastery of the specific content area was an indication of the role she or he was likely to play on the team. The researchers determined that the establishment of a working relationship between co-teachers is the major component influencing the success of such programs. Where mutual trust and respect existed, successful efforts to provide modifications and accommodations were greater. Compatibility in teaching perspectives and effective teaching practices led to greater degrees of effective collaboration and student success. Interestingly, the researchers found that the number of years of experience did not appear to affect the success of co-teaching teams.

One of the more obvious benefits of cooperative teaching between special and regular education teachers is the greater opportunity for special education students to have a more meaningful access to the general curriculum (Magiera, Smith, Zigmond, & Gebauer, 2005; Walsh & Jones, 2004). State and federal academic standards and rigorous content assessments will more likely be met successfully by students with disabilities when they are exposed to the regular curriculum through team teaching. Through effective co-teaching, the strong content skills of the regular class teacher and the learning strategy skills of the special educator blend together to meet the needs and abilities of a wide variety of students. Many schools will look to co-teaching as a way of attempting to meet the requirements of No Child Left Behind that children with disabilities meet the same high standards as their nondisabled peers (Murawski & Diecker, 2004).

Peer Coaching   In peer coaching, at least one other adult observes teacher or staff performance and provides specific feedback. It can be used with teachers, paraeducators, or specialists (e.g., physical therapists). Peer coaching bridges limitations in knowledge or skills, and it facilitates the following types of collaboration:

> *By Experts*—more of a consultation model wherein people with special expertise observe teaching and provide feedback.
>
> *Reciprocal*—professionals observe each other and provide feedback. Participants can be at differing experience levels for a mix of perspectives. Philosophical differences, however, can be a problem (Vail, Tschantz, & Bevill, 1997).

Consulting   Teacher-to-teacher collaboration requires that special educators take a proactive role and seek out situations in which regular educators are willing to develop an ongoing openness of collaboration for the benefit of all students. Ongoing communication should occur on a weekly basis and a journal kept for later reference. Neither the special or regular educator should take the role of expert; both should be there to help the other. Collaboration may be started for the benefit of a particular student, but a trusting relationship can lead to instructional practices and services that benefit all students in a classroom setting (Vargo, 1998).

Because special education teachers cannot be in several regular education classrooms at the same time, paraeducators can be trained to act as surrogates of the special education teacher in working with the regular education teacher. It is important that the special education teacher maintain direct contact with the students on a regular basis (Dover, 2005).

Joint Planning   Educators and support staff, in group sessions, discuss different ways to meet a child's needs in a variety of settings and curricular areas. Sometimes this involves only the curricular needs of students through the joint determination of curricular priorities and the joint assignment of teaching responsibilities.

ASSIST Model   A secondary student instructional support team (ASSIST) is a more formalized joint planning model. It is used primarily at the secondary level and is comprised of both general and special educators across content areas and often includes service and support staff. It requires a close physical proximity cluster of classes and staff. Direct and indirect instructional support can be planned and implemented as required by student needs, whether for small groups or individuals. Time for planning and communication is crucial. Sometimes parallel teaching is the goal, and sometimes content review or learning strategy building is the goal. Having multiple instructional centers in a classroom at the same time leads to the alternative program nickname of "class-within-a-class" (Gable, Manning, Hendrickson, & Rogan, 1997).

The Multidisciplinary Team

As discussed in Chapters 3 and 7, many schools have begun to use multidisciplinary teams with diverse training and skills to identify and focus on individual students' educational needs in regular education before they are referred for formal special education evaluation. The teams may bear different names, such as Child Study Team or Student Assistance Team, and may vary in the number and professional specialty of members. However, they all are similar in function: to identify and attempt regular education alternative solutions to student learning needs other than referral to special education.

A standard arrangement is to meet weekly for a set limited time or number of cases. The first priority is to identify nonspecial education programs, services, and accommodations that may resolve a student's learning difficulties in a particular regular class setting. Only after it is conceded that the alternatives have not been, or will not be, successful is attention focused on the possible need for special education assessment and programming.

Under the 2004 Amendments to the IDEA, the approach of attempting multiple interventions in the regular class environment is referred to as "Response to Intervention." The potential benefits of a multidisciplinary team structure include increased efficiency, greater accuracy in assessment, and the fruitful and creative exchange of ideas, values, knowledge, and experience. All students in kindergarten through grade 12 who need academic and behavioral support to succeed in regular education, but who have not been identified as needing special education or related services, are eligible. Professional development for teachers and other staff to enable them to deliver scientifically based academic instruction and behavioral interventions, to improve their use of computer software, and to provide academic and behavioral assessments may be included in early intervention programs (20 U.S.C. § 1412 [a] [4] [A] [ii]). Under the 2004 Amendments, states may use up to 15% of the federal funds they receive under the IDEA to develop and coordinate these early intervention programs (20 U.S.C. § 1413 [f]).

NEW ROLES FOR EDUCATORS

A number of innovative ideas have been proposed for redefining the roles of both regular and special educators in inclusion schools. Where the history and tradition of a school have bred an environment of professional isolation and unfamiliarity, the first step toward cooperation and collaboration is to build trust. Successful implementation of inclusion presumes that no one staff member has the knowledge and experience to meet the needs of all students. It is critical that school staff think about collaboration and learn to work together rather than continuing to think and act as individuals (Kaff, 2004; Lamar-Dukes & Dukes, 2005; Villa & Thousand, 2003).

Special educators' traditional focus on remedial instruction and skill acquisitions, often in separate settings, has changed to one of joint participation and responsibility across the general curriculum. They now collaborate with regular class teachers and staff to create materials, teaching strategies, and assessments for all students on an individualized basis. The current focus on student academic achievement includes students with disabilities. That dictates that the special educator be integrated into interrelated curriculum development and teaching for learning focusing on curriculum, instructional modifications and accommodations, and new uses of technology and individualized student supports. In recognition of the new and varied roles played by special education teachers in providing direct and indirect support to students in inclusive settings, they are often referred to as *inclusion support teachers* (Lamar-Dukes & Dukes, 2005). The previous paradigm of only specialists educating students with disabilities has resulted in staffing models that are no longer justifiable from a logical perspective (Fisher, Frey, & Thousand, 2003).

Activities for education leaders to consider as possible new roles for special educators to fill while building trust in regular educators include

- team teaching combined classes in which one regular and one special education teacher are jointly responsible for all students (co-teaching);
- providing consultation and training services for teachers of all students, including, for example, consulting with regular teachers about all students with learning problems, whether or not they are identified for special education; and providing training for teachers of all students in social skills, communication skills, the nature of disabilities, and other areas of special expertise or benefit to assist in the successful integration of new students with disabilities into regular class settings;

- consulting on the assessment and grading of special students;
- leading in-service seminars or parent meetings;
- sharing equal responsibility for supervision of lunchrooms and playgrounds;
- supporting regular teachers in parent meetings;
- providing occasional activities for gifted and average students (this can help remove the stigma from resource rooms and special programming);
- sharing responsibility with regular teachers for the planning and development of school policies as well as individual programming.

Regular educators must be able to demonstrate a general understanding of disabilities in children, a sensitivity to their needs for accommodation, an awareness of their own obligations under the law, and especially, the skills to adapt instruction and activities to meet needs of a diverse group of students.

Principals must maintain an understanding of special education legal requirements, IEP implementation, team and collaboration building among staff, and their responsibility to monitor the success of their staff to successfully include students with disabilities into regular classes and activities. They must support and role-model team work and problem-solving approaches. They must treat all support staff, such as service providers and paraeducators, as members of the education team that has a shared duty and responsibility to all students. Both principals and teaching staff will need to develop the skills necessary to direct and supervise the work of paraeducators.

PARAEDUCATORS

Paraeducators are known by a number of other titles (e.g., teacher aides, teacher associates) and have a lengthy history of service to education. Over the years their role has evolved from clerical, housekeeping, and monitoring chores, to teacher support and facilitator, and to educational technicians providing instructional and

support services to a variety of students (French & Pickett, 1997; Giangreco, Yuan, McKenzie, Cameron, & Fialka, 2005). As the needs of students have become more complex and shortages of some teachers, such as bilingual and special education, have not been solved, education has turned more and more to the paraeducator for support.

One of the authors was present when a mother of six volunteered to provide paraeducator services to a third-grade child with autistic tendencies. Most of the school staff were concerned at the thought of attempting to work with an "impossible" child. The volunteer said that "a mother with six children of her own isn't likely to see many completely new things in only one child." The paraeducator participated fully in the IEP meetings and communicated regularly with the parents, teaching staff, and consultants about concerns and successes. Four years later, working with the same paraeducator but not in as close proximity, the boy was fully included in regular seventh-grade classes, was on the school's academic honor roll without grading accommodations, and was the recipient of awards for citizenship and writing poetry.

In collaborative situations, paraeducators often can make or break the success of an inclusive program. Paraeducator specialized training frequently has direct benefits for all students (Giangreco, Edelman, & Broen, 2003; Schepis, Ownbey, Parsons, & Reid, 2000). It is not surprising that the IDEA expressly requires states to ensure that persons serving as paraeducators be appropriately trained, supervised, and properly licensed where required (20 U.S.C. § 1412 [a] [14]).

With the success of a great number of students' education programs dependent, in part, on the quality of skills and ability of a paraeducator to communicate, facilitate, and coordinate, it is surprising that more care is not demanded in their recruitment, training, and assignment. Researchers have identified strong support for improved paraeducator training by parents of students with disabilities (Werts, Harris, Tillery, & Roark, 2004) and by paraeducators themselves (Chopra et al., 2004). The Council for Exceptional Children has issued a position paper that expressly calls for improvement in several areas of the use of paraeducators, including training. The six areas of expressed concern are (a) clarification of paraeducator roles, (b) systematic supervision and evaluation, (c) clarification of legal and ethical responsibilities, (d) development of job descriptions, (e) opportunities for preservice and staff development training, and (f) the training of teachers and specialists in the management of paraeducators (Hilton & Gerlach, 1997).

French and Pickett (1997) have studied related issues of teacher associates for many years and have raised a number of similar issues, which are summarized as follows:

- Teachers supervising paraeducators have little or no preparation for their supervisory task.
- Paraeducators often have little or no training in any phase of the tasks they are assigned.
- A good deal of job role overlap results from the lack of teacher or paraeducator preparation and a clear notion of what the role of paraeducator is to be.
- Paraeducators, as members of the community where the school is located, are often underused as links to the local community.
- Paraeducators, because of interest and experience, are good sources of future teachers, but are too often overlooked as a result of their lack of formal education.

Trautman (2004) has studied many of the same issues related to paraeducator performance and has recommended a planned sequential training program for paraeducators involving preservice, on-the-job, and in-service training for improved performance. Some topics of training that should be covered before a paraeducator starts working with students would include orientation to the school, school schedules, policies, communication practices, special education (e.g., IEP goals, related services), behavior management procedures, instructional methods, disabilities, and confidentiality concerns. In addition to formal training, it would be desirable for paraeducator trainees to observe supervising teachers and other paraeducators in their work settings. It is important in all training to engrain in the

trainee the school's role and responsibility expectations for various staff members.

Not all training needs to be completed before a paraeducator begins service. However, there should be a clear plan of providing the necessities early and the remainder soon after service begins. Because most training of paraeducators occurs on the job, Trautman (2004) has recommended that supervising teachers assume a coaching role. The supervisor can model appropriate skills and tasks, and then provide timely feedback on paraeducator's early use of skills, strategies, and methodologies.

Regular meetings should be planned between paraeducators and their supervising teachers to maintain communication and rapport and to discuss student problems or progress. Boyer and Mainzer (2003) have noted that paraeducators' confidence in their skills when working with special education programs greatly increases in direct correlation with increased meeting times with teachers. It is desirable to document decisions made at meetings so that everyone can approach a child's needs on a consistent and planned basis (Trautman, 2004).

The need for training and reinforcement of skills is continuous regardless of the number of years of paraeducator experience. Trautman has recommended comprehensive long-range training programs using formal course work, workshops, peer mentoring, and web-based training. (See the end of this chapter for suggested paraeducator training web site resources.)

The assignment of duties by supervising teachers should be well-thought out and planned, but the investment of time and effort allows teachers to do those tasks that only licensed educators can and should do (French, 2000).

Paraeducators can play the role of connectors of the school to the parents and the student with disabilities to other students. They often develop close and intertwining relationships with the family and community through common language (e.g., translators) and cultures (Chopra et al., 2004). Parent perceptions of paraeducators are generally quite positive. They see the paraeducator as an important key to their child receiving academic help, keeping their child focused, and assisting with behavior and peer social needs. Parents generally believe that their child's paraeducators should be more actively involved in parent conferences and IEP meetings and should play a more important role in communication among a child's IEP team members (Werts, Harris, Tillery, & Roark, 2004).

Appropriate attention must also be given to the training of substitute paraeducators who fill in for absent staff. It is important for paraeducators to have their work day outlined as specifically as possible so a substitute can follow as normal a schedule as possible (Trautman, 2004).

Giangreco, Edelman, Luiselli, and MacFarland (1997) have pointed out that with over 500,000 paraeducators employed in the schools, teachers and administrators must pay close attention to the function and services they provide. In their study of paraeducators working with students with multiple disabilities placed in the regular classroom, the researchers identified a number of major concerns related to the paraeducators' proximity to children with disabilities. When the paraeducator hovered near the child, even when not necessary, a number of negative results occurred. These included segregation of the student from classmates, interference with the concept of ownership by general educators, and interference with the instruction of other students. As a result of their findings, they recommend several solutions: IEP team awareness of the problem of paraeducator proximity and addressing it through training, both of paraeducators and other team members; use of paraeducators for the entire class and teacher, rather than individual students; and training the paraeducators in how to decrease student dependence on them. Giangreco (2003) has subsequently provided additional suggestions to minimize unintended effects of paraeducator support. Among the additional suggestions were greater use of peer-to-peer teaching methodologies, such as cooperative learning and peer tutoring; seating students with disabilities in the midst of the class; and including students with disabilities in determinations of the type and nature of paraeducator suport they need.

Causton-Theoharis and Malmgren (2005) have recognized the desirability of reducing the inadvertent effect of paraeducators creating social isolation for students with disabilities in regular classrooms. They have identified appropriate training as a potential solution. They investigated the effectiveness of a training program designed to teach paraeducators to facilitate appropriate interactions between students with severe disabilities and their peers. Their study demonstrated that a training intervention of low cost and short duration provided immediate and potentially long-lasting positive results on the interaction rates of students with severe disabilities in inclusive classrooms. The authors recommended that intervention strategies to improve paraeducator assistance in facilitating peer interaction be used in professional development opportunities for paraeducators.

Teachers and principals working with paraeducators are only now beginning to feel experienced in the process. That is probably why little research exists on job expectations from the perspective of paraeducators. In attempting to learn more about paraeducators' perspectives, Riggs (2004) convened a focus group of 35 veteran paraeducators from several states and asked them to list the things they wanted teachers to know about working with paraeducators. The list reflects best practice, but it is revealing:

1. Know the paraeducator's name, background, and interests. Teachers showing an interest in their team members can lead to a more productive and happier paraeducator.
2. Be familiar with district policies for paraeducators. Policies and contract terms concerning work hours, breaks, and supervision responsibilities should not have to lead to unnecessary conflicts.
3. View the teacher and paraeducator as a team. Problems and conflicts should be resolved cooperatively and professionally.
4. Share your classroom expectations with paraeducators. Clear expectations of what to do and what not to do are important.
5. Define specific roles and responsibilities for pareducators and teachers. Sometimes

similar roles need clearly defined distinctions between the teacher and paraeducator roles.

6. It is the teacher's responsibility to direct and supervise paraeducators. Many teachers are unaccustomed and reluctant to supervise adults, especially when the paraeducator may be of the same age or older.

7. Communicate with paraeducators. Formal and informal feedback are critical to success.

8. Recognize that paraeducators have experience and knowledge. Involving paraeducators in planning and decision-making activities establishes mutual respect.

9. As the teacher, take ownership of all students. Each child should feel a relationship with the teacher.

10. Show respect for paraeducators. Showing appreciation and recognizing paraeducator contributions, both formally and informally, are important parts of maintaining the appropriate team climate.

Giangreco, Edelman, and Broen (2003) have recognized the need for more effective planning and implementation of paraeducator programs in school districts. They developed and field-tested a process to assist schools in self-assessing paraeducator practices, identifying priorities, developing implementation plans, and evaluating results. The field tests established the successful utilization of the process in a variety of school settings. Their *A Guide to Schoolwide Planning for Paraeducator Supports* is online, free, and available to schools (see reference list).

Principals should be ready and able to take the cue from researchers' observations and train paraeducators to be more meaningful team players. After all, a significant portion of students' individual contacts with adults at school are with paraeducators.

With research reporting the benefits of paraeducators to students and teachers, it would logically be assumed that teacher preparation programs would spend considerable time teaching preservice special education teachers the knowledge and skills related to working with paraeducators. A study conducted in one state,

however, indicated that newly licensed special education teachers did not perceive they had been adequately trained in paraeducator collaboration, communication, and supervision skills in their preparation programs. An especially telling aspect of the study was that professors in those same teacher training programs expressed the belief that adequate preparations for working with paraeducators had taken place (Wiese, 2004).

Paraeducators should not be used to substitute for licensed teachers and should always work under the direction and supervision of licensed staff (French, 2003). The use of paraeducators to carry out the traditional role of a teacher (to plan, evaluate, diagnose, and prescribe student learning) would violate the IDEA requirement that personnel assigned to work with children with disabilities be appropriately and adequately prepared for their roles.

"HIGHLY QUALIFIED" STAFF

The Elementary and Secondary Education Act of 1965 as amended in January 2002 by the No Child Left Behind Act (NCLB; P. L. 107–110) and the 2004 Amendments to the IDEA present significant personnel challenges to the nation's public schools. As explained in the 2004 Amendments, Congress determined that the 30-year existence of the IDEA had demonstrated that the education of children with disabilities can be made more effective through the provision of "intensive preservice preparation and professional development" for all staff who work with children with disabilities. Requiring school personnel to have the skills and knowledge, including "scientifically based instructional practices" necessary to improve student academic achievement and functional performance would help ensure effective education for those children (20 U.S.C. § 1401 [c] [5] [E]). The result is that schools must assure that their staffs are "highly qualified."

Each state receiving Title I funds for disadvantaged students must ensure that all newly hired teachers of core academic subjects teaching in programs with Title I support must be "highly qualified." By the end of the 2005–2006 school year, *all* teachers of core academic subjects in the public schools of the state were required to be "highly qualified." The phrase "core academic subjects" means English, reading or languages arts, mathematics, science, foreign languages, civics and government, economics, arts, history, and geography. Teachers of courses not considered a core academic subject, such as vocational education, are not required to be "highly qualified."

To be considered "highly qualified" as a teacher, a person must

- hold at least a bachelor's degree from a 4-year institution of higher education; and either
- hold full state licensure as a teacher; or
- demonstrate competence through a rigorous state test in the subject area taught, or majoring in the subject; by earning a graduate degree, or by equivalent course work in that subject; or by obtaining an advanced certificate.

To be considered "highly qualified" as a special education teacher, a person must

- hold at least a bachelor's degree from a 4-year institution of higher learning; and either
- hold full state licensure as a special education teacher, with no licensure requirements waived on an emergency, temporary, or provisional basis; or
- pass the state special education teacher licensing examination.

Special education teachers who provide instruction in core academic subjects in a regular classroom, a resource room, or other educational setting must meet the "highly qualified teacher" requirements for each of the core academic subjects they teach. However, special education teachers who do not provide direct instruction to students in core academic subjects do not have to meet the "highly qualified" standard. Special educators who only provide consultation, adapt curricula, determine appropriate accommodations, and provide other supports to "highly qualified teachers" of core academic subjects do not need to demonstrate their meeting the "highly qualified" teachers' standards (Yell, 2006). Neither do special educators who teach study skills, organizational skills, or support instruction provided by a "highly qualified" teacher.

Special education teachers who exclusively teach students with disabilities who are assessed under alternate state achievement standards are considered "highly qualified" when they hold licensure at least at the elementary level or successfully pass a state exam covering multiple academic subjects.

In an apparent recognition of the difficulty of local schools meeting the "highly qualified" teacher standard in the provision of special education, Congress has prohibited lawsuits by individual students and class actions for the failure to have employees "highly qualified" (20 U.S.C. § 1402 [10] [E]). Congress did not, however, prohibit the use of other administrative remedies (mediation and due process hearings) in challenging a school's use of staff that are not "highly qualified" (20 U.S.C. § 1412 [a] [14] [b]).

The most difficult adjustment for special education teachers will be for those who provide direct instruction in the core academic subjects in special education class settings. They will no longer be able to continue providing direct instruction of core academic subjects to students needing special education unless they meet the definition of "highly qualified" or teach under the direct supervision of "highly qualified" regular education teachers. Some schools and teachers may turn to inclusive programs and team teaching in order to assure special education students access to "highly qualified" teachers for core academic subjects. That may also be an indirect result of holding *all* students accountable for a school's adequate yearly progress (AYP) on testing of standards under the NCLB legislation.

Brownell, Hirsch, and Seo (2004) acknowledge the difficulty of states meeting the demand for "highly qualified" teachers in special education. They expect the demand to be met partially by paying greater attention to and remediation of factors that play a role in teachers leaving the profession (attrition), and partially through better data maintained by schools on personnel characteristics and needs. They contend that the final result should be an improvement in preparation, induction, and professional development programs for special education teachers.

Billingsley (2004) has expressed a similar expectation. She is especially concerned with the high number of new special education teachers who leave teaching or teach in areas other than special education. As a result, Billingsley recommends well-planned comprehensive and responsive induction programs for new special education teachers, clear and deliberate role design and description, positive work conditions and school climate, administrative supports, and necessary professional development opportunities.

All paraeducators hired before January 2002, if their positions are funded by Title I funds or they provide instructional support in Title I school-wide programs, must now meet specified qualifications and all paraeducators hired after January 2002 must meet three specific qualifications when hired. These paraeducators must

- meet a rigorous standard of quality, established through formal assessment of knowledge of and ability to assist in instructing or in readiness activities for reading, writing, or mathematics;
- have completed at least 2 years of study at an institution of higher education; and
- have obtained an associate's or higher degree.

Paraeducators meeting the qualifications must work under the direct supervision of a teacher when providing instructional support activities. Other appropriate duties of a paraprofessional under the NCLB legislation include one-on-one tutoring, assisting with classroom management, assisting in computer instruction, conducting parent involvement activities, providing instructional support in a library or media center, and acting as a translator (Yell, 2006). People who perform only noninstructional roles, such as clerical tasks and supervision, do not have to meet the NCLB definition of a paraeducator.

Related services personnel and paraeducators with only an emergency, temporary, or provisional license may not deliver services to children with disabilities (20 U.S.C. § 1412 [a] [14] [B]).

Many of those involved in education view the new legal requirements as a warning to school districts, as well as states, that the skills, training, and knowledge requirements of school staff, including paraeducators, has been inadequate. More attention must be paid to the training and quality of the staff assigned to work with students with disabilities. Inherent in the entire context of the current IDEA is the need for trained team members to meet the needs of a new system of integrated programs and services. Many skills, not previously exhibited on an extensive level such as collaboration, problem-solving, and communication, must be considered a part of that training.

The mandates to states for improvement of personnel working with students with disabilities appear to be considerably different from what is actually occurring in some states and local school districts. Both state and local school officials are forewarned that they had better be working to improve the quality of training for staff members working with students and on dissemination of research results and best practices ideas. If not, Congress may make the personnel mandates more concrete in the future.

Local schools are prohibited under the IDEA from discrimination in the employment and advancement of qualified staff members with disabilities in programs and services for students with disabilities (20 U.S.C. § 1406).

CONCLUSION

The organization of schools with one teacher, one class, and one classroom may have served America well, but its roots are in the nineteenth century. Back then, a high school education, or less, was considered adequate training for a teacher. Greater efforts at specialized training, mandated dissemination of research results and best practices, and success with a variety of classroom organization models across the nation are signals that the time for change has come.

Like everything else in modern society, education has become more complex. New ways of doing things are required. Collaboration and teaming are but a small part of the overall educational reform movement that will make schools better places to learn and to work. Educational leaders play the key role in bringing about the changes in practice, philosophy, and professional development necessary to best serve the needs of all students. America's educational leaders are up to the task; new delivery systems are being implemented successfully across the country.

VIEW FROM THE COURTS

T. W. v. Unified School District No. 259 (2005; staff members frequently consulted and coordinated with each other and were properly trained). A parent challenged a lower court ruling permitting a school to place a first-grade student with Down Syndrome in a self-contained special education classroom rather than an inclusive classroom setting. The boy had previously been placed in an inclusive kindergarten setting for one semester. The parent complained that the providers of supplementary aids and services (a one-on-one paraeducator, a physical therapist, an occupational therapist, a speech therapist, and an adaptive physical education teacher) were ineffective because they did not coordinate their services with the regular education teacher or special education personnel.

The court noted that the law does not establish a particular level of coordination between service providers and regular and special education staff. Nothing in the law requires that all coordination and collaboration be conducted in regularly scheduled and formal meetings between service providers and staff. The court recognized that informal collaboration and coordination is sometimes done "on the run as they're walking down the hallway." The school placement in a self-contained special education classroom was upheld.

Board of Education v. I. S. (2004; paraeducator's one-on-one services interfered with student's learning and development of independence in an inclusive classroom). An administrative law judge (ALJ) concluded, following a hearing, that the appropriate placement for a 10-year-old child with multiple disabilities was in a private special education school and not an inclusive regular education classroom as the public school proposed. The school appealed the ALJ's decision into federal district court. For a number of reasons, especially the lack of educational benefit received by the girl in the previous inclusive regular classroom setting, the court upheld the ALJ's ruling. One reason expressly given by the court for its agreement that a special education placement was appropriate for the child was the interference with learning that resulted from an assigned one-on-one paraeducator to work with the girl in the inclusive kindergarten setting.

The evidence established that the paraeducator's presence impeded the girl from becoming accustomed to the regular class setting and discouraged her from developing skills of independence and self-reliance. Her opportunities for social interactions with peers were disrupted by the presence of the paraeducator, which was considered to be stigmatizing in the minds of the girl's peers. At times the physical presence of the paraeducator blocked the girl's view of the teacher and instruction. The court upheld the placement of the girl in a private special education school.

RECOMMENDED READINGS

Carroll, D. (2001). Considering paraeducator training, roles and responsibilities. *Teaching Exceptional Children, 34*(2), 60–64. The article provides a broad range of recommendations for schools using paraeducators.

Dieker, L. A., & Little, M. (2005). Secondary reading: Not just for reading teachers anymore. *Intervention in School and Clinic, 40,* 276–283. This article provides strategies for regular and special educators at the secondary level to effectively use reading material in content areas.

Elliott, D., & McKenney, M. (1998). Four inclusion models that work. *Teaching Exceptional Children, 30*(4), 54–58. This article discusses four collaborative and consultative models experienced by the authors.

French, N. K. (2002). Maximize paraprofessional services for students with learning disabilities. *Intervention in School and Clinic, 38*, 50–55. This article, by a nationally recognized expert, provides 20 specific recommendations for implementing successful paraeducator programs.

Giangreco, M. F., Yuan, S., McKenzie, B., Cameron, P., & Fialka, J. (2005). "Be careful what you wish for . . .": Five reasons to be concerned about the assignment of individual paraprofessionals. *Teaching Exceptional Children, 37*(5), 28–34. This article identifies concerns with the use of paraeducators often overlooked by educators and parents and provides considerations for effective use of paraeducators.

Keefe, E. B., Moore, V., & Duff, F. (2004). The four "knows" of collaborative teaching. *Teaching Exceptional Children, 36*(5), 36–42. This article describes how potential co-teacher colleagues can prepare to meet the challenges of co-teaching.

Lamar-Dukes, R., & Dukes, C. (2005). 20 ways to consider the roles and responsibilities of the inclusion support teacher. *Intervention in School and Clinic, 41*, 55–61. The article discusses 20 roles that can be fulfilled by special education teachers in inclusive settings.

Magiera, K., Smith, C., Zigmond, N., & Gebauer, K. (2005). Benefits of co-teaching in secondary mathematics classes. *Teaching Exceptional Children, 37*(3), 20–24. This article discusses the benefits of secondary mathematics teachers team teaching with secondary special education teachers and provides specific recommendations for successful learning.

Mulholland, R. (2005). Woodshop, technology, and reading! *Teaching Exceptional Children, 37*(3), 16–19. This article describes a team teaching model involving hands-on experiences and integrated reading, writing, and mathematics skills.

Murawski, W. W., & Diecker, L. A. (2004). Tips and strategies for co-teaching at the secondary level. *Teaching Exceptional Children, 36*(5), 52–58. The article provides strategies for co-teaching, including checklists for preparation.

Murray, C. (2004). Clarifying collaborative roles in urban high schools: General educators' perspectives. *Teaching Exceptional Children, 36*(5), 44–51. This article discusses common barriers, solutions, and benefits to teacher collaboration in urban high schools.

Walsh, J. M., & Jones, B. (2004). New models of cooperative teaching. *Teaching Exceptional Children, 36*(5), 14–20. This article discusses cooperative teaching and describes four alternative approaches.

Westling, D. L., Cooper-Duffy, K., Prohn, K., Ray, M., & Herzog, M. J. (2005). Building a teacher support program. *Teaching Exceptional Children, 37*(5), 8–13. This article describes a university-sponsored community program designed to assist in collaborative problem solving and providing support for educators involved in inclusive programs.

Wilson, G. L. (2005) This doesn't look familiar! A supervisor's guide to observing co-teachers, *Intervention in School and Clinic, 40*, 271–275. This article provides suggestions for the evaluation of teacher teams and the assessment of co-teaching effectiveness.

Relevant Federal Regulations

Assistance to States for the Education of Children with Disabilities (70 Fed. Reg., 35,833–35, 880 [June 21, 2005]).

34 C.F.R. § 300.18	Highly qualified special education teacher.
.119	Technical assistance and training activities.
.156	Personnel qualifications.
.207	Personnel development.

SELECTED WEBSITES

Code of Federal Regulations–Government Printing Office–National Archives and Record Administration *http://www.gpoaccess.gov/cfr/index.html*

Council for Exceptional Children *http://www.cec.sped.org*

IDEA Practices
   http://www.ideapractices.org

Individuals With Disabilities Education Act Data
   http://www.ideadata.org

Internet Resources for Special Children
   http://www.irsc.org

A Guide to Schoolwide Planning for Paraeducator Supports–Center on Disability and Community Inclusion–University of Vermont
   http://www.uvm.edu/~cdci/parasupport/guide.html

National Resource Center for Paraprofessionals
   http://www.nrcpara.org

Project Para Web Site–Unversity of Nebraska at Lincoln
   http://www.para.unl.edu

PARA Center–a University of Colorado at Denver
   http://www.paracenter.org

Center for Multilingual, Multicultural Resources—University of Southern California
   http://www.cmmr.org

North Central Regional Educational Laboratory
   http://www.ncrel.org/sdrs/

QUESTIONS FOR THOUGHT

1. What content should teacher and principal preparation programs contain in order to prepare their students for a collaborative inclusive school environment?
2. What should a good professional development workshop include in order to improve the skills and knowledge of teachers and principals to become better collaborators in inclusive school programs?
3. What planning elements should a school consider for the implementation or improvement of an inclusion program? Who should be involved in the planning?
4. Was it a policy mistake to create "special education" in the 1970s and allow the creation of the "two-box model"?
5. Why are many educators reluctant to participate in inclusive programs?
6. How well are schools doing in the preparation and training of paraeducators for the important roles they play?

REFERENCES

Assistance to States for the Education of Children with Disabilities. 20 U.S.C. §§ 1401–1487. 34 Code of Federal Regulations, Part 300 (70 Fed. Reg. 35, 833–35, 880 [June 21, 2005]).

Bauwens, J., & Hourcade, J. J. (1997). Cooperative teaching: Pictures of possibilities. *Intervention in School and Clinic, 33*, 81–85.

Billingsley, B. C. (2004). Promoting teacher quality and retentions in special education. *Journal of Learning Disabilities, 37*, 370–376.

Board of Education v. I.S., 325 F. Supp. 2d 565 (D.C. Md. 2004).

Bondy, E., & Brownell, M. T. (1997). Overcoming barriers to collaboration among partners-in-teaching. *Intervention in School and Clinic, 33*, 112–115.

Boyer, L. (2005). Supporting the induction of special educators: Program descriptions of university-school district partnerships. *Teaching Exceptional Children, 37*(3), 44–51.

Boyer, L., & Mainzer, R. W. (2003). Who's teaching students with disabilities? *Teaching Exceptional Children, 35*(6), 8–11.

Brownell, M. T., Hirsch, E., & Seo, S. (2004). Meeting the demand for highly qualified special education teachers during severe shortages: What should policy makers consider? *The Journal of Special Education, 38*, 56–61.

Causton-Theoharis, J. N., & Malmgren, K. W. (2005). Increasing peer interactions for students with severe disabilities via paraprofessional training. *Exceptional Children, 71*, 431–444.

Chalmers, L., & Faliede, T. (1996). Successful inclusion of students with mild/moderate disabilities in rural school settings. *Teaching Exceptional Children, 29*(1), 22–25.

Chopra, R. V., Sandoval-Lucero, E., Aragon, L., Bernal, C., DeBalderas, H. B., & Carroll, D. (2004). The paraprofessional role of connector. *Remedial and Special Education, 25*, 219–231.

Cole, C. M., & McLeskey, J. (1997). Secondary inclusion programs for students with mild disabilities. *Focus on Exceptional Children, 29*(6), 1–15.

Cook, L., & Friend, M. (1995). Co-teaching: Guidelines for creating effective practices. *Focus on Exceptional Children, 28*(3), 1–16.

Council of Chief State School Officers (1996). *Interstate school leaders licensure consortium: Standards for school leaders.* Denver, CO: Author. Available at http://www.ccsso.org (search ISLLC).

Council for Exceptional Children and National Association of Elementary Principals (2001). *Implementing IDEA: A guide for principals.* Arlington, VA: Authors.

Dieker, L. A., & Little, M. (2005). Secondary reading: Not just for reading teachers anymore. *Intervention in School and Clinic, 40,* 276–283.

Dover, W. F. (2005). 20 ways to consult and support students with special needs in inclusive classrooms. *Intervention in School and Clinic, 41,* 32–35.

Fisher, D., Frey, N., & Thousand, J. (2003). What do special educators need to know and be prepared to do for inclusive schooling to work? *Teacher Education and Special Education, 26,* 42–50.

French, N. K. (2000). Taking time to save time: Delegating to paraeducators. *Teaching Exceptional Children, 32*(3), 79–83.

French, N. K. (2003). Paraeducators in special education programs. *Focus on Exceptional Children, 36*(2), 1–16.

French, N. K., & Pickett, A. L. (1997). Paraprofessionals in special education: Issues for teacher educators. *Teacher Education and Special Education, 20,* 61–73.

Gable, R. A., Manning, M. L., Hendrickson, J. M., & Rogan, J. P. (1997). A secondary student instructional support team (ASSIST): Teachers face the challenge of student diversity. *The High School Journal, 81,* 22–27.

Giangreco, M. F. (1996). What do I do now? A teacher's guide to including students with disabilities. *Educational Leadership, 53*(5), 56–59.

Giangreco, M. F. (2003) Working with paraprofessionals. *Educational Leadership, 61*(2), 50–53.

Giangreco, M. F., Dennis, R., Cloninger, C., Edelman, S., Schattman, R. (1993). "I've counted Jon": Transformational experiences of teachers educating students with disabilities. *Exceptional Children, 59,* 359–372.

Giangreco, M. F., Edelman, S. W., & Broen, S. M. (2003). Schoolwide planning to improve paraeducator supports. *Exceptional Children, 70,* 63–79. *A Guide to Schoolwide Planning for Para Educator Supports* is available at http://www.uvm.edu/~cdci/parasupport/guide.html

Giangreco, M. F., Edelman, S. W., Luiselli, T. E., & MacFarland, S. Z. C. (1997). Helping or hovering? Effects of instructional assistant proximity on students with disabilities. *Exceptional Children, 64,* 7–18.

Giangreco, M. F., Yuan, S., McKenzie, B., Cameron, P., & Fialka, J. (2005). "Be careful what you wish for. . .": Five reasons to be concerned about the assignment of individual paraprofessionals. *Teaching Exceptional Children, 37*(5), 28–34.

Goor, M. B., Schwenn, J. O., & Boyer, L. (1997). Preparing principals for leadership in special education. *Intervention in School and Clinic, 32,* 133–141.

Hilton, A., & Gerlach, K. (1997). Employment, preparation, and management of paraeducators: Challenges to appropriate service for students with developmental disabilities. *Education and Training in Mental Retardation and Developmental Disabilities, 32,* 71–76.

Hunt, P., Soto, G., Maier, J., & Doering, K. (2003). Collaborative teaming to support students at risk and students with severe disabilities in general education classrooms. *Exceptional Children, 69,* 315–332.

Individuals with Disabilities Education Act, 20 U.S.C., §§ 1400–1487 (2000).

Kaff, M. S. (2004). Multitasking is multitaxing: Why special educators are leaving the field. *Preventing School Failure, 48*(2), 10–17.

Kochhar, A., & West, L. L. (1996). *Handbook for successful inclusion.* Gaithersburg, MD: Aspen.

Lamar-Dukes, P., & Dukes, C. (2005). Consider the roles and responsibilities of the inclusion support teacher. *Intervention in School and Clinic, 41,* 55–61.

Littrell, P. C., Billingsley, B. S., & Cross, L. H. (1994). The effects of principal support on special and general educators' stress, job satisfaction, school commitment, health, and intent to stay in teaching. *Remedial and Special Education, 15,* 297–309.

Lloyd, S. R., Wood, T. A., & Moreno, G. (2000). What's a mentor to do? *Teaching Exceptional Children, 33*(1), 38–42.

Magiera, K., Smith, C., Zigmond, N., & Gebauer, K. (2005). Benefits of co-teaching in secondary mathematics classes. *Teaching Exceptional Children, 37*(3), 20–24.

Mainzer, R. W., Deshler, D., Coleman, M. R., Kozleski, E., & Rodriguez-Walling, M. (2003). To ensure the learning of every child with a disability. *Focus on Exceptional Children, 35*(5), 1–16.

Mastropieri, M. A., Schruggs, T. E., Graetz, J., Norland, J., Gardizi, W., & McDuffie, K. (2005). Case studies in co-teaching in the content areas: Successes, failures, and challenges. *Intervention in School and Clinic, 40*, 260–270.

Murawski, W. W., & Diecker, L. (2004). Tips and strategies for co-teaching at the secondary level. *Teaching Exceptional Children, 36*(5), 52–58.

Phillips, L., Sapona, R. H., & Lubic, B. L. (1995). Developing partnerships in inclusive education: One school's approach. *Intervention in School and Clinic, 30*, 262–272.

Praisner, C. L. (2003). Attitudes of elementary school principals toward the inclusion of students with disabilities. *Exceptional Children, 69*, 135–145.

Reinhiller, N. (1996). Coteaching: New variations on a not-so-new practice. *Teacher Education and Special Education, 19*(1), 34–48.

Reynolds, M., & Birch, J. (1977). *Teaching exceptional children in all America's schools.* Reston, VA: The Council for Exceptional Children.

Riggs, C. G. (2004). To teachers: What paraeducators want you to know. *Teaching Exceptional Children, 36*(5), 8–12.

Robertson, G., Haines, L. D., Sanche, R., & Biffart, W. (1997). Positive change through computer networking. *Teaching Exceptional Children, 29*(6), 22–30.

Salisbury, C. L. & McGregor, G. (2002). The administrative climate and context of inclusive elementary schools. *Exceptional Children, 68*(2), 259–274.

Santos, K. E., & Rettig, M. D. (1999). Going on the block: Meeting the needs of students with disabilities in high schools with block scheduling. *Teaching Exceptional Children, 31*(3), 54–59.

Schepis, M. M., Ownbey, J. B., Parsons, M. B., & Reid, D. H. (2000). Training support staff for teaching young children with disabilities in an inclusive preschool setting. *Journal of Positive Behavior Interventions, 2*, 170–178.

Sirotnik, K. A., & Kimball, K. (1994). The unspecial place of special education in programs that prepare school administrators. *Journal of School Leadership, 4*, 598–630.

Stanovich, P. J. (1996). Collaboration—The key to successful instruction in today's inclusive schools. *Intervention in School and Clinic, 32*, 39–42.

T. W. v. Unified School District No. 259, 136 Fed. Appx. 122 (10th Cir. 2005).

Taylor, R. L., Richards, S. B., Goldstein, P. A., & Schilit, J. (1997). Teacher perceptions of inclusive settings. *Teaching Exceptional Children, 29*(3), 50–54.

Trautman, M. (2004). Preparing and managing paraprofessionals. *Intervention in School and Clinic, 39*, 131–138.

Vail, C. O., Tschantz, J. M., & Bevill, A. (1997). Dyads and data in peer coaching. *Teaching Exceptional Children, 30*(2), 11–15.

Vargo, S. (1998). Consulting: Teacher-to-teacher. *Teaching Exceptional Children, 30*(3), 54–55.

Vaughn, S., Schumm, J. S., & Arguelles, M. E. (1997). The ABCDEs of co-teaching. *Teaching Exceptional Children, 30*(2), 4–10.

Villa, R. A., & Thousand, J. S. (2003). Making inclusive education work. *Educational Leadership, 61*(2), 19–23.

Villa, R. A., Thousand, J. S., Meyers, H., & Nevin, A. (1996). Teacher and administrator perceptions of heterogeneous education. *Exceptional Children, 63*, 29–45.

Wallace, T., Anderson, A. R., Bartholomay, T., & Hupp, S. (2002). An ecobehavioral examination of high school classrooms that include students with disabilities. *Exceptional Children, 68*(3), 345–359.

Walsh, J. M., & Jones, B. (2004). New models of cooperative teaching. *Teaching Exceptional Children, 36*(5), 14–20.

Weiss, M. P., & Lloyd, J. W. (2002). Congruence between roles and actions of secondary special educators in co-taught and special education settings. *Journal of Special Education, 36*(2), 58–68.

Werts, M. G., Harris, S., Tillery, C. Y., & Roark, R. (2004). What parents tell us about paraeducators. *Remedial and Special Education, 25*, 232–239.

Whitaker, S. D. (2000). Mentoring beginning special education teachers and the relationship to attrition. *Exceptional Children, 66,* 546–566.

Wiese, B. J. (2004). *Knowledge and skills for the utilization and supervision of paraeducators across Iowa: Trends in special education teacher preparation and inservice needs.* Unpublished doctoral dissertation, University of Iowa, Iowa City.

Wood, M. (1998). Whose job is it anyway? Educational roles in inclusion. *Exceptional Children, 64*(2), 181–195.

Yell, M. L. (2006). *The law and special education* (2nd ed.). Upper Saddle River, NJ: Merrill/Prentice Hall.

Young, I. P., & Castetter, W. B. (2004). *The human resource function in educational administration* (8th ed.). Upper Saddle River, NJ: Merrill/Prentice Hall.

CHAPTER 11

DISPUTE RESOLUTION— DUE PROCESS HEARINGS, MEDIATION, AND COMPLAINTS

CHAPTER PREVIEW

Focus

Before 1975, millions of American children with disabilities were systematically denied access to public education. Their parents could protest and negotiate, but they had no clear legal recourse when they were dissatisfied with their school's decisions. The law, in the form of the Individuals with Disabilities Education Act (IDEA), now provides parents with recourse through a variety of dispute resolution processes, including resolution meetings, the state complaint process, mediation, and due process hearings. Those processes also provide assurance that the intent of the IDEA will be carried out.

Parents and, in some limited situations, school districts may request an impartial due process hearing to resolve differences regarding decisions made in the context of providing special education services to students. In practice, these due process hearings are usually requested by parents but are most frequently decided in favor of the schools. They are expensive, time consuming, and emotionally exhausting for both parents and schools. Consequently, hearings and subsequent litigation should be viewed as a last resort in resolving educational disagreements. The alternatives to expensive due process hearings for dispute resolution are used regularly and successfully.

Legal Issues

The IDEA requires that parents receive written notice each time the school proposes (or refuses) to initiate or change a student's identification, evaluation, educational placement, or provision of a free appropriate public education (FAPE). That notice must describe and explain the proposed (or refused) action in detail and must remind parents of their rights, including the right to request mediation or a due process hearing. When a due process hearing is requested, both the parents and the school are guaranteed the right to

- understand the specific nature of the disagreement and each other's position regarding the issue;
- attempt to resolve the disagreement through a resolution meeting or mediation prior to a due process hearing;
- be advised and accompanied at the hearing by a lawyer or experts if they choose;
- present evidence, call and cross-examine witnesses;
- expect an impartial hearing officer;
- prevent the introduction of evidence not disclosed by the opposing side at least 5 business days before the hearing;
- receive a written decision within a specified time after the hearing was requested;
- receive a copy of a verbatim record of the hearing; and
- appeal the hearing decision into court.

When due process hearings are held, the parents may

- have the hearing conducted at a convenient time and place;
- have the child present;
- open the hearing to the public, if they choose to do so;
- have the child remain in the current educational placement (except for some hearings involving discipline) until the dispute is resolved; and
- receive reimbursement for attorney's fees when they prevail.

The law does not require mediation or due process hearings in all dispute situations, only those dealing with the identification, evaluation, educational placement, or provision of FAPE. Nor does the law explicitly define all aspects of the hearing proceedings. Some variations will occur in the process from state to state and among individual hearing officers. In general, due process hearings can be seen as similar to court proceedings, but usually much less formal. Every time there is a request for a due process hearing, the parties must be provided an opportunity for voluntary resolution opportunities, including mediation of the issues in dispute. Parents and organizations may file complaints with the state regarding technical violations of the law. Formal complaints must be investigated and a report of findings must be issued.

Approaches

Most disagreements between parents and schools can be settled without a due process hearing, and it is to everyone's benefit to do so. Preventive school practices include creating a cooperative environment in the school, providing satisfying and meaningful opportunities for parents to become involved in their child's education, and providing and using alternative problem-solving procedures.

As long as the parents and school staff agree to and understand the specific process, a wide variety of alternative dispute resolution processes are available. The appropriate goal of those processes is to have a limited adversarial system that encourages compassion and respect for participants and aids in building trust, mutual respect, and value for each other's contributions.

ALTERNATIVES IN RESOLVING DISPUTES

From its earliest beginnings in the mid-1970s, the authors of the IDEA recognized that parents and schools would have disputes over the provision of special education programs and services. As a result, they provided for due process hearings and appeals into court (Yell, 2006). However, the law does not require that disputes between schools and the parents of children with disabilities be resolved in due process hearings or litigation. It provides those formats only as a last legal recourse (Getty & Summy, 2004). Various less antagonistic and less expensive means of resolving conflicts have been used successfully for decades. School districts have been consistently adopting less formal models as alternatives for parents in dispute resolution. Some schools enter into informal negotiation or informal mediation, or provide trained IEP facilitators and problem solution teams for early dispute resolution.

Schrag and Schrag (2004) have reported a high rate of disputes between parents and schools being resolved through various informal dispute resolution processes. They recommend that greater attention be given to local dispute resolution alternatives rather than those available at the state level. They recommend the resolution of issues as close to the classrooms where they originate as possible.

Educators must remember that not all efforts at dispute resolution are born in or result in hostility. Special education decision making is, after all, a problem-solving process. Working toward the goal of improving educational opportunity for students can open better lines of communication between families and schools and lead to the building of trust. (See Chapter 2 for specific suggestions.)

For instance, the Bureau of Indian Affairs' schools offer an Early Assistance Program (EAP) that serves a resolution facilitation purpose. Under the EAP, a parent or school may request assistance in resolving issues involving a student's FAPE. The Bureau offers information and technical assistance to the parties, and mediation when appropriate. The EAP focuses on a systematic and quick informal resolution process for problems of mutual concern to all parties (Bureau of Indian Affairs, 2002). The philosophy inherent in the process draws upon the preferred model of schools and parents working together in the best interest of the child. That process recognizes the desirability of having trained, impartial persons readily available to assist schools and parents to work through and discuss problems and conflicts as they arise, rather than waiting until the issues become hardened.

The alternatives to informally resolving differences are limited only by the creativity and willingness of the parties to trust one another (Schrag, 2003). Examples of informal dispute resolution include the following:

Negotiation—The parties maintain the child as the focus of their disagreement, recognize that disagreement is healthy, and proceed to continue a positive dialog regarding potential solutions.

Advisory opinion—A third party, selected by mutual agreement, reviews the situation, including the student records and expressed positions of the parties, and issues a nonbinding recommendation for the resolution of differences.

Fact-finding—A neutral third party (may be an expert) reviews the student record, hears the expressed opinions of the parties, and issues an opinion. The opinion can be binding or not, as determined in advance by the parties.

Problem-solving—With the assistance of a case manager, solution team, or process coach, the IEP team identifies the specific issues in dispute, the potential solutions available, the apparent best solution, the amount of time the chosen solution will be attempted, and the assessment process for evaluating the attempted solution.

Ombudsperson—A neutral third party investigates the situation, makes judgments, and issues reports including recommendations. The results are usually nonbinding.

Facilitation—A person, or persons, knowledgeable in the special education process and procedures maintain the focus of the deliberations on the best interests of the child and ensure that participants are respectful listeners and presenters.

Binding arbitration—A neutral third party is presented the student record, as well as relevant facts and arguments, and issues a decision that is binding on the parties. It is extremely difficult to successfully challenge an arbitration decision in the courts.

Mediation—Formal

Some states have successfully provided an opportunity for formal mediation on a voluntary basis for many years (Schrag & Schrag, 2004). Schrag (2003) has reported that national data from a 1999–2000 study indicated that 96% of responding school districts reported that mediation was more desirable and cost effective than due process hearings. In addition to the benefits of less cost and less staff time spent in comparison to due process hearings, mediation can salvage a working relationship between parents and schools (Osborne, 1996).

A mediator, unlike a hearing officer or arbitrator, does not make decisions or rulings. Instead, the role of the mediator is to facilitate communications and improve the likelihood of agreement (Yell, 2006). One state department of education has explained the role of mediator as follows:

The mediator is a neutral third party acting as a facilitator to assist parents and school personnel in reaching an agreement. Although the mediator is in control of the session, he/she does not make the decision on how to resolve the issue(s). The mediator allows the parties to present their positions and attempts to achieve mutual understanding and a solution to the problem in the best interest of the student. The mediator facilitates the process. He or she summarizes positions and helps the parties consider possible alternatives.

. . . . .

The purpose of mediation in special education is to provide an alternative to a due process hearing or complaint procedure investigation as a way to resolve conflicts, clarify issues and stimulate mutual problem solving efforts between parents and school personnel. Even if an agreement is not reached, there is the potential of both parties leaving the session with an enhanced perspective of the issues and with the focus on the student. Most mediations result in better communication between school and parents. This leads to an improved situation for the student.*

The Bureau of Indian Affairs manual on mediation offers the following advice to participants preparing for a successful mediation session (1999):

- Make no other plans for the day or evening of the mediation.
- Put aside personality conflicts and focus on the student's best interest.
- Review all relevant documents, papers, and reports prior to the session.
- Organize your information and any materials before the mediation session.
- Think of possible alternatives or ways of solving the problem.
- Think about what you want to get out of the session.
- Think about what you want the other party to do.
- Think about what you are willing to do.
- Be willing to listen and compromise.

The experiences of a mediator in Missouri evidences the potential benefits of mediation as an alternative dispute resolution process. However, the mediator cautions that the process is only as good as the intent of the parties involved. When the parties do not come to the table in earnest and do not have a desire to work together in the best interest of the child, a dispute resolution process other than mediation will be desirable (Mills & Duff-Mallams, 1999).

---

*From Montana Office of Public Instruction. (1994). *Montana Mediation Process* (pp. 6–8). Logan, UT: Mountain Plains Regional Resource Center. Reprinted by permission.

A vast majority of states have offered formal mediation services anytime parents or a school request it (Schrag, 2003).

State Complaint Process—Formal

Filing a formal complaint with the state education agency is another alternative form of dispute resolution. This alternative is not found in the statutory language of the IDEA. It is found only in the regulations of the U.S. Department of Education, which has listed it since 1999 as one of the parental safeguards that schools must make known and available to parents (34 C.F.R. §§ 300.151; .504[c][5]). Under the regulations, each state must adopt procedures for resolving complaints, either at the state or local school level, with review by the state being available. Complaints must be investigated and followed by a written decision that addresses each issue within 60 days. Both the complainant and the school must have the opportunity to submit information and the school may submit a proposal to resolve the complaint. In keeping with the 2004 Amendments' thrust of encouraging informal solutions, when the parties agree, they may enter into mediation or alternative means of dispute resolution (34 C.F.R. § 300.152[a][3]). Formal complaint decisions must contain findings of facts and conclusions, reasons for the final decision, and procedures for the implementation of corrective action by schools, when needed.

The complaint process is limited to alleged technical and legal violations of the IDEA, such as failure to carry out IEP terms, failure to provide parental safeguards, and refusal to consider some types of services. Disputes involving issues of judgment, such as the appropriateness of IEP goals, may be resolved only through due process hearings or mediation, not the state complaint process.

Complaints may be filed by organizations or individuals under state prescribed procedures and may involve either individual or systemic IDEA issues. The person or organization filing the complaint does not have to have been directly affected by the complained of school actions. Thus, complaints can be filed by an ob-

server, teacher association, or friend (Huefner, 2006). The complaint must outline the alleged violations of the IDEA, the facts on which the statement is based, and a proposed solution to the dispute. The alleged incident may not have occurred more than one year prior to state receipt of the complaint.

When the subject matter of a complaint is also the subject matter of a due process hearing, the state must defer the complaint subject matter decision until the hearing is completed. If an issue raised in a complaint has been the subject matter of a previous due process hearing, the hearing decision is binding.

In a study involving state educational agency experience with the complaint process, Suchey and Huefner (1998) found that parent and school awareness of the complaint procedure had not yet reached a high level, the number of complaints filed had been slowly increasing, and the complaint process had resulted in a reduced number of due process hearings in some states. Schrag and Schrag (2004) reported that the findings in the National Study of Dispute Resolution Use and Effectiveness establish that parents receive a favorable result in the complaint process about 75% of the time compared to only 27% in due process hearings.

Several advantages of the use of state complaint procedures versus the use of mediation and due process hearings were identified by Suchey and Huefner (1998):

- Costs of the complaint procedure and investigation are borne by the state.
- Attorneys are not usually involved.
- Complaints can be used to address system-wide violations of the IDEA, and complaint results are enforceable in court when the state does not enforce its own decision.

Some state educational agencies discourage the use of complaints and, instead, encourage the use of mediation alternatives.

It is felt that the complaint process results in "winners and losers," which generates antagonisms that are not easily overcome. In an effort to avoid a breakdown in communications that may result from the parents' filing of a complaint, the Bureau of Indian Affairs offers its

FIGURE 11-1 *Comparison of Alternative Dispute Resolutions*

Mediation (not arbitration)
Win/win situation—not a compromise
Parties are in control of decision
Cost is time only
Time spent by parties: moderate
No lawyers are involved

Hearing
Win/lose situation
Decision made by outsider
Costly $ $ $ $
Time spent by parties: great
Lawyer involvement likely

Complaint
Win/lose situation
Decision made by state department
of education
Little or no financial cost
Time spent by parties: limited
No lawyers are involved

Early Assistance Program (EAP) to schools and parents prior to the filing of a complaint, just as it does prior to the filing of a request for due process hearing (Bureau of Indian Affairs, 2002).

Figure 11-1 compares some aspects of mediation, hearings, and complaints to help illustrate which is generally more desirable.

THE SHADOW OF DUE PROCESS HEARINGS

Like a mysterious and ever-present threat, the possibility of due process hearings hangs over most inclusive school environments. Few school staff members know exactly what the hearings entail, and fewer still have ever been involved in one, but everyone knows such hearings have a bad reputation. "What makes these hearings happen?", "What goes on in them, anyway?", and especially, "How can I avoid them?" are haunting questions in the back of many educators' minds.

What is the origin of the overwhelmingly negative reputation of due process hearings? Not frequency of occurrence. The number of disputes between parents and schools that actually go to hearing is relatively small. The onslaught of hearing decisions that many educators have feared over the years has failed to materialize. Zirkel and D'Angelo (2002) determined that in the 3-year period of 1998–2000 693 hearing decisions were rendered in the entire country, which averages to 231 hearing decisions per year. That is remarkably few for a nation with nearly 7 million children between the ages of 3 and 21 years identified as being eligible for IDEA services (IDEA Data, 2004).

The number of hearings requested do not necessarily equate to the number of hearings held. Schrag and Schrag (2004) have reported that for the 2000–2001 school year, only 28% of requested due process hearings actually resulted in decisions. Sometimes, hearings are requested to get someone's attention or to use as leverage for seeking settlement. Another study showed that of the 189 hearing requests filed in one mid-western state during a 3-year period, 118 were settled prior to the actual hearing and only 71 (38%) went to hearing (McKinney & Schultz, 1996).

The bad reputation of hearings does not result from schools' continued failure to successfully defend their actions in hearings. Studies among the various states have shown a parent rate of victory between 20 and 43% (Newcomer, Zirkel, & Tarola, 1998). Rickey (2003) found in a review of all 50 hearings in one mid-western state, involving 130 separate issues during a 12-year period, that schools prevailed on 63% and parents prevailed on 34% of the issues. The remaining 3% of the issues resulted in a mixed decision. Zirkel and D'Angelo (2002) determined in a review of all reported hearing decisions in the United States in the 3 years 1998–2000 that schools prevailed 55% of the time, parents 23%, and mixed results were had in 22% of the decisions. Schrag (2003) reported that the Special Education Expenditure Project 1999–2000 data found that 55% of the due process hearings favored schools and about one third (34%) favored parents. Using a different national data set, Schrag and Schrag (2004) determined that parents received a favorable decision in due process hearings only 27% of the time.

It should be no surprise that although parents initiated the vast majority of hearings, they prevail in a relatively small number. Schools have the money and staff resources, as well as the opportunity, knowledge, and experience to provide appropriate education programs for students. When necessary, those same school resources can be used to successfully defend appropriate school actions in a hearing.

The fact is, of course, that schools have time, money, and resources for hearings only at the expense of education programs, and this is where the stigma may originate. Due process hearings drain time, money, and emotional energy from the system that would otherwise be more positively directed toward improving childrens' education. Hearings are expensive in a number of ways. An average hearing may cost thousands of dollars and court appeals many thousands more. Hearings require substantial investments in staff time, thus aggravating resentment at the paperwork already demanded by the IDEA. As if this were not enough, hearings are damaging to community attitudes. The implicit content of every hearing is an accusation of wrongdoing or, at the very least, neglect on the part of the school. The outcry and zealous lobbying of dissatisfied parents is rarely matched or compensated by testimony from the majority of parents who are satisfied. All this tends to result in lower staff morale and to increased resentment toward special education (Getty & Summy, 2004).

A Last Resort

In an early study of parent and school official satisfaction with the due process hearing procedures in Pennsylvania, Goldberg and Kuriloff (1991) found that both parents and school officials concluded that the legal model of dispute resolution present in hearings was ill-suited to resolving educational disputes. Both parents and school officials believed that participation in adversary hearings resulted in unnecessary

antagonism between them. Goldberg and Kuriloff concluded that alternative models of dispute resolution, such as negotiation or mediation, should be used for dispute resolution in special education. It was argued that other forms of alternative dispute resolution could allow educators and parents the opportunity to work together to avoid disruptive, divisive, and costly due process hearing battles. This philosophy has resulted in a persistent congressional effort to identify alternatives that allow schools and parents a variety of options to resolve disputes before going to due process hearing. The continuation of the effort, as found in the 2004 Amendments, provides alternatives for two separate mediation opportunities and an informal problem resolution meeting before a due process hearing is held.

Other hidden costs to the education of a child are generated not by due process hearings themselves, but by fear of them. The avoidance of hearings often becomes an end in itself; a goal that begins to divert time and attention away from the effort to meet students' needs. That also means that because of the fear of due process hearings, a child may not receive an appropriate education (Getty & Summy, 2004). As early as 1979, Jacobs warned:

> Constant adversarial pressure cannot help
> but create in some educators an attitude designed to protect the system rather than the child's best interest to make them reluctant to recommend services which they will be forced to justify at some upcoming hearing. This timidity in professional decision making can . . . place self protection ahead of concern for the best interest of their client. (p. 88)

The key word here is "adversarial." A cooperative attitude toward decision making—in which the parents and school share the best interests of the child as a common goal—is difficult to maintain once adversarial legal procedures have been interjected between the bargaining parties. The situation is similar to that experienced by many divorcing couples who find a relatively amicable separation transformed into a legal war over children and possessions fueled by their emotions and the lawyers they have hired. It is the unfamiliar and exhausting role of adversaries that participants in due process hearings often find profoundly distressing. In the quasi-judicial due process setting, educators find themselves suddenly cast in the role of the villains, the accused, and parents are encouraged by the legal structure and proceedings to view them that way. The child involved cannot help but suffer, no matter what the outcome.

The challenges confronting educators with regard to due process hearings are two-fold. On one hand, it is important to avoid adversarial settings in due process hearings and litigation as much as possible. On the other, it is equally important to avoid sacrificing educational quality for institutional safety. The most productive policy is not to focus on the negative aspect of how to avoid becoming embroiled in hearings, but rather on the positive—how to create a relationship of cooperation and trust between parents and staff in the best interest of the child.

Schrag and Schrag (2004) have reported in the National Dispute Resolution Use and Effectiveness Study that the use of due process hearings by parents and schools is somewhat on the increase in the United States. However, it still remains less than half of the total alternative dispute resolution efforts attempted in special education. Efforts at mediation and use of the formal state complaint process together outnumber the due process hearings requested. Overall, the researchers concluded that due process hearing activity is slowing in the nation relative to population growth. They speculate that this result may arise from a maturation of state and local alternative dispute resolution practices. They predict little growth of the use of due process hearings in the future, other than that resulting from population growth.

Required Process Leading to a Due Process Hearing

The 2004 Amendments to the IDEA have established a number of mandatory steps leading up to the due process hearing. A parent may begin the process when he or she receives a written notice from the school that explains why the school proposes to initiate or change, or refuses a parent request to initiate or change the identification of a child as being eligible for special education, the evaluation of the child, the educational placement of the child, or the provision of FAPE to the child. A school's initiation of the process leading to a hearing would be related only to parental refusal of consent for an initial evaluation or a reevaluation of a child, or to prove its evaluation was appropriate when a parent requests an independent educational evaluation at public expense (34 C.F.R. § 300.502[b][21]). The 2004 Amendments have removed parental refusal of written consent for the initial placement in special education as grounds for a school seeking hearing officer authority through the hearing process (34 C.F.R. § 300.300[b])

All complaints leading to a due process hearing must now be made within 2 years of the date the parent or school knew or should have known about the alleged decision or refusal that forms the basis for the request for due process hearing. An exception to the 2-year statute of limitation exists when state law has an explicit time limit for presenting requests for hearing. Two other exceptions exist: when the parent was prevented from requesting a timely hearing due to misrepresentations made by the school, or when the school withheld information required to be provided the parent.

The state, or local school district, responsible for providing the due process hearing must provide the parent with information regarding free or low-cost legal and other relevant services available in the area.

Notice Format   A parent or school or an attorney representing a party must provide the other party with a due process hearing complaint notice in a specific format, and must forward a copy to the state or local education agency that is responsible for providing the due process hearing. The complaint notice must remain confidential.

The format of the hearing notice must include

- the name and address of the child (or contact information in the case of a homeless child);
- the name of the school the child is attending;

- a description of the nature of the problem related to the child (initiation of change or refusal to initiate a change), including facts related to the problem;
- a proposed resolution of the problem to the extent known and available (34 C.F.R. § 300.508[b]).

States are required to develop and disseminate a model form to assist parties in filing a complete due process hearing complaint notice (34 C.F.R. § 300.509).

No hearing will be held until a complaint notice is filed that meets the above requirements. The content of the notice shall be considered sufficient unless the receiving party provides notice to the sending party and the assigned hearing officer within 15 days that the receiving party believes that the content is in some way deficient. The hearing officer must make a determination on the adequacy of the notice within 5 days, and must immediately notify the parties of the determination in writing. The determination is to be made "on the face of the notice," which means that the hearing officer does not confer with the parties regarding the adequacy of the notice content.

A due process hearing complaint notice can be amended only when the receiving party consents in writing and is provided an opportunity to resolve the problem in an informal resolution meeting (as discussed below), or the hearing officer grants permission for amendment of the notice 5 or more days prior to the scheduled due process hearing.

School Response When the local school has not previously sent a prior written notice of a proposed educational change or refusal of a parent request to the parents, the school must, within 10 days of receipt of the complaint notice, send a response to the due process complaint notice. The response must contain much of the information that would have been included in a prior written notice, had it been sent:

- An explanation of the reasons the school proposed or refused to take the action contained in the complaint notice

- A description of other options considered by the IEP team and the reasons those options were rejected
- A description of each evaluation procedure, assessment, record, or report the school used as the basis for the proposed or refused action
- A description of other factors relevant to the school's proposal or refusal (34 C.F.R. § 300.508[e]).

A school's providing a response to the parent's complaint notice does not preclude it from also challenging the form or content sufficiency of the parent's complaint notice. A copy of the parent procedural safeguards explanations (see Chapter 2) must be provided to the parents "upon the first occurrence of the filing of a complaint notice initiating procedures leading to a due process hearing" (20 U.S.C. § 1415[d]).

In the event the noncomplaining party receiving the notice of a due process hearing complaint is not a school (i.e., a parent when the school challenges the parent's refusal for consent for evaluation), the noncomplaining party must send the other party (i.e., the school) a response that specifically addresses the issues raised within 10 days of receipt of the due process hearing complaint (34 C.F.R. § 300.508[f]).

Resolution Meeting As a prerequisite to the holding of a due process hearing, unless waived in writing by the school and parent or mediation is substituted, a school receiving a complaint notice (or a revised complaint notice) has 15 days to convene a resolution meeting. The meeting will involve the parents and relevant members of the IEP team who have specific knowledge of the situation identified in the complaint notice, as determined jointly by the school and parents. The meeting is obviously required to allow the school and parents another opportunity to resolve the dispute to their mutual satisfaction before existing problems escalate as a result of the advocacy process inherent in due process hearings.

The school must have a representative at the resolution meeting who has decision-making authority for the school. The school's attorney may not be included in the meeting unless the parent is accompanied by an attorney. If a settlement is reached at the resolution meeting, it must be reduced to writing and signed by the parents and the school representative. The agreement will be legally binding and enforceable in any state court with competent jurisdiction or a federal district court. A party may void any executed settlement agreement within 3 business days of the execution of the agreement.

When the school has not resolved the hearing complaint to the satisfaction of the parents within 30 days of the receipt of the notice or amended notice, whichever is later, the parties must proceed to due process hearing.

Unless the parent and school agree to jointly waive the resolution meeting or to use mediation, the failure of a parent filing a due process hearing complaint to participate in the resolution meeting will delay the timelines for the resolution process and due process hearing until the resolution meeting is held (34 C.F.R. § 300.510[b][3]). This regulation provides parents who are satisfied with their child's situation and who don't want the school to change the child's status to an unfair advantage. By filing a due process complaint notice, a proposed change for the student will be halted, and by refusing to participate in the resolution meeting or mediation, no hearing can be held. See the "stay put or status quo" discussion on page 261.

Mediation Opportunities The high success rates of mediation and the generally more favorable maintenance of a working relationship between schools and parents resulted in the 1997 Amendments to the IDEA requiring that states make mediation available when a due process hearing is requested. This change was in part due to congressional recognition of the desirability of nonadversarial methods of dispute resolution (Yell, 2006). The terms of the 2004 Amendments to the IDEA also require that opportunities for mediation between schools and parents be available at all times before a hearing is requested.

The rationale for providing an opportunity for mediation of disputes prior to the filing of requests for due process lies in the belief that the filing of a request for due process hearing solidifies parties' positions and creates an unnecessarily hardened adversarial atmosphere. The belief is that an earlier opportunity for problem-solving mediation is beneficial to maintaining good working relationships between schools and parents. Mediation procedures in both situations must ensure that the process is

- voluntary on the part of the parties;
- not used to deny or delay a parent's right to a due process hearing, or other rights;
- conducted by a qualified and impartial mediator;
- at no cost to the parent;
- held at a location convenient to the parties (34 C.F.R. § 300.506[b]).

Each state must maintain a list of people who are qualified mediators knowlegeable in the laws and regulations related to the provision of special education programs and services. Mediator qualifications under the IDEA exclude employees of educational agencies who provide services or programs to the child, and who have a personal or professional conflict of interest in the dispute. The selection of mediators by the state for specific disputes should be conducted on a random or a mutual agreement selection basis.

When disputes are resolved through mediation, the parties are expected to execute a legally binding agreement that includes, in addition to the educational agreements reached, the following provisions:

- All discussions at the mediation conference shall be confidential and may not be used as evidence in a later hearing or litigation (many states require or recommend a written confidentiality agreement prior to mediation).
- The signatures of both the parent and the school representative, who must have the authority to bind the school, must be obtained.
- The agreement is enforceable in any state court of competent jurisdiction or in a federal district court (many states require or allow enforcement of settlement agreements through state complaints or due process hearings).

The parties must make sure that the written agreement accurately reflects the mutual understanding of the school and the parents. When mediation settlements are haphazardly worded or unclear regarding required actions of the parties, the dispute is likely to fester and result in additional harsh and bitter disputes.

The presence of attorneys at mediation is not discussed in the language of the IDEA and is a detail to be worked out by the parties (Letter to Chief State School Officers, 2000). In an effort to keep mediation informal and the parties talking to each other rather than attorneys talking to each other, some states prohibit the use of attorneys in the mediation process (Yell, 2006). Advocates for parents, other than attorneys, are frequently permitted to attend mediations to provide support for the parents (Schrag & Schrag, 2004).

The reason that the law prohibits the use of mediation discussions as evidence in subsequent hearings or proceedings is to encourage the parties to consider and discuss all aspects of the situation. That way parties can express themselves freely and openly without fear that what they say can later be used against them (Huefner, 2006).

States may offer a process to parents and schools who elect not to participate in mediation to meet with a "disinterested" person from a community parent resource center or a dispute resolution entity who will explain the benefits of the mediation process and encourage the parents' participation. Parents may not be penalized for refusal to participate in mediation.

Conduct of a Hearing

When a hearing cannot be avoided, it is important to be well prepared for it. Part of that preparation must include knowing what to expect. The U.S. Department of Education regulations enacted under the 2004 Amendments provide that a hearing decision must be rendered within 45 days after the conclusion of an unsuccessful effort to resolve disputes through a resolution meeting. The 45-day timeline begins no later than 30 days after the filing of a due process hearing complaint or an amended complaint, whichever is later.

Continuances (specific time extensions) may be granted by the hearing officer at the request of either party. The law does not delineate valid reasons for requesting a continuance, but hearing officers will usually grant requests when "good cause" (e.g., the need for additional time for evaluation or for settlement negotiation) is shown. Each hearing must be conducted at a time and place that are reasonably convenient to the parents.

The conduct of a due process hearing is less formal than a court proceeding and will vary somewhat from state to state (Yell, 2006). The specific procedure is under the control of the hearing officer and usually proceeds as follows:

1. In order for the hearing officer and parties to discuss preliminary issues, such as the potential absence of a witness, objections to evidence, whether the hearing will be open or closed to the public (parent choice), and whether witnesses will be prohibited from being present other than while testifying (sequestered), hearings will be frequently preceded by an informal prehearing conference, either in person or by conference telephone call. Under the direction of the hearing officer, participants may resolve preliminary matters.

2. At the hearing, the hearing officer will make an introductory statement, including introductions of the parties. The hearing officer will describe what due process hearings are, the procedures to be followed, and the issues to be resolved in the hearing.

3. Each party may present a brief oral opening statement. The opening statement explains what that party will attempt to prove through the introduction of evidence and what result is desired. Usually the party requesting the hearing goes first. Opening statements may be waived by either or both parties.

4. The first party presents its evidence including witnesses and documents (usually the party requesting the hearing goes first), with cross-examination permitted by the other party. Witnesses will be administered an oath to tell the truth. Upon objection during the questioning of a witness, the

hearing officer determines and allows evidence that is reliable, probative, and relevant. Most formal trial evidentiary rules, such as hearsay, do not apply to administrative hearings.

5. The second party presents its evidence in the same manner, with cross-examination permitted by the first party.

6. Hearing officers may ask witnesses questions as they deem appropriate.

7. Either party may prohibit, through objection, the introduction of any evidence that has not been disclosed to that party at least 5 business days prior to the hearing. The primary purpose of this evidentiary rule is to lessen the unfairness of surprise evidence.

8. Parties must disclose reports of all evaluations and accompanying recommendations at least 5 business days prior to a hearing, or they may be precluded from introducing the information at the hearing.

9. Both parties are allowed to present brief rebuttal evidence, when desired.

10. Both parties are allowed the opportunity to make closing arguments.

11. Some states allow the filing of written arguments.

12. A party may obtain a verbatim record of the hearing; thus, one must be made. Parents may receive a copy at no cost.

13. No party may raise issues at the hearing that were not filed in the complaint notice (as amended), unless the other party agrees otherwise.

14. The hearing officer adjourns the hearing and must produce written findings and a decision within the allotted remaining time period.

The 2004 Amendments require that hearing decisions must be based on substantive grounds on the issue of whether the child received a free appropriate education. Violations of the many IDEA-required procedures will be relevant only when those violations deprive the child of FAPE because they impeded the child's right to FAPE, significantly impeded the parent's opportunity to participate in decision making regarding FAPE, or resulted in a deprivation of educational benefits to the child. Mere procedural violations without prejudice shown to the student or parents cannot be grounds for rulings against schools (Yell, 2006). Hearing officers and courts, however, may prospectively order schools to comply with procedural requirements when called for by the situation (20 U.S.C. § 1415 [f][3][E]).

Other potentially important points to know about hearings include the following:

- The hearing officer need not decide in favor of either party's recommendation, but may come up with an alternative solution.
- Any party has the right to be accompanied and advised by an attorney and by individuals with special knowledge or training with respect to children with disabilities.
- Parties may compel the attendance of witnesses (subpoena).
- Parents determine whether the child will attend the hearing. The child may be called as a witness or may meet with the hearing officer and attorneys before the hearing session begins.
- Federal statutes and regulations do not indicate whether either party in the hearing has the burden of proof. Some state special education rules provide for the burden of proof on one party or the other. The general rule enforced by the courts is that the burden of proof falls on the party who initiated the hearing (*Schaffer v. Weast*, 2005). Hearing officers most often simply weigh the evidence presented by both sides and decide facts in favor of the stronger or more convincing position.
- Hearing officers must be impartial and may not be employees of the school or state educational agency, and they may not be people with professional or other conflicts of interest. They must possess the knowledge and ability to understand federal and state special education law and interpretation by courts, and must possess the knowledge and ability to render and write decisions in accordance with legal practice.
- Hearing officers may have other titles, such as administrative law judge, dependent upon state law.

- Although the parties in due process hearings are quite often aided by lawyers, one must be cautious in making this choice. Not all attorneys—not even all attorneys regularly representing school districts—are adequately prepared and current on the complexities of special education law.

Appeals

Local hearing decisions, in about half of the states, must first be appealed to a state hearing reviewer or panel (two-tier system) for review before being appealed to a court (Newcomer, Zirkel, & Tarola, 1998). In most situations, the state review involves only a review of the record of the original hearing. For this reason, it is important that a verbatim record of the original hearing be made. If a simple tape-recording system is used in the first hearing, the hearing officer must make sure that the equipment is functioning properly, the voices are clearly audible, adequate blank tapes are available, and speakers verbally identify themselves before speaking. Many states hire licensed court reporters or stenographers for hearings and have professionally prepared transcripts made of the hearing testimony. The state-level review may include the opportunity to present further oral or written arguments and additional evidence when necessary.

Administrative hearing decisions at the state level involving either a one- or two-tier system may be appealed further through civil action in the appropriate state or federal courts. The statute of limitations specifying the time allowed for bringing civil actions under the 2004 Amendments is 90 days from the date of the hearing decision, unless state law provides an explicit time limit for such actions. After the time for filing an appeal has passed without an appeal, the decision is considered final.

Attorney Fees

There is evidence that the hiring of an attorney for representation for due process hearings, by at least one of the parties, lessens the likelihood that the disagreement will ever go to hearing

(McKinney & Schultz, 1996). It is speculated that settlement in appeals becomes more likely because attorneys are accustomed to settling civil cases before they go to trial, and they bring that negotiating philosophy and skill to the special education arena. Thus, in some situations, the risk of creating a more hostile adversarial environment is apparently decreased through the use of attorneys. A prehearing settlement greatly reduces the time and financial resources committed by all parties and lessens the likelihood of damaging the parent-school relationship beyond repair.

Federal courts may award reasonable attorney fees to parents who prevail in due process hearings and subsequent litigation. Fees are prorated when parents prevail only in part. Schools may protect themselves from potential payment of parent attorney fees through the written offering of a proposed settlement more than 10 days prior to a scheduled hearing. If the school offer is not accepted and the hearing officer does not render a decision that is more favorable to the parents than the offer of settlement, attorney fees will not be awarded to parents for legal services provided after the offer was made. This provision of law encourages schools to offer reasonable settlement terms in advance of hearings to encourage resolution of disputes without the necessity of a hearing (Osborne, 2003).

Attorney fees will not be awarded to prevailing parents for any IEP meeting participation unless the meeting was convened as a result of a court or hearing officer action (20 U.S.C. § 1415 [i][3]).

An amendment to the IDEA appearing in the 2004 legislation, perhaps as an effort to discourage litigation, allows local school and state educational agencies to be awarded attorney fees in limited situations when they prevail over a parent's claims (20 U.S.C. § 1415[i][3][B][i]). An attorney of a parent who brings a lawsuit that is determined by the court to be frivolous, unreasonable, or without foundation or a parent attorney who continues to litigate after the cause of action clearly became frivolous, unreasonable, or without foundation may have to pay all or part of the school's attorney fees.

A parent or the attorney of a parent may be required to pay the school's attorney fee, in whole or in part, when litigation was brought by the parent for purposes of harrassment, causing unnecessary delay or increasing the school's cost of litigation.

"Stay Put" (Status Quo)

During the pending proceedings of a due process hearing and court review, unless the school and parent agree otherwise, the child must remain in the "current educational placement." This provision of law is sometimes referred to as the "stay put" or "status quo" provision. The rationale behind this provision is to protect the student from being buffeted back and forth or uprooted from educational settings based on who was winning at any particular stage in due the process hearing proceedings (Huefner, 2006). It maintains stability in the child's educational environment regardless of potential turmoil in other areas of the child's life. When a child is seeking admission to a school for the first time and a dispute arises, the child must be admitted to the school pending completion of due process and court proceedings.

When an initial state hearing officer decision or a subsequent state review decision agrees with the parents' position that a change in placement is appropriate, the change will take place immediately, even though additional court proceedings may be imminent. In some situations where students commit great bodily injury or are involved with drugs or weapons at school or at school events, the "stay put" concept is applied differently so that school officials may have more latitude in dealing with those important safety concerns (see Chapter 9).

Preparation for the Hearing

Although hearings are not a preferred method for resolving disputes, in some situations other alternatives do not exist or have not been successful. When a due process hearing cannot be avoided, it is imperative that parties be prepared.

Almost three decades ago, Ekstrand (1979) provided advice on preparing for due process hearings. The authors of this book, two with a total of nearly 50 years' experience working with special education due process hearings between them, believe that Ekstrand's summary of how to prepare for a due process hearing continues to be excellent advice:

There are two parties to the local level due process hearing: the local school system and the parents. There is no question that preparation by both parties is the most important part of the hearing process. If the local school system and the parents are fully prepared, the hearing will flow smoothly and all necessary information will be presented in an orderly fashion, allowing the hearing officer to make a well-informed decision in the best interest of the child.

The federal rules provide that either party has the right to be represented by counsel. While legal representation is not necessary, the parties can often be greatly assisted in the preparation and conduct of a hearing by an attorney who is familiar with special education due process procedures.

Although the hearing is much less formal than court and judicial procedures, many legal rights are involved. As a result, both parties often are represented by counsel. The local school system is required to inform parents of any available free and low-cost legal and other relevant services when a hearing is initiated or when the parents request this information.

Preparation for the hearing involves gathering and organizing the relevant information so that it can be presented clearly, completely, and concisely. . . . The evidence presented in such a case will usually be in two forms: documents (such as student progress reports) and testimony (statements made by witnesses).

Preparation should start with a review of the child's entire school file. Those records that appear most informative should be selected as evidence to be submitted at the hearing. So that the hearing officer may easily refer to the documents, it is advantageous to put them in chronological order, with a cover summary sheet identifying each one. And if the records are organized properly, a simple reading of them will give the hearing officer a fairly comprehensive chronological history of the child. Further, each document should be marked as an exhibit (for instance, School Exhibit 1, etc., or Parent Exhibit A, etc.) for easy identification during the hearing. . . .

The documents [should] provide the hearing officer with an understanding of the background of the child and educational needs, and finally, a description of the program and services which the party believes will appropriately meet the needs of the child.

Once the documentation is properly organized, it is necessary to determine what witnesses will testify at the hearing. The federal rules state that any party to a hearing has the right to be accompanied and advised by individuals with special knowledge or training with respect to the problems of children with disabilities. Witnesses are not required but are generally necessary to a sufficiently complete presentation of the position of either party. In determining what witnesses will testify, it is recommended, although not necessary and often not possible, that the witnesses have first-hand knowledge of the child.

The child's school history can be described by any appropriate school representative and by the parent. A specialist . . . can then discuss the handicapping conditions and educational needs of the child. Finally, a representative from the proposed school . . . can describe the programs and services available at that school and explain why those meet the child's educational needs. During their testimony, these witnesses should identify any documents or reports substantiating particular aspects of their testimony. . . .

The preparation for the hearing should be completed at least ten days before the hearing date because the federal rules provide that any party to the hearing may prohibit the introduction of any evidence that has not been disclosed to that party at least five days before the hearing. The meaning of the word "disclosed" is not clear, however. Since both school and parents have free access to the child's school file, it could be said that any document in the child's file is automatically disclosed. Yet a better approach to this issue might require parent and school to inform each other, within the time limit, of each document intended for submission at the hearing. This should be done in writing, and if the other party does not have the document, a copy should be provided. The federal rules require, moreover, that "any evidence" must be disclosed. Because testimony is evidence, a strict reading of this provision would seem to mandate the advance disclosure of any statement or testimony of a witness. Practically, this would of course be unreasonable—if not impossible. It would, however, appear that if the parties disclose the names of the witnesses who will testify at the hearing on their behalf and the subject matter of the testimony, the intent and purpose of the provision will be met. It is clear that the purpose of this rule is to avoid a "hearing by surprise," which would be contrary to the very purpose of a full and fair impartial due process hearing.

Proper preparation and disclosure before the hearing will greatly simplify the conduct of the hearing and will provide the complete information necessary for the hearing officer to make a proper decision.*

School District's Defense

An important aspect of a successful school defense at a due process hearing is the important role played by the school's attorney. The role is not played out solely within the walls of the hearing room, however. Providing advice, recommendations, and review of school practices long before any particular conflict arises are also important roles for a school's attorney.

*From "Preparing for the Due Process Hearing: What to Expect and What to Do," by R. E. Ekstrand, 1979, *Amicus*, 4(2), pp. 93–95. Copyright 1979 by the National Center for Law and the Handicapped, Inc. Reprinted by permission.

Education law and special education law are specializations that require great care in the selection of school legal representation. Osborne (1996) has provided this advice in the selection of a school attorney:

As an area of law, special education has become a specialized topic due to the tremendous amount of litigation that has occurred since IDEA was passed in 1975. School officials cannot rely on the school board attorney to defend the school district in a special education lawsuit. Although the school board attorney may be well qualified to handle most of the school district's legal affairs, he or she may not have the specialized knowledge required to adequately litigate a special education case.

School districts should retain a separate attorney to handle all their special education litigation. Many school districts use the services of a large law firm that specializes in education law. A large law firm may have one or two attorneys who further specialize in special education law. If this is the case, school officials need look no further for special education counsel.

However, if the school district is not represented by a large firm with a special education division, a separate attorney for special educational litigation must be located and retained. The attorney chosen should be well versed in education law in general as well as special education law and must have experience in administrative hearing procedures since most of the litigation will be at that level. Furthermore, the attorney should be familiar with educational issues and practices such as evaluation methods, teaching techniques, and various placement options. Naturally, an experienced and talented attorney will cost more; however, there simply is no substitute for experience. To find a qualified attorney to handle a special education lawsuit a school district should solicit referrals from other knowledgeable parties. Since the person representing the school district in a special education lawsuit may need to confer with the school board attorney, that

person would be a logical starting point. The school board attorney may have a ready list of qualified special education attorneys. Special education administrators from other districts would be another source of referrals.

. . . . .

Choosing an attorney is much like choosing a person to fill any open position in the school district. School officials should examine the attorneys' credentials, seek references from other school districts that have used the attorneys being considered, and interview the candidates that appear most qualified. Choosing an attorney is as important as filling any top-level administrative position in the school district. The process should not be taken lightly.*

CONCLUSION

Working with parents to provide students with appropriate educational programming and services is very rewarding when successful. When not successful, the mandated process can become frustrating, irritating, and tiresome. This does not mean that educators can lower their professional devotion when things do not work out. To do so may result in expensive and time-consuming hearings or embarrassing complaint results. Even winning hearing decisions and complaint investigations bring a real threat of losing those things most important in providing quality education services and programs to students (i.e., school resources and parent and community support). Relationships between parents and schools that are fractured by the adversarial system foreshadow adverse challenges for a successful team approach. Resources spent on litigation are resources lost to education programs and students.

---

*From *Legal Issues in Special Education* (pp. 244–45), by A. G. Osborne, Jr., 1996. Boston: Allyn & Bacon. Copyright 1996 by Allyn & Bacon. Reprinted by permission.

Most issues, however, may be worked out through honest, sincere communication and mutual trust. Developing and maintaining good parental working relationships, using consensus-building skills, exploring professional flexibility, and finding creative acceptable solutions are not situational; they are full-time considerations.

Disagreements should be considered a healthy part of the decision-making process. Informal dispute resolution activities such as problem-solving and fact finding, allow for review of alternative perspectives, reflection, and reconsideration in decision making. Some formal dispute resolution processes, such as mediation, help to "level the playing field" and help those with differences of opinions to hear each other. In the final reality of the entire process of developing a special education program for a child, some important issues arise out of honest differences of opinion that may need to go to hearing or court for resolution.

The important thing for educators and parents to remember is that the best interests of the child are served in arriving at mutually satisfactory solutions to disagreements as close to the child's educational setting as possible.

VIEW FROM THE COURTS

S. H. v. State Operated School District (2003; finding of facts). When federal courts review hearing officers' decisions, they generally give deference to the hearing officer's finding of facts. Unless the federal court can identify important evidence in the record of a hearing contrary to that relied upon by the hearing officer, the court should uphold the hearing officer's factual determination. In this case, at the request of the school, the federal district court overturned a hearing officer's factual determination that a school district's proposed IEP did not meet the needs of a kindergarten student with a profound hearing loss. The result was that the child's educational placement in a school for the deaf would be changed. The federal circuit court of appeals reviewed the

district court's ruling after the parent appealed, and reversed the lower court ruling. It found that the hearing officer's findings should not have been overturned without a specific finding of facts contrary to the hearing officer's original findings. The school lost before the court of appeals because the district court had not given appropriate deference to the hearing officer's finding of fact. As a result, the child remained at the school for the deaf as her mother had wanted.

A similar holding was reached in a decision in a different circuit court of appeals involving a preschool child with autism in *County School Board v. Z. P.* (2005).

Vultaggio v. Board of Education (2003) (attorney fees). In this case a parent who prevailed after using a state complaint process sought recovery of attorney fees. The parent's request was rejected under the IDEA by a federal circuit court of appeals because the complaint process was not considered a due process hearing or court litigation that is required for recovery of attorney fees by a prevailing parent.

Schaffer v. Weast (2005; burden of proof in hearings). A Maryland student with a disability was moved from a private school to a public school by his parents in order for him to receive IDEA services. The boy's parents challenged the adequacy of the school's IEP through a due process hearing. The hearing officer ruled that the parents did not meet their burden of proof that the IEP and the process through which it was developed was improper under the IDEA. A federal district court overturned the hearing officer's decision and ruled that the public school had the burden to demonstrate the adequacy of the IEP. The Fourth Circuit Court of Appeals reversed the district court and ruled that the IDEA does not expressly address the issue of burden of proof, and thus, according the standard practice of legal challenges, the burden of proof should fall on the party who initiated the challenge. The U.S. Supreme Court agreed to hear the case on appeal.

The Court ruled that the burden of proof in administrative hearings involving an IEP is placed on the party seeking the relief. Since the parents were found by the hearing officer not to have carried their burden of proving the IEP inappropriate for their son, the school's decision on the IEP was upheld.

The Court did not rule on the question of whether states may by statute or rule apply the burden of proof differently.

RECOMMENDED READINGS

Getty, L. A., & Summy, S. E. (2004). The course of due process. *Teaching Exceptional Children, 36*(3), 40–44. This brief article reviews several areas of IDEA's due process hearings' impact on education.

Goldberg, S. S., & Huefner, D. S. (1995). Dispute resolution in special education: An introduction to litigation alternatives. *Education Law Reporter, 99*, 703–711. This article addresses the use of mediation and hearings in special education and concludes that there may be better ways to resolve disputes than going to hearing.

Letter to Chief State School Officers, 33 IDELR 247 (OSEP, 2000). This official interpretive letter from OSEP provides answers to 20 questions regarding alternative dispute resolution.

Schrag, J. A. (1996). *Mediation in special education: A resource manual for mediators.* Alexandria, VA: National Association of State Directors of Special Education. This excellent pamphlet explains the concept of mediation, provides recommendations and forms, and contains case studies for discussion.

Relevant Federal Regulations

34 C.F.R. Part 300 Assistance to States for the Education of Children with Disabilities (70 Fed. Reg. 35,833–35,880 [June 21, 2005]).

34 C.F.R. § 300.151	Adoption of state complaint procedures.
	.152	Minimum state complaint procedures.
	.153	Filing a complaint.
	.500	Responsibility of public SEA and other agencies.
	.503	Prior notice by public agency; content of notice.
	.504	Procedural safeguard notice.
	.505	Electronic mail.
	.506	Mediation.
	.507	Filing a due process complaint.
	.508	Due process complaint.
	.509	Model forms.
	.510	Resolution process.
	.511	Impartial due process hearing.
	.512	Hearing rights.
	.513	Hearing decisions.
	.514	Finality of decision; appeal; impartial review.
	.515	Time lines and convenience of hearings and reviews.
	.516	Civil action.
	.517	Attorney fees.
	.518	Child's status during proceedings.

SELECTED WEBSITES

Code of Federal Regulations–Government Printing Office
http://www.gpoaccess.gov/cfr/index.html

Council of Exceptional Children
http://www.cec.sped.org

Mediate.com: The World's Dispute Resolution Channel
http://www.mediate.com/

National Association of State Directors of Special Education (NASDSE)
http://www.nasdse.org

Consortium for Appropriate Dispute Resolution in Special Education (CADRE)
http://www.directionservice.org/cadre

National Dissemination Center for Children with Disabilities (NICHCY)
http://www.nichcy.org

Special Needs Advocate for Parents (SNAP)
http://www.snapinfo.org

IDEA Partnerships
   http://www.fape.org/idea/problem_solving

Internet Resource for Special Education
   http://www.irsc.org

Technical Assistance Alliance for Parent Centers (The
Alliance)
   www.taalliance.org

U.S. Department of Education
   http://www.ed.gov

Teaching Research Institute–Western Oregon University
   http://www.tr.wou.edu

Western Regional Resource Center–University of
Oregon
   http://www.rrfcnetwork.org/wrrc

QUESTIONS FOR THOUGHT

1. Why should educators' decisions be reviewed
    through the complaint and impartial due process
    hearing processes?
2. Attorneys are not educators. Why should they
    play such a crucial role in IDEA disputes?
3. Is the IDEA a procedural or a substantive law?
4. Is the money spent on dispute resolution
    processes wasted?

REFERENCES

Bureau of Indian Affairs, Department of the Interior
   (1999). *Conflict resolution in special education
   and Section 504 through mediation.* Logan, UT:
   Mountain Plains Regional Resource Center.

Bureau of Indian Affairs, Department of the Interior.
   (2002). *Procedures for the investigation and resolution of special education complaints: Under the
   Individuals with Disabilities Education Act
   (IDEA).* Washington, DC: Author.

County School Board v. Z. P., 399 F.3d 298 (4th Cir.
   2005).

Ekstrand, R. (1979). Preparing for the due process
   hearing: What to expect and what to do. *Amicus,
   4,* 91–96.

Getty, L. A., & Summy, S. E. (2004). The course of
   due process. *Teaching Exceptional Children,
   36*(3), 40–44.

Goldberg, S. S., & Kuriloff, P. J. (1991). Evaluating the
   fairness of special education hearings. *Exceptional
   Children, 57,* 546–555.

Huefner, D. S. (2006). *Getting comfortable with special education law: A framework for working with
   children with disabilities* (2nd ed.). Norwood, MS:
   Christopher-Gordon Publishers, Inc.

Individuals with Disabilities Education Act. 20 U.S.C.
   §§ 1400–1487 (2000).

Individuals with Disabilities Education Act (IDEA)
   data, Table 1-1. (2004). Washington, DC: U.S. Office of Special Education Programs. Retrieved December 10, 2005, from http://www.ideadata.org.

Jacobs, L. (1979). Hidden dangers, hidden costs.
   Amicus, 4, 86–88.

Letter to Chief State School Officers, 33 IDELR 247
   (OSEP, 2000).

McKinney, J. R., & Schultz, G. (1996). Hearing officers, case characteristics, and due process hearings. *Education Law Reporter, 111,* 1069–1076.

Mills, G. E., & Duff-Mallams, K. (1999). A mediation
   strategy for special education disputes. *Intervention
   in School and Clinic, 35,* 87–92.

Montana Office of Public Instruction. (1994).
   *Montana mediation process for dispute resolution
   under special education.* Logan, UT: Mountain
   Plains Regional Resource Center, Utah State University.

Newcomer, J. R., Zirkel, P. A., & Tarola, R. J. (1998).
   Characteristics and outcomes of special education
   hearing and review officer cases. *Education Law
   Reporter, 123,* 449–457.

Osborne, A. G. (1996). *Legal issues in special education.* Boston: Allyn & Bacon.

Osborne, A. G. (2003). Attorneys' fees under the
   IDEA after Buckhannon: Is the catalyst theory still
   viable? *Education Law Reporter, 175,* 397–407.

Rickey, K. (2003). Special education due process
   hearings: Student characteristes, issues, and decisions. *Journal of Disability Studies, 14,* 46–53.

Schaffer v. Weast, 126 S. Ct. 528 (2005).

Schrag, J. A. (2003). *Dispute resolution refinement
   and innovation.* Presentation to Administative
   Law Judge/Mediator Conference; Iowa Department of Education, Des Moines, IA (July 11,
   2003).

Schrag, J. A., & Schrag, H. L. (2004). *National dispute resolution use and effectiveness study.* The National Association of State Directors of Special Education. Retrieved March 13, 2005, from http://www.directionservice.org/cadre

S. H. v. State Operated School District, 336 F.3d 260 (3d Cir. 2003).

Suchey, N., & Huefner, D. S. (1998). The state complaint procedure under the Individuals with Disabilities Education Act. *Exceptional Children, 64,* 529–542.

Vultaggio v. Board of Education, 343 F.3d 598 (2d Cir. 2003).

Yell, M. L. (2006). *The law and special education* (2nd ed.). Upper Saddle River, NJ: Merrill/Prentice Hall.

Zirkel, P. A., & D'Angelo, A. (2002). Special education case law and empirical trends analysis. *Education Law Reporter, 161,* 731–753.

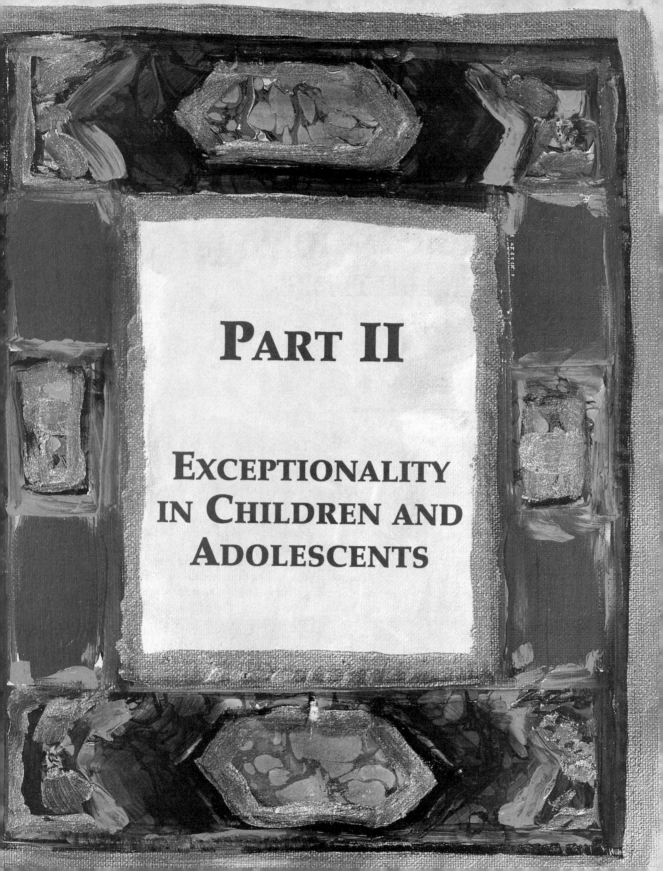

PART II

EXCEPTIONALITY IN CHILDREN AND ADOLESCENTS

CHAPTER 12

HIGH-INCIDENCE DISABILITIES

CHAPTER PREVIEW

Focus

The prevalence of certain disabilities is higher than others. For example, learning disabilities, behavioral disabilities, speech and language disabilities, and mental disabilities have higher prevalence estimates than do others (e.g., autism, orthopedic impairments). These high prevalence disabilities, also called *high-incidence* disabilities, are the focus of this chapter. Administrators and other professionals must be aware of the characteristics of various disabilities in order to meet their child find obligations and to effectively plan appropriate educational programs for students with high-incidence disabilities.

    Students with emotional disturbance/behavioral disorders (E/BD) frequently are referred for special education evaluation because of behaviors that interfere with their achievement or the achievement of other students. Students with E/BD display a variety of behaviors that impact learning and achievement:

- Physical aggression
- Verbal aggression
- Opposition and noncompliance
- Anxiety
- Depression

Students with mental disabilities are a diverse group of children with varied abilities and needs. Characteristics of students with mental disabilities include

- learning characteristics including a slow rate of developmental progress and skill acquisition;

- adaptive skills including limitations in personal, interpersonal, and emotional development; and
- physical characteristics including delayed speech and motor development.

An IEP team may determine that a child has a specific learning disability if he does not achieve commensurate with his age in one or more of the following areas:

- Oral expression
- Listening comprehension
- Written expression
- Basic reading skills
- Reading comprehension
- Reading fluency skills
- Mathematics calculation
- Mathematics problem-solving

Students with speech and language impairments have difficulties in the expression and understanding of language. These disorders include

- speech impairments, including articulation, fluency, and voice disorders; and
- language impairments, including both expressive and receptive disorders.

Inclusion Strategies

Successful inclusion strategies for students with high-incidence disabilities include

- collaborative teaching and multilevel instruction,
- peer support,
- teacher assistance teams,
- classroom and environmental modification,
- modification of content area instruction,
- paraeducator support,
- assistive technology and augmentative/alternative communication approaches, and
- professional consultation.

EMOTIONAL DISTURBANCE/BEHAVIORAL DISORDERS (E/BD)

Federal Definition of E/BD

The federal definition for emotional disturbance is a condition exhibiting one or more of the following characteristics over a long period of time and to a marked degree that adversely affects a child's educational performance:

- An inability to learn that cannot be explained by intellectual, sensory, or health factors
- An inability to build or maintain satisfactory interpersonal relationships with peers and teachers
- Inappropriate types of behavior or feelings under normal circumstances
- A general pervasive mood of unhappiness or depression
- A tendency to develop physical symptoms or fears associated with personal or school problems.

The term includes schizophrenia. The term does not apply to children who are socially maladjusted, unless it is determined that they have an emotional disturbance (34 C.F.R. § 300.8[c][4]).

Many professionals have criticized this definition because it lacks the precision necessary to provide objective eligibility determinations. However, defining emotional and behavioral disorders is difficult because of the variety of conceptual models, problems in evaluating social-interpersonal behavior, variability in age-typical behavior, and the transience of many childhood social or emotional disorders (Kauffman, 2004). Further, many states use the term behavioral disorders instead of the federal category of emotional disturbance. Both terms will be combined in this chapter to address the needs of children with emotional and behavioral needs.

Referral and Initial Assessment

Children with E/BD frequently are referred for special education evaluation because of behaviors that interfere with their achievement or the achievement of other students. These behaviors might be aggressive, noncompliant, acting-out, or antisocial (often called *externalized* behavioral disorders). Or, teachers may be concerned with students who are quiet, anxious, withdrawn, or depressed (often called *internalized* behavioral disorders). Although many students exhibit "disturbing" behaviors at times, it is when their behaviors and emotions become significantly discrepant from those of their peers for an extended period of time that professionals choose to refer students for special education to determine an appropriate educational program (Epstein, Cullinan, Harniss, & Ryser, 1999).

Professionals trying to decide whether a child referred for assessment meets the E/BD definition must examine the five defining characteristics previously mentioned. This determination involves a comprehensive evaluation of multiple factors, including the child's behavioral, cognitive, and social functioning and the influences of non-school factors, such as family and peer group (Wicks-Nelson, & Israel, 2000). Multiple assessment methods are used to ascertain the eligibility and needs of the child, such as interviews, tests, observations, and teacher or parent checklists. The assessment typically includes measures of the child's educational performance, such as achievement or ability tests. Measures of adaptive and social behaviors are also important sources of information.

The most reasonable estimate of the prevalence of E/BD is 3 to 6% of the student population (Kauffman, 2004). However, the identification rate is significantly less than the predicted prevalence. The U.S. Department of Education (2005) estimated that in the 2001–2002 school year, schools identified and served 437,585 children with emotional disturbance, which represented .9% of all students and 8.2% of the total number of students in all disability categories. Identification rates are lower for girls and young women possibly due to internalized types of E/BD (e.g., anxiety, depression), which are not as frequently referred. The overrepresentation of African Americans may be due to both teacher expectations and tolerance regarding behavior and to biased assessment instruments (see Chapter 3). Once identified, an assessment of the student's current performance and needs is included in the Individualized Education Program (IEP). Because emotional disturbance can affect various areas of performance (e.g., academic and social), the student's assessment must cover a variety of domains (Rosenberg, Wilson, Maheady, & Sindelar, 1997). The assessment may include formal or standardized assessments as well as informal measures such as behavior observation or checklists. The assessment of personal and social competence is also an important component of the evaluation. The results are reported in the IEP as the child's Present Levels of Academic Achievement and Functional Performance, and might include classroom observations of on-task behavior and of peer or teacher interaction.

The IDEA requires that the IEP include a statement of how the disability affects the child's involvement and progress in the general curriculum (20 U.S.C. § 1414[d][1][A][i][I]). For students with emotional disturbance, this statement might describe how internalizing or externalizing behaviors impact the student's achievement. A summary of the student's strengths and needs will lead to the development of IEP goals and objectives.

Characteristics of E/BD

Students with E/BD display a variety of behaviors that impact learning and achievement. Characteristics of behavioral disorders may include

- physical or verbal aggression,
- opposition and noncompliance, and
- antisocial or inappropriate social behavior.

Students who are physically aggressive are often involved in fighting, throwing objects, or the destruction of property. They may hurt others when they become angry or upset. Verbally aggressive students may use profanity or threaten adults or peers.

Students with E/BD who are oppositional are often noncompliant, resistant to rules, or nonresponsive to directions. Their opposition may be direct (e.g., verbally challenging, blatant refusal, tantrums) or passive (e.g., not responding to requests or directions). Antisocial behaviors might include inappropriate interactions with peers or adults, such as cursing or taunting. Antisocial behaviors might also include immature responses, such as overreacting or displaying silly or annoying behaviors.

Characteristics of internalized behavioral disorders include anxiety and depression (Edwards & Starr, 1996). Students who display anxious behaviors often seem fearful. They might exhibit nervous behaviors such as fidgeting or nail biting. Students with anxiety disorders may be withdrawn and socially isolated both in the classroom and in non-structured settings, such as the lunchroom or the playground. Similarly, students who are depressed may often be alone and socially isolated. These characteristic behaviors impact and interfere with the education of students with E/BD. Such students are more likely to drop courses, earn lower grade-point averages, be absent from school, be retained at grade level, and fail to graduate than students with other disabilities (U.S. Department of Education, 1998).

Students with E/BD often have difficulty with learning structures employing cooperative or peer approaches. Their behaviors may also interrupt the learning of other students and disrupt the teacher or classroom environment. Unprepared administrators and teachers often view these students as "bad" or "sick" and respond in punitive and punishing ways. This view obscures their [students'] identity as learners, excuses teachers from addressing their needs, and exacerbates their problems by removing them from the supports that they need (Glennon, 1993). Educational programs for students with E/BD must provide specialized instruction in social interactions and personal management, positive behavior management, and supports for involvement in the general education curriculum and classrooms.

Instruction

Students with emotional or behavioral disorders often require instructional goals and objectives dealing with social interactions and personal management. This instruction may involve social skill instruction, self-control instruction, and self-regulatory instruction (Bauer & Shea, 1999; Lewis, Hudson, Richter, & Johnson, 2004).

Social Skill Instruction Students with emotional or behavioral disorders often exhibit social difficulties, including lack of appropriate interactions with adults and peers. These students may need instruction in social skills, which involves identifying and defining the target social skill, modeling the skill, practicing the skill in role plays, providing feedback and reinforcement, and programming for generalization. Examples of social skills curricula for students with E/BD include the *Stop and Think Social Skills Program* (Knoff, 2001), *Connecting with Others* (Coombs-Richardson, 2001), *The PASSPORT Program* (Vernon, 1998), *Getting to Know You* (Hanken & Kennedy, 1998), *Teaching Social Skills to Youth* (Dowd & Tierney, 1997), *Teaching Social Competence* (Knapczyk & Rodes, 1996), *The Tough Kid Social Skills Book* (Sheridan, 1995), *The EQUIP Program* (Gibbs, Potter, & Goldstein, 1995), *The Second Step Program* (Beland & Moore, 1992), *The Boys' Town Social Skills Curriculum* (Wells, 1990), *Skillstreaming* (McGinnis & Goldstein, 1989), and *The Walker Social Skills Curriculum* (Walker, Todis, Holmes, & Horton, 1988). Social skill curricula for students of cultural diversity have also been developed (e.g., Cartledge & Loe, 2001; Rivera & Rogers-Atkinson, 1997).

Although commercial curricula are available, many authors advocate informal or incidental teaching strategies in social skill instruction (Gresham, 1998). For example, a student might role-play giving a compliment as part of a commercially available curriculum, or be directed by the teacher to change a comment such as "Where'd you get that jacket?" into a compliment to a peer (e.g., incidental learning). Skill

building programs have been successful in improving social interaction and reducing aggression (Strain & Timm, 2001). Social skill instruction has been regarded as a critical component of educational programs for students with E/BD.

Self-Control Instruction Children with deficits in self-control can be helped by instruction tailored to improve their capacity to direct and regulate their behavior. Self-control instruction may involve many approaches. Available self-control curricula include *Teaching Self-Control: A Curriculum for Responsible Behavior* (Henley, 2003), *Aggression Replacement Training: A Comprehensive Intervention for Aggressive Youth* (Goldstein & Glick, 1987); *Anger Management for Youth* (Eggert, 1994); and *Think Aloud* (Camp & Bash, 1981). A self-control curriculum is designed to reduce disruptiveness and strengthen emotional and cognitive control (Fagan & Long, 1998). This curricular approach addresses the social and affective deficits of these students that interfere with successful school achievement and life adjustment (Edwards & O'Toole, 1998). For example, a student might be working with a teacher and small group to recognize anger arousal and develop a plan for calming down. Self-control instruction is designed to help students manage their behavior and emotions.

Self-Management Self-management can be described as a set of procedures designed to develop the self-regulation of behavior. Students can also be taught self-regulation procedures to improve their interactions in both social and academic situations (Graham, Harris, & Reid, 1998). Self-management involves self-instruction, self-monitoring, self-evaluation, and self-reinforcement. These procedures promote the development of self-regulated learners. Self-instruction refers to speaking the process aloud and fading speech to a silent or whispered level. The speaking statements may include directions for problem-solving or academic responses. Self-instruction has successfully been used to improve the academic engagement and responding of students with

E/BD (Callicott & Park, 2003). Self-monitoring and self-evaluation involve the student recording occurrences of target behavior and determining the adequacy of the behavior change. Self-reinforcement involves the student choosing the type and schedule for receiving a reward for accomplishing a target behavior. As students learn to self-regulate their behaviors, they increase their level of task engagement and decrease the occurrence of disruptive or off-task behaviors. Self-regulation approaches are considered to be language-based, cognitive-behavioral strategies that assist students in selecting appropriate behaviors. An example of self-regulation instruction is Harris and Graham's *Making the Writing Process Work: Strategies for Composition and Self-Regulation* (1996).

In self-regulation, students identify target behaviors, design a step-by-step strategy to improve the behavior, and monitor their use and the success of the strategy. For example, a student might monitor her use of a "stay on task" strategy during math class. Self-regulation assists students with E/BD to become more independent and successful. Specialized instruction in self-control and social skills is a necessary ingredient in educational programs for students with E/BD (Meese, 1996). The selection of an approach or a specific curriculum depends on the goals and objectives generated for an individual student. These proactive strategies teach appropriate and replacement behaviors or adaptive coping skills (Rutherford & Nelson, 1998).

Behavior Management

Students with E/BD often need assistance in managing their behavior. These students often require intervention plans to promote appropriate behavior and reduce challenging or interfering behavior. The IDEA requires that the IEP team consider positive behavioral interventions, strategies, and supports for children with E/BD to address the behavior that is impeding her or his learning or that of others (20 U.S.C. § 1415[d][3] [B][i]). A behavior intervention plan (BIP) enables teachers and students to specifically determine the target behavior for change, design interventions to promote the change, document changes in the target behavior, and evaluate the success of the change (Bauer & Shea, 1999; see Chapter 9 for a discussion of BIPs).

Johns (2001) reviewed hearings and cases involving BIPs and offered the following recommendations: (a) the BIP should be based on the functional assessment of the student, (b) the BIP should be implemented during times when behavior impedes learning, (c) individuals responsible for implementing the BIP must have access to it, (d) positive behavioral interventions must be part of the BIP and facilitate improvements in behavior, and (e) the BIP must result in meaningful benefit to the student.

Depending on the target behavior, the interventions may involve problem-solving instruction (Hune & Nelson, 2002), social skill instruction (Lane et al., 2003), self-monitoring (Levendoski & Cartledge, 2002), or reinforcement (Sutherland, Wehby, & Copeland, 2000). For example, a student involved with a reinforcement system might earn points for target behaviors such as working quietly and completing assignments. The student then exchanges the points earned for a reward such as personal time (e.g., time on the computer) or school supplies (e.g., pencils, crayons, notebooks). Examples of classwide token economy systems are the *Boys' Town Educational Model* (Connolly, 1995) and *Assertive Discipline* (Canter, 1976; Canter & Canter, 1993).

Supportive Strategies Positive behavioral interventions may also include supportive strategies to assist students who are off-task or engaged in inappropriate behavior. These strategies are designed to quickly eliminate interfering behaviors and redirect the student to more productive and appropriate behavior. These strategies include:

- *Signal Interference:* Any type of nonverbal behavior that communicates to the student that her behavior is inappropriate and reminds her of more appropriate behavior (e.g., finger over lips to be quiet, pointing to chair to sit down).

- *Interest Boosting:* Efforts to boost the student's interest in an activity if she is losing interest or becoming bored (e.g., timing the student as she completes a task, relating the activity to her personal interests).
- *Restructuring:* Changing certain aspects of the assignment to increase the student's motivation to continue (e.g., handing the student a different writing utensil, changing the location of the activity). Alper, Schloss, Etscheidt, and Macfarlane (1995) provide a detailed description of these supportive strategies.

Crisis Management   Students with E/BD are often flooded with intense feelings of embarrassment, frustration, self-doubt, confusion, or anger. They respond to these feelings with behaviors that are disturbed and disturbing (Zionts, 1996). The child's teacher is a helping teacher who responds effectively to the emotional needs of students with E/BD and is an integral component of programs for students with E/BD.

Although the specialized instruction designed to improve social interactions and personal management is intended to prevent emotional crises, teachers must also be prepared for crisis intervention and management. Crisis intervention is an important component of programs for students with E/BD (Dice, 1993; Myles & Simpson, 1994; Meadows, 1996). The crisis or helping teacher must be available to assist students with E/BD during times of crises (Wood & Long, 1991). Examples of crisis intervention models include *A Crisis Intervention Team Model* (Graham, 1994), *Crisis Intervention for Community-Based Individuals with Developmental Disabilities and Behavioral and Psychiatric Disorders* (Davidson, 1995), *The P.L.A.C.E. Crisis Intervention Model: Emotional First-Aid* (Hoggan, 1995), and *Life-Space Interviewing* (James & Long, 1992; Long & Kelley, 1994; Long & Morse, 1996). Although the approaches differ, the steps in crisis intervention typically involve a

discussion of the behavior or incident, the student's perception, the central issue(s), and a plan for resolution. For example, Robinson, Smith, and Miller (2002) successfully incorporated an Anger Control curriculum to decrease inappropriate response to anger by middle school students with E/BD. Crisis intervention enables students to make changes in their behavior through problem-solving with a helping professional.

Medication   Psychopharmacologic medications are often used to treat certain types of E/BD. Lithium and antidepressants such as Prozac, Tofranil, Wellbutrin, and Risperdal have been used effectively as mood stabilizers for students with E/BD (Forness, Kavale, Sweeney, & Crenshaw, 1999). When psychopharmacologic medications are used, administrators and teachers should carefully monitor their use, and understand their side effects.

Related Services   In addition to their instructional program, students with E/BD may require related services in order to benefit from their educational plan. Among the potentially appropriate related services for students with E/BD are counseling services by qualified social workers, psychologists, guidance counselors, or other qualified personnel (34 C.F.R. § 300.34[c][2]). Given the types of social and interpersonal problems experienced by students with E/BD, counseling may represent an important component of a comprehensive intervention program (Maag & Katsiyannis, 1996).

Other related services might include psychological counseling for children and parents (34 C.F.R. § 300.34[c][10][v]). A student's educational and psychological needs may be intertwined, and psychological counseling may be necessary to assist a child with a disability to benefit from special education. Like other related services, psychological services (e.g., psychotherapy) are provided to support the child's special education program as identified in the IEP. Etscheidt (2002) analyzed 63 published decisions issued across seven circuits and 21 states that addressed the provision of psychotherapy services to students with emotional or behavioral disorders. She concluded that psychotherapy may be a related service under the IDEA and may be provided by social workers, school psychologists, guidance counselors, or other qualified personnel. However, psychotherapy that must be provided by a physician (e.g., psychiatric psychotherapy) is excluded as a medical service and would not be the responsibility of the school district. The need for psychotherapy is established by an adequate evaluation, and must be provided if necessary for a child to receive FAPE.

Inclusion Strategies

The successful inclusion of students with E/BD has been difficult to achieve. The majority of students with E/BD continue to receive most of their services in environments that separate them from their peers without E/BD. Approximately 45% of students with E/BD are educated in settings outside of general education for the majority of the day (U.S. Department of Education, 2005). Despite specific provisions in the IDEA to address behavioral concerns, research suggests that many of these students and their teachers do not receive the supports they need to succeed in regular class environments, particularly with increasing academic and behavioral standards (Lewis, Chard, & Scott, 1994). The behavioral and social difficulties of students with E/BD combined with the attitudes and expectations of general education teachers have negatively impacted the success of inclusion efforts (Lewis, Chard & Scott). Additionally, students with E/BD present educators with challenging academic and behavioral problems (Nickerson & Brosof, 2003). In response to these barriers, several strategies for successful inclusion may be identified (Johns & Guetzole, 2004), as described in the ensuing sections.

Collaborative Teaching Collaborative teaching is a cooperative and interactive process between two teachers in the regular education setting to meet the needs of all students, including those with disabilities (Wiedmeyer & Lehman, 1991). Collaborative teaching involves capturing the unique expertise and techniques of several teachers. Activities include shared planning and assignment development, curriculum adaptation, and presentation of diverse techniques and strategies. Edwards (1998) confirmed that curriculum modification was a strategy that helped students with E/BD in the regular classroom. Adapting the content and delivery of the curriculum, combined with behavioral supports, is an effective strategy for students with E/BD in regular classrooms.

Peer Support Systems Enlisting the assistance of peers to support inclusion for students with E/BD is important for several reasons. Peer intervention can foster both academic and interpersonal skills for students with E/BD (Dion, Fuchs, & Fuchs, 2005; Strayhorn, Strain, & Walker, 1993). Modeling, cueing, and monitoring by peers have been successful in improving the interactions of students with E/BD. Peer helpers and peer mediators can assist in friendship-building and in problem-solving or conflict resolution. General education peers have helped students with E/BD manage anger (Presley & Hughes, 2000), modify disruptive behavior (Gable, Allen, & Hendrickson, 1995), and improve socialization (Davis, 1995). Peer-assisted learning strategies have also increased the reading performance of students with E/BD (Falk & Wehby, 2001).

Teacher Assistance Models Several models have been developed to assist general educators in successfully including students with E/BD. These approaches, such as the Effective Behavioral Support model (Sugai & Horner, 1994) and the Problem Solving System (Tilly, Reschly, & Grimes, 1998) ensure that teachers receive assistance in addressing challenging behavior. The models are multidisciplinary, involving the collaboration of students, parents, teachers, support personnel, and administrators.

The key to establishing effective programs for students with E/BD is understanding that the disturbed or disturbing behaviors are symptoms of a disability, similar to the inattention of the student with ADHD or the writing difficulties of the student with learning disabilities. These behaviors are also diagnostic in representing the unique needs of the child. Nickerson and Brosof (2003) highlighted the importance of teaching non-academic skills necessary for inclusion to students with E/BD. An educational program that includes instruction in personal management and social skills, positive behavioral strategies or supports, and adjunct related services (e.g., counseling) will offer students with E/BD an appropriate education in the LRE.

MENTAL DISABILITIES OR RETARDATION

Federal Definition of Mental Disabilities

The federal definition of mental disability or retardation describes the impact of the disability on educational performance: Mental retardation means significantly subaverage general intellectual functioning, existing concurrently with deficits in adaptive behavior and manifested during the developmental period, that adversely affects a child's educational performance (34 C.F.R. § 300.8[c][6]).

This definition is based on the 1973 American Association on Mental Retardation (AAMR) criteria for identification (Grossman, 1973). Defining mental retardation based on the degree of measured intelligence and adaptive behavior is controversial due to the potential bias of IQ testing and to the focus on the deficiencies—rather than the strengths—of individuals.

Referral and Initial Assessment

The question of whether individuals with mental disabilities require special education and related services depends on the severity of the disability. As with other disabilities, student needs may vary from mild to severe. Historically, individuals were classified as educable mentally retarded (EMR) or trainable mentally retarded (TMR) based on IQ scores. In 1992, AAMR proposed a system to define the intensity of support that individuals with mental disabilities require: intermittent, limited, extensive, and pervasive. Students with extensive and pervasive needs have typically been referred for special education services early as infants or toddlers. Students with intermittent or limited needs may have accessed services later in their educational careers.

The assessment of individuals with mental disabilities frequently includes an IQ test and a test of adaptive behavior. The measurement of intellectual functioning is based on standardized IQ tests. Two widely used intelligence tests are the Stanford-Binet Intelligence Scale (Thorndike, Hagen, & Sattler, 1986) and the Wechsler Intelligence Scale for Children—Fourth Edition (WISC-IV) (Wechsler, 2003). The degree of intellectual functioning is often described as mildly, moderately, or severely discrepant from the age-based norm. Children with mild intellectual disabilities have IQ scores of 50 to 70, those with moderate disabilities score in the 35 to 50 range, and those classified as severely or profoundly disabled score below 35 (Heward, 2000).

The evaluation of the child's adaptive behavior is an index of the ability to function independently. It is important to view adaptive behaviors and functional living skills within cultural and environmental contexts, because expectations for independence vary based on the demands or requirements of specific contexts. Frequently used tests of adaptive behavior include the AAMR Adaptive Behavior Scale—School (ABS-S; Lambert, Nihira, & Leland, 1993), the Vineland Adaptive Behavior Scales (Sparrow, Balla, & Cicchetti, 1984), and the Scales of Independent Behavior (SIB; Bruininks, Woodcock, Weatherman, & Hill, 1984).

Assessment for students with mental disabilities should include measures of performance in the general curriculum as well as measures of functional living. Ysseldyke and Olsen (1997) identified domains of essential and desirable outcomes for students with disabilities, which include:

- Academic and functional literacy
- Personal and social adjustment
- Contribution and citizenship
- Responsibility and independence
- Physical health

The assessment data can be gathered by tests, observation, interview, or document review. The focus of the assessment must be on real-life experiences, must measure performance in various domains, and must be continuous (Ysseldyke & Olsen, 1997). The assessment should also document the nature and type of assistive technology used by the child to increase independence. The results of the assessment will provide the IEP team with information necessary to develop goals and objectives for the student and to plan instruction. The U.S. Department of Education (2002) reported that 612,987 students with mental disabilities received services under the IDEA during the 2000–2001 school year.

Characteristics of Mental Disabilities

Students with mental disabilities are a diverse group of children with varied abilities and needs. Drew and Hardman (2000) identified several characteristics of these students:

- Difficulties with learning including generalization and understanding abstract concepts
- Delayed emotional development including limited interpersonal and personal care skills
- Delayed motor development
- Delayed or impaired speech and language development

Often a slower development of adaptive behavior and language deficits result in challenging and difficult behaviors such as aggression and self-injury (Beirne-Smith, Patton, & Kim, 2006). The impact of mental disabilities on the educational performance of students depends on the severity of the disability. Some students will require extensive environmental and educational supports whereas others may require limited, intermittent assistance. The assessment results will guide IEP teams in developing appropriate instructional programs for students with mental disabilities.

Instruction

The curriculum for students with mental disabilities must be based on assessment results and must be individualized, person-centered, and functional (Wehman & Kregel, 1997). Several curricular domains are often included in education programs. The domain of academic and functional literacy may include instruction in academic content (e.g., reading, math, science) as well as instruction for independent living (e.g., personal, community, and work-related skills) (Wolfe & Harriott, 1997). Instruction in the domain of personal and social adjustment may include self-care (e.g., dressing, nutrition, grooming) and socialization (e.g., interpersonal skills). The instruction for students with mental disabilities should focus on skills that they will need for living, working, and leisure (Chandler & Pankaskie, 1997).

The domain of contribution and citizenship may include instruction in self-determination. Self-determination instruction involves enhancing choice, goal-setting, and self-monitoring skills in students with disabilities. To foster independence, the components of self-determination must be infused into all curriculum and instruction (Sale & Martin, 1997). Self-determination also involves the student's exploration of careers and employment. Although the 2004 Amendments to the IDEA require specific transition planning at age 16, the entire educational careers of students with disabilities should prepare them to be productive citizens. The curriculum should help students make independent and meaningful life decisions throughout the schooling process (Hanley-Maxwell & Collet-Klingenberg, 1997).

Instructional approaches for the domain of responsibility and independence may address skills for the home and community. Instruction in the community or school routines promotes generalization and independence

(Dymond, 1997). Travel and mobility training (e.g., using public transportation, traveling in and around the school building) may also be included in this domain. Instruction in financial planning and management (e.g., checking account, credit cards) is also important to the development of responsibility and independence.

In addition to the instructional domains, the educational program for students with mental disabilities may include the provision of several related services. These services are required in order for individuals with mental disabilities to benefit from the educational program.

Related Services

The provision of assistive technology is a related service for many students with mental disabilities. *Assistive technology device* means any item, piece of equipment, or product system—whether acquired commercially off the shelf, modified, or customized—that is used to increase, maintain, or improve functional capabilities of a child with a disability (20 U.S.C. § 1401[1]). *Assistive technology service* means any service that directly assists a child with a disability in the selection, acquisition, or use of an assistive technology device. These devices and services include

- the evaluation of the needs of such child, including a functional evaluation of the child in the child's customary environments;
- purchasing, leasing, or otherwise providing for the acquisition of assistive technology devices by such child;
- selecting, designing, fitting, customizing, adapting, applying, maintaining, repairing, or replacing of assistive technology devices;
- coordinating and using other therapies, interventions, or services with assistive technology devices, such as those associated with existing education and rehabilitation plans and programs;
- training or technical assistance for such child, or, where appropriate, the family of such child; and

- training or technical assistance for professionals (including individuals providing education and rehabilitation services), employers, or other individuals who provide services to, employ, or are otherwise substantially involved in the major life functions of such child (20 U.S.C. § 1401[2])

The determination of whether a child with a disability requires an assistive technology device or service in order to receive FAPE must be made by the IEP team, with the focus on the child's educational needs. The appropriate devices or services must be determined on a case-by-case basis. The district must first screen a student to ascertain whether it is necessary to conduct a formal evaluation of the student's need for assistive technology. If an IEP team determines that a student with a disability requires assistive technology services or devices in order to receive FAPE, then the specific devices and services must be identified in the child's IEP and made available at no cost to the parent.

Examples of areas in which assistive technology devices, products, or systems might be provided include mobility and response (e.g., switches, pointers, positioning equipment), computer access (e.g., universal access, sticky keys, text-to-speech devices, keyguards), communication (e.g., voice output communication aids, talking card readers), vision and hearing (e.g., hearing aids, magnification systems), reading (e.g., electronic dictionary, page fluffers/turners, large print books), writing (e.g., adapted writing implements, writing stabilizer), and math (e.g., adapted calculator, talking calculator); (Purcell & Grant, 2002).

Inclusion Strategies

Access to and progress in the general curriculum is an important consideration for students with mental disabilities. Parents of students with mental disabilities want their children around typical peers as much as possible (Gallagher et al., 2000). Students in inclusive classrooms compared to those in self-contained programs have made significant gains on developmental measures and have realized higher gains in social competence (Fisher & Meyer, 2002). Several approaches have been identified to assist in successfully including students with mental disabilities into general education environments: environmental modification, multilevel instruction, social interaction interventions, and paraeducator assistance.

Environmental Modification Environmental modifications include flexible scheduling, flexible programming, availability of program options, appropriate space, and appropriate materials (Keenan, 1997). Scheduling involves determining the class composition in terms of teachers and students. Flexible programming permits both group and individualized instruction. Program options should permit a continuum of instructional options, from general classroom instruction to one-to-one support. Flexibility in scheduling, programming, and instruction requires appropriate space allotted for individualized centers, small group work, and large group instruction (Keenan).

Multilevel Instruction Functional and valuable life skills can be taught within general education environments (McDonnell, 1998). One strategy to enhance such skill acquisition is multilevel instruction (Wehmeyer, Lance, & Bashinski, 2002). Multilevel instruction is a planning strategy that enables teachers to facilitate the participation of all students in shared class activities. This strategy has been effective with students with mental disabilities because it focuses on developing concepts by using content as a means for teaching specific skills, rather than teaching the content as an end in itself (Perner & Porter, 1998). By including numerous methods of curriculum delivery, the teacher is able to address various levels of ability within the class. A strategy similar to multilevel curriculum is curriculum overlapping (Giangreco, Cloninger & Iverson, 1998), in which students with mental disabilities have distinct learning outcomes in two or more curriculum areas. The selection of outcomes is based on the individual child's needs.

Social Interaction Interventions Social interaction intervention opportunities are designed to enhance the interaction between students with disabilities and their teachers and peers. Garrison-Harrell, Doelling, and Sasso (1997) describe two promising social interaction interventions: cooperative learning and peer networks. Cooperative learning involves grouping students of different ability levels together to accomplish shared goals. General and special educators collaborate in the planning, preparation, and implementation of learning activities. Peer network interventions promote a positive social environment for students with disabilities through assistance and support provided by classmates and peers. The Circle of Friends support network is an example of this type of interaction intervention. By carefully arranging the interaction between students with disabilities and their non-disabled peers, teachers can enhance the quality of the class community for both students with disabilities and their non-disabled peers—an important and intended benefit of inclusion (Ohtake, 2003).

Peer-mediated strategies may also assist in the successful inclusion of students with mental disabilities. Gilberts, Agran, Hughes, and Wehmeyer (2001) found that a self-management strategy combined with peer-mediated instruction was effective in improving skills necessary to survive in general education classrooms (e.g., asking questions, following teacher directions). Peer-mediated strategies may improve the participation of students with mental disabilities in the general education classroom.

Paraeducator Assistance The availability and support of paraeducators is an important component in successfully including students with mental disabilities in general education programs. Simpson, Myles, and Simpson (1997) suggested that paraeducators may assist in a variety of tasks, including management activities, data collection, teacher assistance, and student assistance. Administrators should be familiar with the legal issues pertaining to the need, selection, responsibilities, preparation, and supervision of paraprofessionals (Etscheidt, 2005).

As students with mental disabilities prepare for transition from school, their education programs may feature community-based instruction and vocational skills (see Chapter 8–Secondary School Considerations). These domains should also be addressed in inclusive settings, thereby maximizing interaction with non-disabled peers and adults.

LEARNING DISABILITIES

Federal Definition

The federal definition of the term *specific learning disability* is a disorder in one or more of the basic psychological processes involved in understanding or using language, spoken or written, which may manifest in an imperfect ability to listen, think, speak, read, write, spell, or do mathematical calculations. The term includes such conditions as perceptual disabilities, brain injury, minimal brain dysfunction, dyslexia, and developmental aphasia. The term does not include a learning problem that is primarily the result of a visual, hearing, or motor disability; mental retardation, emotional disturbance; or environmental, cultural, or economic disadvantage (20 U.S.C. § 1401[30]).

Referral and Initial Assessment

The criteria for determining the existence of a specific learning disability are described in 34 C.F.R. § 300.309–300.311. An IEP team may determine that a child has a specific learning disability if he does not achieve commensurate with his age when provided with learning experiences appropriate for the child's age in one or more of several areas: oral or written expression, listening comprehension, basic reading skills, reading fluency and comprehension, or math calculation or problem-solving. The team may not identify a child as having a specific learning disability if the lack of achievement is primarily the result of a visual, hearing, or motor

impairment; mental retardation; emotional disturbance; or environmental, cultural, or economic disadvantage.

The determination of whether a child suspected of having a specific learning disability is a child with a disability is made by the child's parents and a group collectively qualified to conduct individual diagnostic assessments in the areas of speech and language, academic achievement, intellectual development, and social-emotional development. A member of the group must be able to interpret assessment and intervention data, and apply critical analysis to those data. The team must additionally develop appropriate educational and transitional recommendations based on the assessment data, and be qualified to deliver and monitor specifically designed instruction and services to meet the needs of a child with a specific learning disability. The team must include a special education and general education teacher, and other professionals as appropriate. Federal regulations require that a group may determine that a child has a specific learning disability if the child does not achieve commensurate with the child's age when provided with appropriate learning experiences, and when the child fails to achieve a rate of learning to make sufficient progress to meet state-approved standards when assessed with a response to a scientific, research-based intervention process. The child must exhibit a pattern of strengths and weaknesses in performance, achievement, or both relative to intellectual development, and the group must confirm that the child was provided appropriate high-quality, research-based instruction in regular education settings and that the parents were provided data-based documentation of repeated assessments. If the team determines that the child has not made adequate progress under the condition of high-quality instruction delivered by qualified personnel, the child must be referred for evaluation. For a child suspected of having a specific learning disability, the documentation of the team's determination of eligibility must be provided.

The assessment of students with learning disabilities involves a variety of formal and informal tests. Formal tests include measures of intelligence (e.g., *Wechsler Intelligence Scale for Children-III,* Wechsler, 1991) and achievement or diagnostic assessments (e.g., *Kauffman Assessment Battery for Children,* Kauffman & Kauffman, 1983). Informal measures may include classroom observation or interviews.

The U.S. Department of Education (2005) reported that nearly 50% of the 5.75 million students receiving special education services are students with learning disabilities, a number that has increased by 28.5% over the past 10 years.

Characteristics of Learning Disabilities
Mercer (1997) described several characteristics of learning disabilities, including

- a discrepancy between a child's academic potential and his current academic achievement;
- learning difficulties in reading, mathematics, and expressive domains;
- language disorders involving both expressive and receptive abilities;
- perceptual difficulties including auditory and visual discrimination and memory difficulties;
- metacognitive deficits including deficits in self-regulation;
- social-emotional problems including both social skills and self concept; and
- attention problems and hyperactive behavior.

Students with learning disabilities may have one or more of these characteristics, which often impact their educational achievement. The IEP team must design an instructional program to meet the specific learning disabilities of these students.

Instruction

The instructional program for students with learning disabilities often addresses educational needs in reading, mathematics, and oral and written expression.

Reading   Reading instruction for students with learning disabilities should balance skill-building

instruction with authentic literary experiences (Pressley & Rankin, 1994) and should include both direct instruction and strategic instruction (Swanson, 1999). Skill building may include phonemic and phonological awareness (an understanding that sounds of speech are distinct from their meaning and that words are a sequence of sounds) (Chard & Dickson, 1999), comprehension instruction and monitoring (Gertsen & Baker, 1999), and cognitive strategy instruction. Strategy instruction, a step-by-step approach to decoding or comprehension, has been particularly effective with these students. An example of a decoding strategy is DISSECT (Deshler, Ellis, & Lenz, 1996):

D	Discover the content of the word
I	Isolate the prefix
S	Separate the suffix
S	Say the stem
E	Examine the stem
C	Check with someone
T	Try the dictionary

Strategy instruction teaches students a step-by-step, problem-solving procedure for decoding and comprehension in reading. Other instructional approaches such as Peer-Assisted Learning Strategies (PALS) (Fuchs, Fuchs, & Burish, 2000) and Collaborative Strategic Reading (Klingner & Vaughn, 1998) have proven effective in improving reading performance for students with learning disabilities. Goals and objectives for reading may include improving reading fluency and comprehension as well as increasing reading appreciation.

Mathematics   For mathematics, teacher modeling of explicit strategies has been found to be an effective approach for students with learning disabilities. Maccini and Gagnon (2005) described the STAR strategy for solving word problems involving integer numbers:

S	Search the word problem and ask "What do I need to find?"
T	Translate the words into an equation in picture form

A   Answer the problem

R   Review the solution and ask if the answer makes sense.

Computer-assisted instruction (Irish, 2002), manipulatives and Touch Math (Wisniewski & Smith, 2002), and strategic instruction (Jackson, 2002) can be effective instructional tools. Students should be frequently asked to verbalize and describe math tasks.

Oral and Written Expression Providing visual advanced organizers, presenting visual aids, and modeling processes and strategies are effective instructional strategies for oral and written expression (Vaughn, Bos, & Schumm, 2000). For example, students can be taught how to graphically organize ideas for writing through the use of a "webbing" technique. In the center of the web is the main topic or idea, and supporting details are spokes radiating from the center. Teaching alternative handwriting methods, verbalizing or dramatizing the motor sequences of letter forms, or employing multisensory techniques can all improve handwriting.

Educators have developed innovative and effective methods to address the instructional needs of students with learning disabilities. As the number of such students continues to increase, so will efforts to create, validate, and expand methodology to meet their needs.

Related Services

Students with learning disabilities may receive services from a speech clinician or pathologist. Classroom-based models for speech services emphasize the collaboration between the language specialist and the classroom teacher and eliminate the disadvantages of traditional "pull-out" models. The speech clinician serves as a consultant to the classroom teacher, providing direct services to both the student and the educator.

Inclusion Strategies

Although the inclusion of students with learning disabilities has been controversial and produced mixed reports of effectiveness, the number of such students educated in general education classrooms has increased significantly since 1993 (McLeskey, Henry, & Axelrod, 1999). Numerous strategies have been developed to address the needs of students with learning disabilities in general education classrooms, including using assistive technology, modifying content area instruction, employing alternative methodology, and promoting social competence.

Assistive Technology Recent advances in assistive technology may facilitate successful inclusion for students identified as learning disabled. Computer-assisted instruction may provide the greatest assistance (Shea & Bauer, 1994). Students with learning disabilities may have difficulty with the technical aspects of writing (e.g., handwriting, spelling, mechanics, usage). Word processing and prediction programs such as Kispiration, Aurora, Co:Writer, Read and Write, WriteAway, and Write: OutLoud from the National Center for Improving Practices in Special Education through Technology, Media, and Materials (NCIP) (2005) assist students in literacy tasks (Lewis, 1998). Cooperative computer lessons promote both skill building and social interaction (Denti & Tefft-Cousin, 2001).

Modifying Content Area Instruction Modifying content area instruction will also assist in the inclusion of students with learning disabilities into regular education classrooms. Modifications include adjusting the amount or completion time of assignments or adjusting the type of response for the assignment (e.g., oral response in lieu of an essay). Lewis and Doorlag (1999) describe several modifications for content area instruction. In reading, the teacher may wish to reduce the amount or level of reading material or provide instruction support such as tape-recorded texts or peer assistants. For written assignments, extending the time for assignment completion or permitting the use of assistive technology may be helpful. The use of assistive technology, as well as visuals and manipulatives, may also support the student in math assignments.

Teachers must provide ongoing adaptations and accommodations, and anticipate students' difficulties in content curriculum (Klinger & Vaughn, 2002).

Alternative Methodology Alternative methodology can also assist in content area classes. Reciprocal teaching has been found to be an effective comprehension strategy for students with learning disabilities in inclusive settings (Lederer, 2000). Self-regulated strategy instruction for written expression improved achievement for students with learning disabilities in regular education settings (de la Paz, 1999). Etscheidt and Bartlett (1999) recommended that IEP teams discuss supplemental aids and services that can be provided to achieve goals and objectives in the regular education classroom. Sample questions are included in Figure 12-1.

Given the recent emphasis on state and national standards and outcomes, the successful inclusion of students with learning disabilities will require IEP teams to carefully examine the demands of regular classrooms and provide effective assistance to students with learning difficulties.

Promoting Social Competence Another important strategy to promote the successful inclusion of students with learning disabilities into general education classrooms is promoting social competence. In a meta-analysis of the social competence of children with learning disabilities, Nowicki (2003) found that students with learning disabilities are at greater risk for social difficulties than are average-to-high achieving children. Simply placing students in inclusive settings has not resulted in improvement in social functioning for students

FIGURE 12-1 *Sample accommodation questions for educators*

- Does the student need visual aids, large print, or alternative media?
- Could the student be provided process-of-reading guides, or highlighted or tape-recorded texts?
- Could the student be allowed extra time for completion of assignments, have alternative assignments, or be provided a calculator or word processor?
- Could the student have take-home or alternative (e.g. oral) tests?
- Could the student use a study guide during a test?
- Could tests be divided into parts and taken over a series of days?
- Could the student be graded pass/fail or receive IEP progress grading?
- Could the resource teacher and regular teacher use shared grading?
- Could contracting be used?
- Could portfolio evaluations be used?
- Could cooperative learning or reciprocal teaching be incorporated?
- Could the student be assigned a peer partner?
- Does the student need an assignment notebook or home copies of texts?
- Could the student be provided computer-assisted instruction, communication switches, or software?
- Does the student require electronic aids or services?

From S. K. Etscheidt & L. Bartlett (1999). The IDEA amendments: A four-step approach for determining supplemental aids and services. *Exceptional Children*, 65(2), 1–12.

with learning disabilities. Consideration of the social dimensions of inclusive placement will be essential to successful inclusion (Vaughn, Elbaum, & Boardman, 2001). Without social supports, students with learning disabilities report loneliness and social isolation in inclusive placements (Pavri & Luftig, 2000). Teachers must understand and promote social interactions and social competence of students with learning disabilities in inclusive settings (McCay & Keyes, 2002). Social competence can be promoted through such interventions as peer-assisted learning and buddy systems. A speech/language pathologist can assist in designing activities to improve social cognition and effective social behaviors.

SPEECH AND LANGUAGE IMPAIRMENTS

Federal Definition

The federal definition for speech and language impairments is a communication disorder, such as stuttering, impaired articulation, or impairment of language or voice, that adversely affects a child's educational performance (34 C.F.R. § 300.8[c][11]).

Referral and Initial Assessment

The first step in the detection of speech and language impairment is screening. Screening may involve formal and informal measures administered by the speech and language pathologist. The classroom teacher may also be an important participant in the screening process. The screening attempts to detect students whose speech and language difficulties may adversely affect educational performance.

Following the screening procedures, specific speech and language assessments can be administered to determine the child's unique needs. The speech clinician may select certain tests to assess language. The assessment may include a

hearing test, interviews with parents, a review of medical records, and classroom observation.

Characteristics of Speech and Language Impairments

Students with speech and language impairments have difficulties in the expression and understanding of language. There are several types of speech and language disorders, including difficulties with speech production (e.g., articulation), speech rhythm (e.g., fluency), or vocal production (e.g., voice), or voice in communication (Lewis & Doorlag, 1999). Articulation disorders are also very common, and involve difficulty in the production of speech sounds. The difficulties may be mild or significant. Additionally, difficulty with the speed or tempo of speech production may also occur, such as with stuttering. Children may also have unusual pitch or volume in speech, which may interfere with communication.

Children with language disorders have difficulty with the production or understanding of language. A receptive language disorder causes difficulty in understanding spoken language, whereas an expressive language disorder is represented by difficulties in oral communication. Vaughn, Bos, and Schumm (2000) describe the characteristics of children with language disorders. The child with a receptive language impairment frequently asks for information to be repeated or clarified and has difficulty following directions, understanding abstract and inferential language, or understanding multiple meanings of words or phrases. Children with expressive language impairments often communicate less frequently than their peers and have difficulty with correct grammar use, word retrieval, and extended or content-specific dialogue (Vaughn, Bos, & Schumm).

The number of students receiving speech and language services increased by 9.5% from 1991 to 2001 and involved 1,093,808 children or about 18.6% of all students with disabilities receiving services under the IDEA in 2001–2002 (U.S. Department of Education, 2005).

Instruction and Related Services

Speech-language pathology services are provided to students who have speech and language impairments. As with special education, these related services are provided according to the individual child's needs. These services include:

- Identification of children with speech or language impairments
- Diagnosis and appraisal of specific speech or language impairments
- Referral for medical or other professional attention necessary for the habilitation of speech or language impairments
- Provision of speech and language services for the habilitation or prevention of communicative impairments
- Counseling and guidance for parents, children, and teachers regarding speech and language impairments (34 C.F.R. § 300.34[c][15])

Communication services and supports should be evaluated, planned, and provided by an interdisciplinary team with expertise in communication and language form, content, and function, as well as in augmentative and alternative communication (National Joint Committee for the Communication Needs of Persons with Severe Disabilities, 2002). Speech and language services are based on the assessment data and are provided in conjunction with the goals and objectives determined by the student's IEP team. The speech and language clinician guides the development of language programs and services. For articulation impairment, Heward (2002) presents four instructional models that are commonly used: the discrimination model (e.g., learning to listen and detect differences in sounds and imitate production with auditory, visual, and tactual feedback), the phonologic model (e.g., learning to identify and modify patterns of sound production), the sensorimotor model (e.g., learning production through repetition of sounds), and the operant model (e.g., reinforcing the successful production of articulatory responses). The speech clinician selects the approach most suited for the individual child's needs. For fluency and voice disorders, consultation with the child's physician may be warranted.

Educational approaches for language disorders are diverse. Classroom-based models include collaboration between the speech clinician and classroom teachers. The team may develop child-specific approaches or select commercially available programs. Classroom-based programs promote generalization of language skills to other settings (Yaruss & Reardon, 2003). As services move from clinical settings to classroom-based applications, the speech clinician must continue to assume responsibility for program development and progress monitoring (Ehrens, 2000). Mercer (1997) advised that the language intervention curriculum be relevant to the general curriculum, integrate spoken and written language, and focus on generalization.

Currently, speech-language service delivery is characterized by infrequent sessions and clinicians with a large caseload sustained for many years (Ukrainetz & Fresquez, 2003). One possible response to the problem of caseloads is to employ well-trained and appropriately supervised speech-language clinician assistants. As one of the consistently growing categories of disabilities under the IDEA, such assistance in service delivery may be warranted.

Inclusion Strategies

A variety of strategies can be used in general education classrooms to address the needs of students with speech and language impairments. These strategies include the collaborative consultation model, instructional adjustments, and the use of augmentative and alternative communication.

The collaborative consultation model is an effective tool for the inclusion of students with speech and language impairments. In this model, the speech clinician provides consultation to the general education teacher, develops the child's language program, and evaluates the child's language progress. The model is a classroom-based, naturalistic approach to addressing speech and language impairments. Adjustments in the instructional environment can positively influence speech and language skills. One of the barriers to successful inclusion of students with speech and language impairments involves interactional difficulties (Wellington & Wellington, 2002). Smith, Polloway, Patton, and Dowdy (1995) have suggested several strategies to address these difficulties, including increasing receptive language in the classroom, frequently soliciting language from the child with speech or language difficulties, and simulating real-life activities to enhance the use of language.

For students with more severe disorders, the use of augmentative and alternative communication (AAC) may be appropriate. A variety of computer-assisted and alternative methods for communicating may be important components of the child's program.

CONCLUSION

Administrators must be prepared to address the needs of students with high-incidence disabilities whose prevalence continues to increase. High-incidence disabilities include emotional/behavioral disorders, mental disabilities, learning disabilities, and speech/language disorders. The special education and instructional needs of students with emotional/behavioral disorders will focus on social interaction and self-control, whereas students with mental disabilities will require both academic and functional approaches. Students with learning disabilities may benefit from computer-assisted and strategic instruction.

These students may require related services to adjunct the instructional services, including counseling, assistive technology, or speech/language pathology services. Successful inclusion will require teacher training and assistance, multilevel instruction, and peer support.

As the number of students with high-incidence disabilities continues to increase, school leaders must be aware of characteristics and effective practices to ensure appropriate educational programs. Collaborations with all members of the IEP team will ensure the needs of these students can be met in the least restrictive environments.

VIEW FROM THE COURTS

Clyde K. v. Puyallup School District (1994) (behavior disorders and behavior management). The Ninth Circuit concluded that a self-contained placement was the least restrictive environment for a 15-year-old with Tourette's Syndrome and ADHD. The student was enrolled in an inclusive classroom until he assaulted a staff member and was removed under an emergency expulsion order. The district proposed a temporary placement in a self-contained program while the IEP team determined how to address the student's needs. Although the parents had initially agreed to the temporary placement, they later filed for a due process hearing to continue his placement in the inclusive setting.

The district court determined that the self-contained setting was the least restrictive placement because the student was not receiving academic or non-academic benefits in the inclusive placement. Further, despite extensive efforts by school personnel to provide supplementary services to facilitate successful inclusion (e.g., teacher training in Tourette's, a behavior management plan permitting the student to relocate to relieve the symptoms of Tourette's, and behavioral consultation), the student continued to exhibit assaultive and aggressive behavior.

The implications from this case are important. First, school personnel must consider adequate supplemental aides and services to facilitate successful inclusion for students with emotional and behavioral disabilities. Second, if despite those efforts, the placement of the student interferes with the learning of that student or other students, a more restrictive placement may be required.

RECOMMENDED READINGS

Beirne-Smith, M., Patton, J. R., & Kim, S. H. (2006). *Mental retardation: An introduction to intellectual disability* (7th ed.). Upper Saddle River, NJ: Merrill/Prentice Hall. This text provides comprehensive and current information concerning students with mental disabilities and highlights effective classroom practices.

Bentum, K. W., & Aaron, P. G. (2003). Does reading instruction in learning disability resource rooms really work? A longitudinal study. *Reading Psychology, 24*(3), 361–382. This interesting longitudinal study found that reading instruction in a resource room did not contribute to improvement in reading performance and possibly had negative effects on spelling.

Court, D., & Givon, S. (2003). Group intervention: Improving social skills of adolescents with learning disabilities. *Teaching Exceptional Children, 36*(2), 50–55. This article describes a life skills approach to improving the social skills of adolescents. The lessons include developing friendships, assertiveness, and coping with stressful situations.

Drew, C. J., & Hardman, M. L. (2004). *Mental retardation: A life cycle approach* (8th ed.). Upper Saddle River, NJ: Merrill/Prentice Hall. This text presents information addressing the needs of students with mental disabilities with a developmental, multidisciplinary approach.

Gerber, S. (2003). A developmental perspective on language assessment and intervention for children on the autistic spectrum. *Topics in Language Disorders, 23*(2), 74–94. This article discusses developmental influences on the development of language in autistic children.

Hallahan, D. P., Lloyd, J. W., Kauffman, J. M., Weiss, M. P., Martinez, E. A., & Lloyd, J. W. (2005). *Learning disabilities: Foundations, characteristics, and effective teaching* (3rd ed.). Needham Heights, MA: Allyn & Bacon. This text has an abundance of classroom strategies for students with learning disabilities.

Johns, B. H., Crowley, E. P., & Guetzloe, E. (2002). Planning the IEP for students with emotional and behavioral disorders. *Focus on Exceptional Children, 34*(9), 1–12. This article describes a process for developing IEPs addressing behavioral challenges.

Lane, K. L., Gresham, F. M., & O'Shaughnessy, T. E. (2002). Serving students with or at-risk for emotional and behavior disorders: Future challenges. *Education and Treatment of Children, 25*(4), 507–521. This article stresses the need to carefully examine the curriculum for students with E/BD.

Love, R. J. (2000). *Childhood motor speech disability* (2nd ed.). Needham Heights, MA: Allyn & Bacon. This book provides an overview of approaches to speech and language disabilities.

Malian, E., & Nevin, A. (2002). A review of self-determination literature: Implications for practitioners. *Remedial and Special Education, 23*(2), 68–74. This article is an excellent resource for information concerning self-determination and approaches for teachers.

McCormick, L., Loeg, D. F., & Schiefelbusch, R. L. (2003). *Supporting children with communication difficulties in inclusive settings: School-based language intervention* (2nd ed.). Needham Heights, MA: Allyn & Bacon. This text provides a collaborative model for delivering services to students with speech-language difficulties in inclusive setting.

Mercer, C. D., & Mercer, A. (2005). *Teaching students with learning problems* (7th ed.). Upper Saddle River, NJ: Merrill/Prentice Hall. This text provided research-based methods for addressing the needs of students with learning and behavioral problems.

Meyerson, M. J., & Kulesza, D. L. (2006). *Strategies for struggling readers and writers* (2nd ed.). Upper Saddle River, NJ: Prentice Hall. This text provides a variety of strategies for improving literacy skills for students, and includes step-by-step instructions for implementing the lessons.

Nelson, N. W. (1998). *Childhood language disorders in context: Infancy through adolescence* (2nd ed.). Needham Heights, MA: Allyn & Bacon. This text provides practical information concerning assessment and intervention strategies for three developmental levels: early, middle, and late.

Owens, R. E., Metz, D. E., & Haas, A. (2003). *Introduction to communication disorders: A lifespan approach* (2nd ed.). Needham Heights, MA: Allyn & Bacon. This text discusses the impact of communication disorders through personal stories from students.

Richardson, B. G., & Shupe, M. J. (2003). The importance of teacher self-awareness in working with students with emotional and behavioral disorders. *Teaching Exceptional Children, 36*(2), 8–13. This article proposes five key questions to increase a teacher's self-awareness when working with students with E/BD.

Rivera, D. P. (1998). *Mathematics education for students with learning disabilities: Theory to practice.* Austin, TX: PRO-ED.

Stuard, S. K. (2003). Choice or chance: Career development and girls with emotional or behavioral disorders. *Behavioral Disorders, 28*(2), 150–161. This article addresses the unique needs of girls with E/BD and their post-secondary opportunities.

Tournaki, N., & Criscitiello, E. (2003). Using peer tutoring and a successful part of behavior management. *Teaching Exceptional Children, 36*(2), 22–29. This article describes reverse-role tutoring as a means of improving the behavior for students with disabilities.

Wicks-Nelson, R. N., & Israel, A. C. (2000). *Behavior disorders of childhood.* Upper Saddle River, NJ: Prentice Hall. This introductory text provides a good overview of students with E/BD.

Wood, J. W. (2006). *Teaching students in inclusive settings: Adapting and accommodating instruction* (5th ed.). Upper Saddle River, NJ: Merrill/Prentice Hall. This text provides excellent suggestions for educating students with disabilities in inclusive settings.

Relevant Federal Regulations

34 C.F.R. Part 104 (2005). Nondiscrimination on the basis of disability in programs and activities receiving federal financial assistance–Section 504 regulations.

34 C.F.R. Part 300 Assistance to states for the education of children with disabilities (70 Fed. Reg., 35,833–35,880 [June 21, 2005]).

300.111(a)	Child find.
300.8	Child with a disability (definitions).
300.8(c)(4)	Definition of emotional disturbance.
300.8(c)(6)	Definition of mental disabilities.
300.8(c)(10)	Definition of specific learning disability.
300.8(c)(11)	Definition of speech and language imapairments.
300.34(c)(2)	Counseling services as related services.
300.34(c)(10)	Psychological counseling as related service.
300.306	Eligibility determination team.
300.306	Determination of eligibility.
300.308	Additional team members—specific learning disabilities.
300.309	Criteria for determining the existence of a specific learning disability.
300.310	Observation—specific learning disability.
300.311	Written report—specific learning disability.
300.324(a)	Consideration of special factors for IEP.
300.34	Related services (defined).

SELECTED WEBSITES

The Council for Children with Behavioral Disorders (CCBD)
http://www.ccbd.net/

The National Information Center for Children and Youth with Disabilities (NICHCY)
http://www.nichcy.org/

Special Education Resources on the Internet (SERI)
http://www.seriweb.com/

The Council for Exceptional Children (CEC)
http://www.cec.sped.org/

The ARC (Association for Retarded Citizens)
http://www.thearc.org/

The Division for Learning Disabilities (DLD)
http://www.dldcec.org/

The Learning Disabilities Association of America (LDA)
http://www.ldaamerica.org/

The National Center for Learning Disabilities (NCLD)
http://www.ncld.org/

LD Online
http://www.ldonline.org/

The Division for Children's Communicative Disabilities and Deafness (DCDD)
http://education.gsu.edu/dcdd/

The American Speech-Language-Hearing Association
http://www.asha.org/

QUESTIONS FOR THOUGHT

1. Discuss how teacher training and teacher attitude may affect the successful inclusion of students with emotional and behavioral problems.
2. Provide examples of functional skills that may be important instructional goals for students with mental disabilities.
3. Read one article concerning the social construction of learning disabilities. Discuss the article and the implications for school personnel.
4. The information presented in this chapter suggests that the number of students with high-incidence disabilities continues to rise. To what do you attribute this increase in prevalence? What do you predict the future prevalence trends to be? Why?
5. For which of the high-incidence disabilities do you think administrators are most prepared to address? Why? For which are they least prepared and why?

REFERENCES

Alper, S., Schloss, P. J., Etscheidt, S. K., & Macfarlane, C. A. (1995). *Inclusion: Are we abandoning or helping students?* Thousand Oaks, CA: Corwin Press.

American Association on Mental Retardation. (1992). *Mental retardation: Definition, classification, and systems of supports* (9th ed.). Washington, DC: American Association on Mental Retardation.

Bauer, A. M., & Shea, T. M. (1999). *Learners with emotional and behavioral disorders: An introduction.* Upper Saddle River, NJ: Merrill/Prentice Hall.

Beirne-Smith, M., Patton, J. R., & Kim, S. H. (2006). *Mental retardation: An introduction to intellectual disabilities* (7th ed.). Upper Saddle River, NJ: Merrill/Prentice Hall.

Beland, K., & Moore, B. (1992). *Second step program.* Seattle, WA: Committee for Children.

Bruininks, R. H., Woodcock, R. W., Weatherman, R. F., & Hill, B. K. (1984). *Scales of independent behavior.* Chicago: Riverside.

Callicott, K. J., & Park, H. (2003). *Effects of self-talk on academic engagement and academic responding.* Behavioral Disorders, 29(1), 48–64.

Camp, B. W., & Bash, M. A. S. (1981). *Think aloud: Increasing social cognitive skills—a problem-solving program for children.* Champaign, IL: Research Press.

Canter, L. (1976). *Assertive discipline: A take-charge approach for today's educator.* Seal Beach, CA: Canter & Associates.

Canter, L., & Canter, M. (1993). *Succeeding with difficult students: New strategies for reaching your most challenging students.* Santa Monica, CA: Canter & Associates.

Cartledge, G. & Loe, S. (2001). Cultural diversity and social skill instruction. *Exceptionality, 9*(1), 33–46.

Chandler, S. K., & Pankaskie, S. C. (1997). Socialization, peer relationships, and self-esteem. In P. Wehman & J. Kregel (Eds.), *Functional curriculum for elementary, middle, and secondary age students with special needs* (pp. 123–153). Austin, TX: PRO-ED.

Chard, D. J., & Dickson, S. V. (1999). Phonological awareness: Instructional and assessment guidelines. LD on Line. Retrieved December 1, 2005, from *http://ldonline.org/.*

Connolly, T. (1995). *The well-managed classroom: Promoting student success through social skill instruction.* Boys' Town, NE: Father Flanagan's Boys' Home.

Coombs-Richardson, R. (2001). *Connecting with others.* Champaign, IL: Research Press.

Davidson, P. W. (1995). Crisis intervention for community-based individuals with developmental disabilities and behavioral and psychiatric disorders. *Mental Retardation, 33*(1), 21–30.

Davis, C. A. (1995). Peers as behavior change agents for preschoolers with behavioral disorders: Using high probability requests. *Preventing School Failure, 39*(4), 4–9.

de la Paz, S. (1999). Self-regulated strategy instruction in regular education settings: Improving outcomes for students with and without learning disabilities. *Learning Disabilities Research and Practice, 14*(2), 92–106.

Denti, L., & Tefft-Cousin, P. (2001). *New ways of looking at learning disabilities.* Denver, CO: Love Publishing.

Deshler, D. D., Ellis, E. S., & Lenz, B. K. (1996). *Teaching adolescents with learning disabilities: Strategies and methods.* Denver, CO: Love Publishing.

Dice, M. L. (1993). *Intervention strategies for children with emotional or behavioral disorders.* San Diego, CA: Singular.

Dion, E., Fuchs, D., & Fuchs, L. S. (2005). Differential effects of peer-assisted learning strategies on students' social preference and friendship making. *Behavioral Disorders, 30*(4), 421–429.

Dowd, T., & Tierney, J. (1997). *Teaching social skills to youth.* Boystown, NE: Boystown Press.

Drew, C. J., & Hardman, M. L. (2000). *Mental retardation: A life cycle approach.* Upper Saddle River, NJ: Merrill/Prentice Hall.

Dymond, S. K. (1997). Community living. In P. Wehman & J. Kregel (Eds.), *Functional curriculum for elementary, middle, and secondary age students with special needs* (pp. 197–226). Austin, TX: PRO-ED.

Edwards, L. L. (1998). Curriculum modification as a strategy for helping regular classroom behavior-disordered students. In R. J. Wheelan (Ed.), *Emotional and behavioral disorders: A 25-year focus.* Denver: Love Publishing.

Edwards, L. L., & O'Toole, B. (1998). Application of the Self-Control Curriculum with behavior-disordered students. In R. J. Wheelan (Ed.), *Emotional and behavioral disorders: A 25-year focus.* Denver: Love Publishing.

Edwards, G., & Starr, M. (1996). Internalizing disorders: Mood and anxiety disorders. In M. J. Breen & C. R. Fiedler (Eds.), *Behavioral approach to assessment of youth with emotional/behavioral disorders.* Austin, TX: Pro-Ed.

Eggert, L. L. (1994). *Anger management for youth.* Bloomington, IN: National Educational Service.

Ehrens, B. (2000). Maintaining a therapeutic focus and sharing responsibility for student success: Keys to in-classroom speech-language services. *Language, Speech and Hearing Services in Schools, 31*(3), 219–229.

Epstein, M. H., Cullinan, D., Harniss, M. K., & Ryser, G. (1999). The Scale for Assessing Emotional Disturbance: Test-retest and interrater reliability. *Behavioral Disorders, 24*(3), 231–245.

Etscheidt, S. (2002). Psychotherapy services for students with emotional or behavioral disorders: A legal analysis of issues. *Behavioral Disorders, 27*(4), 386–399.

Etscheidt, S. (2005). Paraprofessional services for students with disabilities: A legal analysis of issues. *Research and Practice for Persons with Severe Disabilities, 30*(2), 60–80.

Etscheidt, S. K., & Bartlett, L. (1999). The IDEA amendments: A four-step approach for determining supplemental aids and services. *Exceptional Children, 65*(2), 1–12.

Fagan, S. A., & Long, N. J. (1998). Teaching children self-control: A new responsibility for teachers. In R. J. Wheelan (Ed.), *Emotional and behavioral disorders: A 25-year focus.* Denver: Love Publishing.

Falk, K. B., & Wehby, J. H. (2001). The effects of peer-assisted learning strategies on the beginning reading skills of young children with emotional or behavioral disorders. *Behavioral Disorders, 26*(4), 344–359.

Fisher, M., & Meyer, L. H. (2002). Development and social competence after two years for students enrolled in inclusive and self-contained educational programs. *Research and Practice for Persons with Severe Disabilities, 27*(3), 165–174.

Forness, S. R., Kavale, K. A., Sweeney, D. P., & Crenshaw, T. M. (1999). The future of research and practice in behavioral disorders: Psychopharmacology and its school implications. *Behavioral Disorders, 24*(4), 305–318.

Fuchs, D., Fuchs, L.S., & Burish, P. (2000). Peer-Assisted Learning Strategies: An evidence-based practice to promote reading achievement. *Learning Disabilities Research and Practice, 15*, 85–91.

Gable, A. R., Allen, L. N., & Hendrickson, J. (1995). Use of peer confrontation to modify disruptive behavior in inclusion classrooms. *Preventing School Failure, 40*(1), 25–28.

Gallagher, P. A., Floyd, J. H., Stafford, A. M., Taber, T. A., Brozovic, S. A., & Alberto, P. A. (2000). Inclusion of students with moderate or severe disabilities in educational and community settings:

Perspectives from parents and siblings. *Education and Training in Mental Retardation and Developmental Disabilities, 33,* 199–215.

Garrison-Harrell, L., Doelling, J. E., & Sasso, G. M. (1997). Recent developments in social interaction interventions to enhance inclusion. In P. Zionts (Ed.), *Inclusion strategies for students with learning and behavior problems* (pp. 273–295). Austin, TX: PRO-ED.

Gertsen, R., & Baker, S. (1999). Reading comprehension instruction for students with learning disabilities. National Center for Learning Disabilities. Retrieved December 1, 2005 from: *http://www.ld.org/*

Giangreco, M. F., Cloninger, C. J., & Iverson, V. S. (1998). *Choosing outcomes and accommodations for children: A guide to educational planning for students with disabilities* (2nd Ed.). Baltimore: Paul H. Brookes.

Gibbs, J. C., Potter, G. B., & Goldstein, A. P. (1995). *The EQUIP Program: Teaching youth to think and act responsibly through a peer helping approach.* Champaign, IL: Research Press.

Gilberts, H. G., Agran, M., Hughes, C., & Wehmeyer, M. (2001). The effects of peer-delivered self-monitoring strategies on the participation of students with severe mental retardation in general education classrooms. *Journal of The Association for Persons with Severe Handicaps, 26,* 25–36.

Glennon, T. (1993). *Disabling ambiguities: Confronting barriers to the education of students with emotional disabilities.* In Tennessee Law Review. Knoxville: The University of Tennessee.

Grossman, H. J. (Ed.). (1973). *Manual on terminology in mental retardation.* Washington, DC: American Association on Mental Deficiency.

Goldstein, A. P., & Glick, B. (1987). *Aggression Replacement Training: A comprehensive intervention for aggressive youth.* Champaign, IL: Research Press.

Graham, C. S. (1994). A Crisis Intervention Team Model. In D. G. Burgess & R. M. Dedmond (Eds.), *Quality leadership and the professional school counselor.* Alexandria, VA: American Counseling Association.

Graham, S., Harris, K. R., & Reid, R. (1998). Developing self-regulated learners. In R. J. Wheelan (Ed.), *Emotional and behavioral disorders: A 25-year focus.* Denver: Love Publishing.

Gresham, F. M. (1998). Social skills training: Should we raze, remodel, or rebuild? *Behavioral Disorders, 24*(1), 19–25.

Grossman, H. J. (Ed). (1973). *Manual on terminology and classification in mental retardation.* Washington, DC: American Association on Mental Deficiency.

Hanken, D., & Kennedy, J. (1998). *Getting to know you.* Champaign, IL: Research Press.

Hanley-Maxwell, C., & Collet-Klingenberg, L. (1997). Curricular choices related to work. In P. Wehman & J. Kregel (Eds.), *Functional curriculum for elementary, middle, and secondary age students with special needs* (pp. 155–183). Austin, TX: PRO-ED.

Harris, K. R., & Graham, S. (1996). *Making the writing process work: Strategies for composition and self-regulation.* Cambridge, MA: Brookline Books.

Henley, M. (2003). *Teaching self-control: A curriculum for responsible behavior* (2nd ed.). Bloomington, ND: National Education Service.

Heward, W. L. (2000). *Exceptional children: An introduction to special education.* Upper Saddle River, NJ: Merrill/Prentice Hall.

Hoggan, D. (1995). *The P.L.A.C.E. Crisis Intervention Model: Emotional First-aid.* ERIC Digest 37955Z.

Hune, B. J., & Nelson M. C. (2002). Effects of teaching a problem-solving strategy on preschool children with problem behavior. *Behavioral Disorders, 27*(3), 185–207.

Irish, C. (2002). Using peg and keyword mnemonics and computer-assisted instruction to enhance basic multiplication performance in elementary students with learning and cognitive disabilities. *Journal of Special Education Technology, 17*(4), 29–40.

Jackson, F. B. (2002). Crossing content: A strategy for students with learning disabilities. *Intervention in School and Clinic, 37*(5), 279–282.

James, M., & Long, N. J. (1992). Looking beyond behavior and seeing my needs: A red flag interview. *Journal of Emotional and Behavioral Problems, 1*(2), 35–38.

Johns, B. (2001). Here comes the judge: Lessons from the courts on behavioral intervention plans. Paper presented at the Annual Convention of the Council for Exceptional Children (Kansas City, MO, April 18–21, 2001). Retrieved March 17, 2004 from, *http://www.eric.ed.gov/*

Johns, B. H., & Guetzole, E. C. (2004). *Inclusive education for children and youths with emotional and behavioral disorders: Enduring challenges and emerging practices.* Reston, VA: Council for Exceptional Children.

Kauffman, J. M. (2004). *Characteristics of emotional and behavioral disorders of children and youth* (8th ed.). Upper Saddle River, NJ: Prentice Hall.

Kaufman A. S., & Kaufman, W. L. (1983). *Kaufman assessment battery for children.* Circle Pines, MN: American Guidance Service.

Keenan, S. M. (1997). Program elements that support teachers and students with learning and behavior problems. In P. Zionts (Ed.), *Inclusion strategies for students with learning and behavior problems* (pp. 117–138). Austin, TX: PRO-ED.

Klingner, J. K., & Vaughn, S. (1998). Using Collaborative Strategic Reading. LD OnLine. Retrieved December 1, 2005, from *http://ldonline.org/*

Klinger, J. K., & Vaughn, S. (2002). The changing roles and responsibilities of the learning disabilities specialist. *Learning Disability Quarterly, 25*(1), 19–31.

Knapczyk, D. R., & Rodes, P. (1996). *Teaching social competence.* Pacific Grove, CA: Brookes/Cole.

Knoff, H. M. (2001). *The stop and think social skills program.* Longmont, CO: Sopris West.

Lambert, N., Nihira, K., & Leland, H. (1993). *Adaptive Behavior Scale-School* (2nd ed.). Austin, TX: PRO-ED.

Lane, K. L., Wehby, J., Menzies, H. M., Doukas, G. L., Munton, S. M. & Gregg, R. M. (2003). Social skills instruction for students at risk for antisocial behavior: The effects of small-group instruction. *Behavioral Disorders, 28*(3), 229–248.

Lederer, J. M. (2000). Reciprocal teaching of social studies in inclusive elementary classrooms. *Journal of Learning Disabilities, 33*(1), 91–106.

Levendoski, S. L., & Cartledge, G. (2002). Self-monitoring for elementary school children with serious emotional disturbances: Classroom applications for increased academic responding. *Behavioral Disorders, 25*(3), 211–224.

Lewis, R. B. (1998). Assistive technology and learning disabilities: Today's realities and tomorrow's promises. *Journal of learning disabilities, 31,* 16–25.

Lewis, R. B., & Doorlag, D. H. (1999). *Teaching Special Students in General Education Classrooms* (5th ed.). Upper Saddle River, NJ: Merrill/Prentice Hall.

Lewis, T. J., Chard, D., & Scott, T. M. (1994). Full inclusion and the education of children and youth with emotional and behavioral disorders. *Behavioral Disorders, 19*(4), 277–293.

Lewis, T. J., Hudson, S., Richter, M., & Johnson, N. (2004). Scientifically supported practices in emotional and behavioral disorders: A proposed approach and brief review of current practices. *Behavioral Disorders, 29*(3), 247–259.

Long, N. J., & Kelley, E. F. (1994). The double struggle: "The butler did it." *Journal of Emotional and Behavioral Problems, 3*(3), 49–55.

Long, N. J., & Morse, W. C. (1996). *Conflict in the classroom: The education of at-risk and troubled students* (5th ed.). Austin, TX: PRO-ED.

Maag, J. W., & Katsiyannis, A. (1996). Counseling as a related service for students with emotional or behavioral disorders: Issues and recommendations. *Behavioral Disorders, 21*(4), 293–305.

Maccini, P., & Gagnon, J. (2005). Mathematics strategy instruction (SI) for middle school students with learning disabilities. The Access Center. Retrieved December 1, 2005, from *http://www.k8accesscenter.org/*

McCay, L. O., & Keyes, D. W. (2002). Developing social competence in the inclusive primary classroom. *Childhood Education, 78*(2), 70–78.

McDonnell, J. (1998). Instruction for students with severe mental retardation in general education settings. *Education and Training in Mental Retardation and Developmental Disabilities, 33,* 199–215.

McGinnis, E., & Goldstein, A. P. (1989). *Skillstreaming in early childhood: Teaching prosocial skills to the preschool and kindergarten child.* Champaign, IL: Research Press.

McLeskey, J., Henry, D., & Axelrod, M. I. (1999). Inclusion of students with learning disabilities: An examination of data from reports to Congress. *Exceptional Children, 66*(1), 55–66.

Meadows, N. B. (1996). Behavior management as a curriculum for students with emotional and behavior disorders. *Preventing School Failure, 40*(3), 124–130.

Meese, R. L. (1996). *Strategies for teaching students with emotional and behavioral disorders.* Pacific Grove, CA: Brooks/Cole.

Mercer, C. D., & Mercer, A. (1997). *Students with learning disabilities* (5th ed.). Upper Saddle River, NJ: Merrill/Prentice Hall.

Myles, B. S., & Simpson, R. L. (1994). Understanding and preventing acts of aggression and violence in school-age children and youth. *Preventing School Failure, 38*(3), 40–46.

National Center for Improving Practices in Special Education through Technology, Media, and Materials (2005). Word prediction collection. Retrieved December 1, 2005, from *http://www2.edc.org/NCIP/*

National Joint Committee for the Communication Needs of Persons with Severe Disabilities (2002). Position statement on access to communication services and supports: Concerns regarding the application of restrictive "eligibility" policies. *Communication Disorders Quarterly, 23*(3), 143–144.

Nickerson, A. B., & Brosof, A. M. (2003). Identifying skills and behaviors for successful inclusion of students with emotional or behavioral disorders. *Behavioral Disorders, 28*(4), 401–409.

Nowicki, E. A. (2003). A meta-analysis of the social competence of children with learning disabilities compared to classmates of low and average to high achievement. *Learning Disability Quarterly, 26*(3), 171–188.

Ohtake, Y. (2003). Increasing class membership of students with severe disabilities through contributions to classmates' learning. *Research and Practice for Persons with Severe Disabilities, 28*(4), 228–231.

Pavri, S., & Luftig, R. (2000). The social face of inclusive education: Are students with learning disabilities really included in the classroom? *Preventing School Failure, 45*(1), 8–14.

Perner, D. E., & Porter, G. L. (1998). Creating inclusive schools: Changing roles and strategies. In A. Hilton & R. Ringlaben (Eds.), *Best and promising practices in developmental disabilities* (pp. 317–330). Austin, TX: PRO-ED.

Presley, J. A., & Hughes, C. (2000). Peers as teachers of anger management to high school students with behavioral disorders. *Behavioral Disorders, 25*(2), 114–130.

Pressley, M., & Rankin, J. (1994). More about whole language methods of reading instruction for students at risk for early reading failure. *Learning Disabilities Research & Practice, 9*, 157–168.

Purcell, S. L., & Grant, D. (2002). *Assistive technology solutions for IEP teams.* Verona, WI: IEP Resources.

Rivera, B. D., & Rogers-Atkinson, D. (1997). Culturally sensitive interventions: Social skills training with children and parents from culturally and linguistically diverse backgrounds. *Intervention in School and Clinic, 33*(2), 75–80.

Robinson, T. R., Smith, S. W., & Miller, M. D. (2002). Effect of a cognitive-behavioral intervention on responses to anger by middle-school students with chronic behavior problems. *Behavioral Disorders, 27*(3), 256–271.

Rosenberg, M. S., Wilson, R., Maheady, L., & Sindelar, P. T. (1997). *Educating students with behavior disorders* (2nd ed.). Boston: Allyn & Bacon.

Rutherford, R. B., & Nelson, C. M. (1998). Management of aggressive and violent behavior in the schools. In R. J. Wheelan (Ed.), *Emotional and behavioral disorders: A 25-year focus.* Denver: Love Publishing.

Sale, P., & Martin, J. E. (1997). Self-determination. In P. Wehman & J. Kregel (Eds.), *Functional curriculum for elementary, middle, and secondary age students with special needs* (pp. 43–67). Austin, TX: PRO-ED.

Shea, T. M., & Bauer, A. M. (1994). *Learners with disabilities: A social systems perspective of special education.* Madison, WI: Brown & Benchmark Publishers.

Sheridan, S. M. (1995). *The tough kid social skills book.* Longmont, CO: Sopris West.

Simpson, R. L., Myles, B. M., & Simpson, J. D. (1997). Inclusion of students with disabilities in general education settings: Structuring for successful management. In P. Zionts (Ed.), *Inclusion strategies for students with learning and behavior problems* (pp. 171–196). Austin, TX: PRO-ED.

Smith, T. E. C., Polloway, E. A., Patton, J. R., & Dowdy, C. A. (1995). *Teaching children with special needs in inclusive settings.* Boston: Allyn & Bacon.

Sparrow, S. S., Balla, D. A., & Cicchetti, D. V. (1984). *Vineland Adaptive Behavior Scales.* Circle Pines, MN: American Guidance Service.

Strain, P. S., & Timm, M. A. (2001). Remediation and prevention of aggression: An evaluation of the regional intervention program over a quarter of a century. *Behavioral Disorders, 26*(4), 297–313.

Strayhorn, J. M., Strain, P. S., & Walker, H. M. (1993). The case for interaction skills training in the context of tutoring as a preventive mental health intervention in schools. *Behavioral Disorders, 19*(1), 11–26.

Sugai, G., & Horner, R. (1994). Including students with severe behavior problems in general education settings: Assumptions, challenges, and solutions. In J. Marr, G. Sugai, & G. Tindal (Eds.), *The Oregon Conference Monograph 1994.* Eugene: University of Oregon.

Sutherland, K. S., Wehby, J. H., & Copeland, S. R. (2000). Effects of varying rates of behavior-specific praise on the on-task behavior of students with E/BD. *Journal of Emotional and Behavioral Disorders, 8,* 2–9.

Swanson, H. L. (1999). Intervention research for students with learning disabilities: A meta-analysis of treatment outcomes. National Center for Learning Disabilities. Retrieved December 1, 2005, from *http://www.ld.org/*

Thorndike, R. I., Hagen, E. P., & Sattler, J. M. (1986). *Technical manual for the Stanford-Binet Intelligence Scale* (4th ed.). Chicago: Riverside.

Tilly, W. D., Reschly, D. J., & Grimes, J. (1998). Disability determination in problem solving systems: Conceptual foundations and critical components. In D. J. Reschly, W. D. Tilly, and J. P. Grimes (Eds.), *Functional and Noncategorical Identification and Intervention in Special Education.* Des Moines, IA: Iowa Department of Education.

U.S. Department of Education (1998). *20th Annual Report to Congress on the Implementation of the Individuals with Disabilities Education Act.* Washington, DC: Office of Special Education Programs.

U.S. Department of Education (2002). *24th Annual Report to Congress on the Implementation of the Individuals with Disabilities Education Act.* Washington, DC: Office of Special Education Programs.

U.S. Department of Education (2005). *25th Annual Report to Congress on the Implementation of the Individuals with Disabilities Education Act.* Washington, DC: Office of Special Education Programs.

Ukrainetz, T. A., & Fresquez, E. F. (2003). "What isn't language?": A qualitative study of the role of the school speech-language pathologist. *Language, Speech and Hearing Services in Schools, 34*(4), 284–298.

Vaughn, S., Bos, C. S., & Schumm, J. S. (2000). *Teaching mainstreamed, diverse, and at-risk students in the general education classroom* (2nd ed.). Boston: Allyn & Bacon.

Vaughn, S., Elbaum, B., & Boardman, A. G. (2001). The social functioning of students with learning disabilities: Implications for inclusion. *Exceptionality, 9*(1-2), 47–65.

Vernon, A. (1998). *The PASSPORT Program.* Champaign, IL: Research Press.

Walker, H. M., Todis, B., Holmes, D., & Horton, G. (1988). *The Walker Social Skills Curriculum: The ACCESS Program.* Austin, TX: PRO-ED.

Wechsler, D. (1974). *Manual for the wechsler intelligence scale for children–revised.* New York: Psychological Corporation.

Wechsler, D. (2003). *Manual for the wechsler intelligence scale for children—*(4th ed.). New York: The Psychological Corporation.

Wechsler, D. (1991). *Wechsler intelligence scale for children* (3rd ed.). San Antonio, TX: Psychological Corporation.

Wehman, P., & Kregel, J. (1997). *Functional curriculum for elementary, middle, and secondary age students with special needs.* Austin, TX: PRO-ED.

Wehmeyer, M. L., Lance, G. D., & Bashinski, S. (2002). Promoting access to the general curriculum for students with mental retardation: A multi-level model. *Education and Training in Mental Retardation and Developmental Disabilities, 37*(3), 223–234.

Wellington, W., & Wellington, J. (2002). Children with communication difficulties in mainstream science classrooms. *School Science Review, 63*(305), 81–92.

Wells, T. (1990). *The Boys' Town Education Model.* Boys' Town, NE: Father Flanagan's Boys' Home.

Wilks-Nelson, R. N., & Dsrael, A. C. (2000). *Behavior disorders of childhood.* Upper Saddle River, NJ: Prentice Hall.

Wiedmeyer, D. & Lehman, J. (1991). "The house plan" approach to collaborative teaching and consultation. *Teaching Exceptional Children, 23*(10), 7–10.

Wisniewski, Z. G., & Smith, S. (2002). How effective is Touch Math for improving students with special needs academic achievement on math addition and minute timed tests? EDRS report. Retrieved April 26, 2005, from *http://www.eric.ed.gov/*

Wolfe, P. S., & Harriott, W. A. (1997). Functional academics. In P. Wehman & J. Kregel (Eds.), *Functional curriculum for elementary, middle, and secondary age students with special needs* (pp. 69–103). Austin, TX: PRO-ED.

Wood, M. M., & Long, N. J. (1991). Life space intervention: *Talking with children and youth in crisis.* Austin, TX: PRO-ED.

Yaruss, J. S., Reardon, N. A. (2003). Fostering generalization and maintenance in school settings. *Seminars in Speech and Language, 24*(1), 33–40.

Ysseldyke, J. E. & Olsen, K. (1997). NCEO Synthesis Report 28: *Putting alternate assessments into practice: What to measure and possible sources of data.* Minneapolis, MN: National Center for Educational Outcomes.

Zionts, P. (1996). *Teaching disturbed and disturbing students: An integrative approach* (2nd ed.). Austin, TX: PRO-ED.

CHAPTER 13

LOW-INCIDENCE DISABILITIES

CHAPTER PREVIEW

Focus

This chapter focuses on *low-incidence* disabilities. Although these disabilities may impact a child's educational performance, the prevalence of these disabilities is not as high as those discussed in Chapter 12. The low-incidence disabilities include autism, physical disabilities, visual and hearing impairments, and traumatic brain injury. Administrators and other professionals must be aware of the characteristics of these disabilities in order to meet their child find obligations. School leaders and professionals must also be aware of instructional and inclusion strategies to assure students with low-incidence disabilities receive a free, appropriate education.

Students with autism often display behaviors characteristic of the disability, including

- Disturbances in the development of social and language skills;
- Exaggerated responses to sensations; and
- Difficulties in speech, language, and nonverbal communication development.

Physical or orthopedic disabilities are associated with congenital anomalies, disease, or other causes. Some conditions that may affect students with physical disabilities include the following:

- Cerebral palsy
- Spina bifida
- Muscular dystrophy
- Spinal cord injury

Traumatic Brain Injury (TBI) is an acquired injury to the brain caused by an external physical force that causes functional and social impairments and adversely affects a child's educational performance.

The lack of vision or reduced vision may vary greatly in students and may be influenced by

- the environment,
- other disabilities, or
- the nature of the vision loss.

The curriculum for students with visual impairment or blindness includes

- Reading and writing through the use of Braille,
- Functional skills,
- Interpersonal skills,
- Orientation and mobility training, and
- Instruction in the use of special aids and equipment.

The effects of hearing loss on academic achievement and social competence depend on several factors, including the

- type and degree of hearing loss,
- age of onset,
- familial and social context,
- language opportunities, and
- co-occurrence of other disabilities.

Deafness-blindness is a condition involving concomitant hearing and visual impairment. The education needs and programs of a child with deafness-blindness are unique.

Inclusion Strategies

The successful inclusion of students with low-incidence disabilities requires a variety of supports, including the following:

- Paraeducator availability
- Reduced class size
- Adequate teacher and staff planning time
- Access to related services and assistive technology
- Adequate teacher preparation
- Facilitating positive peer interactions

AUTISM

Federal Definition of Autism

Autism is described as a developmental disability significantly affecting verbal and nonverbal communication and social interaction, generally evident before age 3, that adversely affects a child's educational performance. Other characteristics often associated with autism are engagement in repetitive activities and stereotyped movements, resistance to environmental change or change in daily routines, and unusual responses to sensory experiences. The term does not apply if a child's educational performance is adversely affected primarily because the child has an emotional disturbance. A child who manifests the characteristics of autism after age 3 could be diagnosed as having autism if the criteria are satisfied (34C.F.R. § 300.8[c][1]).

Autism is one of several disabilities related to pervasive developmental disorders (PDD). Asperger Syndrome, involving less significant delays in language and conditions, would also be included. Autism, Asperger Syndrome, and other less-known variations of PDD are described as autism spectrum disorders (ASD). All disabilities within the spectrum are characterized by difficulties in communication, social interactions, and behavior.

Referral and Initial Assessment

According to the Autism Society of America (ASA, 2001), the unique characteristics of autism are often identified before a child's third birthday. Parents may notice that their infant does not cuddle, make eye contact, or respond to affection and touching, or has unusual responses to sensory stimulation from hearing, smelling, tasting, movement, or reaction to pain. The young child with autism may be unable to communicate appropriately, may echo language of others, or may use movement or gestures to communicate. Parents may notice unusual repetitive movements, such as spinning or finger flicking, or a preoccupation or avoidance of certain objects. The child's social interactions may be limited or deficient, even with family members. Because these characteristics are recognized in early development, children with autism are often referred for special education services as infants and toddlers (see Chapter 7).

The Autism Society of America (ASA, 2001) reports that an accurate diagnosis of autism must be based on an evaluation of the child's communication, behavior, and developmental levels. The assessment should be conducted by a multidisciplinary team that might include a neurologist, psychologist, pediatrician, speech-language therapist, or another professional knowledgeable about autism. The U.S. Department of Education reported that 78,747 students with autism were served during the 2000–2001 school year, which represents a 1,354% increase in the number of students with autism served in the last 10 years (U.S. Department of Education, 2002). Students with autism represent 1.7% of all students with disabilities served under the IDEA (U.S. Department of Education, 2005).

Characteristics of Autism

The ASA (2001) describes autism as a severely incapacitating, lifelong developmental disability that typically becomes evident in the first 3 years of life. Children with autism often display certain characteristics including difficulties in social and language skills. Eaves (1997) researched behavior commonly ascribed to children with autism and found three factors. Children often revealed affective or cognitive indifference factors by expression or movement, affective factors displayed in aggression or anxiety, and cognitive factors that resulted in unusual speech or uneven skill development.

Although certain characteristics are associated with autism, children with autism vary tremendously in abilities and needs. The impact of autism on a student's abilities may range from mild to severe. IEP teams need to consider this variability when planning educational programs for students with autism.

Instruction

Various approaches to instruction have addressed the "What to teach" questions for students with autism (Mirenda & Donnellan, 1987). Advocates of a development approach suggest curricular content decisions be based on activities that match the student's cognitive and conceptual abilities. Proponents of an ecological approach require selecting curricular content that will ultimately and directly enhance the ability of students to function in a variety of domestic, recreational/leisure, and vocational environments. Both approaches emphasize the selection of curricular content that is developmentally appropriate and also based on an ecological assessment of potential utility to the student.

An appropriate instructional program for a student with autism would typically address communication-language skills, social skills, behavior management, vocational skills, and community living skills (ASA, 2001). The "How to teach" questions have resulted in a variety of approaches involving behavioral and interactive models. Prominent researchers have concluded that there is not a single, universally best suited and effective method for students with autism (Simpson, 2004). The following sections are examples of instructional approaches for students with autism.

Visual Approaches

TEACCH. The TEACCH approach, developed by Eric Schopler (1997), involves the development of a program based on the child's skills, interests, and needs. Structured teaching is an important component of the TEACCH model and involves organizing the physical environment, developing schedules and work systems, making expectations clear and explicit, and using visual materials. Although independent work skills are emphasized, the program also addresses communication, social, and leisure skills (University of North Carolina, 2006).

Students with autism may have difficulty with organization and sequencing. They may also experience difficulty understanding rules and directions. Visual structures are helpful in assisting students with autism respond appropriately within classroom environments. Structuring the physical environment of the classroom gives students with autism visual cues about how and

where to respond. The schedule of daily activities is also carefully structured. Visual schedules promote student organization, smooth activity transitions, and task engagement. Instructional methods are also organized and systematic. The structure within the curriculum involves work stations and task organization that provides the students with a systematic and successful way to approach each task (e.g., left-to-right sequence, matching numbers, finished work in containers). This structure also minimizes distractions, helps with personal organization, and assists in personal independence.

The TEACCH model has been criticized as being not a teaching or learning system, but a behavioral management system that employs rigid routines, the need for predictability, using objects of obsession as rewards, and a day "filled with charts and other visual aids" that become the focus of the program (Autism-PDD Resources Network, 1997).

Applied Behavioral Approaches

The UCLA Project (Lovaas, 1987). The UCLA project, also described as the Early Intervention Project (EIP), was designed as an intense program involving instruction in the home, school, and community environment an average of 40 hours per week for 3 or more years. Parents work as part of the treatment team and are extensively trained so treatment can take place for almost all of the student's waking hours, 365 days per year.

The treatment is based on operant conditioning and behavioral modification using discrete trial discrimination training. Students are repeatedly presented with a stimulus (e.g., verbal direction to look at the teacher) and are reinforced for a correct response (e.g., eye contact with the teacher). Aggressive and self-stimulatory behaviors are decreased by ignoring or time-out procedures and alternative appropriate behaviors are reinforced. First-year goals target reducing self-stimulatory and aggressive behavior, increasing compliance to verbal requests, improving imitation and play, and introducing family-based treatment.

Typical second-year goals include teaching language, increasing interaction with peers, and introducing community-based treatment in pre-school settings. The third-year goals focus on teaching pre-academic tasks (reading, writing, math) and learning from observing peers. Transition to regular public preschool programs is carefully planned. The number of hours of clinic treatment decreases from 40 to 10 or fewer hours per week during transition.

The Lovaas method claims to produce improvement in about one-half of the cases and to greatly reduce severity in another 42%. Many researchers have criticized the results of Lovaas' studies, citing serious methodological problems (Gresham & MacMillan, 1997), and have advised school districts to resist its adoption or endorsement as a validated treatment for children with autism because it "is at best experimental, is far from providing a cure for autism, and awaits replication before school districts are required to provide it on a wholesale basis" (p. 196). Claiming a cure for autism, the standard 40-hour week and the "one-size-fits-all" model are possible reasons for skepticism.

In response to criticism and skepticism, Smith and Lovaas (1997) suggest that parents of children with autism are knowledgeable about the outcome research and have requested the program "to reduce their children's need for services over the course of the children's lives, not to obtain more than their fair share of help" (p. 214). Parents requesting the program have concluded their children will not benefit from other services offered to them, and have a great personal stake in the adequacy of their children's educational program.

Communication Approaches

The Picture Exchange Communication System (Bondy & Frost, 1994). This system was designed to improve the communication skills of children with autism. After determining the necessary and preferred objects, the child is taught to use the picture to obtain the object.

Auditory Approaches

Auditory Integration Training (AIT). AIT is an approach based on the conclusion that some characteristics of autism occur because of auditory dysfunction. AIT devices play processed music through headphones to reduce some of the auditory problems that may occur in individuals with autism, such as sound sensitivity and auditory processing. Currently, clinical research is not sufficient to support the effectiveness and safety of AIT devices (ASA, 2001).

Interactional Approaches

Social Stories (Gray, 1994). Social stories are used to teach social skills to students with autism. They involve three types of sentences: descriptive, directive, and perspective. Descriptive sentences define a situation, directive sentences tell the student which response is expected, and perspective sentences describe the reactions and feelings of others in a given situation. The stories are presented to the student to guide his or her behavior in various academic and social settings.

Legal Issues

Disputes involving the appropriateness of programs for students with autism represent the fasting growing and most expensive area of litigation in special education (Baird, 1999). Challenges to IEP's proposal for students with autism have included both procedural and substantive issues (Yell & Drasgow, 2000). In an analysis of legal hearings and cases related to IEPs for children with autism, Etscheidt (2003) identified three factors that influenced legal decisions regarding educational programs for students with autism: (a) whether the proposed IEP program goals were consistent with the evaluation data, (b) whether the IEP members were qualified to develop appropriate programs for students with autism, and (c) whether the methodology of the IEP was reasonably tailored to accomplish the goals of the IEP. School districts must propose programs for students with autism that are based on assessment data, developed by qualified professionals and the child's parents, and can be defended as appropriate in meeting the needs of the child.

Related Services

Students with autism may receive an array of related services, including occupational therapy, physical therapy, audiology, or speech and language services. Speech-language pathologists play an increasingly significant role in assessing the communication and social interaction skills of students with autism and in providing applied behavioral approaches to speech development (Prelock, 2001).

Inclusion Strategies

In planning for the successful inclusion of students with autism, Simpson (1995) identified several supports necessary to provide an appropriate program in the general education setting. These supports included:

- *Paraeducator Availability.* The paraeducator may be delegated the responsibility of implementing instructional and management programs, collecting data and charting progress, monitoring progress, assisting teachers with the creation and modifications of materials, and assisting students in a variety of tasks.
- *Reduced Class Size.* In inclusive settings, general educators must work carefully to plan curricular activities for students with autism. Both planning and implementing these activities will require reasonable class loads.
- *Adequate Teacher and Staff Planning Time.* Students with autism require unique instructional and management programs, necessitating that both the regular educator and the special educator have sufficient time to collaborate.
- *Access to Related Service Personnel.* General educators will require consultation with related service personnel for addressing the child's needs. Assistance from psychologists, speech and language therapists, occupational therapists, physical therapists, social workers, special educators, and other professionals may be necessary (Simpson, 1995).

A variety of approaches to improve the academic performance of students with autism in general education settings have been proposed. For example, "priming" (e.g., tasks to be presented in the general education class the following day are taught and rehearsed in order to prepare the student with autism to academically

respond) has been found to decrease problem behavior while increasing academic responding (Koegel, Koegel, Frea, & Green-Hopkins, 2003).

Peer-mediated support strategies have been successful in assisting students with autism in general education settings. These peer-mediated strategies include cooperative learning groups in reading (Kamps, Leonard, Potucek, & Garrison-Harrell, 1995), social initiation from peers (Odom & Strain, 1986; Sasso, 1987), and peer tutoring (Blew, Schwartz, & Luce, 1985). The value of peer-mediated strategies to establish social relationships and generalization of social skills over time is well-documented (Kamps et al., 2002).

Self-management strategies have similarly been successful in promoting inclusion of students with autism. Self-management techniques include following visual schedules (Newman, et al., 1995) and improving social skills (Koegel, Koegel, Hurley, & Frea, 1992) by monitoring the occurrence of specific social skills.

Students with autism have unique characteristics and educational needs. IEP teams must carefully and thoughtfully plan the necessary supports to facilitate successful inclusion.

ORTHOPEDIC IMPAIRMENTS (PHYSICAL DISABILITIES)

Federal Definition of Orthopedic Impairments

Orthopedic impairment is defined as a severe impairment that adversely affects a child's educational performance. The term includes impairments caused by congenital anomaly (e.g., clubfoot, absence of some member), impairments caused by disease (e.g., poliomyelitis, bone tuberculosis), and impairments from other causes (e.g., cerebral palsy, amputation, fracture, or burns that cause contractures) (34 C.F.R. § 300.8[c][8]). Children with orthopedic impairments represent 1.3% of the total number of students served under the IDEA (U.S. Department of Education, 2005).

Referral and Initial Assessment

Students with physical disabilities are referred for special education services when those disabilities adversely affect their educational performance. For many students, the physical disability was present at birth and services were initiated during infancy.

In addition to the parents, the multidisciplinary assessment team for students with physical disabilities includes a variety of educators and health professionals, such as general and special educators, speech clinicians, occupational and physical therapists, school psychologists, social workers, and medical professionals. This diversity is needed to obtain assessment information that will help the team to determine appropriate goals and objectives for the students and to select the methodology, services, adaptive technology, and adaptations necessary to meet those goals.

The multidisciplinary team should review the assessment data and plan the student's IEP. Each area affected by the disability should be addressed. The team develops goals and objectives for each area and specifies the services needed to meet those goals.

Characteristics of Physical Disabilities

Students with physical disabilities do not share common characteristics. Their cognitive, academic, physical, social-emotional, and communication characteristics are specific to their impairments (Ysseldyke & Algozzine, 1990). The following sections represent some common conditions affecting students with physical disabilities.

Cerebral Palsy   Cerebral palsy is the most prevalent physical disability of school-aged children. The National Information Center for Children and Youth with Disabilities (2002) describes cerebral palsy as a condition caused by injury, accident, or illness that results in movement and coordination difficulties. The most common type of cerebral palsy is hypertonia, or spastic cerebral palsy, which is characterized by tight, stiff muscles. Students may move awkwardly or scissor their legs as they walk. In contrast, hypotonia is a type of cerebral palsy

characterized by weak, unsupported muscles in the neck and trunk. Children with this type of cerebral palsy may have reduced movement or require extensive support. Athetosis involves slow, uncontrolled body movements, resulting in mobility difficulties. Ataxia is the inability to make purposeful motor responses, and children with ataxic cerebral palsy have poor balance and poor motor control. Students with cerebral palsy may experience stress or fatigue, which may affect interpersonal interactions and academic development.

Spina Bifida   The National Information Center for Children and Youth with Disabilities (2002) describes spina bifida as an incomplete closure of the spinal column resulting in three types of disorders: spina bifida occulta, in which only a few vertebrae are malformed without damage of the spinal cord; meningocele, in which the protective covering surrounding the spinal cord is displaced but remains intact; and myelomeningocele, the most severe form, in which the spinal cord protudes through the back. Myelomeningocele is often accompanied by hydrocephalus, a condition in which spinal fluid collects in tissues surrounding the brain. Children with spina bifida may have weakness or paralysis below the area of the spine where the incomplete closure occurs, and possibly loss of bowel and bladder control. Students may require catheterization.

Muscular Dystrophy   Muscular dystrophy is characterized by the deterioration of tissues and muscles. By 2 to 6 years of age, children with muscular dystrophy experience muscle difficulties and, typically between ages of 10 and 14, lose the ability to walk (Mastropieri & Scruggs, 2004). A trained physical therapist may be involved to prevent further deterioration of muscle tissue. Goals of movement and purposeful motor function are often included in the child's IEP.

Spinal Cord Injury   A fracture or compression of the vertebrae results in spinal cord injury. Automobile accidents and sports injuries are the most common causes of spinal cord injuries in school-aged children (Heward, 2000). Programs for students with spinal cord injuries often include physical therapy, rehabilitation, and mobility training.

The population of students with physical disabilities has steadily increased. During the 2000–2001 school year, 73,057 students with orthopedic impairments were served under the IDEA (U.S. Department of Education, 2002), and currently represent 1.3% of students with disabilities (U.S. Department of Education, 2005).

Instruction

Because the medical, educational, and related service needs of students with physical disabilities are interrelated, it is important for the multidisciplinary team to work collaboratively in planning an IEP (Heward, 2000). The administrator, as a member of that team, must be aware of the services provided to students with physical disabilities.

Teachers who educate students with physical and health disabilities require specialized knowledge to provide an appropriate education, including evaluation and instructional skills, behavior management skills, case management and coordination skills, and collaboration skills (Heller, Fredrick, Dykes, Best, & Cohen, 1999). These competencies enable teachers to be effective educators, school-based consultants, and co-teachers to ensure an appropriate education for students with physical disabilities. Administrators must ensure that teachers working with students with physical disabilities are qualified and capable of providing an appropriate education program.

Related Services

Students with physical disabilities often require a variety of related services to support their educational program. Depending on the nature and severity of the disability, students may require supplemental assistance to benefit from special education.

Occupational Therapy　Occupational therapy involves services provided by a qualified occupational therapist and includes

- improving, developing, or restoring functions impaired or lost through illness, injury, or deprivation;

- improving the ability to perform tasks for independent functioning if functions are impaired or lost; and
- preventing, through early intervention, initial or further impairment or loss of function (4 C.F.R. § 300.34[c][6]).

The occupational therapist helps improve the child's independence in daily activities by teaching essential motor skills. Therapy may be provided in both the school and home environments.

Physical Therapy　Physical therapy involves services by a qualified physical therapist (34 C.F.R. § 300.34[c][9]) and includes the development and maintenance of motor function and skills, movement, and posture. Physical therapists may develop exercises to improve muscle tone or function, and may also prescribe equipment or assistive devices. The provision of physical and occupational therapy has been shown to facilitate successful inclusion of students with physical disabilities (Szabo, 2000).

School Nurse Services　Students with physical disabilities often have special health care needs that require specialized procedures that are provided by a qualified school nurse or other qualified persons (34 C.F.R. § 300.34[c][13]). Nursing services may include clean intermittent catheterization (CIC) or gastrointestinal and tracheotomy care. State rules governing the delegation of nursing responsibility should be consulted in designing a program for students requiring health services.

Assistive Technology　The IDEA requires IEP teams to consider whether the child requires assistive technology devices and services (34 C.F.R. § 300.324[a] [2] [v]). Parette (1998) identified several assistive technology devices that may help students with physical disabilities, including augmentative communication devices, positioning devices, visual aids, and mobility aids. The IEP team should match the unique needs of the student to the device options, and assure that the device is achieving the desired outcomes for the individual.

The administrator should be familiar with the variety of related services provided to students with physical disabilities. Although the costs and funding sources for such services are important issues, related services must be provided if they are necessary for the child to benefit from special education.

Inclusion Strategies

The provision of related services and assistive technology has facilitated the inclusion of students with orthopedic impairments in general education classrooms. In 2000, about 24% of students receiving services for orthopedic impairments were included in regular education classes more than 60% of the day, whereas 20% were in regular education classes between 21% to 60% of the day, 46% were in regular education classes less than 20% of the day, and 6% were educated in separate environments (U.S. Department of Education, 2005). The challenges facing teachers and administrators involve accessibility, social-behavioral concerns, and the complexity of physical disabilities.

Maintaining Barrier-Free Classrooms and Schools
Schools and classrooms should be evaluated for accessibility to students with physical disabilities. Evaluation should include all physical features of the school and classroom (Lewis & Doorlag, 1999).

The Classroom Ecological Preparation Inventory (CEPI) (Wadsworth & Knight, 1999) was designed to assist in planning successful inclusion for students with physical disabilities and health needs. The CEPI focuses on health and medical concerns, arrangements in the physical environment, assistive equipment needs, and social skill management.

Facilitating Positive Peer Interactions
The attitudes of non-disabled peers affect the successful inclusion of students with physical disabilities. Non-disabled students who have been involved with the inclusion of students with severe disabilities are supportive (York, Vandercook, MacDonald, Heise-Neff, & Caughney, 1992). Students without disabilities benefit from inclusion experiences in learning patience, in helping others, and in developing friendships (Ringlaben & Dahmen-Jones, 1998).

Several strategies can promote positive interactions in inclusive classrooms. Peer networks can promote a positive social environment for students with disabilities through the creation of support systems committed to the development of social competency and friendship (Garrison-Harrell, Doelling, & Sasso, 1997). Additional strategies for promoting social acceptance include the Circle of Friends (Forest & Lusthaus, 1989), Special Friends (Cole, Vandercook, & Rynders, 1988), peer-assistance programs (Mastropieri & Scruggs, 2000), peer social initiation (Kerr & Nelson, 2002), and cooperative learning (Jenkins, Antil, Wayne, & Vadasy, 2003). Teachers need a variety of options to facilitate peer relationships for students with physical disabilities (Mukherjee, Lightfoot, & Sloper, 2000).

Familiarizing with Adaptive and Medical Devices
The inclusion of students with physical disabilities may be facilitated by school personnel learning about the adaptive equipment that these students may be using. Familiarity with augmentative communication systems or mobility devices will enable school personnel to effectively and smoothly integrate students with physical disabilities into the school environment. A survey of teachers indicated that they did not feel adequately prepared to include students with physical disabilities in their classrooms and needed more training in assistive and adaptive equipment (Singh, 2001). Administrators and teachers must also learn about a child's medical needs. Some children may require medical procedures that they may independently administer, whereas others may require the services of a registered nurse (RN) or licensed practical nurse (LPN). Students without disabilities should also be introduced to the child's medical needs and procedures.

TRAUMATIC BRAIN INJURY (TBI)
Federal Definition of TBI

TBI is an acquired injury to the brain caused by an external physical force, resulting in total or partial functional disability, psychosocial impairment, or both, which adversely affects a child's educational performance. The term applies to open or closed head injury resulting in impairments in one or more areas, such as cognition; language; memory; attention; reasoning; abstract thinking; judgment; problem-solving; sensory, perceptual, and motor abilities; psychosocial behavior; physical functions; information processing; and speech. The term does not apply to congenital or degenerative brain injuries, or to brain injuries induced by birth trauma (34 C.F.R. § 300.8[c][12]). Public Law 94–142 did not include TBI as a disability category, but when amended in 1990, the IDEA specified TBI as a new area of eligibility.

Characteristics of TBI   Common symptoms of TBI include seizures, movement or coordination difficulties, attention deficits, and speech disorders. Hill (1999) identified several signs and effects of TBI, including physical and sensory changes; cognitive changes and academic problems; and social, emotional and behavioral problems. Other characteristics include reduced stamina, irregular growth, memory problems, helplessness, apathy (Mira, Tucker, & Tyler, 1992), flat affect, and depression (Tucker & Colson, 1992). The number of students with TBI served during the 2000–2001 school year was 14,844, a 5,958% increase since 1991, making the percentage increase of students in the TBI category the greatest of any disability area in the last 10 years (U.S. Department of Education, 2002). Children with TBI represent 4% of all children served under the IDEA (U.S. Department of Education, 2005).

Instruction

The first step in developing an educational program for students with TBI is carefully planning for the student's reentry to school (Tyler & Mira, 1999). The IEP team must specify the necessary adaptive equipment, while the school staff must receive training about TBI and be prepared for the child's reentry into school. Regional or state specialists in TBI should be involved in IEP planning, and peers should assist in the transition process (Tyler & Mira, 1999).

The IEP team needs to develop educational strategies to meet the specialized needs of the student with TBI. Direct instruction (Glang, Singer, Cooley, & Tish, 1992) and strategy instruction have proved to be effective instructional techniques for students with TBI. Students with TBI may have behavioral problems and require a behavior management plan that includes social skills training and positive peer interaction (Tyler & Mira, 1999)

D'Amato and Rothlisberg (1997) suggest that teachers modify their teaching methods in terms of an "SOS" for students with TBI: structure, organization, and strategies. TBI is associated with disorientation and low tolerance for environmental change. The child requires a structured environment and daily routine. Strategies such as advanced organizers and assignment completion guides can be helpful.

Related Services

Students with TBI may require rehabilitation counseling as a related service. This service is provided by qualified personnel in individual or group sessions that focus specifically on career development, employment preparation, achieving independence, and integration in the workplace and community of a student with a disability (34 C.F.R. § 300.34[c][12]).

Inclusion Strategies

The student with TBI will require modifications in the physical, instructional, and social behavioral dimensions of the school and classroom. In the physical dimension, the student with TBI may benefit from minimized visual and auditory distractions, special seating, and specialized equipment (Smith, Polloway, Patton, & Dowdy, 1995). In the instructional dimension, the student with TBI may require a shortened school day or reduced class load, the assistance of resource personnel (e.g., peers, counselors, therapists), and modified or adjusted curricula (Tyler & Mira, 1993). In the social-behavioral dimension, the teacher should limit the amount of information presented at one time, frequently restate and reinforce rules, and maintain the student's attention (Mira, Tucker, & Tyler, 1992).

For the student with TBI, successful inclusion will require both student-centered and environment-centered strategies. These may include direct training of social skills, training parents to encourage skill generalization, in-service and peer training about TBI, "peer liaisons," and pairing community volunteers with TBI students (Glang, Cooley, Todis, Stevens, & Voss, 1995). The integration of the medical, rehabilitation, and educational perspectives is necessary for the student with TBI to be successfully included in general education classrooms.

Schools must be prepared to deal with the increasing number of students with TBI. Silver and Oakland (1997) outlined a six-step process to enable school districts to become better prepared to meet the needs of students with TBI. These include (a) determining what educators and related services personnel know about TBI, (b) coordinating a consortium of professionals with TBI expertise, (c) developing a policy for referral, (d) developing district-wide in-service, (e) creating a TBI advisory board to provide consultation, and (f) retaining a part-time TBI consultant for ongoing collaboration. The district should also use existing related service personnel, such as the school psychologist, speech and language pathologist, occupational therapist, school counselor, and school nurse. The six-step model should enable the school to more effectively meet the needs of students with TBI.

VISUAL IMPAIRMENTS INCLUDING BLINDNESS

Federal Definition of Visual Impairment

Visual impairment including blindness is defined as an impairment in vision that, even with correction, adversely affects a child's educational performance. The term includes both partial sight and blindness (34 C.F.R. § 300.8[c] [13]).

Characteristics of Visual Impairment

The lack of vision or reduced vision may vary greatly in students and may be influenced by the environment, concomitant disabilities, and type of impairment (Kennedy & Horn, 2004). An understanding of how the student uses vision functionally is more important that the cause of the student's visual impairment in determining educational needs (Vaughn, Bos, & Schumm, 2006).

Instruction

The curriculum for students with visual impairment or blindness includes reading and writing through the use of Braille, functional skills, interpersonal skills, orientation and mobility training, and instruction in the use of special aids and equipment (ERIC, 1992). The IDEA requires the IEP team to "provide for instruction in Braille and the use of Braille unless the IEP team determines, after an evaluation of the child's reading and writing skills, needs, and appropriate reading and writing media (including an evaluation of the child's future needs for instruction in Braille or the use of Braille), that instruction in Braille or the use of Braille is not appropriate for the child" (34 C.F.R. § 300.324[a][2][iii]).

The IEP goals may focus on increasing familiarity with Braille text and word-processing skills. Goals may also address personal and daily living skills domains. Orientation and mobility objectives may focus on independent travel around the school building. Transition planning will be an important component of career education, and includes planning courses of study and post-school assistance.

School personnel will need collaboration with experts in the field of visual impairments to successfully plan IEPs for students. Specifically trained personnel facilitate the development of goals, objectives, and methodology for students with visual impairments.

Related Services

Students with visual impairments may benefit from several related services, including orientation and mobility services and assistive technology. The need for these services is determined by the student's IEP team.

Orientation- and Mobility-Related Services
Students with visual impairments often will

require orientation- and mobility-related services. These services are provided to blind or visually impaired students by qualified personnel to enable these students to attain systematic orientation to and safe movement within their school, home, and community environments. These services include teaching the students

- Spatial and environmental concepts and use of information received by the senses (e.g., sound, temperature, vibrations) to establish, maintain, or regain orientation and line of travel (e.g., using sound at a traffic light to cross the street)
- To use a cane to supplement visual travel skills or as a tool for safely negotiating the environment for students with no available travel vision
- To understand and use remaining vision and distance low-vision aids
- Other concepts, techniques, and tools (34 C.F.R. § 300.34 [c][7])

Assistive Technology Assistive technology is also important in education programs for students with visual impairments. Heward (2000) reported that various curricular materials have been developed for students with visual impairments, including MAVIS (Materials Adaptation for Students with Visual Impairments in the Social Studies) and SAVI (Science Activities for the Visually Impaired). Large-print materials, Braille materials, and tape-recorded materials are also available.

Inclusion Strategies

Historically, students with visual impairments were educated in segregated residential facilities. Even today, proponents for such placements argue that student outcomes show these facilities provide more services than inclusive placement, and are critically essential and justifiable for many students (Bing, 1999). Liberman and Houston-Wilson (1999) reported that part of the slow movement to more inclusive placements for students with visual impairments was due to teacher barriers (e.g., lack of professional preparation), student barriers (e.g.,

parental overprotection), and administrative barriers (e.g., lack of appropriate equipment). Currently, with the aid of supports and strategies, these students are educated in general classroom settings. Strategies that provide support and assistance are classroom adaptations, an instructional assistant, collaboration with support personnel, and family-school-community partnerships (Liberman & Houston-Wilson).

Classroom Adaptations Mastropieri and Scruggs (2004) offer several suggestions for classroom adaptations for students with visual impairments. The modifications include physical cues, alternative landmarks, narration of class activities, and the use of concrete objects and manipulatives during teaching. Clear traffic patterns and seating arrangements must be established.

A variety of curriculum strategies have been developed for students with visual impairments, including the use of activity boxes (Dunnett, 1999) to enhance cognitive and motor development in young children with visual impairments and the use of descriptive video (Cronin & King, 1990). Although excellent materials are available for students with visual impairments, teachers may need to adapt or develop supplemental materials.

Family-School-Community Partnerships Muhlenhaupt (2002) discusses the importance of a family-school-community partnership in planning inclusion for students with visual impairments. Such planning will facilitate successful inclusion in school and in post-school opportunities.

Advances in technology and a variety of related services have facilitated the inclusion of students with visual impairments in general education classrooms. The U.S. Department of Education (2002) reported that 25,975 students with visual impairments were served under the IDEA during the 2000–2001 school year, a 7.9% increase since 1991. Children with visual impairments represent .4% of all students with disabilities served under the IDEA (U.S. Department of Education, 2005).

DEAFNESS AND HEARING IMPAIRMENT

Federal Definition of Deafness and Hearing Impairment

Federal regulations distinguish between children who are deaf and children who have hearing impairment in their definitions. Deafness means a hearing impairment that is so severe that the child is impaired in processing linguistic information through hearing, with or without amplification, which adversely affects the child's educational performance (34 C.F.R. § 300.8[c][3]). Hearing impairment means an impairment in hearing, whether permanent or fluctuating, that adversely affects a child's educational performance but is not included under the definition of deafness (34 C.F.R. § 300.8[c][5]). A child who is deaf cannot respond to speech or auditory stimuli and cannot use hearing to understand speech, even with the assistance of hearing aid or device. This child who is deaf must rely on visual acuity. The child with hearing impairment can respond to speech and auditory stimuli and can use hearing to understand speech, often with the assistance of amplification devices. The U.S. Department of Education (2002) reported that 70,767 students with hearing impairments were served under the IDEA during the 2000–2001 school year, representing a 16.5% increase since 1991. Children with hearing impairments represent 1.2% of all students served under the IDEA (U.S. Department of Education, 2005).

Characteristics of Hearing Impairment The degree to which a hearing loss adversely affects educational performance depends on several factors including the type and degree of hearing loss, the age of onset, social and family contexts, opportunities for early language development, and the effects of other disabilities (Heward, 2000). IEP teams must be aware of these factors when planning instructional programs.

Instruction

The most appropriate approach to instruction for children who are deaf or hearing impaired has been hotly debated for years. Drasgow (1998) suggests that this disagreement over the best approach is not simply a discussion over which language or code is best to use, but rather represents "profound, and often polarized, differences in educational philosophy" (p. 329). Methods are grounded either in a clinical-pathological model or a cultural model. The former views deafness as a disability stemming from a biological deficit and focuses educational goals on overcoming or compensating for hearing loss so that students can learn to speak, read, and write English.

One approach of the clinical model is the oral-aural method, which views speech as essential and incorporates producing and understanding speech and language into all aspects of the child's education. Education methods associated with the clinical oral approach to develop speech and maximize hearing include amplification, auditory training, speech reading, and cued speech-visual representation (Stewart, 1992).

Another approach of the clinical model is the total communication method, which emphasizes the use of both manual communication (e.g., signs and finger spelling) and speech (e.g., speech reading, amplification). Sign systems such as Seeing Essential English, Signing Exact English, and Signed English are called Manually Coded English and are based on English usage. Finger spelling uses different hand positions to represent the letters of the alphabet. The total communication approach, also called simultaneous communication, enables teachers to use the communication methods most appropriate for a particular child at a particular stage of development. Hawkins and Brawner (1997) found that although individualization was at the heart of total communication and it can open several avenues of communication for children who are deaf or hearing impaired, many students are immersed in a form of total communication that does not match their level of linguistic readiness or ability. Further, the authors proposed that combining the visual and spoken mode may cause signers and speakers to alter their messages to accommodate one or the other mode, causing a compromise between the two methods. Moreover, teachers are limited to the number of modes they can simultaneously use.

The cultural model views deafness as a difference, not a disability. This model acknowledges people who are deaf have a unique identity with their own language, history, and social organization. This bilingual-bicultural education approach recognizes American Sign Language (ASL) as the child's natural language and the language of instruction. Thus, the child becomes proficient in two languages: ASL and English (Mahshie, 1995).

The IDEA requires the IEP team to "consider the communication needs of the child, and in the case of a child who is deaf or hard of hearing, consider the child's language and communication needs, opportunities for direct communications with peers and professional personnel in the child's language and communication mode, academic level, and full range of needs, including opportunities for direct instruction in the child's language and communication mode" (34 C.F.R. § 300.324 [a][2][iv]). The IEP team should discuss the options for instruction (McAnally, Rose, & Quigley, 1994) and select an approach based on the child's unique strengths and needs.

Related Services

Students who are deaf or hearing impaired often require audiology as a related service. Figure 13-1 provides a description of audiology services.

Additional related services may include the use of interpreters and television captioning. Jones, Clark, and Soltz (1997) examined the characteristics and practices of sign language interpreters in inclusive education programs. The duties performed by the interpreters included expected activities, such as interpreting in the mainstream academic classroom and vocational classes, as well as noninterpreting activities, such as tutoring, teaching sign language to hearing students, correcting assignments, and other teacher assistance tasks. The researchers suggested that state departments of education should coordinate the development and implementation of guidelines related to the roles and responsibilities of educational sign language interpreters, because using them as teacher's aides was questionable practice. They found that 63% of the interpreters had no certification for sign language interpreting of any kind and suggested an upgrading of training and skills for interpreters if ready access to general education is to be achieved. Hwa-Froelich and Westby (2003) argue that all people working as interpreters need to receive training in the rules and roles of interpreters and must achieve a satisfactory level of competence prior to employment.

Inclusion Strategies

The inclusion of students who are deaf or hearing impaired has been controversial. Nowell and Innes (1997) described the benefits and

FIGURE 13-1 *Audiology services*

- Identification of children with hearing loss
- Determination of the range, nature, and degree of hearing loss, including referral for medical or other professional attention for the habilitation of hearing
- Provision of habilitative activities, such as language habilitation, auditory training, speech reading (lip-reading), hearing evaluation, and speech conservation
- Creation and administration of programs for prevention of hearing loss
- Counseling and guidance of children, parents, and teachers regarding hearing loss
- Determination of children's needs for group and individual amplification, selecting and fitting an appropriate hearing aid, and evaluating the effectiveness of amplification (34 C.F.R. § 300.34 [c][1]).

limitations of inclusion for students who are deaf or hard of hearing. Benefits included the opportunity to live at home, to communicate with the hearing community, and to access academic or vocational programs. Limitations included potential social isolation. In inclusive settings, students who are deaf or hearing impaired may require an interpreter. Some school districts have difficulty obtaining the services of qualified interpreters.

Despite the potential limitations, the U.S. Department of Education (1998) reported that 36% of students who are deaf or hearing impaired receive services in regular education classrooms, 19% are served in resource rooms, and 27% are educated in separate classrooms.

Rose (2002) suggested that there will never be one model of inclusion that will be the solution for all children with hearing impairments. For example, a co-teaching placement model called TRIPOD (Kirchner, 1994) places deaf and hard-of-hearing students in a classroom with a teacher of the deaf and a general education teacher. All teachers and students receive instruction in sign language and issues related to hearing loss. Teaching strategies are shared and co-taught. Although the TRIPOD model offers "the most significant promise for full inclusion," the application of the model is limited to settings where resources and populations are available. Powers (2001) also offered that good inclusion practices for students with hearing impairments involve joint planning by support and mainstream teachers, student involvement in decision making, and in-service training for mainstream teachers. Ten themes contributing to the successful inclusion of students who are deaf include: (a) family involvement, (b) self-determination, (c) involvement in extracurricular activities, (d) establishing friendships, (e) self-advocacy, (f) collaboration and communication with general education teachers, (g) preteaching content learned in general education classrooms, (h) collaboration with early intervention service providers, (i) reading experiences, and (j) high expectations for the students (Luckner & Muir, 2002).

Vaughn, Bos, and Schumm (2006) recommended several accommodations for students who are deaf or hearing impaired. These adaptations include preferential seating, minimization of environmental noise, use of visual media and demonstrations, peer assistance, and monitoring student understanding.

Additional strategies that have been successful in facilitating the inclusion of students who are deaf or hearing impaired in general education classrooms include the following:

- Interactive writing between teacher and student on instant computer access (Holcomb & Peyton, 1992)
- Computer-assisted notetaking (Youdelman & Messerly, 1996)
- Pretutoring (English, 1999)
- Lecture guides (Rees, 1992)
- Writing rubrics (Schirmer, Bailey & Fitzgerald, 1999)

Students who are deaf or hearing impaired should be encouraged to develop self-advocacy and self-determination skills to facilitate the success of their education programs. Marttila and Mills (1995) have developed curricula for enhancing self-advocacy skills.

MULTIPLE DISABILITIES AND DEAFNESS-BLINDNESS

Federal Definition of Multiple Disabilities

Many students have dual or multiple disabilities. Federal regulations define multiple disabilities as concomitant impairments (e.g., mental retardation-blindness, mental retardation-orthopedic impairment), the combination of which causes such severe educational needs that students cannot be accommodated in special education programs designed solely for children with only one of the impairments (34 C.F.R. § 300.8[c][7]). Types of multiple disabilities include mental retardation with physical disabilities (e.g., cerebral palsy, spina bifida, traumatic brain injury), or mental retardation with visual or hearing impairments.

The regulations define deafness-blindness as concomitant hearing and visual impairments, the combination of which causes such severe communication and other developmental and educational needs that students cannot be accommodated in special education programs designed solely for children with deafness or blindness (34 C.F.R. § 300.8[c][2]). Although federal regulations use the deafness-blindness reference, most professionals view these students as having dual sensory impairments or multiple sensory impairments.

The U.S. Department of Education (2005) reported that students with multiple disabilities represented 2.2% of the students served by the IDEA. Approximately 2,640 of those students are served in separate learning environments.

Instruction

The curriculum for students with dual sensory impairments should include components that have been discussed earlier in the text to assist students with visual impairments, hearing impairments, or severe mental disabilities. Skills that are taught should be ecologically based (i.e., needed to function in all the different environments of their daily lives). Marchant (1996) identified the steps to be included in an ecological curriculum development process. These steps include the identification of curricular domains, the determination of the child's natural environments and subenvironments, the selection of IEP goals and skills to be acquired by the student, the identification of environmental or individual adaptations, and the development of an instructional program based on assessment data. The instructional program typically includes orientation and mobility training, a functional vision and hearing program, communication methods, and daily living skills.

Inclusion Strategies

Sall and Mar (1999) identified critical factors associated with the success of inclusion programs for students with deaf-blindness: (a) administrative involvement, (b) teachers' and peers' problem-solving skills, (c) adaptation of materials and activities, and (d) positive attitudes towards inclusion.

Environmental accommodations for students with dual sensory impairments include the use of kinesthetic and tactile materials for instructional presentation and schedules, and use of objects for marking pathways and for communication (Rikhye, Gotheif, & Appell, 1989). Communication partners can also assist students with deafness-blindness (Heller, Ware, Allgood, & Castelle, 1994), and tactile teaching techniques can supplement information obtained through auditory and visual modalities.

CONCLUSION

Students with low-incidence disabilities present unique challenges to the school administrator and school personnel. The successful inclusion of students with autism, orthopedic disabilities, traumatic brain injury, visual impairments, deafness, and blindness requires careful planning by the IEP team. The necessary supports for students with low-incidence disabilities may include teacher training, paraeducator assistance, access to related services and assistive technology, and facilitating peer interactions.

As inclusive programs become more common, administrators and educators will notice an increase in the number of students with low-incidence disabilities in their schools and classrooms. This increase in students with diverse needs will necessitate careful planning of instruction and strategies to facilitate inclusion.

VIEW FROM THE COURTS

Tarah P. v. Fremont School District (1995); (inclusion of student with multiple disabilities). This case involved a 7-year-old child with physical and visual impairments. The district proposed a fully integrated kindergarten program located at a non-district school approximately four miles from her home. The girl's IEP included a one-to-one assistant; occupational, physical, and speech therapy; and access to an augmentative communication device. The parents preferred placement in a neighborhood school for the greatest interaction with non-disabled peers. The district court determined that the least restrictive environment (LRE) mandate did not require the girl's placement in the neighborhood school, because both placements provided mainstreaming to the maximum extent appropriate and possible. However, the district's proposed program was taught by a special education teacher trained in augmentative communication, who could consistently and efficiently modify the classroom curriculum requirements for the girl. The district court framed the issue as a dispute of methodology, and confirmed the school district's responsibility for determining appropriate methodologies for a child. The district-proposed placement would enhance curriculum modifications necessary to provide the child with an appropriate education program.

RECOMMENDED READINGS

Barnes, S. B., & Whinnery, K. W. (2002). The effects of functional mobility skills training for young students with physical disabilities. Exceptional Children, 68(3), 313–324. This article describes the Mobility Opportunities Via Education (MOVE) curriculum for improving mobility for students with physical disabilities.

Blischak, D. M., & Schlosser, R. W. (2003). Use of technology to support independent spelling by students with autism. *Topics in Language Disorders, 23*(4), 293–304. This article provides guidelines for selecting and evaluating assistive technology for students with autism.

Hagood, L. (1997). *Communication: A guide for teaching students with visual and multiple impairments.* Austin, TX: Texas School for the Blind and Visually Impaired. These materials were developed to assist teacher in meeting the needs of students with multiple disabilities, including visual impairments.

Hwa-Froelich, D. A., & Westby, C. E. (2003). Considerations when working with interpreters. *Communication Disorders Quarterly, 24*(2), 78–85. This article provides important information for teachers, staff, and other team members working with interpreters.

Kimball, J. W., Kinney, E. M., Taylor, B. A., & Stromer, R. (2003). Lights, camera, action! Using engaging computer-cued activity schedules. *Teaching Excep-tional Children, 36*(1), 40–45. Although visual schedules have been developed for students with autism, this article describes how cued visual schedules may improve behavior for students with disabilities.

Koegel, R. L., & Koegel, L. K. (1995). Teaching children with autism: Strategies for initiating positive interactions and improving learning opportunities. Baltimore, MD: Paul H. Brookes. This book focuses on social interactions for children with autism.

Livingston, S. (1997). *Rethinking the education of deaf students: Theory and practice from a teacher's perspective.* Portsmouth, NH: Heinemann. This book provides resources for developing literacy skills in deaf students, including methods to read to children with hearing impairments.

McAnally, P. L., Rose, S., & Quigley, S. P. (1999). *Reading practices with deaf learners.* Austin, TX: PRO-ED. This book provides strategies for developing literacy skills in students with hearing impairments.

Miles, B., & McLetchie, B. (2004). *Developing concepts with children who are deaf/blind.* This article promotes activities and routines to support concept development in children who are deaf/blind. National Information Clearinghouse on Children who are Deaf/Blind at http://www. dblink.org/

Perla, F., & O'Donnell, B. (2002). Reaching out: Encouraging family involvement in orientation and mobility. *RE:view, 34*(3), 103–110. This article emphasizes the school-home connection.

Pogrund, R. L., Fazzi, D. L., & Lampert, J. S. (Eds.) (1992). *Early focus: Working with young blind and visually impaired children and their families.* New York: American Foundation for the Blind. This article highlights school practices and information concerning parental education and involvement.

Rose, S. (2002). Inclusion of students with hearing loss in general education: *Fact or fiction? Teacher Educator, 37*(3), 216–229. An excellent review of the controversy surrounding inclusive placements for students with hearing impairments.

Rosenblum, L. P. (2000). Perceptions of the impact of visual impairment on the lives of adolescents. *Journal of Visual Impairment and Blindness, 94*(7), 34–45. This first-person perspective of visual impairments is helpful in understanding educational approaches.

Savage, R. C., & Wolcott, G. F. (1995). *An educator's manual: What educators need to know about students with brain injury.* Alexandria, VA: Brain Injury Association. This information may be accessed at the BIA website http://www.biausa.org/

Specht, K. Q. (1996). *Physical management of students who have sustained a traumatic brain injury: Guidelines and strategies for school personnel.* Alexandria, VA: Brain Injury Association. Another helpful article from the BIA website.

Steward, D., & Kluwin, T. (2001). *Teaching deaf and hard of* hearing students: *Content, strategies, and curriculum.* Boston: Allyn & Bacon. This methodology text highlights the curriculum options for students with hearing impairments.

Tyler, J. S., & Mira, M. P. (1999). *Traumatic brain injury in children and adolescents: A sourcebook for teachers and other school personnel* (2nd ed.). Austin TX: PRO-ED. This sourcebook contains information on the characteristics of TBI as well as helpful educational suggestions.

Vaughn, S., Bos, C. S., & Schumm, J. S. (2006). *Teaching mainstreamed, diverse, and at-risk students in the general education classroom: IDEA 2004 Update Edition (3rd ed.).* Boston: Allyn & Bacon. This textbook addresses a variety of students with diversity, including those with low-incidence disabilities.

Volkmar, F. R., Paul, R., Klin, A., & Cohen, D. (2005). *Handbook of autism and pervasive developmental disabilities.* New York: Wiley & Sons. This two-volume book set provides very comprehensive information concerning autism and PDD.

Wolcott, G., Lash, M., & Pearson, S. (1995). *Sign and strategies for educating students with brain injuries: A practical guide for teachers and schools.* Alexandria, VA: Brain Injury Association. This BIA website source provides basic, yet important, suggestions for teachers and administrators working with students with TBI.

Relevant Federal Regulations

34 C.F.R. Part 104 (2005). Nondiscrimination on the basis of disability in programs and activities receiving federal financial assistance–Section 504 regulations.

34 C.F.R. Part 300 Assistance to states for the education of children with disabilities (70 Fed. Reg., 3,5833–3,5880 [June 21, 2005]).

300.8(c)(2)	Definition of deaf-blindness.
300.8(c)(3)	Definition of deafness.
300.8(c)(5)	Definition of hearing impairment.
300.8(c)(7)	Definition of multiple disabilities.
300.8(c)(8)	Definition of orthopedic impairment.
300.8(c)(12)	Definition of traumatic brain injury.
300.8(c)(13)	Definition of visual impairment.
300.111(a)	Child find.
300.308	Child with a disability (definitions)
300.306	Determination of eligibility.
300.324(a)	Consideration of special factors for IEP.
300.324(a)(2)(iii)	Requirement that the IEP team must consider child's need for Braille services.
300.324(a)(2)(iv)	Requirement that the IEP team must consider the communication needs of the child.
300.324(a)(2)(v)	Requirement that IEP must consider child's need for Assistive Technology devices and services.
300.34(c)(1)	Audiology services as related services.
300.34(c)(6)	Occupational therapy as a related service.
300.34(c)(7)	Orientation and mobility services as related services.
300.34(c)(9)	physical therapy as a related service.
300.34(c)(12)	Rehabilitation counseling as a related service.
300.34(c)(13)	School nurse services as a related service.

SELECTED WEBSITES

Division TEACCH
http://www.teacch.com

Autism/PDD Resources Network (1997)
http://www.autism-pdd.net

Center for Study of Autism (2001)
http://www.autism.com/

Autism Society of America (2001)
http://www.autism-society.org/

Division for Physical and Health Disabilities (DPHD)
http://www.cec.sped.org/

United Cerebral Palsy Association
  http://www.ucpa.org/

Spina Bifida Association of America
  http://www.sbaa.org

World Association of Persons with Physical Disabilities (WAPD)
  http://www.wapd.org/

The American Foundation for the Blind
  http://www.afb.org/

Brain Injury Association of America
  http://www.biausa.org/

DB-Link: National Information Clearinghouse on Children Who Are Deaf-Blind
  http://www.tr.wou.edu/dblink/

Helen Keller National Center for Deaf-Blind Youths and Adults
  http://www.helenkeller.org/national/

National Association of the Deaf
  http://www.nad.org/

National Federation of the Blind
  http://www.nfb.org/

National Information Center on Deafness
  http://www.gallaudet.edu/

Traumatic Brain Injury Resource Guide
  http://www.neuroskills.com/

Traumatic Brain Injury
  http://www.tbiguide.com/

Traumatic Brain Injury Resources
  http://curry.edschool.virginia.edu/sped/projects/ose/categories/tbi.html/

QUESTIONS FOR THOUGHT

1. Successful inclusion of students with low-incidence disabilities such as physical, visual, and hearing impairments requires collaboration and consultation with professionals with expertise in those areas. Discuss how school districts may access or locate such individuals or services.

2. In what ways does the preparation of peers for the inclusion of students with low incident disabilities impact successful inclusion?

3. Define the controversy surrounding the inclusion of students with hearing impairments. Include a discussion of the clinical and cultural perspectives.

4. Define your early education experiences concerning peers with low-incidence disabilities. Were the inclusion strategies presented in this chapter incorporated?

REFERENCES

Autism-PDD Resources Network (1997). *The Realities of TEACCH.* Available at: http://www.autism-pdd.net/teach.html/

Autism Society of America (2001). *How is Autism Diagnosed?* Available at: http://www.autism-society.org/

Baird, M. M. (1999). Legal issues in autism. *Proceedings of the 20th National Institute on Legal Issues of Educating individuals with disabilities.* Alexandria, VA: LRP Publications.

Blew, P. A., Schwartz, I. S., & Luce, S. C. (1985). Teaching functional community skills to autistic children using nonhandicapped peer tutors. *Journal of Applied Behavior Analysis, 18,* 337–342.

Bondy, A., & Frost, L. (1994). The Picture Exchange Communication System. *Focus on Autistic Behavior, 9,* 1–19.

Cole, D. A., Vandercook, T., & Rynders, J. (1988). Comparison of two peer interaction programs: Children with and without severe disabilities. *American Educational Research Journal, 25,* 415–439.

Cronin, B. J., & King, S. R. (1990). The development of the Descriptive Video Service. *Journal of Visual Impairment and Blindness, 86*(12), 503–506.

D'Amato, R. C., & Rothlisberg, B. (1997). How education should respond to students with TBI. In E. D. Bigler, E. Clark, & J. E. Farmer (Eds.), *Childhood traumatic brain injury: Diagnosis, assessment and intervention.* Austin, TX: PRO-ED.

Drasgow, E. (1998). American Sign Language as a pathway to linguistic competence. *Exceptional Children, 64*(3), 329–342.

Dunnett, J. (1999). Use of activity boxes with young children who are blind, deaf-blind, or have severe learning disabilities and visual impairments. *Journal of Visual Impairment and Blindness, 93*(4), 225–232.

Eaves, R. C. (1997). Autistic disorder. In P. J. McLaughlin and P. Wehman (Eds.), *Mental Retardation and Developmental Disabilities* (2nd ed.). Austin, TX: PRO-ED.

English, K. (1999). Inclusion tips for the teacher: Students who are hard of hearing. In R. B. Lewis &

D. H. Doorlag (Eds.), *Teaching special students in general education classrooms* (5th ed.). Upper Saddle River, NJ: Merrill/Prentice Hall.

ERIC (1992). *Visual impairments*. ERIC Digest #E511. Reston, VA: ERIC Clearinghouse on Disabilities and Gifted Education.

Etscheidt, S. (2003). An analysis of legal hearings and cases related to individualized education programs for children with autism. *Research & Practice for Persons with Severe Disabilities, 28*(2), 51–69.

Forest M., & Lusthaus, E. (1989). Circles and maps. In S. Stainback, W. Stainback, & M. Forest (Eds.), *Educating all students in the mainstream of regular education*. Baltimore: Brookes.

Garrison-Harrell, L., Doelling, J. E., & Sasso, G. M. (1997). Recent developments in social interaction interventions to enhance inclusion. In P. Zionts (Ed.), *Inclusion strategies for students with learning and behavior problems*. Austin, TX: PRO-ED.

Glang, A., Cooley, E., Todis, B., Stevens, T., & Voss, J. (1995). *Enhancing social support and integration for students with traumatic brain injury*. Final report. Eugene, OR: Teaching Research.

Glang, A., Singer, G., Cooley, E., & Tish, N. (1992). Tailing direct instruction techniques for use with elementary students with brain injury. *Journal of Head Trauma Remediation, 7*(4), 93–108.

Gray, C. (1994). *The social story kit*. Jenison, MI: Jenison Public Schools.

Gresham, F. M., & MacMillan, D. L. (1997). Autistic recovery? An analysis and critique of the empirical evidence on the early intervention project. *Behavioral Disorders, 22*(4), 185–201.

Hawkins, L., & Brawner, J. (1997). Educating children who are deaf or hard of hearing: Total communication. *ERIC Digest* #559. Reston, VA: ERIC Clearinghouse on Disabilities and Gifted Education.

Heller, K. W., Fredrick, L. D., Dykes, M. K., Best, S., & Cohen, E. T. (1999). A national perspective of competencies for teachers of individuals with physical and health disabilities. Exceptional *Children, 65*(2), 219–234.

Heller, K. W., Ware, S., Allgood, M. H., & Castelle, M. (1994). Use of dual communication boards with students who are deaf-blind. *Journal of Visual Impairment and Blindness*, (July/August), 368–376.

Heward, W. L. (2000). *Exceptional children: An introduction to special education*. Upper Saddle River, NJ: Merrill/Prentice Hall.

Hill, J. L. (1999). *Meeting the needs of students with special physical and health care needs*. Upper Saddle River, NJ: Merrill/Prentice Hall.

Holcomb, T., & Peyton, J. K. (1992). Literacy for a linguistic minority: The deaf experience. *ERIC Digest* #353861. Reston, VA: ERIC Clearinghouse on Disabilities and Gifted Education.

Hwa-Froelich, D. A., & Westby, C. E. (2003). Frameworks of education: Perspectives of southeast Asian parents and Head Start staff. *Language, Speech, and Hearing Services in School, 34*(4), 299–319.

Jenkins, J. R., Antil, L. R., Wayne, S. K., & Vadasy, P. F. (2003). How cooperative learning works for special education and remedial students. *Exceptional Children, 69*(3), 279–292.

Jones, B. E., Clark, G. M., & Soltz, D. F. (1997). Characteristics and practices of sign language interpreters in inclusive education program. *Exceptional Children, 63*(2), 257–268.

Kamps, D., Royer, J., Dugan, E., Kravits, T., Gonzalez-Lopez, A., Garcia, J., Carnazzo, K., Morrison, L., & Kane, L. G. (2002). Peer training to facilitate social interaction for elementary students with autism and their peers. *Exceptional Children, 68, 173–187.*

Kamps, D. M., Leonard, B., Potucek, J., & Garrison-Harrell, L. (1995). Cooperative learning groups in reading: An integration strategy for students with autism and general classroom peers. *Behavioral Disorders, 21*(1), 89–109.

Kamps, D., Royer, J., Dugan, E., Kravits, T., Gonzalez-Lopez, A., Garcia, J., et al. (2002). Peer training to facilitate social interaction for elementary students with autism and their peers. *Exceptional Children, 68,* 173–187.

Kennedy, C. H., & Horn, E. M. (2004). *Including students with severe disabilities*. Boston: Pearson Education Inc.

Kerr, M. M., & Nelson, C. M. (2002). Strategies for addressing behavior problems in the classroom (4th ed.). Upper Saddle River, NJ: Merrill/Prentice Hall.

Kirchner, C. (1994). Co-enrollment as an inclusion model. *American Annals of the Deaf, 139,* 163–164.

Koegel, L. K., Koegel, R. L., Frea, W., & Green-Hopkins, I. (2003). Priming as a method of coordinating educational services for students with autism. *Language, Speech and Hearing Services in Schools, 34*(3), 228–235.

Koegel, L. K., Koegel, R. L., Hurley, C., & Frea, W. (1992). Improving social skills and disruptive behavior in children with autism through self-management. *Journal of Applied Behavior Analysis, 25*, 341–354.

Lewis, R. B., & Doorlag, D. H. (1999). *Teaching special students in general education classrooms* (5th ed.). Upper Saddle River, NJ: Merrill/Prentice Hall.

Liberman, L. J., & Houston-Wilson, C. (1999). Overcoming the barriers to including students with visual impairments and deafblindness in physical education. *RE: view, 31*(3), 129–138. Retrieved May 8, 2006, from http://sas.epnet.com/

Lovaas, O. I. (1987). Behavioral treatment and normal educational and intellectual functioning in young autistic children. *Journal of Consulting and Clinical Psychology, 55*(1), 3–9.

Luckner, J. L., & Muir, S. (2002). Suggestions for helping students who are deaf succeed in general education settings. *Communication Disorders Quarterly, 24*(1), 23–30.

Mahshie, S. (1995). *Educating deaf children bilingually*. Washington, DC.: Laurent Clerc National Deaf Education Center. Retrieved December 1, 2005, from http://clerccenter.gallaudet.edu/

Marchant, J. M. (1996). Deaf-Blind. In P. J. McLaughlin & P. Wehman (Eds.), *Mental retardation and developmental disabilities* (2nd ed.). Austin, TX: PRO-ED.

Marttila, J., & Mills, M. (1995). *Knowledge is power*. Bettendorf, IA: Mississippi Bend Area Education Agency.

Mastropieri, M. A., & Scruggs, T. E. (2000). *The inclusive classroom: Strategies for effective instruction*. Upper Saddle River, NJ: Merrill/Prentice Hall.

Mastropiere, M. A., & Scruggs, T. E. (2004). *The inclusive classroom: Strategies for effective instruction* (2nd ed.). Upper Saddle River, NJ: Pearson.

McAnally, P. L., Rose, S., & Quigley, S. P. (1994). *Language learning practices with children who are deaf* (3rd ed.). Austin, TX: PRO-ED.

Mira, M. P., Tucker, B. F., & Tyler, J. S. (1992). *Traumatic brain injury in children and adolescents: A sourcebook for teachers and other school personnel*. Austin, TX: PRO-ED.

Mirenda, P. L., & Donnellan, A. M. (1987). Issues in curriculum development. In D. J. Cohen, A. M. Donnellan, & R. Paul (Eds.), *Handbook of Autism and Pervasive Developmental Disorders* (pp. 211–226). New York: Wiley.

Mukherjee, S., Lightfoot, J., & Sloper, P. (2000). The inclusion of pupils with a chronic health condition in mainstream school: What does it mean for teachers? *Educational Research, 42*(1), 59–72.

Muhlenhaupt, M. (2002). Family and school partnerships for IEP development. *Journal of Visual Impairment and Blindness, 96*(3), 175–178.

National Information Center for Children and Youth with Disabilities (2002). *Cerebral Palsy Fact Sheet*. Retrieved April 26, 2005, from http://nichcy.org/

National Information Center for Children and Youth with Disabilities (2002). *Spina Bifida Fact Sheet*. Retrieved April 26, 2005 from:http://nichcy.org/

Newman, B., Buffington, D. M., O'Grady, M. A., McDonald, M. E., Poulson, C. L., & Hemmes, N. S. (1995). Self-management of schedule following in three teenagers with autism. *Behavioral Disorders, 20*(3), 190–196.

Nowell, R., & Innes, J. (1997). Educating children who are deaf or hard of hearing: Inclusion. *ERIC Digest* #E557. Reston, VA: ERIC Clearinghouse on Disabilities and Gifted Education.

Odom, S., & Strain, P. (1986). A comparison of peer-initiation and teacher-antecedent interventions for promoting reciprocal social interaction of autistic preschoolers. *Journal of Applied Behavior Analysis, 19*, 59–71.

Parette, H. P. (1998). Assistive technology: Effective practices for students with mental retardation and developmental disabilities. In A. Hilton & R. Ringlaben (Eds.), *Best and promising practices in developmental disabilities*. Austin, TX: PRO-ED.

Powers, S. (2001). Investigating good practice in supporting deaf pupils in mainstream schools. *Educational Review, 53*(2), 181–189.

Prelock, P. (2001). Understanding Autism Spectrum Disorders: The role of the speech-language pathologist and audiologist in service delivery. The American Speech-Language-Hearing Association. Retrieved December 1, 2005, from *http://www.asha.org/*

Rees, T. (1992). Students with hearing impairments. In L. G. Cohen (Ed.), *Children with exceptional needs in regular classrooms*. Washington, DC: National Education Association.

Rikhye, C. H., Gotheif, C. R., & Appell, M. W. (1989). A classroom environment checklist for students with dual sensory impairments. *Teaching Exceptional Children, 22*(1), 44–46.

Ringlaben, R., & Dahmen-Jones, D., (1998). Attitudes about individuals with developmental disabilities. In A. Hilton & R. Ringlaben (Eds.), *Best and promising practices in developmental disabilities.* Austin, TX: PRO-ED.

Rose, M. (2002). *Hearing-impaired children in the mainstream.* Monkton, MD: York.

Sall, N. & Mar, H. H. (1999). In the community of a classroom: Inclusion education of a student with deaf-blindness. *Journal of Visual Impairments and blindness, 93*(4), 197–210.

Sasso, G. M. (1987). Social interactions: Issues and procedures. *Focus on Autistic Behavior, 2*(4), 1–7.

Schirmer, B. R., Bailey, J., & Fitzgerald, S. M. (1999). Using a writing assessment rubric for writing development of children who are deaf. *Exceptional Children, 65*(3), 383–397.

Schopler, E. (1997). Implementation of TEACCH philosophy. In D. J. Cohen & F. R. Volkmar (Eds.), *Handbook of autism and pervasive developmental disorders* (2nd ed., pp. 767–795). New York: Wiley.

Silver, C. H., & Oakland, T. D. (1997). Helping students with mild traumatic brain injury: Collaborative roles within schools. In E. D. Bigler, E. Clark, & J. E. Farmer (Eds.), *Childhood traumatic brain injury: Diagnosis, assessment and intervention.* Austin, TX: PRO-ED.

Simpson, R. L. (1995). Children and youth with autism in an age of reform: A perspective on current issues. *Behavioral Disorders, 21*(1), 7–20.

Simpson, R. L. (2004). Finding effective intervention and personnel preparation practices for students with autism spectrum disorders. *Exceptional Children, 70*(2), 135–144.

Singh, D. K. (2001). Are general educators prepared to teach students with physical disabilities? Paper presented at the Annual Convention of the Council for Exceptional Children (Kansas City, MO., April 18–21, 2001). Retrieved March 16, 2004, from http://www.edrs.com/

Smith, T., & Lovaas, O. I. (1997). The UCLA young autism project: A reply to Gresham and MacMillan. *Behavioral Disorders, 22*(4), 202–218.

Smith, T. E. C., Polloway, E. A., Patton, J. R., & Dowdy, C. A. (1995). *Teaching children with special needs in inclusive settings.* Boston: Allyn & Bacon.

Stewart, D.A. (1992). Initiating reform in total communication programs. *The Journal of Special Education, 26*(1), 68–84.

Szabo, J. L. (2000). Maddie's story: Inclusion through physical and occupational therapy. *Teaching Exceptional Children, 33*(2), 12–18.

Tucker, B. F., & Colson, S. E. (1992). Traumatic brain injury: An overview of school re-entry. *Intervention in School and Clinic, 27*, 198–206.

Tyler, J. S., & Mira, M. P. (1993). Educational modifications for students with head injuries. *Teaching Exceptional Children, 25*(3), 24–27.

Tyler, J. S., & Mira, M. P. (1999). *Traumatic brain injury in children and adolescents: A sourcebook for teachers and other school personnel* (2nd ed.). Austin TX: PRO-ED.

University of North Carolina (2006). Introduction to TEACCH. Retrieved May 8, 2006, from http://www.teacch.com

U.S. Department of Education (2002). *24th Annual Report to Congress on the Implementation of the Individuals with Disabilities Education Act.* Washington, DC: Office of Special Education Programs.

U.S. Department of Education (2005). *25th Annual Report to Congress on the Implementation of the Individuals with Disabilities Education Act.* Washington, DC: Office of Special Education Programs.

Vaughn, S., Bos, C. S., & Schumm, J. S. (2006). *Teaching exceptional, diverse, and at-risk students in the general education classroom* (3rd ed.). Boston: Allyn & Bacon.

Wadsworth, D. E. D., & Knight, D. (1999). Preparing the inclusion classroom for students with special physical and health needs. *Intervention in School and Clinic, 34*(3), 170–175.

Yell, M. L., & Drasgow, E. (2000). Litigating a free appropriate public education: The Lovaas hearings and cases. *The Journal of Special Education, 33*(4), 205–214.

York, J., Vandercook, T., MacDonald, C., Heise-Neff, C., & Caughney, E. (1992). Feedback about integrating middle-school students with severe disabilities in general education classes. *Exceptional Children, 58*, 244–258.

Youdelman, K., & Messerly, C. (1996). Computer-assisted notetaking for mainstreamed hearing-impaired students. *Volta Review, 98*(4), 191–199.

Ysseldyke, J. E., & Algozzine, B. (1990). *Introduction to special education.* Boston: Houghton Mifflin.

CHAPTER 14

OTHER SPECIAL NEEDS

CHAPTER PREVIEW

Focus

School leaders should be aware of other "exceptional" students who may require special services or accommodations in schools. Students who may not qualify for services under the IDEA may qualify for services under Section 504 of the Vocational Rehabilitation Act if they have a disability that substantially limits learning. One purpose of Section 504 is to prevent discrimination of individuals with disabilities in school programs and activities that receive federal financial assistance. Students returning to school from accidents, illnesses, or those with chronic health problems may qualify for 504 services. Frequently, students with attention-deficit hyperactivity disorders (ADHD) also quality for 504 services, which may include classroom accommodations.

Two additional groups of students deserve attention from the school administrator. Students from culturally or linguistically diverse backgrounds currently represent a significant population of children in schools. Classrooms today are populated with students from multiethnic backgrounds, and teachers and administrators must be prepared to meet the needs of culturally and linguistically diverse students.

The unique needs of talented and gifted (TAG) students must also be adequately addressed in our schools. Instructional principles for TAG students suggest that effective programming must involve challenging content presented by effective teachers. These groups of exceptional students present unique challenges and opportunities to public schools.

Inclusion Strategies

Students with disabilities covered by Section 504 may require an array of adaptations or modifications to be successful in general education classrooms. These may include the following:

- Teacher coaching and case managing
- Peer support
- Curriculum modifications

Similarly, students from culturally or linguistically diverse backgrounds may require a variety of accommodations in general education classrooms, including the following:

- Structured peer interactions
- Adequate teacher preparation
- Classroom adaptations including
- curricular modifications
- team teaching

Among the most important inclusion strategies for gifted and talented students will be the diversification and individualization of instruction.

STUDENTS WITH DISABILITIES PROTECTED BY SECTION 504 (INCLUDING ADHD)

Students with disabilities who do not qualify for services under the IDEA may qualify for special education and related services under Section 504 of the Vocational Rehabilitation Act of 1973 (Section 504 of the Vocational Rehabilitation Act, 1973). Students with chronic health conditions, returning to school after a serious illness or injury, or with other disabilities impacting learning may qualify for services under section 504 (Yell, 2006). Often, students diagnosed with ADHD may qualify for 504 services and will receive classroom accommodations to ensure an appropriate educational program.

It is conservatively estimated that 3 to 5% of America's school-age population is affected by ADHD (American Psychiatric Association [APA], 1994). Students are often diagnosed with ADHD according to criteria for inattention, hyperactivity, and impulsivity found in the Diagnostic and Statistical Manual of Mental Disorders (DSM-IV; APA, 1994) or according to criteria from a model developed by Russell Barkley (1990) involving interviews, behavior checklists, questionnaires, and observation. Most educational definitions suggest that ADHD is a developmental disorder involving attention and activity that is evident relatively early in life (before age 7 or 8), persists throughout the life span, involves both academic and social skills, and is frequently accompanied by other disorders. The difficulties in focusing and sustaining attention, controlling impulsive action, and inhibiting hyperactivity and unpredictability impact the educational performance of students with ADHD (Kauffman, 1997). Although the characteristics of ADHD may be noticed by parents or others before the child enters school, the ADHD is often not diagnosed or addressed until the child is school-aged. The core characteristics of ADHD are inattention, impulsivity, hyperactivity, and social problems.

Attention Deficits

A child with ADHD is usually described as having a short attention span and frequent attention shifts. The child is easily distracted and has difficulty concentrating, listening, beginning or completing tasks, and following directions. The child attends to only certain parts of auditory or visual information (e.g., listens to only part of the teacher's directions, looks at only part of the numbers in a math problem) or attends to irrelevant information that interferes with work completion (e.g., listens to noises from outside, looks around the room and not at task materials). The child fails to give close attention to details or makes careless mistakes, has difficulty sustaining attention, does not seem to listen or follow through on instructions, has difficulty organizing tasks, and is forgetful in daily activities (APA, 1994). These characteristics may seriously and adversely affect the educational performance of the student with ADHD.

Impulsivity

Impulsivity is a deficiency in inhibiting behavior or "acting without thinking." The child may blurt out answers before a question is complete, interrupt others, rush through tasks, or ask irrelevant questions. The child seems unable to wait, take turns, or hold back behaviors. The child may exhibit inappropriate or immature behaviors, such as silliness, uncontrolled laughing, or temper tantrums (APA, 1994).

Hyperactivity

Hyperactive children fidget with their hands or feet, run about or climb excessively, talk excessively, or act as if they are "driven by a motor" (APA, 1994). These children are often "on the go" and engaged in physical activity not related to schoolwork (e.g., moving about the classroom, handling materials inside the desk, squirming). The movement is disorganized and unpredictable. Some children may talk rapidly, loudly, or incessantly. They have difficulty controlling movement, particularly in settings requiring sitting or with limited opportunity for activity. The intensity and inappropriateness of the movement impact their classroom performance.

Social Problems

Social difficulties are commonly reported for students with ADHD. The relationship between ADHD and antisocial behavior has been clearly established (Walker, Ramsey, & Gresham, 2004). They are described as having high social impact: They are often talkative, socially busy, annoying, or bothersome (Wicks-Nelson & Israel, 2000). In social situations, these children may be overly sensitive or easily frustrated. Although children with ADHD often exhibit socially inappropriate behavior, teachers' concerns about their students' academic performance most often lead them to refer students for special education (Lloyd, Kauffman, Landrum, & Roe, 1991).

Individuals with ADHD frequently perform poorly in school, drop out, and have continuing difficulties in vocational settings (Raymond, 2004). Therefore, effective educational programs will be essential to students with ADHD.

Students with ADHD may be eligible for services under the IDEA as an Other Health Impairment (OHI). A child with OHI has "limited strength, vitality or alertness, including a heightened alertness to environmental stimuli, that results in limited alertness in the educational environment" due to "chronic or acute health problems such as asthma, attention deficit disorder or attention deficit hyperactivity disorders, diabetes, epilepsy, a heart condition, hemophilia, lead poisoning, leukemia, nephritis, rheumatic fever" that adversely affects a child's educational performance (34 C.F.R. § 300.8[c][9]). Whether covered under the IDEA or Section 504, school leaders must be aware of instruction and accommodation necessary to provide an appropriate education for students with ADHD.

Instruction

The instructional program for students with ADHD requires carefully planned educational interventions that address the physical environment, the classroom schedule, and the curriculum.

Physical Environment Carefully arranging the physical environment of the classroom can assist the child with ADHD. Some effective strategies include arranging the physical environment to permit movement, scheduling breaks throughout the instructional period, and minimizing environmental distractions.

Classroom Schedule Organizing the classroom schedule can be an effective educational intervention. Bender and Mathes (1995) suggested that teachers arrange short units of assignments, set specific times for assignment completion, and vary assignments to reduce distraction and student disinterest.

Curriculum Modification Modifying the curriculum is a necessary educational intervention for students with ADHD. Fowler (2002) recommends guided instruction, hands-on activities, and one-to-one instruction. Additionally, the curriculum can be modified by eliminating irrelevant cues, highlighting relevant information, incorporating an easy-to-more-difficult task sequence, and cueing the student to monitor his or her attention (Zentall, 2005).

Students with ADHD selectively attend to novelty, such as color and changes in size and movement (Fiore, Becker, & Nero, 1993). A variety of novel curriculum modifications can be effective with students with ADHD. A combination of approaches works best to help students with ADHD maintain successful performance in school. In fact, strategies designed to improve attention and memory in students with ADHD have enhanced successful inclusion (Mastropieri & Scruggs, 2004).

Medication

The use of medication for treatment of ADHD is controversial. Medication has proven effective for many children with ADHD. Most experts agree, however, that medication should never be the only treatment used. The parents' decision to place a child on medication is a personal one and should be made after a thorough evaluation of the child has taken place and after careful consideration by both the parents and the physician (Fowler, 1994). Psychostimulants are the medication most widely prescribed for ADHD. These drugs include Ritalin (methylphenidate), Dexedrine (dextroamphetamine), or Cylert (pemoline). Research now suggests that administering the correct dosage of the appropriate drug, carefully monitored, can result in remarkable improvement in behavior and facilitates learning in about 90% of students with ADHD (Kauffman, 1997).

Inclusion Strategies

The majority of students with ADHD can be taught in the regular classroom. Others may require some degree of special education and related services. When appropriate, accommodation strategies should be provided in general education settings. Reading strategies (Ostoits, 1999) and math strategies (Sliva, 2003) have been effectively provided in inclusive general education settings.

Students with ADHD need assistance and support in regular classroom environments. Booth (1998) lists several considerations to support inclusion:

- Provide consistent coaching from all teachers to support organizational skills, time management skills training, study skills training, and test-taking skills.
- Designate one teacher as the advisor/supervisor/coordinator/liaison for the student and the implementation of this plan who will periodically review the student's organizational system and whom other staff may consult when they have concerns about the student, and to act as the link between home and school.
- Permit the student to check in with an advisor to plan and organize each day of the week.
- Form study groups and encourage collaboration among students.
- Increase the frequency of positive, constructive, supportive feedback.
- Create a nonthreatening learning environment wherein the student asks questions and seeks extra help.

Although a variety of accommodation strategies have been identified in the literature, Zentall and Stormont-Spurgin (1993) found that some educators had not and would not implement accommodations that substantively changed the curriculum (e.g., modifying tests, restructuring assignments, allowing alternative response modes such as computers). Similarly, Schumm and Vaughn (1991) found that general education teachers were willing to provide reinforcement and encouragement, but viewed substantive instructional adaptations as undesirable. The researchers suggested that the desirability and feasibility of accommodations be discussed with the regular education teacher prior to implementing inclusion.

The accommodations and modifications for successful inclusion must be desirable, feasible, and efficacious. Strategies such as small group work, consistent instructional methods and strategies, and peer conferences have been acceptable to teachers and have resulted in successful inclusion of students with ADHD in general education classrooms (Ostiots, 1999).

Students with ADHD may be provided modifications and accommodations under either the IDEA or Section 504. In either case, school leaders should be aware of effective practices to ensure appropriate programs.

CULTURALLY AND LINGUISTICALLY DIVERSE STUDENTS (CLD)

School leaders must also be aware of exceptional students from culturally and linguistically diverse backgrounds. Classrooms today are increasingly populated with students from multiethnic backgrounds. According to the National Center for Educational Statistics, about 39% of public school students in 2001–2002 were members of minority groups. About 63% of the student population in large or midsize city schools were minority students, whereas 21% of the student population in small town or rural schools were minority students (National Center for Educational Statistics, 2003a). Between 1972 and 2000, the percentage of African American students rose from 15% to 17% of the school-aged population, and the percentage of Hispanic students rose from 6% to 17%. Another 5% of the student population was comprised of Native American and Asian-Pacific Island students.

Many of these students are not native speakers of English and have limited English proficiency (LEP) or are English language learners (ELL). LEP students represent multiethnic and socioeconomically diverse populations. The number of LEP or ELL students in U.S. schools during 2001–2002 was 3.7 million or 7.9% of the student population. This figure has doubled over the previous 10 years (Land & Legters, 2002) and is projected to increase to 25% to 40% of the school-aged population by the 2030s (National Center for Education Statistics, 2003a; Thomas & Collier, 2002). McCloskey (2002) estimated that 45% of teachers in the United States work with LEP or ELL students in their classrooms.

In 2000, 13% of the school-aged population received services under the IDEA. African American students comprised 14.9% of the IDEA students, and Native Americans were represented as 14.1%. These proportions were higher than for white, non-Hispanic students (10.9%), Hispanic (11.3%), and Asian-Pacific Island children (5.9%; National Center for Educational Statistics, 2003b). The concern for the overidentification of culturally and linguistically diverse students in special education has been well documented (Artiles, Harry, Reschly, & Chinn, 2002; Valles, 1998).

Instruction and Inclusion Strategies

Many professionals have not been explicitly taught to deal with diversity issues during their professional training program (Evans, Torrey, & Newton, 1997). They may not have the cultural consciousness or integrated instructional approaches to meet the needs of students from culturally or linguistically diverse backgrounds (Chamberlain, 2005). Failure to understand second-language acquisition may interfere with teachers' ability to plan appropriate instruction for students with LEP (Rodriguez & Higgins, 2005). Teacher preparation programs must help

preservice teachers learn to address the needs of diverse students. These approaches may involve modeling modified pedagogical strategies, providing cross-cultural field experience, and providing experiences in diverse communities (Major & Brock, 2003).

Datnow, Borman, Stringfield, Overman, and Castellano (2003) reported that programs for linguistically and culturally diverse students should allow for the development of students' native linguistics talents, and should use instructional activities to develop students' competence in language and literacy. Programs should employ a challenging curriculum and portray diverse perspectives contextualized in the experiences of students' homes and communities. Schools need to consider revising curriculum methods of assessment and classroom management tactics in order to fully meet the needs of linguistically and culturally diverse students (Brigaman, 2002). Educators must understand the social, language, learning, and literacy environment of ELL students as well as the use of specific learning and teaching strategies needed to ensure educational success for this population (Cheng, 1998).

The National Center for Culturally Responsive Educational Systems (NCCRES; 2004) proposes that culturally and linguistically diverse students can excel in academic endeavors if their culture, language, heritage, and experiences are valued and used to facilitate their learning and if they are provided access to high-quality teachers, programs, curricula, and resources. Classroom adaptations for students from culturally and linguistically diverse backgrounds include (a) completing an assessment to determine the linguistic, ethnic, and cultural background of the students; (b) selecting curricula to facilitate awareness and understanding of other cultures; (c) teaching awareness and acceptance issues; and (d) adapting the physical environment, instructional materials, and evaluation procedures as appropriate to meet the needs of CLD students (Mastropieri & Scruggs, 2004).

Several approaches to bilingual education have been offered, and scholars debate whether to immerse children in English-speaking classrooms or if non-English languages should be combined within classroom instruction. Although some argue that the most effective programs for LEP students are dual-language and bilingual immersion programs (Thomas & Collier, 2002), all professionals would agree that students who are not fluent in English will require supportive services in classrooms.

Special Education and CLD Students

Schools face high numbers of referrals of culturally and linguistically diverse students to special education and many researchers have concluded that CLD students may be disadvantaged in the assessment and evaluation process (U.S. Department of Education, 2001). Professionals must employ assessment procedures free of cultural or linguistic bias. The IDEA requires that tests and other evaluation materials used for eligibility assessment are selected and administered so as not to be discriminatory on a racial or cultural bias and are provided and administered in the child's native language or other mode of communication (20 U.S.C. § 1414[b][3][A]). Formal testing often employs measures with a norming bias (i.e., minority groups unrepresentative) and content bias (i.e., dominant culture's language used), as well as linguistic and cultural biases resulting from factors affecting test performance (e.g., test time limits; Garcia & Pearson, 1994). Recently, alternative forms of assessment and evaluation for culturally and linguistically diverse students have been proposed. For example, the System of Multicultural Pluralistic Assessment (SOMPA) has been shown to greatly reduce the percentage of culturally and linguistically diverse students in special education (Skaggs, 2001). The Ecobehavioral System for the Contextual Recording of Interactional Bilingual Environments was developed to examine ELL students at risk for developmental disabilities (Arreaga-Mayer, Utley, Perdomo-Rivera, & Greenwood, 2003). Student-centered assessment strategies such as interviews and portfolio development provide a direct link between assessment and instruction for CLD students (Dean, Salend, & Taylor, 1993). Baca and Cervantes (1998) developed a

professional development model called *Exito* for the assessment and instruction of culturally and linguistically diverse students. The content of *Exito* is based on an interactive paradigm of assessment, and has been implemented throughout the country.

Teachers may have a limited knowledge of effective practices for culturally and linguistically diverse learners and may consequently refer these students to special education (Winzer & Mazurek, 1998). Educators have mistakenly labeled certain language-minority students as learning or emotionally disabled due to a lack of knowledge related to English language acquisition (Baca & Cervantes, 1998). Reform in programs for culturally and linguistically diverse special needs students will require collaboration among professional disciplines (e.g., general education, special education, speech/language) and yet school professionals report they have not received appropriate training in collaboration (Roache, Shore, Gouleta, & de Obaldia Butkevich, 2003). It will be necessary to provide professional development to increase collaboration. Professional development programs such as Project CRISP (Culturally Responsive Instruction for Special Populations) may impact teachers' conceptualization of teaching from a multicultural perspective (Voltz, Brazil, & Scott, 2003).

The IEPs for students from culturally and linguistically diverse backgrounds must address learning needs in ways that are responsive to disability, cultural characteristics, and language needs (Garcia & Robertson, 1998; Cloud, 1993). For children with limited English proficiency, the IDEA requires IEP teams to "consider the language needs of the child as such needs relate to the child's IEP" (20 U.S.C. § 1414[d][3][B][ii]). Culturally responsive instruction involves curriculum adaptations that are consistent with students' experiences, cultural perspectives, and developmental ages and involve parents in the selection or development of instructional materials (Garcia & Malkin, 1993).

Parental involvement in programs for culturally and linguistically diverse students with special needs has presented numerous challenges. Families are becoming more diverse in terms of language, socioeconomic status, education, family structure, belief systems, and values (Lynch & Hanson, 1998). The shortage of special education teachers compounds the challenge. In 1999–2000, 10% of students with special needs were taught by non-certified personnel, and the projected need for special educators over the next ten years shows a dramatic increase (U.S. Department of Education, 2001). For the 1999–2000 school year, 86% of special education teachers were white, whereas 11% were African American, 3% were Hispanic, 1% were Asian or Pacific Islanders, and another 1% were Native American (National Clearinghouse for Professionals in Special Education, 2002). Although the population of culturally and ethnically diverse students represents 37% of students in special education, diverse special education teachers represent only 16% of special education teachers. Bilingual and bicultural special education professionals are in great shortage. Campbell-Whatley (2002) identified several factors that contribute to the shortage of diverse educators, such as inadequate outreach and recruitment, limited financial assistance for post-secondary education, and the invalid use of teacher competency exams to measure teaching skills.

Interestingly, research shows that families from culturally or linguistically diverse backgrounds underuse early intervention services, whereas school-age children from CLD backgrounds are overrepresented with mild disabilities (U.S. Department of Education, 2001). Yet families of CLD students exhibit lower levels of participation than European-American families in the special education process due to barriers including (a) limited understanding of linguistic and cultural diversity by professionals, (b) inadequate culturally responsive service delivery systems, and (c) limited English proficiency of the parents and their sense of alienation from the school (Bennett, Zhang, & Hohnar, 1998). Research with the families of African American children with special needs was conducted to determine the relationship between cultural differences and satisfaction with the special education services provided. The level of satisfaction is tied to issues of respect and levels of

comfort (Zionts, Zionts, Harrison, & Bellinger, 2003).

Several authors have offered recommendations for improving the involvement of CLD families in the IEP process. Professionals must be aware of various cultural interpretations of disability and understand cultural family structures and practices (Rogers-Adkinson, Ochoa, & Delgado, 2003). Training sessions for parents prior to IEP meetings (Cloud, 1992), the involvement of bilingual and bicultural guides or translators (Barrera, 1994), and expectations for family participation that are sensitive to families' needs and priorities (Shu-Minutoli, 1995) may result in the development of effective IEP's for culturally and linguistically diverse students.

Legal and Educational Issues

In 1985, the OCR issued "The Office for Civil Rights' Title VI Language Minority Compliance Procedures," which outlines the OCR policy with regard to the education of language-minority students and Title VI compliance standards. In 1991, the OCR issued an update, "Policy Update on Schools' Obligations Toward National Origin Minority Students with Limited-English Proficiency (LEP students)."

The document explains the relevant legal standards for OCR policy concerning discrimination on the basis of national origin in the provision of education services to LEP students at the elementary and secondary level.

When investigating complaints and conducting compliance reviews of school districts regarding equal education opportunity for national-origin minority students who are limited English proficient (LEP), the OCR considers two general issue areas: (a) whether there is a need for the district to provide a special language service program (an alternative language program) to meet the education needs of all language-minority students, and (b) whether the district's alternative language program is likely to be effective in meeting the education needs of its language-minority students. The OCR allows school districts broad discretion concerning how to ensure equal education opportunity for LEP students. However, the OCR advises that school districts follow certain procedures to ensure their programs are serving LEP students effectively:

> (a) identify students who need assistance; (b) develop a program that, in the view of experts in the field, has a reasonable chance for success; (c) ensure that necessary staff, curricular materials, and facilities are in place and used properly; (d) develop appropriate evaluation standards, including program exit criteria, for measuring the progress of students; and (e) assess the success of the program and modify it where needed.

Most important, steps must be taken so that LEP students are not assigned to special education classes because of their lack of English language proficiency, rather than because they have a disability. Title VI is violated if "national-origin minority students are misassigned to classes for the mentally retarded because of their lack of English skills" (OCR, 2000a). The OCR has also issued guidance for the development and evaluation of programs for ELL students (Programs for English Language Learners; OCR, 2000b).

Behavioral Disorders and Culture

Danforth (2000) proposed that programs filled with male, African American, and working class students represent a form of "behavior tracking"—a historical extension of "ability tracking" in public schools. Working class and minority students were tracked and isolated from their middle class peers. Classrooms for students with emotional and behavioral disorders were specifically designed to house students who opposed school authority. These segregated programs represented a social exclusion for economically disadvantaged and minority culture students who opposed conduct codes endorsed by school professionals. Accompanying this school stratification by class, the laws for students with disabilities fortified the presumption that a child's academic or behavioral problems could be attributed to an underlying, individual psychological disorder. As part of

the eligibility process, behavior common to economically disadvantaged and minority students was classified as a disability (Danforth, 2000).

Danforth (2000) suggests that from a critical sociological perspective, oppositional or disruptive behaviors represent social interactions rather than a condition within an individual. He argued that misconduct from historically oppressed and politically marginalized groups may be an artifact of broader social inequities. Based on resistance theory, Danforth (2000) proposed that oppositional behavior may be a student's attempt to craft identity in schools that have historically failed to acknowledge the uniqueness of the individual student. He asserted that a student's resistance is to an "achievement ideology" of schools (e.g., behave, work hard, get good grades, get a good job, make lots of money) that represents an empty and oppressive promise to poor and minority students. Danforth (2000) recommended that teachers examine social divisions or conflicts that exist in classrooms and determine how all students can meaningfully participate in educational programs.

Learning Disabilities and Culture

As early as 1986, scholars proposed that the special education disability described in federal legislation as "learning disabilities" was a social construction created to explain the failure of white middle class children in a way that gave them some protection from the stigma of failure (Sleeter, 1986). Learning disabilities were associated with children from advantaged social groups, whose failure could be explained and not interfere with their eventual ability to attain higher status occupations than "other" low achievers. The proposition that learning disabilities were created by cultural influences continues to receive significant support today, as in Zuriff's (2002) paper *The Myths of Learning Disabilities: The Social Construction of a Disorder*. The author suggests that the LD concept was introduced in the 1960s to describe children of normal cognitive capacity who were having significant difficulties in school due to "problems in the psychological processes needed for academic success" (p. 276). He argues that research shows that process training does not improve cognitive skills or performance, yet the tenet of a processing deficit has remained irresistible to the LD field.

Mental Disabilities and Culture

In an issue dedicated to culturally and linguistically diverse learners with severe disabilities, Meyer (2001) commented that current models and approaches for educating students with disabilities must be accommodated to the values and understandings of diverse cultural groups. Park and Lian (2001) called for increased awareness among educators and service providers of the importance of culturally responsive and sensitive approaches in educating students with severe disabilities. The authors suggested that educators are confronted with critical issues of discrimination and isolation of CLD students with severe disabilities, and a need to articulate strategies for enhancing partnerships with families from diverse cultural or linguistic backgrounds. Indeed, Harry, Rueda, and Kalyanpur (1999) called for a "posture of cultural reciprocity" between parents and educators in order to provide culturally sensitive programs to CLD students.

TALENTED AND GIFTED STUDENTS (TAG)

Talented and gifted (TAG) students represent another "exceptional" group of students in our schools. Among the common attributes of giftedness are

- Motivation and advanced interests;
- Communication skills;
- A well-developed memory;
- Insight and imagination/creativity;
- Advanced ability to deal with symbol systems; and

- Problem-solving, reasoning, and highly developed inquiry (Karnes & Bean, 2001).

Often, school guidance and counseling services are necessary adjuncts for the gifted child, to create an atmosphere where it is "safe" to be different and to address his or her uniqueness, sensitivity, or intensity (Millar & Torrance, 2003). Instructional theory for gifted students is based on instructional principles, which include

- a clear statement of purpose for the child and teacher,
- challenging content, and
- thoughtfully planned and personally relevant curriculum (Coleman & Cross, 2001).

These principles suggest that effective programming for TAG students must involve challenging content presented by effective teachers.

Despite early attention to gifted learners, educational programs for TAG students have been criticized as inadequate and inappropriate. Underachievement of TAG students and the underrepresentation of CLD students in gifted programs are two critical issues.

Underachievement

Davidson and Davidson (2004) concluded that "gifted education is largely haphazard, ineffective, and underfunded; it is more style than substance and rarely produces what gifted kids truly need: work that challenges them to the extent of their abilities" (p. 33). Gifted students often receive the same assignments as the whole class, and over half of the programs offered to TAG students nationwide are pull-out enrichment programs wherein students study only non-curricular material. In fact, one author reports that the school's inadequacy to meet the intellectual needs of gifted students is a primary reason parents choose to home-school their talented children (Rivero, 2002). The U.S. Department of Education reported in 1993 that about half of identified gifted students underachieved in schools (Ross, 1993). This "quiet crisis" of underachievement continues today, as documented by Rimm

(2003). Promising approaches for improving achievement include strengthening teacher-parent collaboration, creating accountability for achievement between teachers, parents, and students, and improving student's study habits and skills (Smutney, 2003).

The Underrepresentation of Minority and Economically Disadvantaged Children in Gifted Education (GE)

The underrepresentation of minority and economically disadvantaged students in TAG programs has been a concern of researchers and educators for several decades. Many authors have proposed that gifted and talented students transcend cultural, linguistic, and socioeconomic factors (Castellano, 2003). Specialists addressing this issue argue that attitudinal barriers result in the underrepresentation of minority children. Authors have suggested that a "pervasive deficit orientation" held by educators hinders access to TAG programs for African American students (Ford, Harris, Tyson, & Trotman, 2002). Educators interpret differences as deficits, dysfunctions, and disadvantages and label children with differences as "at risk" rather than recognizing these differences as strengths. Dr. Mary M. Frasier, founder and director of the Torrence Center for Creative Studies, commented that educators are often biased in their perception of giftedness: "You must have two parents; they must be college educated. You must be White. You must be in the suburbs" (Grantham, 2002, p. 50). Frasier advised that a key to addressing the issue of underrepresentation is a committed administrator who "truly believes that gifted kids from underrepresented groups are out there" (p. 51) and will use nontraditional methods and procedures for identifying and serving those students.

Traditionally, the identification of TAG students has involved testing. School personnel rely on the results of standardized norm-referenced tests to place students in TAG programs. The possibility of cultural bias in IQ tests has been extensively discussed (Onwuegbuzie &

Daley, 2001; Valencia & Suzuki, 2001). If high IQ scores are determinative of placement in TAG programs, African American students may be disadvantaged by the cultural bias now recognized as inherent in standardized measures. Several authors have called for alternative assessment to more reliably and validly identify gifted minority students, such as the use of multidimensional, culturally sensitive instruments (Frazier, Garcia, & Passow, 1995). Placement in TAG programs should not be "driven by racist notions and practices predicated on the unexpressed, presumed intellectual inferiority of African Americans" but rather on multicultural definitions of giftedness (Morris, 2002, p. 62).

Nontraditional assessment of giftedness must involve an understanding of the characteristics of creativity in CLD students. Sandler and Esquivel (2000) suggest that individual learning styles of CLD students must be factored into the assessment process. An instructional environment responsive to unique learning styles will nurture creativity in all children. Kopala (2002) discussed the social and emotional characteristics of gifted CLD students. Failure to identify the talents of CLD students may impact self-esteem, and a child's sense of ethnic identity may be affected if forced to leave a cultural community to develop giftedness. Further, the decision to develop giftedness—and later to pursue career options—is influenced by cultural values. Martorell (2002) discussed bilingualism as a powerful factor in the enhancement of creativity and called for a broadening of the concept of giftedness to include bilingual and language-diverse children.

Inadequate teacher preparation in multicultural and gifted education also contributes to the underrepresentation of minority and economically disadvantaged children in TAG programs. Increasing the number of minority teachers in TAG programs who have been dually prepared in multicultural and gifted education will lead to an increase in qualified CLD students who are selected for TAG programs (Bernal, 2002). The goals and objectives of a multicultural-gifted program would include the following:

- Meet the individual needs of students based on ability
- Meet the cognitive and academic needs regardless of culture, ethnicity, general, or socioeconomic status
- Provide curricular and instructional modifications essential for meeting the needs of highly able students from various socioeconomic, racial, or ethnic backgrounds, and both gender groups
- Structure a learning environment for highly able students that is supportive, nurturing, and affirming
- Guard against underachievement and support students in reaching their potential in school and life
- Train teachers to address the unique needs of gifted students
- Support highly able students to become responsible adults and competent citizens (Ford & Harris, 1999)

The authors recommended integrating gifted and multicultural education and conducting a school self-evaluation of multicultural competence in gifted education.

Inclusion Strategies

Many advocates of TAG programs support homogeneous grouping (i.e., grouping students according to ability for instruction) because a "one size fits all" education system is not effective and hence not equitable (Persson-Benbow, 1998). Such separation is rationalized by empirical support (i.e., homogeneous grouping improves the achievement of high-ability youth) and a belief that students learn better when working with others at their level of competence. The separatists argue that homogeneous grouping also makes teaching easier.

However, the National Association for Gifted Children and other professional organizations support an inclusive program for children with special talents and gifts. A *parallel curriculum* is recommended to develop the po-

tential and ability of gifted learners (Tomlinson et. al., 2002). Teachers develop and incorporate a separate curriculum for gifted learners, but infuse the activities into regular class placements. A variety of adaptations and modifications have been proposed to adequately address the needs of TAG students in inclusive settings:

- Team teaching provides an interdisciplinary perspective on the development, implementation, and evaluation of curriculum for TAG students in regular class placements (Parke, 2003).
- Subject-based acceleration and grade-based acceleration are options to challenge TAG students in inclusive placements. Both in-school and out-of-school options for the gifted child might be considered (Rogers, 2002).
- In addition to acceleration, the curriculum and instruction for gifted children may be differentiated by the use of complexity or the addition of depth or novelty in the existing curriculum (Clark, 2002).
- At the secondary level, the language arts, math, science, and social studies curricula may be adapted within existing content standards to challenge the gifted students to exceed those goals (Little & Ellis, 2003).

Talented and Gifted Students with Disabilities

Many students with physical, learning, or behavioral difficulties possess unique talents and strengths that are often masked by attention to deficits or disability. These *twice exceptional* students were a priority in the 2004 Amendments to the IDEA, which fund projects that addressed the needs of gifted students with disabilities. Historically, the focus of education programs has been on accommodating for the child's disability, thus precluding the recognition of the child's giftedness. For example, in a study by Rizza and Morrison (2003) teachers classified characteristics of students as either gifted or emotional/behavioral disorders (E/BD), but not both. The authors concluded that students with E/BD may not be screened for or receive TAG programming. Amendments to the IDEA have clarified the need for school leaders and professionals to address the academic and social needs of students who are twice exceptional.

Nielsen and Higgins (2005) proposed that services for twice exceptional students include four components: competence, choice, connections, and compassion. Teachers must help students discover their talents, provide meaningful curricular choice, enhance peer support, and show respect for students' uniqueness. Providing adequate time, structure, complexity, and support in academic work will facilitate success for twice exceptional students (Coleman, 2005). Because twice exceptional children have both learning gifts and learning difficulties, strategies to support their social and emotional needs must also be included in school programs (King, 2005). Neu (2003) addressed the need to identify and develop talent in gifted students with disabilities. Restricted special education environments may camouflage talents of students. The curriculum must accommodate their unique gifts while simultaneously compensating for disabilities, a process classed as *dual differentiation* (p. 159). Unless both exceptionalities are addressed, students may be at risk for underachievement and dropping out of school (Seeley, 2002).

For example, giftedness in students with learning disabilities is rarely identified and inadequately addressed (Brody & Mills, 1997). The incidence of learning disabilities in the gifted population is equal to the incidence in the general population (10% to 15%), yet the co-existence of both exceptionalities is rarely recognized:

> Children with the highest IQ ranges often have attention deficit symptoms, sensory integration issues, or both. Some suffer from dyslexia (reading disability), dysgraphia (writing disability), Asperger's syndrome (severe impairment of social interaction), or combinations of symptoms that do not clearly fit any diagnostic category. (Silverman, 2002, p. 533)

Gifted students with learning disabilities may benefit from curricular compacting and differentiation in addition to accommodations for processing challenges (Winebrenner, 2003). Effective interventions for gifted students with ADHD must address both conditions by differentiating curriculum to challenge the student and by promoting self-management of interfering behavior (Yewchuk & Lupart, 2000). Giftedness also co-exists with Asperger's syndrome (AS), a pervasive developmental disorder often discussed as a type of autism. Students with AS have poor social skills, average cognitive skills, and unique interests. Once the dual diagnosis is confirmed, programs must focus both on the social skill deficits and the cognitive abilities of these students.

Montgomery (2003) has edited a book designed to enable elementary and secondary practitioners to identify able pupils with special needs such as ADHD, reading disorders, and Down's syndrome, and to develop a curriculum to maximize their strengths within inclusive settings. Critical ingredients of programs for gifted children with disabilities may include the following:

- Developing self-concept and self-esteem
- Reducing communication limitations
- Fostering high-level, abstract thinking. (Rogers, 2002)

School administrators must be ever-vigilant to identify not only the needs of students with disabilities, but also their strengths. Inclusive placements permit an individualization to meet both needs and strengths of students with disabilities.

CONCLUSION

School administrators and other members of multidisciplinary teams must be aware of other exceptionalities requiring thoughtful planning for successful inclusion in general education. Children with disabilities protected under Section 504 often include students with ADHD. CLD students populate a range of learning environments from early childhood through secondary schools, and talented and gifted students—with and without disabilities—may also necessitate thoughtful planning for successful inclusion. Preservice programs must prepare administrators and school personnel to meet the needs of these growing groups of students, and ongoing professional development inservice opportunities must also be provided.

Programs for CLD students should be contextualized within the student's culture and experiences. School administrators must ensure that teachers of CLD students use appropriate assessment methods to determine the educational needs of CLD students and select appropriate curricula. IEPs for CLD students must meet special needs with methods that are linguistically and culturally responsive.

Gifted students with disabilities are "twice exceptional," yet current assessment practices focus more on deficits than gifts. Programs provide special education services, but not content that supports the development of their creativity and uniqueness. Many gifted students with disabilities will benefit from inclusive placements, whereby both accommodations for special needs and curriculum differentiation for abilities can be simultaneously provided.

Although children with disabilities under the IDEA must be identified and provided an appropriate education in the least restrictive environment, school leaders must also assure that students with ADHD, students from culturally and linguistically diverse backgrounds, and talented and gifted students are also provided effective educational programs. An awareness of these exceptional students and strategies to promote successful inclusion in general education programs will be essential to achieving that goal.

VIEW FROM THE COURTS

Austin Independent School District v. Robert M. (2001; student with "dual exceptionalities"). A high school student with ADHD attended a magnet school for gifted students but skipped numerous classes and failed to do homework assignments. Administrators informed the student and his mother that if attendance and effort did not improve, he would be reassigned to his home high school. The administrators did attempt to reassign the student as behavior problems continued, but the mother convinced the administration to try a 6-week trial period. The student's problems continued, and the magnet school proposed several accommodations. The mother pulled the student from the school, claiming the school district had failed to provide a free, appropriate education.

The district court concluded that when a student "demonstrates the mental ability and the motivation to take advantage of a gifted program, no disability should deprive the child of that opportunity" (35 IDELR 182). However, the student lacked motivation and squandered his opportunity at the magnet school with truancy, misconduct, and irresponsibility. Although the mother claimed the school district failed to accommodate the student's ADHD, the district court concluded that the district offered the student FAPE: "Schools are not required to force or motivate students to take advantage of the education they offer—this is the parents' role. Schools are also not required to spoonfeed students or to maximize their potential. They simply must offer a program that is reasonably calculated to confer an educational benefit upon the student" (35 IDELR 182), which the district provided.

RECOMMENDED READINGS

Austin, V. L. (2003). Pharmacological interventions for students with ADD. *Intervention in School and Clinic, 38*(5), 289–296. This article discusses the use of medication for students with ADHD.

Borland, J. H. (2003). *Rethinking gifted education.* New York: Teachers College Press. This article presents a nice overview of the controversies surrounding the education of TAG students.

David, G. A., & Rimm, S. B. (2004). *Education of the gifted and talented* (5th Ed.). Boston, MA: Allyn & Bacon. This text offers professionals useful background information and resources concerning students who are talented and gifted.

DeDemaray, M. K., Schaefer, K., & DeLong, L. K. (2003). Attention-deficit/hyperactive disorder (ADHD): A national survey of training and current assessment practices in schools. *Psychology in the Schools, 40*(6), 583–597. This article highlights the discrepancies in how school teams approach programs and services for students with ADHD.

Diaz, C. F. (2001). *Multicultural education for the 21st century.* New York: Longman. This information is critical for school leaders in understanding the policies and practices of multicultural programs in public schools.

Duhaney, L. M. G. (2003). A practical approach to managing the behaviors of students with ADD. *Intervention in School and Clinic, 38*(5), 267–279. This article presents several classroom-based strategies for addressing the needs of students with ADHD.

DuPaul, G. J., & Stoner, G. (1994). *ADHD in the schools: Assessment and intervention strategies.* New York: Guilford. The assessment information in this text is useful to practitioners, and the prevalence data may be of interest to school leaders.

Gibbons, P. (2002). *Scaffolding language, scaffolding learning: Teaching second language learners in the mainstream classroom.* Heinemann: New York. This article highlights suggestions for strategies to promote the successful inclusion of CLD students.

Guyer, B. P. (2000). *ADHD: Achieving success in school and in life.* Boston, MA: Allyn & Bacon. This book focuses on the transition from school to post-school opportunities for students with ADHD.

Layzer, C., & Sharkey, J. (2000). Whose definition of success? Identifying factors that affect English language learners' access to academic success and resources. *TESOL Quarterly, 34*(2), 352–368. This journal is a useful resource to school leaders and provides strategies to classroom teachers.

Mathur, S., & Smith, R. M. (2003). 20 ways to collaborate with families of children with ADD. *Intervention in School and Clinic, 38*(5), 311–315. This article highlights establishing a meaningful home-school partnership.

Rief, S. F. (2005). *How to reach and teach ADD/ADHD children: Practical techniques, strategies, and interventions for helping children with attention problems and hyperactivity* (2nd ed.).

West Nyack, NY: The Center for Applied Research in Education. An excellent resources of easily implemented strategies to meet the needs of students with ADHD.

Salend, S. J., Elhoweris, H., & van Garderen, D. (2003). Educational interventions for students with ADD. *Intervention in School and Clinic, 38*(5), 280–288. This article addresses the unique learning style of students with ADHD, including individualization and homework strategies.

Relevant Federal Regulations

34 C.F.R. Part 104 (2005). Nondiscrimination on the basis of disability in programs and activities receiving federal financial assistance–Section 504 regulations.

34 C.F.R. Part 300. Assistance to states for the education of children with disabilities (70 Fed. Reg. 35,833–35,880 [June 21, 2005]).

300.8	Child with a disability (definitions).
300.8(c)(a)	Definition of other health impairments.
300.306	Determination of eligibility.
300.324 (a)(2)	Consideration of special factors for IEP.

SELECTED WEBSITES

Children and Adults with Attention Deficit Disorder (CHADD)
http://www.chadd.org/

National Attention Deficit Disorder Association
http://www.add.org/

Teachers of English to Speakers of Other Languages (TESOL):
http://www.tesol.org/

United States Department of Health and Human Services (DHHS)
http://www.hhs.gov/ocr/lep/

Internet Teaching English as a Second Language (TESL) Journal
http://iteslj.org/

National Foundation for Gifted and Creative Children
http://www.nfgcc.org/

National Research Center on the Gifted and Talented
http://www.gifted.uconn.edu/

National Association for Gifted Children
http://www.nagc.org/

QUESTIONS FOR THOUGHT

1. How does the administrator balance the need to meet state and district standards and benchmarks with the need to present a personally relevant and challenging curriculum to students?
2. What are the advantages and disadvantages of subject-based acceleration?
3. What are the advantages and disadvantages of grade-based acceleration?
4. How might parents of CLD students be involved in the development and delivery of curriculum?
5. How might a language interpreter contribute and/or distract from the school climate?

REFERENCES

American Psychiatric Association (1994). *Diagnostic and statistical manual of mental disorders* (4th ed.). Washington, DC: APA.

Arreaga-Mayer, C., Utley, C. A., Perdomo-Rivera, C., & Greenwood, C. R. (2003). Ecobehavioral assessment of instructional contexts in bilingual special education programs for English language learners at risk for developmental disabilities. *Focus on Autism and Other Developmental Disabilities, 18*(1), 28–40.

Artiles, A. J., Harry, B., Reschly, D. J., & Chinn, P. C. (2002). Over-identification of students of color in special education: A critical overview. *Multicultural Perspectives, 4*(1), 3–10.

Austin Independent School District v. Robert M., 168 F.Supp. 2d 635 (WD TX 2001).

Baca, L., & Cervantes, H. (1998). *The bilingual special education interface* (3rd Ed.). Upper Saddle River, NJ: Merrill/Prentice Hall.

Barkley, R. A. (1990). *Attention-deficit hyperactivity disorder: A handbook for diagnosis and treatment.* New York: Guilford Press.

Barrera, I. (1994). Thoughts on the assessment of young children whose sociocultural background is unfamiliar to the assessor. *Zero to Three*, 9–13.

Bender, W. N. & Mathes, M. Y. (1995). Students with ADHD in the inclusive classroom: A hierarchical approach to strategy selection. *Intervention in School & Clinic, 30*(4) 226–234.

Bennett, T., Zhang, C., & Hohnar, L. (1998). Facilitating the full participation of culturally diverse families in the IFSP/IEP process. *Infant-Toddler Intervention, 8*, 227–249.

Bernal, E. M. (2002). Three ways to achieve a more equitable representation of culturally and linguistically diverse students in gifted and talented programs. *Roeper Review, 24*(2), 82–88.

Booth, R. C. (1998). *List of appropriate school-based accommodations and interventions for a 504 Plan or for adaptations and modifications section of an IEP*. Highland Park, IL: National Attention Deficit Disorder Association.

Brigaman, K. J. (2002). *The culturally diverse classroom: A guide for ESL and mainstream teachers*. Paper presented at the TESOL Convention, 2003. Retrieved March 25, 2004 from, http://www.edrs.com

Brody, L. E., & Mills, C. J. (1997). Gifted children with learning disabilities: A review of the issues. *Journal of Learning Disabilities, 30*(3), 282–296.

Campbell-Whatley, G. D. (2002). Recruiting and retaining of culturally and linguistically diverse groups in special education: Defining the problem. *Teacher Education and Special Education, 26*(4), 255–263.

Castellano, J. A. (2003). *Special populations in gifted education: Working with diverse gifted learners*. Boston: Allyn & Bacon.

Chamberlain, S. P. (2005). Recognizing and responding to cultural differences in the education of culturally and linguistically diverse learners. *Intervention in School and Clinic, 40*(4), 195–211.

Cheng, L. L. (1998). Intervention strategies for CLD students with speech-language disorders. In B. A. Ford (Ed.), *Compendium: Writings on effective practices for culturally and linguistically diverse exceptional learners*. Reston, VA: Council for Exceptional Children.

Clark, B. (2002). *Growing up gifted* (6th ed.). Upper Saddle Rivers, NJ: Merrill/Prentice Hall.

Cloud, N. (1992). Multicultural competencies in early intervention: Training professionals for a pluralistic society. *Infants and Young Children, 4*(3), 49–63.

Cloud, N. (1993). Language, culture and disability: Implications for instruction and teacher preparation. *Teacher Education and Special Education, 16*, 60–72.

Coleman, J. J., & Cross, T. L. (2001). *Being gifted in school: An introduction to development, guidance, and teaching.* Waco, TX: Prufrock Press, Inc.

Coleman, M. R. (2005). Academic strategies that work for gifted students with learning disabilities. *Teaching Exceptional Children, 38*(1), 28–32.

Danforth, S. (2000). Resistance theories: Exploring the politics of oppositional behavior. *Multiple Voices for Ethnically Diverse Exceptional Learners, 4*(1), 13–29.

Datnow, A., Borman, G. D., Stringfield, S., Overman, L. T., & Castellano, M. (2003). Comprehensive school reform in culturally and linguistically diverse contests: Implementation and outcomes from a four-year study. *Educational Evaluation and Policy Analysis, 25*(2), 143–170.

Davidson, B., & Davidson, J. (2004). *Genius denied.* New York: Simon & Schuster.

Dean, A. V., Salend, S. J., & Taylor, L. (1993). Multicultural education: A challenge for special educators. *Teaching Exceptional Children, 26*(1), 40–43.

Evans, E. D., Torrey, C. C., & Newton, S. D. (1997). Multicultural requirements in teacher certification. *Multicultural Education, 4*, 9–11.

Fiore, T. A., Becker, E. A., & Nero, R. C. (1993). Educational interventions for students with attention deficit disorder. *Exceptional Children, 60*(2), 163–173.

Ford, D. Y., & Harris, J. J. (1999). *Multicultural gifted education.* New York: Teachers College Press.

Ford, D. Y., Harris, J. J., Tyson, C. A., & Trotman, M. F. (2002). Beyond deficit thinking: Providing access for gifted African American students. *Roeper Review, 24*(2), 52–58.

Fowler, M. (2004). *Briefing paper: Attention-deficit/hyperactivity disorder.* Washington, DC: National Information Center for Children and Youth with Disabilities.

Frazier, M. M., Garcia, J. H., & Passow, A. H. (1995). Toward a new paradigm for identifying new talent potential. The University of Connecticut: National Research Center on the Gifted and Talented. Retrieved August 25, 2004, http://www.gifted.uconn.edu/

Garcia, S. B., & Malkin, D. H. (1993). Toward defining programs and services for culturally and linguistically diverse learners in special education. *Teaching Exceptional Children, 26*(1), 52–58.

Garcia, G. E. & Pearson, M. (1994). Equity challenges in authentically assessing students from diverse backgrounds. *Educational Forum, 59*(1), 64–73.

Garcia, S. B., & Robertson, P. M. (1998). Collaborative staff development in bilingual special education: Preliminary results of a five-year project. In B. A. Ford (Ed.), *Compendium: Writings on effective practices for culturally and linguistically diverse exceptional learners.* Reston, VA: Council for Exceptional Children.

Grantham, T. C. (2002). Straight talk on the issue of underrepresentation: An interview with Dr. Mary M. Frazier. *Roper Review, 24*(2), 50–51.

Harry, B., Rueda, R., & Kalyanpur, M. (1999). Cultural reciprocity in sociocultural perspective: Adapting the normalization principle for family collaboration. *Exceptional Children, 66*(1), 123–126.

Karnes, F. A., & Bean, S. M. (2001). *Methods and materials for teaching the gifted.* Waco, TX: Prufrock Press.

Kauffman, J. M. (1997). *Characteristics of emotional and behavioral disorders of children and youth* (6th ed.). Upper Saddle River, NJ: Merrill/Prentice Hall.

King, E. W. (2005). Addressing the social and emotional needs of twice-exceptional students. *Teaching Exceptional Children, 38*(1), 16–20.

Kopala, M. (2002). Social and emotional characteristics of gifted culturally diverse children. In G. B. Esquivel & J. C. Houtz (Eds.), *Creativity and giftedness in culturally diverse students.* Cresskill, NJ: Hampton Press.

Land, D., & Legters, N. (2002). The extent and consequences of risk in U.S. education. In S. Stringfield and D. Land (Eds.), *Educating at-risk students.* Chicago, IL: University of Chicago Press.

Little, C. A., & Elis, W. T. (2003). Aligning curricula for the gifted with content standards and exemplary secondary programs. In J. Van Tassel-Baska & C. A. Little (Eds.), *Content-based curriculum for high ability learners.* Washington, DC: National Association for Gifted Children.

Lloyd, J. W., Kauffman, J. M., Landrum, T. J., & Roe, D. L. (1991). Why do teachers refer pupils for special education? An analysis of referral records. *Exceptionality 2*, 113–126.

Lynch, E. W., & Hanson, M. J. (1998). *Developing cross-cultural competence: A guide for working with young children and their families*. Baltimore: Brookes.

Major, E. M., & Brock, C. Y. (2003). Fostering positive dispositions toward diversity: Dialogical explorations of a moral dilemma. *Teacher Education Quarterly, 30*(4), 7–26.

Martorell, M. (2002). Bilingualism and creativity. In G. B. Esquivel & J. C. Houtz (Eds.), *Creativity and giftedness in culturally diverse students*. Cresskill, NJ: Hampton Press.

Mastropieri, M. A., & Scruggs, T. E. (2004). *The inclusive classroom: Strategies for effective instruction* (2nd Ed.). Upper Saddle River, NJ: Merrill/Prentice Hall.

McCloskey, M. L. (2002). President's message: No child left behind? *TESOL Matters, 12*(4), 3.

Meyer, L. H. (2001). Multiculturalism and severe disabilities. *Journal of the Association for Persons with Severe Handicaps, 26*(3), 204–205.

Millar, G. W., & Torrance, E. P. (2003). School guidance and counseling for the underserved gifted: Strategies to facilitate the growth of leaders, thinkers and change agents. In J. F. Smutny (Ed.), *Underserved gifted populations: Responding to their needs and abilities*. Cresskill, NJ: Hampton Press.

Montgomery, D. (2003). *Gifted and talented children with special education needs: Double exceptionality*. Independence, KY: Taylor and Francis.

Morris, J. E. (2002). African American students and gifted education: The politics of race and culture. *Roeper Review, 24*(2), 59–62.

National Center for Culturally Responsive Educational Systems (2004). *Responsive practices*. Retrieved March 24, 2004, from http://www.nccrest.org/

National Center for Educational Statistics (2003a). *Overview of public elementary and secondary schools and districts: School year 2001–2002*. Retrieved March 25, 2004, from http://nces.ed.gov/pub2003/overview03/

National Center for Educational Statistics (2003b). *Status and trends in the education of blacks*. Retrieved March 25, 2004, from http://nces.ed.gov/pubs2003/2003034.pdf

National Clearinghouse for Professions in Special Education (2002). *Study of personnel needs in special education*. Retrieved March 25, 2004, from http://www.special-ed-careers.org/

Neu, T. (2003). When gifts are camouflaged by disability: Identifying and developing the talent in gifted students with disabilities. In J. A. Castellano (Ed.), *Special populations in gifted education: Working with diverse gifted learners*. Boston: Allyn & Bacon.

Nielsen, M. E., & Higgins, D. (2005). The eye of the storm: Services and programs for twice-exceptoinal learners. *Teaching Exceptional Children, 38*(1), 8–15.

Office for Civil Rights (1985). The Office for Civil Rights' title VI Language Minority Compliance Procedures. Retrieved December 7, 2005, from http://www.ed.gov/

Office for Civil Rights (1991). Policy update on schools' obligations toward national origin minority students with limited english proficiency (LEP Students). Retrieved December 7, 2005, from http://www.ed.gov/

Office for Civil Rights (1999). Programs for English *language learners*. Retrieved December 6, 2005, from http://www.ed.gov/

Office for Civil Rights (2000a). *The provision of an equal education opportunity to limited-English proficient students*. Retrieved March 24, 2004, from http://www.ed.gov/about/offices/list/ocr/index.html

Office for Civil Rights (2000b). *Programs for English language learners*. Retrieved March 24, 2004, from http://www.ed.gov/about/offices/list/ocr/index.html

Onwuegbuzie, A. J., & Daley, C. E. (2001). Racial differences in IQ revisited: A synthesis of nearly a century of research. *Journal of Black Psychology, 27*(2), 209–220.

Ostoits, J. (1999). Reading strategies for students with ADD and ADHD in the inclusive classroom. *Preventing School Failure, 43*(3), 129–132.

Park, H. S., & Lian, M. G. J. (2001). Introduction to special series on culturally and linguistically diverse learners with severe disabilities. *Journal of the Association for Persons with Severe Handicaps, 26*(3), 135–137.

Parke, B. N. (2003). *Discovering programs for talent development*. Thousand Oaks, CA: Corwin Press.

Persson-Benbow, C. (1998). Grouping intellectually advanced students for instruction. In J. Van Tassel-Baska (Ed.), *Excellence in educating gifted and talented learners*. Denver, CO: Love Publishing.

Raymond, E. B. (2004). *Learners with mild disabilities: A characteristic approach* (2nd Ed.). Boston: Pearson/Allyn & Bacon.

Rimm, S. (2003). Underachievement: A continuing dilemma. In J. F. Smutney (Ed.), *Underserved gifted populations: Responding to their needs and abilities.* Cresskill, NJ: Hampton Press.

Rivero, L. (2002). *Creative home schooling for gifted children: A resource guide.* Scottsdale, AZ: Great Potential Press.

Rizza, M. G., & Morrison, W. F. (2003). Uncovering stereotypes and identifying characteristics of gifted students and students with emotional/behavioral disabilities. *Roeper Review, 25*(2), 73–77.

Roache, M., Shore, J., Gouleta, E., & de Obaldia Butkevich, E. (2003). An investigation of collaboration among school professionals serving culturally and linguistically diverse students with exceptionalities. *Bilingual Research Journal, 27*(1), 117–136.

Rodriguez, C. D., & Higgins, K. (2005). Preschool children with developmental delays and limited English proficiency. *Intervention in School and Clinic, 40*(4), 236–242.

Rogers, K. B. (2002). *Re-forming gifted education: Matching the program to the child.* Scottsdale, AZ: Great Potential Press.

Rogers-Adkinson, D. L., Ochoa, T. A., & Delgado, B. (2003). Developing cross-cultural competence: serving families of children with significant developmental needs. *Focus on Autism and Other Developmental Disabilities, 18*(1) 4–8.

Ross, P. (1993). *National excellence: A case for developing America's talent.* Washington, DC: U.S. Government Printing Office.

Sandler, F., & Esquivel, G. B. (2000). Learning styles and creativity in culturally diverse children. In G. B. Esquivel & J. C. Houtz (Eds.), *Creativity and giftedness in culturally diverse students.* Cresskill, NJ: Hampton Press.

Section 504 of the Vocational Rehabilitation Act (1973). 20 U.S.C. § 794 *et. seq.*

Seeley, K. (2002). High risk gifted learners. In N. Colangelo and G. A. David (Eds.), *Handbook of gifted education.* Boston: Allyn & Bacon.

Shu-Minutoli, K. (1995). Family support: Diversity, disability, and delivery. *Yearbook in Early Childhood Education, 6,* 125–140.

Schumm, J. S., & Vaughn, S. (1991). Making adaptations for mainstreamed students: General classroom teachers' perspectives. *Remedial and Special Education, 12*(4), 18–27.

Silverman, L. K. (2002). Gifted children with learning disabilities. In N. Colangelo & G. A. David (Eds.), *Handbook of gifted education.* Boston: Allyn & Bacon.

Skaggs, M. C. (2001). Facing the facts: Overrepresentation of culturally and linguistically diverse students in special education. *Multicultural Education, 9*(2), 42–43.

Sleeter, C. E. (1986). Learning disabilities: The social construction of a special education category. *Exceptional Children, 53*(1), 46–54.

Sliva, J. A. (2003). *Teaching inclusive mathematics to special learners, K–6.* Thousand Oaks, CA: Corwin Press.

Smutney, J. F. (2003). *Gifted education: Promising practices.* Bloomington, IL: Phi Delta Kappa Educational Foundation.

Thomas, W. P., & Collier, V. P. (2002). *A national study of school effectiveness for language minority students' long-term academic achievement.* Santa Cruz, CA: Center for Research on Education, Diversity, and Excellence. Retrieved May 8, 2006, from http://www.cal.org/crede/

Tomlinson, C. A., Kaplan, S. N., Renzulli, J. S., Purcell, J., Leppien, J., & Burns, D. (2002). *The parallel curriculum: A design to develop high potential and challenge high ability learners.* Thousand Oaks, CA: Corwin Press.

U.S. Department of Education (2001). *Twenty-third Annual Report to Congress on the Implementation of the Individuals with Disabilities Education Act.* Washington, DC: U.S. Department of Education.

U.S. Department of Education (2005). *25th Annual Report to Congress on the Implementation of the Individuals with Disabilities Education Act.* Washington, DC: Office of Special Education Programs.

Valencia, R. R., & Suzuki, L. A. (2001). Intelligence testing and minority students: Foundations, performance factors, and assessment issues. *Racial and Ethnic Minority Psychology Series.* Thousand Oaks, CA: Sage Publications.

Valles, E. C. (1998). The disproportionate representation of minorities in special education: Responding to the problem. *Journal of Special Education, 32,* 52–54.

Voltz, D. L., Brazil, N., & Scott, R. (2003). *Professional development for culturally responsive instruction: A promising practice for addressing* the disproportionate representation of students of color in special education.

Walker, H. M., Ramsey, E., & Gresham, F. M. (2004). *Antisocial behavior in school* (2nd Ed.). Belmont, CA: Wadsworth.

Wicks-Nelson, R., & Israel, A. C. (2000). *Behavior disorders of childhood* (4th ed.). Upper Saddle River, NJ: Prentice Hall.

Winebrenner, S. (2003). Teaching strategies for twice-exceptional students. *Intervention in School and Clinic, 38* (3), 131–137.

Winzer, M. A., & Mazurek, K. (1998). *Special education in multicultural contexts.* Upper Saddle River, NJ: Merrill/Prentice Hall.

Yell, M. L. (2006). *The law and special education* (2nd ed.). Upper Saddle River, NJ: Merrill/Prentice Hall.

Yewchuk, C., & Lupart, J. (2000). Inclusive education for gifted students with disabilities. In K. A. Heller, F. J. Monks, R. J. Sternberg, & R. F. Subotnik (Eds.), *International handbook of giftedness and talent* (2nd ed.). New York: Elsevier.

Zentall, S. S. (2005). Theory- and evidence-based strategies for children with attention problems. *Psychology in the Schools, 42* (8), 821–836.

Zentall, S. S., & Stormont-Spurgin, M. (1993). Research on the educational implications of attention deficit hyperactivity disorders. *Exceptional Children, 60,* 143–153.

Zionts, L. T., Zionts, P., Harrison, S., & Bellinger, D. (2003). Urban African American families' perceptions of cultural sensitivity within the special education system. *Focus on Autism and Other Developmental Disabilities, 18* (1), 41–50.

Zuriff, G. E. (2002). Are learning disabilities a myth? In M. Byrnes (Ed.), *Taking sides: Clashing views on controversial issues in special education.* Guilford, CT: McGraw-Hill.

APPENDIXES

A EXAMPLES OF EXCERPTS FROM PLEP STATEMENTS
Source: Iowa Department of Education (1998, p. 77). *Their Future . . . our guidance: Iowa IEP guidebook.* Des Moines, IA: Author. Adapted and reprinted by permission.

B EXAMPLES OF GOAL STATEMENTS
Source: Iowa Department of Education (1998, Appendix C). *Their Future . . . our guidance: Iowa IEP guidebook.* Des Moines, IA: Author. Adapted and reprinted by permission.

C EXAMPLES OF MONITORING OBJECTIVES
Source: Iowa Department of Education (1998, p. 82). *Their Future . . . our guidance: Iowa IEP guidebook.* Des Moines, IA: Author. Adapted and reprinted by permission.

D EXAMPLES OF INTEGRATED PLEPS, GOALS, AND MONITORING OBJECTIVES
Source: Iowa Department of Education (1998, pp. 83–84). *Their Future . . . our guidance: Iowa IEP guidebook.* Des Moines, IA: Author. Adapted and reprinted by permission.

E IEP MODEL FORM
Source: Iowa Department of Education, July 1, 2005. Reprinted by permission.

F SAMPLES OF DIFFERENT IEP ANNUAL GOALS AND OBJECTIVES AS PART OF TRANSITION IEPS
Source: Assess for Success: Handbook on Transition Assessment, by P. L. Sitlington, D. A. Neubert, W. Begun, R. C. Lombard, & P. J. Leconte. Copyright 1996 by The Division of Career Development and Transition, a division of the Council for Exceptional Children, pp. 32-40. Adapted by permission.

G INDIVIDUALIZED FAMILY SERVICE PLAN MODEL FORM
Source: Iowa Department of Education (February and May 2004). Reprinted by permission.

H SAMPLE BEHAVIOR/DISCIPLINE FORMS:

H1 BEHAVIOR OBSERVATION FORM
Source: From "Functional Assessment: A Systematic Process for Assessment and Intervention in General and Special Education Classrooms," by M. E. McConnell, D. B. Hilvitz, & C. J. Cox, 1998, *Intervention in School and Clinic, 34*(1): 17. Copyright 1998 by PRO-ED, Inc. Adapted with permission.

H2 FUNCTIONAL ASSESSMENT INTERVIEW FORM
Source: From "Functional Assessment: A Systematic Process for Assessment and Intervention in General and Special Education Classrooms," by M. E. McConnell, D. B. Hilvitz, & C. J. Cox, 1998, *Intervention in School and Clinic, 34*(1): 19. Copyright 1998 by PRO-ED, Inc. Adapted with permission.

H3 BEHAVIORAL INTERVENTION PLAN
Source: From "Functional Assessment: A Systematic Process for Assessment and Intervention in General and Special Education Classrooms," by M. E. McConnell, D. B. Hilvitz, & C. J. Cox, 1998, *Intervention in the School Clinic, 34*(1): 20. Copyright 1998 by PRO-ED, Inc. Adapted with permission.

H4 MANIFESTATION DETERMINATION REVIEW FORM

A EXAMPLES OF EXCERPTS FROM PLEP STATEMENTS

1. In the general education curriculum, students are expected to complete all assignments. John turns in an average of 60% of his math assignments, 50% of his reading and language assignments (on average per week). Of assignments turned in, fewer than 75% are complete. Accuracy of turned-in work fluctuates markedly from less than 10% to 100%.

2. Christine is working on the district's standard to be able to read, understand, and respond to a variety of materials for various purposes. Our focus will be on functional vocabulary. Christine is able to say the sounds of 15 to 26 letters of the alphabet independently (missed v, d, l, r). With a gestural prompt she was able to say the sounds of w, x, y, z, g, l, n. Christine is able to read 19 survival words.

3. Charlie is having difficulties in math. He is unable to meet the general education standards in the area of understanding and applying a variety of problem-solving strategies. He can compute addition problems when using touch math. He has difficulty processing story problems when they are read to him in a one-to-one situation. He does not understand the relationship of the language in the problems and the computation. He needs to learn to set up and solve story problems. He was not able to complete any of the addition or subtraction story problems on the second grade math assessment.

B EXAMPLES OF GOALS

A. *Presence and Participation*
In 32 weeks, when in a 10-minute or longer teacher-directed question-and-answer activity, Jan will raise her hand and volunteer an answer at least two times across three consecutive opportunities.

B. *Accommodation and Adaptation*
In 32 weeks, prior to beginning each new class or activity, Renee will meet with the teacher, ask questions about the activities and content, and identify for herself and the teacher the visual accommodations (e.g., enlarged type, books on tape) that will be needed for her to succeed in the course or activity for 100% of her classes.

C. *Physical Health*
In 32 weeks, during snacks and meals at school, Gigi will independently eat using a spoon and independently drink from a tippy cup with more than 1/2 of the food and liquid going into her mouth, across all meals on 3 consecutive days.

In 10 weeks, when feeding from a bottle, Marion will consume at least 5 ounces of formula per feeding for at least 5 feedings per day across all days.

In 32 weeks, across all settings, Ian will identify 20 major warning words and symbols (e.g., Stop, Poison, Danger, Hazard) with 95% accuracy and will identify appropriate actions to take when these words are seen with 100% accuracy.

D. *Responsibility and Independence*
In 30 weeks, while at school, Peter will appropriately and independently use the toilet when necessary for a period of at least 3 weeks.

In 31 weeks, while at school, Kendra will appropriately use her walker to get to all of her classes within 4 minutes of the tardy bell for 3 consecutive weeks.

In 32 weeks, before snack time, Jacob will prepare a simple snack of his choice and eat it, at school, for 3 consecutive weeks.

In 32 weeks, when a grocery item or items are needed, Marlo will go shopping at the grocery store, pay for her purchases using the nearest dollar strategy and count change ($1.00), on three consecutive trips to the store.

E. *Contribution and Citizenship*
In 30 weeks, across all classroom activities that require taking turns, Joe will wait his turn on 80% of turn-taking opportunities for 3 consecutive data days.

In 32 weeks, when engaged in a cooperative learning activity, Jessie will participate with the rest of the group throughout the entire activity across 5 cooperative learning activities.

F. *Academic and Functional Literacy*
In 31 weeks, when conversing with the Speech Language Pathologist using multiple word phrases, Mandy will use T, D, P, B, and M sounds with 90% accuracy.

In 32 weeks, during 30-minute play sessions, Jerry will independently solve problems in order to play with toys in 4 out of 5 situations presented on 3 consecutive school days.

In 29 weeks, when asked descriptive questions about classroom activities by an adult, Glenn will correctly answer 80% of these questions using appropriate multiple word phrases.

In 32 weeks, when presented with 20 randomly chosen pictures (from a pool of 300 representing basic vocabulary word/concepts), Martin will correctly label 18 of the 20 pictures for 5 consecutive sessions.

In 25 weeks, when presented with serially presented phonemes, Carol will imitate the sounds in order to form words on 9 of 10 presentations across 3 consecutive days.

In 26 weeks, after silently reading a previously unread story from third-grade trade books, Bob will orally retell the story and identify all of the major characters and events for 5 consecutive stories.

In 26 weeks, when presented with a randomly selected passage from third-grade trade 3 books, Felicia will read aloud 120 words correctly in 1 minute with 4 or fewer errors.

G. *Personal and Social Adjustment*
In 30 weeks, when on the playground, Spencer will appropriately play beside other children in all situations for 2 consecutive weeks.

In 30 weeks, when given a direct verbal direction by an adult, Joe will begin to comply with the direction within 10 seconds on 80%

of opportunities for 3 consecutive data days.

In 18 weeks, when confronted with teasing by peers, Rambo will physically remove himself from the situation across all occurrences, times, and settings in school.

In 32 weeks, during teacher-led instruction in all of his classes, Arnold will raise his hand prior to asking a question or offering an opinion 90% of the time for 2 consecutive weeks.

In 32 weeks, in free play situations, Maryann will use appropriate phrases to request an object or activities 70% of the time across 5 consecutive free play situations.

C EXAMPLES OF MONITORING OBJECTIVES

David will write answers to simple addition facts with the sums 0 to 20 (e.g., 4 1 5) in 5 minutes on a worksheet at a rate of 40 correct digits per minute with no errors by October 2007.

Given different board games and 2 to 3 peers, Mary will play cooperatively for 15 consecutive minutes for 10 turn-taking exchanges.

D EXAMPLES OF INTEGRATED PLEPs, GOALS, MONITORING OBJECTIVES

1. PLEP
At 36 months, Abigail is working on developmental skills of early object use and functional play with toys or objects. Abigail is able to perform exploratory schemes (banging, shaking, throwing) as she plays with toys or objects. She applies the same schemes to all objects, but does not demonstrate an understanding of the functions of toys or objects. Abigail has learned to imitate her parents' and other adults' actions when provided with a model of combining two schemes to manipulate a toy in a functional play activity. Abigail's parents want her to play with her toys

without requiring their constant attention and modeling of actions.

When given toys or objects, Abigail will perform five schemes with them (shake, roll, bang, throw, push). She does not combine schemes into a functional play sequence with the toys or objects. Children between 18 to 24 months of age typically play with toys or objects by combining schemes to see a cause-and-effect relationship and to use objects according to their functions. By 36 months, children are beginning to engage in symbolic or pretend play.

Annual Goal
In 36 weeks, when given the opportunity to play with six to eight different toys or objects, Abigail will spontaneously link four discrete schemes according to the toys' or objects' intended functions three times per observation period across five consecutive play times.

Monitoring Benchmarks
Link two discrete schemes
Link three discrete schemes

2. PLEP
John displays difficulties writing his thoughts on paper. He has very creative ideas but does not understand sentence construction or how to develop paragraphs. He needs to use punctuation and capitalization consistently. John received 12 out of 50 points on the district's assessment for expressive writing. He needs to learn to write the four different sentence types (simple, compound, complex, and compound-complex) correctly and integrate them into a paragraph.

Annual Goal
In 36 weeks, John will write at least a six-sentence paragraph using at least three different sentence types scoring 45 out of 50 on the writing rubric.

Monitoring Benchmarks
Write simple sentences
Write compound sentences
Write complex sentences
Write compound-complex sentences

3. PLEP
Michelle is working on the standard general education curriculum to enhance reading fluency. Michelle has difficulty identifying words in isolation. When reading a text, she uses context clues and picture clues to identify words unfamiliar to her. When reading words in isolation, she attempts to dissect the word phonetically, but has difficulty drawing closure to the word and pronouncing the word as a whole. Michelle studied the DISSECT word identification strategy in seventh grade. It appears she still uses this strategy with some limited success.

When asked to read passages from her government textbook, Michelle read at an average rate of 82 words per minute with 96% accuracy in word identification. This compares to a norm of 150 to 200 words per minute with 98% to 99% accuracy for high school juniors. During this reading probe, Michelle stated that she can read faster when she reads aloud. It seems that her literal comprehension also improves when she is able to read aloud. She used a ruler as a guide to enable her to read line by line.

Annual Goal
Given sample passages of at least 200 words from high-school level textbooks, Michelle will read grade level materials at an average rate of 100 words per minute with 98% accuracy or better in word identification.

Monitoring Objectives
Michelle will read a 200-word passage at 90 wpm with 98% accuracy.

Michelle will read a 200-word passage at 95 wpm with 98% accuracy.

E IEP MODEL FORM

Individualized Education Program

DATE: _____ / _____ / _____   **TYPE:** ☐ Initial ☐ Review ☐ Reevaluation ☐ Amendment ☐ Interim

Evaluation was completed within 60 days ☐ yes ☐ no. If no specify the reason for the delay: _____

STUDENT: _____ ☐ M ☐ F

          Last (legal)   First (no nicknames)   M.I.

Birthdate: _____ / _____ / _____   Grade: _____   Teacher/Service Provider: _____

Resident District: _____   Building: _____

Attending District: _____   Building: _____

Attending Area Education Agency: _____   Attending Building Phone: _____

[ ] Parent [ ] Foster Parent [ ] Guardian [ ] Surrogate [ ] Student	Name: _____ Address: _____ _____	Home Phone: _____ Work/Cell Ph: _____ E-mail: _____
[ ] Parent [ ] Foster Parent [ ] Guardian [ ] Surrogate [ ] Student	Name: _____ Address: _____ _____	Home Phone: _____ Work/Cell Ph: _____ E-mail: _____

Duration of this IEP: From _____ / _____ / _____ to _____ / _____ / _____   Reevaluation is due: _____ / _____ / _____

Procedural safeguards were reviewed by: _____ Method: _____

Rights will transfer at age 18: _____ / _____ / _____   Notification: Student _____ / _____ / _____   Parent: _____ / _____ / _____

Persons Present at Meeting/Position or Relationship to Student

_____ Parent   _____ Student

_____ Parent   _____ _____

_____ LEA Rep/Designee _____ _____

_____ Gen Ed Tchr   _____ _____

_____ Sp Ed Tchr   _____ _____

Signature or listing indicates presence at the meeting, not approval or acceptance of the IEP

Outside written input: Name/Agency: _____ Date: _____ / _____ / _____

Required System Data	☐ Assistive technology	☐ Shortened school day	Goal (descrip)	Code	SDO(s)
Ethnicity:	☐ Behavior assessment/plan	☐ Special transportation			
Disability(ies):	☐ Braille instruction	☐ Specially designed PE			
Early childhood code:	☐ Communication plan (Deaf/HH)	Basis for enrollment:			
Time: ☐ Full ☐ Part	☐ Extended school year services	Served status:			
☐ Alternate assessment ☐	☐ Health plan	WEF:	☐ I-Plan _____ / _____ / _____		
Domicile district/building:		Roster change(s):	Final exit:		

Name: _____ Date: _____/_____/_____ Page _____ of _____

Present Levels of Academic Achievement and Functional Performance

Strengths, interests and preferences of this individual _____

_____

Parents' concerns for enhancing their child's education _____

_____

Student and family vision. Include post-high school outcomes in the areas of living, learning, and working based on the needs, interests and preferences of the individual by age 14.

_____

_____

_____

Special considerations to be addressed in developing this IEP. Include or attach appropriate information for any "Yes".

Y	N	Behavior (in the case of a student whose behavior impedes his or her learning or that of others, consider the use of positive behavioral interventions and supports, and other strategies, to address that behavior)	Y	N	Communication and language, particularly if the student is deaf or hard of hearing	Y	N	Limited English proficiency (Consider the language needs related to the IEP)
			Y	N	Braille instruction needs if this student has a visual impairment	Y	N	Assistive technology

Other information essential for the development of this IEP _____

_____

_____

_____

_____

Describe the effect of this individual's disability on involvement and progress in the general education curriculum and the functional implications of the student's skills. For a preschool child, describe the effect of this individual's disability on involvement in appropriate activities. By age 14, describe the effect of this individual's disability on the pursuit of post-secondary expectations (living, learning, and working).

_____

_____

_____

Based on the vision and transition assessments of students ages 14 and older, describe the post secondary expectations for living, learning, and working.

_____

_____

Course of study (By age 14, include target graduation date, graduation requirements and courses and activities needed to pursue the post secondary expectations for living, learning, and working.)

_____

_____

_____

Name: _____ Date: _____/_____/_____ Page _____ of _____

<table>
<tr><td>IEP Results</td><td>Results of the previous IEP dated _____/___/_____</td></tr>
</table>

Goal #:   **Goal code:**   **Goal:**

| **Progress:** Did the child make the progress expected by the IEP team in the last year? (check one)
☐ M   Yes, goal met
☐ I   Goal not met; performance improved
☐ W   No change or poorer performance
☐ X   Insufficient data for decision making | **Comparison to peers or standards:** How does the child's performance compare with general education peers or standards? (check one)
☐ L   Less discrepancy from peers or standards
☐ U   Same discrepancy
☐ M   More discrepancy
☐ N   Comparison to age or grade level peers or standards not appropriate
☐ X   Insufficient data for decision making | **Independence:** Is the child more independent in the goal area? (check one)
☐ G   Greater independence
☐ U   Unchanged independence
☐ L   Less independence
☐ X   Insufficient data for decision making | **Goal status:** Will work in the goal area be continued? (check one)
Discontinue goal area:
☐ S   Success, no further special education needs in goal area
☐ X   Goal area in not a priority for the next year
☐ N   Limited Progress, plateau
☐ M   Moved ☐ D   Dropped out
☐ G   Graduated
Continue goal area
☐ C   More advanced work in goal area
☐ O   Continue as written |

Goal #:   **Goal code:**   **Goal:**

| **Progress:** Did the child make the progress expected by the IEP team in the last year? (check one)
☐ M   Yes, goal met
☐ I   Goal not met; performance improved
☐ W   No change or poorer performance
☐ X   Insufficient data for decision making | **Comparison to peers or standards:** How does the child's performance compare with general education peers or standards? (check one)
☐ L   Less discrepancy from peers or standards
☐ U   Same discrepancy
☐ M   More discrepancy
☐ N   Comparison to age or grade level peers or standards not appropriate
☐ X   Insufficient data for decision making | **Independence:** Is the child more independent in the goal area? (check one)
☐ G   Greater independence
☐ U   Unchanged independence
☐ L   Less independence
☐ X   Insufficient data for decision making | **Goal status:** Will work in the goal area be continued? (check one)
Discontinue goal area
☐ S   Success, no further special education needs in goal area
☐ X   Goal area is not a priority for the next year
☐ N   Limited progress, plateau
☐ M   Moved ☐ D   Dropped out
☐ G   Graduated
Continue goal area
☐ C   More advanced work in goal area
☐ O   Continue as written |

Goal #:   **Goal code:**   **Goal:**

| **Progress:** Did the child make the progress expected by the IEP team in the last year? (check one)
☐ M   Yes, goal met
☐ I   Goal not met; performance improved
☐ W   No change or poorer performance
☐ X   Insufficient data for decision making | **Comparison to peers or standards:** How does the child's performance compare with general education peers or standards? (check one)
☐ L   Less discrepancy from peers or standards
☐ U   Same discrepancy
☐ M   More discrepancy
☐ N   Comparison to age or grade level peers or standards not appropriate
☐ X   Insufficient data for decision making | **Independence:** Is the child more independent in the goal area? (check one)
☐ G   Greater independence
☐ U   Unchanged independence
☐ L   Less independence
☐ X   Insufficient data for decision making | **Goal status:** Will work in the goal area be continued? (check one)
Discontinue goal area
☐ S   Success, no further special education needs in goal area
☐ X   Goal area in not a priority for the next year
☐ N   Limited progress, plateau
☐ M   Moved ☐ D   Dropped out
☐ G   Graduated
Continue goal area
☐ C   More advanced work in goal area
☐ O   Continue as written |

Goal #:   **Goal code:**   **Goal:**

| **Progress:** Did the child make the progress expected by the IEP team in the last year? (check one)
☐ M   Yes, goal met
☐ I   Goal not met; performance improved
☐ W   No change or poorer performance
☐ X   Insufficient data for decision making | **Comparison to peers or standards:** How does the child's performance compare with general education peers or standards? (check one)
☐ L   Less discrepancy from peers or standards
☐ U   Same discrepancy
☐ M   More discrepancy
☐ N   Comparison to age or grade level peers or standards not appropriate
☐ X   Insufficient data for decision making | **Independence:** Is the child more independent in the goal area? (check one)
☐ G   Greater independence
☐ U   Unchanged independence
☐ L   Less independence
☐ X   Insufficient data for decision making | **Goal status:** Will work in the goal area be continued? (check one)
Discontinue goal area
☐ S   Success, no further special education needs in goal area
☐ X   Goal area in not a priority for the next year
☐ N   Limited progress, plateau
☐ M   Moved ☐ D   Dropped out
☐ G   Graduated
Continue goal area
☐ C   More advanced work in goal area
☐ O   Continue as written |

Name: _____ Date: _____ Page _____ of _____

Goal #:	Goal code:	Goal area:

Current Academic Achievement and Functional Performance (Results of the initial or most recent evaluation and results on district-wide assessments relevant to this goal; performance in comparison to general education peers and standards)

_____
_____
_____
_____

Baseline (describe individual's current performance in measurable terms) _____

Measurable Annual Goal: conditions (when and how the individual will perform); **behavior** (what the individual will do); and **criterion** (acceptable level of performance). For students 14 years and older, indicate if this goal is related to post-secondary expectations of: (check all that apply to this goal) ☐ living ☐ learning ☐ working

_____
_____
_____

Evaluation procedures (state how progress toward meeting this goal will be measured and how often progress will be measured) _____

State the district standard and benchmark related to this goal _____

Position(s) responsible for services _____

Major Milestones or Short Term Objectives/Dates Expected (Required for students assessed against alternate achievement standards)	Comments/Progress Notes/Dates Achieved

Progress Report
1 = This goal has been met.
2 = Progress has been made towards the goal. It appears that the goal will be met by the time the IEP is reviewed.
3 = Progress has been made towards the goal but the goal may not be met by the time the IEP is reviewed.
4 = Progress is not sufficient to meet this goal by the time the IEP is reviewed. Instructional strategies will be changed.
5 = Your child did not work on this goal during this reporting period (provide an explanation to the parents).

___/___/___	1 2 3 4 5	___/___/___	1 2 3 4 5	___/___/___	1 2 3 4 5
___/___/___	1 2 3 4 5	___/___/___	1 2 3 4 5	___/___/___	1 2 3 4 5
___/___/___	1 2 3 4 5	___/___/___	1 2 3 4 5	___/___/___	1 2 3 4 5

Name: _____ Date: ___/___/___ Page _____ of _____

Goal #:	Goal code:	Goal area:

Current Academic Achievement and Functional Performance (Results of the initial or most recent evaluation and results on district-wide assessments relevant to this goal; performance in comparison to general education peers and standards)

_____

_____

_____

_____

Baseline (What is this individual's current performance, stated in measurable terms?) _____

Measurable Annual Goal: conditions (when and how the individual will perform); **behavior** (what the individual will do); and criterion (acceptable level of performance). For students 14 years and older, indicate if this goal is related to post-secondary expectations of: (check all that apply to this goal.) ☐ living ☐ learning ☐ working

_____

_____

_____

Evaluation procedures (state how progress toward meeting this goal will be measured and how often progress will be measured) _____

_____

State the district standard and benchmark related to this goal _____

_____

Position(s) responsible for services _____

Major milestones: (Required for students assessed against alternate achievement standards)

1: _____   2: _____

3: _____   4: _____

Progress Report
1 = This goal has been met.
2 = Progress has been made towards the goal. It appears that the goal will be met by the time the IEP is reviewed.
3 = Progress has been made towards the goal but the goal may not be met by the time the IEP is reviewed.
4 = Progress is not sufficient to meet this goal by the time the IEP is reviewed. Instructional strategies will be changed.
5 = Your child did not work on this goal during this reporting period (provide an explanation to the parents).

___/___/___ 1 2 3 4 5   ___/___/___ 1 2 3 4 5   ___/___/___ 1 2 3 4 5

___/___/___ 1 2 3 4 5   ___/___/___ 1 2 3 4 5   ___/___/___ 1 2 3 4 5

___/___/___ 1 2 3 4 5   ___/___/___ 1 2 3 4 5   ___/___/___ 1 2 3 4 5

Name: _____ Date: _____ Page _____ of _____

Special Education Services

Indicate the special education and related services, supplementary aids and services, based upon peer-reviewed research to the extent practicable, that will be provided in order for this individual: 1) to advance appropriately toward attaining the annual goals; 2) to be involved and progress in the general curriculum; 3) to be educated and participate with other individuals with disabilities and nondisabled individuals. 4) to participate in extracurricular and other nonacademic activities; and 5) by age 14, to pursue the course of study and post-high school outcomes (living, learning & working);

Y N Accommodations Y N Linkages/interagency responsibilities Y N Supplementary aids and services
Y N Assistive technology Y N Program modifications Y N Supports for school personnel
Y N Community experiences Y N Specially designed instruction Y N Support or related services
Y N Development of work and other post-high school living objectives Y N Other _____

Describe each service, activity and support indicated above:	Provider(s)& when the service, activity or support will occur	Minutes in Setting
	Beginning Date: Provider(s): Time & frequency/when provided:	___ General education ___ Special education ___ Community per __ Day __ Week __ Month
	Beginning Date: Provider(s): Time & frequency/when provided:	___ General education ___ Special education ___ Community per __ Day __ Week __ Month
	Beginning Date: Provider(s): Time & frequency/when provided:	___ General education ___ Special education ___ Community per __ Day __ Week __ Month
	Beginning Date: Provider(s): Time & frequency/when provided:	___ General education ___ Special education ___ Community per __ Day __ Week __ Month
	Beginning Date: Provider(s): Time & frequency/when provided:	___ General education ___ Special education ___ Community per __ Day __ Week __ Month
	Beginning Date: Provider(s): Time & frequency/when provided:	___ General education ___ Special education ___ Community per __ Day __ Week __ Month
Support Services:	Total minutes per month removed from general education:
	LRE: Removal from GE % plus Time in GE % = 100%

F

Name: _____ Date: ____ / ____ / ____ Page ____ of ____

Special Education Services, continued

☐ Yes ☐ No **Are extended school year (ESY) services required?** If yes, specify the goals that require ESY services and describe the services. _____

☐ Yes ☐ No **Are specialized transportation services required that are related to the disability?** If yes, describe.

    ☐ Special route (outside normal attendance area or transportation not typically provided based on distance from school)

    ☐ Attendant services ☐ Specially equipped vehicle ☐ Other _____

Physical Education: ☐ General ☐ Modified — describe below ☐ Specially designed — requires goal(s)

_____

Indicate how this individual will participate in district-wide assessments

☐ Without accommodations

☐ With accommodations

    Describe accommodations necessary to measure academic achievement and functional performance _____

_____

☐ Through the state alternate assessment. Why can't the individual participate in the general assessment? _____

_____

Why is this alternate assessment appropriate for this student? _____

_____

Least Restrictive Environment Considerations

Address the following questions.

☐ Yes ☐ No Will this individual receive all special education services in general education environments?

If no, explain: _____

_____

☐ Yes ☐ No Will this individual participate in nonacademic activities with nondisabled peers and have the same opportunity to participate in extracurricular activities as nondisabled peers?

If no, explain: _____

_____

☐ Yes ☐ No Will this individual attend the school he or she would attend if nondisabled?

If no, explain: _____

_____

☐ Yes ☐ No Will this individual attend a special school? If yes, attach responses to the special school questions.

Progress reports

Parents: You will be informed of your child's IEP progress _____ times per year. You will receive:

☐ An IEP report with report cards and progress reports   ☐ Updated copies of the IEP goal pages

☐ _____

G   Copies: School, AEA, Parent(s)   **July 1, 2005**

F SAMPLES OF DIFFERENT IEP ANNUAL GOALS AND OBJECTIVES AS PART OF TRANSITION IEPs

College-Bound Student with Mild Disabilities

Statement of Needed Transition Services.

Prior to the IEP meeting, Matt and his teacher met to discuss his assessment results. Based on the results of Matt's assessment, he and his teacher developed the following statement:

> Matt will work with his learning center teacher to develop self-advocacy skills, including the ability to ask for reasonable accommodations and the ability to describe his learning disability in functional terms. Matt will also work with the learning center teacher to learn and apply learning strategies to written assignments in his high school classes as preparation for college. He also needs to explore his areas of vocational interest by contacting members of the community who work in the fields of veterinary medicine, sports, and engineering. Matt also needs to contact a vocational rehabilitation counselor and a representative from the local community college to determine what services might be available to assist him in his transition from high school.

Annual Goals and Monitoring Objectives.

Matt and his teacher developed annual goals and short-term objectives for two of the areas of need identified in the statement of needed transition services. The areas of self-advocacy and learning strategies each had an annual goal and a series of short-term objectives.

Annual Goal: Matt will demonstrate self-advocacy skills by requesting reasonable accommodations in each of his classes.

> *Monitoring Objective:* Matt will select from a list provided by the learning center teacher the reasonable accommodations he needs in each of his classes to maximize his success.

> *Monitoring Objective:* Matt will demonstrate his ability to ask for reasonable accommodations by role playing the situation with 90% effectiveness when rated by a peer and teacher using a teacher-made rating form.

> *Monitoring Objective:* Matt will ask a selected regular education teacher for reasonable accommodations with 90% effectiveness as rated by that regular education teacher using the above-mentioned rating form.

Annual Goal: Matt will apply selected learning strategies related to written communication in the regular classroom.

> *Monitoring Objective:* Matt will select two learning strategies related to written communication that he would like to learn and indicate why.

> *Monitoring Objective:* Matt will demonstrate competence in applying the learning strategies within the learning center by independently completing all of the steps of each strategy as rated by his learning center teacher during two written assignments of his choice.

> *Monitoring Objective:* Matt will generalize the learning strategies to written assignments in his regular classes as indicated by grades of 85% or better in his regular classes.

Student with Mild Disabilities Who Will Attend a 2-Year Technical School

Statement of Needed Transition Services.

Nicole's statement of needed transition services was developed based on her assessment results and planning. It read:

> Nicole has identified the area of graphic arts as her career interest. She will work with her guidance counselor to apply for admission to the area vocational-technical program. Nicole will work with her high school art teacher to assemble a portfolio for submission at the time of application. Nicole has invited the admissions counselor and graphic arts teacher to attend her IEP meeting. She will also arrange a meeting

with a representative from the local technical college to receive admission information for the postsecondary graphic arts program. Nicole needs to work on money management skills in order to meet her goal of living independently. Through special education, Nicole will work on time management and organization skills. She will also complete a review unit on linear measurement.

Annual Goals and Monitoring Objectives.

The annual goals and monitoring objectives included in Nicole's IEP relate to time management and organization skills and measurement.

Annual Goal: Nicole will complete and turn in assignments on time in all of her classes.

> *Monitoring Objective:* Nicole will keep an assignment notebook that lists all of her assignments from her classes and due dates with 100% accuracy as determined by teacher spot-checks of the notebook.

> *Monitoring Objective:* Nicole will complete and turn in to her special education teacher a weekly assignment checklist on which teachers sign off as assignments are turned in with 100% match.

Monitoring Annual Goal: Nicole will demonstrate the use of linear measurement.

> *Monitoring Objective:* Nicole will meet with her art teacher and assemble a list of at least five ways linear measurement is used in graphic arts.

> *Monitoring Objective:* Nicole will use a ruler to draw five lines of different lengths with accuracy to 1/8th of an inch.

Student with Moderate Disabilities

Statement of Needed Transition Services.

During Jamey's IEP meeting, the following statement of needed transition services was developed:

> Jamey needs to explore several career options to affirm his interest in food service.

He also needs to develop job skills through on-the-job training experiences in the community with a job coach. Jamey needs to explore community living options to build his level of confidence in his ability to live on his own. His functional living skills need to be assessed through a community living agency in a realistic setting. Jamey needs to complete an application for a supported living program and be put on a waiting list. He also needs to complete an application for services with Vocational Rehabilitation for transition support as he moves from high school to employment. Jamey also has social skills needs that will be addressed through instruction in his special education class. Another area to be addressed through instruction and community-based experiences is the area of money management. Jamey does not know how much things cost and has no experience budgeting for expenditures.

Annual Goals and Monitoring Objectives.

Jamey's teacher developed annual goals and short-term objectives related to social skill development and money management.

Annual Goal: Jamey will attend a school dance with a date.

> *Monitoring Objective:* Jamey will identify the dates of the upcoming school dances with 100% accuracy.

> *Monitoring Objective:* Jamey will identify a girl he would like to take to the dance.

> *Monitoring Objective:* With his special education teacher, Jamey will role-play asking a girl for a date. He will follow 100% of the steps generated through classroom discussion, as monitored by the teacher on a rating scale based on the steps.

> *Monitoring Objective:* Jamey will ask a girl for a date to the dance using 100% of the steps generated by the class and will self-monitor, using the rating scale after the conversation.

Annual Goal: Jamey will develop a budget based on his potential earnings and expenses.

Monitoring Objective: Jamey will list with 100% accuracy the monthly wages for a position in the food service industry he would like.

Monitoring Objective: Jamey will list with 100% accuracy the fixed costs for living on his own for 1 month.

Monitoring Objective: Jamey will develop a budget that takes into account income and expenses for 1 month and reflects a positive balance.

Student with Severe Disabilities

Statement of Needed Transition Services.

The following statement of needed transition services was developed during Nate's IEP meeting:

> Nate and his parents will contact the Vocational Rehabilitation Office to begin the process of intake for services. Nate and his parents will also contact the County Developmental Disabilities Service Center to begin the process of intake for services. Nate and his parents will contact three supported living centers to determine the options available to Nate for independent living. Nate will continue to work with a job coach in the community in a variety of job settings for 3 hours each day to increase his vocational skills and to determine which job he is most interested in. Nate will also participate in daily living activities in the community such as shopping, laundry, and using public transportation at least 5 hours each week. Nate will continue to participate in the Circle of Friends group and Special Olympics.

Annual Goals and Monitoring Objectives.

Nate's parents and his teacher developed goals and objectives for two of the areas listed in the statement of needed transition services.

Annual Goal: Nate will increase his vocational skills by increasing his production rate.

Monitoring Objective: Nate will increase his production rate on a job related to light industry by 10% over baseline during a 2-week period.

Monitoring Objective: Nate will increase his production rate on a job related to clerical tasks by 10% over baseline during a 2-week period.

Monitoring Objective: Nate will increase his production rate on a job related to the service industry by 10% over baseline during a 2-week period.

Annual Goal: Nate will demonstrate the ability to shop in a grocery store.

Monitoring Objective: Given a picture grocery list with five items on it, Nate will find four out of five items within a 30-minute period in a grocery store near his home during three consecutive visits.

Monitoring Objective: Nate will make a grocery list containing five items from food pictures and/or from coupons.

Monitoring Objective: Nate will purchase a soft drink from a machine independently on 2 consecutive days.

Individualized Family Service Plan
Family Information

Date: _____

Child's name: _____ DOB: _____ ❑ F ❑ M

Child lives with: _____ Relationship to child: _____

Address: _____ City/Zip: _____

Country: _____ Home Phone: _____ Work Phone(s): _____

Best place/time to be reached: ❑ Home ❑ Work Time: _____ Language used in home: _____

How did the family learn about Early ACCESS: _____

Reason for the call to Early ACCESS: _____

Other significant adults involved in your child's life, e.g. grandparent, friend, etc. (name & relationship to child/family): _____

Other children in the family – name(s) and DOB: _____

Check whether any screening or evaluation activities have already been completed: ❑ No ❑ Yes

If yes, dates and by whom: _____

Child's Primary Medical Provider:

Name: _____ Phone: _____

Address: _____ City/State/Zip: _____

Agencies or Programs with whom Family and Child are Currently Involved:

Agency/Program	Address	Contact Person	Phone

Child's Social Security #: _____ Health Insurance: _____

Waiver(s): _____ Medicaid #: _____

Date of Referral to Early ACCESS:	Initial IFSP Meeting Date:
Official Reminders*	
Periodic Review Due By (at least every 6 months):	Annual Review Meeting Due By:
Child Turns 3 On:	Transition Planning Meeting Due By: (at least 90 days before 3rd birthday):

*Documentation for missed timelines must be included in the IFSP

Initial Service Coordinator: _____ Phone: _____

Agency/Address: _____

2/04

Date: _____

☐ Interim IFSP   ☐ Change in Service
☐ Initial IFSP   ☐ Change in S. Coordinator
☐ Periodic Review ☐ Final Exit
☐ Annual Review

Individualized Family Service Plan
Summary of Service

Child's Name: _____ DOB: _____ School District: _____
Address: _____ Phone: _____
Parent Name(s): _____ Intake Date: _____
Service Coordinator: _____ Phone: _____
Staff Position: _____ Agency: _____

Early ACCESS Early Intervention (EI) Services

Service, Code & Outcome #	☐ EI Service ☐ Other Service	☐ EI Service ☐ Other Service
Provided by: (first & last name)		
Discipline (Staff Position & Code)		
Agency:		
Phone:		
Location for providing service*:		
Method – ind or grp – How long – How often (sessions & minutes per wk, mo, yr):		
Start date & projected duration:		
Payment:		
Service, Code & Outcome #	☐ EI Service ☐ Other Service	☐ EI Service ☐ Other Service
Provided by: (first & last name)		
Discipline (Staff Position & Code)		
Agency:		
Phone:		
Location for providing service*:		
Method – ind or grp – How long – How often (sessions & minutes per wk, mo, yr):		
Start date & projected duration:		
Payment:		

*If any EI services are provided in a non-natural environment, justify here:

Parent(s) Signature(s) shows agreement with Early Intervention Service(s) listed above:

Primary Setting Code (Circle one code per update)
IT: 1 2 3 4 5 6 7
Eligibility Code (Circle one at Initial IFSP Meeting Only)
HP TD NE
Gender (Circle at Initial IFSP only)
F M

Race/Ethnicity Code (Circle one at Initial IFSP Meeting Only)
01 02 03 04 05
Final Exit Reason from Early ACCESS/Change Code/Speech Code (circle one)
PMA EFB EOP ENR BND PDS SD01 SD02 SD03
DEC CMK CMN UNK SDP SD04 SD05

Early ACCESS
for Children and Families

Eligible based on: □ **Not eligible**

□ 25% or greater delay including informed clinical opinion

□ Condition/High Probability including informed clinical opinion

Child's Name: _____ **DOB:** _____

Areas Evaluated or Assessed (See below for initial evaluation requirements):	What we found out: (Child's current health and development)	How we found out: (Person, discipline, agency, method & tool used, date, setting. Document reason(s) if 45-day timeline for evaluation is not met here.)	Things to consider when making team decisions: • Brainstorming (ideas) • Recommendations • Family concerns/priorities/resources • Informal and formal support options

The following areas must be addressed for the initial evaluation: developmental areas, including cognitive, physical (including vision and hearing), communication, social or emotional, and adaptive development, and a review of current health status.

2/04

357

Early
A C C E S S
for Children and Families

Individualized Family Service Plan
Work Page

Date: _____ Outcome: # _____

Work Page pertains to - check all that apply:

❑ Initial IFSP Meeting ❑ Interim IFSP
❑ Periodic Review ❑ New Outcome
❑ Annual Review ❑ Transition
❑ Evaluation/Assessment ❑ Meeting Notice

Child's Name: _____ DOB: _____

Child/Family Outcome (Priority): What does the family want to see happen? Why?	How will this be done? Who will help? (Consider family strengths and their informal and formal supports as well as other resources available. Date each addition to the plan for this outcome.)

Tracking our Progress:

Parent Rating:		Date
1. Just started	3. Modifications needed	
2. Still working towards outcome	4. Accomplished outcome and satisfied	
	5. Not completed, no longer a priority	Rating

2/04

H1 BEHAVIOR OBSERVATION FORM

Date	Time	Length of Behavior	What Occurred Prior to the Behavior	Describe Behavior	Outcome of Behavior
9/17/07	1:20–1:30 p.m.	20 to 30 seconds	The students were assigned independent seat work. The teacher gave individual help to students as she walked around the classroom. The teacher stands at Tom's desk.	Tom wads up his paper, then tears it up and scatters the pieces on the floor.	Other students turn to look. The teacher says to Tom, "Get out another sheet of paper and start over." She waits at his desk another 45 seconds.
9/22/07	1:15 p.m.	15 seconds	Verbal instructions were given on how to complete a pre-lab worksheet.	Tom wads up his paper and clenches it in his fist.	Several students turn to look at Tom. The teacher tells him the work must be completed by the end of class or he will have to stay after school.
9/23/07	1:00–1:10 p.m.	25 seconds	The class completed watching a film.	Tom picks up his paper in one hand, then puts his head on his desk and wads up his paper.	The teacher tells him to sit up, straighten out his worksheet, and get to work.
9/24/07	1:15–1:25 p.m.	20 seconds	Students were assigned to answer questions from their book after viewing a teacher demonstration.	Tom takes out a sheet of paper. He starts to write, then wads up his paper and slams his book shut.	A few students giggle. Some turn to look. The teacher says, "Tom, you are wasting time."
9/25/07	1:05–1:15 p.m.	25 seconds	Students completed oral review questions and were given directions to complete a review study guide for a test.	Tom receives his study guide, looks at it, then separates the pages. He then wads up each page, one at a time, loudly.	The teacher tells Tom to take his things and go to the office.

H2 FUNCTIONAL ASSESSMENT INTERVIEW FORM

Student: Tom Clark   Teacher: Jennifer Braun

Team Member's Name   Team Member's Position

Ms. Jones   English Teacher
Mr. Smith   Principal
Ms. Clark   Mother
Ms. Johnson   Case Manager

A. Describe the Behavior

1. What is the behavior?

   Tom destroys his written assignments.

2. How is the behavior performed?

   When given written assignments to be completed independently, Tom wads up and/or tears up his paper. When he is reminded to get to work, he says he does not want to do the work.

3. How often does the behavior occur?

   The behavior occurs on days when written work is to be completed, 3 to 4 days a week.

4. How long does the behavior last when it occurs?

   15 to 30 seconds.

5. What is the intensity of the behavior when it occurs?

   The behavior results in the destruction of paper and detracts from peer work time.

B. Define Setting Events and Environmental Factors That Predict the Behavior (describe the following variables)

1. Classroom structure (physical).

   Science 7 is a classroom with work tables and storage cabinets for lab equipment and materials.

2. Class rules and procedural expectations.

   Students are responsible for the care of all materials, including their work. Written work must be completed before lab work can begin.

3. Instructional delivery (e.g., lecture, cooperative learning, labs).

   Lecture, cooperative group work, discussion, lab activities, and independent seat work.

4. Instructional materials (textbooks, worksheets, hands-on activities).

   Textbook and/or worksheets.

5. How are directions presented?

   Verbal directions are given by the teacher. Some directions are read independently by the students.

6. Assessment techniques (multiple-choice tests, essay tests, rubrics, authentic assessment).

   A multiple choice test is given weekly. One essay question is included in each test. Each test covers a combination of lab work and written work.

C. Define Specific Immediate Antecedent Events That Predict When the Behaviors Are Most Likely to Occur

1. When are the behaviors most likely to occur?

   The behaviors generally occur after the lecture and prior to independent seat work.

2. When are the behaviors least likely to occur?

   The behaviors occur least often when Tom is interacting with his peers and feels a part of the group.

3. Where are the behaviors most likely to occur?

   The behaviors occur frequently in his science class.

4. Where are the behaviors least likely to occur?

   The behaviors are least likely to occur in social settings and in classrooms where Tom is not the only one asked to sit alone.

5. During what activities are the behaviors most likely to occur?

   Behaviors occur most often during independent seat work when he is asked to work alone.

6. During what activities are the behaviors least likely to occur?

   The behaviors occur least often during group activities.

D. Identify Specific Consequences That Follow the Behavior

1. What specific consequence is most likely to immediately follow the behavior?

   Teacher and peer attention. The student receives a "0" for the assignment.

2. What seems to be the effect of the consequence on the student's behavior?

   The effect seems to be somewhat reinforcing in that Tom continues the problem behavior.

3. Does the consequence remove the student from an uncomfortable situation?

   Yes, temporarily. It delays work time and provides attention.

4. Is there consistency between the consequences given by the classroom teacher and the consequences given by the administrators?

   Yes.

5. Is there consistent follow-through with all consequences both in the classroom and in the school office?

   Yes.

H3 BEHAVIORAL INTERVENTION PLAN

Student: Tom Clark   School: Middle School
Date Developed: 9/30/97 Date Implemented: 10/3/97
Grade: 7

Baseline Data Results:
Tom destroyed 5 assignments out of 5 observation days.

Hypothesis Statement:
Tom's behavior is related to frustration brought on by a discrepancy between his skill level and the skill level necessary to complete the assignments. Much of Tom's destructive behavior is related to his isolated seating from his peers in the classroom. Tom feels singled out because he sits at a table by himself.

Type of Interview Plan: Educational × Behavioral _____

Person(s) Responsible for Implementing Plan: Science teacher

Description of the Behavior:

Behavior	Behavior Defined
Tom destroys his written assignments.	Tom wads up and tears up his assignment papers.

Intervention Goal:
To decrease the number of occurrences that Tom destroys his assignments to 0 per week.

Intervention Plan:
1. Seat Tom with a peer who has good on-task behavior. The peer will review directions with Tom and help him get started with assignments.
2. Provide Tom a daily monitoring assignment checklist to improve the following areas of difficulty.

Assignment Checklist

____ I understood teacher directions
____ I asked for help when I needed it
____ I answered all questions
____ I understood the assignment
____ I need more time
____ I turned in my assignment

3. Provide Tom with academic modifications, including:
   a. Extended time to complete and turn in assignments if needed.
   b. Provide Tom with a word definition list to use when completing work-sheet assignments.
   c. Provide peer assistance with some assignments.
   d. Provide additional instructional modifications as needed.
4. Provide directions to Tom in a variety of ways (e.g., verbal, written, direction instructions, and peer assistance).
5. Reinforce Tom's academic productivity and assignment completion.

Sample Behavioral Intervention Plan.

When and Where the Plan Will Be Implemented:
The plan will be implemented in Tom's science class for 3 consecutive weeks beginning 10/3/07.

Intervention Data Collection Summary:

Week 1	Decrease in behavior to three occurrences.
Week 2	Decrease in behavior to two occurrences.
Week 3	Decrease in behavior to one occurrence.

Follow-up and Review Date(s):
Follow-up and review meeting 10/24/07

Comments:
The intervention plan is successful with Tom.
The team agreed to write the interventions outlined in this plan in Tom's IEP.
The team will meet in 3 weeks for another review.

Team Meeting Participants:

Name: _____   Position: _____

361

H4   MANIFESTATION DETERMINATION REVIEW FORM

Name:

Date of Misconduct:

Description of Misconduct:

Part A: Day of Incident Report

Immediate Action (if any):

Date Scheduled for Manifestation Determination Review:
(No later than 10 school days following the decision to take disciplinary action.)

Relevant Members of the IEP Team Invited to Participate in the Manifestation Determination Review:

Part B: Manifestation Determination Review

Participants in Manifestation Determination Review:

Review of Relevant Information:

NOTE: This review must include the child's IEP, any teacher observations, and any relevant information provided by the parents.

Determination Based on Review of Relevant Information:
• Was the misconduct in question caused by or have a direct and substantial relationship to the child's disability?

• Was the misconduct in question the direct result of the local educational agency's failure to implement the IEP?

Part C: Decision

Note: If misconduct was **NOT** a manifestation of the child's disability, disciplinary action such as long-term suspension or expulsion may be taken.

NOTE: A child removed from current placement must continue to receive educational services to enable the child to participate in the general education curriculum; to progress toward meeting IEP goals; and to receive, as appropriate, a functional behavioral assessment and behavioral intervention services to address the misconduct to prevent recurrence.

If misconduct **WAS** a manifestation of the child's disability, a functional behavioral assessment must be conducted and a behavioral intervention plan must be developed or reviewed to address the misconduct.

Name Index

Note: Page numbers in italics indicate figures.

SUBJECT INDEX

Note: Page numbers in italics indicate figures.